CULTS AND NEW RELIGIOUS MOVEMENTS

814 -765-7244 -565- 619

What do we gain from
studying NRMS?

what language should
we use when
discussing l representing
them?

BLACKWELL READINGS IN RELIGION

The Blackwell Readings in Religion series brings together the knowledge of leading international scholars, and each volume provides an authoritative overview of both the historical development and the contemporary issues of its subject. Titles are presented in a style which is accessible to undergraduate students, as well as scholars and the interested general reader.

Published

The Blackwell Reader in Judaism
Edited by Jacob Neusner and Alan J. Avery-Peck

Cults and New Religious Movements
A Reader
Edited by Lorne L. Dawson

CULTS AND NEW RELIGIOUS MOVEMENTS
A READER

Edited by Lorne L. Dawson

Blackwell Publishing

Editorial material and organization © 2003 by Blackwell Publishing Ltd

BLACKWELL PUBLISHING
350 Main Street, Malden, MA 02148-5020, USA
9600 Garsington Road, Oxford OX4 2DQ, UK
550 Swanston Street, Carlton, Victoria 3053, Australia

First published 2003 by Blackwell Publishing Ltd

11   2013

Library of Congress Cataloging-in-Publication Data

Cults and new religious movements : a reader / edited by Lorne L. Dawson.
p. cm. – (Blackwell readings in religion)
Includes bibliographical references and index.
ISBN 978-1-4051-0180-6 (hardback: alk. paper) – ISBN 978-1-4051-0181-3 (pbk. : alk. paper)
1. Cults. I. Dawson, Lorne L., 1954– II. Series.
BP603 .C86 2003
291–dc21   2002038285

A catalogue record for this title is available from the British Library.

Set in 9.5 on 11.5 pt Galliard
by SNP Best-set Typesetter Ltd, Hong Kong
Printed and bound in Malaysia
by Vivar Printing Sdn Bhd

The publisher's policy is to use permanent paper from mills that operate a sustainable forestry
policy, and which has been manufactured from pulp processed using acid-free and elementary
chlorine-free practices. Furthermore, the publisher ensures that the text paper and cover board
used have met acceptable environmental accreditation standards.

For further information on
Blackwell Publishing, visit our website:
www.blackwellpublishing.com

Contents

Acknowledgments   vii

Introduction: The Book and the Subject   1

I   **The Study of New Religious Movements**   **5**

   1   The Scientific Study of Religion? You Must Be Joking!   7
       Eileen Barker

   2   The Continuum Between "Cults" and "Normal" Religion   26
       James A. Beckford

II   **The Nature of New Religious Movements**   **33**

   3   Three Types of New Religious Movement   36
       Roy Wallis

   4   Cult Formation: Three Compatible Models   59
       William Sims Bainbridge and Rodney Stark

III   **New Religious Movements in Historical and Social Context**   **71**

   5   False Prophets and Deluded Subjects: The Nineteenth Century   73
       Philip Jenkins

   6   The New Spiritual Freedom   89
       Robert Wuthnow

IV   **Joining New Religious Movements**   **113**

   7   Who Joins New Religious Movements and Why: Twenty Years
       of Research and What Have We Learned?   116
       Lorne L. Dawson

   8   The Joiners   131
       Saul Levine

CONTENTS

V   **The "Brainwashing" Controversy**   **143**

    9   The Process of Brainwashing, Psychological Coercion, and
       Thought Reform   147
       Margaret Thaler Singer

    10   A Critique of "Brainwashing" Claims About New
       Religious Movements   160
       James T. Richardson

    11   Constructing Cultist "Mind Control"   167
       Thomas Robbins

VI   **Violence and New Religious Movements**   **181**

    12   The Apocalypse at Jonestown   186
       John R. Hall

    13   "Our Terrestrial Journey is Coming to an End": The Last
       Voyage of the Solar Temple   208
       Jean-François Mayer

VII   **Sex and Gender Issues and New Religious Movements**   **227**

    14   Women in New Religious Movements   230
       Elizabeth Puttick

    15   Women's "Cocoon Work" in New Religious Movements:
       Sexual Experimentation and Feminine Rites of Passage   245
       Susan J. Palmer

VIII   **New Religious Movements and the Future**   **257**

    16   Why Religious Movements Succeed or Fail: A Revised
       General Model   259
       Rodney Stark

    17   New Religions and the Internet: Recruiting in a New Public Space   271
       Lorne L. Dawson and Jenna Hennebry

Index   292

Acknowledgments

The editor and publishers gratefully acknowledge the following for permission to reproduce copyright material:

Eileen Barker, "The Scientific Study of Religion? You Must Be Joking!" *Journal for the Scientific Study of Religion* 34, 1995: 287–310.

James A. Beckford, "The Continuum Between 'Cults' and 'Normal' Religion." In Pauline Cote (ed.) *Chercheurs de dieux dans l'espace public*, University of Ottawa Press, 2001: 11–20; reprinted by permission of the publisher.

Roy Wallis, "Three Types of New Religious Movement." In Roy Wallis, *The Elementary Forms of New Religious Life*, Routledge and Kegan Paul, 1984: 9–39; reprinted by permission of Mrs Veronica Wallis.

William Sims Bainbridge and Rodney Stark, "Cult Formation: Three Compatible Models." *Sociological Analysis* 40, 1979: 283–95.

Philip Jenkins, "False Prophets and Deluded Subjects: The Nineteenth Century." In Philip Jenkins, *Mystics and Messiahs: Cults and New Religions in American History*, Oxford University Press, 2000: 25–45; copyright 2000 by Philip Jenkins; used by permission of Oxford University Press, Inc.

Robert Wuthnow, "The New Spiritual Freedom." In Robert Wuthnow, *After Heaven: Spirituality in America Since the 1950s*, Berkeley: University of California Press, 1998: 52–84; copyright © 1998 the Regents of the University of California.

Lorne L. Dawson, "Who Joins New Religious Movements and Why: Twenty Years of Research and What Have We Learned?" *Studies in Religion/Sciences Religieuses* 25, 1996: 141–61.

Saul Levine, "The Joiners." In Saul Levine, *Radical Departures: Desperate Detours to Growing Up*, New York: Harcourt Brace and Company, 1984; copyright © 1994 by Saul V. Levine, reprinted by permission of Harcourt, Inc.

Margaret Thaler Singer, "The Process of Brainwashing, Psychological Coercion, and Thought Reform." In Margaret Thaler Singer, *Cults in Our Midst*, Jossey-Bass, 1995: 52–82.

James T. Richardson, "A Critique of 'Brainwashing' Claims About New Religious Movements." *Australian Religious Studies Review* 7, 1994: 48–56.

Thomas Robbins, "Constructing Cultist 'Mind Control'." *Sociological Analysis* 45, 1984: 241–56.

John R. Hall, "The Apocalypse at Jonestown." In John R. Hall, with Philip D. Schuyler and Sylvaine Trinh, *Apocalypse Observed: Religious Movements and Violence in North America, Europe, and Japan*, Routledge, 2000: 15–43; reprinted by permission of Taylor and Francis Ltd.

ACKNOWLEDGMENTS

Jean-François Mayer, "'Our Terrestrial Journey is Coming to an End': The Last Voyage of the Solar Temple." *Nova Religio* 2, 1999: 172–96.

Elizabeth Puttick, "Women in New Religious Movements." In Bryan Wilson and Jamie Cresswell (eds.) *New Religious Movements: Challenge and Response*, Routledge, 1999: 143–62; reprinted by permission of Taylor and Francis Ltd and the author.

Susan J. Palmer, "Women's 'Cocoon Work' in New Religious Movements: Sexual Experimentation and Feminine Rites of Passage." *Journal for the Scientific Study of Religion* 32, 1993: 343–55.

Rodney Stark, "Why Religious Movements Succeed or Fail: A Revised General Model." *Journal of Contemporary Religion* 11, 1996: 133–46; reprinted by permission of Taylor and Francis Ltd; journal website http:// www.tandf.co.uk/journals.

Lorne L. Dawson and Jenna Hennebry, "New Religions and the Internet: Recruiting in a New Public Space." *Journal of Contemporary Religion* 14, 1999: 17–39; reprinted by permission of Taylor and Francis Ltd; journal website http://www.tandf.co.uk/ journals.

The publishers apologize for any errors or omissions in the above list and would be grateful to be notified of any corrections that should be incorporated in the next edition or reprint of this book.

Introduction:
The Book and the Subject

Most people in North America or Europe have never met anyone who is a member of a "cult," or what scholars prefer to call "new religious movements." Thousands of such groups exist in our societies, but they tend to be so small or last for so short a time that they attract little or no attention. Yet almost everyone has read articles or watched television shows about these groups. In our increasingly secularized and supposedly rational societies our curiosity is peaked by the intense and seemingly peculiar beliefs and practices of the minority of people who choose such alternative worldviews and their accompanying lifestyles. We are often simultaneously drawn to and repelled by their sense of commitment and purpose in life. As social and ideological deviants they are fascinating yet threatening. Their religiosity may seem strangely more real and compelling than the anemic variety of mainstream religion so many of us experience as children and young adults in the churches, synagogues, and temples of our parents. But the beliefs espoused are often subversive of the values and goals to which we have been socialized by the dominant social institutions of our society. Where so often we have been conditioned to the pursuit of happiness through the acquisition of the right job or through romantic love, part of us suspects, as many of the new religions declare, that these ambitions are illusory. Real happiness lies elsewhere. In the words spoken by the leaders of these new religions we often hear distinct echoes of the higher values and sentiments, the spiritual insights, of the great religious figures of the past. Surely there is more to life we all sense at times, and the teachings of Jesus, Mohammed, the Buddha and others, may seem to be more genuinely present in the discourses of these still largely unknown or already scorned men and women than in the sermons and pronouncements of the accepted religious leaders around us. But fear holds us back from exploring these possibilities further and the "cults" in our midst remain just a curiosity. This fear of the unknown and the different is natural and understandable, but it is also exaggerated and in the long run detrimental to both our own spiritual development and that of our societies.

We know about "cults" largely by what the media tells us, and their views have been overwhelmingly negative (see Van Driel and Richardson 1988; Pfeifer 1992). Mirroring the norms of conventional society, and the interests of the powers behind it, the media have preferred to be sensationalistic in their treatment of new religious movements, earning dollars by exploiting our fascination and stoking our fears (see Beckford 1999, and the first chapter of this book). Much of this book is dedicated to correcting this misperception – not from a desire to prejudge the specific merits or faults of any new religious movements, but from a belief in letting the record of reliable research speak for itself. Others will disagree with my choice of readings (see Beit-Hallahmi 2001; Zablocki 2001), and hence my conclusions. The sweeping public stigmatization and often outright condemnation of new religions is based largely on ignorance, and more often than not this ignorance poses a greater threat to our social well-being. I have tried as a social scientist to select the best literature available on the topic from many of the most knowledgeable and distinguished scholars in the field. This selection is limited by the need to use materials that are well written and readily understood by students and non-specialists. Some of the readings have been edited as well, to shorten them and make them even more accessible (the omitted material is indicated by ellipses). Likewise, I have tried to select readings that address most of the major issues raised by the social scientific study of new religious movements: their nature, how they come into being, the social and historical context of their interpretation, the processes by which people convert to them, the rewards and dangers of joining them, and some sense of their future as social organizations as well as the factors that may determine their relative success or failure. This has meant that more space than perhaps is fair is dedicated to debates over controversial issues, most specifically the accusation that converts to new religious movements are "brainwashed," the perplexing incidents of mass violence in which a few groups have been involved, and the occurrence of sexual deviance and abuse in some situations. But these issues have been the focal points of public awareness of "cults," and hence much of the scholarly activity as well.

The study of new religious movements has been conditioned by the problematic character of the subject matter. Soon after the spread of numerous new and unusual religions in the United States in the late 1960s, groups of unhappy parents of young adults who had converted to various "cults" joined forces with some professionals (e.g., lawyers, psychologists, psychiatrists, and social workers), disgruntled ex-members of new religions, and some representatives of other religions (ministers, priests, and rabbis) to create an organized opposition to new religious movements. This "anti-cult movement" tried to have the authorities impose various formal public sanctions on new religions, but they failed. They did succeed, however, in winning the propaganda war that was waged for public opinion, creating a staunch distrust of these groups in the general populace (see Bromley and Shupe 1993, 1994). In the process, the very word "cult" took on a pejorative connotation, leaving social scientists looking for a less prejudicial alternative. From the many suggestions offered, the phrase "new religious movements" has stuck. But it is far from ideal, since some new religious movements are no longer so new, some never were movements, and the religious status of some is a matter of dispute (see Wilson 1992; Richardson 1993; Bednarowski 1995; Dawson 1998: 1–12). The label "cult" is still a technical term in the scholarship on religion, like the terms "church" or "sect." But when used in this book it will be accompanied by scare quotes (i.e., "cults") in acknowledgment of its recent problematic history. In most instances the term new religious movements will be used, and in line with current academic practice it will be abbreviated to NRMs.

The significance of the social scientific study of "cults," however, transcends the public struggles over their legitimacy. Scholars of religion have shown a disproportionate interest in analyzing NRMs because they offer a special opportunity to witness the very birth pangs, growth struggles, and often death throws of religions. They provide immediate access to data about the most basic aspects of religious life that may be instrumental to understanding the rise and spread of the great religious traditions of the past (see Stark 1996). Most notably, as the chapters in this reader display, the study of NRMs has vastly improved our grasp of the nature and complexity of the processes of recruitment and conversion (see chapters 7, 8, 9, 10, 11), as well as the processes of religious innovation and group formation, religious change, and the structure and development of religious institutions (see chapters 4, 6, 16). Likewise it has prompted startling advances in our appreciation of newer concerns, like the gendered character of religious preferences and experiences (see chapters 14, 15) and the origins and nature of religious violence (see chapters 12, 13).

NRMs make the investigation of these basic issues easier for a number of reasons: (1) they offer researchers smaller and more manageable forums for research; (2) they provide an opportunity to acquire a first-hand familiarity with the earliest implementation of religious ideas, plans, and policies, free of the interpretive impact of tradition; and (3), they are likely to present researchers with more extreme types of behavior that are easier to detect and measure, and then extrapolate to less extreme instances (as psychiatrists do, for example, in seeking to understand the inner workings of the mind).

Of course, it is difficult to appreciate any of this or properly understand the readings in this book without some additional knowledge of various actual NRMs Those lacking in some background knowledge of at least a few groups should read this book in conjunction with some of the many fine descriptive studies available on the history, beliefs, and practices of such NRMs as the Church of Scientology, the Unification Church, the International Society for Krishna Consciousness, Soka Gakkai, neo-paganism, the New Age movement, and the Children of God/The Family (e.g., Wallis 1977; Barker 1984; Rochford 1985; Wilson and Dobbelaere 1994; Brown 1997; Berger 1999; Bainbridge 2002). Alternatively, one should at least turn to one of the good collections of descriptive essays on these and many other groups (e.g., Ellwood and Partin 1988; Miller 1995; or Chryssides 1999). For a more comprehensive and systematic overview of the results of the social scientific study of NRMs readers may also wish to consult books like Thomas Robbins's *Cults, Converts and Charisma* (1988) or Lorne L. Dawson's *Comprehending Cults: The Sociology of New Religious Movements* (1998).

References

Bainbridge, William Sims 2002: *The Endtime Family: Children of God*. Albany: State University of New York Press.

Barker, Eileen 1984: *The Making of a Moonie: Choice or Brainwashing?* Oxford: Blackwell.

Beckford, James A. 1999: The Mass Media and New Religious Movements. In B. Wilson and J. Cresswell (eds.), *New Religious Movements: Challenge and Response*. London: Routledge, 103–19.

Bednarowski, Mary Farrell 1995: The Church of Scientology: Lightning Rod for Cultural Boundary Conflicts. In T. Miller (ed.), *America's Alternative Religions*. Albany: State University of New York Press, 385–92.

Beit-Hallahmi, Benjamin 2001: 'O Truant Muse': Collaborationism and Research Integrity. In B. Zablocki and T. Robbins (eds.), *Misunderstanding Cults: Searching for Objectivity in a Controversial Field*. Toronto: University of Toronto Press, 35–70.

Berger, Helen A. 1999: *A Community of Witches: Contemporary Neo-Paganism and Witchcraft in the United States*. Columbia: University of South Carolina Press.

Bromley, David G. and Anson D. Shupe, Jr. 1993: Organized Opposition to New Religious Movements. In D. G. Bromley and J. K. Hadden (eds.), *The Handbook on Cults and Sects in America, Part A* (Religion and the Social Order, vol. 3). Greenwich, CT: JAI Press, 177–98.

Bromley, David G. and Anson D. Shupe, Jr. 1994: The Modern North American Anti-Cult Movement, 1971–1991: A Twenty Year Retrospective. In A. Shupe and D. G. Bromley (eds.), *Anti-Cult Movements in Cross Cultural Perspective*. New York: Garland, 3–31.

Brown, Michael F. 1997: *The Channeling Zone: American Spirituality in an Anxious Age*. Cambridge, MA: Harvard University Press.

Chryssides, George D. 1999: *Exploring New Religions*. London: Cassell.

Dawson, Lorne L. 1998: *Comprehending Cults: The Sociology of New Religious Movements*. Toronto: Oxford University Press.

Ellwood, Robert S. and Harry B. Partin 1988: *Religious and Spiritual Groups in Modern America*, 2nd edn. Englewood Cliffs, NJ: Prentice-Hall.

Miller, Timothy (ed.) 1995: *America's Alternative Religions*. Albany: State University of New York Press.

Pfeifer, Jeffrey E. 1992: The Psychological Framing of Cults: Schematic Representations and Cult

Evaluations. *Journal of Applied Social Psychology* 22 (7): 513–44.

Richardson, James T. 1993: Definitions of Cult: From Sociological–Technical to Popular–Negative. *Review of Religious Research* 34 (4): 348–56.

Robbins, Thomas 1988: *Cults, Converts and Charisma*. Newbury Park, CA: Sage.

Rochford, E. Burke, Jr. 1985: *Hare Krishna in America*. New Brunswick, NJ: Rutgers University Press.

Stark, Rodney 1996: *The Rise of Christianity: A Sociologist Reconsiders History*. Princeton, NJ: Princeton University Press.

Van Driel, Barend and James T. Richardson 1988: Print Media Coverage of New Religious Movements: A Longitudinal Study. *Journal of Communication* 38 (3): 37–61.

Wallis, Roy 1977: *The Road to Total Freedom: A Sociological Analysis of Scientology*. New York: Columbia University Press.

Wilson, Bryan R. 1992: Scientology: A Secularized Religion. In B. R. Wilson, *The Social Dimensions of Sectarianism: Sects and New Religious Movements in Contemporary Society*. Oxford: Clarendon Press, 267–88.

Wilson, Bryan R. and Karel Dobbelaere 1994: *A Time to Chant: The Soka Gakkai Buddhists in Britain*. Oxford: Clarendon Press.

Zablocki, Benjamin 2001: Towards a Demystified and Disinterested Scientific Theory of Brainwashing. In B. Zablocki and T. Robbins (eds.), *Misunderstanding Cults: Searching For Objectivity in a Controversial Field*. Toronto: University of Toronto Press, 159–214.

I

The Study of New Religious Movements

In reading the essays in this book you will learn that "cults" or new religious movements can and should be studied like any other social, cultural, and historical phenomena. Scholars have been accumulating reliable data and developing theories to explain the new religions in our midst and their activities for more than forty years (see Dawson 1998). Many mysteries remain and there is much left to study, but the gaps in our knowledge are the product of limited time, resources, and opportunities. There is nothing intrinsically beyond the pale of comprehension or threatening about "cults" as a subject of inquiry. To the contrary, as stressed by James Beckford in chapter 2, we must learn to accept that most NRMs differ very little in their nature and operation, and in their moral and social failings, from more conventional or mainstream religions (e.g., the Catholic Church or Methodists). Yet the controversy surrounding "cults" makes the study of NRMs unlike the study of these other conventional religions, and most other fields of social scientific research.

The study of NRMs was sparked in part by the emergence of "cults" as a social problem in the late twentieth-century societies of the modern West. Families were angered when their adult sons and daughters left them behind, and abandoned the conventional career paths they were pursuing, to join intense religious groups of unfamiliar origins and orientations. As families and other concerned people began to press the authorities to take action against the new religions – to restrict their activities or suppress them altogether – many scholars of religion saw the need to replace public prejudice or simply fear with a more reliable understanding of these groups and their members. Why were people converting to these new and often strange religions? What were these groups trying to accomplish? What was life in them like? Were they potentially dangerous to society or the individuals in them? In seeking to answer these and many other related questions the sociologists, psychologists, and religious studies scholars who dared to study these groups found themselves embroiled in often heated disputes with other claimants to "the truth." They also found themselves struggling to overcome the stigma associated with studying such reviled groups, amongst their colleagues and the public.

Our first reading, Eileen Barker's "The Scientific Study of Religion? You Must Be Joking!" clarifies the field of contention in which scholars of NRMs must operate. Cults often find their way into the news, and when they do there are commonly several different parties seeking to influence the reaction of the public. Barker, a leading sociologist of religion from England, compares and contrasts the assumptions, objectives, and biases of the different groups trying to shape our understanding of "cults": the NRMs themselves, sociologists of religion, the organized representatives of the anti-cult movement, the media, therapists, and representatives of the legal system (the police, lawyers, and judges). Sometimes the interests of some of these groups converge (e.g., when journalists turn to the anti-cult movement for sensationalistic comments on an NRM), more often they clash (e.g., when the courts want clear and simple answers to complex questions from sociologists acting as witnesses in legal disputes). Any scholar seeking to succeed in the field must be prepared to cope with the frustration and hostility stemming from this clash of interests and information. While the organized opposition to "cults" will seek to undermine the credibility of the scholar because of any positive pronouncements made about NRMs, the cults will be trying to co-opt the scholar and use the same pronouncements as propaganda for their cause. To maintain even the appearance of objectivity in such circumstances requires a fine balancing act.

Likewise any student seeking to understand NRMs must recognize that the views expressed about "cults" will tend to vary systematically according to the personal, and even more the professional or vocational, interests of the persons providing the information. As almost all of the players in the field of contention employ information selectively to suit their purposes, special caution must be exercised to sort the wheat of reliable data and insights from the all-too abundant chaff of hearsay, innuendo, and ridicule.

As indicated in Philip Jenkins's fine discussion of the controversies surrounding NRMs in nineteenth-century America, in chapter 5 of this book, the clash of views over the legitimacy of new religions is not new. Throughout the ages the defenders of the status quo have feared and attacked the proponents of religious innovation. In our second reading, "The Continuum Between 'Cults' and 'Normal' Religion," another leading British sociologist

of religion, James Beckford, argues that the peculiar intensity and scope of today's cult controversy stems in part from several characteristics of life in advanced industrial societies. The extremity of religious commitment displayed by members of contemporary NRMs is perceived as an affront to the sensibilities of modern, rationalized, commodified, and secularized societies. And the clash of sensibilities is accentuated by the sweeping changes in modern means of communication that place the NRMs under an unprecedented measure of scrutiny. In support of the argument Beckford suggests that the intolerance directed at NRMs is largely the result of "skirmishes along a shifting frontier" of points of conflict between the new religions and "various non-religious conditions imposed by state authorities." In other words, the difference between a "normal" and "abnormal" religion often has little to do with any intrinsically religious differences. NRMs must be understood, then, in terms of the broader changes affecting their social context. They are products of, and responses to, the new social pressures to which we are all exposed in late modernity, as well as the age-old spiritual aspirations of humanity (see Dawson 2001).

Students learning about NRMs need to keep both social contexts of contention in mind when reading and studying the literature in the field: consider who is providing the information and why, and recognize that the controversy surrounding NRMs is not so much a clash of strange versus familiar ideas, as a clash of visions of how we should live, and how our societies should be structured.

References

Dawson, Lorne L.1998: *Comprehending Cults: The Sociology of New Religious Movements*. Toronto: Oxford University Press.

——2001: The Cultural Significance of New Religious Movements: The Case of Soka Gakkai. *Sociology of Religion* 62 (3): 337–64.

CHAPTER ONE

The Scientific Study of Religion?
You Must Be Joking!

Eileen Barker

Most of us who have been involved in the study of NRMs during the past quarter of a century or so have enjoyed learning much of interest for the study of religion in general. But several of us have also been bruised and confused, a few of us quite sorely, because of the threat that we have presented to others by our claims to have a more "scientific" – or at least a more balanced, objective, and accurate – or, at very least, a less biased, subjective, and wrong – understanding of the movements than they have.

This has led to a certain amount of navel contemplation about how we might justify our research. *Are* we "doing" a scientific study of religion? What *is* a scientific study of religion? To what extent and why might we claim that we "know better" than some others, including even those who provide the raw data of our research? And, just as importantly, on what matters must we be wary to acknowledge "that whereof we may not speak" – not, that is, as persons claiming to speak as social scientists? . . .

Coming as I do from the London School of Economics, it is not surprising that I have been profoundly influenced by the work of Karl Popper, and if I were forced to select a single criterion that distinguishes a scientific from a pseudo-scientific enterprise, I would chose *to start* with empirical refutability (Popper 1963: 37; 1972: ch 1). But, that said, one needs to continue (as, indeed, Popper

did) by adding a great number of qualifications, especially where the study of society is concerned. Differences between the natural and social sciences that are of relevance in this paper are (a) ontological – concerned with the nature of social reality; (b) epistemological – concerned with how we gain our knowledge of social reality; and (c) ethical and political – how we evaluate our own and others' construction of reality – and what we do about it.

Primary and Secondary Constructions of Social Reality

For the sake of the argument, an analytical distinction needs to be made between primary and secondary constructions of reality. The former comprise the basic data of social science; the latter are accounts of the former. The primary construction of an NRM is the product of direct and indirect interactions between the members of the movement and, to some extent, between members and the rest of society.

Secondary constructions are depictions of the movement that are offered in the public arena by sociologists and others, including the movement itself, *about* the movement. Secondary constructions are, thus, more conscious than primary constructions, although part of the process of the latter may be quite conscious, and the former are by no means always consciously thought through. It should, however, be recognized that the distinction between primary and secondary constructions becomes blurred when one is taking a wider reality into account. Thus, if (as in this paper) we are concerned with "the cult scene," secondary constructions, including those of the sociologist, make a difference and must be considered as part of the primary constructions of *that* social reality.

The concept of social reality is fraught with tensions and paradox. It appeals to both realism and idealism insofar as it is an objective reality, the existence of which no individual members of a social group can wish away any more than they can wish away the existence of a brick wall. At the same time, social reality exists only as ideas in people's heads; if *no one* took it into account (positively or negatively, consciously or unconsciously), it would not exist (Berger and Luckmann 1966). Put another way, although social reality exists independently of the volition of any particular individual, it can exist only insofar as individual human minds are continually recognizing it and acting as the media through which are processed the cultural ideas and meanings, and the roles and expectations that arise from and result in its existence.

This means that, *pace* Wuthnow (1987), if as social scientists we want to understand what is going on, we have no option but to use ourselves as "a medium." A robot cannot do social science; it is not capable of *Verstehen*. It cannot further our understanding beyond the very important ways that logic can further our understanding of what we already know. We need to have some knowledge about the meanings that situations have for individuals. We need to be able to understand how a situation can be perceived.

Of course, others will not perceive it in the same way as we do – *no* two people will perceive a situation in exactly the same way – none of us *ever* has the exact same understanding or perception as anyone else. But – and this is just as important – our perceptions are more or less shared. If they were not shared at all, we would have no society (and no possibility of a social science); and if

they were totally shared, again we would have no society, for there would be no dynamic – no force for change, negotiation, or adjustment to external circumstances.

But these differences between individual perceptions of social reality are not random. The variation will depend upon such factors as people's innate characteristics, their past experiences, hopes, fears, interests, assumptions, values, and expectations and the social position from which they view the reality that confronts them. A new convert will view the NRM from one perspective, seasoned leaders from a different perspective; member's perceptions will differ from nonmembers'; and different groups of nonmembers will perceive the NRM in the light of their own particular interests.

Not only will people *perceive* the movement from different perspectives, they will also *describe* and, perhaps, explain the movement in different ways. Consciously or unconsciously, they will *select* from among the features presented to them. Again, what is included and what excluded in the process of creating their secondary constructions will not be random, but significantly influenced according to their intersts.

The interests of some personally or professionally motivated secondary constructors may lead them to take matters further than a passive reception of their perception. Some, wanting to reinforce an image that has already been delineated, will place themselves in a position that will protect it from disconfirmation and/or supply confirming evidences. Others, wanting to test their secondary construction according to the Popperian criterion, will systematically try to refute their hypotheses. To do this they may actively engage in research which involves as close a scrutiny as possible of the primary construction.

Making a Difference

When I was a student, it was part of the conventional wisdom of the methodology which we were taught that social scientists should be clinically detached observers who noted what was going on but did not allow their observations to affect the data. Such a position is to some extent possible when the scientist is observing through a one-way glass, watching a covertly shot film, or reading diaries or other written materials. But for a number of reasons discussed elsewhere (Barker 1987), I and others have come to believe that such an approach is not only difficult but methodologically inappropriate for the kind of research that is needed for an acceptable secondary construction of NRMs. There is some information that one can acquire only by becoming part of the data and, thus, playing a role in the ongoing social construction of reality. I would even go so far as to say that to remain physically distanced from the data can be methodologically reprehensible – an abrogation of one's responsibility as a social scientist.

But as we step outside the Ivory Tower of academia and become part of the process that we are researching, we are, of course, placing our pristine purity in jeopardy. Most social scientists who have worked "in the field" are aware of the impact that they might have and take this into account when they come to analyze their data. To what extent does the involvement enhance or diminish our "scientific" study of religion? Before addressing this question, let me give some examples to illustrate the variety of ways in which I personally have become conscious that my research was "making a difference."

First of all, just being there can make a difference. When I began studying the Unification Church in the early 1970s, it was a relatively closed community with strong boundaries distinguishing "them" from "us." To have someone living in the community who was not part of "us" threatened and weakened the boundary and, thus, the beliefs and actions associated with a strong-group situation (Douglas 1970). The very fact that a normally impermeable boundary *can* be permeated by an outsider affects the group and its members in a number of concrete ways. For example, one girl left, not because I advised her to do so but, she said, because my anomalous existence as someone who could live both within and without led her to realize that she did not have to make the stark choice between *either* a godly *or* a satanic lifestyle; there could be a middle way which would allow her to pursue an alternative way of serving God without having to deny all that was good about her Unification experience.

At the same time, it is possible that others stayed in the movement, at least for slightly longer than they might otherwise have done, because of the existence of a "professional stranger" (Barker 1987). My presence meant there was someone who would neither report back to the leadership, nor go to the media, but on whom they could off-load their anxieties and frustrations.

Asking questions (in formal interviews, general discussions, or through questionnaire) that no one else has previously asked can lead to an unexpected "raising of consciousness." In the words of one respondent, "It made me take out and look at some of the things I'd been keeping in the pending tray." Sometimes, I was told, the result was a deeper understanding of the theology, but on other occasions the consequence was a growing irritation or suspicion of the leadership. Occasionally a change would be brought about as the result of a group interview offering members the opportunity to discuss openly matters about which they normally kept silent. I gather that a number of fairly radical changes were introduced to an American ISKCON Temple following a day I had spent with a group of female devotees who had not previously shared their feelings of how they were treated by the male hierarchy.

As my research into NRMs progressed, I found myself affecting the situation more consciously. First, I was being asked to mediate between members of movements and their parents, who also formed part of my data. The fact that I could explain the perspective of the movement to nonmembers (and that of nonmembers to members) meant that there was frequently an increased communication and, sometimes, accommodation to the others' points of view as they each reached an increased understanding of how "the other side" saw things.

Then "making a difference" became not merely a result of face-to-face interaction with those individuals who formed part of my data. Publishing books and papers, appearing as a witness in court cases, and making statements in various media about my conception of the NRMs meant that my findings were being presented to a wider audience. Like other scholars, I was offering an alternative perspective that questioned many of the existing secondary constructions and their taken-for-granted assumptions. I was affecting the data not only as part of a methodological procedure, but also as part of a political action.

Once the results of my research became public it became increasingly obvious that they were not to go unchallenged. I had initially contacted the anti-cult movement (ACM) with the somewhat naive belief that, as we were both interested in finding out about NRMs, we might exchange information that could be helpful to us both. My overtures were not merely rejected, the anti-cultists started to launch a full-scale *ad hominem* attack on anything I said or wrote in public; having gone to the NRMs for a significant, though by no means complete part of my research, I was clearly "on the other side." To the astonishment and/or amusement of anyone who knew me, I found myself being labeled a Moonie, a Scientologist, a fundamentalist Christian, or a cult lover – or, by the more benign, an innocent who was being deceived by the movements. *What* I said was rarely questioned – except, curiously enough, for statements for which I had incontrovertible evidence. The first major bone of contention was the membership figures that I publicized, both to the annoyance of the Unification Church (who did not want either their members or the general public to be aware of the very high turnover rates) and to the fury of those members of the ACM who were (and in some cases still are) insistent that the movements use irresistible and irreversible mind control techniques – which would, of course, imply that Unification membership was in the hundreds of thousands if not in the millions, rather than the rather paltry hundreds that I was reporting.

The shift from a methodological to a more politico-ethical involvement in the "cult scene" became even more marked when I reached the conclusion that a considerable amount of unnecessary suffering and unhappinee might be avoided were social scientific constructions of NRMs to compete more robustly in the marketplace. My "Road to Damascus" was an ACM Family Support Group meeting at which an ex-member, whom I happened to know as a thoughtful and honest woman, had been invited to tell her story. It soon became evident that things were not going according to plan. She was resisting the pressure that was being put on her to say how she had suffered, how she had been deceived, and how she had been under the influence of mind control. It was suggested that she had not *really* left the movement and that she was determined to deceive the assembled company. Trying to pour oil on troubled waters, someone asked if she had anything to say that would help the assembled parents. A woman then stood up and shouted "We don't want to hear this; it's just deceit and lies. It's not helpful at all. We don't want to hear any more." At that point I stopped taking notes. Something more, it seemed, needed to be done.

With the support of the British government and mainstream churches, I set up a charity called INFORM (Information Network Focus on Religious Movements) with the aim of providing information that was as objective, balanced, and up to date as possible. In the seven years that have ensued, thousands of relatives and friends of NRM members, ex-members, the media, local and national government, police, social welfare workers, prison chaplains, schools, universities and colleges, traditional religions, and NRMs themselves have contacted the office (located at the London School of Economics) for information and help (Barker 1989a).

I did not consider the founding of INFORM to be part of my research, although it has certainly resulted in my learning a great deal more about the "cult scene." Rather, the aim was to *use* professional knowledge to challenge alternative secondary constructions.

It was not to fight for The Truth in any ideological sense but, minimally, to contest *untrue* statements about NRMs (whether they originate from an NRM or anyone else) . . .

Although INFORM does not see itself as an advice center, it points out the likely consequences of a variety of actions, ranging from joining a new religion to trying to abduct someone from one; it has also been instrumental in mediating between members and their families, and while it certainly does not have a magic wand with which it can solve all problems, the reliability of INFORM's information and its knowledge of the social processes involved in their relationships with the outside world has meant that it has been able to relate to the NRMs in such a way that many of them are willing to cooperate in such matters as putting parents back in touch with their children, or refunding money obtained under duress . . .

It would have been ingenuous to assume that there would not be opposition to an organization such as INFORM. What was unexpected, however, was the virulence with which it has been attacked by a few NRMs, the ACM, some sections of the media, and a small number of individuals with opposing interests. By the late 1980s, it appeared that British anti-cultists were directing more of their resources to trying to discredit us rather than the new religions . . .

The battles continue of course, and while we are making a difference, other people's secondary constructions are also making a difference to "the cult scene" *and* to us. But before giving further consideration to the methodological, ethical, and political implications of such involvement, let us turn to the marketplace and compare the secondary constructs of social science with the competition.

Table 1.1 summarizes some basic differences between six ideal types of secondary constructors: sociologists and others involved in the scientific study of religion, members of the new religions themselves, the anti-cult movement, the media, the legal profession, and therapists (the first four constructors are analyzed in greater detail in Barker 1993a). The types were chosen on the grounds that it

is they who feature most prominently in the competiton with social scientists, but the table could be extended to include the police, the social services, clergy, theologians, educationalists, and any number of other categories of constructors . . .

The sociology of religion

Obviously the particular aims of those concerned with the scientific study of religion will differ from person to person, but most would agree that they wish to present as accurate, objective, and unbiased an account as possible. They will want to describe, understand, and explain social groupings and such phenomena as the power structures, communication networks, and belief systems that enable members to do (or prevent them from doing) things that they could not (or could) do in other social situations. Social scientists will also want to explore and account for the range of different perceptions held by individual actors and to assess the consequences of such differences. The nature of social reality means that the regularities of social science are relative to social space and time in a way that the laws of nature seldom are. Nonetheless, sociological constructions do contain empirically refutable statements, and it is part of the logic of science that the methods and results of its research should be available for public scrutiny: "Our great instrument for progress is criticism" (Popper 1973: 34).

There are those who believe that the task of science is to find out the truth, the whole truth, and nothing but the truth. I disagree. *No one* ever tells the whole truth; no one ever *could*. All secondary constructions consist of both more and less than the primary construction. Although looking for nothing but the truth in the sense that we are committed to accuracy and eliminating falsehoods from both our own and others' constructions, social scientists *select* what will go into our constructions, excluding some aspects that others include, and including further aspects that others exclude.

Not only do social scientists include and exclude for methodological reasons, but also,

Table 1.1 Competing logics in secondary constructions of reality

Secondary constructors	Interest and/or aim	Method	Data selected for inclusion	Data systematically excluded	Mode of communication	Relationship with SoR
Sociology of Religion	Unbiased and objective sociological description, understanding and explanation	Comparison; methodological agnosticism; interview; questionnaire; observation	Individual and social levels; control groups; wider context	Non-empirical evaluation; transcendent variables; definitional essentialism	Scholarly publications; through other secondary constructs	Effect of methods of research; effect of use made of research
NRMs	Primary construction; good PR, promote beliefs	Selective reflection on primary construction	Good behavior; supernatural claims	Bad skeletons; esoteric gnoses	Literature; witnessing	Control of access; use positive evidence
ACM	Warn; expose; control; destroy	Ex-members; parents; media (may be circular)	Atrocity tales	Good behavior; changes for the better	Lobbying; newsletters; media	Use negative data; attack when positive data
Media	Good story; get/keep readers, viewers,	Interview where easy access and/or subject	Topical; relevant; sensational	Everyday; "normal"; unexceptionable	Newspapers, magazines, TV, radio; large public;	Preferred use of ACM where complementary

	and/or listeners	willing to talk; investigative journalism; press releases			short shelf-life; difficult to check or question	interests; SoR used more if new, pithy, sexy and/or sensational
Law	"Justice" according to the law of the land; winning case for individual	Adversarial; confrontational; positive *vs* negative	Evidence presented by the two opposing sides; expert witnesses; legal precedent	Middle ground, not making positive or negative point; what deemed irrelevant to the case; inadmissible evidence	Legal judgments common law; media reports	Impartial expert or whore witness?
Therapy	Help client to get better and to cope with "reality"	Listen, accept, and/or construct client's version of reality	Individual's perception; pragmatic constructs	Other versions of reality	Direct to client; courts; media; professional carers	Competition over importance of "whole" and professional expertise

perhaps paradoxically, because it is only by doing this that an understanding of the primary construction may be transmitted to others. An example I sometimes use to illustrate the importance of *not* replicating the original too precisely is that of an actor playing a bore. The actor is successful in communicating something of the essence of being a bore only insofar as he is not boring. Similarly, in order to communicate something of the essence of an NRM, social scientists have to "interpret" or "translate" the primary constructions so that their audience can understand what may have been incomprehensible when they were looking at the movement itself. Raëlians can tell their parents what it means to them to be a Raëlian, but the parents may be incapable of hearing what is being said. There would be absolutely on point in the sociologist's merely reproducing what the Raëlian says and does – this has to be put in a wider context; both more and less has to be offered to the parent – less, in that we do not tell the parent things that seem irrelevant (that they clean their teeth every morning) – more, in that we add information that relates what they believe and do to the understanding of the parent. For this we need to know not only what Raëlians believe and do, but also what the parent can understand. We are not being selective in the sense that we are being untruthful or keeping back truths; we are representing rather than presenting.

Thus, the constructs of social science *exclude details that do not seem to be of particular interest*. Part of what we decide *is* of interest will depend upon what we and our potential audience consider useful knowledge – either because we believe it will further our general understanding of social behavior, or because we believe that it could be of practical use in implementing our own or society's interests.

Next, the constructs of social science *exclude theological judgments*. The sociology of religion is concerned with who believes what under what circumstances, how beliefs become part of the cultural milieu and are used to interpret people's experiences, and what the consequences of holding particular beliefs may be; but it can neither deny nor confirm ideological beliefs. Social scientists *qua* social scientists have to remain *methodologically agnostic*. The epistemology of an empirical science has no way of knowing whether God, gods, the Devil, angels, evil spirits, or the Holy Spirit have been acting as independent variables; and miracles, by definition, are beyond the purview of science.

Then, social scientists *stipulate* what they mean by particular concepts or use ideal types (Weber 1947: 92) for the purposes of a particular study, but they cannot claim that these definitions are either true or false, merely that they are more or less useful. Of course, concepts are "given" (data) in the sense that they are part of primary constructions and our accounts will *report* what people mean by concepts such as "religion." We also note that different groups use, negotiate, or manipulate definitions to further their own interests (Barker 1994; Douglas 1966) . . .

Most social scientists would agree that they ought to try to *exclude their own subjective evaluations* from the actual collection and analysis of data. . . . Of course, as any methodology book will testify, there are many ways in which our values *do* enter the research and skew the outcome: we cannot interpret the reality that we are studying except by using our own subjective perception; concepts can be value laden; we may be working with unexamined assumptions which have implication for our perception; and so on. But we do try to be aware of and counter such obstacles by various techniques so as to produce descriptions that are as objective as possible in the sense that they are concerned with the object of our study rather than our own or others' subjective beliefs.

But social science not only excludes ideological, definitional, and evaluative concerns, it *includes* interests that extend beyond any NRM under study. Study of the primary construction through interview, questionnaire, participant observation, and the examination of written material needs to be supplemented with data from further sources, all of which may be necessary, but none sufficient for the kind of picture that the sociologist needs to construct

(Barker 1984: 124–33). We may want to check where individual members are "coming from" by speaking to people who have known them both before and after their conversion. Ex-members comprise an invaluable source of further information and for checking the veracity of what members are reporting. It does, however, have to be remembered that no single member (past or present) is likely to know everything that is going on in the movement. The sociological construction of an NRM requires, moreover, information about yet others who have no relationship whatsoever with the movement. This is because a fundamental component of science is the comparative method, which, by putting the NRM in a wider frame of reference, brings *balance* into the equation. In order to able to understand and test "what variable varies with what," the primary construction has to be compared with other primary constructions, using control groups (although this has become distressingly rare in monographs) and techniques such as the statistical manipulation of data about the population as a whole to test for correlations. Such tools of the trade serve, minimally, to eliminate some mistakes that we might otherwise make.

The new religions

NRMs have an interest in gaining new members and, perhaps, political and financial or legal advantage by presenting a secondary construction of their own primary reality in the public domain. As with most organizations, one would expect the movement to select those aspects that show it in a favorable light and be less forthcoming about skeletons in the cupboard. Unlike the social scientist, the NRM will draw on nonempirical revelations to describe and explain at least part of its construction of reality (that, for example, God is responsible for revelations and conversions, and/or that evil forces are responsible for things that go wrong); and it will, of course, be anxious to proclaim the truth of its theological teachings – unless there are esoteric gnoses, in which case these will be kept secret.

Clearly, there is a sense in which an NRM has privileged access to its own reality – but it is also possible to argue that the very fact of their involvement means that members are unable or unwilling to see what is going on with the same detachment as some outsiders (Wilson 1970: ix–xiii). There are, however, members of NRMs such as Mickler (1980, 1992) and Jules-Rosette (1975) who, *as social scientists*, have done excellent work on their own NRMs.

The Anti-cult Movement (ACM)

The ACM includes a wide variety of organizations with members as diverse as anxious parents, ex-members, professional deprogrammers, and "exit counselors." In some ways, the ACM can be seen as a mirror image of the NRM. Both tend to want a clear, unambiguous division between "us" and "them"; but while the NRM will select only good aspects, the ACM selects only bad aspects. Most ACM pronouncements tend to be about "destructive cults," lumping all NRMs together as though they were a single entity, the sins of one being visited on all. Any evidence or argument that could complicate or disprove their negative construction (or reform that may be introduced) is more likely to be ignored or dismissed than denied.

As lobbyists, anti-cultists have to be proactive not only in promoting their constructions but also in denying or dismissing other constructions and denigrating the constructors. Sociological secondary constructions may appear more threatening to the ACM than those of the NRMs, the latter being more likely to agree with the ACM where there are clear boundaries; they can, furthermore, be goaded into reinforcing the anti-cult position by responding to it in an unambiguously negative fashion, exacerbating the process of "deviance amplification" and, thereby, justifying further accusations by the ACM.

Social scientists, members of the media, the legal profession, and therapists have a professional interest in their secondary constructions' achieving their relevant aims, but they do not usually expect to gain much more from their work in the area of NRMs than they would by doing their work well in any other area. When we turn to the ACM and NRMs, however, we find that most of the rank and file membership do their work either on a purely voluntary basis or with little more than living expenses because they believe, sometimes quite passionately, that what they are doing is right – they have a mission to fight evil.

There are, however, also "charismatic leaders" in the NRMs and "leading experts" in the ACM, both of whom may reap enormous financial benefits from having their constructions of reality accepted. Stories about the wealth controlled by Sun Myung Moon, L. Ron Hubbard, or Bhagwan Rajneesh (with his 97 Rolls Royces and collection of Rolex watches) are common enough. What is less well known is the vast amount of money at stake in the fostering of the brainwashing or mind control thesis in ACM secondary constructions. On the one hand, "deprogrammers" and, to a somewhat lesser extent, "exit counselors" can charge tens of thousands of dollars for their services; on the other hand, "expert witnesses" have charged enormous fees for giving evidence about brainwashing in court cases . . .

The sharp "them/us" perspective of the ACM is reflected in the fact that it frequently operates under a cloak of secrecy. Not only the NRMs, but also social scientists may be denied access to allegedly open meetings and refused requests for information or evidence that could corroborate assertions made in ACM constructions of reality. One anti-cultist who repeatedly claims that NRMs use hypnosis to recruit members refuses to tell me which movements he is talking about on the grounds that he does not trust me because I am "on the other side." Other information that is presumably nonconfidential and which one might have though the ACM would want widely disseminated is jealously guarded. The secrecy is, of course, perfectly understandable when it concerns the planning of an illegal kidnapping and deprogramming.

Given its aims, the ACM does not lay stress on either objectivity or balance in its secondary constructions of reality – in fact,

members will frequently admit quite openly that they consider a balanced presentation of the facts counterproductive . . .

As a matter of principle, anti-cultists are likely to refuse to have direct contact with the primary construction itself as a source of information. This is justified by the premise that cults are, almost by definition, bound to practice deception and are probably dangerous. Data for ACM stories tend, therefore, to be collected from anxious parents, disillusioned exmembers, and negative media reports. Often there is a circularity involved in that the anxious parents have been alerted to the negative aspects of their child's movement by anti-cult "atrocity tales" (Shupe and Bromley 1980); the ex-members have been taught by deprogrammers or exit counselors to believe that they were brainwashed and that their whole experience is to be interpreted in negative terms (Lewis 1986; Solomon 1981; Wright 1987); and the media frequently get their stories from the ACM which then uses the fact that the story has appeared in print as proof that it has been independently verified. There have been cases where the media have included rebuttals to a story supplied to them by the ACM, which has then innocently asked why the question was raised in the first place, suggesting that there is no smoke without a fire – even when they themselves had kindled the fire . . .

The media

The overriding interest of the mass media is to get a good story that will keep the loyalty of readers, viewers, and/or listeners and, if possible, to gain new audiences. They are unlikely to be interested in presenting an everyday story of how "ordinary" life in an NRM can be, or even of the rewards that it offers contented members – unless it can expose these as fraudulent, fantastic, or sensational. The media are nearly always working to a tight deadline – very tight compared to the months or years that scholars may spend on their research. They are also limited in the amount of time or space that they have to present their story. Only rarely will the electronic media concentrate on a single topic for more than thirty minutes and only rarely do the printed media allocate mote than a few hundred words.

Pressure of space and time means that members of the media collect their data from sources selected for accessibility and the provision of good quotes. "The grieving mother" or "The man who risked prison to save a helpless victim from the clutches of a bizarre cult" are far more valuable informants than "The mother whose devotee son visits her on a regular basis," "The Moonie who passed his exams with good marks" – or, indeed, the academic who is full of long-winded qualifications. Many (though by no means all) of the media tend, moreover, to be remarkably reluctant to ask members of NRMs for their own versions of reality, and to dismiss press releases from the movements far more readily than they dismiss the information handed out by the ACM. This may seem somewhat surprising to anyone who has researched NRMs and learned what extraordinary statements they themselves are capable of producing; yet on numerous occasions when I have offered to give journalists a contact number for one of the movements, they have dismissed the offer, saying either that they would not get the truth or that their editors would expect them to use a more reliable source.

Unlike social scientists, the media are under no obligation to introduce comparisons to assess the relative rates of negative incidents. Thus, when reporting a tragedy or some kind of malpractice, they note in the headline that the victim or the perpetrator was a cultist, but are unlikely to mention it anywhere in the report if he or she were a Methodist. The result is that even if such tragedies and malpractices are relatively *infrequent* they would still be more visible and, thereby, become disproportionately associated with the NRMs in the public mind.

Not only does the logic of the aims and interests of the media result in their seldom being able to go into the kind of depth or ensure the kind of balance that social science would demand, their social position means that the secondary constructions that they create are both powerful (due do their widespread circulation and interest-appeal) and extremely difficult to check or correct. Complaints and apologies can be made, but they rarely attract as much attention as the original story. Usually it is difficult to track down the story for a second look; a transient television report or a story in a newspaper or magazine long since thrown away leaves an impression but not something that can be scrutinized, and there are seldom references that can be followed up. Even with more balanced programs and articles, it is the more sensationalist images that are likely to stick in the mind. It is only those programs and stories selected by the ACM for quotation that are likely to be preserved for recycling.

The law

The primary interest of the law as represented by a judge and, sometimes, jury, is to ensure that justice is carried out according to the law of the land. No attempt is made to present a complete or balanced picture of a primary construction, but only to point to those aspects that could be of relevance to the case. Indeed, some information (such as previous convictions) that might be pertinent for a more general understanding are ruled out of court as inadmissible evidence. As far as the defense and the prosecution are concerned, their specific interest is to win the case for their clients. Each side will attempt to construct a picture of reality that is advantageous to its own position and disadvantageous to other side. Although is might be argued that, adjudicating between two opposing sides, the judge (or jury) would be able to reach a middle position, there is no guarantee that a middle position is a true position. To begin with, we may ask, middle of what? It is the court that has set the goal posts and the true position might or might not be somewhere (anywhere) between them.

The law does make use of "expert witnesses" who usually present their credentials as representatives of the scientific community, so one might, *prima facie*, expect the expert witness to produce a secondary construction of reality that corresponds to that of the social scientist, but in fact this is not necessarily the case. One reason is that lawyers will invite those witnesses who are known to hold views that support their client's case, but a more fundamental reason is that it is the court that decides what questions will and will not be asked and, thus, answered.

In short, the adversarial procedure is to argue for and against opposing versions of reality, either or both of which may be grossly distorted versions of a primary construction. This might not matter if the procedure were used only for the purposes of the court. But there is plenty of evidence that decisions on one matter are frequently used by others to "prove" a version of reality that may have little relevance, even to what came up in the case (Barker 1989b: 197–201).

Therapists

Like defense lawyers, therapists and counselors have an interest in helping their client. But instead of needing to establish their client's version of reality to score a public victory over an opposing version, they may need to help the client to construct privately a new reality that he or she can live with and feel good about. Practices do, of course, vary enormously – many therapists will try to help the client to reach a clearer understanding of the primary construction in which the client is or was a participant – but it will be a practical construction that has the client at its center, rather than a balanced appraisal of the group as a whole. In fact, therapists who have been interested enough in NRMs to attend the INFORM counseling seminars will, when a particular client is referred to them, ask *not* to be given background information such as a detailed account of the movement in question. This is because they feel that it might interfere with their relationship with the client – it would be a kind of betrayal to hear a point of view other than that of the client.

Let me be quite clear, this is not a criticism of these therapists who play an effective role in their clients' recovery from difficult experiences. It is merely to point out that they have

a different aim from social scientists and will, therefore, use different methods and employ different kinds of knowledge; the secondary construction of the therapist can be different from but complementary to that of the social scientist. Conflicts between the two constructors emerge, however, when counselors and therapists claim to know what a particular movement – or NRMs in general – are like through their client-focused work. This is likely to arise when therapists give evidence as expert witnesses in court or present their stories to the media and/or at public meetings. Again, there would be no conflict if the stories were confined to descriptions of ways in which people might be helped rather than claims being made that these are proven accurate, balanced portrayals of the primary construction as they come from a "professional" source. They are, of course, from a professional source, but, as with the court, the profession is not one that aims primarily to construct an accurate and balanced account.

Two of the main situations in which counselors and therapists have crossed swords with sociologists are (a) over the so-called brainwashing or mind-control thesis (see above) and (b) over allegations of ritual satanic abuse. Studies in the latter area have revealed a considerable body of evidence showing that therapists may not only help clients to construct a secondary version of reality, but some construct a version of reality themselves, and then put considerable pressure on the client to accept it (Mulhern 1984; Richardson et al. 1991; but see also Houston 1993: 9).

Beyond the Ivory Tower

Although social science cannot claim to be as "scientific" as the natural sciences, it is unquestionably more scientific than its competitors. The *logic* of its approach is infinitely superior for producing balanced and accurate accounts of NRMs than is that of any of its competitors. Undifferentiated relativism, as espoused by some of the exponents of deconstructionism and postmodernism, seems to me to be just plain silly. The rules of science (even loosely characterized as in this paper) are not merely a language game; they are an assurance of a minimal, albeit limited, epistemological status. We would be crazy to argue that *anything* goes – some things are patently false, and empirical observation can demonstrate this to anyone with their faculties in good working order. Assuredly, some statements (moral evaluations and claims about the supernatural) are not empirically testable and it would be equally crazy to believe that we could prove or disprove them to someone holding a different opinion. But such statements are not within the purview of social science. I am not suggesting that social science holds a monopoly on The Truth. Far from it. But I am suggesting that the methods of social science (its openness to criticism and empirical testing and, above all, its use of the comparative method) ought to ensure that it produces a more balanced and *more useful* account than that of its competitors for seeing the way things are and the way things might be – *not* for deciding how they ought to be, but for implementing decisions about how they ought to be.

Should social scientists get involved with the use to which their secondary constructions are put and, thereby, become part of the primary construction of the wider "cult scene" not merely for methodological reasons (as discussed earlier), but for ethical or political purposes? Is such involvement compatible with, inimical to, or a question of indifference for the scientific study of religion? What if, in the course of our research, we frequently come across misunderstandings, misinformation, and/or gross distortions that appear to cause unnecessary suffering and are related to a subject that we have been investigating by methods that we believe to be superior to those that have given rise to the errors? What if we find that there are people who, claiming a professional expertise, maintain that they have arrived at certain conclusion using the scientific method, yet they provide no testable evidence, and we suspect that the scientific method not only does not, but could not, produce such conclusions? Should we not . . . fight ignorance, exploitation, and prejudice or

at least correct inaccurate statements in our own field? Or do we just publish our misgivings . . . on the chance that someone else might read what we have written and use it to challenge the alternative versions?

I know of nothing in the scientific enterprise that suggests social scientists *ought* to champion their versions of reality in the marketplace. At the same time, I know of nothing intrinsic to science that would proscribe such involvement. Indeed, those of us who *have* felt drawn to use the secondary constructs of the social scientific study of religion are, rightly or wrongly, of the opinion that we have as much right as anyone (and more relevant knowledge than many) not only to promote the social scientific perspective, but also to question others' secondary constructions when we consider them to be either inaccurate or biased.

But life is not that simple. As we step outside the relative protection of the Ivory Tower, we can find ourselves being affected by our competitors. I have already intimated that, while our presence is welcomed by some, it poses a threat to others. But it poses a threat to us too – not just the unpleasantness of the ways we are sometimes attacked, but a more insidious threat to the very meta-values and methods that can give us the edge over our competitors.

What I want to explore for the rest of this paper are some ways in which the very fact that we become actors in a competitive market means that we come under pressure to incorporate some of our competitors' interests and methods into our own practices. We are in danger of letting our competitors define our agenda.

The means by which the different secondary constructors sell their wares is of crucial significance for their success or failure, and the first hurdle social scientists face is how to set up a stall in a good position in the marketplace. When social scientists have completed their research they are quite likely to publish the results in scholarly books or journals which may sit on dusty shelves with few save other social scientists being aware of their existence. . . . [These writings] might give rise to internal debates, but if we are not heard by outsiders not only may we be missing some valuable feedback, we are also likely to be excluding ourselves from making any difference to "the cult scene."

We may need to be more conscious than is our wont that what we present should come across as being of relevance for the audience we want to reach. I am not suggesting that we fudge our results so that they are acceptable. On the contrary, I am suggesting that, like the actor playing a bore, we need to present our results so that they are understandable and *heard*, whether or not they are welcomed – especially, perhaps, if we suspect that they are not going to be welcomed . . . to those who with no particular axe to grind, are interested in accurate and balanced accounts of NRMs. But how can we make our construction available without jeopardizing the integrity of our account?

Playing their game

The most obvious way to disseminate our version is to cooperate with the mass media, and there are plenty of producers and journalists who are willing, even eager, to use our information. But, as we have seen, their main objective is to have a gripping story. How do we collaborate? On their terms or ours? There is a limit to the number of "on the one hand . . . on the other hands", 'howevers", or "nonetheless's" that they can accommodate. How much of a price must we be prepared to pay? Do we hope, as with the abstract to an article, that the absence of qualification is made up for by the wide and clear dissemination of the main points?

What about our being misquoted? We learn through hard experience which are the more unreliable media – and it is nearly always those who are getting our story second or third hand; few (though some) members of the media deliberately misrepresent their informants. There are, however, some who do deliberately mislead us to "set us up to put us down." We have no control over the editing of what we say – and others say about us. Even in a live broadcast it can be extremely difficult to get across one's actual position if misrepre-

sented or suddenly attacked for something we have never done. We can protest, but most of us tend to be so taken aback that we find ourselves unable to think up an effective response – until we are off-air. Apart form being extremely frustrating and unpleasant, such experiences can make one wonder whether agreeing to take part in any program is not simply counterproductive.

But such behavior is the exception rather than the rule (and antagonistic programs often elicit more letters of support than protest). What is more to the point here is that we do not react to the pressures of media interests or the competition of ACM interests by allowing ourselves to slip into facile generalizations for the sake of a good sound bite, that we do not make cheap jokes at the expense of someone else's beliefs, that we do not pass judgments about which are the "good" and which the "bad" cults – which is not to say that we cannot report that in movement X they carry out child sacrifice, in Y they have weekly sex orgies, and in Z they pray to little green men in flying saucers – so long, of course, that what we say is true and we make it clear that the other 99.9 percent of NRMs do not do such things. The media usually give us an opportunity to put things in context through comparisons, although I have been asked not to quote Luke 14:26, as it results in so many angry denials that Jesus ever said such a thing.

Our relationship with the courts is in some respects like that with the media. It is they who are largely in control of both the content and the context of what is transmitted. It is they who ask the questions. If we do not bow to their interests, they will ignore us and, in all likelihood, turn to our competitors. If our unbiased perspective results in our giving responses in court that are helpful to one side on one occasion but damaging on another occasion, lawyers brand us as "unreliable" or "whore witnesses." There can be temptation to say just what the side that calls us (pays us) wants us to say, collaborating in the suppression of relative information or distorting with sophistry the position of the other side.

Taking sides or sitting on the fence?

A more subtle problem arises when, trying to *appear* balanced, we become unbalanced. Broad-minded and liberal media often ask us to give an objective and balanced point of view in the middle – which usually means halfway between an NRM and the ACM. But, as was intimated when discussing legal constructions, to give a balanced account is not necessarily to be in the middle. Science is not summing two extreme positions and dividing by two. Sometimes one "side" *is* right – but to say so may be seen, even by ourselves, as "taking sides." Indeed, a question that is constantly posed by both competitors and potential buyers is "whose side are you on?" The social scientist's answer might be "the side of accuracy and balance," but we find ourselves being pushed and pulled in a number of directions. Some of us hold back information because we fear that we might be taken to court and, even if we feel confident that we could eventually vindicate what we say, it could still cost us a lot of time and money. Sometimes it is the producer or publisher who does not dare risk a court case and we do not want the hassle of finding a bolder (or perhaps more foolhardy) producer or publisher.

While codes of ethics have been produced by professional organizations (the British Sociological Association has such a code), there are gray areas where our personal feelings may incline us one way rather than another. We may not want to betray confidences about individual informants. This is normally not too great a problem as we can usually find some way to preserve a person's anonymity while incorporating the information if it is of importance. But I have given information to the police or other authorities, such as the Charity Commissioners or the social services, or, occasionally, to the more reputable media when I have learned of criminal or anti-social activities. Has this been a betrayal of trust? Would *not* telling not be a betrayal of another kind of trust? I believe that any citizens in a democratic country, be they social scientists or not, have a duty to other members of society not to allow criminal or harmful behavior to go unquestioned, but it is

not always easy to see how widely one should disseminate this information. One may want to alert the public to potential problems, but one also needs to be aware that, irresponsibly used, such information might lead to greater damage. Evangelical countercultists alerting the public to the dangers of ritual satanic abuse have provided us with a salutary warning (Richardson et al. 1991).

The NRMs we study are likely to want us to take their side – several of them have actually approached social scientists because they believed that, even if we do not do a "whitewash," we shall at least be fairer to them than most other constructors (Barker 1984: 15 1995: 176). To a greater or lesser extent, we have been subjected to "love-bombing," hints of eternal damnation and/or emotional blackmail. Such techniques tend to be countersuggestive for seasoned researchers, and despite the fact that some NRMs many try to convert us, we are unlikely to start promoting their beliefs, proclaiming Moon the messiah or Berg an Endtime prophet. Nonetheless, the very fact that they give us time, that we accept their hospitality (be it a cup of tea or an expenses-paid conference), might make us feel beholden to them. But then, we might feel equally or more beholden to their parents and others whom we also meet in the course of our investigations – and, perhaps, to society as a whole. Certainly, the fact that we are fellow human beings means that as we get to know those whom we are studying as individuals we may make friends (or, conversely, may generate antagonisms). We may come to feel protective and when we see them attacked unfairly come to their defense. There is nothing wrong in this if we are merely introducing into the scene an accurate and balanced version of the NRM reality, but what would be reprehensible according to the canons of science is if, feeling bound by friendship or loyalty to "our" NRM, we promote what we know from our research to be a biased version of the truth.

More frequently, I suspect, we have held back information for the scientifically questionable reason that we felt that the way information would be used would be unacceptable to us. Here I am referring less to a "pull" from the NRM than to a "push" from the ACM or sections of the media. We have learned from experience that the negative aspects we report will be taken out of context and added to the list of "bad things that cults do," while the more positive aspects will be ignored or taken as proof that we have been deceived or bought off. I am, moreover, painfully aware that what I am now writing offers our competitors further evidence that we are not as scientific as we pretend – the dilemma here being that the *suppression* of discussion of such concerns would be the more unscientific pretense.

If we are to be honest and self-critical, we have to admit that several of us have reacted against the selective negativity of the ACM by, sometimes quite unconsciously, making our own unbalanced selections. Having been affronted by what have appeared to be gross violations of human rights perpetrated through practices such as deprogramming and the medicalization of belief, there have been occasions when social scientists have withheld information about the movements because they know that this will be taken, possibly out of context, to be used as a justification for such actions. The somewhat paradoxical situation is that the more we feel the NRMs are having *untrue* bad things said about them, the less inclined we are to publish *true* "bad" things about the movements.

The other side of the same coin is that there are social scientists who have felt that they have had to publish negative material and withhold more positive aspects because they are aware that they are in danger of being defined as cult apologists or accused of being covert members of a movement that they have been studying. I know of two sociologists of religion who have been warned that they would be denied tenure or not be awarded their Ph.D. if they did not make it quite clear that their monographs were *exposés*.

As the converse of "taking sides," we are not infrequently stung by the comment that we insist on sitting on the fence and that we are indifferent to the suffering of others. Most of us have infuriated the media by refusing to give unequivocal answers to questions about who the goodies or, more frequently, the baddies are. (A frustrated journalist once made me the butt of a humorous article entitled *No Room for a View*). But if we are being interviewed as social scientists, we need to declare the limits of our expertise and make it clear that we have no special criterion to choose between opposing theological or moral claims. The meta-values of science require us to use the hypothetical form in answer to ethical or definitional questions. Of course, it is silly to be too pedantic with statements such as "if you consider multiple murder a bad thing, then you will not consider the Manson Family a good thing" or "it all depends what you mean by ritual sacrifice."

And, of course, we have as much right as anyone else to express our beliefs so long as it is quite clear that we are speaking as a private citizen. But, just because most of us are *not* indifferent to what is going on, some of us have taken advantage of the air time to communicate our own values and prejudices. And while we are unlikely to promote a particular theological belief, we are quite likely to start from an assumption that, for example, prophecies will fail. While we are unlikely to make a prescriptive distinction between benign and destructive cults, we do tend to produce examples of behavior that we consider (or believe our audience will consider) either reprehensible or praiseworthy if we want to make a point – especially when we want to question a competitor's claims about the movements. Similarly, when social scientists have been pressed in a court of law to say whether a particular NRM is "really" a religion, they have not always insisted as clearly as they might that science cannot *give* the definition of a real religion. It is only when the court provides a definition, or we use the form "if by religion you mean . . .," that we can say whether, *according to that definition*, the movement is "really" religious.

The loneliness of the long-term researcher

The loneliness, psychological and emotional discomfort, and the intellectual uncertainties of research can become greatly intensified as we move into the competitive market. It is not unusual for the social scientist to wonder why no one else's construction seems to tally with the reality that he or she is perceiving (Asch 1959; Barker 1992: 246–7; 1984: 21–2). Sometimes we long to find others who agree and who might thereby save us from the gnawing doubts which can at times reach a point where it is difficult to be certain even on those matters about which we ourselves must be the best placed to know the truth. Responses to the feeling of isolation vary, but they are seldom conducive to scientific study. A few succumb to the desire to "belong" and become involved with or, very occasionally, join the ACM or an NRM. Others avoid or drop out of the arena altogether. For some of us the emotional discomfort of being branded "the enemy" becomes so disagreeable that we find excuses for not checking out our sources as thoroughly as we might. On a couple of occasions, I have found myself asking colleagues or students to deputize for me at meeting at which I suspected I would be attacked. Although I rationalized this cowardice by saying I was too busy or that those going in my place would cause less antagonism and therefore get a better idea of what was happening, I suspect that the truth was that I would have preferred not to find out what was going on rather than subject myself to the unpleasantness once more.

The situation becomes compounded when a group of social scientists who have been similarly vilified get together and exchange their experiences . . . In some ways we are doing precisely what members of a professional body are expected to do – exchanging information and providing a critique of each other's work. But one can also recognize the process whereby we are creating a cozy little support group within which we collaborate to construct a monolithic image of the ACM, taking insufficient account of the differences and changes within the movement as we collectively confirm our prejudices about "them" (but see Bromley and Shupe 1995). Insofar as we respond to the ACM's response to us in this way, we are in danger of ignoring what it has to say that might be of relevance to our understanding of the NRMs, but also, and more significantly so far as the topic of this paper is concerned, of actually obstructing ourselves from acquiring a fuller understanding of how the ACM operates within the cult scene. The fact that it is unpleasant, or in some cases impossible, to have direct access to certain groups or members of the ACM does not excuse us for characterizing them by the very methods that we accuse them of using in their characterization of us and the NRMs . . .

Conclusion

Social reality is not an unchanging structure; it is an ongoing process that exists only insofar as individuals recognize its existence and act as the media through which it is processed. Whilst some perceptions always overlap, no two people ever share exactly the same vision of reality. All constructions of social reality are more or less affected not only by subjective understandings (previous experiences, values, assumptions, hopes, fears, and expectations), but also by the social position from which the social reality is perceived. Secondary constructions exhibit differences that can be observed to vary systematically and significantly according to the professional or group interests of the constructors.

As social scientists, we are interested in producing accurate and balanced constructions. To achieve this objective, we may believe that, rather than remaining clinically removed, part of our research necessitates an involvement with the people we are studying. This gives rise to the complication that we are likely to affect, and may ourselves be affected by, our data – a complication that becomes even more acute if, as individuals holding certain values, we actively engage in competing in the open market with others who are trying to sell their secondary constructions of the same primary reality.

. . . I do not believe that the idea of a scientific study of religion is utterly ridiculous. I would like to affirm that the exercise of social science is, despite its problems, an important and valuable discipline. We have a method-o-logic that can produce a more accurate and balanced account of social reality than those adopted by other secondary constructors. So far as "the cult scene" is concerned, I have argued that methodologically we ought to "get in there" to find out what's going on, and that politically me may, perhaps even should, "make a difference." We ought to communicate so that we can be *heard*; there is no reason why we should not fight ignorance and misinformation when we see it. Nor is there any reason why, *as citizens*, we should not use the findings of social science to fight bigotry, injustice, and what we conceive to be unnecessary misery.

But if we are to take on this mission, we also need to be careful that we do not throw the baby out with the bathwater or, to mix my metaphors still further, let the political tail wag the empirical dog. We need to be more aware, careful, and true to our meta-values as professional social scientists than has sometimes been the case. We need to recognize that others may start defining our agenda – that we could be starting to select and evaluate according to criteria that violate the interests of social sciences. And when promoting and defending our versions of reality, we must remember that we can claim professional proficiency only within a limited area – that there are many legitimate questions which we cannot and should not address – *qua* social scientists.

If we are to preserve our expertise . . . then we need to sharpen our tools of reflexive awareness, open debate, and constructive critique. We need to keep a constant vigilance not only on the pronouncements that we . . . make in the name of social science, but also on the pronouncements others make in the name of social science . . .

References

Asch, Solomon E. 1959. Effects of group pressure upon the modification and distortion of judgments. *In Readings in social psychology* (3rd edition), edited by Eleanor E. Maccoby et al., 174–83. London: Methuen.

Barker, Eileen. 1984. *The making of a Moonie: Brainwashing or choice?* Reprinted by Gregg Revivals, Aldershot, 1993.

——1987. Brahmins don't eat mushrooms: Participant observation and the new religions. *LSE Quarterly* 1: 127–52.

——1989a. *New religious movements: A practical introduction*. London: HMSO.

——1989b. Tolerant discrimination: Church, state and the new religions. In *Religion, state and society in modern Britain*, edited by Paul Badham, 185–208. Lewiston, NY: Edwin Mellen Press.

——1992. Authority and dependence in new religious movements. In *Religion: Contemporary issues. The All Souls Seminars in the sociology of religion*, edited by Bryan Wilson, 237–55. London: Bellew.

——1993a. Will the real cult please stand up? In *Religion and the social order: The handbook of cults and sects in America*, edited by David G. Bromley and Jeffrey Hadden, 193–211. Greenwich, CT, and London: JAI Press.

——1993b. Behold the New Jerusalems! *Sociology of Religion* 54: 337–52.

——1994. But is it a genuine religion? In *Between sacred and secular: Research and theory on quasi-religion*, edited by Arthur L. Greil and Thomas Robbins, 69-88. Greenwich. CT, and London: JAI Press.

——1995. Plus ça change. In *20 years on: Changes in new religious movements*. Special edition of *Social Compass* 42, edited by Eileen Barker and Jean-François Mayer, 165–80.

Berger, Peter and Thomas Luckmann. 1966. *The social construction of reality*. London: Penguin.

Bromley, David G. and Anson Shupe. 1995. Anticultism in the United States. *Social Compass* 42: 221–36.

Douglas, Mary. 1966. *Purity and danger*. London: Routledge and Kegan Paul.

——1970. *Natural symbols: Explorations in cosmology*. London: Barrie and Rockliff.

Houston, Gaie. 1993. The meanings of power. *Self and Society* 21: 4–9.

Jules-Rosette, Bennetta. 1975. *African apostles*. Ithaca, NY: Cornell University Press.

Lewis, James R.1986. Restructuring the 'cult' experienece. *Sociological Analysis* 47: 151–9.

Mickler, Michael L. 1980. *A history of the Unification Church in the Bay Area: 1960–74*. MA thesis. Graduate Theological Union, University of California, Berkeley.

——1992. The politics and political influence of the Unification Church. Paper given at SSSR, Washington, DC.

Mulhern, Sherrill. 1994. Satanism, ritual abuse, and multiple personality disorder: A sociohistorical perspective. *The International Journal of Clinical and Experimental Hypnosis* 42: 265–88.

Popper, Karl. 1963. *Conjectures and refutations: The growth of scientific knowledge*. London: Routledge.

——1972. *Objective knowledge: An evolutionary approach*. Oxford: Clarendon Press.

Radcliffe-Brown, A. R. 1950. On joking relationships. *Africa* 13: 195–210.

Richardson, James T., Joel Best, and David G. Bromley (eds.) 1991. *The satanism scare*. New York: de Gruyter.

Runciman, W. G. 1969. Siciological evidence and political theory. In *Philosophy, politics and society*, 2nd series, edited by Peter Laslett and W. G. Runciman, 34–47. Oxford: Blackwell.

Shupe, Anson D. and David G. Bromley. 1980. *The new vigilantes*. Beverly Hills, CA: Sage.

Solomon, Trudy. 1981. Integrating the 'Moonie' experience. In *In Gods we trust*, edited by Thomas Robbins and Dick Anthony, 275–94. New Brunswick, NJ, and London: Transaction.

Weber, Max. 1947. *The theory of social and economic organization*. New York: Free Press.

Wilson, Bryan (ed.) 1970. *Rationality*. Oxford: Blackwell.

Wright, Stuart. 1987. *Leaving cults: The dynamics of defection*. Washington, DC: SSSR.

Wuthnow, Robert. 1987. *Meaning and moral order: Explorations in cultural analysis*. Berkeley: University of California Press.

CHAPTER TWO

The Continuum Between "Cults" and "Normal" Religion

JAMES A. BECKFORD

Introduction

While dramatic and tragic events have been unfolding around the world in connection with religious movements as varied as Aum Shinrykyo, the Branch Davidians, the Solar Temple, and Heaven's Gate, a "shadow drama" has been taking place in various countries of Western and Eastern Europe. I am referring to the succession of public inquiries and official reports on religious sects or "cults" which have emerged from France, Germany, Spain, Belgium, and Russia in recent years. There have also been debates in the European Parliament. Some of these reports have recommended draconian measures to deal with what is often perceived as the serious problem of "so-called sects," "destructive cults," or "psychogroups." Levels of anxiety, at least among some citizens and public officials, are high – even about groups as old and well known as the Jehovah's Witnesses and the Mormons.

Public concern about the gas attacks carried out in Japan and the suicides in other places in fully understandable. The case of the Branch Davidians is more complicated because public concern is about the violent actions taken by the US authorities as well as about the reports of authoritarianism, exploitation, and sexual abuse in the group. What I find more difficult to understand is the virtually universal failure to see that these abuses occur in many religious organizations: not just the stigmatized minority movements. Evidence has come to light in recent years of, for example:

Systematic sexual abuse of children in the care of Catholic priests

Brutality in residential institutions for young people run by the Catholic church in various countries

Catholic church policies for transporting young children from Britain and Ireland to Australia under the bogus pretext that they were orphans

Massive financial irregularities in the Catholic Archdiocese of Chicago

Clergy malfeasance of various kinds in many American churches (Shupe 1995)

Sexual improprieties among Methodist clergy in the UK

Financial irregularities in certain Pentecostal churches in the UK

Racism in the Church of England

The exploitation of women in many Christian churches

Collusion between church officials and some of the world's most brutal regimes

This list of examples of scandals, abuses, and problems in mainstream, supposedly respectable Christian churches is far from exhaustive, but it is intended merely to draw attention to the disparity between the levels of public awareness and anxiety about problems in well-established religious organizations and the levels of concern about so-called "cults." Moreover, there are few genuine *controversies* about mainstream churches: merely a perception of scattered problems associated with particular individuals. As a category, churches are not perceived to give rise to difficult moral or legal dilemmas. Indeed, William Bainbridge (1997: 24) refers to them as "conventional religious organizations." Yet, in my view, this categorical distinction between them and so-called cults is exaggerated. There is actually a continuum between the problematic and the unproblematic aspects of all religious collectivities.

From a sociological point of view, it makes very little difference whether the abuses are accidental or consequential on doctrines or ideology.

Admittedly, the most spectacular episodes of violence and collective suicide have occurred in so-called cultic groups, but public animosity against the category of "cult" was strong even before the destruction of the Peoples Temple at Jonestown, Guyana in 1978. In any case, that particular episode and the armed assault on the Branch Davidian compound in Waco, Texas in 1993 should remind us that both of the religious collectivities concerned were developments of more or less respectable Christian denominations. And in the wake of the massive slaughter of religiously identified opponents in such places as the former Yugoslavia and Northern Ireland, who can deny that "ordinary" religion can also be a hazard to life and limb?

The important thing is therefore to understand why and how problems occur on *any* religious collectivity: not just in collectivities categorized *a priori* as cultic. This could be done by analyzing the processes of, for example, exploitation, authoritarian leadership, harassment and abuse, systematic fraud and deception, violence and patriarchy in *all* religious collectivities. Such an approach might even reveal that religious collectivities are not themselves completely distinctive; it might show that religious collectivities are only marginally different from other voluntary organizations in respect of the problems to

which they give rise. This is a heretical thought for a sociologist of religion.

This is not the place to develop this particular argument further (see Beckford 1985a, 1989), so let me turn now to the question of why the problems attributed to "cults" gain a much higher public profile than the much more widespread problems attributable to supposedly conventional religious collectivities.

The Social Sources of Cult Controversies

Allegations that so-called cults brainwash their recruits, exploit them economically, abuse them sexually and, in many other ways, ruin their lives are too well known to need repeating here (Barker 1984, 1989; Beckford 1985b; Richardson 1985, 1991, 1996). I want to suggest that this pattern of accusations and, in particular, its exclusive focus on stigmatized movements can be explained in terms of several characteristics of late twentieth-century life in advanced industrial societies.

Massification and demonization

Firstly, the consolidation of nation-states with relatively stable boundaries and effective measures for monitoring and controlling the activities of their populations had helped to perpetuate the medieval suspicion of people who were migrants, vagrants, wandering holy men and women, or free spirits. Nowadays citizenship is not only the key to eligibility for various obligations and benefits but it is also inseparable from numerous processes of official registration, monitoring, and surveillance. The surface of late modern life may appear to be fragmented or confused, but the underlying forces of standardization, rationalization, and commodification are still powerful. The metaphor of "slipping through the net" conveys the sense that people whose life course does not conform with the "normal" progression through stages of education, training, employment, consumption, sexual relationships, leisure, and welfare have somehow managed to avoid the normal devices for detecting failures in the system or weaknesses of individual motivation.

The fact that members of some minority religious movements choose to order aspects of their lives in accordance with different priorities makes them objects of suspicion because, among other things, their non-conventional ways of living imply that something is wrong with the machinery of "normalization." The public sense of fear and outrage is all the more intense because it is widely believed that late modernity is a time of great individualization and that non-conventional religious practices are therefore unnecessary. But permissible individualization is mostly confined to choice of such things as dress, leisure activities, language, and sexual relations. Departures from the expected patterns of education, employment, and consumption are grounds for suspicion and, in some cases, demonization. It is therefore acceptable to "shop around" for religious ideas, alternative therapies, or spiritual experiences; but it is not acceptable to follow a religious path which involves a break with the publicly approved life course. The fact that some people choose to abandon the path of "normal" education or employment for the sake of non-conventional religious ideals is experienced by others as an affront to their conviction that modern individuals are free, rational decision-makers. In other words, modern living is both massified *and* pervaded by an ideological conviction that individual freedom of choice is stronger than ever.

In these circumstances, claims that new religious movements brainwash their recruits or exploit them unfairly can be interpreted as reactions against the exercise of free will in a register to which the accusers are deaf. Allegations of brainwashing are the modern equivalent of late medieval accusations of witchcraft and demonic possession (Anthony and Robbins 1980; Robbins 1988). The common thread is the claim that reason has been subverted by an external agency.

Communication and controversy

Secondly, the severity of present-day strictures against NRMs is partly a function of the effi-

ciency and rapidity of *communication* in the late twentieth century. In previous eras it was common for unconventional religious groups to operate only in very small geographical areas or to create their own remote communities as refuges from prying eyes. But nowadays it is possible for even small movements, with the help of telecommunications, to reach large audiences scattered over huge areas of the world. By the same logic it is more difficult for such movements to avoid prying eyes because communications among their opponents or critics are equally efficient. So, just as NRMs can capitalize on the advantages of computerized mailing lists and multimedia presentations to spread their message, cult monitoring groups find it relatively easy to collect information about large numbers of NRMs and to compile aggregate statistics. In this sense, the idea that the category of "cult" has become threatening on a large scale has been facilitated by the technology which permits rapid exchange, compilation, and analysis of information between cult monitoring groups, researchers, journalists, and program makers around the world.

The intensity of today's cult controversies has to be understood partly in terms of the simultaneous application of communications technology by NRMs and by their opponents. If global communications have made the human world appear to be a smaller place than previously, they are also making cult controversies more intense.[1] There is no reason why a small world should be less conflictual than a larger one. In other words, we should expect that religious controversies of all kinds will become more intense in the future. Indeed, one might go further and speculate that religion will continue to be a major contributor to global disputes because it is one of the places where the "colonization of the life-world" by "the system" (Habermas 1987) can be challenged.

Secularization and polarization

Thirdly, I suggest that religion is paradoxically likely to remain at the heart of controversies and disputes in the globalized future despite the fact that levels of participation in the activities of formal religious organizations are in decline and that religion exercises relatively little explicit influence over the policies pursued by governments, businesses, or public institutions. How can religion be simultaneously controversial but marginal? Would it not be more sensible to expect that religion would become more bland and uninteresting as more people became religiously "illiterate" or simply unconcerned about it?

My answer is that it is precisely the fact that large numbers of people in advanced industrial societies are ignorant or apathetic about religion most of the time that makes the activities of those who are enthusiastic about their religion potentially more controversial. I am not simply repeating the observation that secularization is compatible with outbursts of religious enthusiasm in marginal places (Wilson 1976). I am arguing that a process of *polarization* is taking place between religiously energetic minorities and religiously apathetic majorities. Moreover, this process of polarization will ensure that, in the midst of secularization, religion will remain controversial. My claim is not that NRMs are throw-backs to an earlier age of religious vitality. On the contrary, I want to suggest that it is a very modern dynamic between active minorities and inactive majorities which is helping to create a new and polarized situation. The public animosity towards NRMs is only one expression of the perverse logic which connects secularization with intense religious controversies. NRMs are simply caught up in a process which affects all religious collectivities.

What Would Make "Cults" Appear to Be "Normal"

What evidence is there to support my argument that the demonization of "cults" is a product of social forces inherent in late twentieth-century advanced industrial societies? One way of answering this question is to calculate how far NRMs would have to change in order to become acceptable. In other words, what would help to make NRMs appear to be normal or acceptable? I was inspired to pursue this

approach by Peter Brown's stunning insight into the political economy of religious toleration in late Roman antiquity:

> Seen from the point of view of the civic notables of the fourth and fifth centuries, the annual paroxysm of the collection of taxes . . . and not religious affairs – however exciting these might be . . . to those who knew about such things, on a supernatural level – was the true elephant in the zoo of late Roman politics . . . In most areas, the system of negotiated consensus was usually stretched to its limits by the task of extracting taxes. It had little energy left over to give "bite" to intolerant policies in matters of religion. (Brown 1995: 41–2)

In short, religious minorities and enthusiasts in late Antiquity could be tolerated if they paid their taxes. Toleration was extended to minority religions for pragmatic reasons: not out of concern for philosophical principles. Is this still the situation? Let me discuss five ways in which toleration is extended these days to NRMs which satisfy various non-religious conditions imposed by state authorities.

1   Toleration depends these days on much more than paying taxes, although movements which are seen to evade their fiscal obligations certainly confirm the modern stereotype of cults as *fraudulent*. The Church of Scientology, for example, has attracted especially harsh criticism for its attempts to qualify for tax privileges on the grounds of being a religious organization in the USA (successfully) or a charity in the UK (unsuccessfully). In both cases, the crucial question is whether Scientology constitutes a religion: and the answer is sought paradoxically from state agencies with responsibility for purely material things. Nevertheless, religious movements seeking to have their religious authenticity affirmed must turn to these secular agencies. Being recognized as religious in the eyes of the US Internal Revenue Service or the Charity Commission in the UK or a court of law in Italy is a necessary but not

sufficient condition for achieving acceptability in the long run.

2   In parts of southern Europe and elsewhere in the world, NRMs are tolerated on condition that their members comply with requirements to perform *military service*. States which offer exemption to categories of religious professionals still tend to demand that NRMs prove their religious authenticity by showing willingness to comply with conscription laws before becoming eligible to apply for exemption.

3   Another condition of NRMs' acceptability in many countries is the abandonment of all claims to *cure* medical problems, especially if therapy forms part of the movements' normal practices. Challenges to, or evasions of, state-licensed medical practices are rarely tolerated. NRMs are under suspicion if their members do not avail themselves of publicly available medical services or personnel.

4   *Education* is less tightly controlled by state agencies than is the provision of health care, but NRMs which prefer to educate their members' children in their own schools are still widely suspected of irresponsibility or ulterior motives. Movements which educate their children from different countries in a single international school are especially suspect. They are accused of trying to hide their children in places where the standards of education and care cannot be easily monitored.

5   A novel condition of acceptability in the UK concerns the *accessibility* to the public of NRMs' worship services. The Broadcasting Act 1990 made it a condition of religious organizations' access to commercial channels of television and radio that their worship services should be publicly advertised and accessible to members of the public without special invitation or the payment of entrance fees. This condition seems to be predicated on two assumptions. The first is that *bona fide* religious organizations presumably have no need to impose restrictions on access to their services; and the second is that the risk of abuse or exploitation is reduced if a religious organization's services are open to public scrutiny.

In short, there is a close parallel between late antiquity and the late twentieth century insofar as toleration of religious minorities in both eras was and is still conditional on their satisfying largely "secular" criteria of religious authenticity. My point is that this dependence on the deployment of non-religious criteria by agencies of the state in order to make decisions about the authenticity of NRMs is virtually inevitable at a time when religion is fragmented and when no single religious organization has control over it (Beckford 1989).

Conclusion: The Normal–Abnormal Continuum

The difference between "normal" and "abnormal" religious groups is not so much a matter of fixed categorical distinctions but more a matter of skirmishes along a shifting frontier, In fact, sociological analysis is best served by substituting "continuum" for "distinctions." Of course, public opinion and some religious interest groups prefer to make categorical distinctions between, say, "real religion" and "destructive cults." But a dispassionate analysis of the social aspects of religion suggests that, within all religious organizations, some practices are accepted as clear evidence of religious authenticity and others are suspected of compromising that authenticity. The criteria of acceptability change over time, often reflecting ethical and ideological changes which take place outside religious organizations.

Moreover, the skirmishes that break out from time to time in connection with the objectionable practices of specific NRMs are rarely conducted in isolation from other grievances. Discussion of particular cases quickly gives way to claims about the entire category of "destructive cults" or "cultism" as a general issue. Continuities between NRMs and other religious organizations are thereby ignored or suppressed for ideological reasons. Sociologists would be better advised to concentrate on analyzing specific dimensions of all religious collectivities without making prior judgments about their church-like or cult-like nature.

Note

1 Disputes in some Christian churches are also intensified by the ease of modern communications and by the relentless search of journalists for sensational stories. See Ammerman (1990) on the conduct of disputes among the souther Baptists in the USA.

References

Ammerman, Nancy (1990) *Baptist Battles: Social Change and Religious Conflict in the Southern Baptist Convention*, New Brunswick, NJ: Rutgers University Press.

Anthony, D. and T. Robbins (1980) "A demonology of cults," *Inquiry Magazine*, September: 9–11.

Bainbridge, William S. (1997) *The Sociology of Religious Movements*, New York: Routledge.

Barker, Eileen V. (1984) *The Making of a Moonie*, Oxford: Blackwell.

Barker, Eileen V. (1989) *New Religious Movements: A Practical Introduction*, London: HMSO.

Beckford, James A. (1985a) "The insulation and isolation of the sociology of religion," *Sociological Analysis*, 46 (4): 347–54.

Beckford, James A. (1985b), *Cult Controversies: Societal Responses to New Religious Movements*, London: Tavistock.

Beckford, James A. (1989) *Religion in Advanced Industrial Society*, London: Routledge.

Brown, Peter (1995) *Authority and the Sacred*, Cambridge: Cambridge University Press.

Habermas, Jürgen (1987) *The Theory of Communicative Action*, Vol. 2, Boston, MA: Beacon Press.

Richardson, James T. (1985) "The "deformation" of new religions: impacts of societal and organizational factors," Pp. 163–75 in T. Robbins, W. Shepherd, and J. McBride (eds), *Cults, Culture and the Law*, Chico, CA: Scholars Press.

Richardson, James T. (1991) "Cult/brainwashing cases and freedom of religion," *Journal of Church and State*, 33: 55–74.

Richardson, James T. (1996) "Brainwashing" claims and minority religions outside the United States: cultural diffusion of a questionable concept in the legal arena," *Brigham Young University Law Review*, 4: 873–904.

Robbins, T. (1988) *Cults, Converts and Charisma*, London: Sage.

Shupe, Anson D. (1995), *In the Name of All that's Holy: A Theory of Clergy Malfeasance*, Westport, CT: Praeger.

Wilson, Bryan R. (1976) *Contemporary Transformations of Religion*, Oxford: Oxford University Press.

II

The Nature of New Religious Movements

The best way to gain knowledge about new religious movements is to read some of the many excellent book-length studies available about specific groups (e.g., Lofland 1977; Wallis 1977; Barker 1984; Rochford 1985; Wilson and Dobbelaere 1994; Lucas 1995; Maaga 1998; Reader 2000; Bainbridge 2002). By way of preparation, the two readings in this section of the book will alert you to several of the most basic features of NRMs, and provide a preliminary sense of the diverse beliefs and practices of these groups. In addition, the readings highlight aspects of the social scientific study of NRMs that we need to keep in mind.

There is little consensus about what constitutes a "cult." This is due in part to the background and agenda of those writing about them (see chapter 1). But it also reflects the problems posed by the great diversity of NRMs operating in contemporary societies. "Cults" come in many shapes, sizes, and styles. The religious imagination knows few bounds, and in an age of global travel, communication, and immigration the religious traditions of the world (both old and new) are being transplanted and transformed in complex and unanticipated ways. To bring a measure of order to seeming chaos, some scholars have tried to classify the thousands of new religions into groups according to their family resemblances. Various NRMs share beliefs and practices that tie them to certain religious

traditions. J. Gordon Melton (1993), for example, distinguishes eight "family groups": (1) the Pentecostal family, (2) the communal family, (3) the Christian Science–Metaphysical family, (4) the spiritualist, psychic, and New Age family, (5) the ancient wisdom family, (6) the magic family, (7) the Eastern and Middle Eastern families, and lastly (8) a category for new and unclassifiable religious groups. This approach to the classification of different types of NRMs is largely historical and descriptive. As such it helps to familiarize us with the range of possibilities, while demonstrating that there is a measure of order and cultural continuity to the seemingly endless variety of new forms of religious life.

But scholars have also found it useful to categorize NRMs in more abstract ways, according to certain common features revealed by their analysis (see Dawson 1997). One of the best known of these alternative schemes of classification is delineated by Roy Wallis in the first reading of this section (chapter 3). Focusing on how NRMs tend to view their relationship with the rest of society, Wallis proposes that there are three different types of new religions: world-rejecting, world-affirming, and world-accommodating. An NRM "may embrace the world, affirming its normatively approved goals and values; it may reject that world, denigrating those things held dear within it; or it may remain as far as possible indifferent to the world in terms of its religious practice, accommodating to it otherwise, and exhibiting only mild acquiescence to, or disapprobation of, the ways of the world" (Wallis 1984: 4). It is these differences in attitude, Wallis suggests, that most fully account for the differences in the organization and behavior of these groups, and how they are treated by the societies in which they exist. In making his case Wallis provides a rich introduction to the specific beliefs and practices of a wide array of new religions and their leaders. He also demonstrates why and how theoretical insights need to be introduced to the study of NRMs, to allow for more manageable and effective comparisons between groups and the development of more general propositions about the nature and functioning of these kinds of religious groups.

These substantive and methodological themes are developed further in the second reading in this section, William Sims Bainbridge and Rodney Stark's essay "Cult Formation: Three Compatible Models" (chapter 4). Substantively, Bainbridge and Stark suggest that we can learn a great deal about the nature of NRMs, individually and as a type of religious organization, by grasping the social and psychological dynamics that may have brought these groups into existence in the first place. The analysis Bainbridge and Stark offer is unique and very engaging. Methodologically, they demonstrate the advantages of exercising some theoretical ingenuity in the face of the great complexity of data available about NRMs. Like Wallis, they employ a few well-crafted ideal types, in this case models of religious innovation, to systematically stipulate a large number of pertinent empirical generalizations about the way NRMs function. They propose three different conceptions of why and how NRMs are formed: (1) the psychopathology model, (2) the entrepreneur model, and (3) the subculture-evolution model. These models are based in turn on a set of even more general theoretical propositions about religions as social systems of exchange in which members and the groups participate to secure certain scarce rewards. In each model the rewards exchanged, and the costs incurred, differ. In

the end, however, Bainbridge and Stark stress, these models are essentially compatible. For it is unlikely that any one model adequately reflects the motivations for starting any specific movement. It is more likely that elements of all three models must be invoked in different combinations to explain the origins of any NRM. The models are not replicas of reality. They are conceptual frameworks for stimulating and guiding empirical research and organizing the results into coherent explanations of religious innovation. The specific explanations derived from their application to actual cases will in turn influence the theoretical process of creating other models, augmenting the capacity of such models to suggest and frame even newer and more specific lines of research. Many of the other readings included in this book were written with the same objective. Researchers in this new field are striving to elevate the study of NRMs beyond the mere description of new religious activities to the development of more generalized principles of explanation for this type of social phenomena.

References

Bainbridge, William Sims 2002: *The Endtime Family: Children of God*. Albany: State University of New York Press.

Barker, Eileen 1984: *The Making of a Moonie: Choice or Brainwashing?* Oxford: Blackwell.

Dawson, Lorne L. 1997: Creating "Cult" Typologies: Some Strategic Considerations. *Journal of Contemporary Religion* 12 (3): 363–81.

Lofland, John F. 1977: *Doomsday Cult: A Study of Conversion, Proselytization and Maintenance of Faith*, enlarged edn. New York: Irvington.

Lucas, Phillip C. 1995: *The Odyssey of a New Religion: The Holy Order of MANS from New Age to Orthodoxy*. Bloomington, Indiana University Press.

Maaga, Mary McCormick 1998: *Hearing the Voices of Jonestown*. Syracuse, NY: Syracuse University Press.

Melton, J. Gordon (ed.) 1993: *The Encyclopedia of American Religions*, 4th edn. Detroit, MI: Gale Research.

Reader, Ian 2000: *Religious Violence In Contemporary Japan: The Case of Aum Shinrikyo*. Honolulu: University of Hawaii Press.

Rochford, E. Burke, Jr. 1985: *Hare Krishna in America*. New Brunswick, NJ: Rutgers University Press.

Wallis, Roy 1977: *The Road to Total Freedom: A Sociological Analysis of Scientology*. New York: Columbia University Press.

Wallis, Roy 1984: *The Elementary Forms of New Religious Life*. London: Routledge and Kegan Paul.

Wilson, Bryan and Karel Dobbelaere 1994: *A Time to Chart: The Soka Gakkai Buddhists in Britain*. Oxford: Clarendon Press.

CHAPTER THREE

Three Types of New Religious Movement

ROY WALLIS

. . . I propose to provide a characterization of . . . three types of new religion, illustrating the characteristics of each type from actual movements which appear to approximate them particularly closely, or to embody features of the type in a sharply visible form.

The World-Rejecting New Religion

The world-rejecting movement, no matter what religious tradition it draws upon, is much more *recognizably* religious than the world-affirming type. It possesses a clear conception of God as at the same time a *personal* entity but yet radically distinct from man and prescribing a clear and uncompromising set of moral demands upon him. For example, in the International Society for Krishna Consciousness (ISKCON) – the saffron-robed devotees of Swami Bhaktivedanta (also known as Prabuphāda), an Indian guru who travelled to America in 1965 to spread devotion to Krishna and the ecstatic practices of his worship, such as chanting the Hare Krishna mantra – Krishna 'is not an idea or abstract principle but a person not unlike every human, however unfathomably greater, more magnificent, opulent and omnipotent he may be' (Reis 1975: 54).

The Children of God derive from a quite different tradition, that of American fundamentalism, adapted to the counter-cultural youth revolt of the 1960s. Founded in 1968 by David Brandt Berg (later known as Moses David, or Mo) in California among the youthful rebels and drop-outs of the West Coast, it subsequently spread nomadically throughout the world. The deity of the Children of God is a variation upon the traditional Judeo-Christian God, highly personalistic even when referred to more impersonally as 'Love' and possessed of the same whims, emotions, arbitrariness, and tendencies to favouritism as any human being.

The Unification Church, whose followers are popularly known as the 'Moonies', also emerged from within the Judeo-Christian tradition. But in this case fundamentalism was syncretized with Asian religious conceptions in Korea where the Reverend Sun Myung Moon, its founder, was born. Although missionaries of the church arrived in America late in 1959, it was not until the late 1960s and early 1970s that it began to expand significantly and to attain an almost unrivalled public notoriety. For all its novel features, however, the deity of the Unification Church is a Heavenly Father, to whom conventional attitudes of prayer and supplication are taken.

The world-rejecting movement views the prevailing social order as having departed substantially from God's prescriptions and plan. Mankind has lost touch with God and spiritual things, and, in the pursuit of purely material interests, has succeeded in creating a polluted environment; a vice-ridden society in which individuals treat each other purely as means rather than as ends; a world filled with conflict, greed, insincerity and despair. The world-rejecting movement condemns urban industrial society and its values, particularly that of individual success as measured by wealth or consumption patterns. It rejects the materialism of the advanced industrial world, calling for a return to a more rural way of life, and a reorientation of secular life to God.

Moses David, leader of the Children of God, observed in disappointment after a visit to Israel, that it:

reminds us more of America than any country we visited with all its busy materialism, its riches, power, and armaments, its noisy traffic and air pollution, and its increasingly materialistically-minded younger generation. (Moses David, 'The promised land?', 4 February 1971)

God's government is going to be based on the small village plan . . . Each village will be virtually completely self-contained, self-controlled and self-sufficient unto itself, like one big happy family or local tribe, just the way God started man out in the beginning. His ideal economy, society and government based on His own created productive land for man's simple necessities.

We're going to go back to those days with only the beautiful creation of God around us and the wonderful creatures of God to help us plow and power and transport what little we have to do to supply our meagre needs. (Moses David, 'Heavenly homes', 21 October 1974)

These sentiments are echoed by the Krishna Consciousness movement in its references to New Vrndāvana, its model agricultural community established in West Virginia, to

show that one need not depend upon factories, movies, department stores, or nightclubs for happiness; one may live peacefully and happily with little more than some land, cows, and the association of devotees in a transcendental atmosphere of Krishna Consciousness. (*Back to Godhead*, 60, 1973: 14)

Jonestown in the Guyana jungle was viewed as a potential rural paradise by Jim Jones's followers in the Peoples Temple. The prospect of a communist agrarian idyll where food would be plentiful, prejudice and discrimination non-existent, and all would share as they had need, was attractive indeed for underprivileged black ghetto-dwellers in northern California, and for white middle-class radicals alike.

Rather than a life pursuing *self-interest*, the world-rejecting sect requires a life of *service* to the guru or prophet and to others who likewise follow him. Through long hours of proselytizing on the street or distributing the movement's literature, through an arduous round of devotional ritual before the deities or unpaid domestic duties for leaders or other members, the devotee will suppress his own desires and goals in expression of his commitment to the greater good of the movement, or love of God and His agent. Reis observes of the Krishna Consciousness devotee that:

Although one has a duty to provide financial support for the maintenance and expansion of the organisation, this is not done for the self, the fragile illusionary ego, but out of love for Krishna and his personal representative, Prabhupāda. (Reis 1975: 159–60)

Such a movement may anticipate an imminent and major transformation of the world. The Children of God, for example, expect a progressive movement toward the prophesied End Time with the rise of the Anti-Christ shortly to occur or even now under way, the confirmation of the Covenant in 1985 and the inauguration thereby of the final seven years of world history. In 1989 the Tribulation will begin as the Anti-Christ demands to be worshipped as God, turning against the saints; and in 1993 Jesus is to return. Many members of the Unification Church, too, regard themselves as living in the Last Days (Edwards 1979: 80–9) in which the Lord of the Second Advent is destined to take up the task which Jesus failed to complete because of his crucifixion. Jesus was able only to establish God's spiritual kingdom on earth when his mission had been to establish both a spiritual *and* a physical kingdom. The Christian tradition has held – in some of its varieties – to a conception of the physical return of Christ at the Second Coming to establish his millennial reign after defeating the forces of evil. Members of the Unification Church see the Reverend Sun Myung Moon as occupying the role of Christ (rather than being Jesus returned), and engaged in a God-directed mission to establish the basis for the physical kingdom of God, and the restoration of the world to His dominion after wresting it from Satan.

The world-rejecting movement expects that the millennium will shortly commence or that the movement will sweep the world, and, when all have become members or when they are in a majority, or when they have become guides and counsellors to kings and presidents, then a new world-order will begin, a simpler, more loving, more humane and more spiritual order in which the old evils and mistakes will be eradicated, and utopia will have begun. These examples illustrate the close link between religious and political aspirations among world-rejecting sects. Their rejection of the world clearly embraces secular institutions. Since their aim is to recover the world for God, they deny the conventional distinction between a secular and a religious realm, the secular must be restored to its 'original' religious character. Their tendency to reject a distinction between the religious and the political also follows from a conception of mundane events as implicated in a cosmic plan, one based on a struggle between God and evil, truth and illusion, now near culmination. Political differences thus mirror cosmic positions in this struggle, with communism typically seen as the Satanic representative on earth. It also follows from this that, with the final struggle so close, the faithful cannot hope to change the world sufficiently one soul at a time. Thus, although they seek to convert among the world's masses, they also address themselves to the influential, who are in a position to affect a much wider range of people and events and thus to meet the pressing cosmic timetable more effectively.

Hence, a number of such movements have cultivated the company of the powerful. Judah quotes a Krishna devotee on the benefits of such a policy:

> So the idea is that the politicians . . . take advice from Krishna Consciousness . . . Just try to conceive for a moment the potency of a political candidate running for office having spiritual advisers who are telling him that his only goal should be to serve Krishna. (Judah 1974: 119)

The Unification Church, too, has sought to gain a role for some of its members as advisers to, and confidantes of, prominent American politicians. The Children of God have also seen themselves as aides and counsellors to rulers and, more especially, to the world-ruler they believe to be about to rise. After Armageddon and the return of Christ, they believe that 'we, the Children of God, shall rule and reign with Him . . .' (Moses David, 'Daniel 7', May 1975).

So active have some groups been in this direction that their claim to a *religious* mission comes to be regarded as little more than a front for political aspirations. Such accusations have been levelled against Sun Myung Moon and the Unification Church, who have been vigorous in their opposition to communism, and their support for anti-communist figures and regimes such as Richard Nixon, and successive South Korean military dictatorships. Jim Jones, founder of the People's Temple, was courted by many Californian politicians. Manson's gory group are not perhaps readily conceived as 'religious', but it appears that Charles Manson did view himself as a composite of Christ and Satan, returned to earth in preparation for the imminent cataclysm of Armageddon (Bugliosi 1977: 581), which would largely consist of a terrible violent revolution of the blacks against the whites in America. Thereafter his political role would emerge. He is said to have believed that the American blacks, having vanquished the whites, would eventually have to turn to him to guide them.

Meanwhile, in such movements, characteristically the faithful have come out of the world until Armageddon or the millennium transpires, setting themselves apart from it, anticipating utopia in the communal life wherein they can keep themselves separated, uncontaminated by the worldly order, able to cultivate their collective spiritual state unmolested. The religious involvement of members is thus a full-time activity. The committed adherent will need to break completely with the worldly life in order to fulfil the movement's expectations, and separation may result in a rift with family and former friends, with conventional education and career. The movement is a 'total institution', regulating all its adherents' activities, programming all of their day but for the briefest periods of recreation or private time. Not only will the member live in the community, normally he will also work for it. Although this may sometimes mean taking a job 'in the world', the risks of this are quite high for a movement that so heartily condemns the prevailing social order. Usually an economic base for the movement will be devised which limits involvement in the world. Often this can be combined with proselytizing, as in the case of the Krishna Consciousness devotees who offer copies of their magazine, books, or flowers, or the Children of God who offer copies of their leader's letters printed in pamphlet form, in return for a donation. Contact with non-members can then be highly routinized and ritualized. It is, anyway, transient; it can be interpreted in terms confirmatory of the movement's beliefs as, for example, when a hostile response is received from someone approached on the street, which serves only to confirm the evil nature of the world; but such forms of fundraising do provide the opportunity for contact with people who may show some interest in, or sympathy with, what they are being offered, and thus provide occasions for conversion.

An alternative approach is to separate economic activity and proselytism, or to establish an independent source of income, for example, farming, as in the case of some Jesus People groups, or various manufacturing activities such as those conducted by the Unification Church. Most movements tend to have multiple economic bases, often also deriving income from the possessions of new members handed over to the collective fund on joining; donations from sympathetic or unwary businessmen; and remittances from parents of members; as well as the street sales and manufacturing enterprises. Despite their rejection of the world and its materialism, members are often encouraged to collect state welfare payments, rent subsidies, child allowances, etc. Two hundred of the Jonestown, Guyana residents were receiving social security benefits.

Street solicitation became a major initial economic resource for many of the youthful world-rejecting new religions (Children of God, Unification Church, ISKCON, The Process) for a variety of pressing reasons. Unlike the world-affirming movements they had no commodity or service to purvey. Unlike earlier generations of world-rejecting movements, this cohort emerged into a world where readily available, cultivatable land for producing their own subsistence had virtually disappeared. What remained was, at best, marginal land impossible to farm satisfactorily without agricultural expertise lacking among the primarily urban-raised membership (Whitworth 1975). While they could support themselves for a time through handing over their resources to a communal fund, most of those recruited were economically marginal and thus had few resources and little capital to offer. Working at conventional jobs for support entailed a consequent loss of time for spreading the word, for proselytizing others. They lacked funds initially for investment in other income-producing enterprises such as forms of manufacture. Hence, what they required was an economic base which needed little capital investment; made use of their only resources – people and enthusiasm; and which, if possible, brought them into contact with potential members. Street solicitation – seeking donations in return for some low-cost item such as leaflets, magazines, candles, or flowers – met this need. Later, when investment capital had been secured by this means, some of these movements invested in viable agricultural land and book publishing (ISKCON), fishing and manufacture (Unification Church), etc., which supplied some of their resources. The Chidren of God continued to combine witnessing and fund-raising through the practice of 'flirty fishing': demonstrating 'God's love' through sex, and encouraging the beneficiaries of their favours to provide financial and other assistance in return (Wallis 1979a: ch. 5).

The Peoples Temple illustrates the pattern of severe economic self-renunciation characteristic of such movements, particularly in their early years:

Finances for People's Temple members were fairly simple: everything went to Jim Jones. Families signed over homes, property, and pay-checks to the temple. To raise additional money for the cult, some members occasionally begged on street corners.

Members who did not live in the church had to tithe a minimum of 25 percent of their earnings. Those living on church property gave everything to Jones, who returned to them a two dollar weekly allowance. (Kerns 1979: 159)

The lifestyle to be found in world-rejecting movements – despite its deviant appearance – is characteristically highly organized and controlled. The need to generate adequate financial support often imposes severe rigours on members, particularly when combined with an ascetic ethic. Thomas Robbins et al. (1976: 115) argue of the Unification Church, for example, that, 'Life in a communal center is disciplined and most of the day is devoted to activities such as "witnessing" on the street, giving and listening to lectures, and attending other functions.'

The rigours of fund-raising in the Unification Church have been described by Christopher Edwards, a former member:

I had been flower selling for a week now. At the end of each afternoon, we would return to the van, exhausted. For dinner – if lucky, we would receive a generous donation of unusable burgers someone had begged from the McDonald's franchise down the road by telling the manager we were poor missionaries. If we weren't so lucky, we might dine on donated stale doughnuts and cold pizza.

Our group was collecting over a thousand tax-free dollars daily.

Each morning we picked up our order of roses from the San Francisco flower district. We slept in vans at night, eight in a row, brothers at one end, sisters at another. When Family members were on the road for several days, we couldn't change clothes or shower. To even change a shirt in this crowded, smelly vehicle could tempt the sisters to fall again, might stir and excite the sexual drives now buried deep within our unconscious.

Night after night we worked until two in the morning, doing bar runs – blitzing, as we called it, coaxing drunks to buy wilted roses for the angry wives awaiting them at home. At 2.30, we would drive to a local park, praying in unison in the darkness . . . After the gruelling ritual ended, we settled down for a night's sleep, a full hour and a half, for we must soon be up for pledge service Sunday morning. (Edwards 1979: 161–2)

Success in fund-raising becomes an indicator of the member's own spiritual condition rather than of his worldly skills. Fund-raising is interpreted by members less as an economic necessity than as a method of spiritual growth (Bromley and Shupe 1979: 123). A Unification Church member reports that:

Fund-raising was a powerful experience for me. I was out on my own and had to make a decision: do I believe in the *Divine Principle* and am I willing to go through this? To me, fund-raising was a very spiritual experience in that it reaffirmed my faith. Every day I had to question what I believed. (Bryant and Hodges 1978: 62)

Daner (1976: 77) asserts that in Krishna Consciousness too, 'A devotee must be prepared to give his entire self to lead a life of day to day obedience and service'. Indeed, in the face of the increasing competition from groups and movements offering forms of 'easy' enlightenment, ISKCON'S magazine, *Back to Godhead*, has laid *increasing* stress on the necessity of spiritual discipline (Reis 1975: 133).

The disciplined character of the communal life may extend to the use of physical sanctions to encourage the achievement of movement requirements. When 'litnessing', i.e. the distribution of literature in return for donations, was a major aim of the Children of God, members who failed to reach the quota set for them were, at times, sent out again after a day on the streets and forbidden to return to the colony (i.e. the commune) until the quota target in literature distributed, or daily financial quota, was met. Synanon is a movement that began life as a communal drug-rehabilitation programme in California, which developed a religious self-conception and philosophy only subsequently. It has thus undergone considerable changes during the course of its development which I shall discuss later, but, during its most explicitly world-rejecting phase, physical violence was occasionally inflicted on deviant members. As the Peoples Temple, too, became more world-rejecting over the course of its development, so physical violence became more normal as a means of social control (Kerns 1979: 157, 185). This was also, of course, the case in Manson's Family. None the less, the demand for discipline only rather infrequently issues in the routine use of violence in new religious movements. The reason is not far to seek. These movements are voluntary communities living usually in densely populated societies with strong central state authorities. They cannot effectively coerce those who can make their wish to dissent or abandon membership known; they cannot normally hope to isolate effectively members who rebel or resist authority; nor can they compete with the means of violence available to the state if they infringe upon the liberties of members to the degree where they call upon its aid. They must retain their following by persuasion – albeit some may see such persuasion as entailing forms of blackmail – or by the instilling of fear at the prospect of departure. Followers must be given reasons to remain when they cannot in general be coerced. And since *enthusiasm* is normally a prerequisite for the survival and growth of the movement, love, rather than fear, is much the more frequent means of persuasion.

The communal lifestyle of the world-rejecting movement exhibits a high level of diffuse affectivity. Members of such movements kiss each other and hug in greeting, hold hands with other members, or call endearments and offer constant encouragement. Typically, this highly visible affectivity is coupled with a strongly puritan moral code which permits it to go no further than public display. Or, when sexual relationships are permitted, it is normally primarily for the purpose of reproduction. Married members of the Krishna Consciousness movement, for example, are allowed to engage in sexual intercourse only at the wife's most fertile point in the monthly cycle, and even then only after extensive ritual preparations. Sexual relationships are subordinated to *collective* rather than private, *personal* ends, so that, in the Unification Church and the early Children of God, members were willing to have marriage partners chosen for them even from among complete strangers. In the Unification Church, moreover, members will normally lead lives of rigorous chastity, often for a number of years before marriage.

Married members of Synanon and the People's Temple, on the other hand, were prepared to divorce their mates and take new spouses at their leader's direction. But even when, as in the later Children of God, the movement has become sexually antinomian, such apparent self-indulgence may in fact itself be largely a matter of service. The liberal sexuality of the Children of God is employed at least in part to win converts and to increase the solidarity and commitment of members, and personal pleasure therefore remains a *secondary* consideration to helping others and serving God.

In this quotation, Moses David stresses the use of sex as a means of 'saving souls' and serving God:

Who knows? – When all other avenues of influence and witnessing are closed to us this may be our only remaining means of spreading the Word and supporting the work, as well as gaining new disciples and workers for the Kingdom of God.

What better way to show them the love of God than to do your best to supply their desperately hungry needs for love, fellowship, companionship . . . affection, a tender loving kiss, a soft warm embrace, the healing touch of your loving hands, the comforting feeling of your body next to theirs – and yes, even *sex* if need be! (Moses David, 'King Arthur's nights: chapter one', 29 April 1976)

Even earlier he had indicated that monogamous marriage was by no means sacrosanct in the Children of God, and could not be permitted to endanger the solidarity of the movement:

We do not minimize the marriage ties as such. We just consider our ties to the Lord and the larger Family greater and more important. And when the private marriage ties interfere with Our Family and God ties, they can be readily abandoned for the glory of God and the good of the Family! . . . partiality toward your own wife or husband or children strikes at the very foundation of communal living – against the unity and supremacy of God's Family and its oneness and wholeness. (Moses David, 'One wife', 28 October 1972)

Moses David is quite explicit about the role sexual relationships can play in generating solidarity in the Children of God, as in his letter reflecting on 'The real meaning of The Lord's Supper!' (Moses David, 1 October 1978):

Boy, there's a hot one for our Family!: One in the flesh, one body, and one in spirit! . . . in our Family we are one body, all the way! Sexually as well, really one Bride of Christ, One Wife, One Body! How much more could you be one body than *we* are, amen? PTL! *We're one all the way!* . . .

Thank God, in our Family . . . we are not only one in spirit but one in body, both in sex and sacrificial service to others.

The Manson Family – to take a yet more extreme case – also employed sexual promiscuity as a means of eliminating the individual ego and subordinating all individual personality and goals to those of the collectivity, as formulated by Charles Manson:

The lack of sexual discrimination among hard-core Family members was not so much gross animalism as it was simply a physical parallel to the lack of emotional favoritism and attachment that Charlie taught and insisted on. As long as we loved one person more than the others, we weren't truly dead [to self] and the Family wasn't one. (Watson 1978: 70)

Manson's Family also employed sexuality instrumentally as a means of attracting converts (Zamora 1976: 79). Through sexuality the Children of God believed they showed God's love, and the Manson Family the love of Charlie (Watson 1978: 68–9).

The life of the world-rejecting movement tends to require considerable subordination of individual interest, will, and autonomy in order to maximize collective solidarity and to eliminate disruptive dissent. Naranjo (1979: 27) reports from her observations that 'members are expected to learn that Synanon places the explicit needs and demands of the community over and above the needs of any individual'. A common theme in world-rejecting movements is that of having been *reborn* on joining the group. A complete break with past desires, interests, statuses, with any past identity, is made by dating one's birth from the moment of joining (as, for example, in the Love Israel movement, a small Seattle-based, counter-cultural, communal, religious group). A new identity will be acquired incorporating as its central features the beliefs, norms and values of the collectivity joined. Typically this nascent identity is signified by the convert taking a new name as in the Children of God, Love Israel, Krishna Consciousness, The Process, and the Manson Family.

The ego or former self must be completely repudiated. The Children of God employ the term 'forsake all' to mean not only the process of handing over all worldly possessions to the movement on joining, but also the renunciation of the past and of all self-interest. Enroth reports from some reflections of a COG 'lit shiner' (i.e. a distributor of the largest number of MO Letters in her area at a time when members were encouraged to maximize their output), her aspiration to do even better: 'I'm sure it's possible to hit 12,000 a week. I know it. *I have to die more to myself* and put more hours in' (Enroth 1977: 51, my emphasis). Even the exclusiveness of the marital bond must be abandoned for the collective good. As Moses David, leader of the Children of God, put it in one of his letters to his disciples: 'it's the last vestige of forsaking all to forsake even your husband and wife to share with others' (Moses David, 'One wife', 28 October 1972; on sex and marriage in the Children of God, see Wallis 1979a: ch. 5). Giving up any exclusive claim upon particular others was an important part of abandoning the self. In similar vein, Watson recounts the beliefs of the Manson Family:

> True freedom means giving up ourselves, letting that [*sic*] old ego die so we can be free of the self that keeps us from one another . . . 'Cease to exist', Charlie sang in one of the songs he'd written. 'Cease to exist, come say you love me.' The girls repeated it over and over – *cease to exist, kill your ego, die* – so that once you cease to be, you can be free to totally love, totally come together. (Watson 1978: 54)

Abnegation of personal identity, or self-renunciation, to this degree renders more comprehensible the awesome mass suicide of Peoples Temple members in Jonestown, Guyana. When the cause and the movement are everything, and the self is nothing, giving one's own life may be a small price for what one has had, or for what may be achieved by the gesture.

When individual identity is so thoroughly tied to a collective identity and subordinated to the will and authority of a leader personifying that collective identity, and threat to the leader or the community is a threat to the self. Life is far less important than protection of the leader, defence of the movement's ideal, or indictment of its enemies. The logical extreme of 'forsaking all' for the common good is not – as Moses David supposes – the abandoning of an exclusive sexual claim upon a spouse, but rather it is the *suicidal act*. Members of the Unification Church and the Children of God

are warned that they may have to die for their movement or their faith:

> We know that some will suffer and some will have to die for Thee and Thy Gospel. You promised it, Lord, but you said 'Great is your reward in Heaven, for so persecuted they the prophets which were before you! (MT 5: 12).' (Moses David, 'The happy ending', February 1979)

The deindividuation, subordination of self, and the correlated sense of rebirth, of complete break with the past are highlighted, in the case of the Manson Family, by a recollection of Tex Watson. A prolonged intimate relationship normally results in the partners acquiring substantial background knowledge of each other, yet Watson observes of the girl specially assigned to him by Manson that, 'During the months that Mary and I were more or less together, I learned practically nothing about her past. The past was non-existent for the Family, something to discard along with all the materialistic middle-class programming and the ego that it had built' (Watson 1978: 61).

A collective identity may be fostered by various means as Rosabeth Kanter (1972) has shown, including a common mode of dress and appearance. This is seen at its clearest in Krishna Consciousness, wherein temple residents wear Indian dress and men shave their heads but for a topknot. Observers often commented on the similarity in dress and appearance of members of the Unification Church in its early years of notoriety. To a considerable extent this was also true of the Children of God who might not all look precisely alike, but for whom there was a considerable commonality in style. Another expression of this deindividuation is to be seen in the practice in the Manson Family of keeping all the clothes not in immediate use in one large pile on the floor (see, for example, Watson 1978: 29). This is echoed in Edwards's (1979: 97) account of induction to the Unification Church:

> I left the shower room house, wearing the crumpled old clothes I had pulled out of the

collective laundry hamper . . . All our clothes were thrown together and we dressed on a first-come, first-serve system, those newest in the Family choosing the shabbiest clothes to show humility and Family leaders picking out the finest as a sign of their status.

Another typical means of fostering and marking collective identity, so usual as almost to be a defining characteristic of the world-rejecting movement, is that of new members handing over on joining all belongings (Unification Church, Children of God, Krishna Consciousness, Manson Family, etc.), or major assets and income (People's Temple). Equally general is the conceptualization of the movement as a family in which other members are closer than any physical brothers and sisters, and in which the leader occupies the status of father with an appropriate authority over his 'children'. By this means movements as diverse as the Love Family (in Seattle), the Unified Family – a designation employed by the Unification Church; the Manson Family, and the Family of Love – a later name taken by the Children of God, have sought to describe the close, emotional bonding and corporate loyalty felt by members of the group.

Movements such as these, mandated by God through the medium of a messiah, prophet or guru to fulfil His demands, tend to be highly authoritarian. The resulting constraints of the communal life and an authoritarian leadership provide a basis for the claim by hostile outsiders that the youthful members have lost their identity, personality, and even their 'free will' in joining. Such claims have formed a major part of the rhetoric of the 'anti-cult' movement (Shupe, Spielmann and Stigall, 1977; Wallis 1977) . . .

The World-Affirming New Religion

The other end of the continuum presents a sharp contrast. The style of the world-affirming movement lacks most of the features traditionally associated with religion. It may have no 'church', no collective ritual of worship, it may lack any developed theology or ethics (in the sense of general, prescriptive principles of human behaviour and intention – although see Tipton 1982 on *est*). In comparison to the world-rejecting movement, it views the prevailing social order less contemptuously, seeing it as possessing many highly desirable characteristics. Mankind, too, is not so much reprobate as needlessly restricted, containing within itself enormous potential power which, until now, only a very few individuals have learned to utilize effectively, and even then normally only by withdrawing from the world, and subjecting themselves to the most rigorous disciplines. Silva Mind Control is a training involving techniques of self-hypnosis and visualization, which is transmitted in 40–48 hours and which:

can train anyone to remember what appears to be forgotten, to control pain, to speed healing, to abandon unwanted habits, to spark intuition so that the sixth sense becomes a creative, problem-solving part of daily life. With all this comes a cheerful inner peace, a quiet optimism based on first-hand evidence that we are more in control of our lives than we ever imagined. (Silva and Miele 1977: 12–13)

The method – which brings one 'into direct, working contact with an all-pervading higher intelligence' (ibid.: 17) – was invented by a Mexican American, Jose Silva, in the 1950s. An advertising leaflet for Silva Mind Control avers that:

In 48 hours you can learn to use your mind to do *anything* you wish . . . There is no limit to how far you can go, . . . to what you can do, because there is no limit to the power of your mind.

Transcendental Meditation (TM) involves – as its name makes clear – a meditational technique taught to those who are initiated in a relatively brief ceremony in which the initiator conveys to the new meditator a 'personal' mantra, in fact selected according to the new meditator's age, on which the individual meditates for twenty minutes each morning and evening. The technique was brought to the West by the Maharishi Mahesh Yogi in the late 1950s, but achieved celebrity mainly as a result of the Beatles becoming initiated and visiting the Maharishi in India in 1968. Although their interest shortly waned, numbers undertaking initiation into TM increased dramatically in the late 1960s and 1970s. (For data on the expansion of TM in the USA, see Bainbridge and Jackson 1981.) A pamphlet published by one of the organizations of Transcendental Meditation announces the super-normal powers to which it provides access:

> The TM-Siddhis programme . . . creates the ability to function from the level of . . . unbounded awareness. Any thought consciously projected from that unbounded awareness will be so powerful, will be so supported by all the laws of nature, that it will be fufilled without problems, without loss of time. (Mahesh Yogi 1977)

Movements approximating the world-affirming type claim to possess the means to enable people to unlock their physical, mental and spiritual potential without the need to withdraw from the world, means which are readily available to virtually everyone who learns the technique or principle provided. No arduous prior period of preparation is necessary, no ascetic system of taboos enjoined. No extensive mortification of the flesh nor forceful control of the mind. At most, a brief period of abstention from drugs or alcohol may be requested, without any requirement even of continued abstention after the completion of a training or therapy period.

est (the italicized initial lower-case form is used even at the beginning of a sentence) is the commonly used designation for Erhard Seminar's Training, an organization which provides a 60-hour training, the purpose of which is 'to transform your ability to experience living so that the situations you have been trying to change or have been putting up with, clear up just in the process of life itself'. While it is one of the less transcendental of the new world-affirming salvational movements,

est is clearly part of the same domain as its more overtly religious counterparts among movements of this type. As will be argued subsequently, movements of this type tend to possess a more secularized and individualized conception of the divine. Moreover, they offer access to supernatural, magical and spiritual powers and abilities which legitimize the attribution to them of the label 'religious'. Participants in the *est* training are not expected to submit to any severe preparatory trials or rigours. They are required merely to observe a series of rules during the 60 hours the training involves (normally spread over two weekends in four approximately 15-hour days). They may not smoke in the training room, eat except at the specified meal break, drink alcohol or take any drug (except as medically prescribed) during the training period and the intervening week. The 'asceticism' involved in securing enlightenment through *est* goes no further than being permitted breaks for smoking or the lavatory only three or four times during each 15–16 hour day; being required to sit in straight-backed chairs during much of the training with the consequent mild physical discomfort; and being obliged to raise one's hand, be acknowledged, and stand to use a microphone before speaking. Persons wishing to be initiated into Transcendental Meditation are asked to cease drug use for fifteen days beforehand.

Just as no rigorous discipline is normally involved, so, too, no extensive doctrinal commitment is entailed, at least not at the outset. There may even be no initial insistence that the adherent *believe* the theory or doctrine at all, as long as he is willing to try the technique and see if it works. Examples are readily available in Transcendental Meditation and in *est*:

> No one is required to declare a belief in TM, in the Maharishi, or even in the possible effects of the technique in order for it to work. *It works in spite of an individual's disbelief or skepticism.* (Robbins and Fisher 1972: 7)

> Q. Do I have to believe the training will work in order for the training to work?

A. No. *est* is not a system of beliefs or techniques to be learned and practised. Some people approach the training with enthusiasm, and some with skepticism – and some with both. Your willingness to be there is all you need. (*Questions People Ask About The est Training*, 1977, no pagination)

Nichiren Shoshu, also known as Soka Gakkai, is a movement of Japanese origin which – although formed prior to the Second World War – only flourished with the return of religious liberty to Japan under the postwar American administration. From 1951, it began an aggressive programme of proselytization which led to rapid expansion in Japan and the conversion of some American service men, often married to members of Soka Gakkai. It was largely as a result of their return to America, bearing their new faith, that it spread to the West (Dator 1969). From interviews, I understand that it was by a similar process that the movement was brought to Britain. Soka Gadkai members believe that by chanting the Lotus Sutra, believed to be the highest and most powerful scripture, and the mantra *Namu Myoho Renge Kyo* ('Adoration be to the Sutra of the Lotus of the Wondrous Law'), Before the *Gohonzon* (a copy of a scroll representing the Buddha, the original of which was inscribed by Nichiren, the thirteenth-century monk, founder of this branch of Buddhism) (White 1970: 30), kept in a household shrine, they can attain personal happiness, economic improvement, and other this-worldly goals as well as spiritual rewards. Individuals drawn into an initial discussion meeting by Nichiren Shoshu proselytizers are customarily told:

These meetings are to get you to experiment with the practice, not to believe in it. The reason for having you come to this meeting is to get you to try and test the practice. We don't expect you to believe in it right away, but we do want you to give it a try. (Snow 1976: 236)

While followers of such movements may object to some limited aspects of the present social order, the values and goals which prevail within it are normally accepted. They have joined such a movement not to escape or withdraw from the world and its values, but to acquire the means to achieve them more easily and to experience the world's benefits more fully. Snow (1976: 67) argues that, for most rank and file members, the philosophy of Nichiren Shoshu of America is:

usually interpreted and defined in terms of the various things which collectively yield a sense of personal satisfaction and well-being in one's everyday life in the immediate here and now. For most, happiness or value creation is thus constituted by the attainment of a semblance of material well-being, family harmony, friends, good health, inner security, and a sense of meaning, purpose and direction.

In world-affirming movements, the social order is not viewed as entirely and irredeemably unjust, nor society as having departed from God as in the world-rejecting case. The beliefs of these movements are essentially individualistic. The source of suffering, of disability, of unhappiness, lies within oneself rather than in the social structure. This view is stated for TM by Forem (1973: 235), but could be duplicated for many movements of this type:

When individuals within a society are tense, strained and dissatisfied with life, the foundation is laid for conflict in its various forms: riots, demonstrations, strikes, individual and collective crimes, wars. But a society composed of happy, creative individuals could not give rise to such outbreaks of discord.

Hence, it follows that producing social change is dependent upon producing individual change. The individual must 'take responsibility' for the circumstances around him and for transforming them:

While it does not as yet provide them with political power, NSA [Nichiren Shoshu of America, the corporate name in America for Soka Gakkai] philosophy does teach that responsibility lies with the individual . . .

rather than despairing or complaining, individuals are encouraged to think about and discuss solutions to the problems they see, chant for them and work in any capacity they can, where they are, to bring about better societal conditions. (Holtzapple 1977: 138)

Transcendental Meditation articulates its version of this theory through the notion of the 'Maharishi Effect', which refers to the social consequences of the practice of TM by a significant proportion of the population (once 10 per cent was aspired to, but, more recently, as the following quotation shows, the movement has lowered its recruitment expectations):

The phenomenon known as the Maharishi Effect is the basis of Maharishi's prediction that every nation will soon become invincible in the growing sunshine of the Age of Enlightenment. This phenomenon has been verified in about 1,100 cities around the world, where it was found that crime, accidents, sickness, and other negative trends fell sharply, as soon as just one per cent of the population began the Transcendental Meditation technique. The Maharishi Effect on a global scale results in ideal societies everywhere and invincibility for every nation. (*World Government News* No. 8, August 1978: 4)

Leading Transcendental Meditators, called 'Governors of the Age of Enlightenment', have been despatched in large numbers to areas of civil crisis. There they in no way participate in relief programmes or in providing physical assistance, but rather engage in meditation and the 'Siddhi programme' (a more advanced set of practices which produce magical abilities, such as levitation), and thus:

Without going out of their comfortable hotel rooms, the Governors of the Age of Enlightenment enliven the ground state of natural law deep within themselves and produce the gentle impulses of coherence which neutralize turbulence and disorder in collective consciousness . . . Violence naturally calms down.

(*World Government News*, issue No. 2, Nov./Dec. 1978, Jan. 1979: 6)

The 'Governors' then educate local leaders in the virtues of TM and the 'Siddhi programme', and secure their assistance in teaching these in that locale. By such means world peace is ensured.

Similarly the Hunger Project sponsored by *est* engages in promotional activities connected with ending starvation in the world, and raises money for that purpose. However, the Hunger Project does not send money to feed the starving, nor otherwise directly provide aid to the underdeveloped world, nor even advocate any particular social or economic remedy:

It is not the purpose of The Hunger Project to feed hungry people . . . but rather to speak to the world on behalf of hungry people . . . Your contribution to the Hunger Project goes directly to generate the most important process on our planet – creating the end of hunger and starvation as an idea whose time has come. (*A shift in the wind* [The Hunger Project Newspaper], 4, February 1979: 15)

The Hunger Project exists to convey to the world that hunger can be ended within twenty years. Its purpose, that is, is to change our *consciousness* about the possibility of ending starvation. World hunger is inevitable only because we believe it to be inevitable. The Hunger Project therefore exists 'to create a context of commitment among a critical mass of people, to create the elimination of death due to starvation as "an idea whose time has come"' (Babbie 1978: 16).

This should not be taken to mean that world-affirming movements never have genuinely reformist aims. A number of groups within the Human Potential tradition have aspirations which combine the personal and the political. Human Potential enthusiasts often see a need for action to effect liberation at the level of social structure as well as that of personal psychology. Such issues as feminism, the ecology, peace, siting of nuclear power stations or nuclear weapons facilities, race, and community action are often part of the agenda of such groups as Re-evaluation Counselling, which devotes resources to publicizing precisely these issues and educating its members and others in their implications. Even a movement such as Scientology has undertaken campaigns for the protection of the civil rights of mental patients, although, as in so much of the activity of this group, it is sometimes difficult to disentangle a disinterested desire for social reform from the pursuit of enhanced power and security for Scientology.

However, characteristically in world-affirming movements, the individual is responsible not only for the environment around him but for everything he is and does. The individual's nature and behaviour is not viewed as a composite of predispositions, situations, and a psychological biography, but simply in terms of free choice at the point of performance. *est*, for example, even views stories about predispositions, situations and psychological biographies as part of the individual's 'act', by means of which he avoids experiencing what is happening to him. The individual is the only one who experiences (for him) what is happening to him, and hence he is responsible for (his experience of) life's vicissitudes for him; even his disasters and his illnesses. The individual therefore chooses his (experience of his) circumstances, his illnesses, etc. And as one chooses to be and to behave, so one can choose to change. Linda Dannenberg (1975: 20) observes from a Silva Mind Control lecture: 'You are free to change . . . and can make anything of yourself that you wish. You will be as happy, sad, beautiful, ugly, rich or poor, relaxed or nervous as you make up your mind to be.'

The spiritual dimension in particular is a matter of individual experience and individual *subjective* reality rather than social reality or even social concern. Moreover, God is not perceived as a personal deity imposing a set of ethical prescriptions upon human society. If God is referred to at all it is primarily as a diffuse, amorphous and immanent force in the universe, but present most particularly within oneself. Mind Dynamics, for example, encour-

ages its followers to bring their minds into states where they produce alpha waves. Its founder argues that 'when you are working dynamically in Alpha you are in touch with Higher Intelligence . . .' (Silva and Miele 1977: 37), although Higher Intelligence may be less than God Himself. For many of these groups and movements, the self is the only God there is, or at least the only one that matters. One observer of the Human Potential Movement notes that, rather than 'God', adherents are likely to refer to 'my ground of being, my true nature, the ultimate energy'; and that, 'The most common image of God is the notion of cosmic energy as a life force in which all partake' (Stone 1976: 102). He also relates the experience of one follower: 'A psychiatric social worker said she formerly used terms like *God* to explain suffering and the source of happiness and love. Subsequent to the *est* (Erhard Seminars Training) training, she did not use these terms so often, sensing that she is god in her universe and thus creator of what she experiences' (Stone 1976: 103). Maharishi Mahesh Yogi, founder and leader of Transcendental Meditation and the Spiritual Regeneration Movement, makes the same point, that 'the inner man is Divine, is fully Divine . . .' (Mahesh Yogi 1962: 7), although he may not always know it consciously (Mahesh Yogi 1962: 14). John-Roger, the American founder of the Movement of Spiritual Inner Awareness, associated with the Insight training, announces to his followers that 'we are the Holy Spirit, we are Gods in manifestation' (John-Roger 1976: 18). According to Ellwood (1974: 107), in Nichiren Shoshu (Soka Gakkai), 'All the promises of religion are made to apply to this world. All divine potential is within man, it is said, and can be unleashed.'

These movements, then, share a view of man as inherently *perfectible*. People possess a potential far beyond their current level of functioning. The key to attaining the level of their potential lies not in modification of the social order or the structure of social opportunity, but in facilitating the transformation of *individuals.* Moreover, such a transformation is believed to be possible on the basis of techniques and theories which can be rather quickly transmitted and learned.

The world-affirming movements emphasize the *present*, what Kurt Back (1972) refers to as the 'mythology of the here and now'. They are often hostile to intellectualization and rational evaluation, seeing these as a defence against, or barrier to, feeling and experience. Understanding, Werner Erhard observes of the *est* training and of life in general, 'is the booby prize'. The world-affirming movement offers immediate and automatic benefits of a concrete kind through the practice of some formula or recipe: chanting 'Namu Myoho, Renge Kyo' (Soka Gakkai); fifteen minutes' meditation on a mantra morning and evening (TM): or merely by 'keeping your soles in the room and taking what you get'(*est*). Holtzapple summarizes these characteristics in the case of Nichiren Shoshu of America (Soka Gakkai):

The emphasis within NSA is on practice, i.e. 'doing', 'acting', not theorizing. The 'benefits' which can be achieved are not just in the future. They are here and now, because any goal can be accomplished through the universal mystic law of cause and effect. The right attitude and right effort automatically lead to the right effect. (Holtzapple 1977: 139)

It follows from this ethos of individual self-realization that collective activities have little or no sacred quality and indeed are likely to have only a small place in the enterprise unless it is particularly centred upon some group-based or interpersonal technique, such as encounter groups; and even here the group is of importance only as a means to self-liberation. *est*, for example, is presented to 250 trainees at a time yet requires minimal interpersonal contact, and indeed develops a thoroughly subjective idealist theory of knowledge and of the world. So subjective is its epistemology that it appears at times to verge on solipsism. Its ontology, as noted above, rests on the claim that 'You're god in your universe. You caused it' (Erhard 1973: n.p.). Scientology, one of the most notorious of the world-affirming new religious movements, was developed by L. Ron Hubbard in America

from his lay psychotherapy Dianetics – presented to the public in 1950 – which briefly attained the proportions of a craze in the USA. Scientology, although it describes itself as a church, has only the most rudimentary of religious practices in any conventional sense. So, too, its activities are principally of an individualistic character, with little value placed upon collective or communal enterprise. Its central activity, 'auditing', is undertaken between an 'auditor' and 'pre-clear' on a one-to-one basis, or even by the pre-clear auditing himself; and even training in the theory and practice of Scientology is organized in such a fashion as to enable the student to pursue his course quite alone. Moreover, involvement in Scientology, too, is oriented primarily to the pursuit of individual goals of success, greater power and ability and personal spiritual attainment (Wallis 1976). Such developments in therapy and spiritual search have been characterized as a 'new narcissism' (Marin 1975; see also Tom Wolfe's amusing essay deflating many of the pretensions of such movements as *est* in Wolfe 1977).

It follows that the world-affirming movement rejects the dualism of the world-rejecting movement, with its concrete conception of the transcendental realm and of the coming transformation of the earth in a physically tangible millennium. Indeed, it rejects the materialist assumptions upon which such a view is predicated. Its philosophy is idealist to the degree that perfection is merely the result of realizing that everything is *already* perfect. John Weldon quotes Werner Erhard from an *est* seminar, expressing a sentiment which, with minor modification, could be found in many other cases:

Life is always perfect just the way it is. When you realize that, then no matter how strongly it may appear to be otherwise, you know that whatever is happening right now will turn out all right. Knowing this, you are in a position to begin mastering life. (Weldon, n.d.: 5)

Three themes can be identified which seem, albeit in varying degrees, to be central to the beliefs and ethos of the world-affirming movement. Although these can be distinguished analytically, they none the less sometimes co-occur empirically, perhaps as major and minor themes within the same movement. There is first the theme of coping with the demands made upon us to succeed in modern capitalist societies, of coping with the dilemmas of *individual achievement*. Underlying much of the rhetoric of 'awareness' and 'realizing potential' is the theme of personal success in securing the valued goals of this world: improved income and personal relationships, greater confidence and self-esteem, enhanced ability to cope with life's vicissitudes (Wallis 1979b). Intelligence will be increased, social capabilities immeasurably improved, psychosomatic illnesses and psychological disabilities eliminated. The Inner Peace Movement, founded in 1964 by Francisco Coll, provides methods for spiritual and psychological growth through the medium of a pyramid sales corporation which encourages recruits to move into leadership roles marketing the movement's product of spiritual growth and inner peace (Scott 1980: 24). Scott argues that 'Success and its achievement ... are emphasized repeatedly in IPM programs and songs' (1980: 73).

> To achieve success, the IPMer is encouraged to develop certain personality attributes, such as being positive, enthusiastic, hard working, assertive, dynamic, motivated, committed, confident and organized ... Given these success concerns, many IPM classes center around success, such as an ALC [American Leadership College] class entitled 'Success, Goals, and Motivation'. Many techniques are designed to show participants what they need to do to obtain success ... (Scott 1980: 74–5)

A small sample of Scientologists completed a questionnaire in Wallis's (1976) study, which included a question asking them what kinds of problems they hoped Scientology would solve for them. Twenty-five of the twenty-nine who answered this question indicated a wide range of problems to which they had been seeking solutions (they could indicate more than one):

Problem	No.
(a) Loneliness	8
(b) Financial	4
(c) Marital	5
(d) Other interpersonal relationships	14
(e) Psychological	15
(f) Physical illness	11

(Adapted from Wallis 1976: 170)

Re-evaluation Counseling was founded in the early 1950s by Harvey Jackins, a one-time associate of L. Ron Hubbard. Re-evaluation Counseling appears to lean heavily upon Dianetic theory and to develop central features of its practice, notably co-auditing – or, as it is called in Re-evaluation Counseling, 'co-counseling' – by lay peers. A member of Re-evaluation Counseling, interviewed by the author, presents this achievement theme in somewhat lower key:

> People who come into Counseling are functioning quite well, but they know they could be functioning better. They know they're just not achieving their potential; they're not doing things as well as they could do; they're not behaving to other people as well as they could. Things aren't just quite right. But to all external intents and purposes, they're doing very well.

In some movements this theme of coping with the expectations of individual happiness and achievement prevailing in the Western world appears in the form of its converse, i.e. the dominant theme is one of the *reduction of expectations* from life to a realistic level. This has its clearest embodiment in *est* which encourages participants to make the most of their present experience, to live for the present rather than future aims or past aspirations. *est* assures its adherents that 'This is all there is', and they might as well enjoy it rather than constantly compare their present condition unfavourably with some other, non-existent state of affairs. Even if they did achieve the new job, wife, home, image they want – *est* informs them with considerable, if mortifying, realism – they would only be happy with it for a couple of days before they began to feel as dissatisfied with that as they are with what they have now. Werner Erhard assures his followers that 'Happiness is a function of accepting what is'. Moreover, 'Life is a rip off when you expect to get what you want. Life works when you choose what you get' (Erhard 1973: n.p.).

A second theme, clearly closely related to the desire to achieve one's full potential, is that of coping with our sense of constraint, of facilitating the desire for liberation from social inhibitions, of breaking free from the bonds of social roles to reach the 'real' person beneath. The individual will be released from conventional ritual; from habitual modes of speech or interaction; from inhibitions acquired in childhood; from repressions of instinctual life; or from a learned reserve. He will thereby be enabled to 'get in touch with' his feelings, his emotions; and encouraged to express the 'authentic' self beneath the social facade; to celebrate spontaneity, sensual pleasure and the indulgence of natural impulse.

The shifting congeries of groups, organizations and activities which form the Human Potential Movement take this to be a fundamental assumption. Human beings possess vast potential by way of ability, awareness, creativity, empathy, emotional expressiveness, capacity for experience and enjoyment, and the like. The pristine human being possesses these characteristics and qualities, but is believed to lose or to repress them as a result of the impact of society and the constraining structures it imposes upon the individual. Oscar Ichazo, founder of Arica, a gnostic school drawing much upon Gurdjieff, but eclectic in its synthesis of concepts and practices, has said that:

A person retains the purity of essence for a short time. It is lost between four and six years of age when the child begins to imitate his parents, tell lies and pretend. A contradiction develops between the inner feelings of the child and the social reality to which he must conform. Ego consciousness is the limited mode of awareness that develops as a result of the fall into society. (Interview with Sam Keen see Keen 1973)

Arica provides practices, exercises, ritual and a conceptual system which will enable the individual to transcend mere 'ego consciousness', and thus to recover some of his capabilities from before the fall. Bernard Gunther, author of two best-selling books on the topic of sensitivity training and a major teacher in the Human Potential Movement, has commented on his own approach as follows:

I guess largely I feel that most people in our culture tend to carry around a lot of chronic tension, and that they tend to respond largely on the basis of *habit* behavior . . . what I call sensory awakening is a method to get people to . . . let go their tension and focus their awareness on various parts of the body. And of experiencing the *moment*, experiencing what it is they are actually doing, as opposed to any kind of concept or conditioned kind of habit behavior (Back 1972: 81).

In his book, *The Human Side of Human Beings*, Harvey Jackins provides an illustration of the interrelated themes of a desire to achieve one's full capacity, held to be vastly greater than is manifested at present, and a belief that this achievement is to be gained through liberation from those constraints upon our powers which society has imposed upon us. Reminiscent of early Dianetics, Jackins (1978: 19–20) argues that,

if any of us could preserve in operating condition a very large part of the flexible intelligence that each of us possesses inherently, the one who did so would be accurately described as an 'all round genius' by the current standards of our culture. This is not, of course, the impression that most of us have been conditioned to accept. We have heard, from our earliest age, that 'Some have it and some don't, Where were you when the brains were passed out?'. 'Don't feel bad, the world needs good dishwashers, too', and similar gems. These impressions and this conditioning, however, seem to be profoundly wrong. Each of us who escaped physical damage to our forebrain began with far more capacity to function intelligently than the best operating adult in our culture is presently able to exhibit.

Successful adults, Jackins calculates, are operating on only about 10 per cent of their 'original resources of intelligence, ability to enjoy life and ability to enjoy other people' (Jackins 1978: 59). Re-evaluation Counseling offers a method which will enable its practitioners to recover this enormous inherent capacity.

Arianna Stassinopoulos, a recruit to Insight, an American self-realization movement which she subsequently introduced to Britain, represented particularly sharply the theme of liberation at a public presentation in London in 1979, when she announced that the purpose of Insight could be summarized as 'getting free'. It offered, she said, freedom from the melodrama which goes on in many of our heads most of the time, the fear, anxiety, guilt and recrimination; the burden of the past which continues to dominate our present responses, and produces exaggerated or inappropriate reactions to current circumstances. Freedom from 'self-limiting images and beliefs' which make us feel we are not terribly worthwhile; which sabotage us at points of crisis, by making us feel we simply cannot do whatever the situation requires. But also, from contrary images of ourselves as perfect, leading to self-judgment, guilt and a burden of blame. It offered freedom from the sense of oneself as victim, as the passive recipient of life's circumstances. Thus, like *est* on which it is substantially based, the Insight training purveys the view that we are 'totally responsible for our lives'. Finally, the training offers, it was claimed, freedom from the limitations imposed by a rationalistic and cerebral culture; realization that the heart is equally an 'energy centre', and thus the opportunity to celebrate one's emotional nature.

A third theme is that of coping with the pervasive loneliness of life in modern society. The desire for liberation, therefore, readily shades over into that of attaining a sense of *intimacy*, of instant if highly attenuated community. In a safe, secure environment – or at least one sufficiently separated from the normal world and normal routine so that rebuff or failure can be effectively isolated from everyday reality – individuals seek not only to discover *themselves*, but to make contact with others, to open themselves to relationships which have hitherto seemed threatening. The activities of these movements may provide opportunities wherein with barriers lowered, participants may find it possible to make contact with others without elaborate and socially sophisticated preliminaries, and indeed without any necessary long-term commitment or enduring responsibilities. Kurt Back (1972: 33) has argued, for example, that 'Encounter groups have become a respectable "lonely hearts club" for newcomers or those without roots in a community.'

Many 'graduates' of the *est* training undertake voluntary work for the movement and Adelaide Bry (1976: 76), a sympathetic commentator, describes how intimacy forms at least one reward of such continued participation:

Working at *est* means instant friends, confidants, and people who sincerely are interested in one another . . . Someone would burst into tears and immediately find both a sympathetic ear and assistance in getting whatever the tears related to. The problems shared were intimate ones – a bad trip with parents, a lover, a boss. Nothing seemed too private, too embarrassing, too crazy to [have to] hide.

As the world-affirming movement does not reject the world and its organization, it will quite happily model itself upon those aspects of the world which are useful to the movement's purpose. The salvational commodity includes a set of ideas, skills and techniques which can be marketed like any other commodity since no sense of the sacred renders such marketing practice inappropriate (as it might, for example in, say, the idea of marketing the Mass, or Holy Communion). The logic of the market is wholly compatible with the ethos of such movements. Thus the salvational product will be tailored for mass-production, standardizing content, instructional method, and price, distributing it through a bureaucratic apparatus which establishes or leases agencies, just as in the distribution of Kentucky Fried Chicken or Ford motor cars. Scientology, for example, possesses a substantial bureaucratic structure which invests a great deal in the collection of statistics, maintenance of records and the implementation of a considerable body of rules. Professional practitioners may operate as employees of the central organizations of the movement, as 'Field Auditors', i.e. relatively independent practitioners teaching and auditing the lower levels of Scientology, or they might establish 'franchises', expected to send a proportion of their receipts to the central organization in return for assistance, preferential discounts and other concessions (Wallis 1976: 127–56).

The Inner Peace Movement is organized on the model of the modern multinational corporation. Like Scientology, it possesses an elaborate fee structure, offering introductory courses as 'loss-leaders' at rates as low as $1.00 per hour, but moving up to as much as $600 for advanced courses. Like Scientology too, it employs modern methods of marketing:

> Besides soliciting business from those already committed, the group makes a major effort to recruit newcomers through newspaper, TV and radio promotions . . . This kind of hard-driving promotional push draws heavily from the corporate business model and systematizes the selling of spiritual growth. (Scott 1980: 38)

The methods of mass instruction employed in universities or mail-order colleges are drawn upon for pedagogic technique by world-affirming movements. The outlets are situated in large cities where the market exists, rather than reflecting an aspiration for a return to the rural idyll. And, as with the sale of any commercial service or commodity, the normal round of life of the customer is interfered with as little as possible. Courses of instruction or practice are offered at weekends or in the evenings, or during periods of vacation. *est* offers its basic training over two consecutive weekends, albeit at the rate of 15–16 hours for each of the four days. TM is transmitted on the basis of an initial lecture, a talk with the initiator explaining it in more detail, an initiation an practice session lasting perhaps a couple of hours, and brief checking sessions

thereafter, a total of probably no more than 12–15 hours. Encounter and other forms of human potential training are usually programmed to take place over a maximum of a fortnight at a time, in the evenings. Although clients may sometimes subtly be encouraged to engage in further participation, full-time involvement and complete commitment are not normally required. Membership is a leisure activity, one of the multiple role-differentiated pursuits of the urban dweller. His involvement will be partial and segmentary rather than total.

Such movements tend to employ quite normal, commercial means for generating income. Their followers are mostly in orthodox employment, and the movement simply sells them a service or commodity for an established price plus local taxes, sometimes even with facilities for time-payment or discounts for cash! Only for the staff of full-time professionals employed by the organization will life normally approximate to any degree the 'total institution' setting of the contemporary world-rejecting religions.

It is evident, then, that in the context of a Christian culture, the world-rejecting movement appears much more conventionally religious than the world-affirming movement. Christianity has tended to exhibit a tension between the church and the world, based in part on the institutional differentiation of Christianity from society, which leads us to expect religious institutions to be distinct in form. This differentiation is much less evident in Hindu and Buddhist culture, where, too, the more immanent conception of God, the idea of each individual as a 'divine spark', and that of the existence of hidden wisdom which will lead to salvation, are also familiar. Many of the world-affirming movements have been to some extent influenced by Hindu and Buddhist idealist philosophies. But they have also drawn substantially upon developments in modern science and psychology for their beliefs and practices – or at least for the rhetoric of their presentation – and, marketing a soteriological commodity in quite highly secularized surroundings, the tendency has been to emphasize the *scientific* character of their ideas and techniques, and to suppress the more overtly religious aspects, although an attitude of pragmatism has informed their practice in this regard. Transcendental Meditation, for example, was first presented in the West in much more explicitly religious terms than it is today (see, for example, Mahesh Yogi 1962), the religious rhetoric being dropped largely on marketing grounds. Robert McCutchan (1977: 146) makes the observation that:

Publications dating from the late fifties are overtly religious and spiritual . . . Other early publications such as *Love and God*, *Commentary on the Bhagavad-Gita*, *The Science of Being* and *Art of Living*, are overtly Hindu and religious. After about 1970, however, the movement focused entirely (at least in terms of its public face) on the scientific verification of psychological, physical, and social benefits of TM. None of the more recent publications even mentioned God, much less Hindu cosmology. Simply, one could say that the Hindu cosmology remained, but expressed in more 'sanitized' language. God became cosmic creative intelligence; *atman* became the pure field of creative intelligence within; *karma* became the law of action and reaction; *Brahman* became the ground state of physics.

Scott (1978: 217) presents evidence of the rationale behind this shift. He reports a conversation between Professor Robert Bellah and an official of the Maharishi International University in which the latter replied to Dr Bellah's inquiry concerning why TM denied its religious nature, by stating that this was for 'public relations reasons'. He also reports a public lecture by Charles Lutes, a leading figure in TM, in which Lutes declared: 'The popularization of the movement in non-spiritual terms was strictly for the purpose of gaining the attention of people who wouldn't have paid the movement much mind if it had been put in spiritual terms.' (See also Spiritual Counterfeits Project, 1976, for a report of the affidavit from which this evidence derives. See also Woodrum, 1977, for an analysis of the phases through which the TM movement has

passed.) TM has even unsuccessfully fought a legal action to defend itself from being declared a religion in New Jersey, since this would inhibit its presentation in public schools. Scientology, on the other hand, was made more explicitly religious when it seemed this would be a useful public-relations device in the face of government hostility an intervention (Wallis 1976; see also the case of Synanon discussed later).

The world-affirming movements could perhaps be conveniently called 'quasi-religious' in recognition of the fact that, although they pursue transcendental goals by largely metaphysical means, they lay little or no stress on the idea of God or transcendent spiritual entities, nor do they normally engage in worship (Soka Gakkai is an exception here, since for this movement worship at the sacred shrine of the *Gohonzon* is a very significant element of its practice). As Donald Stone notes, these movements tend to prefer the term 'spiritual' to 'religious' as a self-description. They straddle a vague boundary between religion and psychology, and which side they are held to fall upon will depend entirely on the nature of the definition of religion employed.

The World-Accommodating New Religion

The world-accommodating new religion draws a distinction between the spiritual and the worldly in a way quite uncharacteristic of the other two types. Religion is not construed as a primarily social matter; rather it provides solace or stimulation to personal, interior life. Although it may reinvigorate the individual for life in the world, it has relatively few implications for how that life should be lived, except that it should be lived in a more religiously inspired fashion. Any consequences for society will be largely unintended rather than designed. While it may strengthen the individual for secular affairs and heighten his enjoyment of life, these are not the justifications for its practice. The benefits it offers are not of the thorough-going instrumental variety to be found in world-affirming movements. Michael Harper, a leader in Charismatic Renewal, has said that:

> Its main strength, and for many its attractiveness, lies in its spontaneity, and in the fact that it is so far comparatively unstructured. It is not basically a protest movement, but a positive affirmation of faith in God and His power to change people and institutions. It is a new style of Christian life. (Quoted in Quebedeaux 1976: 71)

Neo-Pentecostalism, or the Charismatic Renewal Movement, comprises a wide range of bodies, organizations and groups both within and beyond the major denominations (including the Catholic Church), which have flourished since the early 1960s. They typically consist of individuals who, although committed Christians before joining the Renewal Movement, felt something to be lacking in their spiritual loves, particularly an active *experience* of God's power working within them and within the church. Involvement in the Renewal Movement was often motivated by the desire for experience of the power of the Holy Spirit, the most obvious and characteristic sign of which was normally glossolalia, the 'gift of tongues'. It would also be accompanied by enthusiastic participation in worship – other religious activities of a less formally structured and more fully participatory kind than the normal religious services – which they would often also continue to attend, perhaps even more zealously than before. Fichter, speaking of the Catholic Pentecostal movement on the issue of its social consequences, argues that:

> The goal of the renewal movement is personal spiritual reform not organized social reform, but this does not imply the absence of social concern. The movement's basic conviction is that a better society can emerge only when people have become better, yet it would be completely erroneous to interpret this as an individualistic and self-centred attitude. (Fichter 1975: 144)

Nevertheless, while its beliefs and the benefits of practice are personalistically oriented, the form of practice in worship or ritual will characteristically be collective.

At a conscious level at least, the innovatory religious movement with a world-accommodating orientation will be seen not so much as a protest against the world or society, but as a protest against prevailing religious institutions, or their loss of vitality. These are seen to have abandoned a living spirituality, to have eschewed experience for an empty formalism. The new movement restores an experiential element to the spiritual life and thereby replaces lost certainties in a world where religious institutions have become increasingly relativized. The membership of such movements is drawn from the 'religiously musical' middle and 'respectable' working classes, firmly integrated into the prevailing social order, who are not entirely unhappy with it, but who seek none the less some experiential reassurance of their general spiritual values. Movements approximating this type are likely to draw their associational forms from traditional social models of churches or other religious voluntary associations. Religious activities will tend to be regular and frequent but none the less leisure-time commitments.

As I indicated earlier, all actual cases are likely to be mixed in some degree, but the Charismatic Renewal or Neo-Pentecostal Movement embodies this orientation to a significant extent. Meredith McGuire (1975), for example, argues of the former that:

> pentecostal Catholics can be considered a cognitive minority relative to the rest of American society in general because of their insistence on a religion which over-arches all spheres of everyday life. With the rest of society, hoverer, the pentecostal Catholics tend to accept most of the prevailing social and political system, but interpret it within their religious framework. Nevertheless, the pentecostal belief system, with its emphasis upon interior spiritual concerns, has an inherent bias toward accepting the status quo in 'worldly' affairs.

Fichter's survey of American Catholic Pentecostals showed them to be predominantly strongly attached to the church before becoming charismatics and for the most part *even more* so afterwards. Eight out of ten affirmed the Pope to be the infallible Vicar of Christ (Fichter 1975: 25); 76 per cent reported that they attended mass, and 77 per cent that they received Holy Communion *more* than before joining the Charismatic Renewal (ibid.: 30). Fichter argues that the movement originated in the middle classes and that there has been a gradual spread down into the working classes. His sample showed the following distribution (ibid.: 49)

	%
Professional–Managerial	40.5
White collar	29.4
Blue collar	30.1

Bradfield (1975: 98) found 65 per cent of his sample of members of the Protestant Neo-Pentecostal Full Gospel Businessmen's Fellowship to be in professional–managerial occupations (on Catholic charismatics, see also Hammond 1975).

Such movements need not be of Christian origin. Subud, for example – a Muslim mystic movement introduced to the West by an Indonesian, Pak Subuh – seems to fit this category. A slightly greater admixture of world-rejection produces a group like the Aetherius Society (Wallis 1974). The Aetherius Society is a movement founded by a Londoner, George King, in the mid-1950s, on the basis of an eclectic synthesis of ideas drawing heavily upon the Theosophical tradition but modified to the degree that the Masters were now to be found not in the Himalayas, but in space craft. Members engage in rituals designed to transmit energies for the good of humanity, and undertake – at set times of the week and in special pilgrimages and ceremonials – a cosmic battle against the forces of evil. The rest of their time, they, by and large, conduct themselves conventionally as accountants, shopkeepers, housewives, and the like (Wallis 1974). This movement is world-rejecting to the extent that it advances a critique of contemporary greed and materialism which have led to violence and ecological despoliation, and mobilizes its efforts to produce social,

political and environmental changes, albeit by magical means. But the world is ameliorable. Its ills can be remedied if treated in time, and thus the followers of the Aetherius Society do not cut themselves off from the world around them. Their response to the world is one of accommodation, while they pursue their mission of striving to save it from its self-inflicted fate.

An interesting contrast is formed by the Western supporters of the Japanese movement, Soka Gakkai, called in America Nichiren Shoshu of America (NSA), and in Britain Nichiren Shoshu of the United Kingdom (NSUK). In this movement, transition to Western, particularly American, culture has led to substantial changes in style which render it an apparently stable combination of world-accommodating and world-affirming types. While its main message is one of individual self-improvement through the chanting of the movement's *mantra*, it began during the late 1960s to recruit larger numbers of American followers and to undergo considerable adaptation as a result. The early membership of the movement in the USA was among Japanese-Americans, many of whom were GI brides, and in some cases their converted husbands. Proselytization was predominantly among the Japanese community. During the late 1960s, the movement attracted a large number of Caucasian Americans, mostly single, under thirty, and often students or lower white-collar workers (Snow 1976: 133–4).

In the course of this revolution in its social composition, the movement sought self-consciously to accommodate to American society and to ingratiate itself with Americans. The Japanese-born president of the movement in America became a United States citizen, and changed his name to George Williams. Members are encouraged to dress in a respectable middle-class fashion. English is now used, rather than Japanese as formerly, at meetings. The American flag is prominently displayed in movement buildings. NSA participated actively in the American bicentennial celebrations. Thus, by every possible means, it seeks to foster 'the impression that its values, aims, and conduct are in conformity with, or at least not incongruent with certain values, traditions, and normative standards within its community or society of operation' (Snow 1976: 190).

References

Babbie, Earl 1978: 'Unseating the Horseman: World Hunger.' *Downtown Magazine* (November), Honolulu.

Back, Kurt W. 1972: *Beyond Words: The Story of Sensitivity Training and the Encounter Movement.* New York: Russell Sage Foundation.

Bainbridge, William Sims and Daniel H. Jackson 1981: 'The Rise and Decline of Transcendental Meditation.' Pp. 135–58 in Bryan Wilson, ed., *The Social Impact of New Religious Movements.* New York: Rose of Sharon Press.

Bradfield, Cecil D. 1975: 'An Investigation of Neo-Pentecostalism.' Ph.D. dissertation, American University.

Bromley, David G. and Anson D. Shupe, Jr. 1979: *'Moonies' in America: Cult, Church, and Crusade.* Beverly Hills, CA: Sage.

Bry, Adelaide 1976: *est: 60 Hours that Transform Your Life.* New York: Harper and Row.

Bryant, M. Darroll and Susan Hodges 1978: *Exploring Unification Theology.* New York: Rose of Sharon Press.

Bugliosi, Vincent (with Curt Gentry) 1977: *Helter Skelter: The Manson Murders.* Harmondsworth: Penguin.

Daner, Francine Jeanne 1976: *The American Children of Krsna: A Study of the Hare Krsna Movement.* New York: Holt, Rhinehart and Winston.

Dannenberg, Linda 1975: 'Tuning in to Mind Control.' *Family Circle* (August).

Dator, James Allen 1969: *Soka Gakkai: Builders of the Third Civilization.* Seattle: University of Washington Press.

Edwards, Christopher 1979: *Crazy for God: The Nightmare of Cult Life.* Englewood Cliffs, NJ: Prentice-Hall.

Ellwood, Robert S. 1973: *One Way: The Jesus Movement and Its Meaning.* Englewood Cliffs, NJ: Prentice-Hall.

Ellwood, Roberts. 1974: *Religious and Spiritual Groups in Modern America.* Engelwood cliffs, NJ: Prentice-Hall.

Enroth, Ronald 1977: *Youth, Brainwashing and the Extremist Cults.* Grand Rapids, MI: Zondervan.

Erhard, Werner 1973: 'If God had meant man to fly He would have given him wings.' No publisher given.

Fichter, Joseph H. 1975: *The Catholic Cult of the Paraclete.* New York: Sheed and Ward.

Forem, Jack 1973: *Transcendental Meditation: Maharishi Mahesh Yogi and the Science of Creative Intelligence.* New York: Dutton.

Hammond, Judith Anne 1975: 'A Sociological Study of the Characteristics and Attitudes of Southern Charismatic Catholics.' Ph.D. dissertation, Florida State University.

Holtzapple, Vicki Rea 1977: 'Soka Gakkai in Midwestern America: A Case Study of a Transpositional Movement.' Ph.D. dissertation, Washington University (St. Louis).

Jackins, Harvey 1978: *The Human Side of Human Beings: The Theory of Re-evaluation Counselling.* Seattle, WA: Rational Island Publishers.

John-Roger 1976: *The Christ Within.* New York: Baraka Press.

Judah, J. Stillson 1974: *Hare Krishna and the Counterculture.* New York: Wiley.

Kanter, Rosabeth Moss 1972: *Commitment and Community: Communes and Utopias in Sociological Perspective.* Cambridge, MA: Harvard University Press.

Keen, Sam 1973: 'Arica.' *Psychology Today* (July).

Kerns, Phil (with Doug Wead) 1979: *People's Temple, People's Tomb.* Plainfield, NJ: Logos International.

Mahesh Yogi, Maharishi 1962: *The Divine Plan: Enjoy Your Own Inner Divine Nature.* Los Angeles: SRM Foundation.

——1977: *Celebrating Invincibility to Every Nation.* Pamphlet, Oct. 21, Geneva: MERU Press.

Marin, Peter 1975: 'The New Narcissism: The Trouble with the Human Potential Movement.' *Harpers* 25, 1505: 45–56.

McCutchan, Robert 1977: 'The Social and the Celestial: Mary Douglas and Transcendental Meditation.' *The Princeton Journal of Arts and Sciences* 1: 130–63.

McGuire, Meredith 1975: 'Toward a Sociological Interpretation of the Catholic Pentecostal Movement.' *Review of Religious Research* 16: 94–104.

Naranjo, Betty Ann 1979: 'Biobehavioral Belonging: The Reorganization of Behavior and the Reconstruction of Social Reality During Rites of Passage at Synanon.' Ph.D. dissertation, University of California, Irvine.

Quebedeaux, Richard 1976: *The New Charismatics.* Garden City, NY: Doubleday.

Reis, John P. 1975: ' "God is not dead, he has simply changed his clothes . . .", A Study of the

International Society for Krsna Consciousness.' Ph.D. dissertation, University of Wisconsin, Madison.

Robbins, Jhan and David Fisher 1972: *Tranquillity without Pills*. New York: Peter H. Wyden.

Robbins, Thomas, Dick Anthony, Thomas Curtis and Madalyn Doucas 1976: 'The Last Civil Religion: The Unification Church of Reverend Sun Myung Moon.' *Sociological Analysis* 37: 111–25.

Scott, Gina Graham 1980: *Cult and Countercult: A Study of a Spiritual Growth Group and a Witchcraft Order*. Westport, CT: Greenwood Press.

Scott, R. D. 1978: *Transcendental Misconceptions*. San Diego, CA: Beta Books.

Shupe, Anson D., Roger Spielmann and Sam Stigall 1977: 'Deprogramming: the New Exorcism.' *American Behavioral Scientist* 20: 941–56.

Silva, Jose and Philip Miele 1977: *The Silva Mind Control Method*. New York: Pocket Books.

Snow, David Alan 1976: 'The Nichiren Shoshu Buddhist Movement in America: A Sociological Examination of its Value Orientation, Recruitment Efforts and Spread.' Ph.D. dissertation, University of California, Los Angeles.

Stone, Donald 1976: 'The Human Potential Movement.' Pp. 93–115 in Charles Glock and Robert Bellah, eds, *The New Religious Consciousness*. Berkeley: University of California Press.

Tipton, Steven M. 1982: 'The Moral Logic of Alternative Religions.' Pp. 79–107 in Mary Douglas and Steven M. Tipton, eds, *Religion and America*. Boston, MA: Beacon Press.

Wallis, Roy 1974: 'The Aetherius Society: A Case Study in the Formation of a Mystagogic Congregation.' *Sociological Review* 22: 27–44.

—— 1976 *The Road to Total Freedom: A Sociological Analysis of Scientology*. London: Heinemann.

—— 1977 'Salvation from Salvation.' *The Zetetic* 1: 67–71.

—— 1979a *Salvation and Protest: Studies of Social and Religious Movements*. New York: St. Martin's Press.

—— 1979b 'Varieties of Psychosalvation.' *New Society* 50: 649–51.

Watson, Tex 1978: *Will You Die For Me?* Old Tappan, NJ: Revell.

Weldon, John n.d.: *The Frightening World of est* (pamphlet). Berkeley, CA: The Spiritual Counterfeits Project.

White, James W. 1970: *The Sokagakkai and Mass Society*. Stanford, CA: Stanford University Press.

Whitworth, John McKeivie 1975: 'Communitarian Groups and the World.' Pp. 117–37 in Roy Wallis, ed., *Sectarianism: Analyses of Religious and Non-religious Sects*. London: Peter Owen.

Wolfe, Tom 1977: 'The Me Decade and the Third Great Awakening.' Pp. 111–47 in Tom Wolfe, *Mauve Gloves and Madmen, Clutter and Vine*. London: Bantam.

Woodrum, Eric 1977: 'The Development of the Transcendental Meditation Movement.' *The Zetetic* 1: 38–48.

Zamora, William 1976: *Bloody Family*. New York: Kensington.

CHAPTER FOUR

Cult Formation: Three Compatible Models

WILLIAM SIMS BAINBRIDGE AND RODNEY STARK

The origins of the great world faiths are shrouded by time, but cult formation remains available for close inspection. If we would understand how religions begin, it is the obscure and exotic world of cults that demands our attention. This essay attempts to synthesize the mass of ethnographic materials available on cult formation [arguing that] . . . three fundamental models of how novel religious ideas are generated and made social can be seen dimly . . .

The three models of cult formation, or religious innovation, are (a) *the psychopathology model*, (b) *the entrepreneur model*, and (c) *the subculture-evolution model*. While the first has been presented in some detail by other social scientists, the second and third have not previously been delineated as formal models.

Cult formation is a two-step process of innovation. First, new religious ideas must be *invented*. Second, *social acceptance* of these ideas must be gained, at least to the extent that a small group of people comes to accept them. Therefore, our first need is to explain how and why individuals invent or discover new religious ideas. It is important to recognize, however, that many (perhaps most) persons who hit upon new religious ideas do not found new religions. So long as only one person holds a religious idea, no true religion exists. Therefore, we also need to understand the process by which religious inventors are able to make their views social – to convince other persons to share their convictions. We conceptualize successful cult innovation as a social process in which innovators both invent new religious ideas and transmit them to other persons in exchange for rewards.

Religions as Exchange Systems

Human action is governed by the pursuit of rewards and the avoidance of costs. Rewards, those things humans will expend costs to obtain, often can be gained only from other humans, so people are forced into exchange relations. However, many rewards are very scarce and can only be possessed by some, not all. Some rewards appear to be so scarce that they cannot be shown to exist at all. For example, people act as if eternal life were a reward of immense value. But there is no *empirical* evidence that such a reward can be gained at any price . . .

Faced with rewards that are very scarce, or not available at all, humans create and exchange compensators – sets of beliefs and prescriptions for action that substitute for the immediate achievement of the desired reward. Compensators postulate the attainment of the desired reward in the distant future or in some other unverifiable context. Compensators are treated by humans as if they were rewards. They have the character of IOUs, the value of which must be taken on faith. Promises that the poor will be rich following the revolution or that the mortal will be immortal in another world are such compensators.

Just as rewards differ in the value accorded them by humans, so do compensators. Furthermore, compentsators vary in the extent to which they are specific (substituting for specific, limited rewards of moderate value) or general (substituting for a great number of highly desired rewards). A magical "cure" for headaches is a specific compensator, while Heaven is the most general compensator, promising an unlimited stream of future rewards to those humans fortunate or virtuous enough to be admitted. Relatively specific compensators are offered by many kinds of secular institutions, as well as by religion, while the most general compensators seem to require the supernatural agencies postulated by religious doctrines.

We define religions as social enterprises whose primary purpose is to create, maintain, and exchange supernaturally based general compensators (Stark and Bainbridge 1979). We thus eliminate from the definition many non-supernatural sources of compensators, such as political movements. We also exclude magic, which deals only in quite specific compensators and does not offer compensators on the grand scale of Heaven or of religious doctrines about the meaning of life (cf. Durkheim 1915).

We define cults as social enterprises primarily engaged in the production and exchange of novel and exotic compensators. Thus not all cults are religions. Some cults offer only magic, for example psychic healing of specific diseases, and do not offer such *general* compensators as eternal life. Magical cults frequently evolve toward more general compensators and become full-fledged religions. They then become true *cult movements*: social enterprises primarily engaged in the production and exchange of novel and exotic general compensators based on supernatural assumptions.

Often a cult is exotic and offers compensators that are unfamiliar to most people because it migrated from another, alien society. Here we are not interested in these *imported cults* but in those novel cult movements that are innovative alternatives to the traditional systems of religious compensators that are normal in the environment in which the cult originated.

Having briefly described our theoretical perspective and defined key concepts, we are now ready to understand the three models of cult innovation and to see their common propositions.

The Psychopathology Model of Cult Innovation

The *psychopathology model* has been used by many anthropologists and ethnopsychiatrists, and it is related closely to deprivation theories of revolutions and social movements (Smelser 1962; Gurr 1970). It describes cult innovation as the result of individual psychopathology that finds successful social expression. Because of its popularity among social scientists, this model exists in many variants, but the main ideas are the following.

1 Cluts are novel cultural responses to personal and societal crisis.

2 New cults are invented by individuals suffering from certain forms of mental illness.

3 These individuals typically achieve their novel visions during psychotic episodes.

4 During such an episode, the individual invents a new package of compensators to meet his own needs.

5 The individual's illness commits him to his new vision, either because his hallucinations appear to demonstrate its truth, or because his compelling needs demand immediate satisfaction.

6 After the episode, the individual will be most likely to succeed in forming a cult around his vision if the society contains many other persons suffering from problems similar to those originally faced by the cult founder, to whose solution, therefore, they are likely to respond.

7 Therefore, such cults most often succeed during times of societal crisis, when large numbers of persons suffer similar unresolved problems.

8   If the cult does succeed in attracting many followers, the individual founder may achieve at least a partial cure of his illness, because his self-generated compensators are legitimated by other persons, and because he now receives true rewards from his followers.

The psychopathology model is supported by the traditional psychoanalytic view that magic and religion are mere projections of neurotic wish-fulfillment or psychotic delusions (Freud 1927, 1930; Roheim 1955; La Barre 1969, 1972). However, the model does not assume that cultic ideas are necessarily wrong or insane. Rather, it addresses the question of how individuals can invent deviant perspectives and then have conviction in them, despite the lack of objective, confirmatory evidence.

All societies provide traditional compensator-systems which are familiar to all members of the society and which have considerable plausibility, both because their assumptions are familiar and because of the numbers of people already committed to them. Why, then, would some persons reject the conventional religious tradition, concoct apparently arbitrary substitutes, and put their trust in these novel formulations? The psychopathology model notes that highly neurotic or psychotic persons typically do just this, whether in a religious framework or not. By definition, the mentally ill are mentally deviant. Furthermore, especially in the case of psychotics, they mistake the products of their own minds for external realities. Thus their pathology provides them not only with abnormal ideas, but also with subjective evidence for the correctness of their ideas, whether in the form of hallucinations or in the form of pressing needs which cannot be denied.

A number of authors have identified occult behavior with specific psychiatric syndromes. Hysteria frequently has been blamed. Cult founders often do suffer from apparent physical illness, find a spiritual "cure" for their own ailment, then dramatize that cure as the basis of the cult performance (Messing 1958; Lévi-Strauss 1963; Lewis 1971). A well-known American example is Mary Baker Eddy, whose invention of Christian Science apparently was a successful personal response to a classic case of hysteria (Zweig 1932).

In other cases a manic-depressive pattern is found. John Humphrey Noyes, founder of the Oneidia community, had an obsessive need to be "perfect," and in his more elevated periods was able to convince a few dozen people that he had indeed achieved perfection and that he could help them attain this happy state as well. But the times of elation were followed by "eternal spins," depressive states in which Noyes was immobilized by self-hatred (Carden 1969).

Clssical paranoia and paranoid schizophrenia also have been blamed for producing cults. A person who founds a cult asserts the arrogant claim that he (above all others) has achieved a miraculous cultural breakthrough, a claim that outsiders may perceive as a delusion of grandeur. For example, L. Ron Hubbard announced his invention of Dianetics (later to become Scientology) by saying that "the creation of dianetics is a milestone for Man comparable to his discovery of fire and superior to his inventions of the wheel and arch" (Hubbard 1950).

Martin Gardner has shown that the position of the cultist or pseudoscientist in his social environment is nearly identical to that of the clinical paranoid. Neither is accorded the high social status he demands from conventional authorities and is contemptuously ignored by societal leaders or harshly persecuted. Gardner notes that paranoia actually may be an advantage under these circumstances because without it the individual "would lack the stamina to fight a vigorous, single-handed battle against such overwhelming odds" (Gardner 1957).

Many biographies of cult founders contain information that would support any of these diagnoses, and often the syndrome appears to be a life pattern that antedated the foundation of the cult by a number of years. However, the symptoms of these disorders are so close to the features that *define* cult activity that simplistic psychopathology explanations approach tautology. Lemert (1967) has argued that social exclusion and conflict over social status can *produce* the symptoms of paranoia. It may be that some cult founders display symptoms of mental illness as a *result* of societal rejection of their cults. Another problem faced by the psychopathology model is the fact that the vast majority of mental patients have not founded cults.

The simplest version of the model states that the founder's psychopathology had a physiological cause. Religious visions may appear during psychotic episodes induced by injury, drugs, and high fevers. If an episode takes place outside any medical setting, the individual may find a supernatural explanation of his experience most satisfactory (Sargant 1959). Innumerable examples exist. Love Israel, founder of a cult called The Love Family, told us that his religious vision was triggered by hallucinogenic drugs which enabled him to experience a state of fusion with another man who subsequently became a prominent follower. The stories of some persons who claim to have been contacted by flying saucers sound very much like brief episodes of brain disorder to which the individual has retrospectively given a more favorable interpretation (Greenberg 1979).

More subtle variants of the psychopathology model present psychodynamic explanations and place the process of cult formation in a social context. Julian Silverman (1967) outlined a five-step model describing the early career of a *shaman* (sorcerer, witch doctor, magical healer) or cult founder. In the first stage, the individual is beset by a serious personal and social problem, typically severely damaged self-esteem, that defies practical solution. In the second stage, the individual becomes preoccupied with his problem and withdraws from active social life. Some cultures even have formalized rituals of withdrawal in which the individual may leave the settlement and dwell temporarily in the wilderness. The Bible abounds in examples of withdrawal to the wilderness to prepare for a career as a prophet. This immediately leads to the third stage in which the individual experiences "self-initiated sensory deprivation," which can produce very extreme psychotic symptoms even in previously normal persons. Thus begins the fourth stage, in which the

future cult founder receives his supernatural vision. "What follows then is the eruption into the field of attention of a flood of archaic imagery and attendant lower-order referential processes such as occur in dreams or reverie . . . Ideas surge through with peculiar vividness as though from an outside source" (Silverman 1967: 28). In the fifth stage, *cognitive reorganization*, the individual attempts to share his vision with other people. If he fails, he lapses into chronic mental illness, but if he finds social support for his supernatural claims, he can become a successful shaman or cult leader. If his followers reward him sufficiently with honor, the originally damaged self-esteem that provoked the entire sequence will be repaired completely, and the cult founder may even become one of the best-adapted members of his social group.

The theory of revitalization movements proposed by Anthony F. C. Wallace (1956) is similar to Silverman's model but adds the important ingredient of social crisis. Wallace suggests that a variety of threats to a society can produce greatly increased stress on members: "climatic, floral and faunal change; military defeat; political subordination; extreme pressure toward acculturation resulting in internal cultural conflict; economic distress; epidemics; and so on" (Wallace 1956: 269). Under stress, some individuals begin to go through the process outlined by Silverman, and under favorable circumstances, they achieve valuable cultural reformulations which they can use as the basis of social action to revitalize their society. While Wallace advocates a pure form of the psychopathology model, he concludes "that the religious vision experience per se is not psychopathological but rather the reverse, being a synthesizing and often therapeutic process performed under extreme stress by individuals already sick" (Wallace 1956: 273).

The importance of the psychopathology model is underscored by Wallace's suggestion that many historically influential social movements, and perhaps *all major religions*, originated according to its principles. This view is held by Weston La Barre (1972) who says that every religion without exception originated as a "crisis cult," using this term for cults that emerge according to the pattern described by Wallace. Among many examples, he specifically describes even Christianity as a typical crisis cult. Writing in an orthodox Freudian tradition, La Barre identifies the source of a cult founder's vision: "A god is only a shaman's dream about his father" (La Barre 1972: 19). He says the shaman is an immature man who desperately needs compensation for his inadequacies, including sexual incapacity, and in finding magical compensations for himself, he generates compensators for use by more normal persons as well (La Barre 1972: 138).

Claude Lévi-Strauss, an exchange theorist as well as a structuralist, emphasizes that the shaman participates in an economy of meaning. Normal persons want many kinds of rewards they cannot obtain and can be convinced to accept compensators generated by fellow citizens less tied to reality than they. "In a universe which it strives to understand but whose dynamics it cannot fully control, normal thought continually seeks the meaning of things which refuse to reveal their significance. So-called pathological thought, on the other hand, overflows with emotional interpretations and overtones, in order to supplement an otherwise deficient really" (Lévi-Strauss 1963: 175). In shamanism, the neurotic producer of compensators and the suffering normal consumer come together in an exchange beneficial to both, participating in the exchange of compensators for tangible rewards that is the basis of all cults.

The Entrepreneur Model of Cult Innovation

The *entrepreneur model* of cult innovation has not received as much attention from social scientists as the *psychopathology model*. We have known for decades that the psychopathology model could not explain adequately all cultic phenomena (Ackerknecht 1943), but attempts to construct alternate models have been desultory. Of course, it is difficult to prove that any given cult founder was psychologically normal, but in many cases even rather lengthy biographies fail to reveal significant evidence of pathology. While the psychopathology model focuses on cult founders who invent new compensator-systems initially for their own use, the entrepreneur model notes that cult founders often may *consciously develop new compensator-systems in order to exchange them for great rewards*. Innovation pays off in many other areas of culture, such as technological invention and artistic creativity. If social circumstances provide opportunities for profit in the field of cults, then many perfectly normal individuals will be attracted to the challenge.

Models of entrepreneurship have been proposed to explain many other kinds of human activity, but we have not found adequate social-scientific models specifically designed to explain cult innovation. Journalists have documented that such a model would apply well to many cases, and our own observations in several cults amply confirm that conclusion. Therefore, we shall sketch the beginnings of an entrepreneur model, with the understanding that much future work will be required before this analytic approach is fully developed. The chief ideas of such a model might be the following.

1 Cults are businesses which provide a product for their customers and receive payment in return.
2 Cults are mainly in the business of selling novel compensators, or at least freshly packaged compensators that appear new.
3 Therefore, a supply of novel compensators must be manufactured.
4 Both manufacture and sales are accomplished by entrepreneurs.
5 These entrepreneurs, like those in other businesses, are motivated by the desire for profit, which they can gain by exchanging compensators for rewards.
6 Motivation to enter the cult business is stimulated by the perception that such business can be profitable, an impression likely to be acquired through prior involvement with a successful cult.
7 Successful entrepreneurs require skills and experience, which are most easily

gained through a prior career as the employee of an earlier successful cult.

8 The manufacture of salable new compensators (or compensator-packages) is most easily accomplished by assembling components of pre-existing compensator-systems into new configurations, or by the further development of successful compensator-systems.

9 Therefore, cults tend to cluster in lineages. They are linked by individual entrepreneurs who begin their careers in one cult and then leave to found their own. They bear strong "family resemblances" because they share many cultural features.

10 Ideas for completely new compensators can come from any cultural source or personal experience whatsoever, but the skillful entrepreneur experiments carefully in the development of new products and incorporates them permanently in his cult only if the market response is favorable.

Cults can in fact be very successful businesses. The secrecy that surrounds many of these organizations prevents us from reporting current financial statistics, but a few figures have been revealed. Arthur L. Bell's cult, Mankind United, received contributions totalling four million dollars in the ten years preceeding 1944 (Dohrman 1958: 41). In the four years 1965–1959, the Washington, DC, branch of Scientology took in $758,982 and gave its founder, L. Ron Hubbard, $100,000 plus the use of a home and car (Cooper 1971: 109). Today Scientology has many flourishing branches, and Hubbard lives on his own 320-foot ship. In 1973 a small cult we have called The Power was grossing $100,000 a month, four thousand of this going directly to the husband and wife team who ran the operation from their comfortable Westchester County estate (Bainbridge 1978). In addition to obvious material benefits, successful cult founders also receive intangible but valuable rewards, including praise, power, and amusement. Many cult leaders have enjoyed almost unlimited sexual access to attractive followers (Orrmont 1961; Carden 1969).

The simplest variant of the entrepreneur model, and the one preferred by journalists, holds that cult innovators are outright frauds who have no faith in their own product and sell it through trickery to fools and desperate persons. We have many examples of cults that were pure confidence games, and we shall mention examples of fraud in three kinds of cult: audience cults, client cults, and cult movements.

Audience cults offer very specific and weak compensators, often no more than a mild, vicarious thrill or entertainment, and they lack both long-term clients and formal membership. *Client cults* offer valued but relatively specific compensators, frequently alleged cures for particular diseases and emotional problems, and they may possess a relatively stable clientele without counting them as full members of the organization. *Cult movements* deal in a much more elaborate package of compensators, including the most general compensators based on supernatural assumptions, and they possess committed membership. In terms of their compensators, these three levels of cults can be described conveniently in traditional language: audience cults provide *mythology*; client cults add serious *magic*; cult movements give complete *religion*.

In 1973, Israeli prestidigitator Uri Geller barnstormed the United States presenting himself as a psychic who could read minds and bend spoons by sheer force of will. As James Randi (1975) has shown, Geller's feats were achieved through trickery, and yet untold thousands of people were fascinated by the possibility that Geller might have real psychic powers. The whole affair was a grand but short-lived audience cult.

Medical client cults based on intentional fraud are quite common. A number of con artists not only have discovered that they can use the religious label to appeal to certain kinds of gullible marks, but also have learned that the label provides a measure of protection against legal prosecution (Glick and Newsom 1974). In many of these cases it may be impossible to prove whether the cult founder was sincere or not, and we can only assume that many undetected frauds lurk behind a variety of client cults. In some cases the trickery is so blatant that we can have little doubt. Among the most recent examples are the Philippine psychic surgeons Terte and Agpaoa, and their Brasilian colleague, Arigo. These men perform fake surgery with their bare hands or brandishing crude jackknives. In some cases they may actually pierce the patient's skin, but often they merely pretend to do so and then spread animal gore about to simulate the results of deep cutting. Through a skillful performance they convince their patients not only that dangerous tumors have been removed from their bodies, but also that the surgeon's psychic powers have instantaneously healed the wound. But their failure actually to perform real operations in this manner must be clear to the psychic surgeons themselves (Flammonde 1975).

Arthur L. Bell's cult movement was a fraud based on the traditional Rosicrucian idea that a vast benevolent conspiracy prepares to rule the world and invites a few ordinary people to join its elite ranks. Bell claimed only to be the Superintendent of the Pacific Coast Division, in constant communication with his superiors in the (fictitious) organizational hierarchy. In this way he was able to convince his followers that they were members of an immensely powerful secret society, despite the fact that the portion of it they could see was modest in size. Like several similar fraudulent movements, Bell's cult did not originally claim religious status, but only became a "church" after encountering legal difficulty (Dohrman 1958).

In order to grow, a cult movement must serve real religious functions for its committed followers, regardless of the private intentions of the founder. Many older cults probably were frauds in origin, but have been transformed into genuine religious organizations by followers who deeply believed the founder's deceptions.

But fraud need not be involved in entrepreneurial cult innovation. Many ordinary businessmen are convinced of the value of their products by the fact that customers want to buy them, and cult entrepreneurs may likewise accept their market as the ultimate standard of value. Many cult founders do appear to be convinced by testimonials from satisfied customers that their compensator-packages are valuable. This was probably the case with Franz Anton Mesmer, who saw astonishing transformations in his clients, apparently the beneficial results of his techniques, and who found in them ample evidence of the truth of his theories (Zweig 1932; Darnton 1970). Practitioners of all client cults frequently see similar evidence in favor of their own ideas, no matter how illogical, because all such cults provide compensators of at least some strength (Frank 1963).

Another source of confidence for the cult innovator is his experience with other cults. Early in their careers, innovators typically join one or more successful cults, and honestly may value the cults' products themselves. However, the innovator may be dissatisfied with the older cults and come to the sincere opinion that he can create a more satisfactory product. Despite their often intense competition, cult leaders frequently express respect and admiration for other cults, including the ones with which they themselves were previously associated. For example, L. Ron Hubbard of Scientology has praised Alfred Korzybski's General Semantics, and Jack Horner of Dianology has praised Hubbard's Scientology.

Once we realize that cult formation often involves entrepreneurial action to establish a profitable new organization based on novel culture, we can see that concepts developed to understand technological innovation should apply here as well. For example, a study of entrepreneurship and technology by Edward B. Roberts (1969) examined the cultural impact of the Massachusetts Institute of Technology, the preeminent center of new technological culture. Over 200 new high-technology companies had been founded by former MIT employees who concluded they could achieve greater personal rewards by establishing their own businesses based on what they had learned at MIT. The current cult equivalent of MIT is Scientology, studied by one of us in 1970. Cultic entrepreneurs have left Scientology to found countless other cults based on modified Scientology ideas, including Jack Horner's Dianology, H. Charles Berner's Abilitism, Harold Thompson's Amprinistics, and the flying saucer cult described in the ethnography *When Prophecy Fails* (Festinger et al., 1956). Scientology, like MIT, is a vast storehouse of exotic culture derived from many sources. Social scientists studying patterns of cultural development should be aware that an occasional key organization can be an influential nexus of innovation and diffusion.

Future research can determine the most common processes through which entrepreneurial cult founders actually invent their novel ideas. We suspect the main techniques involve the cultural equivalent of recombinant DNA genetic engineering. Essentially, the innovator takes the cultural configuration of an existing cult, removes some components, and replaces them with other components taken from other sources. Often, the innovator may simply splice pieces of two earlier cults together. In some cases, the innovator preserves the supporting skeleton of practices and basic assumptions of a cult he admires, and merely grafts on new symbolic flesh. Rosicrucianism affords a sequence of many connected examples (McIntosh 1972; King 1970). In creating the AMORC Rosicrucian order, H. Spencer Lewis took European Rosicrucian principles of the turn of the century, including the hierarchical social structure of an initiatory secret society, and grafted on a veneer of symbolism taken from Ancient Egypt, thus capitalizing on public enthusiasm for Egyptian civilization current at that time. His headquarters in San José, California, is a city block of simulated Egyptian buildings. Later, Rose Dawn imitated Lewis in creating her rival Order of the Ancient Mayans. In great measure, she simply replaced AMORC's symbols with equivalent symbols. Instead of Lewis's green biweekly mail-order lessons emblazoned with Egyptian architecture and Egyptian hieroglyphics, she sold red biweekly mail-order lessons decorated with Mayan architecture and Mayan hieroglyphics.

The highly successful *est* cult is derived partly from Scientology and well illustrates the commercialism of many such organizations in contemporary America. Werner Erhard, founder of *est*, had some experience with Scientology in 1969. Later, he worked for a while in Mind Dynamics, itself an offshoot of José Silva's Mind Control. After Erhard started his own cult in 1971, he decided to emulate Scientology's tremendous success and hired two Scientologists to adapt its practices for his own use. We should note that conventional businesses, such as auto companies and television networks, often imitate each other in pursuit of profit. Erhard's research and development efforts were rewarded, and by the beginning of 1976, an estimated seventy thousand persons had completed his $250 initial seminar (Kornbluth 1976).

We suggest that cult entrepreneurs will imitate those features of other successful cults which seem to them most responsible for success. They will innovate either in nonessential areas or in areas where they believe they can increase the salability of the product. In establishing their own cult businesses they must innovate at least superficially. They cannot seize a significant part of the market unless they achieve product differentiation. Otherwise they will be at a great disadvantage in direct competition with the older, more prosperous cult on which theirs is patterned. The apparent novelty of a cult's compensator-package may be a sales advantage when the public has not yet discovered the limitations of the rewards that members actually will receive in the new cult and when older compensator-packages have been discredited to some extent. Much research and theory-building remains to be done, but the insight that cults often are examples of skillful free enterprise immediately explains many of the features of the competitive world of cults.

The Subculture-Evolution Model of Cult Innovation

While the *psychopathology* and *entrepreneur* models stress the role of the individual innovator, the *subculture-evolution model* emphasizes group interaction processes. It suggests that cults can emerge without authoritative leaders, and it points out that even radical cultural developments can be achieved through many small steps. Although much social-psychological literature would be useful in developing this model, we are not aware of a comprehensive statement on cult innovation through subcultural evolution, so again we will attempt to outline the model ourselves.

1 Cults are the expression of novel social systems, usually small in size but composed of at least a few intimately interacting individuals.

2 These cultic social systems are most likely to emerge in populations already deeply involved in the occult milieu, but cult evolution may also begin in entirely secular settings.

3 Cults are the result of sidetracked or failed collective attempts to obtain scarce or nonexistent rewards.

4 The evolution begins when a group of persons commits itself to the attainment of certain rewards.

5 In working together to obtain these rewards, members begin exchanging other rewards as well, such as affect.

6 As they progressively come to experience failure in achieving their original goals, they will gradually generate and exchange compensators as well.

7 If the intragroup exchange of rewards and compensators becomes sufficiently intense, the group will become relatively encapsulated, in the extreme case undergoing complete social implosion.

8 Once separated to some degree from external control, the evolving cult develops and consolidates a novel culture, energized by the need to facilitate the exchange of rewards and compensators, and inspired by essentially accidental factors.

9 The end point of successful cult evolution is a novel religious culture embodied in a distinct social group which must now cope with the problem of extracting resources (including new members) from the surrounding environment.

In writing about juvenile delinquency, Albert K. Cohen (1955) described the process of *mutual conversion* through which interacting individuals could gradually create a deviant normative structure. This process may result in criminal behavior, but it may also result in the stimulation of unrealizable hopes and of faith in the promise of impossible rewards. Thus, *mutual conversion* can describe the social process through which people progressively commit each other to a package of compensators which they simultaneously assemble. It begins when people with similar needs and desires meet and begin communicating about their mutual problems. It takes place in tiny, even imperceptible exploratory steps, as one individual expresses a hope or a plan and receives positive feedback in the form of similar hopes and plans from his fellows. "The final product . . . is likely to be a compromise formation of all the participants to what we may call a cultural process, a formation perhaps unanticipated by any of them. Each actor may contribute something directly to the growing product, but he may also contribute indirectly by encouraging others to advance, inducing them to retreat, and suggesting new avenues to be explored. The product cannot be ascribed to any one of the participants; it is a real 'emergent' on a group level" (Cohen 1955: 60.)

Cohen says all human action "is an ongoing series of efforts to solve problems" (1955: 50). All human beings face the problem of coping with frustration because some highly desired rewards, such as everlasting life, do not exist in this world. Through mutual conversion, individuals band together to solve one or more shared problems, and the outcome presumably depends on a number of factors, including the nature of the problems and the group's initial conceptualization of them. We suspect a cultic solution is most likely if the people begin by attempting to improve themselves (as in psychotherapy) or to improve their relationship to the natural world, and then fail in their efforts. Criminal or political outcomes are more likely if people believe that other persons or social conditions are responsible for their problems.

The quest for unavailable rewards is not reserved for poor and downtrodden folk alone. Many elite social movements have been dedicated to the attainment of goals that ultimately proved unattainable. One well-documented example is The Committee for the Future, an institutionally detached little organization that formed within the network of technological social movements oriented toward spaceflight. Founded in 1970 by a wealthy couple, the CFF was dedicated to the immediate colonization of the moon and planets and to beginning a new age in which the field of man's activity would be the entire universe. The biggest effort of the CFF, Project Harvest Moon, was intended to establish the first demonstration colony on the moon, planted using a surplus Saturn V launch vehicle. Ultimately, high cost and questionable feasibility prevented any practical accomplishments. In struggling to arouse public support, the CFF held a series of open conventions at which participants collectively developed grand schemes for a better world. Blocked from any success in this direction, the CFF evolved toward cultism. The convention seminars became encounter groups. Mysticism and parapsychology replaced spaceflight as the topic of conversation. Rituals of psychic fusion were enacted to religious music, and the previously friendly aerospace companies and agencies broke off with the Committee. Denied success in its original purposes, and unfettered by strong ties to conventional institutions, the CFF turned ever more strongly toward compensators and toward the supernatural (Bainbridge 1976).

Cults are particularly likely to emerge wherever numbers of people seek help for intractable personal problems. The broad fields of psychotherapy, rehabilitation, and personal development have been especially fertile for cults. A number of psychotherapy services have evolved into cult movements, including those created by some of Freud's immediate followers (Rieff 1968). Other independent human service organizations may also be susceptible to cultic evolution. The best-known residential program designed to treat drug addiction, Synanon, has recently evolved into an authoritarian cult movement that recruits persons who never suffered from drug problems.

Two important factors render cultic evolution more likely. First, the process will progress most easily if there are no binding external constraints. For example, psychiatrists and psychologists who work in institutional settings (such as hospitals or universities) may be prevented by their conventional commitments from participating in the evolution of a cult, while independent practitioners are more free. Second, the process will be facilitated if the therapist *receives* compensators as well as gives them and thus participates fully in the inflation and proliferation of compensators.

A good example is The Power, founded in London in 1963, which began as an independent psychotherapy service designed to help normal individuals achieve super-normal levels of functioning. The therapy was based on Alfred Adler's theory that each human being is impelled by subconscious *goals*, and it attempted to bring these goals to consciousness so the person could pursue them more effectively and escape inner conflict. The founders of The Power received the therapy as well as gave it, and frequent group sessions brought all participants together to serve each other's emotional needs. The Power recruited clients through the founders' pre-existing friendship network, and the therapy sessions greatly intensified the strength and intimacy of their social bonds.

As bonds strengthened, the social network became more thoroughly interconnected as previously distant persons were brought together. The rudiments of a group culture evolved, and many individuals contributed ideas about how the therapy might be improved and expanded. Participants came to feel that only other participants understood them completely, and found communication with outsiders progressively more difficult. A *social implosion* took place.

In a social implosion, part of an extended social network collapses as social ties within it strengthen and, reciprocally, those to persons outside it weaken. It is a step-by-step process. Social implosions may be set off by more than one circumstance. In the case of The Power, the implosion was initiated by the introduction of a new element of culture, a "therapy" technique that increased the intimacy of relations around a point in the network. Correlated with the implosion was a mutual conversion as members encouraged each other to express their deepest fantasies and to believe they could be fulfilled. The Adlerian analysis of subconscious goals was ideally designed to arouse longings and hopes for all the unobtained and unobtainable rewards the participants had ever privately wished to receive. The powerful affect and social involvement produced by the implosion were tangible rewards that convinced participants that the other rewards soon would be achieved. Concomitant estrangement from outside attachments led The Power to escape London to the isolation of a ruined seaside Yucatan plantation. Remote from the restraining influence of conventional society, The Power completed its evolution from psychotherapy to religion by inventing supernatural doctrines to explain how its impossible, absolute goals might ultimately be achieved. When the new cult returned to civilization in 1967, it became legally incorporated as a church (Bainbridge 1978).

Since non-religious groups can evolve into religious cults, it is not surprising that cults also can arise from religious sects – extreme religious groups that accept the standard religious tradition of the society, unlike cults that are revolutionary breaks with the culture of past churches. An infamous example is The People's Temple of Jim Jones that destroyed itself in the jungles of Guyana. This group began as an emotionally extreme but culturally traditional Christian sect, then evolved into a cult as Jones progressively became a prophet with an ever more radical vision. Of course, either the psychopathology or entrepreneur models may apply in this case. But the committed members of the sect probably contributed to the transformation by encouraging Jones step-by-step, and by demanding of him the accomplishment of impossible goals. Even when a single individual dominates a group, the subculture-evolution model will apply to the extent that the followers also participate in pushing the group toward cultism. In this case, the needs of the followers and their social relationships with the leader may have served as a *psychopathology amplifier*, reflecting back to Jones his own narcissism multiplied by the strength of their unreasonable hopes.

Conclusion

Each of the three models identifies a system of production and exchange of compensators. In the *psychopathology model*, a cult founder creates compensators initially for his own use, then gives them to followers in return for rewards. In the *entrepreneur model*, the cult founder sets out to gain rewards by manufacturing compensators intended for sale to followers. The *subculture-evolution model* describes the interplay of many individual actions in which various individuals at different times play the roles of producer and consumer of novel compensators.

While the models may appear to compete, in fact they complement each other and can be combined to explain the emergence of particular cults. After a cult founder has escaped a period of psychopathology, he may act as an entrepreneur in promoting or improving his cult. An entrepreneur threatened with loss of his cult may be driven into an episode of psychopathology that provides new visions that contribute to a new success. The subculture-evolution model may include many little episodes of psychopathology and entrepreneurial enterprise participated in by various members, woven together by a complex network of social exchanges . . .

References

Ackerknecht, Erwin H. 1943. "Psychopathology, primitive medicine and primitive culture." "*Bulletin of the History of Medicine* 14: 30–67.

Bainbridge, William Sims. 1976. *The Spaceflight Revolution*. New York: Wiley.

—— 1978. Satan's Power. Berkeley: University of California Press.

Bainbridge, William Sims, and Rodney Stark. *Forth-*

coming. "Sectarian tension." *Review of Religious Research*.

Carden, Maren Lockwood. 1969. *Oneide: Utopian Community to Modern Corporation*. Baltimore, MD: Johns Hopkins University Press.

Cohen, Albert K. 1955. *Delinquent Boys*. New York: Free Press.

Cooper, Paulette. 1971. *The Scandal of Scientology*. New York: Tower.

Darnton, Robert. 1970. *Mesmerism and the End of the Enlightenment in France*. New York: Schocken.

Dohrman, H. T. 1958. *California Cult*. Boston, MA: Beacon Press.

Durkheim, Emile. 1915. *The Elementary Forms of the Religious Life*. London: Allen and Unwin.

Evans, Christopher. 1973. *Cults of Unreason*. New York: Dell.

Festinger, Leon, H. W. Riecken, and S. Schachter. 1956. *When Prophecy Fails*. New York: Harper.

Flammonde, Paris. 1975. *The Mystic Healers*. New York: Stein and Day.

Frank, Jerome D. 1963. *Persuasion and Healing*. New York: Schocken.

Freud, Sigmund. 1962 (1930). *Civilization and its Discontents*. New York: Norton.

—— 1964 (1927). *The Futue of an Illusion*. Garden City, NY: Doubleday.

Gardner, Martin. 1957. *Fads and Fallacies in the Name of Science*. New York: Dover.

Glick, Rush G., and Robert S. Newsom. 1974. *Fraud Investigation*. Springfield, IL: Thomas.

Greenberg, Joel. 1979. "Close encounters – all in the mind?" *Science News* 115: 106–7.

Gurr, Ted Robert. 1970. *Why Men Rebel*. Princeton, NJ: Princeton University Press.

Hubbard. L. Ron. 1950. *Dianetics, The Modern Science of Mental Health*. New York: Paperback Library.

King, Francis. 1970. *The Rites of Modern Occult Magic*. New York: Macmillan.

Kornbluth, Jesse. 1976. "The Fuhrer over est" *New Times*, March 19: 36–52.

LaBarre, Weston. 1969. *They Shall Take up Serpents*. New York: Schocken.

—— 1972. *The Ghost Dance*. New York: Dell.

Lemert, Edwin. 1967. "Paranoia and the dynamics of exclusion." Pp. 246–64 in Edwin Lemert, *Human Deviance, Social Problems and Social Control*. Englewood Cliffs, NJ: Prentice-Hall.

Lévi-Strauss, Claude. 1963. "The sorcerer and his magic." Pp. 161–80 in Claude Lévi-Strauss, *Structural Anthropology*. New York: Basic Books.

Lewis, Ioan M. 1971. *Ecstatic Religion*. Baltimore, MD: Penguin.

Lofland, John, and Rodney Stark. 1965. "Becoming a world-saver: a theory of conversion to a deviant perspective." *American Sociological Review* 30: 862–75.

McIntosh, Christopher. 1972. *Eliphas Lévi and the French Occult Revival*. New York: Weiser.

Messing, Simon D. 1958. "Group therapy and social status in the Zar cult of Ethiopia." *American Anthropologist* 60: 1120–6.

Orrmont, Arthur. 1961. *Love Cults and Faith Healers*. New York: Ballantine.

Randi, James. 1975. *The Magic of Uri Geller*. New York: Ballantine.

Regardie, Israel. 1971. *My Rosicrucian Adventure*. St. Paul, MN: Llewellyn.

Rieff, Philip. 1968. *The Triumph of the Therapeutic*. New York: Harper.

Roberts, Edward B. 1969. "Entrepreneurship and technology." Pp. 219–37 in Willian H. Gruber and Donald G. Marquis (eds.), *Factors in the Transfer of Technology*. Cambridge, MA: MIT Press.

Roheim, Geza. 1955. *Magic and Schizophrenia*. Bloomington: Indiana University Press.

Sargant, William. 1959. *Battle for the Mind*. New York: Harper and Row.

Silverman, Julian. 1967. "Shamans and acute schizophrenia." *American Anthropologist* 69: 21–32.

Smelser, Neil J. 1962. *Theory of Collective Behavior*. New York: Free Press.

Stark, Rodney. 1965. "A sociological definition of religion." Pp. 3–17 in Charles Y. Glock and Rodney Stark, *Religion and Society in Tension*. Chicago, IL: Rand McNally.

Stark, Rodney, and William Sims Bainbridge. 1979. "Of churches, sects, and cults: preliminary concepts for a theory of religious movements." *Journal for the Scientific Study of Religion* 18: 117–31.

—— 1980 "Networks of faith: interpersonal bonds and recruitment to cults and sects." *American Journal of Sociology* 85: 1376–95.

—— 1980 "Towards a theory of religion: religious commitment." *Journal for the Scientific Study of Religion* 19: 114–28.

Wallace, Anthony F. C. 1956. "Revitalization movements." *American Anthropologist* 58: 264–81.

Wallis, Roy. 1977. *The Road to Total Freedom: A Sociological Analysis of Scientology*. New York: Columbia University Press.

Zweig, Stefan. 1932. *Mental Healers*. New York: Viking.

III

New Religious Movements in
Historical and Social Context

This reader examines the social scientific response to the latest wave of public controversy about NRMs. One of the things this research has revealed is that the recent controversy is very reminiscent of earlier religious controversies, and yet significantly different as well (as suggested by chapter 2). It is important to understand these similarities and differences. The two readings in this section were chosen to provide some of the broader interpretive context for understanding the contemporary situation, and hence the significance of the cult controversy. In chapter 5, Philip Jenkins evocatively describes some of the many similar episodes of social strife surrounding "new religions" in America in the nineteenth century. He notes the close and surprising parallels to current events and concerns. In chapter 6, Robert Wuthnow helps us to understand how the recent upsurge in new religious activity is related to major new shifts in the religious and spiritual sensibilities of Americans. Today's controversy stems from the rise of new social and spiritual concerns, orientations, and opportunities.

It is wise to realize, as Jenkins documents in "False Prophets and Deluded Subjects: The Nineteenth Century," that new religions have inspired fear and evoked harsh criticism for many centuries. Disputes between established and new religions are a constant of human history, though the disputes have been more numerous and significant at different times.

Christianity, and most of the other so-called world religions (e.g., Buddhism and Islam), began as extremely small groups steeped in controversy (e.g., Stark 1996). As Christianity was established the early Church Fathers waged a prolonged cultural war against what they deemed to be other heretical groups, and much of European history has been marked by struggles between opposed sets of religious "fanatics" (e.g., during the Protestant Reformation). Later, many religious minorities fled to America to secure their freedom (e.g., the Pilgrims), only to begin to persecute other religious minorities that they feared were subversive of their own new societies (e.g., the Quakers).

In the eighteenth and nineteenth centuries the expanding American frontier proved to be a fertile environment for religious innovation and the new ideas stimulated many social conflicts (e.g., the Mormons). More specifically though, it is important for people to realize that the very language and issues used to criticize "cults" today have their historical roots in the campaigns of negative propaganda directed at groups like the Catholics, Mormons, and Freemasons in the nineteenth century. Catholics, for example, were once accused in America of the same bizarre and threatening activities that the anti-cult movement now uses to discredit the Unification Church (i.e., the Moonies), the International Society for Krishna Consciousness, The Family, and other new religions (see Swatsky 1978; Bromley and Shupe 1979; Kent 1987). To borrow a famous phrase, the study of the controversy over "cults" suggests that "the more things change, the more they stay the same."

But while there is continuity in the defensive ways in which societies tend to react to new religions, it is equally important to realize that each new wave of religious innovation is the result, in part, of a societal response to the changed conditions of life. Religious changes tend to happen in conjunction with larger social changes. They are not simply caused by them. Rather it is more accurate to say that religious changes are simultaneously both the product of larger processes of social change, adaptive responses to these changes in society, and in some cases actual causes of social change. The relationship is dialectical and complex. But to understand the NRMs in our midst we must grasp how being religious in general has changed as a result of changes in the structures and values of the rest of society. In chapter 6, Robert Wuthnow traces the changes in the spiritual life of Americans since the 1960s, when the current surge of new religious activity began. Using interviews and survey data, Wuthnow creates a vivid impression of the changing religious sensibilities of Americans, isolating some of the reasons for change: the impact of the increased anonymity, mobility, and consumer orientation of life, the influence of the civil rights and feminist movements, and rising levels of education and prosperity. Wuthnow argues that Americans have turned increasingly from a spirituality of "dwelling," based on identification with a geographically fixed community, to a spirituality of "seeking," free of many traditional constraints. NRMs are the beneficiaries of a new religious environment marked by a historically unique emphasis on "freedom of choice" (as opposed to mere "freedom of conscience") and the pursuit of unconventional sources of spiritual enlightenment (i.e., other

religions and quasi-religious sources of inspiration and practice).

As Wuthnow's analysis suggests, the NRMs and our responses to them, whether positive or negative, often reflect our involvement in larger processes of social change that we only vaguely discern. Sociology shows that our lives are often shaped by social forces beyond our immediate control, by changes in the division of labor, the distribution of wealth, the exercise of political power, or the values, norms, and motivations to which we are socialized. These changes usually have unanticipated consequences. Wuthnow delineates why some Americans would be favorably disposed to what the NRMs had to offer, and most readers will likely recognize the ways in which their own lives have been gripped by the tensions and shifts in sensibilities he discusses. This realization will help bring home the greater significance of studying these small religious groups and the strife surrounding them. They often act as cultural barometers, warning us of changes occurring outside our range of awareness.

References

Bromley, David G. and Anson D. Shupe, Jr. 1979: The Tnevnoc Cult. *Sociological Analysis* 40 (4): 361–6.

Kent, Stephen A. 1987: Puritan Radicalism and the New Religious Organizations: Seventeenth-Century England and Contemporary America. In R. F. Tomasson (ed.), *Comparative Social Research*, vol. 10. Greenwich, CT: JAI Press, 3–46.

Stark, Rodney. 1996: *The Rise of Christianity*. Princeton, NJ: Princeton University Press.

Swatsky, Rodney. 1978: Moonies, Mormons, and Mennonites: Christian Heresy and Religious Toleration. In M. D. Bryant and H. W. Richardson (eds.), *A Time for Consideration: A Scholarly Appraisal of the Unification Church*. New York: Edwin Mellen Press, 20–40.

CHAPTER FIVE

False Prophets and Deluded Subjects: The Nineteenth Century

PHILIP JENKINS

> In what civilized country do evidences of religious fanaticism more abound?
>
> Frederick M. Davenport, *Primitive Traits in Religious Revivals*

Modern opposition to cults and cultlike behavior has deep historical roots. The modern cult stereotype is a complex construction, drawing on concepts originally developed to confront several quite distinct religious groups that would over time merge into one barely differentiated attack. When a modern critic attacks a deviant religious group as a cult, the images evoked are ultimately a mélange of rumors and allegations variously made against Catholics, Masons, Mormons, Shakers, radical evangelicals, and others. Anticult rhetoric encapsulates the whole history of American religious polemic. In the 1870s and 1880s, attacks on deviant religions developed something very like their modern form, owing in large part to the emergence of the mass circulation press in those years and the rise of exposé journalism.[1]

At every point, the stereotypes applied to modern "Moonies" and "Hare Krishnas" find parallels dating back many centuries. Perhaps the persistence of these charges just means that the deviant behaviors in question have always existed, that small religious groups have always engaged in the familiar sorts of violent and exploitative behavior. However, the continuity of rhetoric does have a consistent internal logic. Given that claims to perfection or superior sanctity automatically arouse suspicions of hypocrisy, it is not surprising that we so regularly find the same stereotype of religious fanaticism. Basically, anyone claiming mystical or charismatic authority is likely to be viewed as a rogue or a maniac, and his or her followers are portrayed as unstable dupes ready to perform any action, however degraded or criminal. As America has been so richly productive of prophets and visionaries, it is only to be expected that so many would be denounced as dangerous charlatans.

Prophets and Fanatics

The contemporary image of the cult leader who seduces his fanatical followers into destructive conflict with the established authorities is centuries old; it is even mentioned in the New Testament. In the European Middle Ages, a recurrent nightmare figure was the *prophetas*, the charismatic leader who decided that he (it was usually a man) had a special revelation from God to uproot the current political and ecclesiastical order and initiate a new order of righteousness, commonly by force of arms. Prophets were also accused of sexual unorthodoxy, of orgies or plural marriage. These deviant practices were sometimes justified by antinomian ideas, the view that moral laws had been repealed by the new revelation.[2] The sexually promiscuous messiah leading his armed devotees to a fortress in the wilderness was a stereotypical figure in Europe centuries before the image reappeared in Utah or Texas.

Such military millenarians arose sporadically throughout the medieval centuries, culminating in the great Anabaptist risings of the sixteenth century. In 1534, the prophet Jan of Leyden introduced communism and polygamy in the German city of Münster, in a Utopian regime enforced by the ruthless violence of the "saints," the Children of God. The experiment was destroyed with utmost ferocity by the established order of lords, bishops, and patricians. The Anabaptist sects became over time a far gentler breed, whose modern heirs are found among the Amish and Mennonites, but Jan of Leyden and his like were cited for centuries afterwards as the logical outcome of religious excess. The names of the Münster prophets had the same resonance in the seventeenth or eighteenth centuries that Jim Jones and David Koresh have for modern ears.

The equation seemed obvious: claims of personal revelation led to violent subversion and unrestrained sexuality, which if unchecked would destroy the social order. Lacking a central mechanism to regulate religious belief and practice, society would be at the mercy of fanatics, prophets, and imposters. The full consequences of unregulated religious debate emerged during the English Civil Wars of the 1640s, when the government lost control of public preaching and printing. The result was an upsurge of every kind of extreme and heretical belief. The crisis reached its blasphemous climax in 1656 when Quaker James Nayler staged a messianic entry into the city of Bristol with himself as Christ, mounted on a donkey, while faithful women followers strewed his path with branches and cried, "Hosanna to the son of David."

Though the word "cult" would have meant little to Nayler's contemporaries, this generation was in fact creating the first anticult literature in English. In 1646, orthodox Protestant writer Thomas Edwards published his encyclopedic *Gangraena* ("gangrene"), which provided "[a] catalogue . . . of many of the errors, heresies, blasphemies and pernicious practices of the sectaries of this time." In the process, he offered a list of almost every extreme and esoteric belief that would resurface in America over the next two centuries. Already Edwards was attacking Ranters and antinomians, pantheists and nudists, communists and perfectionists, self-anointed prophets and disorderly women.[3] Like their counterparts in later centuries, conservatives were reluctant to credit that such extravagant beliefs could have been held seriously, or spread without deceit, so Edwards and his like borrowed from the contemporary true crime literature to depict sect leaders as confidence tricksters, thieves, and sexual exploiters.

In understanding these outbreaks, critics like Edwards turned to the writings of the Church Fathers, who had confronted so many heresies in the early Christian centuries – to authors like Irenaeus, Eusebius, and Augustine. They found there the vocabulary required to combat the newly labeled "fanatics" and "enthusiasts." These epithets had a long history. The fanatic exemplified the sort of mindless devotion expected of the adherent of the temple, or *fana* (as in Samuel Butler's reference to "our lunatic, fanatic sects"), while the enthusiast literally claimed to be filled with the power of God, or of a god. Both words, "fanatic" and "enthusiast," have become debased in later speech ("fanatic" is the origin of "fan"), but at the time, they conveyed an all-too-serious threat. Well into the eighteenth century, "fanatic" was the normal word for describing those Protestant sects and preachers who lay outside the established Anglican Church, including Presbyterians, Baptists, and Congregationalists.

From earliest times, the English colonies in America likewise saw themselves as imperiled by subversive religious doctrines and sects of dubious sanity. The most alarming was the Quaker, or Friends, movement of the 1650s, the spiritual kin of James Nayler: the Friends argued that Christ was found in the Inner Light that guided each believer. Outsiders observing their enthusiastic worship style dubbed them "Quakers," which was an insulting epithet, rather like later smear words such as Shaker, Methodist, Mormon, and Moonie. As radical democrats, the Quakers rejected tokens of social hierarchy and challenged the power of clergy by vocally disrupting the formal services of the "steeple houses." Equally shocking, their most active preachers were often women. Between 1659 and 1661, four members of the sect were hanged on Boston Common.

Subversive images recurred during the Great Awakening of the 1730s and 1740s, when the ordained clergy were challenged by revivalists asserting that only those properly filled with the Spirit could lead the churches. The stress on direct revelation opened the way to the emergence of charismatic leaders, some of whom created scandal by their wild excesses, and revived shades of Münster. And when some evangelical leaders created their own communes and religious settlements, rumors about orgiastic celebrations and polygamy soon followed. In Pennsylvania, the Moravian leader Count Zinzendorf, who held daring ideas about sex and spirituality, was a special target for charges that he exploited his female disciples: his enemies christened him the *Herzens Papa*, or "Hearts' Daddy."[4] Like its successor revivals over the next two centuries, the Great Awakening was also criticized for encouraging bizarre and enthusiastic behavior. In the second great revival, which reached its height in 1799 and 1800, we hear of believers driven into ecstatic trances, convulsions, and jerks – wild frenzies that supposedly endangered their sanity. Conservatives charged that abandoning restraints in this way opened female believers to wild sexual excesses, so that the legendary camp meetings were criticized as orgies of debauchery.

Awful Disclosures: America, 1830–1870

American suspicions of fringe religious movements escalated rapidly during the 1830s and 1840s, as simultaneous campaigns against Catholics, Freemasons, and Mormons provided rich new materials for conceptualizing religious exploitation. The anti-Papist image had colonial roots, but was amplified by the presence of significant numbers of Catholic immigrants from the 1830s onwards. Virulent anti-Papist propaganda in American newspapers and pamphlets depicted lay Catholics as ignorant puppets, whose priests were sexually exploitative and conspiratorial. All the later anticult images were present here: Catholics exemplified mindless obedience to a deceitful religious leader, and authority was founded upon bloodthirsty enforcement. These ideas were long-lived. A Sinclair Lewis character noted in 1927 that the Church "requires you to give up your honesty, your reason, your heart and soul," while some years later the *Harvard Journal* described the Legion of Decency as a "Catholic organization, with its regimental draft of blindly obedient underlings on the one hand, and its Machiavellian pontiff on the other."[5]

This alien religion proselytized vigorously, drew naive young people into its web, and lured them to renounce their careers and prospects in order to enter celibate and totalistic religious communities. Convents and religious houses, which were found in all major American cities by the Civil War era, seemed as glaring an offense to personal freedom and intellectual liberty as the cult houses and headquarters of the 1970s. The notion of "escaping" from a religious community first appeared in the context of Catholic convents. Some of the bloodiest urban riots of the antebellum period erupted when citizens tried to liberate nuns from their supposed captivity or else to seek evidence of their crimes. Particularly sought after were the secret tunnels said to link the dwellings of priests and nuns, and the hidden cemeteries in which were buried the murdered babies resulting from these liaisons.

Also foreshadowing modern trends, the anti-Catholic movement paraded defectors from this evil organization, purported former nuns and priests whose firsthand accounts confirmed the worst charges about the sexual exploitation said to be rampant behind the walls of convents and rectories. These ideas surfaced in the sensational *Awful Disclosures of Maria Monk* (1836), which told of life in a Quebec convent and is the prototype for all subsequent defector memoirs. The book portrayed nuns as sex slaves, and its lurid depictions of flagellation added to its strong sadomasochistic appeal. Later bestsellers in this prurient tradition included *The Priest, the Woman and the Confessional* (1875), by the apostate priest Charles Chiniquy, who described the sexual exploitation of women parishioners by lustful priests. It was in the early 1890s that the American Protective Association propaganda campaign reached its height, with its tales of convent life as "grotesque ceremonies, orgies of sex and sadism" at the hands of "licentious and lecherous priests . . . seeking to lure young and innocent girls into sin."[6] Even in the mid-twentieth century, every issue of the *Converted Catholic Magazine* recounted horror stories of Catholic misdeeds, which included sinister associations with every dictatorship and massacre in modern history. Through the 1940s, there was a substantial industry in lecture tours by purported former nuns recounting pornographic fantasies to entranced Protestant audiences.

Anti-Catholicism can be seen as the largest and most potent anticult movement in American history. Several mass political movements aimed to destroy Catholic power, from the Nativists and Know-Nothings of the mid-nineteenth century to the American Protective Association (APA) of the 1890s and the Ku Klux Klan of the 1920s, and each crusade had a sizable impact on the national politics of its day. Each and its scurrilous press, which rehearsed stories of the Inquisition, the seditious secret oaths taken by the Knights of Columbus, the conspiratorial nature of the Jesuit order, and always, of course, the promiscuous nuns and lecherous priests. Reading the lurid charges presented in propaganda sheets like *The Menace* was enough "to make any boy wonder if the priest kept beautiful young girls tied up in the confessional booths, and if there was really an arsenal in the church basement."[7] The most damaging feature of APA propaganda was the publication of bogus statements and documents allegedly derived from Catholic sources, which warned that Catholics planned to exterminate all American Protestants as heretics.

In the mid-nineteenth century, anti-Catholic rhetoric and folklore merged with the polemic against other scapegoat groups,

namely Freemasons and Latter-Day Saints. As David Brion Davis has shown, the movements against these three menaces drew on very similar images: "If Masons, Catholics, and Mormons bore little resemblance to one another in actuality, as imagined enemies they merged into a nearly common stereotype."[8] According to their enemies, Masons and Mormons, like Catholics, belonged to a sinister false religion with clandestine methods and secret goals of secular power. Each was a closed secretive organization that maintained order and discipline through the threat of violence. The anti-Masonic movement erupted in 1826 because the group had supposedly kidnapped and murdered William Morgan, a defector who had threatened to reveal their secret rituals, with all their threats of bloody vengeance. The condemnation of the movement reached its height in the next decade, when an Anti-Masonic political party became a national political force.[9]

Anti-Mormon literature integrated the anti-Catholic charges with the older image of the *prophetas*, who claimed to be motivated by special direct revelations from God and who replaced the Christian scriptures with his own invented texts. These attacks drew on the popular Orientalism of the day, framing Joseph Smith in terms of the Prophet Muhammad, whom contemporary Christians saw as the prototypical religious impostor.[10] Muhammad was viewed as a self-proclaimed prophet or messiah who attracted a blindly obedient following prepared to die or kill for the new cause. His divine messages opened a new age of sexual excess, allowing the leader and his key followers sexual access to any woman follower. Finally, this new movement was transformed into a worldly kingdom, as followers carved out a secular realm. Joseph Smith himself drew the Muslim analogy, warning in 1838 that he "will be to this generation a second Mohammed, whose motto for treating for peace was 'The Alcoran or the sword.'" His movement became "the Islam of America."[11] Muslim analogies became more pronounced in 1852 when the new sect overtly declared its doctrine of polygamy. Polygamy became a prominent element in the anti-Mormon critique, both because it represented the most flagrant violation of conventional morality and because polygamy, like Catholic nunneries, offered such scope for prurient imaginations.

Flawed Utopias

Every element of the modern anticult polemic was a familiar component of American culture by about 1840, and the critique was powerfully reinforced from the upsurge of outré religious groups between about 1830 and 1860. Apocalyptic notions gave rise to the new Adventist churches, and millenarian ideas reached new intensity nationwide with the great revival of 1857. Mesmerist and Swedenborgian mystical notions were well established by the 1830s: these contributed to the new spiritualist movement, which emerged following the accounts of supernatural visitations at Hydesville, in New York state, in 1848.[12]

Common in the religious thought of the time was a sense of utopianism, the idea that humanity could achieve perfection in this life without postponing that prospect to heaven or the Day of Judgment. Perfectionist ideas were implemented in utopian communes, which tried to reform the human condition through new patterns of property ownership, sexual relationships, and changes in diet and healing methods. One celebrated colony was established by John Humphrey Noyes on the principle that the second coming had already occurred. His group practiced community of property and experimented with ideas of complex marriage, dismissing monogamy as "idolatrous love." In 1847, the commune took up residence at Oneida, in New York state, where it flourished into the 1880s; at its height, the membership reached almost three hundred.

Alongside the noble experiments of these exciting years, there were more worrying developments on the religious fringe. Scandal followed Robert Matthews, the Prophet Matthias, who declared himself the incarnated Spirit of Truth, and who gathered a band of dedicated followers in the New York City of the 1830s. Partly on the strength of his similar

name, Matthias consciously identified himself with the sixteenth-century Anabaptist Jan Mathys, one of the leaders of the revolutionary commune in Münster. The New York affair ended in disaster, when Matthias was charged with swindling and murdering one of his followers.[13] Together with the sensational publicity about the Mormons, the case of Matthias revived ancient ideas of the prophet as exploiter and false teacher.

Still more enduring, and more widespread, were the charges against the Shaker movement. Established in the United States since the late eighteenth century, the communal and celibate Shakers enjoyed their greatest period of expansion during the religious fervor of the 1840s. By 1860, perhaps six thousand members were scattered among nineteen settlements. The more converts there were, however, the more grounds for controversy. Shakers attracted popular hatred for much the same reasons as modern-day cult groups. Their religious system was believed to be anti-Christian, with its extreme veneration of prophetic founder Mother Ann Lee, whom critics painted as a drunkard and lecher. And Shaker rituals were dismissed as unorthodox and blasphemous, with services that involved ritual dancing, and enemies charged that secret ceremonies were carried out in the nude.

Most damaging (said critics) were the effects of membership on individuals and families. Families joined the Shaker communities en masse, but individuals resisted losing control of their children to the elders, who inflicted extreme physical punishments on them. When a member of a family tried to defect, the issue arose of his or her access to the children who remained within the sect; property signed over to the Shakers was another tender issue. Defectors fought to regain access to their children and, in so doing, aroused public sympathy for their cause by publishing harrowing accounts of Shaker misdeeds: obviously, these documents made no attempt at objectivity and painted the worst possible picture. During the first half of the century, these sensational conflicts regularly appeared in local newspapers across the country, but mainly in the Shaker heartland in the northeast.

The Shakers' most determined enemy was Mary Dyer, who was with her husband a member of the community from 1799 to 1815, and who left ("escaped") after the collapse of her marriage, and the deaths of two of her children. Her printed revelations of Shaker atrocities went into several editions, the most comprehensive of which appeared in 1847. She placed Ann Lee in the long succession of religious impostors that began with the serpent in the garden of Eden, and progressed through Simon Magus and Muhammad. Despite the sect's affected piety and egalitarianism, Dyer claimed that Shaker communities were slave societies, in which the leaders and elders lived richly, and violated rules against drunkenness and sexual vice, while ordinary believers became serfs once they had signed over their property. Families were divided, so that spouse was not able to talk to spouse or parent to child. The elite enforced their rule through physical violence, backed with sweeping threats of hellfire for any who should leave. Throughout, Dyer's story is substantiated by affidavits from former Shakers who had lost their families and goods to the sect, and who testified that youngsters were savagely beaten. Dyer also described the secret sexual practices of the Shaker leadership, who purportedly enhanced their pleasure by means of electric charges. Shakers were accused of employing both electricity and mesmeric spiritual powers for their secret ends, and Mesmerism was cited as the means by which they recruited converts and broke their wills. In summary, "this Shaker system is a combination of paganism, atheism and a spurious gospel, by means of which every member of the community is made a lanced spy upon the rest . . . The subordinate members are taught that it is a duty to keep within the bounds of those revelations which their leaders blasphemously pretend to receive from the Deity."[14]

Fighting the Sects, 1870–1890

Though controversy had always surrounded marginal religious groups, it was during the 1870s and 1880s that an accumulation of scandals and exposés led to a public reaction against fringe religions and a demand for official restrictions. The assault was sufficiently intense and widespread to permit us to speak of a cult scare, or at least a national anticult reaction. No one book offers the kind of generic denunciation of fringe religions that would become so commonplace in the 1920s or 1970s, but the concatenation of scandals produced an impression of a broad social threat. Between 1875 and 1887, public attacks on religious deviance were intense enough to foreshadow the outbreaks of the "cult wars" that would occur in the 1920s, The 1940s, and the late 1970s (see table 5.1).[15]

The new hostility to marginal groups partly reflected real evidence about fraud and criminal practice in these quarters, but political leaders were also more prepared than hitherto to enforce a degree of Christian religious orthodoxy. Both Evangelicalism and revivalism were riding high, and the Protestant ethos of this time saw few difficulties in using the law to enforce public morality. Between 1864 and 1874, evangelicals sponsored a lively campaign to pass a constitutional amendment that would have formally declared the United States a Christian nation.[16] Despite the rhetoric of religious freedom, toleration was extended only grudgingly to groups outside the Judaeo-Christian tradition. Toleration did not comprehend Native American religious upsurges like the Ghost Dance movement, which was brutally suppressed in 1890. As late as the 1920s, the federal Bureau of Indian Affairs was actively seeking the suppression of Native American religion and fighting manifestations of "paganism."[17]

The Mormon crisis

One major target among the new religions was the Church of Jesus Christ of Latter-Day Saints. Although their settlement in Utah would soon be seeking statehood, the religion was bedeviled by attacks on its bloodthirsty record. Between 1856 and 1858, the US government had fought a literal war against the sect, a conflict marked by guerrilla operations

Table 5.1   Cults and cult scandals, 1875–1888

1875	Theosophical Society founded.
	Charles Nordhoff publishes *The Communistic Societies of the United States.*
	Ann Eliza Young, *Wife No. 19, or The Story of a Life in Bondage.*
	Charles Chiniquy, *The Priest, the Women and the Confessional.*
	Mary Baker Eddy, *Science and Health.*
1877	Execution of Mormon bishop John Lee for his part in the Mountain Meadows massacre.
	Fanny Stenhouse, *Tell it All: The Story of a Life's Experience in Mormonism.*
	Publication of *Mormonism Unveiled.*
	H. P. Blavatsky, *Isis Unveiled.*
1878	Formation of the Anti-Polygamy Society.
1879	US Supreme Court decides case of *Reynolds v. US*
	J. H. Noyes flees the Oneida colony.
	Alleged human sacrifice in Pocasset, Massachusetts.
	First Church of Christ, Scientist, founded.
	First publication of *The Watch Tower.*
1881	Assassination of President Garfield by Charles Guiteau.
1882	Federal Edmunds Act criminalizes polygamy.
	Fanny Stenhouse, *An Englishwoman in Utah.*
	Jennie Anderson Froiseth edits *The Women of Mormonism.*
	Society of Psychical Research formed.
1883	Joseph Pulitzer acquires the *New York World.*
1884	Madame Blavatsky's associates accuse her of faking mediumistic phenomena.
1885	Society of Psychical Research condemns Blavatsky in its "Hodgson Report."
1887	Arthur Conan Doyle publishes *A Study in Scarlet.*
	Federal Edmunds-Tucker Act introduces more intrusive procedures to detect and suppress polygamy.
	Preliminary Report of the Seybert Commission published.
1888	Margaret Fox describes deception in origins of Spiritualist movement.
	Reuben Briggs Davenport, *The Death-Blow to Spiritualism.*
	H. P. Blavatsky, *The Secret Doctrine.*

and punitive raids. The most notorious event was the Mountain Meadows massacre of 1857, in which 120 emigrants on a wagon train, both men and women, were killed by Mormon paramilitaries. The incident was eclipsed by the worse horrors of the struggle between abolitionist and slaveholding supporters in Bleeding Kansas and then the Civil War itself, but the massacre cast a long shadow. In 1872, Mark Twain's popular book, *Roughing It*, reminded readers of the crime, when "the whole United States rang with its horrors." Twain also told of the Mormons' Destroying Angels, the Danites, who were "set apart by the Church to conduct permanent disappearances of obnoxious citizens": generally, Utah was "a luscious country for thrilling evening storier about assassinations of intractable Gentiles."[18] The Mountain Meadows slaughter was again in the headlines in the mid-1870s, when Bishop John Lee went on trial for ordering the attack; Lee was eventually executed in 1877. One explosive element of the case was the charge that real guilt should be assigned to Brigham Young, for whom Lee was serving as a scapegoat, "an official assassin of the Mormon church under the late Brigham Young." One 1904 account of Young's rule in Utah highlighted "the Mountain Meadow massacre – the reign of terror in Utah – the doctrine of human sacrifice . . . the facts of polygamy."[19]

Anti-Mormon tracts appeared at an accelerating rate from the early 1870s, with sensational books on polygamy like *Wife No. 19: A Complete Exposé of Mormonism*, by "Brigham Young's Apostate Wife." A later edition of this book bore the elaborate title *Life in Mormon Bondage*, and promised "a complete exposé of its false prophets, murderous Danites, despotic rulers and hypnotized deluded subjects," which is a fair epitome of the whole tradition of anticult polemic. Drawing from anti-Catholic stereotypes, a Massachusetts paper described Mormonism as founded upon "the ambition of an ecclesiastical hierarchy to wield sovereignty, to rule the souls and lives of its subjects with absolute authority, unrestrained by any civil power."[20]

Charges that Mormon death squads and Danites wrought bloody vengeance upon the movement's enemies were sufficiently well-known to provide the basis of the first Sherlock Holmes story, *A Study in Scarlet*, which appeared in 1887 and is perhaps the first example of the use of a cult setting in a mystery story. Conan Doyle's story relies on the anti-Mormon tracts that publishers had poured out over the previous two decades, especially the autobiographical memoir published by Fanny Stenhouse.[21] *A Study in Scarlet* depicts a region living under a reign of religious terror: "To express an unorthodox opinion was a dangerous matter in those days in the Land of the Saints." The Church's secret enforcement arm "appeared to be omniscient and omnipotent, and yet was neither seen nor heard. The man who held out against the Church vanished away, and none knew whither he had gone or what had befallen him . . . To this day in the lonely ranches of the West, the name of the Danite

Band or the Avenging Angels is a sinister and ill-omened one." Conan Doyle added another twist to the mythology of polygamy when he charged that Church leaders kidnapped women for their harems.

The polygamy question now led to one of the most sweeping episodes of religious persecution in American history. From 1862, federal antipolygamy laws threatened the whole legal basis of the religion and invalidated Utah laws sanctioning multiple marriage. After the Civil War, the federal government had even less tolerance for regions claiming the right to defend local traditions that violated national law. Appealing to this centralizing principle, critics of polygamy cited the practice as Utah's "peculiar institution," a phrase that recalled southern slavery. In 1878, Protestant women formed an Anti-Polygamy Society, explicitly modeled on the old Anti-Slavery Society. The traditional religious critique of polygamy was now reinforced by a feminist assault on the male subjugation of women.[22]

The religious freedom issue found its way to the US Supreme Court, which had recently ruled in 1871 that "[t]he law knows no heresy, and is committed to the support of no dogma, the establishment of no sect." However, that case, *Watson v. Jones*, had concerned a theological squabble within an established denomination, namely the Presbyterians; the laissez-faire principle was not extended to new sects. In 1879, the Court overruled objections that antipolygamy statutes violated the constitutional freedom of religion, affirming in the case of *Reynolds v. US* the principle that religious freedom extended only to belief, not to action. "Congress was deprived of all legislative power over mere opinion, but was left free to reach actions which were in violation of social duties or subversive of good order."

New federal measures fought polygamy with draconian policies that made serious inroads into traditional constitutional and legal protections, and that brought the federal government deep into the business of enforcing religious orthodoxy. The Edmunds Act of 1882 declared polygamy a felony and made

polygamous "unlawful cohabitation" a mis-
demeanor. The law disfranchised polygamists,
excluded them from public office or jury
service, and banned most Mormons from participating in the government of a territory in
which they made up 85 percent of the population. Polygamist exclusion was enforced by
test oaths, and in 1887, a new law demanded
that wives testify against their husbands.
Mormon leaders were arrested or forced to
flee, and some 1,300 men were convicted
under the Edmunds law. The Church of the
Latter-Day Saints was disincorporated and its
property escheated to the United States. The
crisis ended only in 1890, when Mormon
President Wilford Woodruff declared that he
had received a revelation ending polygamy at
least as earthly practice (Mormon men could
still enjoy plural wives in the afterlife). This
change of doctrine paved the way for Utah's
admission as a state in 1896, though the traditional anti-Mormon polemic would often
resurface in the new century.

Attacking the communes

The communes were also attracting critical
interest in these years. Since the 1840s, various
communes had been rent by accusations that
they were being usurped by dictatorial and
authoritarian self-appointed spiritual elites.
Even in the liberated Transcendentalist group
at Fruitlands, women members charged that
overweening male leaders trampled their
rights. In 1875, Charles Nordhoff, in *The
Communistic Societies of the United States*,
published sympathetic accounts of groups as
diverse as the Zoarites, Icarians, and Shakers.
Nordhoff nevertheless raised troubling questions about the fate of the individual will and
personality in such settings and about the lack
of privacy. He also described one of the harrowing group criticism meetings by means of
which the Oneida group maintained internal
order.[23] Though still a long way from the
charges of brainwashing that would be
directed against the cults of the 1970s, critics
of the communes cited Nordhoff's account to
show that group pressure could produce dis-

turbing changes in personality – and possibly
mental instability.

Of much more concern to the critics was the
liberated sexual ambience at Oneida, which
encouraged the idea that "commune" was
simply a code word for group sex. By 1870, the
press was denouncing the commune for its
depravity: surveying press reports about themselves, the Oneida community's news sheet
reported, "The word filth, with its derivatives
filthy, filthiness, etc, occurs nine times; abomi-
nation, abominable, etc, six times; depravity,
depraved, etc, six times; lust four times; blasphemy three times; licentiousness three times;
bestial, foul, and horrible, each twice."
Pubescent youngsters were encouraged to
enter freely into the communal sex life, and
community head J. H. Noyes was often the one
to offer sexual initiation to girls of twelve or
thirteen. Given the contemporary age-of-
consent laws, this was not necessarily criminal
in itself, but there was always the danger of
other sex-related charges, like fornication. By
1879, the clergy and media were pressing for
prosecution: using an ominous analogy, a Syracuse newspaper saw "the Oneida Community
as far worse in their practices than the polygamists of Utah."[24] In response, Noyes suddenly
abdicated from Oneida and fled to Canada.

Two years later, the commune received
more scandalous publicity when one of its
alumni assassinated President Garfield. The
culprit, Charles Guiteau, had been a member
of the Oneida group from 1860 to 1866,
leaving in part because of the impossibility of
finding sexual partners. In 1867 he launched
a moralistic campaign against Oneida and its
alleged vices. Adding to the "cult" element of
the assassination, Guiteau was a profound
believer in spiritualism, and he blamed the
spirits for motivating him to undertake the key
decisions of his life, including the attack on
Garfield. In the ensuing trial, Guiteau's religious fanaticism was cited as a textbook
example of the conditions likely to drive a
person to violent insanity.[25]

Other commune leaders were haunted by
sexual allegations. One such was Thomas Lake
Harris, whose career on the religious fringe
spanned the second half of the nineteenth

century. Originally a spiritualist and a Swedenborgian minister, he operated a series of communes from 1850 onwards and led a sect known as the Brotherhood of the New Life, which he ruled autocratically as "Man, Seer, Adept, and Avatar." Harris preached a complex sexual mysticism that presumed the existence of both masculine and feminine divine spirits: believers were urged to find their spiritual "counterparts" with whom they would beget spiritual offspring. Though commune members apparently lived in strict chastity, tales of orgies, wife swapping, ritual nudity, and child molestation followed the Brotherhood from the late 1860s onwards. Also criticized was the practice of breaking up earthly families and removing children from their parents. Perhaps to escape the scrutiny of the New York newspapers, Harris's group migrated to northern California in 1875, but through the 1880s, the sect was riven by personal feuds, in which each faction publicly denounced its rivals as fanatics. A delighted press picked up the ensuing scandals, reporting on orgies in the Santa Rosa commune and charging that Harris used his hypnotic powers to control his followers and victims. In 1892, the San Francisco *Wave* stated that "his religion is just a trifle worse than Mormonism . . . the place is an idealized house of sin, a den of iniquitous debauchees, whose only religion is the satisfaction of the passions, where there are no ties of affection, and where both sexes of one family bed together like dogs in a kennel."[26]

The crisis of spiritualism

Another new religious system that now found itself under attack was spiritualism, which predictably boomed following the Civil War, as thousands of grieving families sought to contact their lost loved ones. Religious critics had long attacked the movement as criminal necromancy, charging that spirit manifestations were the work of deceptive demons. The new critique was strictly secular and practical, branding spiritualism as a blatant confidence trick. The movement was discredited by copious evidence of fraudulent mediums, particularly the racket in spirit photography, in which photographic images were crudely retouched to suggest the presence of a ghost. The pioneer of this process went on trial in 1869. In 1882, the Society for Psychical Research was formed, and it publicized the extensive evidence of trickery and deception it found among the vast majority of the mediums it examined. Deriding mediums became a literary cliché: in 1883, Twain's *Life on the Mississippi* offered a transcript of a seance in which the medium characteristically spoke in utter generalities, omitting any concrete fact that might have proved the truth of communication from the beyond. By the 1880s, spiritualism had to a large extent lost its niche in high society, and a Henry James character could scoff at the progressive subculture of Boston's "witches and wizards, mediums and spirit rappers, and roaring radicals."[27]

The reaction against spiritualism culminated with several developments from 1887 to 1888. The most damaging involved Margaret Fox, one of the two girls who had been at the center of the original visitation at Hydesville forty years previously. On joining the Catholic Church, Fox published a full confession of "this horrible deception" perpetrated by her sister and herself. The mysterious knocks and clicks had been quite material things, which the girls had done by rapping with their feet, or manipulating the joints in their toes and fingers. Margaret demonstrated the whole technique to a journalist for Pulitzer's *New York World*, for whom she was able to summon forth answers from the great beyond. Among other things, she produced the spirits of Napoleon Bonaparte and Abraham Lincoln, and Napoleon obligingly stated, through rapping, that he had known the journalist well, eighty years before. Although she would later recant her recantation, the whole affair was ruinous. In 1888, a sensational New York trial resulted in the imprisonment of medium Ann O'Delia Diss Debar, for attempting to defraud a client.[28]

About the same time, the University of Pennsylvania published the results of an investigative commission that had been established with funds left by Henry Seybert, who had wished to see the truth of spiritualist claims established for the public record. The Seybert commission was made up of ten open-minded scholars, who worked for three years witnessing some of the best-known mediums of the day. Even under these optimum conditions, spiritualism could not be verified: "In every case with but one exception the result was either a blank seance, a positive failure, or a deliberate cheat." Margaret Fox easily convinced the commission that she had been faking her claims, and shortly afterwards the Fox story was reported in a book with the optimistic title *The Death-Blow to Spiritualism*. It was no such thing, and a new Nationalist Spiritualist Alliance of Churches was formally organized in 1893, but the movement's popularity reached a low ebb at the turn of the century.[29] In 1898, an Episcopalian critic claimed to "see in spiritualism nothing but useless and profitless imposition, deceit and trickery, accompanied by most mercenary motives. Moreover, even if these mediums are influenced by spiritualistic powers, they are the forces of darkness, not of the light."[30]

Theosophy

A similar skepticism extended to sects with practices akin to spiritualism, like Theosophy. The Theosophical Society was formed in New York City in 1875 by Helena P. Blavatsky and Henry Olcott, both of whom had a long-standing interest in seances and mediumship: the two leaders met when both came to the defense of two allegedly bogus mediums. As outlined in Blavatsky's influential books *Isis Unveiled* (1877) and *The Secret Doctrine* (1888), the Theosophical movement integrated spiritualist ideas with a great deal of Hindu and Buddhist thought, including the theories of karma and reincarnation. The movement also offered an extensive history of human civilizations dating back millions of years through the time of Atlantis, incorporating the stories of many lost races and civilizations. Blavatsky claimed to have obtained her wisdom in hidden lamaseries in Tibet and central Asia, where she had found secret texts like the (imaginary) *Stanzas of Dzyan*. She also relied on material channeled from great supernatural Masters, members of the Great White Brotherhood, a select club that included Jesus, the Buddha, Confucius, Mesmer, and Cagliostro, as well as real-life occultists she had consulted over the years.

Theosophy was enjoying a global boom by the early 1880s and its ideas would have a profound influence on all subsequent occultism, but the movement entered a period of crisis in 1884 with a series of scandals. There were the usual mediumistic tricks and equally embarrassing was the leadership's use of letters supposedly channeled from higher spiritual realms. The contents of these letters provided all-too-convenient ammunition for internal factional squabbles. Blavatsky's other difficulties involved the living Masters, whom she had exalted into mythological supernatural beings: "Mahatmas, who . . . could hold the Mount Meru on the tip of their finger, and fly to and fro in their bodies at their will, and who were . . . more gods on earth than a God in Heaven could be." The discovery that these individuals were all too human led to general disappointment among the group's followers, but critics were delighted.[31]

Theosophy also suffered from troubling charges of literary fraud and plagiarism, of the sort that were continually directed against the Mormon scriptures. Reviewers pointed out that if in fact ascended Masters or Mahatmas had assisted Blavatsky in writing her great spiritual texts, then they had a nasty tendency to plagiarism. One scholar claimed to demonstrate that everything in the pioneering Theosophical text *Isis Unveiled* was derived from a corpus of about a hundred books, all avaiable to the supposed channeller, Madame Blavatsky. The Masters also demonstrated a remarkable ignorance of Indian culture and tended to rely on modern popularizations. In 1898, the magazine *Contemporary Literature* attacked the founder of Theosophy in a biting article entitled "Madame Blavatsky and Her Dupes."[32]

The Media and the Cults

During the latter years of the nineteenth century, the climate for the new sects became chillier as the news media became more sensational in tone, finding rich material in the religious fringe. When, for instance, a murder case could be linked to religious extremism, it was interpreted as the outcome of cult fanaticism rather than simple insanity. In 1879, a brutal child murder in Pocasset, Massachusetts, was reported in a contemporary pamphlet, *The Victim of a Father's Fanaticism!* According to this account of "the Pocasset fanatics . . . Charles Freeman, the 'second Adventist,' imagining himself another Abraham, slays his little daughter, offering up his darling child as a human sacrifice!"[33]

American journalism experienced a revolution in the 1880s, inaugurated by Joseph Pulitzer's acquisition of the *New York World* in 1883. The Pulitzer press pioneered the modern era of crusading exposés, the "new journalism," also known less flatteringly as "yellow journalism." The tradition was pushed to even greater lengths after William Randolph Hearst bought the *New York Journal* in 1895. The phenomenal success of the *World* and the *Journal* inspired other press lords across the nation: the number of daily newspapers in the United States rose from 574 in 1870 to 2,600 by 1909, their combined circulation from 2.6 million to 24.2 million. Both Hearst and Pulitzer chains made campaigns against cults and bogus religions a staple of their coverage, so that any new claims to divine inspiration could expect to be greeted with the debunking zeal that had been directed against Theosophy and spiritualism. Happy was the newspaper that had within its market area an eccentric commune ready to be investigated and exposed during slow news periods. Some papers developed a minor specialization in cult debunking, above all the *New York World*, but also the *Los Angeles Times* and the *San Francisco Examiner* (the *Examiner* was another Hearst organ). In the first decade of the new century, the *Brooklyn Daily Eagle* successively declared war upon Christian Science, the Emmanuel Movement, and the Watch Tower Society.[34]

The media found a continuing stream of ludicrous and scandalous material in various sects, some of which recalled the great days of communal expansion.[35] One controversial figure was John Alexander Dowie, who practiced spiritual healing until in 1895, when he was denounced by the *Chicago Tribune* for unlicensed practice of medicine. By 1901, he had founded a theocratic commune at Zion City, Illinois, and declared himself Elijah the Restorer; he believed that the earth was flat and was described as a "paranoiac swindler." The affairs of Zion City offered lively scandal to the press until the settlement was finally burned to the ground in 1937.[36]

Just as eccentric as Dowie was Dr. Cyrus R. Teed, who adopted a range of quasi-Hindu and reincarnationist beliefs. He also preached that the world was hollow and that we are living within it. Teed developed a colony of true believers at the Church Triumphant in Florida, where he took the messianic name Koresh, recalling the Hebrew title of the biblical king Cyrus. He survived until 1906, becoming something of a tourist attraction in the Fort Myers area, where his sect survived into the 1940s. After his death, his disciples kept watch over his body in expectation of his resurrection, giving up only when he showed unmistakable signs of decomposition. The same story about followers expecting a deceased messiah to arise is told of several other groups in this era, suggesting that the motif had become a media cliché: it had been applied to Ann Lee and also appears in the context of Thomas Lake Harris and Benjamin Purnell.[37]

Apart from depicting cult leaders as cranks, news stories also reinforced images of sexual excess and immorality. Even the new sect of Christian Science was blamed for dividing families and encouraging vice, and by 1890, "the odium of increasing divorce and domestic alienation the land over was often attributed to Christian Science."[38] The lurid publicity surrounding the Mormon polygamists was reinforced by other instances of "love cults" and "sex cults," often involving underage girls. One such affair in Oregon culminated in 1906 when the outraged relatives of a young victim murdered a self-proclaimed Elijah the Prophet, after he had drawn dozens of local girls and women into his messianic cult.[39]

Much more substantial was the House of David group, which provided a remarkable link with the most extreme sectarian movements of the eighteenth century. The movement traced its spiritual ancestry to the revelations of Joanna Southcott, the English prophetess of the 1790s, who claimed to be the first in a sequence of Divine Messengers who would usher in the End Times. By the 1890s, the Flying Rollers (or Israelites) had formed a communal settlement headed by Michael Mills of Detroit. At the turn of the century, however, Mills went the way of many other messiahs and was convicted of the statutory rape of a young colony member during a religious rite. The publicity ignited a scandal that forced the colony out of Detroit amidst threats of lynching, and newspaper headlines about "A Bestial Religion" and the "Long-Haired Prince of Darkness."[40] Not for the last time, the Detroit and Chicago newspapers could rejoice at the presence of the House of David in their readership area.

At just the same time as the Mills affair, the *Los Angeles Times* determined on a crusade against its own local cultists, namely the Theosophical commune Katherine Tingley had founded at Point Loma, near San Diego. In 1901, accusing the Theosophists of conducting "weird orgies," the paper offered headlines like "Outrages at Point Loma Exposed by an Escape" and "Women and Children Starved and Treated Like Convicts. Thrilling Rescue." The *Times* reported how at midnight the pilgrims, "in their nightrobes, each holding a torch," went to a sacred spot on the Point Loma peninsular where "gross immoralities were practised by the disciples of spookism."[41] Tingley successfully sued the paper for libel and used the threat of legal sanctions repeatedly against later challenges from other powerful papers, including the *New York World*. Even so, the affair illustrates the emergence of what had come to be a potent cliché of cults and communes, which in the public mind already evoked "gross immoralities" and "thrilling rescues."

The intensity of the criticism directed against fringe religions did not necessarily impede their growth or discourage the emergence of ever

newer ones... The 1880s were an exciting time of growth for the new movements promising spiritual healing, which coalesced into the church of Christian Science and the various schools of New Thought, while occult and Theosophical groups also prospered. But all the emerging movements faced deep hostility from the media and other critics, who now lumped the new creeds together under the suspicious title of "cult."

Notes

1 Robert N. Bellah and Frederick E. Greenspahn, eds., *Uncivil Religion* (New York: Crossroad, 1987); David H. Bennett, *The Party of Fear*, 2nd edn. (New York: Vintage, 1995).

2 For military messiahs in the Bible, see Acts 5:36–7 (RSV). Norman Cohn, *Pursuit of the Millennium*, 3rd end. (London: Paladin, 1970).

3 Thomas Edwards, *Gangraena* (London, 1646); Jerome Friedman, *Blasphemy, Immorality, and Anarchy* (Athens: Ohio University Press, 1987).

4 Joseph J. Kelley, *Pennsylvania: The Colonial Years 1681–1776* (Garden City, NY: Doubleday, 1980), 221. Sydney E. Ahlstrom, *A Religious History of the American People* (New Haven, CT: Yale University Press, 1972). For the European reaction against religious enthusiasm in these years, see Hillel Schwartz, *The French Prophets* (Berkeley: University of California Press, 1979); Michael Heyd, *Be Sober and Reasonable* (Leiden, Netherlands: E. J. Brill, 1995).

5 Jenny Franchot, *Roads to Rome* (Berkeley: University of California Press, 1994); *Harvard Journal* April 16, 1934; John T. McGreevy, "Thinking on One's Own," *Journal of American History* 84 (1997): 97–131.

6 In *The Truth About the Catholic Church* (Girard, KS: Haldeman Julius, 1926), former monk Joseph McCabe recounted many scandals involving drunkenness and sexual license, while as late as 1962, former priest Emmett McLoughlin published his study of *Crime and Immorality in the Catholic Church* (New York: Lyle Stuart, 1962). David G. Bromley, ed., *The Politics of Religious Apostasy* (Westport, CT: Praeger, 1998).

7 Marcus Bach, *They Have Found a Faith* (Indianapolis, IN: Bobbs-Merrill, 1946), 14; Donald L. Kinzer, *An Episode in Anti-Catholicism* (Seattle: University of Washington Press, 1964).

8 David Brion Davis, "Some Themes of Counter-Subversion," in *From Homicide to Slavery* (New York: Oxford University Press, 1986), 137–54.

9 Bennett, *The Party of Fear.*

10 M. Aikin, *Memoirs of Religious Impostors* (London: Jones and Co., 1822).

11 Fawn Brodie, *No Man Knows My History*, revd. end. (New York: Vintage, 1971), 230–1; Bruce Kinney, *Mormonism: The Islam of America* (New York: Fleming H. Revell, 1912); Gary L. Ward, ed., *Mormonism I: Evangelical Christian Anti-Mormonism in the Twentieth Century* (New York: Garland, 1990); Fuad Sha'ban, *Islam and Arabs in Early American Thought* (Durham, NC: Acorn, 1991).

12 Jon Butler, "The Dark Ages of American Occultism," in *The Occult in America*, ed. Howard Kerr and Charles L. Crow (Urbana: University of Illinois Press, 1983), 58–78; Jon Butler, *Awash in a Sea of Faith* (Cambridge, MA: Harvard University Press, 1990); Anne Braude, *Radical Spirits* (Boston: Beacon Press, 1991); Robert L. Moore, *In Search of White Crows* (New York: Oxford University Press, 1977); Arthur Wrobel, ed., *Pseudo-Science and Society in Nineteenth-Century America* (Lexington: University Press of Kentucky, 1987). For the British experience, see Alison Winter, *Mesmerized* (Chicago, IL: University of Chicago Press, 1998).

13 Paul E. Johnson and Sean Wilentz, *The Kingdom of Matthias* (New York: Oxford University Press, 1994).

14 Mary Marshall (i.e., Mary M. Dyer), *The Rise and Progress of the Serpent from the Garden of Eden to the Present Day* (Concord, NH: 1847). The quote is from 147; the use of electricity is described on 184–5; Mesmerism on 221. Mary M. Dyer, *A Portraiture of Shakerism* (Concord, NH: 1822). Lawrence Foster, *Religion and Sexuality* (New York: Oxford University Press, 1981).

15 Though see ... William Oxley, *Modern Messiahs and Wonder Workers* (London: Trubner and Son, 1889).

16 Isaac Kramnick and R. Laurence Moore, *The Godless Constitution* (New York: Norton, 1996).

17 Kathleen Egan Chamberlain, "The Native American," in *Religion in Modern New Mexico*, ed. Ferenc M. Szasz and Richard W. Etulain (Albuquerque: University of New Mexico Press, 1997). James Mooney, *The Ghost Dance* (North Dighton, MA: JG Press, 1996).

18 Mark Twain, *Roughing It* (Chicago, IL: F. G. Gilman, 1872); J. H. Beadle, *The History of Mormonism* (Toronto: A. H. Hovey, 1873); Gary L. Bunker and Davis Bitton, *The Mormon Graphic Image, 1834–1914* (Salt Lake City: University of Utah Press, 1983).

19 *The Mormon Menace, being the confession of John Doyle Lee, Danite, an official assassin of the Mormon church under the late Brigham Young* (New York: Home Protection Publishing, 1905); *Mormonism Unveiled; or, The life and confessions of the late Mormon bishop, John D. Lee. ... Also the true history of the horrible butchery known as the Mountain Meadows massacre* (St. Louis, MO: Bryan, Brand, 1877); Juanita Brooks, *The Mountain Meadows Massacre*, revd. edn. (Norman: University of Oklahoma Press, 1970); T. B. H. Stenhouse, *The Rocky Mountain Saints* (Salt Lake City, UT: Shepard Book Co., 1904).

20 Ann Eliza Young, *Wife No. 19, or The Story of a Life in Bondage* (Hartford, CT: Dustin, Gilman, 1875); Jennie Anderson Froiseth, ed., *The Women of Mormonism* (Detroit, MI: C. G. G. Paine, 1882). The book *Life in Mormon Bondage* discussed here was basically a reprinting of *Wife No. 19* and was published by Philadelphia's Aldine Press in 1908. The quotation from the Massachusetts paper is from Ann Taves, "Sexuality in American Religious History," in *Retelling U.S. Religious History*, ed. Thomas A. Tweed (Berkeley: University of California Press, 1997), 45.

21 Fanny Stenhouse, *Tell It All: The Story of a Life's Experience in Mormonism* (Hartford, CT: A. D. Worthington, 1877); Fanny Stenhouse, *An English woman in Utah ... Including a full account of the Mountain Meadows massacre, and of the life, confession and execution of Bishop John D. Lee* (London: S. Low, Marston, Searle and Rivington, 1882).

22 Taves, "Sexuality in American Religious History," 45.

23 For Fruitlands, see Anne C. Rose, *Transcendentalism as a Social Movement* (New Haven, CT: Yale University Press, 1981), 125–8; Louis J. Kern, *An Ordered Love* (Chapel Hill: University of North Carolina Press, 1981). Charles Nordhoff, *The Communistic Societies*

of the United States (London: J Murray, 1875), 287–98.

24 The survey of hostile press reports is from Spencer Klaw, *Without Sin* (New York: Penguin, 1993), 163; the Syracuse paper is quoted in ibid, 245.

25 Harry Houdini, *A Magician Among the Spirts* (New York: Harper, 1924), 187–8; Charles E. Rosenberg, *The Trial of the Assassin Guiteau* (Chicago, IL: University of Chicago Press, 1976).

26 Herbert W. Schneider and George Lawton, *A Prophet and a Pilgrim* (New York: Columbia University Press, 1942); "Respiro," *The Man, the Seer, the Adept, the Avatar*, 2nd edn. (London, E. W. Allen, 1897); Thomas Lake Harris, *Brotherhood of the New Life* (Santa Rosa, CA: Fountain Grove Press, 1891). The quote from the Wave is from Schneider and Lawton, 556.

27 Barbara Goldsmith, *Other Powers* (New York: Knopf, 1998); Howard Kerr, *Mediums, and Spirit-Rappers, and Roaring Radicals* (Urbana: University of Illinois Press, 1972); Houdini, *A Magician Among the Spirits*.

28 Houdini, *A Magician Among the Spirits*.

29 "In every case with but one exception" is from Houdini, *A Magician Among the Spirits*, 195; *Preliminary report of the Commission appointed by the University of Pennsylvania to investigate modern spiritualism* (Philadelphia, PA: J. B. Lippincott, 1887); Reuben Briggs Davenport, *The Death-Blow to Spiritualism* (1888; New York: G. W. Dillingham, 1897); Elijah Farrington and C. F. Pidgeon, *Revelations of a Spirit Medium* (St. Paul, MN: Farrington, 1891); David P. Abbott, *Behind the Scenes with the Mediums* (Chicago, IL: Open Court, 1907); William Jackson Crawford, *Hints and Observations for those Investigating the Phenomena of Spiritualism* (New York: E. P. Dutton, 1918).

30 Arthur H. Barrington, *Anti-Christian Cults* (Milwaukee, WI: Young Churchman, 1898), 29–30.

31 Peter Washington, *Madame Blavatsky's Baboon* (New York: Schocken Books, 1995); K. Paul Johnson, *Initiates of Theosophical Masters* (Albany: State University of New York Press, 1995); K. Paul Johnson, *The Masters Revealed* (Albany: State University of New York Press, 1994); Joscelyn Godwin, *The Theosophical Enlightenment* (Albany: State University of New York Press, 1994); Michael Gomes, *The Dawning of the Theosophical Society* (Wheaton, IL: Theosophical Society, 1987); Bruce F. Campbell, *Ancient Wisdom Revived* (Berkeley: University of California Press, 1980); Robert S. Ellwood, "The American Theosophical Synthesis," in Kerr and Crow, eds., *The Occult in America*, 111–34. The quote is from Blavatsky, in K. Paul Johnson, "Imaginary Mahatmas," *Gnosis* 28 (summer 1993): 28. Blavatsky made an enormous contribution to the Western mythology depicting Tibet as a mystic paradise: see Donald S. Lopez, *Prisoners of Shangri-La* (Chicago, IL: University of Chicago Press, 1998).

32 Cited in Barrington, *Anti-Christian Cults*, 101. Edmund Garrett, *Isis Very Much Unveiled: Being The Story Of The Great Mahatma Hoax* (London: Westminster Gazette, 1894). For other contemporary attacks on Theosophy, see Aidan A. Kelly, ed., *Theosophy II* (New York: Garland, 1990).

33 *Poor Little Edith Freeman: The Victim of a Father's Fanaticism!* (Philadelphia, PA: Barclay and Co., 1879).

34 For campaigns by the *Brooklyn Eagle*, see *The Emmanuel Movement: A Brief History of the New Cult* (Brooklyn: *Brooklyn Daily Eagle*, 1908); William H. Muldoon, *Christian Science Claims Un-Scientific and Un-Christian . . . Eddyism, its healings and fallacies investigated* (Brooklyn: *Brooklyn Daily Eagle*, 1901) . . .

35 Robert S. Fogarty, *All Things New* (Chicago, IL: University of Chicago Press, 1990); Donald E. Pitzer, ed., *America's Communal Utopias* (Chapel Hill: University of North Carolina Press, 1997); Timothy Miller, *The Quest for Utopia in Twentieth-Century America: 1900–1960* (Syracuse, NY: Syracuse University Press, 1998).

36 Martin E. Marty, *Modern American Religion I: The Irony of It All* (Chicago, IL: University of Chicago Press, 1986), 234–4.

37 "This Hollow World: Koreshans," *Newsweek*, December 6, 1948, 26; Elmer T. Clark, *The Small Sects in America* (New York: Abingdon, 1949), 147–50; Hugo Hume, *The Superior American Religions* (Los Angeles: Libertarian Publishing, 1928); Fogarty, *All Things New*; James E. Landing, "Cyrus Reed Teed and the Koreshan Unity," in Pitzer, ed., *America's Communal Utopias*, 375–95. For expectations concerning Ann Lee, see Marshall, *The Rise and Progress of the Serpent*.

38 Josephine Woodbury, *War in Heaven*, 3rd edn. (Boston, MA: Samuel Usher, 1897), 43.

39 Stewart H. Holbrook, "Oregon's Secret Love

Cult," *American Mercury*, February 1937, 167–74. The *American Mercury* was H. L. Mencken's publication, and it delighted in exposing the follies of the fringe religions.

40 Anthony Sterling, *King of the Harem Heaven* (Derby, CT: Monarch Books, 1960), 63; Robert S. Fogarty, *The Righteous Remnant* (Kent, OH: Kent State University Press, 1981), 37–40.

41 The account of "outrages" at Point Loma is from Emmett A. Greenwalt, *The Point Loma Community in California* (Berkeley: University of California Press, 1955), 67–76; "the disciples of spookism" is quoted in Carey McWilliams, "Cults of California," *Atlantic*, March 1946, 105–10.

CHAPTER SIX

The New Spiritual Freedom

ROBERT WUTHNOW

Shirley Knight turned twelve in 1960. Her parents had divorced when she was seven. When she was little, they took her to church every Sunday, but it was usually a different church each Sunday. They thought it was important for her "to explore what was out there." In fourth grade, she attended a Catholic boarding school, and in fifth grade, a private school run by Quakers. In sixth grade, she went through confirmation class at an Episcopal church and in seventh and eighth grade attended Sunday school at the Methodist church. During high school, she attended a Christian Science church.

Shirley's spiritual odyssey continued when she went to college at a large state university. Some students from a fundamentalist Protestant group befriended her, but Shirley soon felt uncomfortable with them. By the end of her freshman year, she was attending services at the Catholic Student Union, attracted by the beauty of its rituals. During her sophomore year she studied in Italy, where she learned more about Catholicism. A course in Buddhism the following year broadened her horizons, and she was soon reading books about other world religions. After graduation she moved in with her boyfriend, who was "into yoga and very spiritual." Within a year she had broken up with him. She had also worked at seven different jobs.

One day Shirley was sitting at work feeling sorry for herself, thinking, as she recalls, that

"nothing is working for me," when a new customer walked in and struck up a conversation. Shirley married him two weeks later. He was involved in Alcoholics Anonymous and interested in Sufism. They spent their honeymoon visiting spiritual retreat centers in Europe. Coming home disappointed, they settled in Virginia and became active in Alcoholics Anonymous. Shirley recalls that she loved the group because the people in it were "so spiritual."

After a decade in Virginia, Shirley, her husband, and two children moved to the Southwest, where they joined an Adult Children of Alcoholics group, and Shirley started taking classes from a Jungian therapist. Through the Waldorf school that her children attended, she became interested in the teachings of Rudolf Steiner, called anthroposophy, and soon began driving to a retreat center on weekends to learn more about it. At the moment, she summarizes her religious beliefs by asserting that they focus on "spiritual freedom and moral imagination."

For people like Shirley, the 1960s and 1970s provided new opportunities to expand their spiritual horizons. The 1960s began with Christian theologians declaring that God was dead; it ended with millions of Americans finding that God could be approached and made relevant to their lives in more ways than they had ever imagined. Campus ministries forged new brands of politicized spirituality.

Evangelical churches and conservative denominations grew quietly in the suburbs. After the Second Vatican Council, Catholics began hearing mass in English and participated more actively than before in Sunday services.[1] New religious movements of Asian origin, such as Zen and Hare Krishna, spread in metropolitan areas, as did the humanistic spirituality of such groups as Esalen, EST, and Scientology.[2] So-called underground churches and Jesus freak organizations emerged, and monasteries and religious communes began to attract new followings. For many people, it was difficult to know which spiritual path to follow.

In retrospect, the 1960s had a dramatic impact on American spirituality. Research indicates that many people were influenced by the turmoil of these years to adopt a freewheeling and eclectic style of spirituality.[3] In addition to baby boomers like Shirley Knight who matured during the 1960s, many older Americans participated in the religious changes of this period, and many younger Americans have been influenced by it indirectly, thus giving the period much wider significance than can be understood by considering generations or cohorts alone.[4] What has not been adequately considered is how activists in the 1960s and their subsequent critics reshaped Americans' understanding of freedom itself, and how this new understanding contributed to . . . the rise of a spirituality of seeking.

New Horizons

Adam Westfield is especially articulate about how the 1960s shaped his views of spirituality. Born in 1942, he grew up in New England, attended a private secondary school, graduated from an elite university, and then embarked on a career in business. Looking back on his childhood, he says his parents taught him the importance of family, trying hard, and being good, but left him to discover spiritual values on his own. He senses a strong shift in the attention given to religion in his family history. "I think my parents' generation had a much more intensive sort of religious pre-history [than I did]," he explains. "My father had been brought up

in Massachusetts and had gone to church two or three times a day. My mother's family had all been preachers in the Unitarian church. I think by the time I came along they were both a little weary. They certainly didn't evangelize their children."

Being conditioned to seek spirituality on his own, he was eager to break out of the subculture in which he was raised. For a long time, however, "I was not aware that there were any other cultures at all," he says. His first awareness came when his parents took him on a trip that included driving through a large city. His father had a small statue of a black Buddha in a cabinet at home, so when the boy spotted a black person for the first time on the trip, he shouted, "Look, Dad, it's the Buddha!" In retrospect, he says, "It's amazing. I lived in a time capsule, sort of Lake Wobegon, a place that time forgot. Everybody was white, and there were forty families that just sort of lived together [in my town] from 1942 to 1960. It's amazing."

As a child, Adam associated religion with a kind of stodgy, tight-lipped, strictly disciplined New England asceticism. It was a spirituality of dwelling that blended imperceptibly into the fabric of the town. Only after college did he start to reflect on the meaning of his own spirituality. He attributes his new interest in spirituality to the more open setting in which he was working. Many of the people were black. One of his closest friends was Jewish. Adam started to realize that whatever spiritual path he took, he would have to come to terms with the racial and religious prejudices in his background.

During the 1960s his spirituality was deeply influenced by the civil rights movement. Adam appreciated the freedom to explore new ways of expressing his spirituality. During the Vietnam war he had to confront impulses toward violence for which his middle-class upbringing had not prepared him. Turmoil in his marriage was also to affect his spirituality. He remains involved in a church, but his spirituality is quite different from that of his parents.

Other people describe different avenues to experiencing new spiritual freedoms. Nancy Nystrom, like many teenagers during the

1960s, experienced the turmoil of the decade as conflict within her own life. Her parents were devout Catholics. During the 1950s they raised her in a secure home embellished with the trappings of organized religion. Her first memories are of Catholic statues "all over the house," of saying the rosary and the Lord's Prayer with her mother, and of conversations about God, sin, and divine punishment. She remembers being terrified of God. "I had a naturally curious mind," she says, "but I was afraid to move, afraid to explore. I felt doomed, helpless, powerless." For her, a spirituality of dwelling felt constraining.

When she was in seventh grade, Nancy quit attending the Baptist church her parents now attended despite their objections. "I hated the church, the minister, and God," she recalls. But in eleventh grade her parents sent her to a Catholic high school, and Nancy started thinking again about God. The principal told her it was more important to be spiritual in her daily life than to attend mass and confession. Everyone was friendly to her, and for two years she found a temporary home that made her feel secure: "I just wanted to *belong*." Still, thoughts about God reminded her of her childhood fears, so she postponed any serious investigation of spirituality until she was in college.

"During the hippie era, I began on my own to read a little about Eastern religions," she recalls. "I doubted Christianity, and I still felt very estranged from God, but I believed in reincarnation. My brother was reading a lot about the occult, and that got me interested in numerology and Tarot. I read the Seth books by Jane Roberts. Seth was allegedly a spirit guide. I never just embraced these ideas automatically. I had a lot of questions, but I believed some of the things, like the idea that each person has a spirit guide who is available if you want them. I also started going to a spiritualist. And I thought a lot about the Ten Commandments. I wasn't sure they were from God, but I did feel they were a kind of code imprinted on me and that they were a good way to live."

The main result of these explorations was an enhanced sense of freedom. Nancy recalls, "I somehow felt *freer*. I felt as if I had more control over my own life. I felt released from the shackles. I still couldn't quite get a grasp on my life, but I was free of the angry God and hypocritical church experiences of my childhood." She still feels this way. She no longer seeks counsel from spiritualists. She knows herself better than she did before and finds it easier to make up her own mind. "There's just something inside my soul that says God is good." She says organized religion did not help her discover that; she needed to find it on her own. To be in charge this way is liberating. Images of freedom come easily to her. Sometimes she imagines herself floating like a balloon. When she prays, she imagines herself freeing her thoughts to rise like little balloons toward God.

Nancy's journey began in reaction to a family and church environment that she found patriarchal and constraining. But she was also a product of her times. Indeed, her parents paved the way. Like a growing number of people in the 1950s, her parents switched denominations – from Catholic to Baptist – in hopes of finding a spiritual home more to their liking. Nancy was put off by both denominations' claims to having absolute truth. She decided that if it were possible to switch, it was possible to do without organized religion entirely. She was also raised to believe that things could be improved if people thought for themselves rather than clinging to the past. Her parents favored the civil rights movement and voted for John F. Kennedy. Nancy says the social reforms of the 1960s "turned up a little flame" inside her that said she should be "part of making things right." The Vietnam war made her angry because she did not think it was making things right. Eastern religions and the hippie culture were a breath of fresh air. She admits she was naive, but she found them liberating because they appealed to the best in human nature.

Understanding the New Freedoms

A decade earlier, few observers of American religion had foreseen the kinds of spiritual exploration in which Shirley Knight,

Adam Westfield, and Nancy Nystrom engaged during the 1960s. Schooled to think that spirituality depended on the tight-knit bonds of ethnic and religious attachments, they saw only the likelihood of spirituality diminishing as these attachments weakened. Indeed, the 1950s' revival in established religion was regarded as a temporary phenomenon because of the social forces working against it.[5] Intense, introspective spiritual searching was the last thing anyone expected; as Abraham Heschel lamented, speaking of Christians and Jews alike, "The self is silent; words are dead, and prayer is a forgotten language."[6]

The upsurge of interest in spirituality in the late 1960s is all the more impressive when viewed against these predictions of declining interest in spirituality. The new quest for the sacred blossomed despite the break-down of social arrangements that had given religion its communal base. The fact that it could blossom this way attests to the fact that spirituality was indeed shifting from an attachment to place and becoming increasingly eclectic.

Although the 1960s was an unusual decade, filled with radical ideas and shocking behavior, it corrected some of the aberrations that the previous decade had brought to spirituality. The clinging to safe, respectable houses of worship in which a domesticated God could be counted on to provide reassurance was being challenged by religious movements that reasserted some of the mystery that had always been part of conceptions of the sacred. Americans in the fifties chose largely to remain where they were, opting for security rather than risking their faith in a genuine search for spiritual depth; however, in the 1960s many Americans, having learned that they could move around, think through their options, and select a faith that truly captured what they believed to be the truth, took the choice seriously, bargaining with their souls, seeking new spiritual guides, and rediscovering that God dwells not only in homes but also in the byways trod by pilgrims and sojourners.

The sixties questioned middle-class, white-bread definitions of who God was and of where God could be found, making it more uncertain how to be in touch with the sacred.

In this process, more Americans drew inspiration from the struggles of the poor, from the rich spiritual traditions of African Americans, from other world religions, from rock music and contemporary art, and from changing understandings of gender and sexuality. If the result was more complex, it was at least more true to the broad variety of human experience.

The mood of the sixties was also indebted to nearly a century of US and European commentary on the growing anonymity of modern life, ranging from Karl Marx and Ferdinand Toennies to Sinclair Lewis's *Babbitt* to William Whyte's *Organization Man* and David Riesman's *Lonely Crowd*. In these depictions, the spiritual homes – Marx's "heart of a heartless world" – that had provided warmth, succor, and identity in the past were becoming increasingly sparse as a result of large-scale industry, the assembly line, the bureaucratic workplace, the city, and finally the suburb. Whereas it had once been possible to have a distinct, nuanced, public sense of who one was as a result of living in a particular neighborhood or attending a certain parish, now, according to these interpretations, one had only a numbing feeling of anonymity. In the suburb of the 1960s, just as in the factory of the 1890s, each person was an interchangeable part, all fundamentally the same in outward appearances. Whatever distinctive characteristics of spirit set the individual apart from others were largely invisible to those same others. The growing desire to escape was thus less of an inclination to leave home for the sheer sake of gaining one's independence than of wanting to flee the stale sameness of modernity that was threatening to engulf one's very soul.

The religious efflorescence of the 1960s was also rooted in longstanding traditions of freedom in American religion. These traditions not only emphasized the right of individuals to choose their own faith but also provided a set of arguments about the basis of this right. For instance, Thomas Jefferson had offered two grounds for the free exercise of religion that remained part of thinking in the United States two centuries later (despite some changes in understandings of basic terms). One was that the human spirit was naturally inclined to think freely, to be curious, to examine alternatives, and to be influenced by arguments and opinions. The other was that any conviction arrived at short of such free exploration was somehow less than genuine. It was, in Jefferson's view, similar to being coerced, and thus tending "only to beget habits of hypocrisy and meanness."[7] Although these arguments focused mostly on preventing the state from interfering with religious expression, they were also associated in Jefferson's mind with the need for people to be free of religious influences that might encourage them to pay homage to one church or pastor rather than seeking another more in keeping with their deepest moral convictions.

Throughout the 1960s, interpreters of the religious scene supplied connections between what was happening among US youth and larger, historical frameworks. Rather than viewing the new experimentation as a complete break with the past, these interpreters saw continuity with important features of Western religion.[8] These interpretations nevertheless presumed that people were still searching for spiritual homes, albeit different ones from those of their congregations or families.

Indeed, much of what attracted public attention were experiments, such as communes, underground churches, and student groups, that fit this conception of the pressing need for new spiritual homes.[9] Freedom was understood as a desire not so much to discard all forms of religious organization as to move from organized religion to new religious communities. Freedom would thus at least be constrained by such leavening influences as the need to get along with each other and to get things done. Religious tradition could embrace some of these alternatives.

It was less clear whether religious leaders could embrace a new mentality that placed less emphasis on community of any king. People who were searching on their own were assumed to be potential members either of alternative communities or of established religious organizations. The possibility that they might remain permanently on the road was less desirable, particularly because the source of their seeking was taken to be alienation from institutions they did not like. Nobody quite understood that they were also being pulled by a freedom they did like, nor that this freedom was quite compatible with the increasingly fluid environment in the United States.

It is possible with hindsight to see not only that freedom was at the heart of the spiritual quest of many Americans during the 1960s but also that the meaning of freedom was changing. Western religious thought has generally held that individuals choose among various courses of action and therefore must have freedom to exercise this choice. Because individuals are likely to choose evil, however, some means of guiding their choices must also be present. Conscience is an inner voice guiding individual choice. It restrains individual choice by reminding people of their social responsibilities or by reflecting time-worn social norms. The key to understanding how the 1960s reshaped ideas of spiritual freedom lies in the difference between freedom of conscience and freedom of choice.

Conscience speaks authoritatively about right and wrong. It does not connote shades of gray as much as it does obedience or disobedience to clear standards. It is thus, as the sociologist Emile Durkheim emphasized in his classic treatise on religion, a feature of community.[10] Individuals who live in homogeneous communities with authoritative standards of right and wrong can be mentored by an internalized voice. This voice is binding, meaning that freedom lies in the right to voluntarily obey or disobey rather than having to conform to some arbitrarily imposed or coercive standard. Freedom of conscience implies an absence of external intrusion into such communities. The sacred space is morally inviolable, and yet it provides freedom within its boundaries for individual talents and convictions to be expressed as long as primary loyalty to the community is maintained.[11]

In contrast, freedom of choice becomes important when individuals must make their way among multiple communities. Decisions are required about entry and exit into particular communities and about whether to participate in any community. Under such conditions, the internal voice decides less between right and wrong and more between better and worse. Freedom to choose implies having available an array of options. The ability to make good choices depends on exercising the right to weigh these various options.

Norman Mailer's essay on the "hipster," which in many ways presaged the mood of the 1960s, illustrates the emerging emphasis on freedom of choice. A person of character, Mailer wrote, is not so much one who can distinguish between good and bad as one who can realize possibilities in the face of growing uncertainty. To make choices is the hallmark of freedom because every situation poses "a new alternative, a new question" and because emphasis is placed "on complexity rather than simplicity." True freedom comes from liberating oneself from the repressive "superego" of the community and from developing one's own moral imagination through a process of experimentation.[12]

The Rights Revolution

For many people, these new ways of thinking about spiritual freedom can be traced to the civil rights movement. Government was the agent most capable of intruding on taken-for-granted freedoms of conscience. In the 1960s, government was perceived as a threat by many who thought it was interfering in their local communities, but it also offered new freedoms to those who felt unable to express themselves adequately. The civil rights movement, calling on government to protect freedom of conscience and being resisted for the same reasons, became one of the prominent places in which freedom was redefined – and in ways that would influence not only civic discourse but also understandings of spirituality.

In 1958, Martin Luther King Jr.'s book *Stride toward Freedom* appeared, quickly selling more than sixty thousand copies and receiving favorable publicity in nearly all religious and secular periodicals. King argued that principles of freedom found in Christianity and in the US democratic tradition needed

to be rediscovered and extended so that all Americans could enjoy the fruits of liberty. His argument reflected a progressive view of history in which the forces opposing freedom would eventually succumb to those favoring it but not without the active efforts of interested parties. Indeed, King saw a special role for African Americans to fulfill in bringing the claims of freedom to the forefront of public attention.[13]

Although King resorted sparingly to the idea of conscience, he did call on all Americans to heed the "national conscience" in working together for racial justice. Freedom was thus associated explicitly in his treatise with freedom from oppression, with the attainment of individual and collective dignity, with civic responsibility, and with the spiritual health of the nation. The quest for freedom was a way of ridding the United States of evil and of elevating its status as a "colony of heaven" in which all people were "one in Christ."

King's understanding of freedom emphasized the internalized voice of right and wrong that was common to a spirituality of dwelling with God. It was rooted in communal traditions within Christianity and in understandings of US democracy to a greater extent than in the restless desire to experience alternative lifestyles as a way of discovering new concepts of morality. In a broad sense, freedom was vitally important to the civil rights movement, as activists participated in freedom marches and fashioned themselves as freedom fighters. Yet its meanings were deliberately framed to give it continuity with US political and religious ideals. Politically, it was a feature of democracy, an inalienable right to live without restrictions arbitrarily imposed because of race, color, or creed. Spiritually, it was rooted in a conception of brotherhood that implied a responsibility to treat others with equal respect and to respect the common values on which that brotherhood was established.

King's idea of freedom was thus constrained by a commitment to equal rights, justice, and love of the common good. It was also the type of freedom best understood within a communal or corporate context such as that in which a spirituality of dwelling was found. In his "I Have a Dream" speech King in fact repeatedly invoked metaphors of dwelling. He spoke often of African Americans living as exiles in their own land, shunted onto an island of poverty in a sea of prosperity. Freedom meant full participation in a place where human rights were inalienable and happiness could be pursued; it meant that all of God's children could sit down at the table together, join hands, and sing together of their beloved land.[14]

Freedom especially meant the opportunity, as theologian Joseph Washington, Jr. added, "to enjoy the fruits and shoulder the responsibilities of the American society."[15] It was often described as the same kind of assimilation that European Americans had experienced – not a loss of ethnic identity, but the chance to build homes and communities and to pursue personal ideals without restrictions imposed by other groups. In the view of most religious leaders, true freedom was enhanced by being part of a religious community that respected the dignity of all persons. The essential mark of spiritual freedom was thus the right not to pick and choose but to be included in "the household of faith."[16]

But the questions that some civil rights activists were raising about "the establishment" gradually became occasions for thinking about deeper meanings of liberation. As the 1960s unfolded, spiritual liberation came increasingly to mean a quest that deliberately took one outside social institutions. Cynicism resulted in questions being raised about the common values in which freedom of conscience was grounded. Other writers encouraged young people to "go into the wilderness" to confront themselves and to spend time meditating about the mysteries of life. They should be, Jack Kerouac had written, "mad to live, mad to talk, mad to be saved, desirous of everything at the same time."[17]

For many of the people we talked to, the civil rights movement was indeed their point of departure, teaching them that diversity is good and that personal exploration is desirable. A woman who still attends church but who expresses her spirituality through a wider variety of social service activities attributes the decisive shift in her orientation to a summer camp she attended in 1961, when she was a junior in high school. The camp, sponsored by several of the churches in her area, was an attempt to bring the civil rights movement to the local level by putting teenagers from predominately white neighborhoods into mixed racial settings for the first time. She says the interaction began to "open" her consciousness. A few years later she participated in a summer work program sponsored by the American Friends Service Committee. She learned a lot, not only from the inner-city residents she was helping but also from fellow volunteers. "They were quite liberal in social philosophy," she remembers. She began to realize how important it is "to understand where different people are coming from," and she was inspired by the people she met who were disadvantaged.

Gradually this woman came to believe that there are good people wherever you go. She began to think that denominational differences and doctrines were less important than serving others. She was especially influenced by the Friends' teaching that, as she puts it, "God can speak through anyone; there's not just somebody appointed by God to carry out his will, but God works through everyone." Over the years, she has followed these inclinations, switching from church to church, sometimes remaining uninvolved, expressing detachment from theological arguments, and feeling that she is seeking God in her own way.

Jim Sampson provides the clearest example of how the civil rights movement started to reshape people's ideas about the meaning of freedom itself. Jim is a retail clothing salesman in his late fifties. When he was a teenager, King preached at the African American church Jim attended with his family in Philadelphia. The sermon had a deep impact on Jim because he had been raised to take what people of faith said with utmost seriousness. The spirituality Jim was raised with is best characterized as a spirituality of dwelling. He says his earliest memory having to do with religion is simply that "religion was everywhere." It was on the lips of his grandmother, with whom he spent a great deal of time. "She would stand with her hands folded behind her, look up, pace up and down the hallway, and talk to the Lord," Jim remembers. He recalls in detail the Baptist church he went to several times a week as a child: the foyer, the double doors leading into the sanctuary, the arrangement of the pews, the pulpit, and the cross behind it. All his friends went to the church.

What Jim remembers most about King's sermon was its emphasis on God's love for all people. He says it pricked his conscience. A few weeks later, Jim's conscience was pricked again, this time by his own pastor's preaching. "I really came in touch with my spirituality – with my purpose here on earth," he recalls. The Christian message of love and redemption became his own. "Part of my core values," he says.[18] At this point in his life, Jim understood spiritual freedom largely as the freedom that comes to a person whose conscience is guided by deep immersion within a Christian community. Describing this understanding as "freedom in Christ," he explains that he felt clearer about what was right and what was wrong. King became a tangible symbol of what was right, an "icon," somebody who Jim wanted to follow. But several years would pass before the opportunity came.

When Jim graduated from high school, he had no money to attend college, so he took a job working for a carpenter. Within months he was drafted. After two years in Vietnam, he returned to find his neighborhood engulfed by the civil rights movement. Jim still believed in "God and country," as he puts it, but he immediately joined one of the civil rights demonstrations. Protesting for the freedom of his people seemed like the right thing to do.

Jim says the civil rights movement affected his spirituality mainly by fueling his anger. During one of the protest marches, police turned off the street lights, causing the marchers to panic, and then beat many of the marchers with clubs. Jim's uncle, one of the deacons at his church, was in the hospital for days. After this episode, Jim sided increasingly with the militant wing of the movement being led by Bobby Seale, H. Rapp Brown, and Malcolm X. He started questioning whether the core values he had learned in church were right.

After King was assassinated, Jim's anger turned to cynicism. Then his cynicism deepened when the only job he could find – as part of a new affirmative-action program sponsored by the city – was washing trucks. Having been unable to achieve freedom in one way, he increasingly turned to seeking it in another. For the next several years he tried to enjoy life as much as possible, even though it was often difficult. On two occasions he and his girlfriend sought an abortion. Eventually they married and had a son, but his wife left him a few years later.

Jim recalls this period as being so traumatic that he was unable to face most of the people he knew. He interacted less with his family, found new friends, and quit going to church. He says his core values did not change. But he did come to think of spirituality in a new way. Rather than associating it with his place in the church, he thinks of it in connection with the wider array of choices he has made. "I'm just as comfortable with Muslims or Catholics as I am with Baptists," he observes. "I feel that God is in all of us. I'm open to more ideas." The greatest change, he says, was that he found trying to be obedient to God oppressive. It became necessary for him to "push out the boundaries."

Apart from the civil rights movement, the 1960s promoted a mood of openness that encouraged people to respect diversity and thus to move freely among different lifestyles and worldviews. Many of the people we talked to took pride in having triumphed over their parents' religious, ethnic, and racial prejudices. Having gotten to know people of other backgrounds, having lived through or learned about the civil rights movement, and in many cases having married someone from a different faith were decisive experiences. They felt that life was better as a result.

Adam Westfield is one example. Even though he came from a long line of educated and professional people, he believes there was much prejudice to be overcome. "My father was definitely bigoted," he admits, "and my mother would never say things particularly, but I do remember her saying, 'It would probably be better if you didn't marry a Catholic or a Negro.' What's interesting about that comment is that Jews weren't even on the chart. I ended up marrying a Catholic, and I felt pretty good about it." Moving toward a more tolerant outlook on life was especially meaningful for him.

Another way in which people started to open out was by experiencing and reflecting on the struggle for equality between women and men, a movement that had grown independently of the struggle for civil rights but that often drew on the same sources for inspiration. The spiritual implications of this struggle were often profound because people came to believe that the teachings of their own religious traditions were fundamentally biased against women. People who came to this conviction were thus compelled to reject some of their religious assumptions and to think how to find inspiration in new interpretations or in other traditions.[19]

Adam Westfield is again an example. Asked how the feminist movement had influenced him, he remarks, "The religious texts – I don't think it's just the Torah and I don't think it's just the Bible – have really done women an incredible disservice. And that's such an understatement. In my heart I know that women are my equal in the same way that I know and feel that a black person is my equal, or that a Jew is my equal, or whatever. I feel it. I feel it really passionately and deeply. So I'm very sympathetic with any feminist activity. I would call myself a feminist to the extent that a man can."

A woman in her late forties – a life-long member of a Lutheran church – also remembered the vivid impact feminist thinking played in her spiritual development. "Talking once with our minister we got onto the topic of how God may view women. The discussion turned to the fact that it was women who first discovered that Christ had risen from the tomb. That led to the fact that it was Mary, again a woman, who first knew of the coming of the Christ child. But even more interesting was the story of the shepherds. He indicated that in those days the shepherds were also

young women!" As a result, she feels more like she has a part in God's scheme.

As the sixties progressed, millions of Americans came to be influenced by changing understandings of gender and by a new interest in feminist views of spirituality. In one important respect, feminist spirituality reinforced the more familiar emphasis on freedom of conscience, especially by focusing greater attention on the internal voices of which conscience was composed and often by insisting that these voices be informed by egalitarian and cooperative social relationships.[20] Yet, in another sense, they also contributed to the growing emphasis on freedom of choice. Choice of lifestyles and careers, as well as the right to participate equally in religious services and institutions, played a role in reshaping understandings of freedom. More important, religious symbols themselves became fungible, severed from automatic connections with their meanings because their patriarchal imagery was being questioned.[21] Increasingly, it proved possible – even necessary – to be intentional about the ways one chose to embrace the sacred.[22]

The Fluidity of Life

Whether they applauded or lamented the changes taking place, social observers in the 1960s and early 1970s uniformly emphasized the fact that life was becoming complex in ways that challenged the viability of established institutions. Theologian Michael Novak (prior to becoming a "neoconservative") wrote that communication technology was destroying the ability to live within stable geographic places. Instead, "the camera zooms in, pulls back, superimposes, cuts away suddenly, races, slows, flashes back, flicks ahead, juxtaposes, repeats, spins." Our very sense of reality, he argued, becomes more fluid.[23]

Social theorists who in the 1950s had written of the need to construct strong institutions in order to keep the terror of chaos at bay were now reinterpreted.[24] If institutions were truly human constructions, then they needed to be questioned, debunked, and perhaps replaced. Facing up to the terror would liberate us. We might be able to withstand more chaos than we had imagined. Institutions, above all, existed not so much to get the work done as to perpetuate a myth that work was being done. Social life was largely a fiction of smoke and mirrors. Once people realized that, they could create their own realities.

But the emphasis that many Americans placed on questioning established social conditions was itself rooted in social conditions. Freedom of choice was the rallying cry of consumers even more than it was of civil rights activists and hippies. Indeed, it is interesting to recall the enormous expansion in consumerism that took place during the 1960s; it has been overshadowed by the political unrest of the period but may have had consequences that were equally profound. At the end of World War II, consumer products were invariably scarce, and the corner grocery or local hardware store remained at the core of retailing. By 1960, retailing had already expanded enormously, including the invention of large chains, such as Korvette's, which took in more than $150 million in that year. In 1954, a Chicago businessman, Ray Kroc, had witnessed a new idea on a trip to California that would revolutionize the way Americans ate, and by 1960 more than two hundred McDonald's restaurants had spread across the country and were rapidly being joined by other fast-food chains. Over the next three decades, more than eight thousand McDonald's would be added. Americans learned two important lessons from these developments: one, that you could shop around for some of the essential services that had always been provided at home, and, two, that not only was it valuable to obtain services at a good price but convenience – especially in the amount of time it took – was a valuable commodity itself. Above all, Americans were deliberately being taught to shop as never before. The generation who came of age during the 1960s was the first cohort of young people to have been reared in a fully commercialized consumer society and to have been exposed to television advertising since birth. Between 1950 and

1960 national expenditures on advertising had doubled, and between 1960 and 1970 they doubled again.[25]

Religious entrepreneurs started to imitate the strategies of advertisers and retailers. Drive-in churches and drive-through confessionals made headlines as innovative, if bizarre, adaptations of business ideas to the religious world. Less visibly, clergy shortened sermons to accommodate the time demands of their parishioners, religious bookstores began to appear, the bookstore chains that developed in shopping malls started to carry Bibles and inspirational books, and college campuses started to provide tracts and sign-up sheets for religious organizations as a cafeteria-style approach to promoting religious interests along with other student activities.[26] Spirituality, like hamburgers, was increasingly something one could get quickly and in a variety of places.

If the consumer revolution encouraged Americans to choose, so did new ideas about the family. In May 1960, the Food and Drug Administration approved Enovid as an oral contraceptive. By the end of 1961 more than four hundred thousand women were taking the Pill. This figure rose to 1.2 million a year later and reached 2.3 million by the end of 1963.[27] Journalists heralded the development as a new era of freedom for women. Religious leaders recognized its moral implications but could scarcely have predicted its wider social impact. During the 1950s, the average time between confirmation class and birth of first child for US young people had been only seven years; by the end of the 1960s, in large measure because of the new contraceptive technologies, this period had more than doubled to fifteen years. Since the time between confirmation and parenthood has always been one in which young people could drop out of established religion and turn their attention to other things, the doubling of this period was of enormous religious significance.

In a study of Presbyterians, the effects of these social developments were much in evidence: young adults who became religiously uninvolved were significantly more likely than those who stayed "churched" to remain single or to divorce, to have no children, to move more often, and to live farther away from their extended families.[28] More broadly, there appears to be a relationship between the loss of family or community ties and a propensity toward eclecticism in one's attitudes and activities. For instance, research on musical consumption and artistic taste shows that eclecticism in these areas has increased steadily, that it reaches higher levels among single or divorced people than among married people (taking account of age differences), and that it is reinforced by geographic mobility.[29]

Thus, if the 1950s had sanctified the nursery and the family room, the 1960s encouraged those who had been reared in these places to explore the wider world. Whereas the fertility rate had been 3.8 children per woman in 1957, by 1973 it was only 1.9, the lowest it had been is US history. During the same period, the number of young women who remained unmarried increased by a third, and the divorce rate soared. Other trends also signaled a more "liberated" orientation toward family: the proportion of first births occurring outside of marriage rose from 5 percent in the late 1950s to 11 percent in 1971; a spectacular eightfold increase occurred during the 1960s in the number of household heads who were reported as living apart from relatives while sharing their living quarters with an unrelated adult "partner" of the opposite sex; and the number of persons reporting in surveys that they had engaged in premarital sexual relations increased, as did homosexual activity.[30]

Accompanying these changes in lifestyle was an enormous rise in exposure to new ideas and information. College training was perhaps the major source of such exposure. Between 1960 and 1970, college enrollments jumped from 3.6 million to 8.6 million students.[31] Another way of gauging the impact of this expansion is through the declining numbers of Americans who had not graduated from high school: in 1950, fully two-thirds (66 percent) fell into this category; by 1970, fewer than half (48 percent) did; and by 1990, the proportion was less than a quarter (22 percent).[32] Young women, whose numbers on campuses tripled

during the 1960s, were particularly influenced by these changes. In contrast to their mothers, whose twenties were spent mostly at home raising small children, young women in the sixties and seventies were much more likely to be living in dormitories or apartments and studying literature and the social sciences or preparing for careers in the professions.[33]

Opening out was being promoted actively by government and business as well. A "mobile, fluid labor force" was championed by employers who wanted workers willing to move as new jobs and markets demanded. Realizing from the war effort that goods and services needed to be brought together in more complex ways than ever before, policymakers approved a new forty-one thousand mile interstate highway system in 1956, and oversaw its construction during the next decade and a half. As teamsters and vacationers scrambled to benefit from these new resources, it should not have been surprising that new rumblings of the spirit would be expressed in books such as Jack Kerouac's *On the Road* or in the music of the Rolling Stones.

The emphasis on choice and exploration would have made little difference, however, had it not been for another important factor. Prosperity made it possible for growing numbers of Americans to take advantage of the new opportunities available to them. The relative prosperity of the 1960s is evident in the fact that per capita income grew by more than 3 percent each year between 1960 and 1975 (adjusted for inflation), compared with growth of less than 2 percent annually during the following fifteen years. Another indicator of how this growth affected people is that families living below the poverty line fell from 22 percent of the population in 1960 to only 12 percent in 1975; in comparison, most of the growth in the subsequent period benefited the rich.[34]

Rising prosperity meant that people like Shirley Knight, Adam Westfield, and Nancy Nystrom had opportunities to explore new spiritual horizons that their parents and grandparents did not have. Young people who matured during the 1960s were able to take classes in college that exposed them to other religious traditions. Many of them traveled, sometimes to places that sparked their religious imaginations. Many were able to major in the humanities or social sciences, rather than specializing in subjects that may not have exposed them to new ideas about religion.

The Confrontation With Evil

Although it is generally pictured as a time of hedonism and self-exploration, the 1960s was even more a decade in which Americans who had tried to build a safe world in the 1950s came to terms with the continuing reality of evil. They did so not in a profoundly theological way but through public events and personal traumas that could scarcely be ignored.[35] If meaninglessness and boredom were (as commentators argued) the wellsprings of youthful unrest, concern about suffering primed the pump. Indeed, new interest in freedom was inspired as much by a desire to understand and alleviate suffering as it was by sheer self-indulgence.

Adam Westfield remembers how the death of President Kennedy affected him. When Kennedy was elected, Adam recalls, "he was all tan and he looked amazing. He was one of us who had gone out and done it, and was leading the Free World, and we could too. I am different in my ambitions and my view of the world because of him." Kennedy's death was a serious psychological blow. "When he died, we were all numb. It was a huge event." But Adam also says "it seemed random." Thus, the deaths of King and Bobby Kennedy had a more radical effect on his thinking.

Most of the people we interviewed who remembered the deaths of the Kennedys and of King spoke of the shock to their values. In an instant, the familiar world was shattered, and the fantasy world of better tomorrows came to an end; in its place was the frightening reality of a world capable of generating evil. A woman who turned fourteen the day Kennedy was killed puts it well: "I was brokenhearted when he died. How could the world kill this man who was supposed to bring

so much good to the world? I really believed that he was going to bring good. It was horrible. Everything went crazy."

Almost three decades later, Nancy Nystrom breaks down and cries as she describes how she felt when she heard that King had been shot. Such emotion can be understood only in relation to the spiritual meaning with which the civil rights movement was charged. Nancy was typical of many younger people who believed that God's work must somehow be done through social reforms because it was not being accomplished by the churches. Working hard on behalf of human betterment became a kind of religion for her. When these efforts met with violent resistance, the basis for that religion had to be rethought. "I wondered," she recalls, "what is prevalent? Good or evil?"

Military service during the war in Vietnam was another way in which young people came to a growing recognition of evil. Adam Westfield had always been taught to defend his country. When he was drafted in 1968, he came to realize that there was evil within himself. He explains, "I don't think there's any sensitive and caring human being who goes into basic training and doesn't get changed dramatically. What the Army does is it makes you anonymous. It shaves off all your hair, it keeps you from sleeping, so it really turns you into a nonperson, which is really alarming. One person had told me before I went in, 'They'll break you.' And they do. That's what military discipline does. I also discovered two things. It's fun to march. You walk along and it's fun. It feels good: click, click, click. It's this deep human thing, for boys anyway, fun to march. The other thing is they give you this really light little thing made out of aluminum or something, with a handle on it, and you carry it around like a little briefcase, and it can fire four hundred bullets a minute. You push the trigger and you hit the target a hundred yards away or two hundred yards away. That was great; I loved it. It struck me that men like to kill, that it's fun. That's a scary thought that doesn't leave you – that I have that in me."

Discovering evil – in the society or in yourself – may not lead to a new interest in spirituality. But, for many of the people we interviewed, this discovery started them on a journey that led away from the simple religious truths they had learned as children or, in other cases, the simple secular pleasures they had taken for granted as children. For Adam Westfield, this was the start of his quest to learn how to be tolerant, how to wage peace, and how to encourage what he calls "moral civic action." In her book, *Dakota*, Kathleen Norris draws an even stronger connection between the confrontation with evil and the possibilities for liberation. "For one who has chosen the desert and truly embraced the forsaken ground," she writes, "it is not despair or fear or limitation that dictates how one lives. One finds instead an openness and hope that verges on the wild."[36]

The person we interviewed who best illustrates the wild hope that Norris describes is Diane Mason. A woman in her forties who runs a mental-health clinic, Diane was deeply influenced by the evil she witnessed in the 1960s and early 1970s. She was sixteen when her brother came home from Vietnam. He was drinking and using drugs, trying hard to forget the killing. Shortly after he was arrested for disturbing the peace, the church where her parents taught Sunday school asked them not to come back.

Diane says she didn't lose her faith in God, but she did lose confidence in the church. From that point on, she decided to live by her own rules. She experimented with drugs until she graduated from high school. In college, she majored in drama because it was an outlet for her desire to be creative. Before she graduated, her restlessness took her in a rusty Volkswagen bus to the Florida Keys, where she lived for a year. During the year she decided she wanted to have a baby. She met a man, got pregnant, and eventually came home to live with her parents. Diane was exercising her freedom to explore spirituality as well. She took courses in world religions in college, read books about Tibetan Buddhism, and learned to meditate. She dabbled with the psychic

teachings of Edgar Cayce, talked with friends about Native American spirituality, and read the Bible. Whenever people asked her her religious preference, she said, "Christian and Buddhist – and Jewish and everything else."

But a spirituality that emphasized freedom to choose anything did not end simply in dabbling or self-indulgence. Through these years, Diane was haunted by her brother's mental anguish. As he went from hospital to hospital, she became increasingly interested in learning what she could do to help. At first she volunteered at a crisis-intervention center. She took courses in psychology and toyed with the idea of becoming a social worker. For a brief time she held an office job at a clinic. Eventually she worked her way up to her present position. Most of her work now involves networking – she solicits donations to keep the clinic afloat, brings health professionals together, and provides services for people like her brother.

The lesson that Diane gained from trying to make choices about her spirituality – and about her life – was that the most important aspect of spirituality is doing. She isn't sure what to believe. Nor is she sure that what one believes matters. Her spirituality frees her to do good. "I just believe that we are what we do," she asserts. "I live my spirituality. It's in everything I do. The reason I exist in this reality is to make it better." The connection between this view of spirituality and the pain she witnesses in people like her brother is that helping to alleviate this pain energizes her. "I've watched how their faith has helped them survive," she says. "It gets them through the night. I see miracles. I see people come alive." She summarizes, "I mostly see God through the work of other people. And my work is acknowledging the God in others." In many ways Diane Mason's spiritual journey has been characterized by choices she made mainly to find out where they would lead. She has exercised a great deal of freedom in making these choices. Yet her view of God became so inclusive that she was led to see God even in the people she was trying to help. She hopes that her work is helping to liberate them. She knows it is helping to liberate her.

Spirituality Takes Wing

The most significant impact of the 1960s for many people's understandings of spirituality was a growing awareness that spirituality and organized religion are different and, indeed, might run in opposite directions. Although many Americans continued to participate in churches and synagogues, younger people increasingly pursued spirituality in other venues, and even the religiously involved found inspiration from a wider variety of sources. Underlying these changes was the shift in fundamental understandings of freedom that I described earlier.

Whereas freedom of conscience had once emphasized an absence of intrusions into one's place of worship, freedom of choice now gave the spiritual quest increased importance and encouraged seekers to make up their own minds in matters of the heart. The poet Maya Angelou, experiencing a spiritual awakening during the 1960s, wrote lyrically of the exhilaration associated with this new sense of freedom: "I am a big bird winging over high mountains, down into serene valleys. I am ripples of waves on silver seas. I'm a spring leaf trembling in anticipation."[37]

Academicians were among the first to challenge the monopoly of established religion and to suggest why the faithful might want to look elsewhere. The groundwork for these attacks had been laid a generation earlier by theologians wrestling with the need to modernize in order to accommodate changing social realities. Dietrich Bonhoeffer had written of a "religionless Christianity," which would be free of the political entanglements that characterized the European churches for so many centuries.[38] Harvey Cox, living in Berlin just prior to writing *The Secular City*, read Bonhoeffer's works and was deeply influenced by them. Cox argued that "dereligioning" was a good thing because it freed people from oppressive moralities and made them think hard about their own spirituality.

Others took up similar themes. In a lecture given at Harvard Divinity School, Robert Bellah asserted that "the biblical tradition provides insufficient resources to meet the desperate problems that beset us." Rather than clinging obstinately to this tradition, he suggested, Americans needed to understand the wisdom of Native Americans, the experience of nothingness expressed in Zen Buddhism, the prophetic elements in African and African American cultures, and the encounters with Mother Earth in primitive and shamanistic religions.[39] Combining Christian and Marxist imagery, philosopher Norman Brown encouraged Americans to "leave the place where we belong. The Proletariate has no fatherland, and the son of man no place to lay his head. Be at home nowhere."[40]

Critics within organized religion were not attempting to debunk Christianity or Judaism but to show . . . that religion had become sacrilegious, worshiping customs and organizations rather than the Creator. Their imagery was of a spiritual home, but one too neat to be lived in. They wrote of chains and confinement, intolerance, nationalism, closed systems, authoritarianism, and heavy-handedness. To live within a sacred habitat was to be tribalistic and thus to dwell among people of limited imagination. It was reminiscent of Nazism and similar to communism. Its familism was too secure, bestowing "on all its members an unquestioned place and a secure identity," answering questions before they were raised.[41] Whatever the new era was hailing, it would be open to all manifestations of truth. It would be tolerant, respecting the insights of all peoples and faiths; it would give people room to doubt, to express their views, and to explore new horizons.[42]

Clergy, too, were becoming increasingly worried that congregations were not doing enough to attack the status quo. In a cross-denominational survey of clergy in California conducted in 1968, more than half (52 percent) agreed that "Protestant churches have become too aligned with the status quo in the United States to become major agents of social reform." Nearly this many (43 percent) agreed that "as long as the churches persist in regarding the parish or the local congregation as their normative structure, they will not confront life at its most significant point."[43] Hoping that parishioners would remain loyal to the faith even if they were disillusioned with their churches, these clergy often played a hand in the changes that were taking place. Nancy Nystrom, we saw, was influenced by the priest at her high school who counseled students to love their neighbors instead of dutifully attending mass. Another Catholic woman who had dropped out of the church found support from a priest at a marriage-encounter weekend who told her, "Many of theology's greatest ideas have come from people who were not part of the church."

Many of the people we talked to had thus come to find special meaning in the contrast between spirituality and religion. For them, spirituality was a broader term that signaled the value of drawing insights from many sources, whereas religion was simply the particular institutional manifestation of different traditions. Adam Westfield explains the distinction in these terms: "if one could ever be so smart as to understand Moses and Buddha and Lao Tsu and the Bantu elders from many centuries ago, I think you could come very close to a common human spirituality and the fundamental goodness of man." Religion, to him, means something like denominationalism, whereas spirituality is more the core of different religions. Spirituality, he says, "is closer to nature and closer to oneness with the planet."

Such broadening has been evident in other studies as well. One study tracked down a large number of adults who had participated in confirmation classes at churches in the 1960s. It found that after two decades fewer than a third remained in their denomination, while nearly half (48 percent) had become "unchurched." Of the unchurched, a relatively small portion (8 percent) claimed to be entirely without religious interests. Most still entertained some religious views, participated occasionally in organized religion, but largely pursued spirituality in their own ways. Indeed, they legitimated their spiritual eclecticism by identifying themselves as religious liberals and by espousing universalistic views of salvation and individualistic orientations toward theo-

logical authority. Nine out of ten thought it possible to be a good Christian or Jew without attending religious services; eight out of ten thought individuals should arrive at their own beliefs independent of any religious organizations; and seven out of ten thought all religions are equally good ways of finding ultimate truth.[44]

Other evidence points to the wide variety of ways spirituality was being pursued.[45] According to a 1977 Gallup Poll, 4 percent of the population said they currently practiced Transcendental Meditation, 3 percent practiced yoga, 2 percent said they were involved in mysticism, and 1 percent claimed membership in an Eastern religion. Among people under age thirty and among college graduates, these figures were approximately twice as high as in the population as a whole.[46] In addition to Eastern religions, many Christian groups provided alternative styles of worship that would alter how people perceived their relationship to congregations. One woman who was in college at the time remembers joining a group called the Church of the Open Doors. She reports, "We went to people's houses and met there rather than at church itself. We were trying to get closer to what Jesus's teachings really were as opposed to all of the trappings of organized church. And we had many interesting discussions. One that stood out in my mind was how much you would help someone you didn't know, someone you saw with car trouble or something, whether you would chance being taken advantage of yourself to stop and help the person and what was the right thing to do."[47]

The impact of some of these changes was clearly evident in 1978, when a national study of religious participation was conducted. Of the people in that study who had been born between 1944 and 1960, nearly half were single or divorced, a majority had lived in their present community fewer than five years, more than two-thirds had changed residences in the past five years, two-thirds had stopped participating in religious organizations for a period of at least two years, and only 13 percent currently attended a church or synagogue weekly. The fact that only one in eight was an active churchgoer was especially striking, given the fact that 66 percent had attended regularly as children. Dissatisfaction with established religion was evident in attitudes as well as in behavior: three quarters agreed that "most churches and synagogues today have lost the real spiritual part of religion," and a majority felt that "most churches and synagogues today are too concerned with organizational, as opposed to theological or spiritual issues."[48]

The study also revealed a little-suspected fact about the religious defection that was taking place among young people: in addition to the liberalizing influences of the classroom and the counterculture, defection was most likely among young people who were being severely affected by the dislocations of social change: semiskilled workers, sales and service workers, divorced persons, African American men, people who had moved more often, and those earning lower incomes.[49] The longer-term significance of these developments was also suggested in the study. Of those in the 1944–1960 birth cohort who had children, only half were exposing their children to formal religious training of any kind, compared with 86 percent who themselves had received religious training as children. Significant exposure was even lower: only 34 percent were sending their children to Sunday school classes, whereas 63 percent had themselves attended such classes . . .

Ultimately the freedom that triumphed in the 1960s was freedom to feel one's own feelings and to experience one's own sensibilities. How one might deliberately go about seeking a relationship with the sacred also underwent serious rethinking. Americans still believed that deliberate effort was valuable. But prayer and Bible reading rooted in habit were no longer as highly valued. Devotional routines that reinforced unthinking loyalty to family and church diminished in importance compared with those that encouraged people to think for themselves. New translations and paraphrases of the Bible proliferated, attracting readers who wanted to think about cant phrases in new ways. Many people saw value in learning about other world religions as ways of sharpening insights about their own. Devo-

tional practice took on added meaning for those who sought to include breathing techniques, exercise, chanting, or emotional work, all in an effort to make spirituality a "whole person" activity.

But devotional practice in another sense was devalued. People were told they needed to escape the security of their religious enclaves and to participate fully in the world. Like Jim Sampson and Diane Mason, they learned that the sacred could also be found in secular society. In work or at play, it was possible to experience moments of transcendence without knowing any special creeds or performing any religious rituals. Thus, one could read Cox's *Secular City*, for example, and find no mention of prayer, meditation, family devotions, or Bible reading. Ordinary work and play were sufficiently sacred to remind the enlightened of God's kingdom. Similarly, ethicist Gibson Winter's *Being Free* encouraged Americans to be critical of technology on religious grounds, but it was enough to form a critical attitude rather than having to adopt an alternative lifestyle or to engage in devotional practices.[50] Faced with the realities of secular society, critics as different as Charles Reich and Theodore Roszak argued that consciousness should (and probably would) be transformed, but doing anything special to communicate with the sacred received little attention.[51]

In the most widely read treatises, therefore, subjectivity was elevated as a central concern, opening the way for increased attention to the interior life . . . But intentional action toward social or personal transformation was often implicitly devalued. Writers pondered feelings of alienation and meaninglessness and counseled readers that life could be better if they only released their inner thoughts from bondage. And, in this respect, the new arguments were not so different from the advice of positive thinkers and thought-reform specialists of the past. Americans did not have to sacrifice comfortable lifestyles as long as they paid attention to how they felt about their lives. The specific spiritual disciplines found in Transcendental Meditation, Zen Buddhism, kundalini yoga, and various "human potential" groups attracted widespread attention but were generally marginalized in popular interpretations as esoteric practices. They were depicted as magical cures that would soon disappoint their devotees or as the teachings of gurus whose dress and language set them apart from mainstream culture. Devotional practice could thus be experimented with as part of a counterculture but just as easily abandoned once the counterculture was no longer in vogue.

Nancy Nystrom illustrates these understandings. She feels her spirituality is stronger than her parents' because she has had to struggle harder with hers. Over the years, she has gotten over most of her previous hatred of the church. She imagines she might even start attending church again in the future; it would feel good, she thinks, to worship with other people. In the meantime, she thinks a lot about God and about spirituality. Various activities prompt her to do so: listening to classical music, conversations with a friend. But she does not actively do anything to cultivate her sense of spirituality. Other than her "thought balloons," she does not pray. Her view of freedom is heavily imbued with the value of being in control, so prayer seems to her like asking God to serve as a crutch. Meditation is more interesting but not something she practices regularly. She explains that God is always present, so it makes sense just to meditate "when the spirit moves me." Sometimes she talks to God in the bathtub, and sometimes she prays just as a way of doing something nice for someone else. The way spirituality influences her daily life is thus to quiet her thoughts. She feels less impatient when things go wrong and more capable of making them go right.

The Limits of Freedom

By the end of the 1970s, many of the new religions that had been formed during the preceding decade were being described as "cults." The mass suicide that took place in Guyana in November 1978 among the followers of religious leader Jim Jones fueled the tendency to view religious experiments as bizarre, anti-

social movements led by misguided, charismatic figures. In this interpretation, people forsook the faith of their parents, escaped the uncertainties of their own lives, and allowed themselves to be brainwashed by authoritarian cult leaders. The result was submersion in a totalitarian community that resembled a theocratic family, only with higher walls against the outside world.

There were plenty of examples, especially from former cult members and from so-called deprogrammers, to support this interpretation. More common, however, was a form of religious experimentation that involved short-term exposure to a variety of leaders, ideas, and spiritual disciplines. Typical accounts of spiritual journeys took the form: "I tried everything from A to Z," perhaps followed by a list starting with aikido and ending with Zen. But much of the impetus to experiment was short-lived; experimentation staggered to a halt once the Vietnam war ended and the economic downturn accompanying the oil embargo of 1973 forced young Americans to become serious about finding jobs and paying their bills. Yet the idea that spirituality needed to be pursued on one's own and perhaps even in tension with social institutions did not die easily. A decade later most Americans still thought it was important to arrive at their religious values on their own and to be skeptical of accepting the words of religious authorities.

The lingering question from the standpoint of organized religion, of course, is why the churches and synagogues did not oppose – or oppose more vehemently – a cultural development that was to contribute so greatly to the weakening of religion's traditional monopoly over spirituality. The answer can be found only partly in liberal tendencies in mainline theology or in inadequate organizational responses to demographic shifts. Moderate mainline denominations, Catholics, Jews, and evangelical Protestants also participated in the redefinition of spirituality that took place in the 1960s. The reason for this participation was organized religion's own desire to promote intense spiritual conviction in the face of a rising tide of secularism, scientific agnosticism, and implicit indifference bred from taking spirituality for granted as part of one's lineage and community. In order to mobilize increased commitment, religious leaders opted for two seemingly innocent proposals: that the faithful could gain knowledge only by being exposed to a variety of arguments and counterarguments, and that faith was ultimately a matter of inner conviction more than of rational or scientific persuasion.

As they endorsed the ancient teaching that "the truth shall make you free," religious leaders took an important step toward accommodating the growing cultural diversity of the period. No longer able to prevent parishioners from learning about spirituality in ways other than those prescribed by established religious bodies, the leaders of these organizations chose, in effect, to argue that their own traditions did not stand in the way of freedom but offered true freedom. Americans who heard this message often took it quite literally, acting as if the truth on which freedom depended was less important than the exercise of freedom itself. In the future, organized religion would thus be able to compete with other media that also offered spiritual freedom, but its leaders would have to work harder to say what freedom entailed, and they would find themselves engaged in a broader arena of competition from which there was no return.

Individuals who left their spiritual homes also found it difficult to return to them or to find alternatives. Some of the people we interviewed were trying to make the world their home, thus maximizing their freedom to pick and choose. When the whole universe is perceived as God's home, there is enormous freedom to roam; but no particular place can ultimately be more sacred than any other. For example, Wilma Nichols believes God loves everybody. "Would he reject anyone from his house?" she asks. "God has a limitless capacity for forgiveness, so I doubt it." Looking back on her Catholic upbringing, she says it was a necessary first step, like learning the multiplication tables. There was security and order, "but I had to reject it as a young adult." Searching for spirituality on her own was a taxing experience, so she is glad to have found

friends who share her journey. Nevertheless, she still imagines herself living in a huge house that she continues to explore. "I have an abiding feeling that new doors are still waiting to be opened." She adds, "There are lessons in spirituality to be learned outside those avenues that advertise themselves as spiritual places."

Other people had returned to a sacred space more narrowly defined where they could feel safe and secure. To an outsider, they sometimes appear to have rejected the pronounced freedom offered by the 1960s, but it is clear that even their search for a spiritual home was influenced by the idea of choice. One man illustrates these influences with particular clarity. Todd Brentwood was attending a Catholic high school in the late 1960s. He recalls that these were "turbulent times" in the church as well as in the society. The result was a "big change" in the school that led him to become "more liberal" and "antiestablishment" in his thinking. Although he had been active in the church since infancy, he now found himself confused. "I couldn't really tell what the church's teachings were." When he went away to college, he found himself without spiritual support. "There was no rail that I could hang onto for spiritual guidance. Everything had to come from me." His response was to embrace a *carpe diem* view of life. "Everything was transitory. Get it while you can. Gather ye rosebuds while ye may, for tomorrow ye may die." He played college basketball, studied, worked at UPS, and enjoyed life.

By the late 1970s, Todd was at a turning point. Deciding that the purpose of life is to achieve happiness for oneself, he had become part of the Me Generation. He became a coach because basketball made him happy. At the high school where he worked, he taught his students to question authority and to dream their own dreams. But he was lonely. His marriage had ended in divorce. His *carpe diem* attitude made it hard to pursue – or to take pleasure in – long-term projects because acquiring the skills for these projects was contrary to keeping his options open from day to day. He also began to realize that he desperately missed his mother, who had died when he was thirteen. He wanted a home, spiritually as well as socially.

Like a growing number of Americans, Todd sought a spiritual home in an evangelical church. It offered fellowship (his new girlfriend attended there) and a compelling message about Jesus as the answer to life's questions. But Todd's new commitment was not a repudiation of his freedom. Indeed, his choice illustrates that conservative Christians were also influenced by the liberating themes of the time. Although he became a "born-again" Christian, Todd did so on his own terms. He says he retained his critical, questioning attitude toward what he heard at the church but was able to participate because the service gave him "a good feeling inside." As he read the Bible and developed a stronger belief in Jesus, he was propelled mainly by the "inner happiness" that resulted. This happiness allowed him to ease up on himself a bit. He decided that "Christian morals" – broadly defined – provided a good basis for life and that he should "find the path the Lord wants you to take." This attitude gave him a new sense of freedom. Unlike churchgoers who he says are "just programmed," he feels he has a "more open approach to things." His favorite book is Stephen Covey's *Seven Habits of Highly Successful People*. He likes it because it emphasizes "your inner self" and gives him confidence that the right decisions in life are consistent with the "moral fiber" that runs through the Christian approach to life.

For people like Todd Brentwood, evangelical Christianity is a new home that offers security in a world gone wild. But it is a commitment that rests lightly on their shoulders. The moral certainty it provides is almost self-legitimating: when Todd makes decisions he now does so with the feeling that he's probably doing God's will. And going to church is a way to feel good and to make friends rather than a deep, enduring commitment to truth. Just being there gives him "peace of mind" and makes him "lighthearted." Todd says his spiritual journey "has mostly to do with individuals," even though he admits the church had an "indirect" effect. He says Christianity

isn't a religion; it is just a way of life based on love. In his daily life, it helps him to relax and be himself.

If my argument is correct, then, the 1960s did not simply introduce new religions that encouraged Americans to be more eclectic in their spirituality; rather, during the 1960s the nature of freedom itself was contested and redefined. The freedom that living in a secure community of like-minded individuals offered was gradually replaced by a freedom to exercise choice in a marketplace of ideas and lifestyles. Freedom of choice was attractive to those who in fact were confronted with an immense array of alternatives. Yet most people recognized that some choices are less healthy than others and that exercising choice for its own sake is not always the most desirable alternative. As a way of reining in freedom of choice, a new emphasis was also placed on the dangers of external constraints, such as those imposed explicitly by government or implicitly by technology. In the process, freedom came to be more subjective. In spirituality, freedom of conscience thus came to mean paying attention to the inner voices of feelings, and freedom of choice meant exposing oneself to alternative experiences that would help develop these voices.

The concept of freedom that emerged during the 1960s proved to be unstable because it did not sufficiently take into account the social forces shaping it. It made freedom largely into a matter of lifestyle, subjective opinion, and choice. The grand narrative of religious and philosophical tradition was replaced by personalized narratives of exploration and expression. As critics have observed, it was not clear how a society could be ordered in these terms. People needed reasons to limit their choices other than the sheer fact that they were exhausted or broke.

Freedom of choice was also unworkable in the terms that visionaries of the 1960s had themselves articulated it. People could not be motivated simply by a historical narrative that envisioned ever greater freedom and sophistication. Coming to terms with the evil embedded in US society required more than a critique of the 1950s; it required a realistic appraisal of what life could be engineered to be. It was not possible to have biblical faith without religion, nor was it likely that people would continue to speak of God if they had no reason to speak to God. They would have to work harder to incorporate insights from African Americans and feminists instead of simply talking about them. The need was not for a different metaphysical canopy that valued freedom less. It was to discover through practical living how to maintain spiritual freedom without losing the essence of spirituality itself.

Were it only that the 1960s encouraged Americans to value their religious freedom or to leave the homes of their upbringing in search of more fulfilling spiritual mansions – were this all that took place – the 1960s would be of only passing interest. Instead, the 1960s brought together a quest for spiritual freedom with rapidly changing social conditions – a quest that had a wide variety of unanticipated results. Rather than either becoming more secular or starting new religious organizations, Americans after the 1960s had to think hard about what it meant to be spiritual. Their freedoms and their circumstances combined in ways that encouraged them to experiment, and these experiments opened up new possibilities that were more puzzling than they had imagined.

Notes

1 The Second Vatican Council was favorably received among American Catholics, more than two-thirds of whom said they approved of the changes effected by the Council. Andrew M. Greeley, *The American Catholic: A Social Portrait* (New York: Basic Books, 1976), p. 130.

2 Charles Y. Glock and Robert N. Bellah, eds., *The New Religious Consciousness* (Berkeley: University of California Press, 1976).

3 Research on changing religious patterns during the 1960s is presented in Robert Wuthnow, *The Consciousness Reformation* (Berkeley: University of California Press, 1976), and in Robert Wuthnow, *Experimentation in American Religion* (Berkeley: University of California Press, 1978). For a narrative overview, see Robert S. Ellwood, *The Sixties*

Spiritual Awakening: American Religion Moving from Modern to Postmodern (New Brunswick, NJ: Rutgers University Press, 1994).

4 On baby-boomer religion, see Dean R. Hoge, Benton Johnson, and Donald A. Luidens, *Vanishing Boundaries: The Religion of Mainline Protestant Baby Boomers* (Louisville, KY: Westminster/John Knox, 1994), and Wade Clark Roof, *A Generation of Seekers: The Spiritual Journeys of the Baby Boom Generation* (San Francisco, CA: Harper San Francisco, 1993).

5 For the most part, middle-class Americans seemed less intent on practicing a deep personal piety than did members of working-class communities, as did third-generation Americans compared with first- or second-generation immigrants. See Lenski, *The Religious Factor*, pp. 57–60. Movement into the middle class and the erosion of ethnic ties were thus expected to result in increased secularity – not necessarily associated with absolute declines in church membership but with the movement toward the bland, comfortable, conformist faith that Herberg (*Protestant, Catholic, Jew*) found among third-generation Americans.

6 Heschel, *Man's Quest for God*, p. xi . . .

7 Thomas Jefferson, *Revisal of the Laws: Drafts of Legislation, A Bill for Establishing Religious Freedom*, 1776, Section I.

8 For example, Winter likened the new religious movements to the mendicant experiments of the Middle Ages; Gibson Winter, *Being Free: Reflections on America's Cultural Revolution* (New York: Macmillan, 1970), pp. 93–6. Cox noted the similarity between youth rock festivals and earlier "feasts of fools"; Harvey Cox, *The Feast of Fools: A Theological Essay on Festivity and Fantasy* (New York: Harper and Row, 1969).

9 Edward E. Plowman, *The Underground Church* (Elgin, IL: David C. Cook, 1971).

10 Durkheim, *Elementary Forms of the Religious Life*.

11 Friedman, whose widely read *Capitalism and Freedom* was published just prior to the upheaval of the late 1960s, explained the connection between conscience and freedom when he wrote that free people are "proud of a common heritage and loyal to common traditions" and when he warned that the chief threat to the "rare and delicate plant" of freedom is "the concentration of power"; Milton Friedman, *Capitalism and Freedom*

(Chicago, IL: University of Chicago Press, 1962), p. 2.

12 Norman Mailer, "The White Negro: Superficial Reflections on the Hipster," in *Legacy of Dissent*, ed. Nicolaus Mills (1957; reprint, New York: Touchstone, 1994), esp. pp. 168–71.

13 Martin Luther King, Jr., *Stride toward Freedom: The Montgomery Story* (New York: Harper and Row, 1958).

14 Martin Luther King, Jr., "I Have a Dream," August 28, 1963; electronic text prepared by National Public Telecomputing Network (NPTN).

15 Joseph R. Washington, Jr., *Black Religion: The Negro and Christianity in the United States* (Boston, MA: Beacon Press, 1964) p. 257.

16 Ibid, p. 266.

17 Jack Kerouac, *On the Road* (New York: Viking Press, 1957), p. 6.

18 "All of a sudden church took on a whole different meaning for me," Jim explains. "I was doing things because *I* wanted to do them. I started seeing myself in a different light. I guess that's the best way to say it. In other words, at that time I accepted the fact that I had a divine purpose for existing, that the Lord was actively involved in my life, that I mattered. It was just a spiritual consciousness. I felt a relationship with the Lord, an ongoing, close relationship."

19 Among the many studies that have described these influences, two that provide especially revealing information from interviews and firsthand observation are Mary Jo Weaver, *New Catholic Women* (Bloomington: Indiana University Press, 1995), and Cynthia Eller, *Living in the Lap of the Goddess: The Feminist Spirituality Movement in America* (New York: Crossroad, 1993).

20 Carol Gilligan, *In a Different Voice: Psychological Theory and Women's Development* (Cambridge, MA: Harvard University Press, 1982); Mary Field Belenky et al., *Women's Ways of Knowing: The Development of Self, Voice, and Mind* (New York: Basic Books, 1986).

21 Elizabeth A. Johnson, *She Who Is: The Mystery of God in Feminist Theological Discourse* (New York: Crossroad, 1993); Christie Cozad Neuger, ed., *The Arts of Ministry: Feminist-Womanist Approaches* (Louisville, KY: Westminster/John Knox, 1996); Sara Maitland, *A Big-Enough God: A Feminist's Search for Joyful Theology* (New York: Holt, Rinehart and Winston, 1995); Elisabeth Schussler Fiorenza, *Bread Not Stone: The Challenge of Feminist Biblical Interpretation* (Boston: Beacon Press, 1995)

22 It is important not to exaggerate the impact of feminist spirituality at the grassroots level however. Among our interviewees, a majority claimed to have been influenced in some way by feminist thinking, but its impact was much more in reinforcing convictions about equal opportunities for women, rights, and freedom of choice than about concepts of God, theology, or religious practice. Women who said they had been particularly influenced by it also emphasized how it had empowered them to become stronger individuals and thus to feel more confident about their own decisions . . .

23 Michael Novak, *The Experience of Nothingness* (New York: Harper and Row, 1970), p. 4.

24 These shifts are evident in popular interpretations of the writings of Peter Berger and Thomas Luckmann; in Bellah, "No Direction Home"; and in the works of scholars such as Norman O. Brown, R. D. Laing, Theodore Roszak, and Herbert Marcuse.

25 US Bureau of the Census, *Statistical Abstract . . . 1992*, p. 559.

26 In 1958, there were approximately twenty-seven hundred bookstores across the country, and more than half reported only modest sales; by 1977, more than ten thousand bookstores were in operation, those with modest sales made up less than a third of the total, and chain stores were rapidly taking a large share of the market. Paul D. Doebler, "Growth and Development of Consumer Bookstores since 1954 – An Update through 1977," in *Book Industry Trends: 1980*, ed. John P. Dessauer et al. (Darien, CT: Book Industry Study Group, 1980), pp. 43–56.

27 David Kennedy, *Birth Control in America* (New Haven, CT: Yale University Press, 1970).

28 Hoge, Johnson, and Luidens, *Vanishing Boundaries*, p. 74.

29 Personal communication from Paul DiMaggio at Princeton University and Timothy Dowd at Emory University.

30 Paul C. Glick, "A Demographer Looks at American Families," *Journal of Marriage and the Family* 37 (1975): 15–26.

31 Wuthnow, *Restructuring*, p. 155.

32 US Bureau of the Census, *Statistical Abstract . . . 1992*, p. 143.

33 In addition to exposing people to new ideas and broadening their horizons, schooling also

significantly increased the likelihood that people would continue to be influenced by a wide variety of cultural sources.

34 US Bureau of the Census, *Statistical Abstract . . . 1989*, p. 424. If baby boomers were the direct beneficiaries of this prosperity, they were not the only segment of the population to gain new freedom. The decline in poverty levels lifted millions of families to a point where they could maintain homes, purchase televisions, and think about educating their children. This was also the period in which older people came to expect that retirement would provide opportunities to explore new horizons. Between 1960 and 1975, for instance, average life expectancy for older men increased by about a year and for older women by more than two years; over the same period, the proportion of men working past age sixty-five declined from about a third to only a fifth, and fewer than one in ten older women was gainfully employed. The fact that older Americans had more disposable income and lived increasingly in their own homes or in retirement communities also offered their children greater freedom to adopt new lifestyles and new styles of consumption. Even if, as some research suggests, inter-generational interaction remained strong in terms of paying visits and giving gifts, the pattern of interacting with significant others was shifting in a manner similar to the shift in in spirituality – from association rooted in a single geographic place to more intentional, sporadic contact within a more dispersed social space.

35 One survey found that four people in ten thought a lot about "why there is suffering in the world" – as many as who thought this much about personal happiness and more than those who thought about purpose in life or life after death. Bay Area Survey, in Charles Y. Glock, *Perspectives on Life in America Today, 1973* [machine-readable data file] (Berkeley: Survey Research Center, 1975); my analysis.

36 Norris, *Dakota*, p. 122.

37 Maya Angelou, *Wouldn't Take Nothing for My Journey Now* (New York: Random House, 1993), p. 76.

38 Dietrich Bonhoeffer, *Letters and Papers from Prison* (1953; reprint, New York: Macmillan, 1962).

39 Bellah, "No Direction Home," p. 74.

40 Norman O. Brown, *Love's Body* (New York: Vintage Books, 1968), p. 262.

41 Harvey Cox, *The Secular City: Secularization and Urbanization in Theological Perspective*, 2nd edn. (New York: Collier Books, 1990), p. 9.

42 The city was an especially attractive metaphor. For white, middle-class Americans, it connoted not squalor but opportunity. It was a place not of degradation but of affluence. The city was style more than substance. It meant freedom from tradition, impersonality – even anonymity – in the sense that one could escape the watchful eye of parents and neighbors. It was less a place than a flow of communication and ideas and people. Its diversity forced people to think and to know their own minds more fully. Advocates of spiritual seeking did not describe the city as a sacred abode, certainly not as a city of God. It was, rather, a place to visit, as on a weekend trip from the suburbs, or to read about and to be amused by. The city as metaphor was everywhere; one did not have to be there to participate in it.

43 Harold E. Quinley, *The Prophetic Clergy: Social Activism among Protestant Ministers* (New York: Wiley, 1974), p. 61.

44 Hoge, Johnson, and Luidens, *Vanishing Boundaries*, pp. 73–87.

45 People who valued the freedom to explore spirituality in their own way had no trouble doing so. For example, by 1982 the American public was spending more than $700 million on religious books – a market that would more than double during the next decade and that was largely in the hands of commercial and independent publishers rather than denominational presses. In addition, the market for self-help, inspiration, psychology, and recovery books was growing even more rapidly. US Bureau of the Census, *Statistical Abstract . . . 1992*, p. 235. The more eclectic style in reading habits was already becoming evident in the 1960s and 1970s, when only two top-selling books (other than the Bible) dealt with spirituality from what might be considered an orthodox perspective (both were by C. S. Lewis – *Mere Christianity* and *The Screwtape Letters* and both sold approximately 1.5 million copies in this period). In comparison, at least ten bestsellers during these years focused on issues that might have been considered "spiritual" in a broader sense and specifically challenged or offered alternatives to conventional theology – among them, William Golding's *Lord of the Flies* (7 million copies), Kahlil Gibran's *The Prophet* (5 million), Alex

Comfort's *Joy of Sex* (4 million), Albert Camus's *The Stranger* (3 million), Richard Bach's *Jonathan Livingston Seagull* (3 million), Hal Lindsey's *Late Great Planet Earth* (2.3 million), Elisabeth Kübler-Ross's *On Death and Dying* (2.1 million), and Eldridge Cleaver's *Soul on Ice* (1.3 million).

46 George H. Gallup, Jr., *Religion in America: 1978* (Princeton, NJ: Gallup Organization, 1978), p. 52. The larger impact of Eastern spirituality was to popularize practices that could be pursued piecemeal and on one's own. Unlike the emphasis in Judaism and in Christianity on "householders," for example, Buddhism has traditionally stressed withdrawal from household duties as a means of attaining spiritual insight; indeed, the term *monk* is often synonymous in Asian languages with "home leaver" . . .

47 Organized religion showed some of the effects of these wider explorations. For example, despite the relative affluence of these years, organized religion did not experience the financial growth it had during the 1950s and early 1960s; indeed, in per capita and inflation-adjusted dollars, the amount given in 1968 was higher than in any subsequent year for the next decade and a half. Caplow et al., *Recent Social Trends*, p. 289. Also, in comparison with the growth in numbers of clergy that had occurred in the 1950s, the 1960s showed virtually no net growth, and only toward the end of the 1970s, when women gained entry to seminaries, did these numbers begin to increase again. At this point, however, most of the growth in seminary enrollments was occurring in specialized ministry programs rather than in training for traditional pastoral duties in congregations. Thus, by 1980, when approximately five hundred thousand ordained clergy were counted in the US Census, only about half were serving in parishes.

48 Gallup Unchurched American Study (Gallup, *Religion in America: 1978*), my analysis of persons age eighteen through thirty-four . . .

49 Among semiskilled workers, only 3 percent attended church weekly, compared with 24 percent of managers and executives, 8 percent of sales workers, 2 percent of service workers, 4 percent of divorced persons, 2 percent of black males, 8 percent of persons who had moved three times in the past five years, 7 percent of those earning less than $10,000 annually.

50 Winter, *Being Free*.

51 Theodore Roszak, *The Making of a Counter Culture: Reflections on the Technocratic Society and Its Youthful Opposition* (Garden City, NY: Doubleday, 1969); Charles A. Reich, *The Greening of America* (New York: Random House, 1970).

IV

Joining New Religious Movements

Few people have had any direct contact with an NRM or even know someone who has been involved with one. Yet it is not uncommon for people to think that they have a pretty good idea why people join such groups. Their opinions, moreover, are almost always negative. The common stereotype is that recruits are either social losers seeking a safe haven from the hardships of this world or naive souls being taken advantage of by others. Either way two factors tend to remain constant: the religious experience under consideration is not genuine and the individuals are being manipulated by a cunning and probably unscrupulous cult leader. The leader is likely motivated, it is usually presumed, by some desire for greater wealth, sexual benefit, or power, and the group employs some process of mind control or brainwashing to win and keep the allegiance of its converts (e.g., Pfeifer 1992; Richardson 1992). These are the assumptions commonly reinforced by most media accounts of NRMs and their activities (e.g., Van Driel and Richardson 1988; Beckford 1999). But the public is receptive to these simplistic and highly critical characterizations because they fit our prejudices about unknown and seemingly deviant groups. The strangeness of the beliefs and practices of many NRMs, especially when reported out of context, combined with the fervent character of the faith espoused by converts, makes people feel uncomfortable. The groups are stigmatized by the rest of society as a natural protection against dealing with ideas and experiences that are subversive of the status quo. As chapter 5 establishes, there is nothing new in the critical reception given to new religions. But in modern democratic societies dedicated to the protection of certain basic rights and freedoms, and interested in the promotion of the tolerance of differences, great care must be taken to prevent the suppression of such groups out of ignorance and fear.

The popular stereotypes about who joins NRMs receive some support from the historical and social scientific study of groups in the past. Many unconventional religious groups recruited their members disproportionately from the more underprivileged sectors of society. Sectarian religious groups from the late nineteenth and early twentieth centuries, like the Jehovah's Witnesses or the Seventh Day Adventists, first attracted most of their members from economically deprived people who turned to these religions, in part at least, as a social protest against the dominant society and the mainstream Christian denominations identified with that society. But some other NRMs of the past, like Theosophy (discussed in chapter 5), tended to recruit their members from the more prosperous and elite members of society, so great care must be taken in making generalizations. The NRMs with which we are chiefly concerned, those rising to prominence since the 1960s, are a case in point. They have drawn their membership primarily from the privileged baby-boomers and other relatively prosperous generations born since the 1950s.

The two readings in this section of the book each provide reliable information about three important aspects of joining NRMs: the process by which someone converts to a contemporary NRM, the social profile of such converts, and their possible psychological motivations. There is much more to be learned about all three topics, but enough information is in hand to convince most scholars that the popular stereotypes are quite inaccurate. The evidence of social scientific research runs contrary to the views espoused by most anti-cult organizations (e.g., American Family Foundation, Watchman Fellowship, Inc.). The information and insights provided by these readings are also relevant to the debate over whether recruits to NRMs are "brainwashed," but that more specific and highly controversial issue will be dealt with separately in the next section of the book.

In chapter 7, "Who Joins New Religious Movements and Why," Lorne Dawson summarizes and synthesizes what we have learned about the three key issues noted above from decades of study of those who have joined NRMs. The data available are used to sort the propositions made by scholars by their degree of empirical support, differentiating between the most and least substantiated claims. There is a pattern to how people come to join NRMs, and we can identify who is most likely to join, and even why, to some extent. For every generalization, however, it is carefully noted that there are often significant exceptions. NRMs are susceptible to the kind of systematic sociological treatment that fosters the development of theory (e.g., Dawson 1999; Bromley 2002), but they are remarkably diverse in their form and functioning. Clearly, people are driven to join NRMs out of some personal need, and these needs are rooted in some identifiable social conditions. We need to develop a better grasp of both factors, but as Dawson argues, we know much more than is commonly appreciated (see, for example, Tipton 1982; Barker 1984; Palmer 1994;

Wilson and Dobbelaere 1994). Minimally, as Dawson demonstrates, we now know that the background of most converts prevents them from being cast as socially marginal or deprived individuals. On the contrary, as Stark and Bainbridge (1985: 395) stress, contemporary NRMs "skim more of the cream of society than the dregs."

In chapter 8, "The Joiners," by the Canadian psychiatrist Saul Levine, we are given a more refined insight into the circumstances surrounding the conversion of nine hypothetical individuals in the late 1970s and early 1980s. These typical conversion accounts are based on a rich body of data Levine accumulated from hundreds of clinical interviews with members and ex-members of NRMs. In line with the research findings summarized by Dawson, these converts are young, fairly well educated, and from relatively well-off and stable families. They show no more signs of psychological abnormality, Levine asserts, than the general population of adolescents and young adults. In fact most of them appear to have been quite active and accomplished. They share, however, a particular psychological dilemma born of certain features of our fast-paced, fragmented, and indulgent society, and it is their struggle with this dilemma that accounts for their often shocking and unexpected conversions. These conversions, Levine proposes, represent radical attempts to resolve certain common and yet difficult problems of maturation. Most young people eventually work out the issues for themselves. But these young men and women are "peculiarly stalled" by the very strength of their family ties. They are unable to figure out who they are or what the future holds for them. In the midst of their quiet frustration a future arrives that promises them a way to separate from their families and explore their own nature, while remaining surrounded by a supportive and highly structured group. In Levine's words: "Out of the blue, the Hare Krishnas, Divine Light Mission, Healing Workshop, Children of God, or Armed Guard offers on a silver platter every ingredient that has been missing from their unhappy youth." Whatever the merits of Levine's specific psychiatric diagnosis, this reading is important because it puts a very human face to those who have joined NRMs. We can all identify to some degree with these young people and their search for greater certainty in life

References

Barker, Eileen 1984: *The Making of a Moonie: Choice or Brainwashing?* Oxford: Blackwell.

Beckford, James A. 1999: The Mass Media and New Religious Movements. In B. Wilson and J. Cresswell (eds.), *New Religious Movements: Challenge and Response.* London: Routledge, 103–19.

Bromley David G. 2002: Dramatic Denouements. In D. G. Bromley and J. G. Melton (eds.), *Cults, Religion and Violence.* Cambridge: Cambridge University Press, 11–41.

Dawson, Lorne L. 1999: When Prophecy Fails and Faith Persists: A Theoretical Overview. *Nova Religio* 3 (1): 60–82.

Palmer, Susan J. 1994: *Moon Sisters, Krishna Mothers, Rajneesh Lovers: Women's R[...] Religions.* Syracuse, NY: Syracuse U[...] Press.

Pfeifer, Jeffrey E. 1992: The Psychological Fram[...] of Cults: Schematic Representations and Cult Evaluations. *Journal of Applied Social Psychology* 22 (7): 531–44.

Richardson, James T. 1992: Public Opinion and the Tax Evasion Trial of Reverend Moon. *Behavioral Sciences and the Law* 10 (1): 53–64.

Stark, Rodney and William Sims Bainbridge 1985: *The Future of Religion: Secularization, Revival and Cult Formation.* Berkeley: University of California Press.

Tipton, Steven 1982: *Getting Saved From the Sixties.* Berkeley: University of California Press.

Van Driel, Barend and James T. Richardson 1988: Print Media Coverage of New Religious Movements: A Longitudinal Study. *Journal of Communication* 38 (3): 37–61.

Wilson, Bryan and Karel Dobbelaere 1994: *A Time to Chant: The Soka Gakkai Buddhist in Britain.* Oxford: Clarendon Press.

CHAPTER SEVEN

ιο Joins New Religious ents and Why: Twenty Years of Research and What Have We Learned?

LORNE L. DAWSON

The headlines read '48 Found Dead in Doomsday Cult' and '50 From Quebec Cult Found Slain'.[1] On the evening of Tuesday, October 4, 1994, the members of a small new religious movement called The Order of the Solar Temple (*Temple Solaire*) committed mass suicide (though murder–suicide is a possibility as well) by shooting or asphyxiating themselves and burning their homes to the ground, almost simultaneously, in three different locations (Morin Heights, Quebec, and the villages of Cheiry and Granges-sur-Salvan, Switzerland).[2] The following evening, like millions of other Americans and Canadians, I tuned in to ABC's popular and award-winning news-commentary program, *Nightline*. Characteristically, the host, Ted Koppel, was already interviewing three 'cult experts' about the Solar Temple tragedy and I hoped to gain a better understanding of what happened. To my dismay, but not to my surprise, two of the 'experts' in question were drawn from the American anti-cult movement, while the third was a Canadian journalist. Over the next half hour Mr. Koppel posed the questions always asked in these situations, What could make someone end their lives in this way? How could someone come to join such a group in the first place? What do we know about the mysterious leader of the cult? He had posed similar questions just over a year earlier to similar 'experts' with regard to the stand-off and eventual massacre of the Branch Davidians, under David Koresh, in Waco, Texas. The answers received to these questions this evening seemed as pat and pre-programmed as they did then. They were largely devoid of specifics, speculative and polemical. We were informed, with little in the way of direct reference to the actual beliefs and practices of the Solar Temple, that the group was like all other 'destructive' and 'apocalyptic' cults. In passing, one of the 'experts' made specific reference to two other new religious movements, the Unification Church of the Reverend Sun Myung Moon and John-Roger's MSIA (pronounced Messiah). Curiously though, neither group has ever been associated with either violence or suicide in any form. Nevertheless, these experts assured us that the members of such dangerous cults are recruited through deception and the sophisticated use of techniques of 'mind-control'. The cunning and charismatic leaders of these groups exploit the psychological weaknesses and idealistic aspirations of their recruits, it was implied, in order to satisfy their own desires for material wealth and power. Yet, these experts acknowledged, we really do not know very much about this cult leader or his followers. By the end of the interview, those viewing the program had probably confirmed the prejudices most Americans and Canadians harbour against 'cults'. These prejudices have been bolstered by the sheer reiteration of the pejorative observations and charges favoured by the media for the last twenty years. Little real insight was obtained into the true nature of the circumstances leading to the Solar Temple tragedy or the nature of the diverse cult activity present in contemporary Western society.

Listening to these 'experts' I could not help wondering whether viewers, no matter how uninformed, still would be satisfied with such platitudinous responses. Might they not ask: Why do we seem to know so little about these groups, especially in the wake of the Jonestown massacre of 1978 and the Koresh debacle in 1993? How can these groups continue to ply their trade, if their sins are so transparent? Whatever the reason for a measure of healthy scepticism, it should be surprising for all to discover that much of the recent public debate over cults has ignored or avoided a substantial and growing body of academic literature on the beliefs, practices, failings and significance of cults (i.e. what sociologists prefer to call new religious movements or NRMs). An established array of empirical information and explanatory insights, directly pertinent to the issues at hand, can be found in this literature. But, as my own direct and indirect experience with the media, my colleagues and students confirms, the message is not getting out. All too often traditional religious studies scholars themselves remain too ignorant of the 'facts', and as a consequence they run the risk, in our secular age, of allowing all religious expressions being tarnished by the fall-out from the campaign of misinformation carried on against the alternative and minority religions in our midst.

Of course journalists face considerable constraints of time, space and competition in fashioning their stories about new religions. They are necessarily guided by the commercial demand to attract readers and often lack expertise in the subject. But as other stories continue to be newsworthy a marked improvement in the quality of reporting and commentary usually can be detected. Such does not appear to be the case (with rare exceptions) when it comes to 'cult stories'.[3] Summarizing their longitudinal and comprehensive analysis of print media coverage of cults in America, Van Driel and Richardson observe that 'although not uniformly negative, [it] can best be described as 'a stream of controversies' with little attention to the history or human side of the new religions'.[4]

One of the most prominent issues in the cult controversy is, who joins new religious movements and why? The popular conception of the situation is riddled with stereotypes. In some instances those who join are thought to be young, idealistic and gullible people duped by cunning cult recruiters. In other instances they are maladjusted and marginal losers who have found a safe haven in the controlled life of a cult. Simultaneously it is also often asserted 'that everyone is susceptible to the lure of these master manipulators.'[5] In the popular press and the anti-cult literature all three positions are combined in ways which manage to cover all eventualities. The question at hand is, what do we really know about who joins NRMs and why? What do systematic studies reveal, as opposed to the anecdotal evidence on which the media and anti-cultists rely? Over the last twenty years a fairly reliable body of data has accumulated. This article draws together and organizes this dispersed material to clarify the micro-structural availability of people to cult involvement. What do we know about how people become *interested* in new religious movements, and the *social attributes* of those who choose to join?

No attempt will be made in this limited context to address directly four other closely related issues: (1) the specific features of the biographic availability[6] of individuals to conversion,[7] (2) the macro-structural availability of people to cult involvement (i.e. the broad social conditions thought to set the stage for the emergence of NRMs),[8] (3) the charge that cults secure and maintain their followers through 'brainwashing' or 'mind control',[9] and (4) the mental health of those involved with NRMs.[10] Indirectly, of course, much will be said that is relevant to a determination of these issues, but answering the question at hand is a necessary preliminary step.[11]

How Do People Get Involved With New Religious Movements?

Much that we now know about who, how and why people join NRMs stems from attempts made to apply and criticize the influential model of conversion advanced by John Lofland and Rodney Stark.[12] This model grew out of field research into what was then a small and obscure deviant religion dubbed the 'Divine Precepts' by Lofland and Stark. The group was in fact the early Unification Church (i.e. the Moonies). Gathering the accounts of converts to this cult, and observing the attempts made at recruitment, Lofland and Stark formulated a seven-step model of the process of conversion. Briefly, this model stipulates that for persons to convert to a cult they must (1) experience enduring, acutely felt *tensions* in their lives, (2) within a *religious problem-solving perspective* (as opposed to a psychiatric or political problem-solving perspective), (3) which leads them to think of themselves as a *religious seeker*. With these three 'predisposing conditions' in place, the person must then (4) encounter the cult to which they convert at a *turning point* in their lives, (5) form an *affective bond* with one or more members of the cult, (6) reduce or eliminate *extracult attachments* and (7) be exposed to *intensive interaction* with other converts. With the completion of the latter four 'situational contingencies,' the new convert can become a 'deployable agent' of the cult. It is the cumulative effect of all of these experiences, Lofland and Stark believed, that produces a true conversion. Each step is necessary, but only the whole process is sufficient to produce a 'total convert.'

Over the years this model has been tested repeatedly, in different contexts, with mixed results. In the study of a quite large NRM imported to America from Japan, Nichiren Shoshu Buddhism (also known by the name of its lay organization, Soka Gakkai), David Snow and Cynthia Phillips found reason to be conceptually and empirically suspicious of the applicability of all but two of the seven steps of the Lofland–Stark model of conversion.[13]

Arthur Greil and David Rudy, to cite another example, arrived at a similar conclusion after scrutinizing the data on conversion available from ten case studies of widely divergent NRMs.[14] Alternatively, Merrill Singer and to some extent Willem Kox, Wim Meeus and Harm't Hart found almost all aspects of the model to be relevant to the study of the Black Hebrew Nation, on the one hand, and Dutch adolescents who had converted to either the Unification Church or the Pentecostal Church, on the other hand.[15] Debate over the merits of the theory has become complex, with clashes of opinion over every aspect of the model. For instance, as a result of their research into Nichiren Shoshu in America, Snow and Phillips are quite dismissive of two aspects of Lofland and Stark's model. They reject the claims that potential converts must experience enduring and acutely felt tensions and some 'turning point' in their lives (e.g. failing out of school, experiencing a divorce, undertaking a long trip). In a study of the same NRM in Britain, however, Wilson and Dobbelaere found that many members at least say they experienced chronic or acute crises in their lives and a turning point.[16] The disparity can be explained in many ways. But these kinds of divergent results suggest, as Kox et al. propose, that the steps outlined by Lofland and Stark do not represent so much an integrated and cumulative model of the actual process of conversion as a fairly adequate statement of some of the key 'conditions' of conversion (with the understanding that these conditions may vary independently and that their significance may vary for different religions and in different circumstances).

While many scholars have clearly overgeneralized the relevance of Lofland and Stark's findings, the research their model inspired has consistently confirmed some of these 'conditions' and led to the formulation of some reasons why they may vary. The empirical and theoretical insights in question constitute the body of what we can confidently say about why people become involved with NRMs. In order, roughly, of the degree of empirical support that exists for them, the microstructural availability of people to cult involvements is conditioned by the following seven generalizations.

In the first place, studies of conversion and of specific groups have found that recruitment to NRMs happens primarily through pre-existing social networks and interpersonal bonds. Friends recruit friends, family members each other and neighbours recruit neighbours. Contrary to public belief and the assertions of many proponents of the 'brainwashing' theory of cult conversion, the figures available support neither the proposition that everyone is equally susceptible to recruitment, nor that most converts are recruited through individual contacts in public places. Groups such as the Unification Church, Krishna Consciousness and Children of God have been scourged for their aggressive and persistent forays into airports, parks and the streets to disseminate literature and proselytize. Yet the evidence strongly indicates that these recruitment drives are usually dismal failures.[17] Rather, the majority of recruits to the majority of NRMs come into contact with the groups they join because they personally know one or more members of the movement.[18]

The results of Wilson and Dobbelaere's recent and quite comprehensive study of Nichiren Shoshu in Britain, are characteristic:

> Only 6 per cent of those in our sample had encountered [the Nichiren Shoshu] through the impersonal agencies of the media – through exhibitions, concerts, the movement's own publicity, or the various media accounts of the organization which had appeared in Britain. Ninety-four per cent met the movement through social interaction. Friends represented the largest category of people who introduced members, amounting to some 42 per cent; 23 per cent were brought into contact with it through their partners or family members. The remainder were first presented with information by acquaintances, work or student colleagues most particularly, but 14 per cent owed the encounter to casual acquaintances.[19]

Even the anti-cultist Margaret Singer supports the proposition that most converts are recruited through social networks.[20] She cites a figure of 66 per cent. Like much of the anti-cult literature, though, she does not provide us with any reliable information about the source of this claim, and she does not seem to see any inconsistency between this claim and another made on the same page, namely that 'All of us are vulnerable to cult recruitment'.

In the study of NRMs, however, there are always exceptions to every rule. Eileen Barker denies that existing personal networks account for the majority of converts to the Moonies in Britain.[21] But her claim is somewhat ambiguous since she notes that networks do account for over a quarter of the British membership and in a footnote she provides evidence that they also account for a third of the membership in the rest of Europe. Moreover, she does not clearly identify an alternative way in which the largest number of recruits are derived. By implication it would appear that the she has in mind 'by-chance' encounters between recruiters and individuals in the streets.

Second, as some of even the harshest critics of the Lofland–Stark model reaffirm, Lofland and Stark were correct in specifying the importance of affective ties in inducing recruits to join.[22] Again, Wilson and Dobbelaere's findings with regard to the Nichiren Shoshu in Britain are typical: over a third of their respondents stressed 'the quality of the membership' as the primary reason for their initial attraction to the group. Wilson and Dobbelaere provide numerous quotations from their questionnaires and interviews redolent with praise for the vibrancy, warmth, openness, joy and positive outlook of the members people first encountered. In general, case studies of individuals who joined NRMs or of the groups themselves commonly reveal the crucial role of affective bonds with specific members in leading recruits into deeper involvements.[23]

Third, and equally strongly, from the same studies it is clear that the intensive interaction of recruits with the rest of the existing membership of the group is pivotal to the successful conversion and maintenance of new members. In fact, as Janet Jacobs discovered, a perceived loss of such intensive interaction often plays a key role in the deconversion or apostasy of members of NRMs.[24] On these three points there is little disagreement in the literature. Other findings are subject to greater variation and dispute, yet their frequency of fit with specific groups and situations is still quite significant.

Fourth, cult involvement seems to be strongly correlated with having fewer and weaker extra-cult social ties.[25] Part of the reason for the disproportionate representation of adolescents and young adults in NRMs is simply that this segment of the population is relatively free of countervailing social and economic obligations and commitments. They have the time and the opportunity to indulge their spiritual appetites and experiment with alternative lifestyles. The more freedom one has in these regards the more likely one is to accept the 'invitation' of a cult recruiter to dinner, a lecture, a meditation session or whatever.[26]

Fifth, and similarly, cult involvement seems to be strongly correlated with having fewer and weaker ideological alignments. Most researchers now discount Lofland and Stark's suggestion that converts to NRMs were probably pre-socialized to adopting a religious problem-solving perspective. The data actually suggests that the 'unchurched,' as Stark and Bainbridge call them,[27] are more likely to join. In many cases, lack of prior religious education and family life seems to leave young people more open to alternative spiritual explanations of the world and its hardships.[28] More will be said about this in discussing the social attributes of converts.

Again, however, there are clear exceptions to this generalization. As Richardson and Stewart and Steven Tipton suggest,[29] in the case of many neo-Christian (e.g. the Unification Church) and Jesus movements we may be dealing with the phenomenon of 'returning fundamentalists.' Recruits to these groups often do seem to have been raised in strict religious households from which they have lapsed or rebelled as adolescents. Similarly, it would seem that recruits to the Catholic Charismatic Renewal and its offshoots are overwhelmingly from Catholic backgrounds.[30]

Sixth, while 'seekership', the active search for religious answers to one's problems, does not seem to be as necessary to all conversions to NRMs as Lofland and Stark thought, it does precede many conversions.[31] People inclined to be interested in even the possibility of joining an NRM have been reading related religious and philosophical literature and giving some serious thought to the so-called 'big questions' (e.g. What is the meaning of life? Is there a God? Is there life after death?). This does not necessarily mean that the converts in question have fully adopted a 'religious problem-solving perspective'. But similar findings are reported in Rochford's study of Krishna Consciousness,[32] Wilson and Dobbelaere's study of Nichiren Shoshu,[33] and Jones's study of the Church Universal and Triumphant:[34] at the time of their conversion to the NRM a little less than half of the members were either actively practising a religion other than that in which they were raised or previously they had been members of one or more other non-traditional religious groups.

Seventh, as Stark and Bainbridge stress,[35] in seeking to account for the conditions of conversion we should be careful not to neglect the obvious. NRMs provide many kinds of 'direct rewards' to their members. They commonly offer such positive inducements as affection and heightened self-esteem, esoteric and exoteric knowledge that provides a sense of power and control over one's life, as well as simple material and social aid, security, new career opportunities and forms of prestige. In fact, as Roy Wallis notes,[36] sometimes the rewards of participating in the new reality constructed by the group may become more important than satisfying 'the ends such participation was originally intended to procure'.

The degree to which any or all of these factors are involved in recruitment to any NRM is subject to variation. As Snow and Phillips and Snow et al. have empirically demonstrated,[37] the degree to which successful recruitment requires that potential converts have weak extra-cult ties and/or ideological alignments depends on how deviant and particularistic the group in question is, as well as the extent of the commitment demanded by the group. If joining an NRM does not entail a dramatic transformation of one's values and lifestyle, as in the case of Scientology, then the need to sever extra-cult bonds is reduced. Obversely, if there is a pronounced difference between the orientation and activities of the new religion and the family and friends of the recruit, as in the case of Krishna Consciousness, then the weakening of prior ties plays a more crucial role in the conversion process. Similarly, for groups stigmatized by the dominant society a strategy of isolation may be used to neutralize the stigma. This strategy may also be induced by the extent to which a group insists it has the exclusive path to truth and salvation. The more particularistic a religion is, the more it will demand a sharp separation from the world and from the convert's past social and ideological attachments. Finally, the more complete the level and type of commitment demanded by a group, as in such communal groups as the Unification Church and Krishna Consciousness, The more likely it is that new members will be recruited through contact in public places rather than through interpersonal bonds and social networks. This latter linkage may explain why Barker's findings for the Unification Church in Britain seem at odds with the strong role of social networks in recruitment detected by most other studies of NRMs.

Various combinations of these factors limit who is structurally available to join NRMs. Relative to the small number of people who do join such groups, though, the delimitation is still insufficient. It is necessary therefore to see these social factors against a backdrop of yet more contingent and situational factors. For example, recruitment can be influenced by the degree and type of hostility to NRMs present in the dominant culture, the presence or absence of missionaries and the presence of competitor groups.[38] It makes a world of difference whether an NRM arises in the relaxed and experimental atmosphere of contemporary California or the highly conformist environment of Ireland or Iran. Contrasting Japan and the United States, Wilson points out that we must be careful not to assume even that new religions fulfil the same function in dif-

ferent cultural and historical circumstances.[39] To the convert it often seems miraculous that a representative of a new religion happens to be at hand at the crucial moment of doubt and/or decision in their lives. If other similar kinds of groups, competitor religions or functional equivalents to religion (e.g. some cathartic encounter therapy group, revolutionary political movement, or idealistic social service organization) are present instead, then the conversion in question might never happen.[40]

Adding another spin to the contingent conditions, as Wilson proposes, we must consider 'that, in some measure, movements may *awaken* needs in particular individuals, giving them increased specificity in the terms of the movement's own ideology, and so defining the situation for prospective adherents, supplying both the sense of needs and the means of its fulfilment.'[41] New religions, like many new commercial enterprises, are in the business of 'consciousness raising' about needs and their satisfaction.

What are the Social Attributes of Those Who Join New Religious Movements?

It is difficult to specify a reliable social profile of typical cult converts. Two things are clear from the numerous studies undertaken of conversion to NRMs: (a) because of the different recruitment strategies of different cult leaders and/or the heavy reliance of NRMs on social networks to secure new recruits, each new religion tends to attract a rather homogeneous group of followers; (b) but the overall membership of NRMs is much more heterogeneous than commonly anticipated, since group tends to attract somewhat different kinds of followers.[42] Nevertheless, it is still possible to make some broad and important generalizations.

First the membership of most NRMs are disproportionately young. Barker[43] found that 50 per cent of the membership of the Unification Church in Britain were between 21 and 26 years old. The average age at which people joined the movement was 23 years old. At the time she wrote, Rochford[44] reported that 56 per cent of the membership of Krishna Consciousness was between 20 and 25 years old, and more than 50 per cent had joined before their 21st birthday.[45] More recently, Wilson and Dobbelaere[46] found that while the membership of Nichiren Shoshu in Britain were also young, they are relatively not as young. Their extensive survey revealed that 68.2 per cent of the membership were under the age of 34 and 88.4 per cent were under the age of 44. With rare exceptions, though, the new religions of today are a game for young people and, relative to the population, middle-aged and old people are markedly underrepresented.

As some of the NRMs of the 1960s have aged, these figures have shifted.[47] But many people drop out of these organizations by the time they are middle aged. This is especially true of NRMs that are more communal in structure and more exclusive in their commitments. The demands they make on members often conflict with the demands of family life and raising children. There is some reason to believe that the new religions that are more segmented and plural in their commitment expectations (like Scientology, Eckancar, Nichiren Shoshu, etc.) will maintain a better spread in the age distribution of their members as the groups grow older. For example, on the basis of an admittedly limited sample, Wallis[48] found that the average age of recruitment to Scientology in Britain was about 32 years old. While Wilson and Dobbelaere report a mean age for starting the practice of Nichiren Shoshu of 31 years old, and Carl Latkin et al., Lewis Carter and Susan Palmer, place the average age of followers of Bhagwan Shree Rajneesh in the mid-30s.[49] In another instance, the Church Universal and Triumphant seems to be aging along with its leadership (approximately 53 per cent of the membership is between 40 and 60 years old).[50]

Second, with few exceptions studies have found that recruits to NRMs are on average markedly better educated than the general public. Wallis[51] reports that 56.7 per cent of the Scientologists he studied had either professional training or college/university degrees (29.7 per cent were university graduates). Likewise, Wilson and Dobbelaere[52] found that 24 per cent of the large sample of the membership of Nichiren Shoshu in Britain had attended university, when in 1990 only 8 per cent of the population had a university education. In the case of the Church Universal and Triumphant, Jones[53] actually found one quarter of her respondents to have completed an advanced technical or professional degree (e.g. MBA, MSW, MD, or Ph.D.). Latkin et al.[54] likewise report that 64 per cent of the members of Rajneeshpuram had at least a college degree, and a further random sample of 100 members uncovered 24 per cent with a masters degree and 12 per cent with a doctorate of some sort. Even Rochford[55] discovered that 65 per cent of his sample of very young Krishna devotees had at least one year of college. Stark and Bainbridge[56] cite comparable findings from studies of other groups. Why do NRMs tend to attract the better educated? Wilson and Dobbelaere, and others, suggest the answer is fairly obvious: 'To be properly understood, the teachings [of most NRMs] demand literate intelligence, a willingness to study, and lack of fear in the face of unfamiliar concepts and language'.[57]

Third, and not surprising given the educational levels, recruits to NRMs are also disproportionately from middle- to upper-middle class households, the advantaged segments of the population. The figures for Scientology, the Unification Church, the International Society for Krishna Consciousness, the followers of Rajneesh and the Church Universal and Triumphant, all closely concur.[58] The fathers of converts come primarily from the professional, business executive, or administrative segments of the occupational world; skilled or unskilled manual labourers are clearly underrepresented.

Fourth, on questions of sex there seems to be some dispute. Machalek and Snow[59] suggest there is an overrepresentation of women in NRMs. At some points, Stark and Bainbridge do as well.[60] But the evidence, as Stark and Bainbridge themselves admit, is highly variable. In the past females were disproportionately present in fringe religions (e.g. Christian Science in the 1920s was 75 per cent female),[61] and Wilson and Dobbelaere found about 59 per cent of the Nichiren Shoshu in Britain to be female.[62] Latkin et al. and Palmer also report a disproportionate number of females in the Rajneesh movement.[63] Barker (1984: 206), however, reports a two-to-one ratio in favour of men for the Moonies in Britain, while Wallis's sample of Scientologists is 59 per cent male.[64] Rochford, Lucas and others imply that there is little substantial discrepancy between the sexes in the groups they studied.[65] On the whole, it would seem that while some cults may attract more of one sex than the other, there is no strong evidence that women are any more susceptible to joining NRMs than men.[66]

It does appear, though, that many groups undergo a kind of developmental shift in their sex ratios as they mature. Krishna Consciousness began life in America as a largely male phenomenon, but this imbalance in sexual representation has been corrected as the movement has become an order of 'householders' and not strictly priestly ascetics.[67] In Korea and Japan, prior to its emergence in America, the Unification Church actually appealed more to women, as did the Rajneesh movement in its beginnings in India.[68] These imbalances also adjusted with time. Reliable membership figures, though, especially ones that differentiate between the sexes, are hard to come by.

Fifth and lastly, there is some ambiguity about the religious background of recruits to NRMs as well. On the one hand, with the limited evidence available, Stark and Bainbridge conclude: 'Church membership and membership in a conservative denomination are preventives against cultism. The unchurched and those affiliated with the more secularized denominations are more open to cult involvement.'[69] The levels of participation in NRMs of American Protestants, Catholics and Jews varies from group to group. On the whole, though, Stark and Bainbridge think that Protestants are underrepresented, reflecting the strength of right-wing evangelicalism in the United States, while

Catholic participation is roughly proportionate to their numbers in the population. Jews are another matter. They are extraordinarily overrepresented. Latkin et al.,[70] for example, found the following distribution in religious backgrounds for the Rajneesh movement: 30 per cent Protestant, 27 per cent Catholic, 20 per cent Jewish, 14 per cent 'none,' 4 per cent Hindu or Buddhist, 4 per cent 'other'. More startlingly, Steve Tipton,[71] in studying the San Francisco Zen Centre, found that 50 per cent of the members were Jewish.[72] Why the overrepresentation? Stark and Bainbridge point to the many indicators of the heightened secularization of the American Jewish community, relative to other religious groups.[73] Support for this stress on the relatively 'unchurched' character of converts to NRMs comes from the British followers of Nichiren Shoshu. 'Fully 76 per cent of [Wilson and Dobbelaere's] respondents said that they had not belonged to any religious organization before they joined.'[74] In fact 47 per cent declared that previously they had not been religious at all, leading Wilson and Dobbelaere to call into question the contention that religious 'seekership' is a necessary precondition for conversion.[75] Latkin et al. report that only 40 per cent of the members of Rajneeshpuram saw themselves as religious before joining, and Jones's survey of the Church Universal and Triumphant revealed a slight overrepresentation of religious 'nones' (12.67 per cent). But, in the latter instance, seekership would seem to be a significant factor since 49 per cent of the sample claimed one or more previous associations with other nontraditional religions after childhood (e.g. Rosicrucians, Theosophy, various Hindu and Buddhist groups).[76] Of course, more information is needed about the kinds of associations claimed to interpret the real meaning of this data.

On the other hand, Rochford found that the American followers of Krishna came from fairly religious households.[77] More than 50 per cent of his sample said religion was stressed in their childhood homes; 77 per cent received formal religious education as children; and about 50 per cent attended religious services regularly, while another 30 per cent attended irregularly. Now as in the case of the British members of Nichiren Shoshu, at the time of conversion, most had lapsed in the practice of their childhood faith and only 25 per cent were practising some other religion. But the contrast with Stark and Bainbridge's conclusion remains pronounced. As Stark and Bainbridge themselves note,[78] though without accounting for it, Barker also found Moonies in England to be ' drawn from families with unusually strong religious convictions'.

Why Do People Join New Religious Movements?

I cannot pretend to any definitive answers to this question. In fact, as specified in the introduction, limitations of space prevent me from considering all of the pertinent factors. Most notably, for example, there is no opportunity to discuss the possible impact of such broad social changes as the breakdown of mediating structures in advanced capitalist societies or the processes of secularization, both of which are thought to influence the macro-structural availability of people to cult involvements.[79] Here, in line with the preceding discussion, we only can comment on some of the more prominent assessments of some of the micro-structural factors affecting availability of people to cult involvements. In this vein, there are essentially two kinds of explanatory options currently available: various psychological speculations and types of rational choice theorizing. At present the former is far more pervasive, developed and empirically grounded. The latter option, while promising, is still new and rather experimental, and a proper introduction would warrant an additional essay.[80] So in this context I confine my comments to a brief summary of two of the better-known psychological analyses. While inevitably speculative, each of these accounts is recommended by the scope and subtlety of the empirical studies from which they derive. Developed independently, they nevertheless suggest a similar profile of converts to cults.

In her much-acclaimed book *The Making of a Moonie*, the British sociologist Eileen Barker states that the Moonies she came to know often seemed idealistic people, coming from fairly happy, conventional and highly 'respectable' families that placed a higher value on public service and doing one's duty than simply making money. They had grown up in sheltered environments, in which they were encouraged to be overachievers at school and in other activities. But their emotional development seems to have been retarded and they failed to experience the usual crises of adolescence until a later point in life than most of their peers. Consequently, it seems that many of them experienced 'disappointments, hurt and disillusionment' when they 'first ventured out into the world'. They may have found the transition to life at university or on the job and away from home more difficult and frustrating than expected. The implication is that they may have joined the Unification Church to at least temporarily re-establish themselves in a more satisfying set of circumstances (i.e. more structured and idealistically motivated).[81]

After interviewing and observing hundreds of young members of various NRMs, the Canadian psychiatrist Saul Levine presents much the same profile but in greater detail.[82] Without endorsing his reading of the dynamics of conversion, his detailed account is instructive. Levine emphatically asserts that he found 'no more sign of pathology among [the members and ex-members of NRMs that he studied] than . . . in any youthful population.' He also notes that the joiners he met were largely children of privilege; they were 'good kids from good backgrounds'.[83] Yet they engaged in the kind of 'radical departures' that are highly disturbing to their families and friends. These radical departures are extraordinary, but seen from the right perspective, he argues, they make sense. 'They are desperate attempts to grow up in a society that places obstacles in the way of the normal yearnings of youth.'[84] The young people who join NRMs, he believes, are distinguished by their curious inability to effect the kind of separation from their families consonant with passage into young adulthood.[85] They are psychological 'children' trapped in a dilemma that our fragmented and indulgent society may have induced. They wish to sever the parental bond and achieve independence, but they lack a sufficient sense of self to do so. On the one hand, the prospect of relinquishing the overly close tie they do have, in 'reality or fantasy', with their mothers and fathers is terrifying; it instills a great fear of personal 'depletion'. On the other hand, the self they display, whether seemingly normal or rebellious, feels 'fraudulent'. Such young people feel trapped: they can neither live with nor without their parents. All the while, though, as the children mature their parents' foibles are becoming apparent, turning them into 'fallen idols'.

Symptomatically, Levine says, joiners usually have not experienced any mature romantic relationships and they lack the kind of intimate peer relationships in which teenagers 'probe, analyze, confess, explore, and lay bare their very souls to one another'.[86] While the social supports their parents had been able to call upon on in their youth for guidance (e.g. churches, ethnic communities, patriotic activities and a liberal-arts education) have either disappeared or now appear 'plastic' and unreal. Enduring this kind of acutely felt tension, these young people yearn for a quick fix to their sense of isolation and confusion. They seek a sense of full belonging and purpose in life, independent of their families, but without engaging in the struggle to achieve true 'mutual understanding' between individuals or the serious 'analysis' of their situation required to find and shape their own identity. With so little real self-esteem in place, they are seeking to avoid, for a time at least, the responsibility of making choices. Then at a moment of crisis, a 'turning point' in Lofland and Stark's terminology, they encounter the missionaries of one or another NRM offering just such an alternative path to (or temporary detour from) maturity.

If there is some plausibility to Levine's theory, then in the end, as Barker stresses, the radical departure in question is in some respects not a departure at all. Moonies, for instance, 'do not appear to be rejecting the values that were instilled into them during their childhood; they appear, on the contrary, to have imbibed these so successfully that they are prepared to respond to the opportunity (which society does not seem to be offering them) to live according to those very standards.'[87] Arthur Parsons and Susan Palmer are led to like conclusions by their interactions with the Moonies.[88] The pattern may well vary for other NRMs, but Palmer found elements of it in each of the seven NRMs she studied and her findings are reminiscent of the views Tipton expresses in *Getting Saved from the Sixties* This perspective certainly accords with the consistent finding that most of the people who join NRMs leave voluntarily within about two years.[89] It works less well for understanding those groups that attract older followers to begin with and are less exclusive in their demands for commitment and less communal in organization (e.g. Scientology, Nichiren Shoshu, Eckancar). Tipton, Robbins and Bromley, and Palmer, however, have developed various theories that encompass these kinds of NRMs as well; theories that are similar in key respects and compatible with the speculations of Levine and Barker.[90] In various ways too complicated to broach at this juncture, these theories suggest that NRMs provide a safe haven for social and psychological experimentation with various new 'rites of passage' in order to defuse the anomie generated by a pervasive sense of moral ambiguity in modern culture.

These speculations are just that, speculations. In the end it is difficult to assess their generality. The empirical insights provided above, while more prosaic, are more reliable. I must caution, however, that while this information helps us to delimit who is more likely to join an NRM, the delimitation is still insufficient, given the small numbers of actual converts. Certainly the data run counter to many of the assertions and stereotypes of the pubilc and the anti-cult movement. But from a social scientific perspective, a crucial and easily overlooked element of mystery remains about why people choose to be religious, especially in so radical a manner.

Taking us back to where we began: Does all of this help us to better understand the tragedy of the Solar Temple? Paradoxically, the answer is both yes and no. In the end, I cannot honestly say that I am much closer to really understanding why these people chose to end their lives. This is frustrating. But I am hopeful that we can raise the level of public understanding of who joins NRMs and why, well beyond that provided by the media in the days following this frightening reminder of the continued power of the religion in our lives. On the one hand, I think it is important to establish how unexceptional in some respects cult involvements are in order to assure or even renew our respect for the religious choices people make, no matter how seemingly foreign to our sensibilities. On the other hand, if the assessments of Barker, Levine, and others hold true, then it is equally important to establish how exceptional the Solar Temple and its apocalypse are in comparison with most other NRMs. In these exceptional cases some other social-psychological processes are at work that we need to ferret out, perhaps through more detaied comparative analyses with the Peoples Temple massacre at Jonestown and the Branch Davidian conflagration at Waco.[91] Like all social phenomena, the specific dynamics in each case are subject to almost infinite variation. But with diligence, as the history of the social sciences strongly suggests, we should be able to discern certain generic social processes that we need to better understand.[92]

Notes

1   The headlines are from *The Toronto Star* and *The Globe and Mail*, respectively, on Thursday, October 6, 1994.
2   Eventually 53 bodies were found, and then, much to the surprise of everyone, on December 21, 1995, 16 more followers committed ritualistic suicide in a French forest near the Swiss border (see Massiomo Introvigne, 'Ordeal by Fire: The Tragedy of the Solar Temple', *Religion*, 25, 4 (1995): 267–83, and Susan J. Palmer, 'Purity and Danger in the

Solar Temple', *Journal of Contemporary Religion*, 11, 3 (1996): 303–18).
3   See, for example, Danny Jorgensen, 'The Social Construction and Interpretation of Deviance – Jonestown and the Mass Media', *Deviant Behavior*, 1, 3–4 (1980): 309–32, and Randy Lippert, 'The Construction of Satanism as a Social Problem in Canada', *Canadian Journal of Sociology*, 15, 4 (1990): 417–39.
4   Barend Van Driel and James T. Richardson, 'Print Media Coverage of New Religious Movements: A Longitudinal Study,' *Journal of Communication*, 38, 3 (1988): 37.
5   The quotation is from Margaret T. Singer with Janja Lalich, *Cults in Our Midst: The Hidden Menace in Our Everyday Lives* (San Francisco, CA: Jossey-Bass, 1995), P. 17. Similar views are expressed in dozens of books; for example, Ted Patrick and Tom Dulack, *Let Our Children Go!* (New York: E. P. Dutton, 1976); Ronald Enroth, *Youth, Brainwashing, and the Extremist Cults* (Grand Rapids, MI: Zondervan, 1977); Steven Hassan, *Combatting Cult Mind-Control* (Rochester, VT: Park Street Press, 1988); and Colin A. Ross, *Satanic Ritual Abuse: Principles of Treatment* (Toronto: University of Toronto Press, 1995).
6   The terms structural and biographic availability are borrowed from Richard Machalek and David A. Snow, 'Conversion to New Religious Movements', in David G. Bromley and Jeffrey K. Hadden, eds., *Religion and the Social Order, Vol. 3: The Handbook on Cults and Sects in America, Part B* (Greenwich, CT: JAI Press, 1993), pp. 53–74.
7   See, for example, Steven M. Tipton, *Getting Saved from the Sixties* (Berkeley: University of California Press, 1982); Saul V. Levine, *Radical Departures: Desperate Detours to Growing Up* (New York: Harcourt Brace Jovanovich, 1984); David Chidester, *Salvation and Suicide: An Interpretation of Jim Jones, The Peoples Temple, and Jonestown* (Bloomington: Indiana University Press, 1988); and Wade Clark Roof, *A Generation of Seekers: The Spiritual Journey of the Baby Boom Generation* (San Francisco, CA: Harper-Collins, 1993).
8   See, for example, Robert Bellah, 'New Religious Consciousness and the Crisis of Modernity', in Charles Glock and Robert Bellah, eds., *The New Religious Consciousness* (Berkeley: University of California Press, 1976), pp. 333–52; Benton Johnson, 'A Sociological

Perspective on New Religions', in Thomas Robbins and Dick Anthony, eds., *In Gods We Trust: New Patterns of Religious Pluralism in America* (New Brunswick, NJ: Transaction, 1981), pp. 51–66; Thomas Robbins, *Cults, Converts, and Charisma* (Newbury Park, CA: Sage, 1988); and Lorne L. Dawson, *Comprehending Cults: The Sociology of New Religious Movements* (Toronto: Oxford University Press, 1998).

9 There is a voluminous literature about the 'brainwashing' charge (e.g. the books cited in note 5). The best analyses are Dick Anthony and Thomas Robbins, 'Brainwashing and Totalitarian Influence,' *Encyclopedia of Human Behavior* (San Diego, CA: Academic Press, 1994), vol. 1, pp. 457–71; James T. Richardson, 'A Social Psychological Critique of 'Brainwashing' Claims about Recruitment to New Religions', in Bromley and Hadden, eds., *Handbook on Cults and Sects*, pp. 75–97; and Dawson, *Comprehending Cults.*

10 See E. Burke Rochford, Jr., Sheryl Purvis and NeMar Eastman, 'New Religions, Mental Health, and Social Control', in Monty Lynn and David Moberg, eds., *Research in the Social Scientific Study of Religion* (Greenwich, CT: JAI Press, 1989), vol. 1, pp. 57–82; and James T. Richardson, 'Clinical and Personality Assessment of Participants in New Religions', *International Journal for the Psychology of Religion*, 5 (1995): 145–70.

11 Many of these and other related readings can be found in Lorne L. Dawson, ed., *Cults in Context: Readings in the Study of New Religious Movements* (Toronto: Canadian Scholars Press, 1996).

12 John Lofland and Rodney Stark, 'Becoming a World-Saver: A Theory of Conversion to a Deviant Perspective', *American Sociological Review*, 30, 6 (1965): 863–74.

13 David Snow and Cynthia Phillips, 'The Lofland–Stark Conversion Model: A Critical Reassessment', *Social Problems*, 27, 4 (1980): 430–47.

14 Arthur Greil and David Rudy, 'What Have We Learned from Process Models of Conversion? An Examination of Ten Case Studies', *Sociological Focus*, 17, 4 (1984): 305–23.

15 Merrill Singer, 'The Social Context of Conversion to a Black Religious Sect', *Review of Religious Research*, 29, 4 (1988): 177–92, and Willem Kox et al., 'Religious Conversion of Adolescents: Testing the Lofland and Stark

Model of Religious Conversion', *Sociological Analysis*, 52, 3 (1991): 227–40.

16 Bryan Wilson and Karel Dobbelaere, *A Time to Chant: The Soka Gakkai Buddhists in Britain* Oxford: Clarendon Press, 1994).

17 With regard to the Moonies see the figures provided in Eileen Barker, *The Making of a Moonie: Choice or Brainwashing* (Oxford: Blackwell, 1984), pp. 141–8, and Marc Galanter, *Cults: Faith, Healing, and Coercion* (New York: Oxford University Press, 1989), pp. 140–1.

18 For example: Michael Harrison, 'Sources of Recruitment to Catholic Pentecostalism', *Journal for the Scientific Study of Religion*, 13, 1 (1974): 49–64; James Beckford, *The Trumpet of Prophecy: A Sociological Study of Jehovah's Witnesses* (New York: Oxford and Halsted Press, 1975); John Lofland, *Doomsday Cult: A Study of Conversion, Proselytization and Maintenance of Faith* (New York: Irvington, 1977): William Sims Bainbridge, *Satan's Power: Ethnography of a Deviant Psychotherapy Cult* (Berkeley: University of California Press, 1978); David A. Snow, Louis A. Zurcher, Jr. and Sheldon Ekland-Olson, 'Social Networks and Social Movements: A Microstructural Approach to Differential Recruitment', *American Sociological Review*, 45, 5 (1980): 787–801; Rodney Stark and William Sims Bainbridge, *The Future of Religion: Secularization, Revival and Cult Formation* (Berkeley: University of California Press, 1985); E. Burke Rochford, *Hare Krishna in America* (New Brunswick, NJ: Rutgers University Press, 1985); Carl Latkin, Richard Hagan, Richard Littman and Norman Sundberg, 'Who Lives in Utopia? A Brief Report on the Rajneeshpuram Research Project', *Sociological Analysis*, 48, 1 (1987): 73–81; Susan Jean Palmer, *Moon Sisters, Krishna Mothers, Rajneesh Lovers: Women's Roles in New Religions* (Syracuse, NY: Syracuse University Press, 1994); and Phillip C. Lucas, *The Odyssey of a New Religion – The Holy Order of MANS from New Age to Orthodoxy* (Bloomington: Indiana University Press, 1995).

19 Wilson and Dobbelaere, *A Time to Chant*, p. 50.

20 Singer, *Cults in Our Midst*, p. 105.

21 Barker, *The Making of a Moonie*, pp. 95–100.

22 For example, Snow and Phillips, 'The Lofland–Stark Conversion Model'; Greil and Rudy, 'What Have We Learned From Process Models of Conversion?'; Stark and

Bainbridge, *The Future of Religion*; and Kox et al., 'Religious Conversion of Adolescents.'

23 For example, Harrison, 'Sources of Recruitment to Catholic Pentecostalism'; Enroth, *Youth, Brainwashing, and the Extremist Cults*; Lofland, *Doomsday Cult*; Bainbridge, *Satan's Power*, Barker, *The Making of a Moonie*; Rochford, *Hare Krishna in America*; Palmer, *Moon Sisters, Krishna Mothers, Rajneesh Lovers*; Saul V. Levine, *Radical Departures*; and David E. Van Zandt, *Living in the Children God* (Princeton, NJ: Princeton University Press, 1991).

24 Janet Liebman Jacobs, *Divine Disenchantment: Deconverting from New Religions* (Bloomington: Indiana University Press, 1989).

25 For example, Lofland, *Doomsday Cult*; Stark and Bainbridge, *The Future of Religion*; and James V. Downton, *Sacred Journeys: The Conversion of Young Americans to Divine Light Mission* (New York: Columbia University Press, 1979).

26 Snow etal., 'Social Networks and Socia Movements'.

27 Stark and Bainbridge, *The Future of Religion*.

28 Ibid., and Snow and Phillips, 'The Lofland-Stark Conversion Model'.

29 James, T. Richardson and Mary W. Stewart, 'Conversion Process Models and the Jesus Movement', *American Behavioral Scientist*, 20, 6 (1977): 819–38, and Tipton, *Getting Saved from the Sixties*.

30 Mary Jo Neitz, *Charisma and Community: A Study of Religious Commitment within the Charismatic Renewal* (New Brunswick, NJ: Transaction, 1987).

31 For example, Roger Straus, 'Changing Oneself: Seekers and the Creative Transformation of Life Experience', in John Lofland, ed., *Doing Social Life* (New York: Wiley and Sons, 1976), pp. 252–73; Robert W. Balch, 'Looking Behind the Scenes in a Religious Cult: Implications for the Study of Conversion', *Sociological Analysis*, 41, 2 (1980): 137–43; David Bromley and Anson Shupe, Jr., 'Just a Few Years Seem Like a Lifetime: A Role Theory Approach to Participation in Religious Movements', in *Research in Social Movements, Conflict and Change*, vol. 2 (Greenwich, CT: JAI Press, 1979); T. Poling and J. Kenny, *The Hare Krishna Character Type: A Study in Sensate Persinality* (Lewiston, NY: Edwin Mellen, 1986); and Brock K. Kilbourne and James T. Richardson, 'Paradigm Conflict,

Types of Conversion, and Conversion Theorise,' *Sociological Analysis*, 50, 1 (1989): 1–21.

32 Rochford, *Hare Krishna in America*, p. 54.

33 Wilson and Dobbelaere, *A Time to Chant*, p. 88.

34 Constance A. Jones, 'Church Universal and Triumphant: A Demographic Profile', in James R. Lewis and J. Gordon Melton, eds., *Church Universal and Triumphant in Scholarly Perspective* (Stanford, CA: Centre for Academic Publication, 1994), pp. 49–50.

35 Stark and Bainbridge, *The Future of Religion*.

36 Roy Wallis, *The Elementary Forms of New Religious Life* (London: Routledge and Kegan Paul, 1984), p. 122.

37 Snow and Phillips, ' The Lofland–Stark Conversion Model', and Snow et al., 'Social Networks and Social, Movements'.

38 Stark and Bainbridge, *The Future of Religion*.

39 Bryan Wilson, 'The New Religions: Preliminary Considerations', in Eileen Barker, ed., *New Religious Movements: A Perspective for Understanding Society* (New York: Edwin Mellen, 1982), p. 24.

40 See Levine, *Radical Departures*.

41 Wilson, 'New Religions: Preliminary Considerations', p. 25.

42 For example, Latkin et al., 'Who Lives in Utopia?'; Poling and Kenny, *The Hare Krishna Character Type*, and Palmer, *Moon Sisters, Krishna Mothers, Rajneesh Lovers*.

43 Barker, *The Making of a Moonie*, p. 206.

44 Rochford, *Hare Krishna in America*, p. 47.

45 J. S. Judah reported comparable findings ten years earlier in *Hare Krishna and the CounterCulture* (New York: John Wiley, 1974).

46 Wilson and Dobbelarere, *A Times to Chant*.

47 For Krishna Consciousness, for example, see Palmer, *Moon Sisters, Krishna Mothers, Rajneesh Lovers*, p. 39.

48 Roy Wallis, *The Road to Total Freedom: A Sociological Analysis of Scientology* (New York: Columbia University Press, 1977).

49 Latkin et al., 'Who Lives in Utopia?'; Lewis F. Carter, *Charisma and Control in Rajneeshpuram* (Cambridge: Cambridge University Press, 1990); and Palmer, *Moon Sisters, Krishna Mothers, Rajneesh Lovers*.

50 Jones, 'Church Universal and Triumphant,' p. 42. The findings of H. R. Alfred, 'The Church of Satan', in Charles Y. Glock and Robert N. Bellah, eds., *The New Religious Consciousness* (Berkeley: University of California Press,

1976), and Earl Babbie and Donald Stone, 'An Evaluation of the *est* Experience by an National Sample of Graduates', *Bioscience Communications*, 3 (1977): 123–40, also lend support to this observation.

51 Wallis, *Road to Total Freedom*, p. 163.

52 Wilson and Dobbelaere, *A Time to Chant*, pp. 121–4.

53 Jones, 'Church Universal and Triumphant,' pp. 43–4.

54 Latkin et al., 'Who Lives in Utopia?'

55 Rochford, *Hare Krishna in America*, pp. 48–50.

56 Stark and Bainbridge, *The Future of Religion*, pp. 406–10.

57 Wilson and Dobbelaere, *A Time to Chant*, p. 123, and Stark and Bainbridge, *The Future of Religion*.

58 Scientology: Wallis, *The Road to Total Freedom*; Unification Church: Barker, *The Making of a Moonie*; Krishna Consciousness: Rochford, *Hare Krishna in America*, Poling and Kenny, *The Hare Krshna Character Type*, Palmer, *Moon Sisters, Krishna Mothers, Rajneesh Lovers*; Rajneesh movement: Latkin et al., 'Who Lives in Utopia?' Carter, *Charisma and Contorl in Rajneeshpuram*, Palmer, *Moon Sisters, Krishna Mothers, Rajneesh Lovers*; and Church Universal and Triumphant: Jones, 'Church Universal and Triumphant.'

59 Machalek and Snow, 'Conversion to New Religious Movements'.

60 Stark and Bainbridge, *The Future of Religion*, pp. 413–17.

61 Ibid., p. 413.

62 Wilson and Dobbelaere, *A Time to Chant*, pp. 42–3.

63 Latkin et al., 'Who Lives in Utopia?' and Palmer, *Moon Sisters, Krishna Mothers, Rajneesh Lovers*.

64 Wallis, *The Road to Total Freedom*, p. 165.

65 Rochford, *Hare Krishna in America*, and Lucas, *The Odyssey of a New Religion*.

66 See Palmer, *Moon Sisters, Krishna Mothers, Rajneesh Lovers*.

67 Ibid., p. 32.

68 Ibid., pp. 62, 90.

69 Stark and Bainbridge, *The Future of Religion*, p. 400.

70 Latkin et al., 'Who Lives in Utopia?'

71 Tipton, *Getting Saved from the Sixties*.

72 Rochford, *Hare Krishna in America*, notes a slight overrepresentation of Jews as well.

73 Stark and Bainbridge, *The Future of Religion*, pp. 402–3.

74 Wilson and Dobbelaere, *A Time to Chant*, p. 79.

75 Ibid., p. 88.

76 Jones, 'Church Universal and Triumphant,' pp. 49–50.

77 Rochford, *Hare Krishna in America*, pp. 51–7.

78 Stark and Bainbridge, *The Future of Religion*, p. 404.

79 See note 8 above.

80 See, for example: Rodney Stark and William Sims Bainbridge, *A Theory of Religion* (New York: Peter Lang, 1987); C. David Gartrell and Zane K. Shannon, 'Contacts, Cognitions, Conversion: A Rational Choice Approach', *Review of Religious Research*, 21, 1 (1985): 32–48; Lorne L. Dawson, 'Self-Affirmation, Freedom, and Rationality: Theoretically Elaborating 'Active' Conversions', *Journal for the Scientific Study of Religion*, 29, 2 (1990): 141–63; and Rodney Stark and Laurence R. Innaccone, 'Rational Choice Propositions about Religious Movements'. in David G. Bromley and Jeffrey K. Hadden, eds., *Religion and the Social Order, Vol. 3: The Handbook on Cults and Sects in America, Part A* (Greenwich, CT: JAI Press, 1993), pp. 242–61. Less overtly, an element of rational choice is also present in Stephen A. Kent's 'Slogan Chanters to Mantra Chanters: A Mertonian Deviance Analysis of Conversion to Religiously Ideological Organizations in the Early 1970s', *Sociological Analysis*, 49, 2 (1988): 140–18.

81 Brock Kilbourne, 'Equity or Exploitation? The Case of the Unification Church', *Review of Religious Research*, 28, 2 (1986): 143–50, also documents the role of youth idealism in predisposing people to joining the Moonies.

82 Levine, *Radical Departures*.

83 Ibid., p. 4.

84 Ibid., p. 11.

85 Ibid., pp. 31–8, 46–7, 61.

86 Ibid., p. 35.

87 Barker, *The Making of a Moonie*, pp. 210–11.

88 Arthur Parsons, 'Messianic Personalism: A Role Analysis of the Unification Church', *Journal for the Scientific Study of Religion*, 25, 2 (1986): 141–61, and Palmer, *Moon Sisters, Krishna Mothers, Rajneesh Lovers*, pp. 92, 100.

89 Barker, *The Making of a Moonie*; Levine, *Radical Departures*; Stark and Bainbridge, *The Future of Religion*; Jacobs, *Divine Disenchantment*; Galanter, *Cults*; Palmer, *Moon Sisters*,

Krishna Mothers, Rajneesh Lovers, and Stuart A. Wright, *Leaving Cults: The Dynamics, of Defection*, Monograph Series, 7 (Washington, DC: Society for Scientific Study of Religion, 1987).

90 Tipton, *Getting Saved from the Sixties*; Thomas Robbins and David Bromley, 'Social Experimentation and the Significance of American New Religions: A Focused Review Essay', in Monty Lynn and David Moberg, eds., *Research in the Social Scientific Study of Religion* (Greenwich, CT: JAI Press, 1992), vol. 4, pp. 1–28; and Palmer, *Moon Sisters, Krishna Mothers, Rajneesh Lovers*.

91 In the morass of highly variable literature two stellar studies of these groups stand out: David Chidester, *Salvation and Suicide – An Interpretation of Jim Jones, The Peoples Temple, and Jonestown* (Bloomington: Indiana University Press, 1988), and Stuart A. Wright, ed., *Armageddon in Waco – Critical Perspectives on the Branch Davidian Conflict* (Chicago, IL: University of Chicago Press, 1995)

92 On discerning generic social processes in general, read Helen Rose Ebaugh, *Becoming an EX* (Chicago, IL: University of Chicago Press, 1988), and Robert Prus, *Symbolic Interaction and Ethnographic Research* (Albany: State University of New York Press, 1996), ch. 5. For an initial attempt to tackle the generic aspect of this particular concern, see Thomas Robbins and Dick Anthony, 'Sects and Violence: Factors Enhancing the Volatility of Marginal Religious Movements', in Wright, ed., *Armageddon in Waco*, pp. 236–59.

CHAPTER EIGHT

The Joiners

SAUL LEVINE

Dennis Ericson's radical departure was among the first I came to know about. In 1969, when I was working among draft dodgers and deserters in Toronto and other cities in Canada, Dennis was a 20-year-old sophomore studying engineering at the University of Cincinnati. He had no trouble with technical courses, but had to work hard to maintain his grades in the required dose of literature and history. Dennis's stocky figure and sandy hair, cropped short even in those long-haired days, resembled those of his father, Jack. Mr. Ericson had worked as a design engineer since his retirement, as a colonel, from the US Army. Ivy Ericson worked as a loan adviser in a bank. An older brother had already graduated with a degree in engineering, and it was a family joke that one day the three men would hoist a sign: Ericson & Sons, Engineers.

The family lived in a pleasant suburb of San Diego. In keeping with their traditionally conservative professions and with their middle-class, Protestant backgrounds, they supported President Nixon and the Vietnam War effort wholeheartedly. Like other students of his day, Dennis anticipated being drafted to serve in Vietnam, and he and his family seemed to be in fundamental agreement that serving one's country was not only an obligation, but also a correct and honorable one.

Dennis had no tolerance for antiwar groups such as Students for a Democratic Society and the Student Nonviolent Coordinating Committee; he had considered joining the Young Republicans.

This seamless agreement in principle showed a slightly frayed edge in practice. Dennis on several occasions confided to his parents a certain eagerness to be drafted, and was surprised to find his urge met with nervous amusement. The Ericsons supported the war but didn't want their son to serve in Vietnam.

Dennis had not, however, confided the full extent of his concerns or the underlying reasons for his urge to join the army. Raised in a career-oriented home and enrolled in a career-oriented course of study, he was nevertheless becoming increasingly unsure of the direction in which he was headed. He was bored with his friends, his activities, his studies, himself. Talking about the months just prior to receiving his draft notice, he said, "All I knew then was that I needed some excitement or adventure in my life. I could get into terrific arguments on campus about the war, but for me it was all a mental game. I wished that I believed what I said." Joining up, he felt, might relieve his overwhelming sense of tedium.

When the draft notice did arrive, Dennis abruptly, to his own and his family's confusion, changed his mind. He joined other draft dodgers in a commune in Vancouver. Within weeks he had left this group to become a member of Healthy Happy Holy

Organization, usually called "3HO." This spiritual-rehabilitation group followed Yogi Bhajan, an Indian teacher of Tantric and Kundalini Yoga in the United States and Canada.

Philip Holtzman at 21 was the success story all parents wish for their children. He was an excellent student, a star athlete, and popular with both boys and girls; he had a steady girl, Marcie, with whom he was quite taken. During the summer of 1978 this tall boy with tightly curling red hair was living at home in Denver after completing his sophomore year at the University of Colorado. He had taken a variety of arts and science courses, had made the dean's list both years, but felt unready to declare a major. Hoping to come upon some one thing that interested him particularly, he planned to take a year's leave of absence from school to travel and work abroad, and his parents, Sam and Ellen, encouraged the idea. They had no doubt that their older son could take on this new venture with the same responsibility he had always shown; to them, this challenging year was to be an extension of his education.

Education was a central value to the Holtzmans. Sam was a prominent physician. Ellen was a high-school librarian studying for her doctorate in library science. Phil's two younger brothers and a sister were all doing well in school, though not quite at the level of their older brother. Like Phil, his parents were what one would call "well-rounded" people. They regularly attended the local symphony and the theater, and found time for tennis and jogging.

Dr. Holtzman had been brought up in an Orthodox Jewish home in New York City; Yiddish was his parents' native tongue. Mrs. Holtzman came from a Conservative, quite devout Jewish background. Although neither grew up to be deeply religious, they felt strongly about their commitment to Judaism and to Israel. They attended Sabbath services at a Reform temple sporadically, never missed the High Holy Day services, and had seen to it that all of their children received religious training and read some Hebrew.

This "ideal" family was further flavored with idealism. In their own words, they had always encouraged their children to "make a contribution," to "leave the world better than they found it." Their only tension with Phil stemmed from the fact that he had been unable to translate this idealism within the context of their religion. As Phil put it, "I never felt much identification with Judaism or Israel. Mom and Dad got annoyed whenever I spoke this way, but I couldn't help it. Actually, I felt that this was the only area in which I disappointed them. I knew I was Jewish, but I didn't feel much else about it."

That summer, abroad, this model youth made his radical departure into the mysticism and narrow intellectualism of an Orthodox Jewish seminary, a yeshiva in Jerusalem.

Jennifer Green was a 19-year-old beauty. She wore her glistening black hair tied back simply from her perfectly oval, creamy-complexioned face. Her gray eyes sparkled with laughter – "bubbly" laughter, as her mother described it. Jennifer showed the sort of native talent that is peculiarly gratifying to parents. She was a gifted pianist, and the Greens took justifiable pride in their expectation that she would go on to a career as a concert pianist.

The whole family had participated in her talent, even to the extent of moving from their home in the Midwest to Houston, where a sought-after teacher had consented to supervise her training. By the winter after her graduation from high school in 1972, their efforts seemed about to pay off: Jennifer had auditioned for and been accepted by two conservatories, Curtis and Juilliard.

The Greens, however, showed signs of family strain. Allen Green, an accountant and tax consultant employed by a well-heeled clientele, was a busy man whose recipe for getting along with his wife and daughter was to lie low. Linda Green was preoccupied with a campaign to achieve "self-realization" – an endeavor that had led her to espouse at various times Gestalt, Rolfing, Esalen, Bioenergetics, and other therapeutic schemes. Jennifer's older brother, Jason, was completing his doctoral thesis in behavioral modification. Indeed, this faith, for that was what their fervor for therapy seemed to amount to, was practiced by everyone in the family except Mr. Green. From the time Jennifer was 15, Mrs. Green had been convinced that her beautiful, talented daughter needed professional help; and it was true that Jennifer, for all her appeal to her schoolmates, had tended to isolate herself from other children her age. At her mother's behest, she was in group, family, or individual therapy for the next four years, while Mrs. Green harped on the refrain "Develop yourself".

But Jennifer seemed to lose the strands of whatever self she was supposed to be developing. By the time she was accepted by a conservatory, she was only going through the motions in her music; she could work at it, but took no pleasure in practice. Her mother was too adamant to notice. As Jennifer explained, about this period prior to her departure, "My mother was on a tear all the time about my career and the latest guru who would cure my woes."

Jennifer found her "guru" on her own through an ad in a psychology magazine: Kurt, the charismatic leader of the Healing Workshop, a therapeutic commune and another variety of radical departure.

Suzanne Marquette, 18 in 1975, lived with her family in Minneapolis, where she had completed a year of junior college, though with little interest and declining grades. This, and the fact that this pretty, diminutive blond had never had a boyfriend and didn't participate in the active social life her friends enjoyed, might have concerned her parents were it not for the special circumstances of their daughter's life. Suzanne had one overriding passion: figure skating. She was extremely talented and had since the age of five devoted thousands of hours to what she considered one of the higher art forms.

Her mother, Barbara, was deeply involved in that pursuit, chaperoning her daughter to practice, shows, and competitions and always being extremely supportive of her continuing progress. Peter Marquette, Suzanne's father, was perhaps too distracted by his own pursuits to contribute to those of his daughter. He owned a small but thriving printing business, and evidently had to be there morning, noon, and night – the sort of driven man one would call a "workaholic."

Suzanne also had that air of constant busyness. She did everything with a competence and thoroughness unusual in a girl that age. Besides the demands of skating, she did volunteer work at a nursing home and was very helpful around the house. She was particularly tender with her tow-headed twin brothers, whom, though they were only four, she coaxed along on the ice until they were really quite good skaters. "Maybe I was too busy in those days," Suzanne was to tell me later. "I don't know – when I wasn't helping out around the house or at the nursing home, I knew that I had to be skating. And it didn't feel like a burden; I mean I had done that most of my life, and that was just the way things were."

Ice-skating had, indeed, become a career choice as well as a recreation. Suzanne planned to turn professional during the coming fall, when she was scheduled to try out for a well-known ice show in Santa Monica, California. Acceptance into the troupe would mean going on tour. "I was busy but I wasn't involved in things," she explained. "For some reason I knew I couldn't wait to get away on tour, even though I was getting tired of skating."

Lying on the beach in Santa Monica the day of the audition, Suzanne was approached by members of the Unification Church. Sometime in the next three days, and after a most successful audition, she had thrown the years of practice to the wind. She had become a Moonie.

Other young men and women who shocked family and friends with their radical departures were more troublesome to their parents than Dennis, Phil, Jennifer, and Suzanne were.

Nancy Lewis was in constant conflict with her parents over her choice of career and her behaviour in general. Her parents had wanted her to go to a small business college not far from their home in northern New Jersey to learn a marketable skill. Nancy, with some contempt for her father's job as a rug salesman, was convinced he saw everything as marketable, even her. She had complied with their wish for one term, then dropped out in favor of informal drama classes run by a New York City actor her father labeled "a loser." Her mother seemed no less crass to Nancy. Mrs. Lewis often remarked on how hard they had worked, how much they had earned, to make her life a happy one.

Nancy's perceptions were not entirely wrong; her parents were not sophisticated and were too often preoccupied with maintaining their middle-class standard of life. The Lewises were nominally Methodist and had sent their three daughters – Nancy was the middle one – to Sunday school, but they themselves rarely attended church. They had few cultural interests. Although their split-level development house was scrupulously cared for, it did not reflect Nancy's idea of creative expression. Mrs. Lewis shopped for supermarket specials on Saturdays; Mr. Lewis watched the ball game and worked around the house on Sundays. All through the week both parents worked hard but unimaginatively to maintain the financial and household standards that, to both of them, stood between them and the much poorer backgrounds both had come from. They were rightly proud of their achievement, but Nancy found their ordinariness dreary. Lillian and George Lewis resented Nancy's apparent ungratefulness.

Nancy responded with what she later called her "grande artiste" front – the belief that she, unlike her parents, was creative, sensitive, cultured. She escaped her house as often as possible to hang out with the guys at "the Elm," smoke a few joints, spend the night with a boyfriend her parents called "a no-good bum," or pick up someone new. She thought these people at least appreciated her creativity, but in fact she was locally known as an "easy lay," which she perhaps inadvertently advertised with overdramatic costuming that accentuated her full breasts and hips.

This desultory sort of life continued for three years without Nancy getting a job, moving away from home, or, as far as the Lewises could see, getting any closer to an acting career. In the winter of 1976, now 22

years old, Nancy looked forward to some relief from the stresses of home life in the form of a two-week vacation in Fort Lauderdale with her close friend, Flo. There she met and joined the Children of God, her radical departure.

Equally bitter but less comprehensible and certainly less likable was Fred Vitelli, a smug young man who by the age of 20 had long since decided that school was "bullshit" and those who remained there "browners." He spoke of others, all others, with contempt weighted with obscenity. If one could ignore his manner, Fred was otherwise attractive: over six feet tall, well built, and with sensual features.

He spent much of his time high or stoned on drugs. He had been suspended from public high school in a wealthy Chicago suburb on two occasions. He had completed secondary education at a private school that specialized in "problem" children, but had refused to apply for college. He had also been in chronic, if minor, trouble with the law – possession of marijuana, reckless driving. Mr. Vitelli, at his wife's pleading for the "baby" in this large family, always bailed Fred out of trouble.

Anthony and Maria Vitelli were one of those couples who by working together in what was originally a small family business – making trophies and commemorative plaques – built their enterprise into a major national concern. They were able to give Fred a Porsche when he was only 17, with the conditional message that the gift was proof of their love but would be taken from him unless he stopped abusing drugs and improved his schoolwork. Fred didn't keep his end of the bargain, but before the Vitellis could reclaim the costly sports car Fred had totaled it. His driver's license was revoked.

By the fall of 1979, parents and son had made another deal. Fred was to go to Europe for a few months, using his own money (which was in fact an accumulation of cash gifts from relatives, not earnings), on condition that he begin college when he returned. Brazen and cocksure on the surface, he intended to spend the forthcoming months stoned, then return to "make a killing" in his family's or some other business. His parents were worn out by this son, unwilling to take him into their business, uncertain of what else to do, yet hopeful that three months on his own would give him the maturity he lacked.

Fred didn't return. In Rome one autumn day he found his radical departure: a militant leftist group of anarchists who called themselves the Armed Guard.

Jamie Gould, 26 years old, was the oldest of the radical departers in this representative sample. His father, John, had made millions as a stockbroker and then moved with his wife to the Bahamas, a location they saw as combination tax haven, retirement home, and center for wheeling and dealing. After a long marriage, they had separated just before Jamie's birthday that year of 1977, and Joanne Gould had begun to divide her time between her own house on Barbados and a villa on the Riviera both provided by her husband. Jamie expected a trust fund worth $4 million when he turned 30. While awaiting this largesse he was free to use the substantial income from the trust as he wished, and he also received a monthly allowance from his father that was expressly to support a lavish brownstone house in New York City.

After graduating from Northwestern University with an arts degree and being accepted into law school, Jamie had turned his back on education. This brief flirtation with becoming a lawyer was one example of his lifelong pattern of transient enthusiasms followed by inertia. The pattern was not unlike that of Mrs. Gould, who suffered from endless fits and starts – collecting Chinese porcelain, sponsoring a local hostorical society, organizing through her church a drive to aid famine victims, participating in political demonstrations, raising Persian cats. People had often remarked that Jamie and his mother looked alike, with their almost mahogany hair and precisely chiseled features.

Between bouts of optimism, Jamie's aimlessness was crushing. He had no job and no longstanding interests; a girl who lived with him in the luxury of his brownstone was seen as a sexual convenience.

Jamie's parents called him regularly, using a three-way connection, a "conference call,"

but conversation was largely perfunctory. The Goulds' main concern, or so it appeared to Jamie, was that he wore an earring in one ear. Their hesitancy about criticizing him any more deeply than that was in contrast to the outspokenness of their older son, John Jr., who had become a lawyer. John Jr. was furious at Jamie's total apathy, but his anger didn't really bother Jamie. "I just felt that my brither was a pain. If he wanted to work so hard that was his business, but I felt that I had the bread, why not enjoy it?"

Neither Jamie nor his parents seemed able to overcome the physical and emotional distance from which their cash currency of love was disbursed. "In a strange way," Jamie told me, "I think that money paralyzed me" – until he joined the Church of Scientology, a quasi-religion, quasi-psychology which follows the bizarre teachings of L. Ron Hubbard.

Kathy O'Connor, unlike Jamie, had been very close to her family, until the age of 23. Although she lived in Montreal and they lived in a rural area some miles north of the city, she had visited them often. She was a senior nurse at a university medical centre, and was described by those who knew this five-foot-five freckle-faced young woman as "warm," "cheerful," "energetic," and "humane." Fellow nurses especially used the word "wholesome" to sum up Kathy's personality.

The O'Connor family itself might have been described that way. Katherine O'Connor was a bustling, brisk woman who not only had cared for her four daughters with unflappable good cheer, but also had seemed to feed the whole neighborhood's kids while they were growing up. She was always involved in this or that minor crisis among her numerous relatives. Her personal dedication to Catholicism was equally cheerful; she believed that it held all the instructions for managing whatever life might deliver.

Charles O'Connor was a public-works administrator for the Montreal city government, and donated time and effort as a scoutmaster. Charles and Katherine were well satisfied that they had devoted their lives to charity, one in the public sphere, the other in service to the family.

But Kathy's relationship with her parents had taken a nose dive the year, 1970, she fell in love with Michael, a young Protestant intern at her hospital. Kathy and Michael both called what had happened between them "love at first sight"; their love was exuberantly sexual. The O'Connors were unable to accept the blatant way in which the two lovers made clear that they were living together. Their three other daughters, one younger and two older than Kathy, were already married, within their faith, to men of whom the family wholeheartedly approved. They could foresee nothing but problems in a mixed marriage, and blamed what was to them their daughter's sinful behavior on her straying from her faith.

Kathy said to me in retrospect, "They wanted what was best for me. It's true they didn't like Michael's religion, but they also resented his liberal politics. I was happy to leave Montreal after our wedding."

The newly married couple moved to New Orleans, where Michael entered an arduous residency in surgery. Kathy saw little of her husband during those months; she couldn't find a senior nursing position; the other residents' wives struck her as shallow people.

After less than half a year of marriage, Kathy left her husband and career to join the Maharaj Ji and his Divine Light Mission.

I was struck by Ethan Browning's intensity when I first met him. He wasn't particularly handsome, though his slight, tanned body emitted energy and his wide hazel eyes were appealing. He was shy, or perhaps reserved is a better way to describe him, for he had learned his manners so well that little spontaneity came through. He used a vocabulary astonishing in one so young.

Ethan, at 16, was the youngest of the joiners in this sample. He was the only child of Stuart Browning, a vice president of a major oil company, and his wife, Patricia, who devoted herself to Ethan's upbringing and to Episcopal church activities. Ethan was in the tenth grade at a special high school for gifted students. Rather a loner, he had only one close friend, also a restrained, bookish boy.

Quiet as he was, Ethan did engage in activities that others saw as social. He was the top chess player in his school and regularly participated in competitions. He was an avid and skilled sailor, both solo and as crew in races. A flutist as well, he was given most of the solo parts in the school ensemble to which he belonged. While he did extremely well in school, he learned so easily that he didn't need to devote a great deal of time to his studies. In his ample spare time, he read voraciously, several books at a time, in subjects as diverse as history, science, and philosophy.

The Browning household was comfortable, if somewhat austere. The year before Ethan's departure in 1976 the family had sold their large home in the suburbs and purchased a well-appointed town house in Boston from which they could walk to work, school, and church. They felt that with Ethan so uninvolved with the suburban lifestyle, they could easily live in the city. Mealtime at the Brownings was polite, a time of well-regulated conversation on a variety of intellectual topics. It held a special place within the family's ordered routine, especially for Ethan, perhaps the most orderly of all, who particularly enjoyed formal debate with his father over dinner.

Ethan never participated, however, in his parents' Episcopal church activities, not even accompanying them to Sunday services. He had said for years that he was an atheist. This bothered the Brownings. Ethan could be obstinately opinionated, and though his parents recognized obstinacy as almost a family trademark, this particular expression of it made them uncomfortable. Their church was central to their lives.

"I knew that at the age of 16, I wasn't a happy person," Ethan confided to me later. "I wasn't suicidal or even depressed, but I felt that something was missing from my life. I learned so much and did so well, yet nothing contented me. I felt there had to be more to my life."

Eathan found what was missing in his radical departure into the Hare Krishna.

Different as these joiners were in personality, talent, and interests, there are similarities among them. Whereas a person who succumbs to a radical departure is as likely to be a girl as a boy, she or he is not likely to be younger than Ethan Browning, 16, or older than Jamie Gould, 26. Those few years from adolescence to early adulthood are about the only time in our society when people *can* depart. Younger than 16 they are too dependent on their families, both emotionally and economically. Older than 26 they are likely to have responsibilities of their own – jobs, families – that they cannot easily abandon.

For a similar reason, radical departures are made almost exclusively by as yet unmarried youngsters from the middle- or upper-middle class, or from among the decidedly rich. Less affluent young people have neither the luxury nor the leisure to depart from obligations; they must pay their own way and often help their families too. Those who make radical departures do not have to pay their own way, nor do their families rely on support from their children. Jennifer Green's family even paid for her membership in the Healing Workshop, as Phil Holtzman's family paid for his year abroad and Suzanne Marquette's family supported her skating.

Thus, although I have seen one boy as young as 14 and occasional joiners in their 30s, radical departures are, with few exceptions, a phenomenon of late adolescence and early adulthood – the only time when there is the luxury and the leisure suddenly to drop out of usual pursuits.

Because of their age and economic situation, the vast majority of these young people are well educated; most are in their college years when they make their decision to leave their traditional paths. Almost all are white. The connection between race and radical departure is indirect, partly because of the underrepresentation of other groups in the middle class, and partly a result of the fact that joiners look especially for groups made up of members almost exactly like themselves.

Cults such as the Peoples Temple, which was made up of adults and entire families, most of them black, rarely attract those youths who make radical departures. Indeed, such groups are themselves a rarity; adults who look for impassioned causes or religions seldom depart from other responsibilities in order to satisfy their need, nor do they ordinarily leave home to live communally. That these young people do leave home is all the more extraordinary in that almost all of them come from intact families. Reviews of all the statistics that have been gathered about radical departures indicate that the divorce rate in joiners' families is considerably below the national rate.

But these are constraints on who *can* become a radical departer, and not an explanation of who *chooses* to depart. Obviously, few of all those affluent youths who might give up education, career, family, and friendships to immerse themselves in the Hare Krishna, the Children of God, the Armed Guard, or the Healing Workshop do so. To understand what it is about them that is different from their contemporaries who struggle on in the larger society, it is necessary to take a look at what is happening internally during the decade from 16 years old to 26.

The school years up to about the age of 12 are ordinarily a time of quite smooth progress. By his birthday each year, a child had grown an inch or so taller, reads at a grade level higher than the year before, and conducts himself with measurably greater sophistication. In the following six years, adolescents may grow five inches between one birthday and the next. Their bodies change shape so radically and rapidly that they have to look at themselves in the mirror constantly to see who they are and how they like it. They may leap in a single bound from reading Judy Blume to enjoying Dostoevsky. And as far as behavior is concerned, parents, and they themselves, hardly know what to expect from hour to hour, much less from month to month.

These physical, emotional, and intellectual changes are biological in nature, a result of built-in programs of maturation over which children have no control. Nature dumps on them, so to speak, the makings of adulthood but doesn't necessarily tell them what to make of it. That's the job of society, the nexus where nature and nurture meet to produce what each culture considers to be the best way to realize the potential of the next generation.

Middle-class culture strongly believes that to be a successful adult, a child must during these years separate from his family and establish his individualism from both a practical and a psychological standpoint.

Teenagers have long since come partway along this road to autonomy. Infants, as far as can be told, have no clear sense that their internal world is distinct from the external world, so that their wishing for milk and their mother providing milk arise from a union that encompasses both of them. As babies become able to get some distance from their mother – literal physical distance as they learn to crawl and emotional distance as they discover that their wish and her fulfillment aren't always in accord – they begin to construct a self-awareness separate from that of their parents.

By toddlerhood what they are up to can clearly be seen. Toddlers test out all sorts of distinctions between themselves and others – who wants to wear what, eat what, touch what, and go to bed when – that will serve as markers of their separate estate. Realistically though, pre-schoolers know themselves to be dependent on parents and wisely don't push their differences too far. Indeed, they look out for their own safety by establishing bonds with their parents in the form of identifications ("Don't I look like Mommy?") and behaviors that their parents will love them for ("I'm a good boy!"). When by the age of 5 or 6 the bonds are safely tied, and yet the child has sufficient distance to enjoy a modicum of self-reliance, a time of peace descends. There is perhaps no nicer time within a family than when the children are all of school age but not yet into the upheavals of adolescence.

When the latter stage is reached, the maneuvers to see who's who resume. By then, the child is working from a position of much greater strength. He has self-care skills: selecting clothes, earning money, pursuing interests independently, and regulating his own life through the whole panoply of negotiations that have, over the years, replaced mere infantile demands. The bonds that assure him he is loved extend beyond mother and father to relatives, neighbors, teachers, and, above all, his peers. His identifications are derived from these actual relationships and also from fantasy – folk heroes, fictional characters, and public leaders.

From these practical and psychological achievements most children derive sufficient self-esteem to begin the process of detachment from their childhood relationship with their parents. How detachment is conducted depends on the quality of the attachment. Those who feel most dependent on parents may the more fiercely launch themselves away. Those who derive pleasure already from a degree of independence may separate from their parents and construct new kinds of bonds with barely a ripple.

Of middle-class adolescents, for example, only about half go through the emotional storms and nasty rebellions many associate with these years. Of the 50 percent who show evidence of turmoil, again only half have worse than moderate problems with their families, their peers, and, above all, with themselves. On the other hand, lack of any apparent rebelliousness can indicate a failure to face the dilemmas of growing up. Radical departures are made by children who, outwardly at least, show this whole range from no rebellion at all to quite troublesome behavior.

The word "rebellion" summons forth images of unleashed criticism, challenges to parents standards, angry confrontation, and anti-social or dangerous behavior. There is no word that easily substitutes, so I will have to speak of rebellion when I really mean something that can be, and often is, entirely acceptable and even likable. A child who announces his weekend plans instead of asking permission is rebelling. So is a boy who wants his family to switch to nonphosphate detergents, and a girl who says she can do a better job of fixing the lawn mower than her father can. A child is rebelling when he or she discovers Thoreau, true love, or meditation and thinks the older generation knows nothing of such things. Most teenagers enact much of their rebellion en masse: they dress to irritate, but they all dress the same. Rebellion is a process of distinguishing and distancing oneself from one's parents by probing for difference and disagreement; there need be nothing awful about it.

As teenagers grow up into young adults their separation is a mutual endeavor. Over time, children's demands for autonomy are matched by parents' willing relinquishment of control. Children come to see themselves more independently, but parents also have to readjust their view of themselves. Mothers and fathers have deeply participated in their child's self for many years. His or her looks, accomplishments, and personality are not just items to take pride in, but partially define who they are too. Women in particular have often lived for and through children. As parents let a son or daughter loosen childhood bonds, they lose something of themselves, and must work to restore it.

Given a long and gradual development toward maturity, parents don't find their task so hard. To be sure, it is difficult at times to have those nice kids who have eaten our cookies and "borrowed" our tools for so many years disagree with our politics ("You're going to vote for *who?*") and, in general, skirt our influence in many everyday matters ("Oh, Mom, you wouldn't understand"). But on the whole most families have the humour to survive a certain amount of criticism in return for the freedom to develop new interests of their own and the gratification of having raised children who can now conduct their own lives. That's as it should be, but it isn't always that way.

No radical departer – not the nine I am using to illustrate the general predicament or any of the hundreds of others I have known – has thus gradually been able to separate from his or her family to everyone's mutual satisfaction. Few have been able to engage their peers in their own form of rebellion, or have sought safety in numbers by rebelling among peers. Some, like Dennis Ericson, enter their 20s without ever having disagreed with their families. They haven't rebelled at all. Others, like Nancy Lewis, don't find ways to control their own lives. They rebel to no effect. And all of them, without exception, are still so closedly tied to their parents either in reality or in fantasy that I will often use the word "children" to refer to joiners in spite of their chronological age. Each has been felled by some obstacle that others their age manage to scramble over, even if it bruises both them and their families for a while.

The process of formulating one's identity is, of course, never over. One is forever having to reformulate oneself to catch up, so to speak, with the changing context as one pursues a career, gets married, becomes a parent, suffers tragedies, grows older. Change is so rapid during adolescence, however, that the task of identity formation then is more demanding than it is likely ever to be again. Also, society demands it of teenagers whether they like it or not.

Parents withdraw support. They no longer wish to supervise children's homework or to chaperone them everywhere. Even if they wish to, they can no longer control children's aggressive and sexual impulses. So adolescents are forced to a degree of independence. They must arrange their own social lives, care for their own bodies, make many of their own decisions, and begin to earn their own money. They are now too muscularly strong for others to subdue easily; they must take over the control of their physical aggression. Both sexes were able to manage the rather mild sexuality of childhood; now sexual impulses are insistent, unpredictable, and sometimes quite unmanageable.

Parents also make it clear to high-school students that adult responsibilities loom ahead. By 16, students know that their present academic industry will determine which college they can hope to attend. By 18, they are asked to make tentative choices of college curriculum and to articulate their reasons for that choice. Most of them are expected to leave home. By 21, they are required to narrow their career choice either by declaring a major or, if they have gone to junior college, by entering the work force. These challenges are unlike those of childhood: they smack of permanence.

There is some suggestion that families of radical departers are hesitant to withdraw support or relinquish control. Fred Vitelli's father protected his son from the consequences of his delinquencies. Mr. Gould paid Jamie's way even into his mid-20s. Jennifer

Green's mother masterminded both her daughter's psyche and her piano career.

At the same time that parents are withdrawing support and control, their sons and daughters are withdrawing the unconditional love for and faith in parents that typifies earlier childhood. But children can't continue into adulthood loveless and faithless. They seek intimacy with others – friends and lovers. Instead of relying on the belief system that was on loan to them during childhood, they now formulate ideologies that will serve the unique person each has come to be.

Of those radical departers toward the upper end of the age group, who might have been expected to enjoy intimacy with a lover, only Kathy O'Connor had a relationship that was more than exploitive or tentative, and her marriage didn't last out the year. Some joiners have no friends at all. They are convinced that peers couldn't possibly understand them – a conviction that certainly precludes intimacy. Those who go through the motions of a social life often use the word "plastic" to describe their relationships. They have no sense of deep connection or even of genuineness with their friends, and can't use their affection and admiration as sources of self-esteem.

No radical departers I have studied felt committed to a value system at the time of their joining. Indeed, to all of them, nothing they were doing made any sense, nor did the activities of others. One could sum up their desolation by saying that radical departers feel they belong with no one, believe in nothing.

This is a risk that is incurred by all adolescents as they sever themselves from childhood. By denigrating the family from whose love and values they have derived the very core of their self-esteem, they may also devalue whatever "good" portion of their self relied on family approval. In other words, they may reject a part of themselves as they reject their parents, and thus find themselves unlovable and of no significance. The trick of withdrawing from the curriculum of a family self is to have built an extracurricular self that is equally laudable.

Most teenagers do have moments of grave doubt: no one likes them, they're ugly, everything's stupid, what's the sense of even trying?

But these are moments only, and give way more and more to positive feelings of accomplishment, significance, and worth. Those who will join radical groups behave as though so great a portion of whatever they have found good about themselves has been built on parental ties that were they to sever them they would be terribly depleted, if not entirely empty. Every joiner I have spoken with was, at the time of his or her departure, at a low of self-esteem so devastating that there seemed to be no self at all.

Teenagers want – and it is required of them – a self of their very own, unique, authentic, and separate from the selves of parents. By coincidence, the tasks that children must tackle to differentiate, rearrange, and fortify their sense of self all begin with *I*: Independence, Individuation, Impulse control, Industry, Intimacy, Ideological commitment, and, of course, Identity itself. One might call these the years of the I.

This preoccupation with internal and private psychological issues has led adults to accuse youth of an excess of narcissism. Self-involvement is, however, a trademark of the times. "Develop yourself," Mrs. Green admonished Jennifer, and that theme of self-realization, self-actualization, liberation, and autonomy is echoed throughout the middle class. The message can make individuals ruthlessly oblivious of the needs of others, and blind to the fact of all people's mutual dependency. No wonder youth is selfish, since society demands that it be so.

Worse, by stressing the early achievement of an independent self parents may be out of step with the psychological realities of adolescent development. There seems plenty of evidence from the young people I have worked with, especially those who have made radical departures but also those who have not, that the self is for years tentative and in constant flux. They themselves don't think it can bear much scrutiny.

By demanding that the self be "actualized" prior to reaching the 20s, society is handing children a double-edged sword. With so much attention focused on the self, they tend to protect their fragility with selfishness, egotism, and the kind of acting out Nancy Lewis attempted with her theatrics and precocious "liberation." At the same time, the assumption that they should have no fragility to hide convinces these children that no one else experiences doubt and pain. All nine of these representative radical departers kept their distress secret because they felt "no one would understand."

Again, a modicum of such loneliness is to be expected in adolescence. All through one's life one harbors some core that one knows to be unreachable by others. But adolescents learn that with the effort of reaching out and inviting others to do the same, sufficient intimacy can be found to ease loneliness. Joiners seem to long for a belonging with others that requires no such effort at mutual understanding. Unlike those who, among less judgmental peers at least, become able endlessly to probe, analyze, confess, explore, and lay bare their very souls to one another over these years, radical departers hold aloof while hoping for some unconditional mutual capitulation in which others would not ask a single question. This is their version of belonging.

Joiners' version of belief is equally unconditional. To them an ideology should, without the effort of their own analysis, offer every answer absolutely.

To some extent, longing for the Answer is an inevitable consequence of intellectual maturation. Younger children are poor debaters: something is either true or false, right or wrong, and if there is an argument it is won by the person with the loudest voice. Adolescents can step outside themselves to see issues from various vantage points, and each view, they realize, contains some truth. In Ethan Browning's school for gifted children, this talent was formalized in a debating club to which Ethan belonged, and was a point of pride at home, where right opinions were considered the offspring of free inquiry.

This intellectual experience can be heady, and it can be unsettling. How, if different things have different meanings to different people, can there be any meaning at all? What, down deep, do *I* really believe? *Who am I? Where am I going?* And *why?*

One can catch Ethan Browning at just that moment of unsettling awareness. His extensive reading had given him histories of the Crusades and the Inquisition, Oriental philosophies, Kafka, Emerson, and *Death of a Salesman*. This array of distraught and dissenting humanity was discussed around his family's civilized dinner table as though it were so many specimens to be dissected. Certainly there was something "missing": some heart of the matter that was ultimately undissectible.

This was not the Brownings' particular fault. What is merely intellectual discussion among adult members of the middle class may be a desperate search for practical and personal applications among their sons and daughters.

Perhaps too much has been made of the "generation gap"; most parents are far more able to appreciate their children's concerns than their children give them credit for. But a rapidly changing world really does alter perceptions abruptly, particularly for the young, who will have to track their future among shifting sands. For Kathy O'Connor's parents, Catholicism had answers for pain and suffering, but as a nurse Kathy came face to face with the appalling reality of moral dilemmas – the "right to die" and the "right to life" – for which there seemed no answers. Jack Ericson had as a soldier defended the Western world from totalitarianism; in what way was that parallel to the ideological issues (if they were that) in Southeast Asia? To the Holtzmans, a liberal arts education was the key to every sort of success, but by 1978, when Phil has completed two years of college, liberal arts students faced unemployment after graduation.

The sureties that guided parents no longer seem reliable to children who came of age during recent decades. Half of all marriages now end in divorce. These are the days of dioxin, the population explosion, downward mobility, and the threat of nuclear war. Moreover, these are children of the electronic age.

It must often look to them as if adults' daily concerns – which brand of toaster to choose, whether to buy more life insurance, how to get into the best college – are sheer insanity. How can parents, who once seemed so strong and wise, not be *doing* something to make the world safe for their children?

They are, of course, doing the best they know how. They understand the many reasons why they can't cut through the Gordian knot of ethical and practical dilemmas with one neat slice of an answer. To a 16-year-old, however, parents begin to look like fallen idols. This is especially so among the families from whom radical departers come, and it is owing to the mixed messages they give.

While organizing rescue for starving Africans, Jamie Gould's mother enjoyed her porcelains and Persian cats. While espousing honesty, churchgoing Mr. Browning was observed by Ethan to be fudging his income tax. Mrs. Green flirted with radical dreams while pushing the orthodox virtues of daily four-hour piano practice for Jennifer. Middle-class children are often raised with a gloss of idealism that their parents hope they will have the sense not to take too literally as they reach adulthood.

Most do have that good sense. As they separate, adolescents put their parents through their paces: they challenge, provoke, argue, and criticize. They adopt moral stances of their own, which are both extreme, to make a point, and tentative, to test the waters. But the common result is that they gradually define the boundaries of their own and their parents' capabilities and limitations, keep whatever portions of the family's value system seem workable to them, add snippets of personal ideals that seem to be proved out through their own experimentation, and come through the trial without any prolonged crisis of belief. They become willing, in other words, to face the personal and public moral dilemmas that no ideology can guarantee against.

In contrast, joiners look to belief as a way to avoid any personal dilemma at all. Feeling so little self-esteem, they can't shoulder the responsibility of perhaps making a wrong moral choice and thereby feeling more worthless still. They hope for an ideology that will bolster the "good me," that part of them which is admirable to themselves. They long to be purged of all badness, to be pure – and this their parents cannot do for them.

Parents have, in fact, few outward clues that might warn them of an impending departure. Joiners closely guard the secret of their inner desolation. Even as their unhappiness mounts to critical proportions they may continue to, as so many put it, "go through the motions" of whatever has been their accustomed life. Only in the few months – sometimes mere weeks – before their departure do families notice a visible decline in buoyancy that marks their inner sinking. Before then, they have seemed to be in a steady state. And that's what should be the giveaway.

While other children, tumultuously or uneventfully, are piecing togehter their separate selves, those who will join radical groups are peculiarly stalled. Whatever they are like, they have been that way for years. Others are learning to say "I know who I am"; these children gain no notion of what a self might feel like. Most young adults begin to need others and to feel needed, love others and feel loved; potential joiners remain bereft. While their peers are becoming increasingly captivated by all sorts of interests, they become weighted with tedium or aimlessly adrift. By the time the overwhelming proportion of adolescents enters the 20s, these young men and women have a sense of optimism and enthusiasm for their future. Radical departers have been unable to conceive of a future for themselves.

And then the future presents itself. Out of the blue, the Hare Krishna, Divine Light Mission, Healing Workshop, Children of God, or Armed Guard offers on a silver platter every ingredient that has been missing from their unhappy youth.

V

The "Brainwashing" Controversy

In many ways the public controversy over "cults" has been a dispute over the claim that NRMs recruit and retain their members through processes of brainwashing, mind-control, or coercive persuasion. This accusation has been the focal point of the criticisms leveled at NRMs by the anti-cult movement and the subject of debate in the numerous legal cases, both criminal and civil, involving NRMs (e.g., Anthony and Robbins 1992; Young and Griffiths 1992; Anthony and Robbins 1995; Richardson 1995; Richardson and Ginsburg 1998). The idea of brainwashing was invoked to account for the seemingly sudden conversion of many young people to NRMs out of legal necessity. The first amendment to the Constitution of the United States guarantees freedom of religious expression to American citizens. When the families of converts elicited the help of the American courts to forcibly remove their (adult) children from various NRMs, in the 1970s and 1980s, they needed a good reason to convince judges to override this constitutional guarantee. With the help of some psychologists and psychiatrists (e.g., Singer 1979; Clark et al. 1981), the lawyers struck upon the idea of arguing that these young adults were not competent to control their lives, and as victims of "brainwashing" they needed to be put under the temporary legal protection of their parents.

For most Americans brainwashing was a term associated with the fate of a handful of American prisoners during the Korean War in the early 1950s. These American prisoners had been subject to elaborate and often brutal programs of thought reform by their North Korean captors to persuade them to publicly denounce the United States and its war efforts. After several American prisoners made such statements in propaganda films, their behavior was attributed to techniques that had cunningly stripped them of their identity and made them vulnerable to manipulation. This mysterious process of psychological transformation became popularly known as brainwashing (see Anthony and Robbins 1994 for more details). Victims of brainwashing were thought to have lost their power to act freely and in their own best interests. Moreover, it was assumed, they had been psychologically harmed by the process. At first many judges were successfully persuaded that converts to NRMs had been brainwashed, and young believers were forcibly removed from groups by "deprogrammers" – self-styled anti-cult crusaders who could be hired to reverse the effects of brainwashing (e.g., Patrick and Dulack 1976; Bromley 1988). But as more reliable scholarly studies of NRMs became available the supposition of brainwashing became scientifically suspect and in the late 1980s the courts became unsympathetic to such claims. By then, however, the concept had been repeated so often in the media that few people could hear the word "cult" without immediately associating it with the highly derogatory process of "brainwashing."

Today most scholars studying NRMs reject the notion, preferring to account for the behavior of members of NRMs through the use of more conventional social scientific concepts like deconditioning and resocialization (e.g., Preston 1981; Wilson 1984). Converts join NRMs of their own free will, and they stay in such movements because it is somehow to their liking or advantageous. While they are members/individuals are likely to be subject to intense pressures to learn new ways of thinking and living, but these aspects of life in NRMs are in line with more traditional forms of religion. In our relatively secular modern societies we are not accustomed to such strident expressions of religiosity. Recognizing the continuity, however, the American courts eventually refused to hear testimony about brainwashing in NRMs for fear of paving the way for the persecution of other religions. A handful of scholars remain unconvinced, and moving against the tide of scholarly opnion they have sought to reform and revive the notion of brainwashing (e.g., Zablocki 2001; Kent 2001). In Europe as well, where the controversy over NRMs only really began to heat up in the late 1990s, after the mass murder–suicides of the Solar Temple cult in 1994 and 1995, the concept has also taken on a new life in various governmental investigations of the "cult threat" (e.g., Richardson and Introvigne 2001).

The readings in this section can only serve as an introduction to this complex topic, yet they were chosen to provide as much breadth of perspective as possible. Chapter 9, "The Process of Brainwashing, Psychological Coercion, and Thought Reform," is drawn from the book *Cults in Our Midst* (1995) by the psychologist Margaret T. Singer. She is the best-known exponent of the brainwashing thesis with regard to NRMs, and she provided expert testimony in many legal cases involving NRMs in the United States. The reading provides a straightforward statement of her position, clearly describing her conception of the history, nature, and consequences of the brainwashing process.

As the editor of this volume it should be noted that I am unconvinced by Singer's arguments (see Dawson 1998, 2001). But I agree, at least in part, with Thomas Robbins when he states in chapter 11 that "the debate over cultist brainwashing will necessarily be inconclusive" because the "contending parties ground their arguments on differing assumptions, definitions, and epistemological rules." Thus I would invite readers of this text to assess for themselves the merits of Singer's argument and those of the two critics that follow. Given the strong public bias against NRMs, I suggest keeping two questions in mind when reading Singer's work: What evidence (i.e., reliable research) is actually provided to support her specific claims? Can the processes of brainwashing, as described and applied to NRMs by Singer, be fairly differentiated from more conventional and accepted practices of religious education and discipline?

The second reading in this section, chapter 10, "A Critique of 'Brainwashing' Claims About New Religious Movements," by the sociologist James T. Richardson, provides a clear and simple summary statement of the case against accepting the brainwashing thesis. He is a leading scholar of NRMs and the chapter is an abbreviated version of a longer argument (see Richardson 1993). It quickly surveys the range of concerns most sociologists of religion have with Singer's thesis, highlighting some of the pertinent academic research literature (see Dawson 1998: 102–27; Anthony 2001). You may note that Singer's discussion attempts at points to preempt some of the very doubts that Richardson raises, because they are so commonly expressed by critics of the brainwashing argument.

In the final and most fascinating reading, chapter 11, "Constructing Cultist 'Mind Control'," Thomas Robbins, another prominent scholar of NRMs, takes the debate to another level. In line with earlier readings in this text, Robbins increases our understanding of the real issues at stake by placing the debate over brainwashing in a larger interpretive context. He does this in two ways: first, he delineates the underlying sources of social tension between all NRMs and the dominant society and explains why, given the constitutional guarantee of the "free exercise of religion," attempts at the social control of deviant religion are being driven towards the "medicalization" of the "cult problem" in the guise of the accusation of brainwashing; second, he demonstrates how the debate over brainwashing can be reduced in many ways to issues of interpretive perspective. What is evidence of abuse and manipulation from a "critical external perspective" can also be interpreted as evidence of intensity of religious commitment and authentic spiritual development from an "empathic internal perspective." In the end, he cogently argues, it is very difficult to say which perspective is more accurate, without simply reinvoking assumptions, framed in agonistic rhetorics, that are obviously prejudicial. The conflict over cults entails a clash of values that cannot be resolved by scientific research alone.

Whatever perspective one favors, it is important to realize that the accusations of brainwashing, and the debate over this charge, have had some very real and deleterious consequences for people's lives. Individuals and groups (both NRMs and anti-cult organizations) have had their plans and activities grievously disrupted, and experienced serious criminal and financial penalties as a result of legal and legislative actions prompted by brainwashing claims. The issues at stake can be clarified significantly by reliable social scientific research. But the matter is not strictly academic. The resolution of the debate cannot be reasonably and justly separated from its legal and political implications.

References

Anthony, Dick 2001: Tactical Ambiguity and Brainwashing Formulations: Science or Pseudo-Science? In B Zablocki and T. Robbins (eds.), *Misunderstanding Cults: Searching For Objectivity in a Controversial Field*. Toronto: University of Toronto Press, 213–317.

Anthony, Dick and Thomas Robbins 1992: Law, Social Science and the "Brainwashing" Exception to the First Amendment. *Behavioral Sciences and the Law* 10 (1): 5–27.

——1994: Brainwashing and Totalitarian Influence. In *Encyclopedia of Human Behavior*, vol. 1. San Diego, CA: Academic Press, 457–71.

——1995: Negligence, Coercion and the Protection of Religious Belief. *Journal of Church and State* 37 (3): 509–36.

Bromley, David G. 1988: Deprogramming as a Mode of Exit from New Religious Movements: The Case of the Unificationist Movement. In D. G. Bromley, (ed.), *Falling From the Faith: Causes and Consequences of Religious Apostasy*. Newbury Park, CA: Sage, 185–204.

Clark, John, M. D. Langone, R. E. Schacter, and R. C. D. Daly 1981: *Destructive Cult Conversion: Theory, Research, and Treatment*. Weston, MA: American Family Foundation.

Dawson, Lorne L. 1998: *Comprehending Cults: The Sociology of New Religious Movements*. Toronto: Oxford University Press.

——2001: Raising Lazarus: A Methodological Critique of Stephen Kent's Revival of the Brainwashing Model. In B. Zablocki and T. Robbins (eds.), *Misunderstanding Cults: Searching For Objectivity in a Controversial Field*. Toronto: University of Toronto Press, 379–400.

Kent, Stephen A. 2001: Brainwashing Programs in The Family/Children of God and Scientology. In B. Zablocki and T. Robbins (eds.), *Misunderstanding Cults: Searching For Objectivity in a Controversial Field*. Toronto: University of Toronto Press, 349–78.

Patrick, Ted and Tom Dulack 1976: *Let Our Children Go!* New York: E. P. Dutton.

Preston, David L. 1981: Becoming a Zen Practitioner. *Sociological Analysis* 42(1): 47–55.

Richardson, James T. 1993: A Social Psychological Critique of "Brainwashing" Claims About Recruitment to New Religions. In D. G. Bromley and J. K. Hadden (eds.), *The Handbook on Cults and Sects in America, Part B* (Religion and the Social Order, vol. 3). Greenwich, CT: JAI Press, 75–97.

——1995: Legal Status of Minority Religions in the United States. *Social Compass* 42 (2): 249–64.

Richardson, James T. and Gerald Ginsburg 1998: "Brainwashing" Evidence in Light of Daubert: Science and Unpopular Religions. *Current Legal Studies* 1: 265–88.

Richardson, James T. and Massimo Introvigne 2001: "Brainwashing" Theories in European Parliamentary and Administrative Reports on "Cults" and "Sects." *Journal for the Scientific Study of Religion* 40 (2): 143–68.

Singer, Margaret T. 1979: Coming Out of the Cults. *Psychology Today* (Jan.): 72–82.

—— 1995: *Cults in Our Midst: The Hidden Menace in Our Everyday Lives.* San Francisco, CA: Jossey-Bass.

Wilson, Stephen R. 1984: Becoming a Yogi: Resocialization and Deconditioning as Conversion Processes. *Sociological Analysis* 45 (4): 301–14.

Young, John L. and Ezra E. H. Griffiths 1992: A Ctitical Evaluation of Coercive Persuasion as Used in the Assessment of Cults. *Behavioral Sciences and the Law* 10 (1): 89–101.

Zablocki, Benjamin 2001: Towards a Demystified and Disinterested Scientific Theory of Brainwashing. In B. Zablocki and T. Robbins (eds.), *Misunderstanding Cults: Searching For Objectivity in a Controversial Field.* Toronto: University of Toronto Press, 159–214.

CHAPTER NINE

The Process of Brainwashing, Psychological Coercion, and Thought Reform

MARGARET THALER SINGER

Leaders of cults and groups using thought-reform processes have taken in and controlled millions of persons to the detriment of their welfare. Sometimes such influence is called coercive persuasion or extraordinary influence, to distinguish it from everyday persuasion by friends, family, and other influences in our lives, including the media and advertising.

The key to successful thought reform is to keep the subjects unaware that they are being manipulated and controlled – and especially to keep them unaware that they are being moved along a path of change that will lead them to serve interests that are to their disadvantage. The usual outcome of thought-reform processes is that a person or group gains almost limitless control over the subjects for varying periods of time.

When cultic groups using this level of undue influence are seen in the cold light of day, uninformed observers often cannot grasp how the group worked. They wonder how a rational person would ever get involved. Recently, because of the media attention garnered by the actions of certain groups, the world has become somewhat more aware of thought reform, but most people still don't know how to deal with situations of extraordinary influence.

A number of terms have been used to describe this process, including *brainwashing,* *thought reform, coercive persuasion, mind control, coordinated programs of coercive influence and behavior control,* and *exploitative persuasion* . . . Perhaps the first and last terms convey something of the crux of what I will be describing in this chapter.

When I ask ordinary people what they think brainwashing is, they correctly grasp that it refers to the exploitative manipulation of one person by another. They usually describe a situation in which a person or group has conned others into going along with a plan put in place by the instigator. *Conned* has a widely understood meaning in our informal conversation and our streets, which is why it is generally difficult to manipulate street-smart kids. They already know to look for a double agenda, calling it a con game, snow job, scam, jiving someone, putting someone on, and many other names.

A certain type of psychological con game is exactly what goes on in a thought-reform environment. A complex set of interlocking factors is put into place, and these factors, either quickly or slowly, depending on the situation and the subject, bring about deep changes in the mind-set and attitudes of the targeted individual. Through the manipulation of psychological *and* social factors, people's attitudes can indeed be changed, and their thinking and behavior radically altered.

Historical Examples of Brainwashing

. . . In just the last sixty years, the world has seen numerous examples of how easily human conduct can be manipulated under certain circumstances.

During the 1930s purge trials in the former Soviet Union, men and women accused of committing crimes against the state were maneuvered into both falsely confessing to and falsely accusing others of these crimes. The world press expressed bewilderment and amazement at the phenomenon but, with few exceptions, soon lapsed into silence.

Then in the late 1940s and early 1950s, the world witnessed personnel at Chinese revolutionary universities implement a thought-reform program that changed the beliefs and behaviors of the citizens of the largest nation in the world. This program, which Mao Tse-tung wrote about as early as the 1920s, was put into place when the communist regime took power in China on October 1, 1949. Chairman Mao had long planned how to change people's political selves – to achieve "ideological remolding," as he called it – through the use of a coordinated program of psychological, social, and political coercion. As a result, millions of Chinese citizens were induced to espouse new philosophies and exhibit new conduct.

The term *brainwashing* was first introduced into the Western world in 1951, when American foreign correspondent Edward Hunter published a book titled *Brainwashing in Red China*. Hunter was the first to write about the phenomenon, based on his interviews of both Chinese and non-Chinese coming across the border from China into Hong Kong. His translator explained to him that the communist process of ridding people of the vestiges of their old belief system was called colloquially *hse nao*, which literally means "wash brain," or "cleansing the mind."

The 1950s also brought the Korean War. North Korea's intensive indoctrination of United Nations' prisoners of war showed the world the extent to which captors would go to win converts to their political cause. The Korean program was based on methods used by the Chinese, combined with other social and psychological influence techniques.

Later in the same decade, Cardinal Mindszenty, the head of the Roman Catholic Church in Hungary and a man of tremendous personal forcefulness, strength of convictions, and faith in God, ended up being so manipulated and processed by his Russian captors that he – like the earlier purge trial victims – both falsely confessed and falsely accused his colleagues.

These extremes of social and psychological manipulations of thought and conduct were, and sometime still are, disregarded by Americans because the events occurred far away and could be dismissed as merely foreign propaganda and political acts. Such reasoning is a variation of the "not me" myth: not in our land could such a thing happen. But later, certain events occurred in California that forced many to see that extremes of influence and manipulation were possible in the United States, too.

In 1969, Charles Manson manipulated a band of middle-class youths into believing his mad version of *Helter Skelter*. Under his influence and control, his followers carried out multiple vicious murders. Not long after, the Symbionese Liberation Army (SLA), a ragtag revolutionary group, kidnapped newspaper heiress Patricia Hearst and abused her psychologically and otherwise. The SLA used mind manipulations as well as gun-at-the-head methods to coerce Patty into compliance. They manipulated and controlled her behavior to the extent that she appeared with them in a bank robbery and feared returning to society, having been convinced by the SLA that the police and the FBI would shoot her.

This series of events from the 1930s to the present demonstrates that individual autonomy and personal identity are much more fragile than was once commonly believed. And that certain venal types have gotten hold of and perfected techniques of persuasion that are wreaking havoc in our society . . .

Packaged Persuasion

Several years ago, a colleague and I interviewed a young couple at the request of their attorneys. The couple, who had once been good citizens and loving parents, had been accused of a spanking that allegedly led to their son's death. While they were members of a cult in West Virginia with a female leader, their 23-month-old son allegedly had either hit or pushed the leader's grandchild during play. The parents were ordered to get the child to apologize; otherwise, according to the irate leader, no one would go to heaven. The boy was beaten with a wooden board by his father, with his mother in the room, for more than two and a half hours. The boy's blood poled in the bruises in his buttocks and legs, and he died. In court, I described how the leader had slowly gained control of the members of her group and how the beating evolved from her teaching and control.

In another case, Ron Luff, a former Navy career petty officer with a series of recommendations for excellent conduct and performance, was convinced by his cult leader to follow that leader's orders. These orders were to help the leader kill an Ohio family of five, including three young daughters, dump the bodies into a lime pit in a barn, then go off on a long wilderness trek with the leader and his two dozen followers. Ron Luff was found guilty of aggravated murder and kidnapping and sentenced to 170 years in prison. The cult leader, Jeffrey Lundgren, was sentenced to die in Ohio's electric chair. Both cases are on appeal at the time of this book's writing.

People repeatedly ask me how cult leaders get their followers to do such things as give their wives to a child-molesting cult leader, drop out of medical school to follow a martial arts guru, give several million dollars to a self-appointed messiah who wears a wig and has his favorite women dress like Jezebel, or practice sexual abstinence while following a blatantly promiscuous guru. Because of the great discrepancies between individual's conduct before cult membership and the behavior exhibited while in the cult, families, friends, and the public wonder how these changes in attitude and behavior are induced.

How cult leaders and other clever operators get people to do their bidding seems arcane and mysterious to most persons, but I find there is nothing esoteric about it at all. There are no secret drugs or potions. It is just words and group pressures, put together in packaged forms. Modern-day manipulators use methods of persuasion employed since the days of the cavemen, but the masterful con artists of today have hit upon a way to put the techniques together in packages that are especially successful. As a result, thought reform, as a form of influence and persuasion, falls on the extreme end of a continuum that also includes education as we typically see it, advertising, propaganda, and indoctrination . . .

There is a mistaken notion that thought reform can only be carried out in confined places and under threat of physical torture or death. But it is important to remember that the brainwashing programs of the forties and fifties were applied not only to military or civilian prisoners of war but also to the general population. In all our research, I and others who study these programs emphasize over and over that imprisonment and overt violence are not necessary and are actually counterproductive when influencing people to change their attitudes and behaviors. If one really wants to influence others, various coordinated soft-sell programs are cheaper, less obvious, and highly effective. The old maxim "Honey gathers more flies than vinegar" remains true today.

Attacking the Self

There is, however, an important distinction to be made between the version of thought reform prevalent in the 1940s and 1950s and the version used by a number of contemporary groups, including cults, large group awareness training programs, and assorted other groups. These latter-day efforts have built upon the age-old influence techniques to perfect amazingly successful programs of persuasion and change. What's new – and crucial – is that these programs change attitudes by attacking essential aspects of a person's sense of self, unlike the earlier brainwashing programs that primarily confronted a person's political beliefs.

Today's programs are designed to destabilize an individual's sense of self by undermining his or her basic consciousness, reality awareness, beliefs and worldview, emotional control, and defense mechanisms. This attack on a person's central stability, or self-concept, and on a person's capacity for self-evaluation is the principal technique that makes the newer programs work. Moreover, this attack is carried out under a variety of guises and conditions – and rarely does it include forced confinement or direct physical coercion. Rather, it is subtle and powerful psychological process of destabilization and induced dependency.

Thankfully, these programs do not change people permanently. Nor are they 100 percent effective. Cults are nor all alike, thought-reform programs are not all alike, and not everyone exposed to specific intense influence processes succumbs and follows the group. Some cults try to defend themselves by saying, in effect, "See, not everyone joins or stays, so we must not be using brainwashing techniques." Many recruits do succumb, however, and the better organized the influence processes used, the more people will succumb.

What is of concern, then, is that certain groups and training programs that have emerged in the last half-century represent well-organized, highly orchestrated influence efforts that are widely successful in recruiting and converting people under certain conditions for certain ends. My interest has been in how these processes work, in the psychological and social techniques that produce these behavioral and attitudinal changes. I am less interested in whether the content of the group centers around religion, psychology, self-improvement, politics, lifestyle, or flying saucers. I am more interested in the widespread use of brainwashing techniques by crooks, swindlers, psychopaths, and egomaniacs of every sort.

How Thought Reform Works

Brainwashing is not experienced as a fever or a pain might be; it is an invisible social adaptation. When you are the subject of it, you are not aware of the intent of the influence processes that are going on, and especially, you are not aware of the changes taking place within you.

In his memoirs, Cardinal Mindszenty wrote, "Without knowing what had happened to me, I had become a different person." And when asked about being brainwashed, Patty Hearst said, "The strangest part of all this, however, as the SLA delighted in informing me later, was that they themselves were surprised at how docile and trusting I had become . . . It was also true, I must admit, that the thought of escaping from them later simply never entered my mind. I had become convinced that there was no possibility of escape . . . I suppose I could have walked out of the apartment and away from it all, but I didn't. It simply never occurred to me."

A thought-reform program is not a one-shot event but a gradual process of breaking down and transformation. It can be likened to gaining weight, a few ounces, a half pound, a pound at a time. Before long, without even noticing the initial changes – we are confronted with a new physique. So, too, with brainwashing. A twist here, a tweak there – and there it is: a new psychic attitude, a new mental outlook. These systematic manipulations of social and psychological influences under particular conditions are called *programs* because the means by which change is brought about is coordinated. And it is because the changes cause the learning and adoption of a certain set of attitudes, usually accompanied by a certain set of behaviors, that the effort and the result are called *thought reform.*

Thus, thought reform is concerted effort to change a person's way of looking at the world, which will change his or her behavior. It is distinguished from other forms of social learning by the conditions under which it is conducted and by the techniques of environmental and

Table [9.1]   Criteria for thought reform

Conditions (Singer)	Themes (Lifton)	Stages (Schein)
1 Keep the person unaware of what is going on and the changes taking place.		1 Unfreezing.
2 Control the person's time and, if possible, physical environment.	1 Milieu control.	
	2 Loading the language.	
	3 Demand for purity.	
3 Create a sense of powerlessness, covert fear, and dependency.	4 Confession.	
4 Suppress much of the person's old behavior and attitudes.		
5 Instill new behavior and attitudes.	5 Mystical manipulation.	2 Changing.
	6 Doctrine over person.	
6 Put forth a closed system of logic; allow no real input or criticism.	7 Sacred science.	
	8 Dispensing of existence.	3 Refreezing.

interpersonal manipulation that are meant to suppress certain behavior and to elicit and train other behavior. And it does not consist of only one program – there are many ways and methods to accomplish it.

The tactics of a thought-reform program are organized to

- Destabilize a person's sense of self.
- Get the person to drastically reinterpret his or her life's history and radically alter his or her worldview and accept a new version of reality and causality.
- Develop in the person a dependence on the organization, and thereby turn the person into a deployable agent of the organization.

Thought reform can be profitably looked at in at least three ways (summarized in table [9.1]). Robert Lifton has recognized eight themes of thought reform, I have identified six

conditions, and Edgar Schein has named three stages. The themes and stages outlined by Lifton and Schein focus on the *sequence of the process*, while the circumstances I have outlined suggest the *conditions needed* in the surrounding environment if the process is to work.

Singer's six conditions

The following conditions create the atmosphere needed to put thought-reform processes into place. The degree to which these conditions are present increases the level of restrictiveness enforced by the cult and the overall effectiveness of the program.

1   Keep the person unaware that there is an agenda to control or change the person.
2   Control time and physical environment (contacts, information).
3   Create a sense of powerlessness, fear, and dependency.

4 Suppress old behavior and attitudes.
5 Instill new behavior and attitudes.
6 Put forth a closed system of logic.

The trick is to proceed with the thought-reform process one step at a time so that the person does not notice that she or he is changing. I will explain more fully how each step works.

(1) *Keep the person unaware of what is going on and how she or he is being changed a step at a time*. Imagine you are the person being influenced. You find yourself in an environment to which you are forced to adapt *in a series of steps,* each sufficiently minor so that you don't notice the changes in yourself and do not become aware of the goals of the program until late in the process (if ever). You are kept unaware of the orchestration of psychological and social forces meant to change your thinking and your behavior. The cult leaders make it seem as though what is going on is normal, that everything is the way it's supposed to be. This atmosphere is reinforced by peer pressure and peer-modeled behavior, so that you adapt to the environment without even realizing it.

For example, a young man was invited to a lecture. When he arrived, he noticed many pairs of shoes lined against the wall and people in their stocking feet. A woman nodded at his shoes, so he took them off and set them with the others. Everyone was speaking in a soft voice, so he lowered his voice. The evening proceeded with some ritual ceremonies, meditation, and a lecture by a robed leader. Everything was paced slowly and led by this man, with the rest quietly watching and listening. The young man also sat docilely, even though he wanted to ask questions. He conformed to what the group was doing. In this case, however, at the end of the evening when he was asked to come back to another lecture, he said, "Thanks, but no thanks," at which two men quickly ushered him out a back door, so others wouldn't hear his displeasure.

The process of keeping people unaware is key to a cult's double agenda: the leader slowly takes you through a series of events that on the surface look like one agenda, while on another level, the real agenda is to get you, the recruit or member, to obey and to give up your autonomy, your past affiliations, and your belief systems. The existence of the double agenda makes this process one of *noninformed consent.*

(2) *Control the person's social and/or physical environment; especially control the person's time.* Cults don't need to have you move into the commune, farm, headquarters, or ashram and live within the cult environment twenty-four hours a day in order to have control over you. They can control you just as effectively by having you go to work every day with instructions that when not working – on your lunch hour, for example – you must do continuous mind-occupying chanting or some other cult-related activity. Then, after work, you must put all your time in with the organization.

(3) *Systematically created a sense of powerlessness in the person.* Cults create this sense of powerlessness by stripping you of your support system and your ability to act independently. Former friends and kinship networks are taken away. You, the recruit or follower, are isolated from your ordinary environments and sometimes removed to remote locations. Another way cults create a sense of powerlessness is by stripping people of their main occupation and sources of wealth. It is to achieve this condition that so many cultic organizations have members drop out of school, quit their jobs or give up their careers, and turn over their property, inheritances, and other resources to the organization. It is one of the steps in creating a sense of dependency on the organization and a continuing sense of individual powerlessness.

Once stripped of your usual support network and, in some cases, means of income, your confidence in your own perceptions erodes. As your sense of powerlessness increases, your good judgment and understanding of the world are diminished. At the same time as you are destabilized in relation to your ordinary reality and worldview, the cult confronts you with a new, unanimously (group-)approved worldview. As the group attacks your previous worldview, causing you distress and inner confusion, you are not allowed to speak about this confusion, nor can you object to it, because leadership constantly suppresses questions and counters any resistance. Through this process, your inner confidence is eroded. Moreover, the effectiveness of this approach can be speeded up if you are physically tired, which is why cult leaders see to it that followers are kept overly busy.

(4) *Manipulate a system of rewards, punishments, and experiences in such a way as to inhibit behavior that reflects the person's former social identity.* The expression of your beliefs, values, activities, and characteristic demeanor prior to contact with the group is suppressed, and you are manipulated into taking on a social identity preferred by the leadership. Old beliefs and old patterns of behavior are defined as irrelevant, if not evil. You quickly learn that the leadership wants old ideas and old patterns eliminated, so you suppress them. For example, the public admission of sexual feelings in certain groups is met with overt disapproval by peers and superiors, accompanied by a directive to take a cold shower. An individual can avoid public rebuke on this topic by no longer speaking on the entire topic of sexuality, warmth, or interest in another human being. The vacuum left is then filled with the group's ways of thinking and doing.

(5) *Manipulate a system of rewards, punishments, and experiences in order to promote learning of the group's ideology or belief system and group-approved behaviors.* Once immersed in an environment in which you are totally dependent on the rewards given by those who control the setting, you can be confronted with massive demands to learn varying amounts of new information and behaviors. You are rewarded for proper performance with social and sometimes material reinforcement; if slow to learn or noncompliant, you are threatened with shunning, banning, and punishment which includes loss of esteem from others, loss of privileges, loss of status, and inner anxiety and guilt. In certain groups, physical punishment is meted out.

The more complicated and filled with contradictions the new system is and the more difficult it is to learn, the more effective the conversion process will be. For example, a recruit may constantly fail at mastering a complicated theology but can succeed and be rewarded for going out to solicit funds. In one cultic organization, the leadership introduces the new recruits to a complicated dodge-ball game. Only long-term members know the complex and ever-changing rules, and they end up literally leading and pushing the new recruits through the game. This, then, is followed by a very simple exercise in which members get together to "share." Older members stand up and share (that is, confess) some past bad deed. The new members, who failed so badly at the bewildering dodge-ball game, now can feel capable of succeeding by simply getting up and confessing something about their past that was, by group standards, bad.

Since esteem and affection from peers is so important to new recruits, any negative response is very meaningful. Approval comes from having your behaviors and thought patterns conform to the models put forth by the group. Your relationship with peers is threatened whenever you fail to learn or display new behaviors. Over time, an easy solution to the insecurity generated by the difficulties of learning the new system is to inhibit any display of doubt and, even if you don't understand the content, to merely acquiesce, affirm, and act as if you do understand and accept the new philosophy or content.

(6) *Put forth a closed system of logic and an authoritarian structure that permits no feedback and refuses to be modified except by leadership approval or executive order.* If you criticize or complain, the leader or peers allege that *you* are defective, not the organization. In this closed system of logic, you are not allowed to question or doubt a tenet or rule or to call attention to factual information that suggests some internal contradiction within the belief system or a contradiction with what you've been told. If you do make such observations, they may be turned around and argued to mean the opposite of what you intended. You are made to feel that you are wrong. In cultic groups, the individual member is always wrong, and the system is always right.

For example, one cult member complained privately to his immediate leadership that he doubted he'd be able to kill his father if so instructed by the cult, even though that act was to signify true adherence to the cult's system. In response, he was told he needed more courses to overcome his obvious weakness because by now he should be more committed to the group.

In another case, a woman objected to her fund-raising team leader that it would be lying to people to say cult members were collecting money for a children's home when they knew the money went to the leader's headquarters. She was told, "That's evidence of your degraded mentality. You are restoring to our leader what's rightfully his, that's all!"

Another woman who wanted to go home to see her dying grandmother was refused her request. "We're strengthening you here," she was told. "This request is a sign of your self-ishness. We're your new family, and we're right to not let you go."

The goal of all this is your conversion or remolding. As you learn to modify your former behaviors in order to be accepted in this closed and controlled environment, you change. You affirm that you accept and understand the ideology by beginning to talk in the simple catchphrases particular to the group. This "communication" has no foundation since, in reality, you have little understanding of the system beyond the catchphrases. But once you begin to express your seeming verbal acceptance of the group's ideology, then that ideology becomes the rule book for the subsequent direction and evaluation of your behavior.

Also, using the new language fosters your separation from your old conscience and belief system. Your new language allows you to justify activities that are clearly not in your interests, perhaps not even in the interests of humankind. Precisely those behaviors that lead to criticism from the outside world because they violate the norms and rules of the society as a whole are rationalized within the cult community through use of this new terminology, this new language.

For example, "heavenly deception" and "transcendental trickery" (terms used by two of the large cultic groups) are not called what they are – lying and deceptive fund-raising. Nor is the rule "do not talk to the systemites" called what it is – a way to isolate members from the rest of the world.

Lifton's eight themes

Paralleling Singer's six conditions are the eight psychological themes that psychiatrist Robert Lifton has identified as central to total-istic environments, including the communist Chinese and Korean programs of the 1950s and today's cults. Cults invoke these themes for the purpose of promoting behavioral and attitudinal changes.

(1) *Milieu control.* This is total control of communication in the group. In many groups, there is a "no gossip" or no "nattering" rule that keeps people from expressing their doubts or misgivings about what is going on. This rule is usually rationalized by saying that gossip will tear apart the fabric of the group or destroy unity, when in reality the rule is a mechanism to keep members from communi-cating anything other than positive endorse-ments. Members are taught to report those who break the rule, a practice that also keeps members isolated from each other and increases dependence on the leadership.

Milieu control also often involves discour-aging members from contacting relatives or friends outside the group and from reading anything not approved by the organization. They are sometimes told not to believe any-thing they see or hear reported by the media. One left-wing political cult, for example, maintains that the Berlin Wall is still standing and that the "bourgeois capitalist" press wants people to think otherwise in order to discredit communism.

(2) *Loading the language.* As members con-tinue to formulate their ideas in the group's jargon, this language serves the purpose of constricting members' thinking and shutting down critical thinking abilities. As first, trans-lating from their native tongue into "groups-

peak' forces members to censor, edit, and slow down spontaneous bursts of criticism or oppositional ideas. That helps them to cut off and contain negative or resistive feelings. Eventually, speaking in cult jargon is second nature, and talking with outsiders becomes energy-consuming and awkward. Soon enough, members find it most comfortable to talk only among themselves in the new vocabulary. To reinforce this, all kinds of derogatory names are given to outsiders: wogs, systemites, reactionaries, unclean, of Satan.

One large international group, for example, has dictionaries for members to use. In one of these dictionaries, *criticism* is defined as "justification for having done an overt." Then one looks up *overt* and the dictionary states: "overt act: an overt act is not just injuring someone or something; an overt act is an act of omission or commission which does the least good for the least number of dynamics or the most harm to the greatest number of dynamics." Then the definition of *dynamics* says: "There could be said to be eight urges in life . . ." And so, one can search from term to term trying to learn this new language. One researcher noted that the group's founder has stated that "new followers or potential converts should not be exposed to [the language and cosmology of the group] at too early a stage. 'Talking whole track to raw meat' is frowned upon."

When cults use such internal meanings, how is an outsider to know that *the devil disguise*, *just flesh relationships*, and *polluting* are terms for parents? That an *edu* is a lecture by the cult leader or that a *mislocation* is a mistake? A former cult member comments, "I was always being told, 'You are being too horizontal.'" Translated, this meant she was being reprimanded for listening to and being sympathetic to peers.

A dwindling group in Seattle, the Love Family, had a "rite of breathing." This sounds ordinary, but in fact for some members it turned out to be a lethal euphemism. The leader, a former California salesman, initiated this rite, in which members sat in a circle, passing around and sniffing a plastic bag containing a rag soaked with toluene, an industrial solvent. The group called the chemical "tell-u-all."

(3) *Demand for purity.* An us-versus-them orientation is promoted by the all-or-nothing belief system of the group: we are right; they (outsiders, nonmembers) are wrong, evil, unenlightened, and so forth. Each idea or act is good or bad, pure or evil. Recruits gradually take in, or internalize, the critical, shaming essence of the cult environment, which builds up lots of guilt and shame. Most groups put forth that there is only one way to think, respond, or act in any given situation. There is no in between, and members are expected to judge themselves and others by this all-or-nothing standard. Anything can be done in the name of this purity; it is the justification for the group's internal moral and ethical code. In many groups, it is literally taught that the end justifies the means – and because the end (that is, the group) is pure, the means are simply tools to reach purity.

If you are a recruit, this ubiquitous guilt and shame creates and magnifies your dependence on the group. The group says in essence, "We love you because you are transforming yourself," which means that any moment you are not transforming yourself, you are slipping back. Thus you easily feel inadequate, as though you need "fixing" all the time, just as the outside would is being denounced all the time.

(4) *Confession.* Confession is used to lead members to reveal past and present behavior, contacts with others, and undesirable feelings, seemingly in order to unburden themselves and become free. However, whatever you reveal is subsequently used to further mold you and to make you feel close to the group and estranged from nonmembers. (I sometimes call this technique *purge and merge.*) The information gained about you can be used against you to make you feel more guilty, powerless, fearful, and ultimately in need of the cult and the leader's goodness. And it can be used to get you to rewrite your personal history so as to denigrate your past life, making it seem illogical for you to want to

return to that former life, family, and friends. Each group will have its own confession ritual, which may be carried out either one-on-one with a person in leadership or in group sessions. Members may also write reports on themselves and others.

Through the confession process and by instruction in the group's teachings, members learn that everything about their former lives, including friends, family, and nonmembers, is wrong and to be avoided. Outsiders will put you at risk of not attaining the purported goal: they will lessen your psychological awareness, hinder the group's political advancement, obstruct your path toward ultimate knowledge, or allow you to become stuck in your past life and incorrect thinking.

(5) *Mystical manipulation*. The group manipulates members to think that their new feelings and behavior have arisen spontaneously in this new atmosphere. The leader implies that this is a chosen, select group with a higher purpose. Members become adept at watching to see what particular behavior is wanted, learning to be sensitive to all kinds of cued by which they are to judge and alter their own behavior. Cult leaders tell their followers, "You have chosen to be here. No one has told you to come here. No one has influenced you," when in fact the followers are in a situation they can't leave owing to social pressure and their fear. Thus they come to believe that they are actually choosing this life. If outsiders hint that the devotees have been brainwashed or tricked, the members say, "Oh, no, I chose voluntarily." Cults thrive on this myth of voluntarism, insisting time and again that no member is being held against his or her will.

(6) *Doctrine over person*. As members retrospectively alter their accounts of personal history, having been instructed either to rewrite that history or simply to ignore it, they are simultaneously taught to interpret reality through the group concepts and to ignore their own experiences and feelings as they occur. In many groups, from the days of early membership on, you will be told to stop paying attention to your own perceptions, since you are "uninstructed," and simply to go along with and accept the "instructed" view, the party line.

The rewriting of personal history more often than not becomes a re-creating, so that you learn to to fit yourself into the group's interpretation of life. For example, one young man recently out of a cult reported to me that he was "a drug addict, violent, and irresponsible." It soon became clear from our discussions that none of this was true. His drug addiction amounted to three puffs of marijuana a number of years ago; his violence stemmed from his participation on a high school wrestling team; and his irresponsibility was based on his not having saved any money from his very small allowance as a teenager. However, the group he had been in had convinced him that these things represented terrible flaws.

(7) *Sacred science*. The leader's wisdom is given a patina of science, adding a credible layer to his central philosophical, psychological, or political notion, He can then profess that the group's philosophy should be applied to all humankind and that anyone who disagrees or has alternative ideas is not only immoral and irreverent but also unscientific. Many leaders, for example, inflate their curricula vitae to make it look as though they are connected to higher powers, respected historical leaders, and so forth. Many a cult leader has said that he follows in the tradition of the greatest – Sigmund Freud, Karl Marx, the Buddha, Martin Luther, or Jesus Christ.

(8) *Dispensing of existence*. The cult's totalistic environment clearly emphasizes that members are part of an elitist movement and are the select of the world. Nonmembers are unworthy, lesser beings. Most cults teach their members that "we are the best and only one," saying, in one way or another, "We are the governors of enlightenment and all outsiders are lower beings." This kind of thinking lays the foundation for dampening the good consciences members brought in with them and allows members, as agents or representatives of a "superior" group, to manipulate nonmembers for good of the group. Besides reinforcing the us-versus-them mentality, this

thinking means that your whole existence centers on being in the group. If you leave, you join nothingness. This is the final step in creating members' dependence on the group.

Numerous former cult members report that, when they look back at what they did or would have done at the command of the group, they are appalled and stricken. Many have said they would have killed their own parents if so ordered. Hundreds have told me of countless deceptions and lies, such as short-changing donors on the street, using ruses to keep members from leaving, and urging persons who could ill afford it to run their credit cards up to their limit in order to sign up for further courses.

Schein's three stages

Next, we consider the stages people go through as their attitudes are changed by the group environment and the thought-reform processes. These were labeled by psychologist Edgar Schein as the stages of "unfreezing, changing, and refreezing."

(1) *Unfreezing*. In this first stage, your past attitudes and choices – your whole sense of self and notion of how the world works – are destabilized by group lectures, personal counseling, reward, punishments, and other exchanges in the group. This destabilization is designed to produce what psychologists call an identity crisis. While you are looking back at your own world and behavior and values (that is, unfreezing them), you are simultaneously bombarded with the new system, which implies that you have been wrong in the past. This process makes you uncertain about what is right, what to do, and which choices to make.

As described earlier, successful behavioral change programs are designed to upset you to the point that your self-confidence is undermined. This makes you more open to suggestion and also more dependent on the environment for cues about "right thinking" and "right conduct." Your resistance to the new ideas lessens when you feel yourself teetering on an edge with massive anxiety about

the right choices in life on the one side, and the group ideas that offer the way out of this distress on the other side.

Mary groups use a "hot seat" technique or some other form of criticism to attain the goal of undercutting, destabilizing, and diminishing. For example, "Harry" had been in the Army, was approaching his late twenties, and was always very sure of himself. But when he joined a Bible cult, the leaders said he wasn't learning fast enough to speak in tongues. He was told that he was resistant, that this was a sign of his evil past. He was told this over and over, no matter how hard he tried. Before long, Harry seemed to lose confidence in himself, even in his memories of his Army successes. His own attitude about himself as well as his actual behavior was unfreezing.

(2) *Changing*. During this second stage, you sense that the solutions offered by the group provide a path to follow. You feel that anxiety, uncertainty, and self-doubt can be reduced by adopting the concepts put forth by the group or leader. Additionally, you observe the behavior of the longer-term members, and you begin to emulate their ways. As social psychology experiments and observations have found for decades, once a person makes an open commitment before others to an idea, his or her subsequent behavior generally supports and reinforces the stated commitment. That is, if you say in front of others that you are making a commitment to be "pure," then you will feel pressured to follow what others define as the path of purity.

If you spend enough time in any environment, you will develop a personal history of experience and interaction in it. When that environment is constructed and managed in a certain way, then the experiences, interactions, and peer relations will be consistent with whatever public identity is fostered by the environment and will incorporate the values and opinions promulgated in that environment.

Now, when you engage in cooperative activity with peers in an environment that you do not realize is artificially constructed, you do not perceive your interactions to be coerced.

And when you are encouraged but not forced to make verbal claims to "truly understanding the ideology and having been transformed," these interactions with your peers will tend to lead you to conclude that you hold beliefs consistent with your actions. In other words, you will think that you came upon the belief and behaviors yourself.

Peer pressure is very important to this process:

- If you say in front of others, you'll do it.
- Once you do it, you'll think it.
- Once you think it (in an environment you do not perceive to be coercive), you'll believe that you thought it yourself.

(3) *Refreezing*. In this final phase, the group reinforces you in the desired behavior with social and psychological rewards, and punishes unwanted attitudes and behaviors with harsh criticism, group disapproval, social ostracism, and loss of status. Most of the modern-day thought-reform groups seek to produce smiling, nonresistant, hardworking persons who do not complain about group practices and do not question the authority of the guru, leader, or trainer. The more you display the group-approved attitudes and behavior, the more your compliance is interpreted by the leadership as showing that you now know that your life before you belonged to the group was wrong and that your new life is "the way" . . .

The degree to which a group or situation is structured according to these conditions, themes, and stages will determine the degree to which it is manipulative. Not all cults or groups that use thought-reform processes implement their mind-bending techniques in the same way or to the same extent. The implementation varies both within individual groups and across groups. Often, the peripheral members will have no awareness of the kinds of manipulations that go on in the upper or inner levels of a particular group or teaching. Thought reform is subtle, fluid, and insidious – and sometimes hard to identify,

particularly for the novice or the overly idealistic. But when it is present, it has powerful repercussions.

Producing a New Identity

As part of the intense influence and change process in many cults, people take on a new social identity, which may or may not be obvious to an outsider. When groups refer to this new identity, they speak of members who are transformed, reborn, enlightened, empowered, rebirthed, or cleared. The group-approved behavior is reinforced and reinterpreted as demonstrating the emergence of "the new person." Members are expected to display this new social identity.

However, the vast majority of those who leave such groups drop the cult content, and the cult behavior and attitudes, and painstakingly take up where they left off prior to joining. Those who had been subjected to thought-reform processes in the Far East, for example, gradually dropped the adopted attitudes and behaviors and returned to their former selves as soon as they were away from the environment. We see from years of research with prisoners of war, hostages, battered wives, former cult members, and other recipients of intense influence that changes made under this influence are not stable and not permanent. The beliefs a person may adopt about the world, about a particular philosophy, and even about himself or herself are reversible when the person is out of the environment that induced those beliefs.

We might ask ourselves – and surely many former cult members have – how a person can display reprehensible conduct under some conditions, then turn around and resume normal activities under other conditions. The phenomenon has been variously described as doubling or as the formation of a pseudopersonality (or pseudoidentity), superimposed identity, a cult self, or a cult personality. What is important about these labels is that they call attention to an important psychological and social phenomenon that needs to be studied more carefully – namely, that ordinary persons, with their own ideas and attitudes, can be rapidly turned around in their social identity but later can recover their old selves and move forward.

By this, I am not saying that people in cults or groups that use thought-reform processes are just faking it by role-playing, pretending, or acting. Anyone who has met a former friend who's been transformed into a recruiting zealot for a New Age transformational program, for example, knows that something more profound than role-playing is operating as that old friend defends her or his new self and new group, speaking single-mindedly, spouting intense, firmly stated dogma. This is not play-acting. It is far more instinctive and experienced as real.

Doubling, or the formation of a pseudo-personality, has become a key issue. It is a factor that ultimately allows cult members to leave their groups and permits us to understand why exit counseling works as a means of reawakening a person who has been exposed to thought-reform processes. The central fact is this: the social identity learned while a person is in a thought-reform system fades, much as a summer tan does when a person is no longer at the beach. The process is far more complicated than this analogy, of course, but I want to emphasize that cult thinking and behaviors are adaptive and not stable.

It is the cult environment that produces and keeps in place the cult identity. Some persons stay forever in the group, but the vast majority leave at some point, either walking away or being lured out by family and friends. An understanding of thought-reforming phenomena is vital to learning more about the role that group social support or pressure plays for all of us. It is important not only for families with relatives in cultic groups but also for ex-members wondering if there are psychological and social theories to explain what happened to them, and for everyone who wants to learn something about how we all operate.

Notes

p. 154, *For example, "heavenly deception" and*: Barker, *The Making of a Moonie*, p. 22; D. G. Bromley and A. D. Shupe, Jr., *Strange Gods: The Great American Cult Scare* (Boston: Beacon Press, 1981), pp. 171–72; R. Enroth, *Youth, Brainwashing and the Extremist Cults* (Grand Rapids, Mich.: Zondervan, 1977), p. 115; Larson, *Larson's New Book of Cults*, pp. 163, 259, 441; Mather and Nichols, *Dictionary of Cults, Sects, Religions and the Occult*, p. 55.

pp. 154–57, *psychiatrist Robert Lifton*: Lifton, *Thought Reform and the Psychology of Totalism*, pp. 419–25.

p. 155, *the group's founder has stated*: R. Wallis, *The Road to Total Freedom* (New York: Columbia University Press, 1976), p. 106.

pp. 157–58, *psychologist Edgar Schein*: Schein, Schneier, and Barker, *Coercive Persuasion*.

p. 158, *We see from years of research*: Lifton, *Thought Reform and the Psychology of Totalism*; R. Ofshe, "Coercive Persuasion and Attitude Change," in E. F. Borgatta and M. L. Borgatta (eds.), *Encyclopedia of Sociology*, Vol. 1 (New York: Macmillan, 1992).

p. 158, *The phenomenon has been . . . described*: R. J. Lifton, *The Future of Immortality and Other Essays for a Nuclear Age* (New York: Basic Books, 1987), pp. 195–208; L. J. West, paper presented at the American Family Foundation Conference, Arlington, Va., May 1992.

CHAPTER TEN

A Critique of "Brainwashing" Claims About New Religious Movements

James T. Richardson

Introduction

Many young people have been involved with new religious movements (NRMs) – sometimes pejoratively called "cults" – over the past several decades in American and other Western societies. These young people have often been among the most affluent and better educated of youth in their societies, which has contributed to controversies erupting about the meaning of such participation. Parents, friends, and political and opinion leaders have attempted to understand the phenomenon, and develop methods to control activities of such groups (Beckford 1985; Barker 1984).

Joining NRMs, which may appear quite strange in their beliefs and organizational patterns, is interpreted by some as an act of ultimate rejection of Western cultural values and institutions – including religious, economic, and familial ones. This "culture-rejecting" explanation has been difficult for many to accept, prompting a search for other explanations for involvement, a search raising serious ethical issues.

An appealing alternative explanation has been so-called "brainwashing" theories (Bromley and Richardson 1983; Fort 1983). According to those espousing these ideas, youth have not joined NRMs volitionally, but have been manipulated or forced into participating by groups using powerful psychotechnology practiced first by communist,

anti-Western societies. This psychotechnology allegedly traps or encapsulates young people in NRMs, allowing subsequent control of their behavior by leaders of the groups, through "mind control."

These techniques were originally developed, according to these claims, in Russian purge trials of the 1930s, and later refined by the Chinese communists after their assumption of power in China in 1949, and then used by them with POWs during the Korean War of the early 1950s (Solomon 1983). Now these techniques are allegedly being used by NRM leaders against young people in Western countries, who are supposedly virtually helpless before such sophisticated methods (Richardson and Kilbourne 1983).

When questioned about obvious logical and ethical problems of applying these theories to situations without physical coercion (such as participation in NRMs), proponents have a ready answer. They claim that physical coercion has been replaced by "psychological coercion," which is supposedly more effective than simple physical coercion (Singer 1979). These ideas are referred to as "second generation" brainwashing theories, which take into account new insights about manipulation of individuals. Supposedly, physical coercion is unnecessary if recruits can be manipulated by affection, guilt, or other psychological influences.

These theories can be considered ideas developed for functional reasons by those who have a vested interest in their being accepted, such as parents of members, therapists, and leaders of competing religious groups. The ideas plainly are a special type of "account" which "explains" why people join the groups and why they stay in them (Beckford 1978). Whatever the origin, and no matter that the veracity of such accounts is questionable, these ideas about NRM participation have become commonly accepted.

For instance, De Witt (1991) reports that 78 percent of a random sample of 383 individuals from Nevada said they believed in brainwashing, and 30 percent agreed that "brainwashing is required to make someone join a religious cult." A similar question asked of a random sample of 1,000 residents in New York prior to the tax evasion trial of Reverend Moon (Richardson 1992) revealed that 43 percent agreed "brainwashing is required to make someone change from organized religion to a cult." Latkin (1991) reported that 69 percent of a random sample of Oregon residents who were asked about the controversial Rajneesh group centered in eastern Oregon agreed that members of the group were brainwashed.

These notions about "brainwashing" and "mind control" have pervaded institutional structures in our society as well, even if they are problematic. Such views have influenced actions by governmental entities and the media (Van Driel and Richardson 1988; Bromley and Robbins 1992). The legal system has seen a number of efforts to apply brainwashing theories as explanations of why people might participate in new religions. Several civil actions have resulted in multimillion dollar judgments against NRMs allegedly using brainwashing techniques on recruits (Anthony 1990; Richardson 1991, 1995).

Thus it appears that ideas about brainwashing of recruits to new religions have developed a momentum of their own in several Western societies. These notions are impacting society in many ways, including limitations on religious freedom (Richardson 1991). Thus, we need to examine the brainwashing thesis more closely, in order to see if it is an adequate explanation of the process whereby people join and participate in NRMs, and to examine the underlying ethics of offering such explanations of religious participation.

Critique of "Brainwashing" Theories

Brainwashing theories serve the interests of those espousing them, which is a major reason they are so readily accepted. Parents can blame the groups and their leaders for what were probably volitional decisions to participate by their sons and daughters. Former members can blame the techniques for a decision to participate which the participant later regrets. Deprogrammers can use brainwashing theories as a justification for their new "profession" and as a quasi-legal defense if they are apprehended by legal authorities during attempted deprogrammings, which often have involved physical force and kidnapping. Societal leaders can blame the techniques for seducing society's "brightest and best" away from traditional cultural values and institutions. Competitive religious leaders as well as some psychological and psychiatric clinicians attack the groups with brainwashing theories, to bolster what are basically unfair competition arguments (Kilbourne and Richardson 1984).

Thus it is in the interest of many different entities to *negotiate an account* of "what happened" that makes use of brainwashing notions. Only the NRM membership, which is usually politically weak, is left culpable after these negotiated explanations about how and why a person joined an NRM. All other parties are, to varying degrees, absolved of responsibility (Richardson, van der Lans, and Derks 1986).

The claim that NRMs engage in brainwashing thus becomes a powerful "social weapon" for many partisans in the "cult controversy." Such ideas are used to "label" the exotic religious groups as deviant or even evil (Robbins and Anthony 1982). However, the new "second generation" brainwashing theories have a number of logical and evidentiary problems, and their continued use raises profound ethical issues.

Misrepresentation of classical tradition

Modern brainwashing theories sometimes misrepresent earlier scholarly work on the processes developed in Russia, China, and the Korean POW situation (Anthony 1990). These misrepresentations are as follows. First, the early classical research by Schein et al. (1961) and Lifton (1963) revealed that, contrary to some recent claims, the techniques were generally ineffective at doing more than modifying behavior (obtaining compliance) even for the short term. Such theories would seem less useful to explain long-term changes of behavior and belief allegedly occurring with NRM participation.

Second, the degree of determinism associated with contemporary brainwashing applications usually far exceeds that found in the foundational work of Lifton and of Schein. Anthony and Robbins (1992) contrast the "soft determinism" of the work of Lifton and of Schein with the "hard determinism" of contemporary proponents of brainwashing theories such as Singer and Ofshe (1990). The "hard determinism" approach assumes that humans can be turned into robots through application of sophisticated brainwashing techniques, easily becoming deployable "Manchurian Candidates." Classical scholars Lifton and Schein seemed more willing to recognize human beings as more complex entities than do some contemporary brainwashing theorists.

Third, another problem is that classical scholars Lifton and Schein may not be comfortable with their work being applied to non-coercive situations. Lifton (1985: 69) explicitly disclaims use of ideas concerning brainwashing in legal attacks against so-called cults, and earlier (1963: 4) had stated: ". . . the term (brainwashing) has a far from precise and questionable usefulness; one may even be tempted to forget about the whole subject and return to more constructive pursuits." The work of Schein and of Lifton both evidence difficulty in "drawing the line" between acceptable and unacceptable behaviors on the part of those involved in influencing potential subjects for change (Anthony and Robbins 1992). Group influence processes operate in all areas of life, which makes singling out one area like NRMs for special negative attention quite problematic. Such a focus cannot be adopted on strictly logical, scientific, or ethical grounds.

Ideological biases of brainwashing theorists

Contemporary applications of brainwashing theories share an ideological bias in opposition to collectivistic solutions to problems of group organization (Richardson and Kilbourne 1983). In the 1950s many Westerners opposed collectivistic communism; in the 1970s and 1980s many share a concern about communally oriented new religions. Another ideological element of contemporary applications concerns the ethnocentrism and even racism which may be related to their use. The fact that a number of new religions are from outside Western culture and were founded and led by foreigners should not be ignored in understanding the propensity to apply simplistic brainwashing theories to explain participation and justify efforts at social control.

Limited research base of classical work

Research on which the classical models are based is quite limited (Richardson and Kilbourne 1983; Anthony 1990). Small non-representative samples were used by both Lifton and Shein, and those in the samples were presented using an anecdotal reporting style, derived from clinical settings, especially with Lifton's work. As Biderman (1962) pointed out, Lifton only studied 40 subjects in all, and gave detailed information on only 11 of those. Shein's original work was based on a sample of only 15 American civilians who returned after imprisonment in China. This work may be insightful, but it does not meet normal scientific standards in terms of sample size and representativeness.

Predisposing characteristics and volition ignored

Contemporary applications of brainwashing theories to NRM recruitment tactics typically ignores important work on predisposing characteristics of NRM participants (Anthony and

Robbins 1992). The techniques of brainwashing supposedly are so successful that they can transform a person's basic beliefs into sharply contrasting beliefs, even against their will. This aspect of brainwashing theory is appealing to proponents who have difficulty recognizing that an individual might have been attracted to a new and exotic religion perceived by the recruit as offering something positive for themselves.

Sizable numbers of participants are from higher social class origins in terms of education level and relative affluence, a finding raising questions about application of brainwashing theories as adequate explanations of participation. Both Barker (1984) and Kilbourne (1986) have found that there are predisposing characteristics for participation in the Unification Church – such as youthful idealism. Thus, the brainwashing argument would seem to be refuted, even if such data are often ignored.

Brainwashing proponents also conveniently ignore volitional aspects of recruitment to new religions. Brainwashing theorists such as Delgado (1982) turn predispositions and interest in exotic religions into susceptibilities and vulnerabilities, adopting an orientation toward recruitment which defines the potential convert in completely passive terms, a philosophical posture that itself raises serious ethical problems. Most participants are "seekers", taking an active interest in changing themselves, and they are often using the NRMs to accomplish planned personal change (Straus 1976, 1979). There is growing use of an "active" paradigm in conversion/recruitment research which stresses the predispositional and volitional character of participation. This view is derived from research findings that *many participants actually seek out NRMs to accomplish personal goals* (Richardson 1985a). This nonvolitional view ignores an important aspect of classical work in the brainwashing tradition. For instance, Lifton's (1963) work clearly shows the voluntaristic character of much of the thought reform which went on in China (his last chapter discusses voluntaristic personal change).

Therapeutic effects of participation ignored

Brainwashing theorists usually claim that participation in NRMs is a negative experience, claims countered by many lines of research. Participation seems to have a generally positive impact on most participants, an often-replicated finding which undercuts brainwashing arguments, but is usually ignored by proponents of such theories. Robbins and Anthony (1982) summarized positive effects which have been found, listing ten different therapeutic effects, including reduced neurotic distress, termination of illicit drug use, and increased social compassion. One review of a large literature concerning personality assessment of participants concluded (Richardson 1985b: 221): "Personality assessments of these group members reveal that life in the new religions is often therapeutic instead of harmful." Kilbourne (1986) drew similar conclusions in his assessment of outcomes from participation, after finding, for instance, that members of the Unification Church felt they were getting more from their participation than did matched samples of young Presbyterians and Catholics.

Psychiatrist Marc Galanter, who has done considerable assessment research on participants in some of the more prominent NRMs, has even posited a general "relief effect" brought about by participation (Galanter 1978). He wanted to find out what about participation leads to such consistent positive effects, in order that therapists can use the techniques themselves. McGuire (1988) found that many ordinary people participate in exotic religious groups in a search of alternatives to modern medicine, and many think themselves the better for the experience. To ignore such scholarly conclusions seems ethically quite questionable.

Large research tradition and "normal" explanations ignored

There has been a huge amount of research done on recruitment to and participation in the new religious groups and movements, research almost totally ignored by brainwashing theorists. This work, which is summarized in such reviews as Greil and Rudy (1984), Richardson (1985a), and Robbins (1985), applies standard theories from sociology, social psychology, and psychology to explain why youths join such groups. These explanations seem quite adequate to explain participation, without any "black box" of mystical psychotechnology such as offered by brainwashing theorists.

Examples of such "normalizing" research include Heirich's (1977) study of the Charismatic Renewal Movement, Pilarzyk's (1978) comparison of conversion in the Divine Light Mission and the Hare Krishna, Straus's (1981) "naturalistic social psychological" explanation of seeking religious experiences, Solomon's (1983) work on the social psychology of participation in the Unification Church, and the examination of process models of conversion to the Jesus Movement (Richardson, et al. 1979). The ethics of ignoring such work, while propounding empirically weak notions such as brainwashing and mind control, seem questionable.

Lack of "success" of new religions disregarded

Another obvious problem with brainwashing explanations concerns assuming (and misinforming the public about) the efficacy of the powerful recruitment techniques allegedly used by the new religious groups. Most NRMs are actually quite small: the Unification Church probably never had over 10,000 American members, and can now boast only 2,000 to 3,000 members in the US; the American Hare Krishna may not have achieved even the size of the Unification Church . . . Most other NRMs have had similar problems recruiting large numbers of participants.

A related problem concerns attrition rates for the new religions. As a number of scholars have noted, most participants in the new groups remain for only a short time, and most of those proselytized simply ignore or rebuff recruiters and go on with their normal lives (Bird and Reimer 1982; Barker 1984; Galanter 1980). Many people leave the groups after being in them relatively short periods

(Wright 1987; Skonovd 1983; Richardson et al. 1986).

An example of one well publicized group . . . is The Family (formerly the Children of God) which has had over 57,000 young people worldwide join it over the group's 25 year history. However, the group has only about 3,000 adult members worldwide at this time, which could be construed to mean they have a serious attrition problem!

These histories of meager growth and/or rapid decline raise serious questions about the efficacy of brainwashing explanations of participation. Such powerful techniques should have resulted in much larger groups, a fact conveniently ignored by brainwashing proponents, who seem intent on raising the level of hysteria about NRMs, through misleading the public about their size and efficiency in keeping members.

"Brainwashing" as its own explanation

A last critique of brainwashing theories is that they are self-perpetuating, through "therapy" offered those who leave, especially those forcibly deprogrammed. As Solomon (1981) has concluded, those who are deprogrammed often accept the views which deprogrammers use to justify their actions, and which are promoted to the deprogramee as reasons for cooperating with the deprogramming. These views usually include a belief in brainwashing theories. One could say that a successful deprogramming is one in which the deprogrammee comes to accept the view that they were brainwashed, and are now being rescued. Solomon's finding has been collaborated by other research on those who leave, including by Lewis (1986), Lewis and Bromley (1987), and Wright (1987). The social psychological truth that such ideas are *learned interpretations or accounts* undercuts truth claims by brainwashing theorists.

Conclusions

The preceding critique indicates that brainwashing theories of participation in new religions fail to take into account considerable data about participation in such groups. However, many people still accept such theories, and high levels of concern about the "cult menace" exist, in part because of the promotion of ideologically based brainwashing theories of participation. Serious attention should be paid to alternative explanations which demystify the process of recruitment to and participation in the new religions.

Motivations for accepting such empirically weak theories as "brainwashing" should be examined. Also, those who propound brainwashing theories of participation need to examine the ethics of promoting such powerful "social weapons" against minority religions. When such theories are used to limit people's religious freedom and personal growth, then the society itself may suffer.

References

Anthony, D. 1990. "Religious Movements and Brainwashing Litigation: Evaluating Key Testimony." Pp. 295–344 in T. Robbins and D. Anthony (eds.), *In Gods We Trust*. New Brunswick: NJ: Transaction Books.

Anthony, D. and T. Robbins 1992. "Law, Social Science and the 'Brainwashing' Exception in the First Amendment." *Behavioral Sciences and the Law* 10: 5–30.

Barker, E. 1984. *The Making of a Moonie: Choice or Brainwashing?* Oxford: Blackwell.

Beckford, J. 1978. "Accounting for Conversion." *British Journal of Sociology* 29 (2): 249–62.

——1985. *Cult Controversies: The Societal Response to the New Religious Movements*. London: Tavistock.

Biderman, A. 1962. "The Image of 'Brainwashing'." *Public Opinion Quarterly* 26: 547–63.

Bird, F. and W. Reimer 1982. "A Sociological Analysis of New Religious and Para-religious Movements." *Journal for the Scientific Study of Religion* 21 (1): 1–14.

Bromley, D. and J. T. Richardson (eds.) 1983. *The Brainwashing/Deprogramming Controversy: Sociological, Psychology, Legal, and Historical Perspectives*. New York: Edwin Mellen.

Bromley, D. and T. Robbins 1992. "The Role of Government in Regulating New and Non-conventional Religions." In J. Wood and D. Davis (eds.), *The Role of Government in Monitor-*
ing and Regulating Religion in Public Life. Waco, TX: Baylor University.

Delgado, R. 1982. "Cults and Conversion: The Case for Informed Consent" *Georgia Law Review* 16: 533–74.

DeWitt, J. 1991. "Novel Scientific Evidence and the Juror: A Social Psychological Approach to the *Frye*/Relevancy Controversy." Doctoral Dissertation in Social Psychology, University of Nevada, Reno.

Fort, J. 1983. "What is Brainwashing and Who Says So?" In B. Kilbourne (ed.), *Scientific Research and New Religions: Divergent Perspectives*. San Francisco, CA: American Assoc. for the Advancement of Science, Pacific Division.

Galanter, M. 1978. "The 'Relief Effect': A Socio-biological Model of Neurotic Distress and Large Group Therapy." *American Journal of Psychiatry* 135, 588–91.

——1980. "Psychological Induction in the Large-Group: Findings from a Modern Religious Sect." *American Journal of Psychiatry* 137: 1574–9.

Greil, A. and D. Rudy 1984. "What Have We Learned About Process Models of Conversion? An Examination of Ten Studies." *Sociological Analysis* 54 (3): 115–25.

Heirich, M. 1977. "Change of Heart: A Test of Some Widely Held Theories About Religious Conversion." *American Journal of Sociology* 85 (3): 653–80.

Kilbourne, B. 1986. "Equity or Exploitation? The Case of the Unification Church." *Review of Religious Research* 28: 143–50.

Kilbourne, B. and J. Richardson 1984. "Psychotherapy and New Religions in a Pluralistic Society." *American Psychologist* 39 (3): 237–51.

Latkin, C. 1991. "Vice and Device: Social Control of Intergroup Conflict." *Sociological Analysis* 52: 363–78.

Lewis, J. 1986. "Reconstructing the Cult Experience: Post-Involvement Attitudes as a Function of Mode of Exit and Post-Involvement Socialization." *Sociological Analysis* 46: 151–9.

Lewis, J. and D. Bromley 1987. "The Cult Withdrawal Syndrome: A Case of Misattribution of Cause?" *Journal for the Scientific Study of Religion* 26 (4): 508—22.

Lifton, R. 1963. *Thought Reform and the Psychology of Totalism*. New York: Norton.

——1985. "Cult Processes, Religious Liberty and Religious Totalism." Pp. 59–70 in T. Robbins, W. Shepherd, and J. McBride (eds.), *Cults, Culture and the Law*. Chico, CA: Scholars Press.

Lofland, J. 1978. " 'Becoming a World-saver' Revisited." In J. Richardson (ed.), *Conversion Careers*. Beverly Hills, CA: Sage.

McGuire, M. 1988. *Ritual Healing in Suburban America*. New Brunswick, NJ: Rutgers University Press.

Pilarzyk, T. 1978. "Conversion and Alienation Processes in the Youth Culture." *Pacific Sociological Review* 21 (4): 379–405.

Richardson, J. T. 1985a. "Active versus Passive Converts: Paradigm Conflict in Conversion/ Recruitment Research." *Journal for the Scientific Study of Religion* 24: 163–79.

Richardson, J. T. 1985b. "Psychological and Psychiatric Studies of New Religions." In L. Brown (ed.), *Advances in the Psychology of Religion*. New York: Pergamon Press.

——1991. "Cult/Brainwashing Cases and Freedom of Religion." *Journal of Church and State* 33: 55–74.

——1992. "Public Opinion and the Tax Evasion Trial of Reverend Moon." *Behavioral Sciences and the Law* 10: 53–64.

——1993. "The Concept of 'Cult': From Sociological–Technical to Popular–Negative." *Review of Religious Research* 34: 348–56.

——1995. "Legal Status of Minority Religions in the United States." *Social Compass* 42 (2): 249–64.

Richardson, J. T. and B. Kilbourne 1983. "Classical and Contemporary Brainwashing Models: A Comparison and Critique." Pp. 29–45 in D. Bromley and J. Richardson, op cit.

Richardson, J. T., J. van der Lans, and F. Derks 1986. "Leaving and Labeling: Voluntary and Coerced Disaffiliation from Religious Social Movements." In K. Lang and G. Lang (eds.), *Research in Social Movements, Conflict and Change* 9. Greenwich, CT: JAI Press.

Richardson, J. T., M. Stewart, and R. Simmonds 1979. *Organized Miracles*. New Brunswick, NJ: Transaction.

Robbins, T. 1985. "Government Regulatory Powers and Church Autonomy." *Journal for the Scientific Study of Religion* 24: 237–51.

——1988. *Cults, Converts and Charisma: The Soci-*

ology of New Religious Movements. Newbury Park, CA; Sage.

Robbins, T. and D. Anthony 1982. "Deprogramming, Brainwashing, and the Medicalization of Deviant Religious Groups." *Social Problems* 29: 283–97.

Robbins, T., D. Anthony, and J. McCarthy 1983."Legitimating Repression." Pp. 319–28 in D. Bromley and J. T. Richardson, op cit.

Schein, E., I. Schneier, and C. Becker 1961. *Coercive Persuasion*. New York: Norton.

Singer, M. 1979. "Coming Out of the Cults." *Psychology Today* 12: 72–82.

Singer, M. and R. Ofshe 1990. " Thought Reform Programs and the Production of Psychiatric Casualties." *Psychiatric Annals* 20: 188–93.

Skonovd, N. 1983. "Leaving the Cultic Religious Milieu." Pp. 91–105 in D. Bromley and J. T. Richardson, op cit.

Solomon, T. 1981. "Integrating the 'Moonie' Experience: A Survey of Ex-members of the Unification Church." In T. Robbins and D. Anthony (ed.), *In Gods We Trust*. New Brunswick, NJ: Transaction.

Solomon, T. 1983. "Programming and Deprogramming the 'Moonies': Social Psychology Applied." Pp. 163–81 in D. Bromley and J. T. Richardson, op cit.

Straus, R. 1976. "Changing Oneself: Seekers and the Creative Transformation of Life Experience." In J. Lofland (ed.), *Doing Social Life*. New York: Wiley.

——1979. "Religious Conversion as a Personal and Collective Accomplishment." *Sociological Analysis* 40: 158–65.

——1981. "A Social-Psychology of Religious Experience: A Naturalistic Approach." *Sociological Analysis* 42: 57–67.

Van Driel, B. and J. T. Richardson 1988. "Print Media Coverage of New Religious Movements: A Longitudinal Study." *Journal of Communication* 36 (3): 37–61.

Wright, S. 1987. *Leaving the Cults: The Dynamics of Defection*. Washington, DC: Society for the Scientific Study of Religion.

CHAPTER ELEVEN

Constructing Cultist "Mind Control"

THOMAS ROBBINS

Who am I to say that's crazy
Love will make you blind
In the church of the poison mind
Culture Club

Introduction

Facts and values are badly entangled in controversies over "cults." Can it be plausibly maintained that the analysis of social processes in terms of "brainwashing" or "coercive persuasion" is primarily an objective scientific matter which can be detached from judgmental ideological and policy considerations? Concepts such as "brainwashing" or "mind control" are inherently normative. Szasz (1976: 10) notes, "We do not call all types of personal or psychological influences 'brainwashing.' We reserve this term for influences of which we disapprove." The application of such concepts to a given group necessarily stigmatizes that group; however, the stigma is frequently primarily *connotative*. It does not derive directly from what is actually empirically established about the group in question but from the choice of terminology or the interpretive framework from which empirical observations are considered.

This essay will examine the rhetorical conventions, underlying assumptions, interpretive frameworks, and epistemological rules which make possible the brainwashing allegations against cults, i.e., an exercise in demystification. It is *not* our contention that authoritarian and "totalistic" sects do not present some difficulties for American institutions or that there aren't "abuses" in a number of areas perpetrated by some groups, or that legal measures and controls may not sometimes be appropriate. We do assume, however, that there is a certain relativity to "social problems" which may be viewed as *social movements* striving to define certain aspects of reality as problematic and requiring social action (Mauss 1975). "It is the conflict over the 'definition of reality' that provides the heart of any 'social problem'" (Wolf-Petrusky 1979: 2).[1] A "Politics of reality" operates (Goode 1968). Allegations of brainwashing and coercive mind control on the part of cults are thus essentially *interpretive* and involve assumptions and frames of reference which interpenetrate the "objective facts." Finally, it is our view that the overwhelming popular, legal, and scholarly focus on the *processes by which individuals become and remain committed to cults* is misleading in the sense that it shifts attention away from what we consider the ultimate sources of social and professional hostility to cults. We see the issue of coercive persuasion in cults as an ideological "superstructure" which mystifies an underlying "base" entailing threats posed by today's movements to various norms, groups, and institutions.

Underlying Sources of Tension

Beckford (1979), Robbins and Anthony (1982), Shupe and Bromley (1980), and others have discussed the underlying sources of tension between contemporary religious movements and various groups and institutions which appear to be ranged against them. These factors may be briefly summarized: (1) Groups such as Hare Krishna or the Unification Church may be said to be *incivil* religions which claim a monopoly of spiritual truth and legitimacy and in so doing contravene American civil religion *qua* "religion of civility" (Hammond 1981; Cuddihy 1978; Robbins 1984b). (2) Such groups are frequently communal and *totalistic* and thus additionally contravene the norm of personal autonomy (Beckford 1979) and the value of individualism, which is central to modern Western culture. (3) Groups such as Scientology or the Unification Church are highly *diversified and multifunctional* and therefore compete with and threaten many groups and structures in modern society (Robbins 1981, 1984a). (3a) Close-knit, totalistic "cults" operate as family surrogates and thus disturb the parents and relatives of converts (Bromley et al. 1983; Schwartz and Kaslow 1979), who are also concerned with converts' termination of conventional career goals. (3b) Dynamic religious movements diminish the pool of young persons available to participate in conventional churches and denominations; moreover, religious movements elicit an intense and diffuse commitment from converts which contrasts with the limited commitment of most churchgoers (Shupe and Bromley 1980). (3c) Gurus and new movements compete with certified secular therapists and healers; moreover, the latter are increasingly taking advantage of opportunities as counselors, rehabilitators and quasi-deprogrammers of "cult victims" and families traumatized by the "loss" of a member to a close-knit movement (Robbins and Anthony 1982). The conflict between "cults" and "shrinks" also has an ideological dimension involving the conflict between the socially adjustive ethos of mental health and the various deviant visions of transcendence, apocalyptic transformation, mystery and ecstacy (Anthony and Robbins 1980; Anthony et al. 1977). (4) The totalism and multifunctionality of some movements encourages a strong dependency on the part of devotees, who may be subject to *exploitation* (Robbins 1981; Thomas 1981). (5) Finally, the totalism, diversification, and transformative visions of cults burst the normative bounds of a largely "secular" culture, and in particular, repudiate the expected differentiation of secular and religious spheres of action (Anthony and Robbins 1980). Some new religions do not "know their place."

These troublesome aspects of "cults" *would cause concern even if individuals entered and remained in cults voluntarily.* However, in the context of the constitutional guarantee of "free exercise of religion," it is difficult to constrain or control deviant religious movements. There is a paradox to freedom: one cannot be truly free unless one is free to surrender freedom. However, this consideration, and civil libertarian objections to action against cults, can be obviated if it is established that in fact the involvement of converts in offending movements is *involuntary* by virtue of "coercive" tactics of recruitment and indoctrination plus consequent psycopathology and converts' diminished rational capacity. The "cult problem" is thus "medicalized" (Robbins and Anthony 1982). Cultist claims to "free exercise of religion" are neutralized by the implication that cultist religion is not really *free* because cults "coerce" their members into joining and remaining and because the latter may lose their capacity for decision-making.[2] Discourse on cults is thus displaced to models of conversion and persuasion, and disputes over how persons enter and leave (or don't leave) cults. In effect, what is considered is not so much the nature and goals of these groups but their procedures of recruitment and indoctrination (Beckford 1979).

In the bulk of this essay we will discuss the assumptions and conventions of reasoning and rhetoric which constitute the "issue" of "forced conversion" in religious movements. We will discuss the following: (1) the simultaneous employment of critical external perspective to analyze and evaluate processes within cults and an empathic internal perspective to interpret processes entailing the seizure, "deprogramming," and "rehabilitation" of devotees; (2) "epistemological manicheanism," which imputes absolute truth to the accounts of hostile apostates and nullifies the accounts of present cult converts as insincere or delusory; (3) the use of a broad and only tenuously bounded concept of "coercion"; (4) the assumption that it is intrinsically "coercive" or reprehensible for movements to recruit or "target" structurally available or "vulnerable" persons; and (5) exaggeration of the extent and effect of deception utilized as a recruiting tactic by some groups.

Epistemological Issues: Internal and External Interpretive Frameworks

Many elements involved in controversies over alleged cultist brainwashing involve *transvaluational conflicts*. Behaviors and processes which might otherwise be seen mainly as indications of intense religious commitment, zeolotry, and dogmatic sectarianism are reinterpreted as signs of pathological mind control. Repetitive chanting, "obsessive prayer," repetitive tasks, evocations of sin and guilt, and "intense peer pressure" are viewed as "coercive" (or even "hypnotic") processes which paralyze free will and enslave the devotee (e.g., State of New York 1981). Speaking in tongues is considered by some clinicians as an aspect of coercive mind control (Mackey 1983). Cult-induced psychopathology and "thought disorders" are inferred from a convert's unconcern with conventional career goals, stereotyped and dogmatic responses to questions (Delgado 1977), and from an alleged pattern of absolutist and polarized thinking which impairs cognition such that "the thinking process is limited to a black–white totalistic perspective where everything external to the cult is evil and everything within is good" (Rosenzweig 1979: 150–1.

Any social process can be evaluated from two perspectives: an empathic *internal* or actors' phenomenological perspective or an *external* critical observer's perspective. As we have seen, evocations of sin and guilt, repetitive chanting, and "obsessive prayer" are interpreted as "coercive processes" which destroy free will, although the application of an alternative perspective would yield different interpretations.

It is arguable that the case against cults with respect to brainwashing is grounded in the simultaneous employment of a *critical external perspective* to interpret processes within religious movements, and an *empathic internal perspective* to evaluate activities in which movement participants are pressed to de-convert and guided in the negative reinterpretation of their experiences in stigmatized movements. However, it is also arguable that defenses of cults against mind-control allegations tend to entail the combination of a critical external perspective on deprogramming and an empathic "inner" or phenomenological perspective on processes within controversial new movements.

Defenders of controversial religious groups have protested the radical transvaluation implicit in some applications of external perspectives. A civil liberties lawyer criticizes "the name calling which is typical of programs of denigration."

> A religion becomes a cult; proselytization becomes brainwashing; persuasion becomes propaganda; missionaries become subversive agents; retreats, monasteries, and convents become prisons; holy ritual becomes bizarre conduct; religious observance becomes aberrant behavior; devotion and meditation become psychopathic trances. (Gutman 1977: 210–11)

Another legal writer maintains that arguments in support of deprogramming essentially transvalue the *intensity of faith* in inferring psychopathology or coercion from items such as total involvement in a movement, unconcern with public affairs, dualistic thinking, etc. Converts who "subordinate their reason to imperatives of faith" and "demonstrate the depth of their commitment by insisting upon their beliefs as ultimate concerns, should not find the intensity of their faith being used as proof of their incompetence" (Shapiro 1978: 795).

In legal terms, Shapiro is arguing that the use of allegations of polarized thinking or unconcern with public affairs as rationales for state intervention violates the *absolute* quality of freedom of belief. But, whatever the legalities, clinicians may still insist that certain behavioral and thought patterns are objectively coercive or pathological or constitute mind control, notwithstanding legal constraints on the use of such allegations or the traditional quality of behavior such as glossolalia. On the other hand, some sociologists have argued that the behavioral and linguistic patterns from which clinicians have inferred a general "depersonalization" or a basic alteration of personality may really be indicative of *situationally specific role behavior* (Balch 1980). The different conceptual frameworks of sociologists, civil libertarian lawyers, and students of religion produce different interpretations of the same phenomenon.

It is important to note that conflicts of internal vs. external perspectives also emerge with respect to *counter-cult activities*. A clinical psychologist who supports the practice of deprogramming comments, "Although lurid details of deprogramming atrocities have been popularly supplied by cults to the press, the process is nothing more than an intense period of information giving" (Singer 1978: 17). Alternatively, deprogramming has been *externally* viewed as coercive persuasion (Kim 1978) or even something akin to exorcism (Shupe et al. 1978).

Many elements involved in controversies over alleged cultist brainwashing entail transvaluational conflicts related to alternative internal vs. external perspectives. The display of affection toward new and potential converts ("love bombing"), which might be interpreted as a kindness or an idealistic manifestation of devotees' belief that their relationship to spiritual truth and divine love enables them to radiate love and win others to truth, is also commonly interpreted as a sinister "coercive" technique (Singer 1978). Yet successfully deprogrammed ex-devotees have enthused over the warmly supportive and "familial" milieu at post-deprogramming "rehabilitation" centers such as the Freedom of Thought Foundation (e.g., Underwood and Underwood 1979). Could this also be "love bombing"? One study indicates that processes

of deprogramming, intervention, and therapy appear to exert influence on ex-cultists in the direction of assisting them to reinterpret their experiences in terms of brainwashing (Solomon 1981). In this connection, the literature of sociology is replete with "external" conceptualizations of psychotherapy as a persuasive process, a process of thought reform, a context of conversion, a context of negotiation and bargaining in which the greater power of the therapist is crucial, or a social control device (Frank 1980; Schur 1980).

The case against cults with respect to alleged brainwashing tends to be grounded in *the simultaneous employment of a critical external perspective to evaluate and analyze processes within movements and an emphatic internal perspective to interpret the activities outside of religious movements through which devotees are physically coerced, pressed to de-convert, or guided in the reinterpretation of cultist experiences.* Likewise, the polemical defense of cults tends to combine a critical external perspective on deprogramming and anti-cult activities with an emphatic internal orientation toward what goes on in cults (e.g., Coleman 1982). Since so many cult issues involve transvaluational conflicts, one's evaluation of conflicting claims may be largely a function of one's *a priori* interpretive framework or perspective.

Epistemological Manicheanism

An additional aspect of the epistemological dimension of cult-brainwashing controversies is the issue of *who is a credible witness*. This is the problem of evaluating the conflicting testimonies of present devotees and apostates. Some critics of cults seem to embrace a kind of epistemological manicheanism whereby the accounts of recriminating ex-devotees are acceptable at face value while the accounts of current devotees are dismissed as manifesting false consciousness derivative from mind control or self-delusion.[3] However, defenders of cults have been criticized – perhaps justly – for too readily discounting the testimonies of ex-converts because they are allegedly under the influence of new anti-cult reference groups or their recriminations against cults are self-justifying, while naively accepting the accounts of current devotees (Zerin 1982c). Doubts have been cast on the accounts of fervent devotees (Schwartz and Zemel 1980), and knowledgeable circumspection has also been urged with respect to the accounts of ex-converts whose interpretations have been influenced by deprogrammers, therapists, parents, and anti-cults activists (Beckford 1978; Solomon 1981) and whose current interpretations may function to disavow deviant stigma and facilitate social and familial reintegration. Epistemological manicheanism often characterizes both fervent indictments and defenses of cults. One's analysis can too easily be predetermined by one's implicit epistemological exclusionary rule.[4]

Construction of Coercive Persuasion Claims Through Assumptions and Definitions

It is our view that debates about mind control and brainwashing in cults are inherently inconclusive. Arguments on either side depend upon arbitrary or *a priori* assumptions, interpretive frameworks, and linguistic conventions. Our argument does not imply that reprehensible manipulative practices and strong peer pressures are not present in the proselytization and indoctrination repertoires of some movements. However, it is implied that certain key issues are assumptive, definitional, or epistemological, and thus in a sense *ideological* and not susceptible to decisive empirical resolution. Propositions may sometimes hinge on the arbitrary use of terms.

Coercion

Arguments to the effect that religious movements "coerce" their participants to remain involved generally depend upon broad conceptions of "coercion" which need not be tangible (e.g., physical), and of which the "victim" need not be aware (Ofshe 1982). Thus, a bill passed by the New York State legislature identified an individual's subjection to "a systematic course of coercive persuasion"

as a necessary condition legitimating the appointment of a guardian over a member of a communal group. "Systematic coercive persuasion" may be inferred from a variety of indices specified in the bill, including "control over information" or the "reduction of decisional capacity" through "performance of repetitious tasks," "performance of repetitious chants, sayings or teachings," or the employment of "intense peer pressure" to induce "feelings of guilt and anxiety" or a "simplistic polarized view of reality" (State of New York 1981).

Can persons be "coerced" by repetitious chanting or by peer pressure in a formally voluntary context? Perhaps, but what has emerged is a *relatively broad and unbounded conception of coercion* which transvalues as reprehensible "coercive" activities which have otherwise been viewed as innocuous religious staples (e.g., repetitious chanting). What pressure cannot be viewed as "coercive" along these lines?

In general, no distinction between "coercive" and "manipulative" processes seems to be made by critics of cults. Disparate processes and pressures arising in cults are labeled "coercive." It is arguable, however, that in common linguistic usage, the term "coercive" is employed to denote a situation in which an order and a threat are communicated such that the "coercee" is *aware that he is being pressured* and that his action is involuntary. Subtle manipulative influence via information control or seductive displays of affection (i.e., Moonist "love bombing") would ordinarily he viewed as *manipulative* rather than coercive processes. Thus, Lofland and Skonovd (1981) distinguish between the manipulated ecstatic arousal or "revivalist" techniques of the "Moonies" and true "coercive conversion" or brainwashing. "Coercion," however, has a stronger negative connotation of the overriding of free will, and is thus an ideologically superior term. Broad conceptions of coercion inevitably have rhetorical and ideological significance because they generalize a negative connotation to disparate situations and groups, which become psychologically and morally equivalent. Formally voluntary associations such as religious movements are sometimes acknowledged to embody a different form of coercive persuasion compared to POW camps, but are then viewed as essentially equal in coerciveness or even *more coercive* than the latter because seductive cultist proselytizing may indeed sometimes be more effective than the techniques used to indoctrinate prisoners. On the other hand, it is arguable that seductive appeals are often more effective than persuasion of captives in part because they are *less coercive* and thus do not elicit the crystallization of a prisoners' adversary culture or resentment syndrome.

The concept of "coercive persuasion" has, in fact, been used in some significant research. A respected model of c.p. is the one developed by Edgar Schein and his colleagues (1961). Schein argues that if the notion of coercive persuasion is to achieve objectivity, it must be seen as transpiring in a wide range of – often culturally valued – contexts, e.g., conventional religious orders, fraternities, mental hospitals, the army. Coercive persuasion is generally stigmatized only when its *goal* is detested, e.g., producing communists or Moonies.

Schein's analysis strives for stringent ideological neutrality. Nevertheless, he may have contributed somewhat to a subjective and stigmatizing use of the concept of coercive persuasion by downplaying an essential distinction between forcible physical restraints (e.g., as in the prisoners of war he studied) and the more voluntaristic contexts to which he aspired to generalize the concept. Notwithstanding this effect, it is important to realize that assumptions about free will are external to Schein's model and some other models (Solomon 1983). "Coercively persuaded" subjects are not necessarily helpless robots (Shapiro 1983).

In rhetorical applications of c.p. models an unexamined and arbitrary assumption is often made with regard to the *involuntary* nature of the involvement of persons involved in movements allegedly utilizing coercive persuasion. References to "forced conversions" and similar notions arise (e.g., Schwartz and Isser 1981), although the inference as to absence of volition is not warranted by the mere technical applicability of c.p. models (Shapiro 1978,

1983; Solomon 1983). Interesting in this respect is the use by Singer (1979) and Zerin (1982a) of the vocabulary of "technologies" of coercive persuasion employed by cults, as if influence processes in cults involved precise instruments or machines operating automatically on passive cogs. In short, arguments as to the involuntary quality of involvements are often supported more by connotative imagery and rhetorical reification than by sophisticated applications of models of coercive persuasion or thought reform.

Models of "coercive persuasion," "brainwashing," and "thought reform" *vary in the stringency of their existential criteria* (Richardson and Kilbourne 1983). Sargent (1961) interprets religious revivals as a form of brainwashing. Schein (1961) model is the broadest and is clearly applicable to cults, as well as to college fraternities, reputable religious orders, etc. Lifton's well-known model (1961) of "thought reform" is applicable to various cults (Richardson et al. 1972; Stoner and Parke 1977: 272–6), and is probably applicable to any authoritarian and dogmatic sect. Recently, Lofland and Skonovd (1981) have argued that Lifton's criteria embody "ideological totalism," which is a broader phenomenon than true brainwashing or coerced conversion. The latter, according to Lofland and Skonovd, is delineated by the more stringent criteria employed by Somit (1968), which would exclude practically all formally voluntary groups. Given the array of diverse models of varying restrictiveness, *cults can "brainwash" and be "coercive" depending upon which model is employed*. Polemicists tend to conflate different models or shift back and forth between models (Anthony, in preparation).

Finally, neither the growing number of studies reporting that the Unification Church and other cults exhibit substantial voluntary defection rates (Skonovd 1981; Barker 1983; Beckford 1983; Ofshe 1976), nor studies indicating that there is a substantial "failure rate" in cultist indoctrination and recruitment (Barker 1983; Galanter 1980), can settle the debate about cultist coercion. Voluntary defectors and non-recruits can be said to lack the "vulnerability" traits which allow coercive pressures in cults to operate (Zerin 1982a). The basic issue is largely definitional and is not susceptible to empirical resolution.

Targeting the "vulnerable"

One of the characteristics of cultist recruitment and proselytization which is widely excoriated is the alleged tendency of cults to exploit the "vulnerability" of young persons who are lonely, depressed, alienated, or drifting away from social moorings. Cultist mind control is held to be differentiated from respectable, innocuous monasticism by the reluctance of the latter to "concentrate, as do religious cults, on the weak, the depressed, or the psychologically vulnerable" (Delgado 1977: 65). "Cult recruiters tend to look for the 'loners,' the disillusioned or floundering ones and those who are depressed" (Schwartz and Kaslow 1979: 21).

The above allegations concerning the nature of cultist recruitment are not false. Social movements in general tend to recruit individuals who are "structurally available" and who are not integrated into "countervailing networks" which would operate to inhibit recruitment in a new movement (Snow et al. 1980). This is the case with respect to those "authoritarian" movements in which participation is *exclusive* in the sense that "core membership may even be contingent upon the severance of extra-movement interpersonal ties" (ibid: 796). Movement organizations of this type tend to proselytize in public places and to recruit relatively unattached persons who are "more available for movement exploration and participation because of the possession of unscheduled or discretionary time and because of the minimal countervailing risks or sanctions" (ibid: 793). In contrast, groups with less exclusive participation patterns exhibit a greater tendency to "attract members primarily from extramovement interpersonal associations and networks, rather than from public places, i.e., existing members recruit their preconversion friends and associates." Although some stigmatized "cults" such as the Divine Light Mission of Guru Maharaj-Ji (Downton 1979) appear to be of this latter variety and to

have recruited largely from existing interpersonal networks, it appears likely that relatively authoritarian and totalistic groups such as Hare Krishna or the Unification Church recruit many unattached individuals whose lack of binding ties and commitment render them structurally available.[5]

It is arbitrary, however, to stigmatize this mode of recruitment as coercive or reprehensible. Clearly social movements and proselytizing religious sects will "target" the more "vulnerable" potential participants. Young persons occupying transitional and ephemeral statuses (e.g., students) bereft of consolidated careers, salaries, dependents, spouses, and children, and not harmoniously nestled into other affiliative structures such as fraternities or clubs, will surely be prime "targets." Such individuals have *less to lose* in joining a communal sect or a messianic movement than other persons. A greater proportion of "available" persons relative to unavailable persons recruited to a movement would seem to this writer to be indicative of a *voluntary* rather than a "forced" quality of participation. Some sort of hypnotic or "coercive" device might be indicated if a disproportionate number of "unavailable" middle-age executives with large families, numerous dependents, and satisfying social affiliations were recruited.[6]

It also seems rather plausible that unhappy or "alienated" persons who are dissatisfied with either themselves or "the system" are more likely to be recruited to messianic movements than complacent "pharisees." The special importance of messianic religion for "miserable sinners" is a rather traditional evangelical theme. While some persons may be more "vulnerable" to cultist involvement than others (Zerin 1982b), it seems arbitrary to view the "targeting" of such persons as illegitimate or as indications of the involuntary or irrational quality of involvement.[7]

Demonology of deception

The role of deception in the proselytizing of cults is receiving increasing emphasis in allegations of cultist mind control. There appears to be some tendency to *treat deception as a functional equivalent to the raw physical coercion which is used to initially bring individuals into POW or concentration camps.* The absence of the physical coercion, which is a defining attribute of classic brainwashing contexts such as POW camps, is thus neutralized as an indicator of voluntariness or lack of coercion.

The writings of Richard Delgado on cults express succinctly a clear and coherent conception of the crucial role and significance of deception of in cultist mind control:

The process by which an individual becomes a member of certain cults appears arranged in such a way that knowledge and capacity, the classic ingredients of an informed consent, are maintained in an inverse relationship: when capacity is high, the recruit's knowledge of the cult and its practices is low; when knowledge is high, capacity is reduced. (Delgado 1980: 28).[8]

The potential recruit, attending his first meeting, may possess an unimpaired capacity to make rational choices. "Such persons, if given full information about the cult and their future life in it, might well react by leaving. For this reason, the cult may choose to keep secret its identity as a religious organization, the name of its leader or messiah, and the more onerous conditions of membership until it perceives that the victim is 'ready' to receive this information. These details may then be parceled out gradually as the newcomer, as a result of physiological debilitation, guilt manipulation, isolation, and peer pressure, loses the capacity to evaluate them in his ordinary frames of reference" (Delgado 1980: 28–9). The necessary conditions for voluntariness are *knowledge* and *capacity*; however, the cult convert "never has full capacity and knowledge at any given time; one or the other is always impaired to some degree" (ibid: 29). In short, gross deception lures the victim on to the premises where he is fairly quickly relieved of his mental capacity. It is claimed that by the time the veil of deception drops, the disoriented convert is not in a position to take advantage of his knowledge (see also Schwartz and Zemel 1980).

Let us examine some issues arising from Delgado's formulation. First we need to consider the question of *generality*. How typical is Delgado's account?

Let us examine *three examples*. (1) Firstly, it would be difficult for someone to become involved with the Hare Krishna sect *without knowing at the very outset that he had encountered a very eccentric and somewhat regimented communal sect*. The Krishnas are known to solicit funds deceptively, donning wigs and business suits to solicit in airports (Delgado 1982). Such ruses are employed for the purpose of soliciting funds – not warm bodies. Devotees seem relatively straightforward with respect to acknowledging the stringent membership requirements and they do not place intense pressure on marginal hangers-on who attend festivals at the Krishna Temple to become encapsulated in the communal sect.[9] A six-month screening period allows persons who cannot take the discipline to self-select themselves out (Bromley and Shupe 1981).

(2) During the middle 1970s one of the most controversial cults in the northeast was the Church of Bible Understanding (COBU), formerly the Forever Family.[10] Several members were deprogrammed and rehabilitated at the Freedom of Thought Foundation in Tucson, Arizona. Members of this movement wore large buttons saying GET SMART GET SAVED. They would accost one on the streets and inquire. "Do you know the Lord?" The author was invited to visit the loft which a large number of devotees were occupying. After "hanging around" the group for a few days, certain properties of the group were rather obvious (and, in the opinion of the writer, would have been readily apparent to anyone). Though not as well-organized as the Krishnas or "Moonies," the sect was regimented and authoritarian. Large numbers of converts lived in decidedly unhygienic conditions in lofts from which they were later evicted on health grounds. The members were expected to take odd jobs and relinquish their pay to the leaders, who researched and publicized available jobs. The group focused on the Bible and had an eccentric exegetical technique of "color coding" scriptural passages. Doubtless, there

were salient aspects of the movement's lifestyle and interactional process which escaped the writer during his brief observation. What is significant, however, is that *a number of rather unpleasant aspects of the group were immediately apparent.* These were not elaborately or effectively concealed. It would be impossible to be fooled into thinking that this was a discussion club or a respectable church outreach program. Recruits were presumably individuals who were willing to sacrifice amenities and "take risks" of various sorts to pursue truth and salvation.

(3) Finally, the writer attended a three-day indoctrination workshop sponsored by the Unification Church in 1974. There was a salient element of deception: the link to Reverend Sun Myung Moon was not emphasized, and the writer was struck by the absence of pictures of the leader of the movement, whom the writer already knew to be an object of devotion to followers. But other elements of the workshop were relatively straightforward. There was not real concealment of the eccentric "religious" character of the group. Lectures commenced on the first day and dealt with the nature and relationship of God and man, and other matters derived from church doctrine. The regimented character of the movement could easily be inferred from the disciplined and ascetic quality of the workshop; men and women were separated; participants were awakened at 7:00 for calisthenics. There were 5–8 hours of lectures each day. There was clearly a manipulative quality to the workshop, although it seemed relatively crude and heavy-handed.[11] But *extreme deception entailing concealment of the basic nature of the group simply did not seem to have been the case.*

It does not seem likely that deception in the above groups was of sufficient magnitude to account for the initial involvements of participants. The latter would likely be aware of the eccentric, authoritarian, and ascetic aspects of these groups from the outset.

Another implication of Professor Delgado's analysis needs to be considered. It is clear that Delgado believes that the pre-convert *loses his or her "capacity" during the period in which he is denied knowledge, i.e., deceived.* How long is

that period? In the above examples, which involved very authoritarian communal sects, thorough deception as to the nature of the movement and its internal milieu was not really accomplished. It seems to be the case, however, that some Moonist groups, particularly the "Oakland Family" operation at Booneville, California, utilized a greater degree of deception than that experienced by the writer in New York (Bromley and Shupe 1981). But how long does deception last? No estimates this writer has heard involve a period longer than three weeks. The question thus arises as to *whether a person can actually "lose capacity" during this period?* Conceivably, there might be methods involving brutality and torture which could "break" a person in a matter of weeks or even days. But these methods are not used. Scheflein and Opton (1978) argue that cults do not really utilize *extreme* brainwashing or coercive persuasion methods: "Some might do so if they could, but they cannot, for dehumanization is excruciatingly painful. Most people who were not prisoners, or tied to the group by strong bonds of loyalty, or by lack of anywhere else to go, would leave" (ibid: 60).[12]

Given the likelihood that unmotivated persons will shun a stringently regimented authoritarian milieu, supporters of mind-control allegations are heavily dependent upon claims with regard to deception. Yet it is problematic whether deception is as widespread, extreme, or significant as the influential Delgado model suggests. Cultist deception is really a (reprehensible) foot-in-the-door tactic and cannot plausibly provide the motivation for a person to tolerate otherwise objectionable conditions.[13]

One additional point is worth noting. The Moonist indoctrination center at Booneville, California once utilized deception to a degree which exceeds the manipulation experienced by the author at another Moonist indoctrination center. As Bromley and Shupe (1981) note, the *modus operandi* of the Unification workshop at Booneville has been generalized by opponents of cults and by the media to "cults" in general. Indeed, the pervasive *general stereotype* of the deceptive cult which lures unwary youth to totalistic communes under false premises is largely based on the Unification Church, and in particular, its operation at Booneville (Bromley and Shupe 1981; Robbins and Anthony 1980). The overgeneralization of the Booneville Moonist *modus operandi* to contemporary deviant religious movements in general has been partly a product of fortuitous circumstances (Bromley and Shupe 1981) and partly a deliberate tactic of anti-cultists (ACLU 1977) to exploit the notoriety of the Moon sect. The allegation of widespread cultist mind control is thus constructed in part through an overgeneralization of the extreme deceptive proselytization of one group.[14]

Conclusion

While the manipulative and heavy-handed recruitment and indoctrination practices of some groups cannot be gainsaid, arguments imputing extreme mental coercion, mind control, and brainwashing to cultist practices tend to depend upon arbitrary premises, definitions, and interpretive and epistemological conventions. Arguments in this highly subjective area are too often mystifications which embellish values and biases with the aura of value-free science and clinical objectivity.

As acknowledged in this essay, there are many difficulties and conflicts associated with cults. *These conflicts would be legitimate objects of concern even if commitments to troublesome movements were acknowledged to be voluntary.* Rhetorical mystiques about mind control have the consequence of implying that cultist involvements are involuntary and that devotees are not fully capable of making rational choices. In consequence, these arguments serve as a rationale for legitimating social control measures which treat devotees *as if they were mentally incompetent* without formally labeling them as such and without applying rigorous criteria of civil commitment (cf., State of New York 1981).

The debate over cultist brainwashing will necessarily be inconclusive. The contending parties ground their arguments on differing assumptions, definitions, and epistemological

rules. Nevertheless the debate will continue. The medicalized "mind control" claim articulates a critique of deviant new religions which not only obviates civil libertarian objections to social control but also meets the needs of the various groups which are threatened by or antagonistic to cults: *mental health professionals*, whose role in the rehabilitation of victims of "destructive cultism" is highlighted; *parents*, whose opposition to cults and willingness to forcibly "rescue" cultist progeny are legitimated; *ex-converts*, who may find it meaningful and rewarding to reinterpret their prior involvement with stigmatized groups as basically passive and unmotivated; and *clerics*, who are concerned to avoid appearing to persecute religious competitors. An anti-cult coalition of these groups is possible only *if medical and mental health issues are kept in the forefront* (Robbins and Anthony 1982) and if the medical model is employed in such a way as to disavow the intent to persecute minority beliefs and to stress the psychiatric healing of involuntary pathology.

As argued above, the debate over whether cult devotees are "coerced" via "mind control" and "psychologically imprisoned" will necessarily be inconclusive. To some degree one can choose from an array of brainwashing/coercive/persuasion/ thought reform models with existential criteria of varying stringency, and, by then selecting appropriate background assumptions, imagery, and epistemological rules, "prove" whatever one wishes. The argument will persist, however, because it articulates an "acceptable" indictment of cults which is arguably compatible with respect for religious liberty, and which avoids a direct confrontation with the underlying issue of the limits of "church autonomy" in the context of the increasing diversification of the functions (e.g., educational, political, healing, commercial) of various kinds of religious groups. Because they use "mind control," it has been argued that cults can be set apart from other religious organizations (Delgado 1977), which arguably are not threatened by constraints on cults. Medicalization of deviant religion compartmentalizes issues involving "cults" and obscures some of the underlying conflicts and broader implications of conflicts over contemporary movements. A shift of focus will be necessary to transcend the inconclusive psychologism of debates over brainwashing. Such a shift will not isolate cults as a special theoretical compartment but will reconsider the uneasy general boundary of church and state in the 1980s.[15]

Notes

The author wishes to thank Dick Anthony, whose collaboration with the writer over a number of years contributed to the development of perspectives which are reflected in this essay.

1 Dr. Wolf-Petrusky's unpublished paper, "The Social Construction of the 'Cult Problem'," represents a pioneering formulation, which bears some similarities to the present analysis. However, the present writer's analysis of the construction of anti-cult claims through *a priori* premises, epistemological rules and definitional parameters diverges somewhat from Dr. Wolf-Petrusky's natural history approach, which follows Mauss (1975) more closely. The present writer has only been slightly influenced by the earlier work of Dr. Wolf-Petrusky.

2 Interestingly, the medical model is less salient in conflicts over cults in France and West Germany where norms of civil liberties and religious tolerance are weaker and deviant cults can be directly attacked as anti-social and culturally subversive (Beckford 1981).

3 A recent survey distributed by anti-cult activists (Conway and Siegleman 1982) of psychopathological symptoms among ex-converts made no attempt to include "returnees" or ex-cultists who had returned to their religious groups in their sample. Schwartz and Zemel (1980) suggest that converts' allegations of lack of deception in their recruitment are not credible because acknowledgment of deception would be cognitively dissonant with their present fervent belief. The authors do not apply a cognitive dissonance argument to the claims of recriminating ex-cultists for whom a lack of deception and manipulation may be dissonant with their present disillusionment, anger, and activism.

4 It is worth noting in this connection that several recent studies (Skonovd 1981; Wright 1983) have indicated that there are substantial numbers of ex-cultists who do *not* recriminate against cults or interpret their experiences in terms of brainwashing in the manner of those embittered deprogrammed apostates whose testimonies and allegations have been widely publicized. The absolute contrast of devotees' and ex-devotees' accounts is an appearance which arises from the fact that more public attention has been focused on a subset of ex-devotees who have usually been deprogrammed and have become assimilated to an anti-cult subculture or social network (Solomon 1981).

5 Snow et al. (1980) present data comparing Hare Krishna with the less totalistic Nicheren Shoshu movement, which supports their argument. A more recent study of Hare Krishna by Rochford (1982) came up with somewhat different findings. Krishna recruitment patterns varied from city to city, and overall, there was significant recruitment from social networks. See Wallis and Bruce (1982) for a conceptual critique of the "structural availability" concept.

6 Interestingly, *elderly* persons also appear to be prime "targets" for cults (see, for example, ABC-TV's *20/20* program, November 24, report on an eternal life cult). Elderly persons, like young persons, are often poorly integrated into the occupational structure. Such marginality *qua* "rolelessness" may enhance one's susceptibility to the appeals of extraordinary groups.

7 The concept of "vulnerability" seems to have an interesting affective connotation, i.e., one isn't considered "vulnerable" to something positive such as a promotion. The implicit imagery is mildly medicalistic, i.e., a "vulnerable" person is like a weakened organism whose defenses against germs have been impaired.

8 See also Delgado (1977, 1982).

9 The author conducted preliminary participant observation among Hare Krishnas in 1969–70 in Chapel Hill, North Carolina. A close colleague and collaborator conducted observation in Berkeley during 1970–2.

10 F. E. Galler, "Inside a New York Cult," *New York Daily News* series (Jan. 1–4, 1979). The author briefly observed this group in the middle 1970s.

11 For a description of the workshop as observed by the author, see Robbins et al. (1976).

12 Some cult critics have acknowledged that it is *social bonds* which "incapacitate" a devotee to leave the group. By the time a neophyte Moonie is undeceived as to the identity of the

group he has joined, he is "bonded" to the group and its members one cannot leave (Edwards 1983). But do we generally consider social bonds to nullify free will, e.g., is someone who loves his spouse a "prisoner" in his or her marriage?

13 A Superior Court judge in San Francisco recently issued a 30-page opinion granting summary judgment for the defendants in a case in which two former "Moonies" sued the Unification Church for "false imprisonment" (through mental coercion) and fraud. The ex-converts had initially been deceived as to the identity of the group, and claimed that by the time the deception was lifted (after 2–3 weeks) they had become psychologically dependent upon the group and were not capable of choosing to leave voluntarily. The court found that, initial deception notwithstanding, the plaintiffs' lengthy subsequent involvement with the church was essentially voluntary; moreover, coercive persuasion without force or threat of force was not sufficient to establish actual imprisonment. See *Molko and Leal vs. Holy Spirit Association For The Unification of World Christianity, et al.*, California Superior Court. City and County of San Francisco, Department No. 3, Order No. 769–529. The facts of this case, involving both deception and alleged "coercive persuasion," closely correspond to the model used by Delgado (1982) in proposing a civil remedy for cultist mind control.

14 See Schwartz and Kaslow (1982) for a description of a "typical" cultist recruitment scenario, which appears in fact to be a description of the Notorious Moonist "Camp K" at Booneville, California; which, in our view, is of limited generality.

15 It has recently been argued (Robbins 1984a) that a general crisis of church and state is emerging in the United States because of three converging factors: (1) the increasing state regulation of "secular" organizations, from which "churches" are exempt; (2) the increasing functional diversification of religious groups which increasingly perform functions similar to those of secular organizations; and (3) the failure of the liberal ideal of providing goods, services, and meanings essential to enhance the "quality of life" under state auspices. As religious groups such as evangelicals or cults strive to "fill the gap" they increasingly become embroiled in conflicts with other groups and institutions (e.g., minorities who feel dependent upon public services). The debate over "mind control" obscures the linkage between controversies over cults and other "church autonomy" conflicts.

References

American Civil Liberties Union 1977. *Deprogramming: Documenting the Issue.* New York.

Anthony, Dick. Monograph on Cults and Coercist Persuasion. In Preparation.

Anthony, Dick and Thomas Robbins. 1980. "A Demonology of Cults." *Inquiry* 3, 15: 9–11.

Anthony, Dick, Thomas Robbins, Madalyn Doucas, and Thomas Curtis. 1977. "Patients and Pilgrims: Changing attitudes toward psychotherapy of converts to Eastern mystical converts." *American Behavorial Scientist* 20, 6: 861–86.

Balch, Robert W. 1980 "Looking Behind the Scenes in a Religious Cult." *Sociological Analysis* 41 (2): 137–43.

Barker, Eileen. 1983. "Resistable Coercion: The significance of failure rates in conversion and commitment to the Unification Church." Forthcoming in D. Anthony, J. Needleman, and T. Robbins eds. *Conversion, Coercion and Commitment in New Religious Movements.* Unpublished.

Beckford, James. 1978. "Through The Looking-glass and out the other side: Withdrawal from Reverend Moon's Unification Church." *Archives de Sciences des Religions* 45 (1): 71–83.

—— 1979. "Politics and the anticult movement." *Annual Review of the Social Sciences of Religion* 3: 169–90.

—— 1981. "Cults, controversy and control: A comparative analysis of the problems posed by new religious movements in the Federal Republic of Germany and France." *Sociological Analysis* 42, 3: 249–63.

—— 1983. "Conversion and apostasy." Forthcoming in D. Anthony, J. Needleman, and T. Robbins eds. *Conversion, Coercion and Commitment in New Religious Movements.* Unpublished.

Bromley, David and Anson Shupe. 1981. *Strange Gods: The Great American Cult Hoax.* New York: Beacon Press.

Bromley, David, Bruce Busching, and Anson Shupe. 1983. "The Unification Church and the American Family: Strain, Conflict and Control." In E. Barker ed. *New Religious Movements: A Perspective for Understanding Society.* 302–11.

Coleman, Lee. 1982. "Psychiatry: The Faith Breaker." Pamphlet.

Conway, Flo and Jim Siegleman. 1982. "Information Disease: Cults have created a new mental illness." *Science Digest* 90 (1): 86–92.

Cuddihy, John M. 1978. *No Offense: Civil Religion and The Protestant Taste.* New York: Seabury Press.

Delgado, Richard. 1977. "Religious Totalism: Gentle and Ungentle persuasion." *Southern California Law Review* 51: 1–99.

——1978. "Investigating Cults." *New York Times*, Op-ed. (Dec. 27, 1978): A27.

——1979–80. "Religious Totalism as Slavery." *New York University Review of Law and Social Change* 9: 51–68.

——1980. "Limits to Proselytizing." *Society* 17 (March/April): 25–32.

——1982. "Cults and Conversion: The Case for Informed Consent" *Georgia Law Review* 16 (3): 533–74.

Downton, James. 1979. *Sacred Journeys: The Conversion of Young Americans to the Divine Light Mission.* New York: Columbia University Press.

Edwards, Chris. 1983. "The Nightmare of Cult Life." Lecture at Central Michigan University, January 25.

Frank, Jerome. 1980. *Persuasion and Healing.* New York: Schocken.

Galanter, Marc. 1980. "Psychological Induction Into the Large-group: Findings from a Modern Religious Sect." *American Journal of Psychiatry* 137: (112).

Goode, Eric. 1968. "Marijuana and the Politics of Reality." *Journal of Health and Social Behavior* 10: 83–94.

Hammond, Phillip. 1981. "Civil Religion and New Movements." In Robert Bellah and Phillip Hammond eds. *Varieties of Civil Religion.* New York: Harpers, 1981.

Kim, Byong-Suh. 1978. "Deprogramming and Subjective Reality." *Sociological Analysis* 40 (3): 197–208.

Lifton, Robert. 1961. *Chinese Thought Reform and the Psychology of Totalism.* New York: Norton.

Lofland, John and Norman Skonovd. 1981. "Conversion Motifs." *Journal for the Scientific Study of Religion* 20 (4): 373–85.

Mackey, Aurora. 1983. "The truth about cults." *Teen Magazine* vol. 27, no. 4 (April): 12–14 and 97.

Mauss, Armand. 1975. *Social Problems as Social Movements.* Philadelphia: Lippincott.

Ofshe, Richard. 1976. "Synanon: The people's business." Pp. 116–38 in C. Glock and R. Bellah eds. *The New Religious Consciousness.* Berkeley: University of California Press.

——1980. "The social development of the Synanon cult: The managerial strategy of organi-

zation transformation." *Sociological Analysis* 41 (2): 109–27.

——1982. "Regulating diversified social movements." Seminar presentation at the Graduate Theological Union, April.

——1983. "The role of out-of-awareness of influence in the creation of dependence on a group: An alternative to brainwashing theories." Forthcoming in D. Anthony, J. Needleman, and T. Robbins, *Conversion, Coercion and Commitment in New Religious Movements.* Unpublished.

Richardson, James and Brock Kilbourne. 1983. "Classical and contemporary applications of brainwashing models: A comparison and critique." In D. Bromley and J. Richardson, *The Brainwashing–Deprogramming Controversy.* Toronto: Mellon.

Richardson, James, Robert Simmonds, and Mary Harder. 1972. "Thought Reform and the Jesus Movement." *Youth and Society* 4: 185–200.

Robbins, Thomas. 1979. "Cults and the therapeutic state." *Social Policy* 10 (1): 42–6.

——1979–80. "Religious movements, the state and the law." *New York University Review of Law and Social Change* 9 (1): 33–50.

——1981. "Church, state and cult." *Sociological Analysis* 42 (3): 209–25.

——1984a. "Religious Movements and the Intensification of Church/State Tensions." *Society* 21 (4): May/June.

——1984b. Incivil religions and religious deprogramming. Presented to the Midwest Sociological Society, Chicago.

Robbins, Thomas and Dick Anthony. 1980. "The limits of 'coercive persuasion' as an explanation for conversion to authoritarian sects." *Political Psychology* 2 (1): 22–37.

——1981. "Harrassing cults." *New York Times*, Op-ed (Oct. 16): A31.

——1982. "Brainwashing, deprogramming and the medicalization of deviant religious groups." *Social Problems* 29, 3: 283–97; 2 (2): 22–6.

Robbins, Thomas, Dick Anthony, Madalyn Doucas, and Thomas Curtis. 1976. "The Last Civil Religion: Reverend Moon and the Unification Church." *Sociological Analysis* 37 (2): 111–25.

Rochford, E. Burke, Jr. 1982. "Recruitment strategies, ideology and organization in the Hare Krishna movement." *Social Problems* 29 (4): 399–410.

Rosenzweig, Charles. 1979. "High demand sects: Disclosure legislation and the free exercise clause." *New England Law Review* 15: 128–59.

Sargent, William. 1957, *Battle of the Mind.* Garden City, NY: Doubleday.

—— 1961. *Battle for the Mind*. London: Heinemann.

Scheflein, Alan and Edward Opton. 1978. *The Mind Manipulators*. New York: Paddington.

Schein, Edgar, I. Schneir, and C. H. Barker. 1961. *Coercive Persuasion*. New York: Norton.

Schur, Edwin. 1980. *Politics and Deviance*. Englewood Cliffs, NJ: Prentice-Hall.

Schwartz, Lita and Natalie Isser. 1981. "Some involuntary conversion techniques." *Jewish Social Studies* 43 (1): 1–10.

Schwartz, Lita and Florence Kaslow. 1979. "Religious cults, the individual, and the family." *Journal of Marital and Family Therapy* 6: 301–8.

—— 1982. "The cult phenomenon: Historical, sociological, and familial factors contributing to their development and appeal." Pp. 3–30 in F. Kaslow and M. Sussman eds. *Cults and the Family* (special double issue of *Marriage and Family Review* 4 (3–4).

Schwartz, Lita and Jacqueline Zemel. 1980. "Religious cults: Family concerns and the law." *Journal of Marital and Family Therapy* 6: 301–8.

Shapiro, Eli. 1977. "Destructive cultism." *American Family Physician* 15 (2): 80–3.

Shapiro, Robert. 1978. "Mind control or intensity of faith: The constitutional protection of religious beliefs." *Harvard Civil Rights–Civil Liberties Law Review* 13: 751–97.

—— 1983. "On persons, robots and the constitutional protection of religious beliefs." *So. Cal. Law Review* 56 (6): 1277–1318. A shorter version of this paper is forthcoming in T. Robbins, W. Shepherd, and J. McBride, *The Law and the New Religions*. Chico, CA: Scholars Press.

Shupe, Anson, Roger Spielmann, and Sam Stigall. 1978. "Deprogramming: The new exorcism." Pp. 145–60 in J. Richardson ed. *Conversion Careers*. Sage.

Shupe, Anson and David Bromlev. 1979. "The Moonies and the anti-cultists: Movement and countermovement in conflict." *Sociological Analysis* 40: 325–34.

—— 1980. *The New Vigilantes*. Beverley Hills, CA: Sage.

Singer, Margaret. 1978. "Therapy with Ex-Cult Members." *National Association of Private Psychiatric Hospitals Journal* 9 (4): 14–18.

—— 1979. "Coming out of the Cults." *Psychology Today* 12 (8): 72–82.

Skonovd, L. Norman. 1981. Apostasy: The Process of Defection from Religious Totalism. Unpublished Ph.D. dissertation, University of California-Davis (sociology).

Snow, David, Louis Zurcher, and Sheldon Eckland-Olsen. 1980. "Social networks and social movements." *American Sociological Review* 45: 787–801.

Solomon, Trudy. 1981. "Integrating the Moonie experience." Pp. 275–94 in T. Robbins and D. Anthony, *In Gods We Trust*. Transaction.

—— 1983. "Programming and deprogramming the Moonies." In D. Bromley and J. Richardson, *The Brainwashing–Deprogramming Controversy*. Toronto: Mellon.

Somit, Albert. 1968. "Brainwashing." Pp. 138–43 in vol. 2 of D. Sills ed. *International Encyclopedia of the Social Sciences*. New York: Macmillan.

State of New York. 1981. "An act to amend the mental hygiene law, in relation to the appointment of temporary guardians." In assembly, March 31.

Stoner, Carroll and Jo Anne Parke. 1977. *All Gods Children: The Cult Experience – Salvation or Slavery*. Radnor: Chilton.

Szasz, Thomas. 1976. "Some call it brainwashing." *New Republic* (March 9).

Thomas, W. John. 1981. "Preventing non-profit profiteering: Regulating religious cult employment practices." *Arizona Law Review* 23: 1003–29.

Underwood, Barbara and Betty Underwood. 1979. *Hostage to Heaven*. New York: Potter.

Wallis, Roy and Steve Bruce. 1982. "Network and Clockwork." *Sociology* 16 (1): 102–7.

Wolf-Petrusky, Julie. 1979. "The social construction of the Cult Problem." Paper presented at the annual meetings of the "Association for the Study of Religion," Boston, 1979.

Wright, Stuart A. 1983. "Post-involvement attitudes of voluntary defectors from controversial new religious movements." Presented to the Society for the Scientific Sociology of Religion, Knoxville, TN.

Zerin, Margery. 1982a. *The Pied Piper Phenomenon: Family Systems and Vulnerability to Cults*. Dissertation. The Fielding Institute.

—— 1982b. Review of F. Kaslow and M. Sussman eds. *Cults and the Family*, 1982, Haworth, pp. 7–9 in *Cultic Studies Newsletter* 1 (1).

—— 1982c. "Reply to Dr. Robbins," *Cultic Studies Newsletter*, forthcoming.

VI

Violence and New Religious Movements

Popular awareness of NRMs is probably most closely associated with a handful of incidents of mass violence involving "cults" that have occurred over the last several decades (see table). The controversies surrounding NRMs readily attract media attention, but nothing matches the negative publicity generated by the episodes of murder–suicide discussed in this section of the book. For many today the very word "cult" most quickly calls to mind the grisly image of the Branch Davidian compound in Waco, Texas, engulfed in flames at the end of the single largest police action in US history. For 51 days the FBI lay siege to the compound following the deadly shootout between the Davidians and the agents of the Bureau of Alcohol, Tobacco, and Firearms. As the world watched through daily media reports, the FBI slowly tightened the noose on the Davidians. In the end, 74 "cult" members, men, women, and children, died in the conflagration. In the face of the fear and mistrust created by such tragic events scholars have tried to gain an accurate picture of what happened in each of the episodes of cult-related violence and to learn about the social and psychological processes that precipitated the violence.

Contrary to popular suspicions, NRMs are not prone to violence (see Melton and Bromley 2002). In fact violent behavior may well be more rare amongst NRMs than the general population – at least in America.

At any given time there are many thousands of NRMs operating in the world. Yet only a tiny handful of these groups has systematically reverted to violence to serve its ends, and with one exception (Aum Shinrikyo), this violence has been directed primarily at the group's own members. From the scholarly perspective, however, the rarity of these occurrences simply increases the importance of understanding what went so horribly wrong in these religions. We must come to grips with the causes of violence in each case in order to derive broader principles through comparative analysis that might help to prevent future tragedies. To do this effectively we cannot rest content with vague and alarmist talk of mad and corrupt cult leaders and brainwashed and helpless followers. There are no "destructive cults," just NRMs that come to be destructive. In each instance, we now appreciate, the violence stems from a complex interaction of factors that set a cycle of deviance amplification in place that heightens the possibility of extreme behavior. But these factors need not result in violence, if appropriate measures are taken. The internal beliefs and practices of some NRMs raise the suspicions of the outside world, while simultaneously leading the members of these groups to be fearful of and hostile towards the larger society. With time, interactions based on mutual fear can induce a measure of paranoia that takes on a life of its own, severely aggravating the

Cult tragedies

NRM	Location and year	Number of deaths	Research literature
Peoples Temple	Jonestown, Guyana, November 1978	918 (mostly suicide)	Hall (1987, 2000a); Chidester (1988); Maaga (1998)
Branch Davidians	Waco, Texas, April 1993	80 (murder–suicide)	Tabor and Gallagher (1995); Wright (1995); Hall (2002)
Solar Temple	Switzerland, Québec, and France, October 1994, December 1995, March 1997	53 (murder–suicide); 16 (suicide); 5 (suicide)	Mayer (1999); Introvigne (2000); Hall and Schuyler (2000); Introvigne and Mayer (2002)
Aum Shinrikyo	Tokyo, Japan, May 1995	12 (murdered on subway and 1000s injured); 23 (or more) previous murders	Lifton (1999); Reader (2000); Hall and Trinh (2000); Reader (2002)
Heaven's Gate	San Diego, California, March 1997	39 (suicide)	Hall (2000b); Balch and Taylor (2002)
Movement for the Restoration of the Ten Commandments	Uganda, March 2000	780 (murder–suicide)	News sources, and Mayer (2001); Melton and Bromley (2002)

misinterpretations and distrust that mark the relations between some NRMs and the rest of society (e.g., Dawson 1998, 2002; Richardson 2001). With informed judgment, however, the agents of social control in our societies can break or at least retard this cycle of mounting tension and avert its worst consequences (e.g., Kliever 1999; Rosenfeld 2000).

The readings provided in this section of the book simply open the door to understanding some of the incidents of mass violence and the interpretive issues they raise. In chapter 12, "The Apocalypse at Jonestown," John Hall provides us with an excellent case study of the first and still the largest instance of cult-related violence in modern times. In November of 1978, 913 members of the Peoples Temple

committed mass suicide by drinking poison at their small religious compound, called Jonestown, deep in the jungle of Guyana, South America. Earlier in the day some of their members had assassinated a US congressman and several members of his entourage following their investigative visit to Jonestown. The Peoples Temple, which had begun in the 1960s, was a fairly successful new Christian group dedicated to racial integration and service to the poor in the United States: It was also, however, very much under the control of its creator, the highly charismatic and rather unstable Reverend Jim Jones. The church espoused an unusual blend of socialist and apocalyptic beliefs, mixed with the often extreme and sometimes illegal aspirations and

actions of its leader. In the wake of some negative publicity Jones had built Jonestown in
Guyana to escape persecution by his enemies,
both real and perceived. He and his followers
sought to fashion a religious utopia free from
outside interference. But their troubles, both
within and without the organization, only
worsened with the move and tragedy soon
ensued.

Hall's chapter provides an overview of every
aspect of this movement, its history and
nature, its accomplishments and failings, as
well as the precise circumstances of its violent
demise. His analysis pinpoints some of the
"necessary preconditions" for the group's self-
destruction in terms of six internal features of
the group. He argues, however, that its violent
end depended more on the impact of three
additional "precipitating factors" born of the
efforts of the group's opponents (i.e., some
of the relatives of members and some
ex-members). Many other groups share the
preconditions he delineates for the Peoples
Temple, but they have never contemplated
undertaking an act of "revolutionary suicide."
In the face of perceived persecution, the
people of Jonestown rehearsed their collective
suicide. Through Hall's careful and complete
analysis we can begin to understand how "the
souls that Jones had lifted to a new self-respect
and vision of hope could decide that it was
better to die for their beliefs, and with their
community, than to stand by and witness the
defeat of their dreams and the destruction of
their new extended family" (Dawson 1998:
156).

In chapter 13, " 'Our Terrestrial Journey is
Coming to an End': The Last Voyage of
the Solar Temple," Jean-François Mayer provides another excellent case study, this time of
the Solar Temple. The Solar Temple and the
Peoples Temple were markedly different
groups. The latter, for example, drew most of
its members from the underprivileged blacks
of America's inner cities, though the organization was led by a coterie of middle-class,
relatively young, well educated, and disaf-
fected white women. The former group, in
contrast, drew its members from the middle
to the upper classes, from middle-aged professional couples, with French-speaking and
predominantly Catholic backgrounds, in
Europe and Québec. Yet, in the end, their
fates were much the same.

The Solar Temple was a small but very prosperous group, founded in Switzerland, that
believed itself to be the contemporary embodiment of a long mystical and esoteric tradition
within Christianity. They claimed to be the
spiritual descendants of the Knights Templar,
a wealthy medieval order of warrior monks
whose members were ultimately convicted of
heresy and burned to death by the Catholic
Church. They infused this mystical tradition
with other ideas drawn from New Age
philosophies, homeopathic systems of healing,
and prophecies of ecological doom. In the
year or so prior to its demise the group had
experienced internal turmoil and attracted
some negative publicity. But no one foresaw
the ritual death of 53 of its members in three
different locations over the course of one day
in October of 1994. Why the deaths happened
remains more obscure than in the case of
the Peoples Temple. But as Mayer's analysis
reveals, these deaths were carefully planned
and justified in terms of the ideology of the
group. His essay provides a detailed account
of the nature and history of the group, as well
as the events leading up to the tragedy. He
uses the statements that the leaders of the
group left behind to provide insight into the
worldview of the Solar Temple, documenting
their seemingly sincere belief that their deaths
were only a "transit" to a higher plane of existence, and in service of a greater purpose to
which they had dedicated their lives. Whatever
our own lack of comprehension or sheer skepticism of this purpose, it is telling that some
remaining members later repeated the ritual
suicide twice in order to join their departed
colleagues. If nothing else, it is clear that the
bonds forged in the Solar Temple were
remarkably strong.

With some insight into at least two of the
episodes of mass violence involving NRMs in
hand, readers may wish to consult a few of the
efforts made to isolate a set of common factors
facilitating the turn to violence in NRMs.
The onset of violence is influenced by both

external and internal factors, working in different combinations in each of the cases. In a well-known initial analysis Thomas Robbins and Dick Anthony (1995) concentrate on three crucial endogenous variables: (1) a strong commitment to apocalyptic belief systems and millennial visions of the imminent end of the world; (2) a strong investment in charismatic, and even more messianic, forms of leadership; and (3) becoming socially isolated and encapsulated. Each of these conditions has unanticipated behavioral consequences that support the eventual legitimation of acts of violence. But no one of these factors is sufficient to foster the violence, since they are shared by many other nonviolent religious groups as well. These are necessary factors for the emergence of violence. It is their combined effect, however, that can be lethal, especially for groups who sense that their mission has failed or that they are being persecuted.

These ideas have been developed further by Robbins and Anthony (e.g., Anthony and Robbins 1997; Robbins 2002) and others (Dawson 1998, 2002), and David Bromley (2002) provides a sophisticated overview of the social dynamic by which "cults" descend into violence, tracing the ways in which relatively minor sources of conflict or latent tensions escalate into situations where either a religious movement or some segment of the dominant social order think that "the requisite conditions for maintaining their core identity and collective existence are being subverted" and that the only tolerable response is "a project of final reckoning" to restore "what they avow to be the appropriate moral order" (Bromley 2002: 11).

References

Anthony, Dick and Thomas Robbins 1997: Religious Totalism, Exemplary Dualism and the Waco Tragedy. In T. Robbins and S. Palmer (eds.), *Millennium, Messiahs, and Mayhem*. New York: Routledge, 261–81.

Balch, Robert W. and David Taylor 2002: Making Sense of the Heaven's Gate Suicides. In D. G. Bromley and J. Gordon Melton (eds.), *Cults, Religion and Violence*. Cambridge: Cambridge University Press, 209–28.

Bromley, David G. 2002: Dramatic Denouements. In D. G. Bromley and J. G. Melton (eds.), *Cults, Religion and Violence*. Cambridge: Cambridge University Press, 11–41.

Chidester, David 1998: *Salvation and Suicide: An Interpretation of Jim Jones, the Peoples Temple, and Jonestown*. Bloomington: Indiana University Press.

Dawson, Lorne L. 1998: *Comprehending Cults: The Sociology of New Religious Movements*. Toronto: Oxford University Press.

——2002: Crises of Charismatic Legitimacy and Violent Behavior in New Religious Movements. In D. G. Bromley and J. G. Melton (eds.), *Cults, Religion and Violence*. Cambridge: Cambridge University Press, 80–101.

Hall, John R. 1987: *Gone From the Promised Land: Jonestown in American Cultural History*. New Brunswick, NJ: Transaction Books.

——2000a: *Apocalypse Observed: Religious Movements and Violence in North America, Europe, and Japan*. New York: Routledge.

——2000b: Finding Heaven's Gate. In J. R. Hall, *Apocalypse Observed: Religious Movements and Violence in North America, Europe, and Japan*. New York: Routledge, 149–82.

——2002: Mass Suicide and the Branch Davidians. In D. G. Bromley and J. G. Melton (eds.), *Cults, Religion and Violence*. Cambridge: Cambridge University Press, 149–69.

——and Philip Schuyler 2000: The Mystical Apocalypse of the Solar Temple. In J. R. Hall, *Apocalypse Observed: Religious Movements and Violence in North America, Europe, and Japan*. New York: Routledge, 111–48.

——and Sylvaine Trinh 2000: The Violent Path of Aum Shinrikyo. In J. R. Hall, *Apocalypse Observed: Religious Movements and Violence in North America, Europe, and Japan*. New York: Routledge, 76–110.

Introvigne, Massimo 2000: The Magic of Death: The Suicides of the Solar Temple. In C. Wessinger (ed.), *Millennialism, Persecution, and Violence*. Syracuse, NY: Syracuse University Press, 138–57.

Introvigne, Massimo and Jean-François Mayer 2002: Occult Masters and the Temple of Doom: The Fiery End of the Solar Temple. In D. G. Bromley and J. G. Melton (eds.), *Cults, Religion and Violence*. Cambridge: Cambridge University Press, 170–88.

Kliever, Lonnie 1999: Meeting God in Garland: A Model of Religious Tolerance. *Nova Religio* 3 (1): 45–53.

Lifton, Robert Jay 1999: *Destroying the World to Save It: Aum Shinrikyo, Apocalyptic Violence, and the New Global Terrorism.* New York: Henry Holt.

Maaga, Mary McCormich 1998: *Hearing the Voices of Jonestown.* Syracuse, NY: Syracuse University Press.

Mayer, Jean-François 1999: "Our Terrestrial Journey is Coming to an End": The Last Voyage of the Solar Temple." *Nova Religio* 2: 172–96 (chapter 13, this volume).

——2001: Field Notes: The Movement for the Restoration of the Ten Commandments of God. *Nova Religio* 5 (1): 203–10.

Melton, Gordon J. and David G. Bromley 2002: Challenging Misconceptions about the New Religions–Violence Connection. In D. G. Bromley and J. G. Melton (eds.), *Cults, Religion and Violence.* Cambridge: Cambridge University Press, 42–56.

Reader, Ian 2000: *Religious Violence in Contemporary Japan: The Case of Aum Shinrikyo.* Honolulu: University of Hawaii Press.

——2002: Dramatic Confrontations: Aum Shinrikyo Against the World. In D. G. Bromley and J. G. Melton (eds.), *Cults, Religion and Violence.* Cambridge: Cambridge University Press, 189–208.

Richardson, James T. 2001: Minority Religions and the Context of Violence: A Conflict/Interactionist Perspective. *Terrorism and Political Violence* 13 (1): 103–33.

Robbins, Thomas 2002: Sources of Volatility in Religious Movements. In D. G. Bromley and J. G. Melton (eds.), *Cults, Religion and Violence.* Cambridge: Cambridge University Press, 57–79.

Robbins, Thomas and Dick Anthony 1995: Sects and Violence: Factors Enhancing the Volatility of Marginal Religious Movements. In S. Wright (ed.), *Armageddon in Waco.* Chicago, IL: University of Chicago Press, 236–59.

Rosenfeld, Jean E. 2000: The Justus Freemen Standoff: The Importance of the Analysis of Religion in Avoiding Violent Outcomes. In C. Wessinger (ed.), *Millennialism, Persecution, and Violence.* Syracuse, NY: Syracuse University Press, 323–44.

Tabor, James and Eugene Gallagher 1995: *Why Waco?* Berkeley: University of California Press.

Wright, Stuart (ed.), 1995: *Armageddon in Waco: Critical Perspectives on the Branch Davidian Conflict.* Chicago, IL: University of Chicago Press.

CHAPTER TWELVE

The Apocalypse at Jonestown

JOHN R. HALL

Two years to the day after the 19 April 1993 conflagration at the Branch Davidians' Mount Carmel compound near Waco, Texas, a bomb destroyed the federal building in Oklahoma City, Oklahoma, killing at least 167 people and injuring hundreds more. Two years after that, in April 1997, jury selection finally began in the trial of Timothy McVeigh, the man eventually convicted of the bombing. Anticipating the upcoming trial, the *New Yorker* magazine's "Talk of the Town" section led with a piece where Scott Malcomson (1997) recounted his visit to "Elohim City," a dirt-poor white-separatist Christian fundamentalist community in the Ozarks. Over supper after church on Sunday, the sect's founder, Robert G. Millar, mentioned to Malcomson that he had met a Pastor Jones in the 1950s, "a good pastor," he called him. Did the *New Yorker* writer remember Jones? "Oh yes, the man in Guyana," Malcomson replied, ending his piece, "Yes, I remembered him."

Thus readers encountered yet another allusion to the first mass suicide in modern times. Jonestown was the communal settlement founded by Peoples Temple in the small, poor, socialist country of Guyana, on the Caribbean coast of South America. On 17 November 1978, a congressman from California, Leo Ryan, arrived there on an investigative expedition, accompanied by journalists and some sect opponents who called themselves the "Concerned Relatives." The next day, Ryan

and four other people – three newsmen and a young defector – were murdered at an airstrip several miles from Jonestown as they prepared to depart with more than a dozen defectors that the visitors had brought out of the jungle utopian community. While this carnage unfolded, back at Jonestown, the Temple's white charismatic leader, Jim Jones, orchestrated a "revolutionary suicide" where the members of the agricultural community – mostly black, some white – drank a deadly potion of Fla-Vor Aid laced with poison. Counting the murders at the airstrip, 918 people died.[1]

Well before Timothy McVeigh's trial, "Jonestown" had become so infamous as the ultimate "cult" nightmare that Malcomson could invoke the mere name of its leader as a chilling conclusion to his story about an isolated, radically anti-establishment religious community of true believers. In his short, sophisticated *New Yorker* report, Malcomson symbolically aligned Waco, the Oklahoma City bombing, and Jonestown with the racist survivalist sect he had visited, all without saying much of substance about any of these episodes. He offered no reflection on even the most immediately intriguing question raised by Elohim leader Robert Millar's mention of Jim Jones: why was a right-wing racist fundamentalist praising the founder of Peoples Temple, a left-wing religious movement dedicated to racial integration?

The power of Malcomson's piece hinges on the mention of Jim Jones, but the rhetorical form of this mentioning depends on glossing any understanding of what happened at Jonestown. Instead, it plays to a generalized collective memory that has enshrined Jones in popular culture as the image incarnate of the Antichrist, and Peoples Temple as the paragon of the religious "cult.' Fed by a flood of news articles, a film, a television docudrama, more than twenty books, and countless oblique allusions, this collective memory now floats free from what, in a simpler era, historians liked to think of as facts. But when we search for the sources of this memory, they trace back to the "Concerned Relatives," the organization that had opposed Peoples Temple in the first place, and to the representatives of the media whom the Temple opponents drew into the ill-fated journey to Jonestown. After the murders and mass suicide, the Concerned Relatives became the outsiders with the most knowledge about a group that had carried out an appalling act of mass suicide. Indeed, because the Concerned Relatives had consistently sought to raise the alarm against Peoples Temple before 18 November 1978, they could take the mass suicide as a sad validation of their concerns. But by the same token, popular accounts of Jonestown depended heavily on the accounts of the Concerned Relatives, and these accounts tended to suppress a crucial question. Did the actions of the Concerned Relatives and the media in any way contribute to the grisly outcome of events in which they were not only observers, but also participants?

Given the tragic deaths, the cultural opponents had a vital interest in denying that their actions had any consequences. This interest may help account for their consistent promotion of a doctrine of *cult essentialism*, whereby the dynamics of religious movements are treated as wholly internal, and unaffected by interaction with the wider social world. Such an analysis would free the cultural opponents and the media from any responsibility for incidents of religious-movement violence. But precisely because the proponents of cult essentialism themselves participated in the events, it is important to give their actions consideration along with other factors that may have contributed to the outcome of murder and mass suicide.

In the absence of this analysis, Jonestown becomes, as Roland Barthes wrote of myths more generally, "a story at once true and unreal" (Barthes 1972: 128). In this case, the story is one of a sick and fiendish man who plotted the deaths of those who would expose his sham community, capping the murder of opponents with the ritualized ceremonial murder of followers, many of them perhaps well-intentioned, but too naive or powerless to break the hold of Jim Jones, a man sufficiently obsessed with his orchestration of events to die of an apparently self-inflicted gunshot to the head.

Treatment of Peoples Temple as the *cultus classicus* headed by Jim Jones, psychotic megalomaniac *par excellence* drifts on a sea of memory, only loosely tied to any moorings of history. Still, like other myths that maintain their power, the one signified by "Jonestown" must be culturally powerful, and perhaps even necessary, for it remains evocative even today. In Barthes's terms, the power of Jonestown is the power of the unreal to offer a meaningful narrative of an event that is otherwise difficult to reconcile with the world as we understand it. The myth of Jonestown has a long half-life because it serves vital needs *not* to understand the murders and mass suicide historically. In effect, the myth of Jonestown displaces history by suppressing alternative narratives that might debunk ideology. Only when this ideological lens is broken can we search for historical explanations.

Devil, psychopath, con artist, Antichrist, Jim Jones was also a discomforting critic of American society, embraced by followers as a prophet, redeemer, and friend. His strongest countercultural images borrowed old Protestant ideas about the Church of Rome as the whore of Babylon, ideas that themselves come from deeper apocalyptic wellsprings of Western thought. But Jones transmuted these ideas into a new religious dispensation: of the United States as Babylon, the Apocalypse as race and class warfare that would engulf a society trapped in its own hypocrisy. An unrelenting iconoclast, Jones sought to forge a militant movement of people committed to the vision of a utopian alternative to a racist, class-dominated, imperialist society. Peoples Temple thus carried a double onus: it was a countercultural communal group and a militant anti-American social movement.

Communalism *per se* has long been viewed as a way of life alien to mainstream America. Legitimate organizations such as religious orders and the military may rightly require submission to collective authority, but in public discourse, the collectivism of countercultural organizations flies in the face of the dominant American ideology that embraces capitalism, individualism, and the nuclear family, and it is thus vulnerable to becoming coded as antidemocratic and subversive (cf. Alexander and Smith 1993).

Like other religious social movements, Peoples Temple practiced a communal socialism. Yet unlike most countercultural hippie communes and utopian communal groups of the 1960s and early 1970s, Peoples Temple located its communalism in a leftist political vein of crude communism. Jones simultaneously evoked apocalyptic imagery that appealed to members of his audience steeped in the codes of religious rhetoric, and used the political language of class and race to amplify latent resentment among those drawn to his cause. By this dual strategy, he forged a religious radicalism that attracted true believers to a movement framed in militant opposition to American capitalist society. Because Jones so sharply opposed the predominant ideology, that ideology requires that his movement and its demise be misunderstood.

The Jonestown myth can be deconstructed if we ask a straightforward question: "why did the murders and mass suicide occur?" To answer this question without recourse to the lens of ideology brings into view a complex relationship between Peoples Temple and the established social order. As we will see, the carnage in Guyana was not simply the product of the politically infused apocalyptic mentality that took hold within Peoples Temple. Nor can it be explained as wholly the result of Jim Jones's demented manipulations. Jones was

more complex than the caricature of him, and Peoples Temple was both utopia and anti-utopia. "Jonestown" was the disastrous outcome of a protracted conflict between Peoples Temple and a loosely institutionalized but increasingly effective coalition of opponents. But the myth of Jonestown has had consequences of its own. It did not simply arise *after* apocalyptic history. It has contributed *to* apocalyptic history.

Jim Jones and the Origins of Peoples Temple

Peoples Temple began, like many American religious groups, in the mind of a self-styled prophet. James Warren Jones was born in east central Indiana in the time of the Great Depression on 13 May 1931. The only child of poor white working parents (his mother was later rumored to have Indian ancestors), Jones grew up with a strong sense of resentment toward people of wealth, status, and privilege. Exposed as a child to a variety of Protestant churches – from the mainstream Methodists to the pacifist Quakers and the holiness-movement Nazarenes – Jones found himself especially impressed by the religious enthusiasm, revival-style worship, and speaking in tongues that he encountered in the fellowship of the then-marginal Pentecostalists, where he later described finding a "setting of freedom of emotion."

During his high school years Jim Jones preached on the streets in a factory neighborhood of Richmond, Indiana, to an audience of both whites and blacks. In the summer of 1949, he married Marceline Baldwin, a young nurse from a Richmond family of Methodists and Republicans. Marcie was shocked, Jim later recounted, when he revealed the views that he seems to have taken from his mother, namely his sympathies with political communism and his disdain for the "sky god."

In 1951 Jim and Marcie Jones moved to Indianapolis. Although Jim Jones was barely twenty years old at the time, he quickly became a preacher and created a volatile mix of theology and practice. Exposed variously to the Methodists' liberal social creed, communist ideology, and the broadly apocalyptic vision of the Pentecostalists, Jones would promote racial integration and a veiled communist philosophy within a Pentecostal framework that emphasized gifts of the spirit, especially faith healing and the "discerning" of spirits. He displayed a knack for preaching, and he learned some tricks already in use in the mid-South Pentecostal revival circuit: how to convince audiences of his abilities in matters of "discernment" and faith healing by sleights of hand, spying, and fakery. Jones was hardly the first faith healer on the circuit to cause elderly ladies confined too wheel-chairs to rise up and walk again, though he may have been the first to come up with the idea of having a perfectly sound leg bone placed in a plaster cast so that it could be removed after a faith healing. Yet for all the deceit, some followers swore that the young minister had the gift of healing, and independent observers later acknowledged that hokum aside, Jones could produce results with a person whose condition "had no major physiological basis."

On the grounds of his religious chicanery alone, Jones would have been hard to distinguish from other self-styled Pentecostalist faith healers of his day. But the audiences attracted by Jones's gifts of the spirit encountered something far different from other tent-camp evangelists and small-time preachers who operated in the mid-South.

Organizationally, Jones started in Indianapolis with a small church called Community Unity. His first important break came when visitors from the Pentecostalist Laurel Street Tabernacle in Indianapolis took in his services following a successful revival appearance that he had made in Detroit, Michigan. In September 1954 some of the visitors invited Jones to preach at Laurel Street. Jones created a stir by bringing blacks to the service of the racially segregated church, but after his preaching and healing performance a substantial segment of the Tabernacle voted with their feet, leaving their congregation in order to walk with Jones. Together, on 4 April 1955, they established Wings of Deliverance, the corporate vehicle of what was later named Peoples Temple.

In his ministry, Jones extended the always-strong Pentecostalist ethic of a caring community toward racial integration, and he initiated urban ministry programs more typically associated with the social gospel of progressive middle-class Protestant denominations like the Methodists. Peoples Temple became a racially integrated self-help community of believers in practical service under the umbrella of a church. Out of this unlikely amalgamation of disparate ideas and practices, Jones gradually built the church into a communalistic social movement. Beginning as a somewhat unconventional preacher, he increasingly took on the mantle of a prophet who warned of an impending capitalist apocalypse and worked to establish a socialist promised land for those who heeded his message.

The movement grew up around the Jones family itself. Already by 1952 Jim and Marcie had adopted a ten-year-old girl. Then in 1955, they capitalized on Marcie's nursing experience, bringing an older follower to live in their own home, thereby establishing a nursing home under a formula whereby their ever-widening family could be supported in part by cash payments from outside. In the late 1950s the couple adopted children who had been orphaned by the Korean War, initiating what they would call their multi-ethnic "rainbow family." Two years after the birth of their natural son Stephan Gandhi Jones in 1959, the Joneses became the first white couple in Indianapolis, and perhaps in the state of Indiana, to adopt a black child. At the time, when the civil rights movement was just gaining steam in the US, Jones remarked, "Integration is a more personal thing with me now. it's a question of my son's future."

For all the dynamism of Jones's early family-centered ministry, however, he was hardly original in developing strategies, practices, and organizational forms. Instead, Jones was something of a living syncretist sponge who could absorb ideas, people, and their energies from the most diverse sources into the development of his organization.

Most importantly, Jones connected to the legacy of blacks's search for redemption in the United States. Several times in the late 1950s, he visited the Philadelphia Peace Mission of the American black preacher Father M. J. Divine, who, in the 1920s and 1930s, had established himself at the center of a racially integrated religious and economic community. Father Divine himself stood in a long tradition of "black messiahs" who promoted migration from the Old South Black Belt after the American Civil War. The cultural sources are even deeper, going back to the time of slavery, and from it, to cultural memories drawn from the Bible. "The rhetoric of this migration" from the South, as James Diggs has noted, "was often reminiscent of antebellum Black nationalism, with its talk of escape from the land of bondage and quest for a promised land" (quoted in Moses 1982: 135). Like the biblical Jews under Moses, nineteenth-century black ministers had sometimes portrayed the collective suffering of their people and their quest for redemption as part of a higher religious purpose to history. Collective migration could serve as a vehicle to this purpose, for example, in the departure of "exodusters" from the South to settle in Oklahoma and Kansas during the latter part of the nineteenth century. In the early twentieth century, Marcus Garvey took up the theme anew with his back-to-Africa movement (which never repatriated a single US black to Africa while Garvey operated in the US). And then there was Father Divine. During the 1930s, he dabbled with the Communist Party but, more centrally, he relocated the destination of back-to-Africa dreams by setting up his peace missions in major Eastern US cities and establishing "The Promised Land" – rural, interracial cooperative communities – in upstate New York (Weisbrot 1983).

Jim Jones borrowed much from the Peace Mission model (and stole some of its members). Like Father Divine, he took to a patriarchal style of organization, with himself at the center, surrounded by a staff that included a heavy concentration of attractive, white women. Like Divine, Jones took to being called "Father," or sometimes, "Dad." Over

the years, he would vacillate between operating an urban human-service ministry akin to Divine's peace missions and establishing an exurban settlement in California not unlike the black messiah's upstate New York communities. But Jones's mission eventually took a more radical direction: emigration to escape the degradation of racism and class inequality in the United States. Again borrowing from Divine, the community that Peoples Temple founded in Guyana – Jonestown – would sometimes be called the Promised Land.

In the 1950s and 1960s, Jones shaped Peoples Temple in Indianapolis as an extended family that offered the shelter of communal fellowship from an uncertain world beyond. Like Divine, Jones worked to develop Peoples Temple as an agent of social action, establishing care homes for the elderly, running a free restaurant to feed the hungry, and maintaining a social service center to help people get their lives back together. In time, the unconventional congregation attracted the notice of the Christian Church (Disciples of Christ), which had long been committed to a social ministry. By 1960, Peoples Temple had affiliated with the Disciples, and in 1964 Jones was officially ordained a minister.

Peoples Temple thrived in Indianapolis, but it also gained a certain notoriety. Jones was more political than Father Divine, and he seemed to go out of his way to precipitate public controversies, seizing on opportunities to dramatize how racial segregation in Indianapolis extended even to its hospitals and its cemeteries. Indianapolis was not a progressive place and bitter resistance to integration surfaced in some quarters. By publicly challenging segregationist policies from the 1950s onwards, Jones enhanced his own status as a civil-rights leader. Seeing the benefit of having reactionary opponents, he also sometimes staged incidents which made him, his family, and his church look like the targets of racist hate crimes. Nonetheless, some of the harassment was real, and Jones does not seem to have held up well under the pressure. In the face of the public tensions, his doctor hospitalized him for an ulcer during the fall of

1961. After his release, Jones began to seek a way out of Indianapolis. Leaving his congregation in the care of associate pastors, he and his family visited British Guiana (Guyana before independence from colonial rule), and then lived for two years in Brazil.

California Heyday

Even as Jones returned to Indianapolis in 1964, he already was laying the groundwork for a collective migration by his most committed followers. Tired of racial intolerance in Indiana and citing fears of nuclear holocaust, in the summer of 1965 they moved to the hamlet of Redwood Valley, near the quiet northern California town of Ukiah, in the Russian River valley. About seventy families, half white, half black, made the journey.

The congregation established itself slowly, comprising only 168 adult members by 1968. In 1969 the Temple completed its own church building, enclosing a swimming pool they had previously built on the Joneses' land just south of Redwood Valley. But Jim Jones failed to make much headway in drawing converts from the various apostolic fundamentalist congregations in the Ukiah area, and he became increasingly matter-of-fact in discussing secular socialism with his own congregation. He also pointedly criticized black ministers still promoting spiritualistic theologies of heavenly compensation for suffering during life, proposing to replace it with an alternative model: the activist church as social movement. On this platform Peoples Temple gradually attracted a wide range of people: working and middle-class blacks, hippies, socially concerned progressive professionals, fundamentalist Christians, former tenant farmers from the South, political activists and militants, street people, delinquents, and the elderly. These diverse sources fed an organization that began to grow rapidly. In the early 1970s, the Temple established a "human services" ministry of "care" homes for juveniles and the elderly, set up churches in San Francisco and Los Angeles, and began operating a fleet of buses to carry followers to church functions attended by thousands of people.

The corporation of people

The care homes, like many other Temple enterprises, worked to the benefit of the organization in multiple ways. Like private-sector operators, the Temple was able to use care-payment income to leverage real estate investments that expanded the care-home operations and increased the property holdings of the organization. It could also use the care homes to employ Temple members. In turn, because people were willing to work so hard for "the Cause," the homes produced substantial profits. The Temple treated these profits as organizational income rather than the income of individual operators, but it neglected to pay taxes, even though the money would have been considered "unrelated business income" falling outside the "nonprofit religious organization" tax-exempt category of the Internal Revenue Service. Beyond the strictly financial benefits, the care-home operations became the nucleus for promoting a collective life and communal orientation more widely among followers. The people served by the care homes were more than clients; they participated as active members of the movement itself.

By its heyday in the mid-1970s, the Temple had established multiple streams of income, from petty church fundraisers and offerings at services, to a radio ministry, the care homes, and the salaries, social security checks, and real estate donated by members who "went communal." The money added up. After the mass suicide in 1978, a court-appointed receiver was able to consolidate $10 million of Temple assets, even though he couldn't recover all the defunct organization's holdings. Before the disastrous end, Jones had once said, "I have made the poor rich." But this isn't quite right. If the value of the receiver's Temple assets were allocated among the 913 members who died in Guyana, it would have come to around $12,000 per person, less if allocated among the total number of Temple members. The Temple thrived on the basis of expanding real-estate investments, a care-home business largely supported by state welfare payments, economies of scale of communal consumption, the labor of committed members supported by the group, and a whole host of evangelical fundraising techniques. But no one got rich. Effectively, Jones forged a collective organization that was wealthier than the sum of its individual parts.

Peoples Temple was devoted to some distinctly anti-establishment ends, but the success of the operation largely depended on disarmingly conventional means, from the petty fundraisers to corporate entrepreneurship, rationalized methods of administration that served a large membership, and active coordination with external organizations such as welfare agencies and the Social Security Administration. On the whole, the Temple avoided the sorts of shady practices that sometimes have plagued both evangelical religious organizations and the care-home industry. Just as clearly, the group sometimes operated outside the law, certainly in failing to report care-home income, and perhaps in its transfers of assets to off-shore bank accounts. Yet at least the quest for profits through tax avoidance and off-shore banking share an understandable rationale with more legitimate organizations that engage in similar practices.

The collectivist reformation

Where Peoples Temple deviated much more dramatically from conventional social practice was in its members' high rates of tithing, unsalaried labor, and donation of real and personal assets. In turn, these differences were part of a more profound difference: replacing individualism and the family unit with the communal equation of an organization that pooled the economic resources of its most highly committed members, and in return, offered them economic security, an extended collectivist "family," and the opportunity to participate in a politically meaningful social cause larger than themselves. Balancing that equation, the Temple demanded commitment, discipline, and individual submission to collective authority.

Social control and the social monitoring required to prevent "freeriders" who fail to do their share are issues faced by all organizations of any significant size, from corporations stores, schools, and monasteries, to mental hospitals, prisons, and armies (Hechter 1987). But in most organizations, procedures of monitoring and control tend to be legitimated by legal authority, contract, or long-established convention. By contrast, counter-cultural communal organizations face more formidable issues of control, because they are quasi-familial yet voluntary groups with much weaker capacities to claim authority over their members.

Historically, the most successful communal groups have promoted solidarity and commitment through practices such as wearing uniforms, sharing a communal table, regulating sexual relationships, and monitoring members' behavior through techniques such as confession (Kanter 1972). Among the wide variety of communal groups, ones with apocalyptic orientations have a particularly strong basis to legitimate their demands for members' commitment, for they frame their existence in relation to a society at large construed as the embodiment of evil (Hall 1988). In such sects, the "end of the world" is taken as a central tenet. But the content of collective demands on members depends on how the apocalyptic group construes its position in relation to the end times . . . A key issue concerns whether the group locates itself *before* or *after* the end of the current epoch. Before the dawn of the new era, a pre-apocalyptic "warring sect" will exhibit a high degree of solidarity in pursuing the battle of Armageddon, that last and decisive struggle between the forces of good and evil. On the other hand, a post-apocalyptic "other-worldly sect" detaches itself from the evil society held to be in its last days, retreating to an isolated heaven-on-earth where the time of this world is treated as part of the past (Hall 1978).

In these terms, Jim Jones sometimes invoked other-worldly images of Peoples Temple as an ark of survival, but during its California years the Temple had higher stakes of commitment than the typical other-worldly sect. This was, first, because it operated in urban and small-town settings where control was not enhanced by physical isolation, and second, because religious rhetoric masked a supposedly secret political antagonism toward the established order signaled by the Temple's posture of alignment with political communism. Thus, an odd juxtaposition emerged: Peoples Temple developed its regime of social control within the framework of an organization that had the external appearance of a conventional church. Internally, however, control increasingly operated in ways more often found in militant political movements and clandestine warring sects.

Authority ultimately derived from the careful legitimation of Jim Jones's proclaimed charismatic mission as a socialist prophet. In practical terms, he enhanced his position by staging demonstrations of his paranormal powers and cultivating a network of personal relationships that was sometimes tinged with sexual domination of both women and men. Jim Jones was bisexual, and sex became something like a currency that he used, supposedly, "for the cause." With it, Jones gave some people intimacy and controlled or humiliated others. The first offspring of his sexual unions was Stephan, the child born in Indiana in 1959 to his legal wife Marcie. In California, Jones fathered Carolyn Layton's son Kimo Prokes, and he was widely believed to be the father of John Victor Stoen, born in 1972 to Grace Stoen, wife of Temple attorney Tim Stoen.

Beyond social control based on personal relationships and charismatic projection, the Temple adopted practices derived from wider cultural sources: first, pseudo-Pentecostalist practices of "discernment" that Jones transformed into a vehicle of intelligence gathering used by Temple staff to monitor members; second, a military-drill security unit like those found more widely in black American culture of the day; third, techniques derived from the 1970s social-work and counseling-psychology culture of California, and, fourth, a fundamentalist Christian ethic of punishment for wrongdoing. These practices helped sustain collective authority that was legitimated in an even more fundamental way by the widespread distribution of relatively equal benefits of group life. In turn, by giving the broad base of participants a stake in the organization, Peoples Temple created a broad interest in maintaining social control (cf. Hall 1988). The leadership was able to consolidate a pervasive apparatus of monitoring in which rank-and-file participants provided information on their own and others' personal problems, sexual conduct, social relationships, degree of commitment to the Temple, and deviant or criminal activities. In turn, Temple staff used this information for collective intervention in individuals' lives and their social relationships. They conducted individual and group counseling sessions, and they held public meetings for "catharsis," where Jim Jones sometimes publicly humiliated backsliders and asked the assembled populace to determine punishments that included paddlings and boxing matches for wrongdoers. The assembled collective itself participated in the practices that sustained organizational authority.

Many of the Temple techniques of monitoring, counseling, and social control were borrowed from the wider society. But there was a critical difference: however pervasive the webs of social control in society at large, they do not become consolidated in a single apparatus. Peoples Temple, on the other hand, amalgamated control in the hierarchy of a total institution that enveloped its participants in a single web of surveillance, even though many Temple members freely participated in the wider world through school and jobs. As in any social order, the burden of this regime fell more heavily on the less committed than on loyal members who followed the rules. From inside the Temple, monitoring, catharsis sessions, and physical punishment seemed necessary to maintain standards of acceptable conduct and prevent internal dissension from taking hold. But from outside, all this came to be viewed as manipulation, physical abuse, and brainwashing.

Politics and public relations

Social control in the Temple gained a special edge through its connection to the group's disciplined struggle against injustice in the wider society. Compared with both conventional churches and retreatist communal groups of its day, Peoples Temple was an anomaly, a highly organized radical religious collective that pursued activist politics within the society at large. Perversely, the Temple used textbook public-relations (or PR) techniques to protect an apocalyptic socialist movement opposed to the capitalist society where practices of public relations had originated.

In the political climate of California during the 1970s, shaped by the counterculture and the anti-Vietnam war movement, the Temple used PR strategies within a broad political coalition committed to racial integration, social and economic justice, peace, and other progressive and radical causes. Because of its discipline, the Temple could turn out the troops. Members demonstrated against the *Bakke* decision by the California Supreme Court when it outlawed a University of California affirmative-action procedure. They joined a coalition denouncing apartheid in South Africa. Temple staff met with the Jewish Community Relations Council about combating the increase in Nazi propaganda in the Bay area. And the Temple supported gay rights, depicting the antigay stances of advertising celebrity Anita Bryant as "giving birth to a new wave of fascism . . . spreading its poison in attacking anything that's not straight, white and conservative."

More concretely, the Temple provided a ready supply of political workers to the Democratic Party. By 1975 Peoples Temple was sufficiently adept at conventional party politics to become a formidable force in the left-liberal political surge that propelled democrat George Moscone into office as mayor of San Francisco. A year later the Temple reaped the political rewards. Temple attorney Tim Stoen was called from his position as assistant district attorney in Mendocino County to prosecute voter fraud for the San Francisco district attorney, and Mayor Moscone appointed Jim Jones to the San Francisco Housing Authority Commission. At the end of the year, the San Francisco *Chronicle* quoted Jones as favoring "some kind of democratic socialism."

The attractions of the Temple

By any standard, Peoples Temple was a deviant organization in American society. Its spartan regimen of social control depended on practices of humiliation and emotional and physical abuse abhorrent to norms of mainstream American culture. Yet the dubious practices of Peoples Temple do not seem sufficient to explain the solidarity of its members and cannot in themselves explain how the organization was able to thrive and grow. What was it about Peoples Temple that attracted tens of thousands to its services and led to the active participation of over one thousand people?

In part, the group's success was the consequence of the ways it exploited conventional pathways of action in the wider society. The Temple operated as a church, and drew on the legitimacy of churches. Its staff became accomplished at organizational coordination, public relations and political stratagems that largely mimicked conventional practices. And as in other organizations, public and private, they channeled resources from the state welfare system into the material benefits that the Temple offered.

Yet these conventional features and benefits came in an alien utopian package that presumably would have put people off, had they not been willing to embrace a radical alternative to their previous life circumstances. Peoples Temple differed dramatically from conventional organizations in the wider society, including the vast majority of its religious organizations. It was first and foremost a highly unusual testament to an alternative mode of ethnic relations, a racially integrated community of people who lived daily life together. In a striking way, the Temple also reconfigured the various available missions of the local church as a social institution (cf. Becker 1999) by radicalizing the social gospel through a congregational communal formula of "apostolic socialism" and direct social ministry, combined with a leftist political agenda in the wider society. This model attracted people from many stations in society, even secular political leftists who might have been expected to take the view of Karl Marx and

Frederick Engels in the *Communist Manifesto* that "social Utopias" amount to "castles in the air."

However, if Peoples Temple was atypical as a religious congregation, it was hardly the typical social utopia either. Most communitarian groups that developed "worldly utopian" alternative models of society – New Harmony in Indiana during the nineteenth century, the Farm in Tennessee during the American countercultural wave of the 1960s and 1970s – did so at some remove from the society-at-large (Hall 1978). On the other hand, during its California heyday, Peoples Temple became an unusual hybrid: an urban-based, relatively autonomous communalistic organization that was nevertheless complexly connected to the wider society, and to the state, corporate, political, and media institutions of that society. By contrast with worldly utopian communal groups, Peoples Temple developed what may be called a "collectivist bureaucracy." Through their joint efforts, Temple staff organized the lives of everyday members in a way fully articulated with the complex governmental and capitalist order around them. Yet by this collective enterprise, the Temple increased the autonomy of its individual members from that external order, giving them time and direction to channel their energies in politically activist ways.

No one should gainsay the reprehensible features of Peoples Temple public relations, politics, and social control. Yet rejection of the reprehensible should be accompanied by recognition that the Temple's practices – both those widely regarded as legitimate and other more questionable ones – are hardly foreign to the wider world. Nor should we deny the organization's appeal during its California years. Peoples Temple was distinctive in its capacity to chart a pathway of expansion within the wider society under the auspices of a utopian vision and innovative form of social organization that harnessed the energies of many people of good will. From multiple walks of life, its members came together in a community that transcended the operative institutions, cultural boundaries, and social divisions of the existing social order.

Gone to the Promised Land

The organizational and political successes of Peoples Temple by the mid-1970s give cause to wonder why Jim Jones did not move directly into the realm of politics, as other activist leaders of religious social movements have done. But the question is moot because the Temple became embroiled in controversy and migrated en masse to Guyana. Indeed, these developments reveal the precarious nature of Peoples Temple's political successes, for those successes depended on the public-relations facade that hid the Temple's more radical and dubious aspects from the wider society.

Within the shell of a church, Jones called his followers to what Max Weber called an "ethic of ultimate ends." He sought to recruit highly committed individuals, and he insisted that followers pursue the cause of Peoples Temple selflessly, tirelessly, and without compromise. It is a measure of the total commitment Jones demanded that he invoked a doctrine originally developed by Black Panther Party member Huey Newton, namely, that the slow suicide of life in the ghetto ought to be displaced by "revolutionary suicide." The life of the committed revolutionary would end only in victory against economic, social, and racial injustice, or in death. In keeping with this thesis, the Temple expected Jones's followers to give up their previous lives and become born again to a collective struggle that had no limits. This radical ethos both deepened the gulf between Peoples Temple and the wider society, and served as the ideological point of departure for the uncompromising posture that the Temple developed during its protracted conflict with increasingly organized apostates and their allies, who became equally committed to their own cause of opposition.

Forging a regime of militant activism, Jones attracted the very "persecution" that he both feared and prophesied. Eventually, the Temple leadership uncovered information which, they thought, confirmed Jones's dire prophecies that the group would not be able to survive in the United States. Jones and over a thousand followers thereupon undertook a collective emigration to Guyana, leaving the path of militant political struggle within the United States behind.

While Peoples Temple remained in the United States, it operated *in* the world. Yet Jones never expected acceptance *from* the world. In Indianapolis, he promised followers that the Temple would protect them from a hostile society, yet he also projected the belief that his racially integrated congregation would have to leave their present surroundings. Like Moses and the ancient Jews searching for a land of "milk and honey" or the Puritans who fled to North America from religious persecution in England to found a "city on a hill," Jones sought redemption for his followers in collective religious migration to a promised land by leading his congregation to California. But there, Jones's promised land soon took a new form: the creation of a sanctuary outside the United States itself. Beginning in 1972 and 1973, Jones used internal defections and small incidents of external "persecution" in California as the warrant to establish Peoples Temple's "promised land" – an "agricultural mission" eventually called Jonestown – in a remote corner of Guyana, an ethnically diverse country with a socialist government on the northern, Caribbean, coast of South America.

At its inception, Jonestown was just a pioneer camp. But even before the site was established in early 1974, a memo by Temple attorney Tim Stoen suggested that the Temple should methodically prepare for collective migration from the US by consolidating its finances and other affairs. The plan was to remain in California "until first signs of outright persecution from press or government," then "start moving all members to mission post." In practice, the Temple followed the basic thrust of this plan. The initial party of settlers devoted most of their efforts toward construction of enough housing and other facilities to accommodate a large influx of newcomers, while Temple operatives in Guyana's capital of Georgetown used their public relations and political skills (and sexual allure) to establish secure political alliances with members of the patrimonial socialist regime of the country's black prime minister, Forbes Burnham.

Jonestown remained a small outpost until Peoples Temple undertook the collective migration of some 1,000 people during the summer of 1977. Unlike the mid-1960s migration to California to escape Hoosier racism, Jones did not justify this migration solely on the basis of his personal perceptions about a hostile environment. The migration unfolded as a move in an escalating conflict between Peoples Temple and an emerging coalition of external opponents.

Over the years, members had occasionally left Peoples Temple, but they had never actively turned against the organization. A handful of outside critics of the Temple, who questioned Jones's faith healing and other unusual practices, remained relatively isolated. But this all changed toward the end of 1975, when Deanna and "Mert" Mertle, two high-ranking members of the Temple leadership, departed, leaving a series of unresolved conflicts in their wake, including a dispute over an unrecorded deed to a property that the couple had signed over to the Temple. In February 1976, the Mertles changed their names to Al and Jeannie Mills, symbolizing that they were new people now that they had left the Temple. Eventually, the Mertles/Millses made contact with others who were leaving the Temple. Among them was Grace Stoen, who in July 1976 drove from Redwood Valley to Lake Tahoe with a Temple bus mechanic, Walter "Smitty" Jones, leaving behind her husband, Temple attorney Tim Stoen, and her son, four-year-old John Victor Stoen.

By the autumn of 1976 a handful of these apostates coalesced into a small group, and the Mills's teenage daughter Linda decided to follow the rest of her family out of the Temple. Linda's exit reduced the issues of contention between the Millses and the Temple and strengthened the family's separation from the group. At the time, there was a wider tide of public concern about "cults" like Sun Myung Moon's Unification Church and the Hare Krishnas (Shupe, Bromley, and Oliver 1984). In this climate the reunited Mills family began to see Peoples Temple as a cult. They followed the public controversies about families seeking court-ordered conservatorships for custody over relatives lost to strange messiahs, and they gravitated toward the centerpiece of anticult movement activism: the "coercive persuasion" explanation of conversion and commitment. As one Mills daughter explained to her sister, "We were all brainwashed in there, Linda. The one thing we have learned is not to blame ourselves for the things Jim made us do."

The apostates did not simply reinterpret their own experiences and actions. They sought to bring the Temple to a public accounting. David Conn, a long-time critic of the Temple and a confidant of the opponents who had come together around the Mertles/Millses and Grace Stoen, brokered the crucial contact. In early 1977, Conn put the apostates in touch with his daughter's boyfriend, George Kleinman a reporter for the Santa Rosa *Press-Democrat*. In turn, George Kleinman put the opponents in touch with a Customs Service agent in the US Treasury Department. The agent met with thirteen Temple opponents and assured them that a full-scale investigatory effort would be directed at Peoples Temple, involving all levels of government.

Around the same time, journalists for conservative media magnate Rupert Murdoch's *New West* magazine decided to write a story on Peoples Temple because of political efforts to unseat a political patron of Jones and the Temple: liberal San Francisco mayor George Moscone. Initially, the *New West* reporters didn't know about the apostates and didn't have any viable source of information about life inside Peoples Temple. Lacking sources, in June 1977 they got the San Francisco *Chronicle* to publish a story about how the Temple was trying to suppress the story they were working on. By this "ploy," as one of the reporters called it, they managed to hook up with the defectors. After gaining inside information in this way, *New West* published an exposé series which generated a flood of negative newspaper accounts, beginning in July 1977, just weeks before the election vote over whether to recall Mayor Moscone. The oppo-

nents appeared in these stories as apostates and relatives courageous enough to expose the group, despite their fear of reprisals. The narratives overwhelmingly depicted Peoples Temple through an anticult lens that raised questions about supposed financial ripoffs, extravagant living and hair-raising practices of psychological catharsis, physical punishment, and brainwashing.

At the time of the exposés, Peoples Temple had already initiated the collective migration to Guyana, and it was widely believed that they had done so in anticipation of the *New West* story. But the exodus had a more complex genesis in Temple concerns during early 1976 about an alignment that they perceived emerging among former members, reporters, and the federal government.

In the years of preparing for a migration to Guyana, the Temple had gone to considerable lengths to keep "black people's money" out of the hands of the US Internal Revenue Service (IRS). By the standards of poor people, they had created substantial collective wealth. Beyond maintaining Peoples Temple in California, the Temple used the resources to finance Jonestown and to prepare for a possible migration. To pursue these activities they shifted millions of dollars into overseas bank accounts beyond the reach of authorities in the United States. In 1976, the Temple leadership took steps to resolve its tax situation with the IRS by applying for tax-exempt status as a religious communal group. However, as the year wore on, they became increasingly worried that their application had inadvertently triggered an IRS investigation into their care-home financial practices, political involvements, and what the government might deem "private benefits" that the group provided to its communal members. Then in early March 1977, the IRS notified the Temple that their application for tax-exempt status had been turned down.

Soon thereafter, and well before the inside sources met with *New West* reporters, David Conn, the confidant of the Temple opponents, did something that had the unintentional consequence of heightening the Temple's long-standing concerns about its tax status. In late

March, he met with American Indian Movement (AIM) leader Dennis Banks, whom Conn hoped to warn about the hidden side of Peoples Temple. But unbeknownst to Conn, Jim Jones had loaned Banks $19,000 to bail his wife out of prison, and Banks was a close and indebted Temple ally. At the meeting with Banks, Conn revealed a great deal about what he knew of the Temple: the defectors' stories of faked healings, beatings, property extortion, threats and intimidations, the fact that he was working with a reporter, and the existence of the US Treasury investigation (initiated through the contact between opponents and the Customs Service agent that reporter George Kleinman had brokered). When Dennis Banks passed on what David Conn had told him to the Temple leadership, they mistakenly supposed their opponents' "treasury agent" (that is, the Customs Service agent) to be connected with the Temple's tax situation. Faced with what they regarded as a serious governmental threat to their organization, Temple leaders launched urgent final preparations for mass departure to Guyana. In the glare of the media spotlight, the collective migration began in earnest in July of 1977. By September, the population of Jonestown had mushroomed to around a thousand people, around 70 percent blacks, 30 percent whites. A steady trickle of immigrants continued to arrive through October of 1978.

The Concerned Relatives and the "Concentration Camp"

There is no way of knowing how Jonestown would have developed as a communal settlement in the absence of the increasingly polarized conflict with its opponents. The migration to Guyana did not cut the Temple off from controversy; it simply shifted the dynamics of the struggle. The opponents continued to offer reporters revelations about the Temple and they fed information about "nefarious acts" to a wide range of government authorities, including the San Francisco Police Department, the Customs Bureau, and the Federal Communications Commission.

Their central concern was the fate of Jonestown's residents.

The flood of negative press stories that accompanied the collective migration to Jonestown during the summer of 1977 heightened the anxieties of Jones's opponents and stirred concerns among relatives who might otherwise have been less involved. The strangest and most notorious case concerned the "child god": John Victor Stoen. Legally he was the son of defector Grace Stoen and her husband, Temple attorney Tim Stoen. But Jim Jones claimed that he was the biological father of John Stoen, and the boy was indeed raised socially within Peoples Temple as the son of Jim Jones. Three months after Grace had set off with Smitty Jones in July 1976, Tim Stoen, John's legal father, signed a notarized power of attorney for his son, appointing Jim Jones and others "to take all steps, exercise all powers and rights, that I might do in connection with said minor." The four-and-a-half-year-old was trundled off to Guyana, to live at the agricultural community. Grace Stoen came to recognize that her abandonment of John Victor Stoen to an identity within a collective organization contradicted basic social mores in the wider society that she had rejoined, and in February 1977 she began to assert her interest in getting the child to come back and live in San Francisco. In response, the Temple declared that the legal father, Tim Stoen, would go to Guyana to live with John. If Grace decided to press the issue, the Guyanese courts would surely side with the resident parent. Soon thereafter, Grace went to court to file for divorce and custody.

The resulting struggle became the most celebrated among a series of contestations that eventually raised the question of whether adults at Jonestown lived there of their own free will. The conflict intensified in the summer of 1977 when Tim Stoen went over to the camp of Temple opponents. After a California court granted custody to Grace Stoen on August 26, her lawyer traveled to Guyana. When people at Jonestown refused to hand over John Stoen, the lawyer went to the Guyanese courts and obtained an arrest order for the child and a court summons for Jim

Jones. Jones learned of these court actions on 10 September, and he responded with a highly dramatized state of siege in Jonestown. Reaffirming his biological paternity of John Stoen, he threatened death: "I related to Grace, and out of that came a son. That's part of the deal. The way to get to Jim Jones is through his son. They think that will suck me back or cause me to die before I'll give him up. And that's what we'll do, we'll die." Jones's staging of the crisis was by all accounts intense, but it quickly abated; through intensive political and legal maneuvering, Temple staff managed to vacate the Guyanese court order by successfully arguing that Grace Stoen had never revoked a standing grant of custody to a Temple member living at Jonestown.

The Stoen custody battle was a particularly complex case that brought to the fore basic legal and social issues surrounding communal versus conventional societal definitions of parenthood and family. But this was not the only such case, nor were custody struggles the only frontiers of conflict engulfing Peoples Temple. The increasingly organized network of opponents grew in numbers and activities. Participants initiated court proceedings in both the US and Guyana to seek legal custody of other Jonestown children, and they made "welfare and whereabouts" requests for the US State Department to have its embassy in Guyana check on their relatives in Jonestown. One distraught father embarked on a desperate and ineffective scheme to kidnap his adult daughter from Jonestown. Once Tim Stoen came over to their side, the opponents began to use political pressure and public relations, the same methods that Peoples Temple had employed so effectively in the United States. Calling themselves the "Concerned Relatives," they launched a highly visible campaign against Peoples Temple: they wrote to members of Congress, met with State Department officials, and organized human rights demonstrations.

Despite the intensity of the Concerned Relatives' manifold efforts, they were largely unsuccessful. The Stoen custody case became bogged down in legal issues in the Guyana courts, and the US State Department insisted on due process, refusing to take sides in a matter still proceeding through the courts of a foreign country. On other fronts, multiple governmental investigations in the US failed to come up with significant prosecutable offenses. And when US embassy officials in Guyana checked up on the "welfare and whereabouts" of Jonestown residents for their relatives, they found people living an austere third-world lifestyle who nevertheless "expressed satisfaction with their lives," as one embassy consul reported after a visit to the jungle community. In the absence of evidence that supported the opponents' charges of mass starvation and people living in bondage, the consul later observed, "The Concerned Relatives had a credibility problem, since so many of their claims were untrue" (Hall 1987: 217, 234).

Overall, the campaign against Peoples Temple backfired. But the meager results on legal and governmental fronts did have an important consequence: the frustrated opponents sought other avenues of remedy. Increasingly, they amplified and generalized their public charges against Peoples Temple.

In turn, even though the opponents failed in their direct goals, the Jonestown leadership took the campaign of opposition as inspiration for an increasingly apocalyptic posture, reinforcing the siege mentality that had started to take hold of the community during the September 1977 custody crisis over John Stoen. Most ominously, they began to elaborate the concept of "revolutionary suicide" that Jones had borrowed years earlier from Black Panther leader Huey Newton. The writer of a March 1978 Temple letter to members of Congress warned, "I can say without hesitation that we are devoted to a decision that it is better even to die than to be constantly harassed from one continent to the next. I hope that you can protect the right of over 1,000 people from the US to live in peace." A woman who defected from Jonestown in May of the same year, Debbie Blakey, told an embassy official and the Concerned Relatives that Jonestown was developing plans to carry out a mass suicide, murdering any resisters. In turn, the Concerned Relatives repeatedly publicized the

Temple's diehard threats of death and suicide as a way of raising the alarm against Jonestown. "When you say you are 'devoted' to this decision," they asked rhetorically, "does that mean it is irreversible?" (Hall 1987: 229).

In a public petition, the Concerned Relatives also portrayed Peoples Temple as "employing physical intimidation and psychological coercion as part of a mind-programming campaign" in violation of the United Nations human rights declaration of 1948 (Hall 1987: 229). This petition effectively raised new issues about Jonestown. Legally, adults at the jungle community had the right to avoid contact with their relatives if they so chose. However, if their mail was censored, if they were intimidated, if they couldn't travel, then it could be argued that they had neither free will nor free access to the outside world. In the words of one of the Concerned Relatives, the residents of Jonestown had become "mind-programmed." By small steps, the struggles by the Concerned Relatives to gain custody over particular children and access to particular relatives became refocused into an effort to "dismantle" what they eventually portrayed as a "concentration camp" (Hall 1987: 232–3). The Concerned Relatives demanded nothing less than that Jonestown cease to exist as a bounded communal society. In effect, they gambled that they could bring Jonestown to a public reckoning without precipitating the extreme acts of violent resistance that the community had threatened. On the other side, the leadership of Peoples Temple would want to know what were the prospects for people who had staked their lives on emigration to a foreign country thousands of miles from California, only to find their opponents hell-bent on shutting down the community they had sacrificed so much to build. Contradictory fears and postures fed the conflict over whether Jonestown was to survive.

Frustrated in both their legal efforts and their attempts to get the US State Department and its embassy to take their side in the tangle of disputes, yet propelled by the belief that Jim Jones had to be stopped, the Concerned Relatives increasingly pinned their hopes on political intervention. In Washington, DC,

they had already attracted the support of Leo Ryan, a US congressman from San Mateo, California, known to be sympathetic to the US anticult movement. In December 1977, Congressman Ryan wrote US Secretary of State Cyrus Vance, asking him "to investigate what action might be taken in connection with Mr. Jones." The State Department responded by describing the situation as a legal controversy that did not warrant any "political action without justification." Ryan rejected this view. In May of 1978, as the Concerned Relatives became increasingly frustrated with their lack of success in the courts and with the State Department, Ryan wrote to Peoples Temple, "Please be advised that Tim Stoen does have my support in the effort to return his son from Guyana." Then he began to work with members of the Concerned Relatives to organize a visit to Jonestown.

Mission to Jonestown

The expedition that Leo Ryan led to Jonestown was publicly billed as the 'fact-finding effort" of a congressional delegation, but this public facade obscured a working alliance between Ryan and the Concerned Relatives. As preparations unfolded, no other congressman would join Ryan on the trip, and for this reason the expedition failed to meet congressional criteria as an official congressional delegation. Another California congressman, Don Edwards, advised that taking the trip under such conditions "was not the right thing to do." Edwards later recalled, "I said congressmen are ill-advised to take such matters into their own hands." But Ryan pressed ahead anyway, accompanied unofficially by a number of Concerned Relatives and some journalists.

Diverse motives shaped the planned trip. At least two opponents, Tim Stoen and Steve Katsaris, wanted to retrieve their relatives "by force if necessary," as Stone put it. A less clandestine strategy hinged on the view of some opponents that conditions at Jonestown were desperate. In this scenario, the presence of visiting relatives together with outside authorities would break Jones's discipline and precipitate a mass exodus. The press had agendas too. A freelance journalist, Don Harris, organized an NBC crew to cover a story about a congressman and ordinary citizens traveling to Guyana to investigate the plight of their relatives trapped in a jungle commune.

Given the participation of a congressman and the newsmen, the expedition promised to confront Jones with the choice of either submitting to external scrutiny and possible intervention, or precipitating a flood of bad press and governmental inquiry. When Peoples Temple staff first learned of Ryan's plans, they sought to negotiate conditions about press coverage and the composition of the congressional delegation. Ryan considered the negotiations a delaying tactic, and on 14 November 1978, accompanied by the group of Concerned Relatives and the news reporters, he boarded the Pan American Airlines flight from New York to Guyana's capital, Georgetown. The group would try to gain access to Jonestown once they arrived. But in Georgetown, Ryan met further resistance. With time running out before he would have to return to the US, on 17 November he flew with the reporters and a subgroup of the Concerned Relatives to Port Kaituma, a small settlement near Jonestown. From there, a dump truck brought Ryan, the US ambassador to Guyana, and Temple lawyers Charles Garry and Mark Lane up the muddy road to Jonestown, where they conferred with Jim Jones. Faced with the prospects of news reports about a congressman and relatives barred from entering a jungle compound that had been called a concentration camp, Jones acquiesced to the visit of the Concerned Relatives and most of the journalists.

At Jonestown, Jim Jones already had coached his community for days about how to respond to the visitors. On the evening that Ryan and the others arrived, Jonestown gave them an orchestrated welcome at the main pavilion, serving up a good dinner and musical entertainment from "The Jonestown Express." But during the festivities, a message was passed to NBC reporter Don Harris: "Help us get out of Jonestown." The note was signed "Vern Gosney." On the reverse side was the name "Monica Bagby." The next day, Jonestown staff tried to occupy the visitors with public-relations activities, but Ryan and embassy staff began to make arrangements for Gosney and Bagby to leave. NBC reporter Don Harris then tipped off Leo Ryan's assistant, Jackie Speier, about members of the Parks family, who also might want to leave. Jones pleaded with the Parks family not to depart with his enemies; he offered them $5,000 to cover transportation back to the US if they would wait several days and go on their own. But they decided to leave with Ryan. "I have failed," Jones muttered to his lawyer, Charles Garry. "I live for my people because they need me. But whenever they leave, they tell lies about the place."

As the dump truck was loaded for departure, Ryan told Jones that he would give a basically positive report: "If two hundred people wanted to leave, I would still say you have a beautiful place here." Ryan talked about the need for more interchange with the outside world. Suddenly he was assaulted by a man brandishing a knife. Blood spurted across Ryan's white shirt. Within seconds, Temple attorneys Charles Garry and Mark Lane grabbed the assailant, a man named Don Sly, the former husband of a Concerned Relative. Jones stood impassively by. Ryan was dishevelled but unhurt: Sly had accidentally cut himself, not the congressman.

"Does this change everything?" Jones asked Ryan. "It doesn't change everything, but it changes things," Ryan replied. "You get that man arrested." Then the US embassy deputy chief of mission, Richard Dwyer, led Ryan to the departing truck and they piled in with the reporters, the four Concerned Relatives, and the Jonestown people who had decided to leave with the entourage. The truck lurched into low gear and down the muddy road toward the nearby Port Kaituma airstrip.

Gone from the Promised Land

All told, sixteen defectors, mostly whites, departed under the auspices of a US congressman whom the Jonestown leadership regarded as allied with their opponents. One of the apostates parted saying that the community was nothing but "a communist prison camp." From Jones's viewpoint, the episode was certain to be used by the Temple's opponents to fuel further accusations, more media scrutiny, and increased intervention in the affairs of Jonestown by external legal authorities. These were the circumstances in which the Jonestown leadership translated revolutionary suicide into a final decisive act against their opponents, sending sharpshooters to the airstrip in pursuit of the dump truck.

When the truck reached the Port Kaituma airstrip and Ryan's group started boarding two planes, a Jonestown man posing as a defector suddenly pulled out a loaded pistol in the smaller plane and fired it. Simultaneously, a tractor came up pulling a flatbed trailer carrying men from Jonestown. When the trailer had pulled to about thirty feet from the larger plane, the men picked up rifles as if by signal and started shooting at the people still clustered outside the plane. After a seeming eternity of gunfire, the tractor pulled away, leaving behind ten people wounded, and five dead bodies: Congressman Leo Ryan, Don Harris and two other newsmen, and defector Patricia Parks.

By directing the airstrip attack on Leo Ryan and his entourage, Jones and his followers constructed a situation of such overriding stigma that their enemies would surely prevail in their plan to "dismantle" Jonestown. The Jonestown leadership chose to finesse this outcome. Back at the pavilion, Jim Jones told the assembled residents of Jonestown that they would no longer be able to survive as a community. With a tape recorder running, Jones argued, "If we can't live in peace, then let's die in peace." Medical staff set up cauldrons of Fla-Vor Aid laced with cyanide and tranquilizers.

A total of 913 members of the community became caught up in the orchestrated ritual of mass suicide that ensued. How many people willingly participated? The question will always be open to debate. Certainly young children could not have understood the consequences of drinking the poison, and during the suicide council a woman named Christine Miller pleaded against Jones's proposal. But many people supported the plan: mothers willing to have their infants killed, elderly people telling Jones they were ready to go, the sharpshooters who had killed the congressman. Amidst low wails, sobbing, and the shrieks of children, they all came up to take the "potion," then moved out of the pavilion to huddle with their families and die. Whatever their individual sentiments, the people of Jonestown departed their own promised land through an improvised ritual of collective death. As people lined up to die, Jones preached to the believers and the doubters assembled in the Jonestown pavilion. Invoking Huey Newton's words, he assured them, "This is a revolutionary suicide. This is not a self-destructive suicide." In the confusion, two black men slipped past the guards. At the very end, Jim Jones and a close aide, Annie Moore, died by gunshots to the head, wounds consistent with suicide. Annie had scribbled a last sentence to the note she left: "We died because you would not let us live in peace." During the mass suicide, the community's two American lawyers, Charles Garry and Mark Lane, had been sequestered at a perimeter house, and after their guards left to join the suicide ritual, Garry and Lane plunged into the jungle. One elderly woman slept through the event. Everyone else died.

After Jonestown

What is the cultural significance of Jonestown? The answer to this question hinges on highly contested questions about why the mass suicide occurred. With a basic narrative of the group's history at hand, we can consider these questions. A general list of *necessary preconditions* – without which the murderous attack and mass self-destruction would not have occurred – might reasonably focus on the *internal features* of a group that could undertake such acts, specifically:

- a charismatic religious social movement;
- an apocalyptic ideology;
- a form of social organization adequate to maintain solidarity;
- legitimacy enough among followers to exercise collective social control over the affairs of the community;
- sufficient economic and political viability;
- life within strong social boundaries in cognitive isolation from society at large.

Without these circumstances, minor incidents of violence might occur within a countercultural communal movement or in a conflict between it and external adversaries, but it is difficult to imagine that they would trigger violence on a large scale.

These preconditions well describe Peoples Temple. Yet if the preconditions are particularly conducive to violence, they are hardly sufficient. Numerous apocalyptic and quasi-apocalyptic religious communities – from Mother Ann Lee's Shakers to contemporary "heavens on earth" like Seattle's Love Family and the Krishna farm in West Virginia (Hall 1978) – have all these *internal* characteristics without experiencing anything remotely like murder of enemies followed by collective suicide. Thus, strongly bounded apocalyptic religious movements may be especially prone to external violence and mass suicide, but that outcome is extremely rare compared to the number of groups adequately described by the list of preconditions. There must be specific additional *precipitating factors* that would result in murders and mass suicide.

In contemporary circumstances, the necessary precipitating factors would seem to be the . . .

- mobilization of a group of cultural opponents who possess a high degree of solidarity;
- the shaping of news media coverage through the cultural opponents' frame of interpretation about "cults";
- the exercise of state authority.

If through the operation of these factors, the apocalyptic group's very capacity to persist comes into question, it would be under these conditions (and in a strong explanation, these conditions alone) that group leaders might unleash aggression toward detractors and use the device of mass suicide to cut off any external exercise of authority over the group.

How well does this general causal explanation capture the circumstances that led up to the murders and mass suicide at Jonestown? Clearly, the proximate cause of murder and mass suicide was the refusal of Jim Jones, his staff, and the loyalists among his followers to brook compromise with opponents whom they believed (with some reason) were out to bring Jonestown as a community to an end. Rather than submit to external powers that they regarded as illegitimate, they chose to stage the airstrip murders as revenge and shut out their opponents by ending their own lives.

After the fact, the narrative structure of myth carved the stigma of this massive carnage into infamy. Jones became a megalomaniacal Antichrist; Peoples Temple, a cult of brainwashed robots; the Concerned Relatives, tragic heroes who valiantly tried but failed to save their loved ones. However, the mythic structure of this narrative depends on a particular analytic claim: that the avoidable carnage was solely a consequence of the acts of Jones and his accomplices. It is by lifting the mantle on this claim that we come to the heart of the apocalypse at Jonestown.

Without the airstrip attack on Ryan and the others, the mass suicide would have lacked a credible rationale, whereas in the context of the airstrip murders Jones presented collective death as the only honorable collective choice in the face of certain subjugation to external authority. In other words, the Jonestown leadership constructed the murders and mass suicide as a unity, but that unity was predicated upon the airstrip attack. The attack itself was not an act of random violence: other than the perhaps accidental killing of a young girl who defected, the gunfire seems to have been carefully targeted toward individuals whom Jonestown principals regarded as their opponents in the ongoing struggle. It was a preemptive strike that snatched victory from opponents, albeit by fulfilling their most nightmarish prophecies.

Given the targets, the attack itself has to be understood as an extreme escalation of an intense conflict between the Concerned Relatives and Peoples Temple. This conflict had already unfolded for more than a year in the press, the courts, the US State Department, in the conduct of espionage on both sides, and in strategic actions that had previously come close to direct confrontation. Under these circumstances, it seems incontrovertible that the expedition of Congressman Ryan, the Concerned Relatives and journalists, and especially their departure with sixteen Jonestown residents, was the precipitating factor in the murderous attack. As a specific event, the mass suicide must be seen as a consequence of the expedition.

It is not easy to answer the question of what would have happened had the expedition not taken place at all, or not turned out as it did, since there are so many alternative scenarios. Conducting "mental experiments" to consider "what would happen if . . ." is a delicate matter. Yet as Geoffrey Hawthorne (1991) has argued, the consideration of alternative scenarios can deepen an analysis if the counterfactual hypotheses are neither so distant from the course of events as to be irrelevant nor so unstable in their dynamics as to make prediction unreliable. With these guidelines in mind, it is possible to push toward a deeper – though necessarily tentative – understanding of the murders and mass suicide.

On the one hand, had the Concerned Relatives not formed an organized group, and had they not achieved some success in their substantial efforts to bring a critical mass of journalistic coverage and a US congressman to their side, it seems unlikely that the mass suicide would have occurred. Indeed, when they first formed, the Concerned Relatives understood their own powerlessness and sought out sympathetic news reporters precisely as patrons who would help them. After Jones and his followers migrated to Jonestown, the opponents took concerted actions through legal and administrative channels, but these actions failed to advance their cause, and

it was because they became frustrated with their prospects within institutional channels of conflict resolution that they turned to publicity campaigns in the media and the political intervention of a congressman's "fact-finding" expedition.

Clearly then, the actions of the apostates and relatives were crucial to catalyzing the dynamic of conflict between Peoples Temple and the outside, and this conflict is a necessary component of any explanation of the mass suicide that actually occurred. It is impossible, however, to say with certainty whether a mass suicide would have occurred without the Ryan expedition. Certainly there are plausible scenarios in which a mass suicide would *not* have taken place. For example, the opponents might have won some legal battles, gained better access to visitation with relatives, and won other concessions without confronting the Temple with complete subordination to external authority. Even more likely, given time, the entire enterprise at Jonestown might have collapsed from internal dissension, as the vast majority of communal groups do (cf. Kanter 1972). In light of these possibilities, the murders and mass suicide were in no way inevitable.

On the other hand, it is also apparent that even without the Ryan trip, the conflict between the Concerned Relatives and the Temple was extremely intense, and the Concerned Relatives were willing to pursue it even in the face of threatened violent responses. They might have gained other victories to which the leadership at Jonestown would likely have responded with violence. For example, had Grace and Timothy Stoen won legal custody over John Victor Stoen, a different violent confrontation – and mass suicide – might have ensued. In other words, within the broad channels of contestation between Peoples Temple and the Concerned Relatives, the potential for violence could have been unleashed in more than one scenario.

The question of John Victor Stoen's biological paternity is the remaining major mystery of the tragedy. Much anecdotal evidence suggests that Jim Jones was his biological father: his paternity was affirmed in an affidavit by Tim Stoen in 1972 only days after the boy's birth (Hall 1987: 127–8), and taken as fact both within the Temple and by certain people outside the group well before the issue became folded into the conflict between the Temple and its opponents. Tim Stoen only denied Jones's claim publicly much later, when he took the side of Grace Stoen in the custody battle. To date, the evidence is not conclusive, but the weight of it leans to the paternity of Jim Jones.

If Jones was indeed the biological father, then a central atrocity claimed by the Concerned Relatives during their campaign against the Temple that Jones amounted to the kidnapper of a child would lose much of its moral (though not legal) force. Thus one significant element of the opponents' brief against Peoples Temple would turn out to have been based on a public construction of reality that differed from privately held knowledge. Resolving this question might sharpen our opinions about the moral high ground held by the two sides. At the time, however, it would have resolved neither the cultural conflict between communalism and familial individualism nor the struggle over whether the adult people of Jonestown had the right to live in isolation from the direct intervention of opponents who sought to dismantle their community. And it probably would not have altered the commitments of the true believers at Jonestown to extreme violence, should their opponents prevail in subordinating them to external social and legal authority.

A second controversy – about government agencies – is even murkier. The Concerned Relatives triggered some governmental investigations of Peoples Temple. But other government initiatives *preceded* the emergence of the Concerned Relatives as an organized group, and the inquiries of various government agencies fed on one another. In particular, the US government had diplomatic and strategic concerns about the socialist government of Guyana, and its embassy in Georgetown sent operatives on monitoring visits to the Jonestown settlement. Because the United States government might have been able to prevent the tragedy, and also because government offi-

cials and representatives may have acted in ways that propelled it, there has been considerable speculation about the government's role. One book weaves some well established facts together with highly questionable inferences to raise the question of whether Jonestown was a "CIA medical experiment" (Meiers 1988). Whatever the truth of the matter, such accounts cannot be easily assessed because the US government has suppressed information about its dealings with Peoples Temple, partly on the basis of the sensitivity of its geopolitical interests. If remaining government files on Peoples Temple can be examined, they may well yield significant reassessments of its history (the same holds for the NBC video "outakes" from its Jonestown coverage, which the network has refused to make public).

Whatever comes of the search for more information, causal analysis of available evidence substantially revises the popular myth of Jonestown. Without question, the apocalypse at Jonestown was an immense tragedy. The Concerned Relatives, Leo Ryan, and the press will no doubt continue to be portrayed as tragic heroes in the affair. Yet there is a deeper tragedy. It is now evident that the opponents' own actions helped to precipitate a course of events that presumably led to the fulfillment of their own worst fears. The murders and mass suicide cannot be adequately explained except as the outcome of an escalating conflict between two diametrically opposed groups: Peoples Temple and the Concerned Relatives.

Other religious groups important to American religious history – the Pilgrims and the Mormons, for example – previously met with pitched opposition from relatives and public detractors, yet they managed to persist and to succeed in ways important for the culture of American religion. By contrast, Peoples Temple was a dramatic failure. Yet even so, the history of the movement reflects many of the tensions and contradictions of American culture. Its members sought to participate in an integrated community that transcended persistent racism in the United States. In a society where the practice of religion is largely segregated from everyday socioeconomic organization and practice, the group infused its members' working lives and social relationships with new "religious" meaning. These aspects neither justify nor compensate for the tragic conflict that Jones long cultivated. But the seldom-acknowledged accomplishments of Peoples Temple stand as stark reminders that the US has failed to achieve anything like a societal community based on racial integration, equal opportunity, and economic justice. Jonestown, we now know, came at the time when the liberal and left social movements that had been active in American politics during the 1960s and 1970s were losing their influence. Ronald Reagan soon followed, proclaiming a pride-filled "morning in America."

There is considerable irony in all this. Much of the criticism of Peoples Temple focused on the group's practices: faked healings, money-making schemes, glorification of a prophet, intimidation and punishment, public relations, and political manipulations. This *auto-da-fé* could only proceed by placing on Jim Jones and Peoples Temple the stigma of bearing evils that are widespread and sometimes institutionalized in the wider society. Unfortunately Jones was hardly a creative man. On the contrary, however crudely, he mimicked and sometimes intensified practices that he drew from the wider culture. Jones established an organization with alien *ends*, to be sure, but that organization owed its success in no small part to the fact that its cultural inventory of *means* mostly came from the wider world. Thus the Temple's realm of opposition to the world at large was often enough but a mirror of it, and sometimes a grotesque reflection of its seamier side. After the mass suicide, those who loaded the moral burden of evil onto Jonestown symbolically cleansed the wider society, but this ritual exorcism left behind elements of Jonestown culture still alive in our world – in techniques of social control, religious practices, politics, and public relations. The "negative cult" of Jonestown thus stands as an ominous monument to an arsenal of manipulations that persist in wider institutional practices. To isolate this arsenal, its boundaries must be drawn more widely than the jungle commune.

A different irony was reflected in the future of memory. Jonestown fulfilled the most dire warnings of its opponents. After the murders and mass suicide, Peoples Temple became the quintessence of the "cult," stereotypically portrayed as an organization that drains both property and free will from its members and "brainwashes" them into a "group mind." Yet these issues have nothing specific to do with Peoples Temple's sustained and increasingly violent interpretation of revolutionary suicide as a doctrine of struggle against an established social order. Instead, they stem from a more general cultural reflection of communalism as a form of life alien to capitalist democratic society. The tragedy of Jonestown thus became an opportunity for scapegoating a broader form of social organization that is not inherently associated with mass suicide. Here, the conflict that produced Jonestown was recapitulated at the core of its mythical reconstruction, for the demonization of communalism as "other" reinforces the ideology of individualism, thus providing the grounds for further antagonism between communalists and their cultural opponents . . .

Note

1 Unless otherwise indicated, information for this chapter is drawn from . . . Hall (1987). See also Hall (1990), Moore (1985), Chidester (1988), Moore and McGehee (1988), and Maaga (1998).

References

Alexander, Jeffrey C. and Philip Smith 1993: "The Discourse of Civil Society: A New Proposal for Cultural Studies." *Theory and Society* 22: 151–207.

Barthes, Roland 1972: *Mythologies*. New York: Hill and Wang.

Becker, Penny 1999: *Congregations in Conflict*. New York: Cambridge University Press.

Chidester, David 1988: *Salvation and Suicide: An Interpretation of Jim Jones, the Peoples Temple, and Jonestown*. Bloomington: Indiana University Press.

Hall, John R. 1978: *The Ways Out: Utopian Communal Groups in the Age of Babylon.* London: Routledge and Kegan Paul.

—— 1987: *Gone from the Promised Land: Jonestown in American Cultural History.* New Brunswick, NJ: Transaction Books.

—— 1988: "Social Organization and Pathways of Commitment: Types of Communal Groups, Rational Choice Theory, and the Kanter Thesis." *American Sociological Review* 53: 679–92.

—— 1990: "The Apocalypse at Jonestown." Pp. 269–93 in T. Robbins and D. Anthony, eds. *In Gods We Trust*, 2nd edn. New Brunswick, NJ: Transaction.

Hawthorne, Geoffrey 1991: *Plausible Worlds: Possibility and Understanding in History and the Social Sciences.* New York: Cambridge University Press.

Hechter, Michael 1987: *Principles of Group Solidarity.* Berkeley: University of California Press.

Kanter, Rosabeth Moss 1972: *Commitment and Community: Communes and Utopias in Sociological Perspective.* Cambridge, MA Harvard University Press.

Maaga, Mary McCormich 1998: *Hearing the Voices of Jonestown.* Syracuse, NY: Syracuse University Press.

Malcomson, Scott 1997: "Keep Out." *New Yorker*, April 7: 39.

Meiers, Nichael 1988: *Was Jonestown a CIA Medical Experiment?* Lewiston, NY: Edwin Mellen Press.

Moore, Rebecca 1985: *A Sympathetic History of Jonestown.* Lewiston, NY: Edwin Mellen Press.

Moore, Rebecca and Fielding McGehee, III (eds.) 1988: *New Religious Movements, Mass Suicide, and Peoples Temple.* Lewiston, NY: Edwin Mellen Press.

Moses, William Jeremiah 1982: *Black Messiahs and Uncle Toms: Social and Literary Manipulations of a Religious Myth.* University Park: Pennsylvania State University Press.

Shupe, Anson D., Jr., David G. Bromley, and Donna L. Oliver 1984: *The Anti-cult Movement in America: A Bibliography and Historical Survey.* New York: Garland.

Weisbrot, Robert 1983: *Father Divine and the Struggle for Radical Equality.* Urbana: University of Illinois Press.

CHAPTER THIRTEEN

"Our Terrestrial Journey is Coming to an End": The Last Voyage of the Solar Temple

Jean-François Mayer

Translated by Elijah Siegler

We, Loyal Servants of the Rosy Cross, declare that, as we left one day, we will return stronger than ever . . . for the Rosy Cross is immortal . . . Like Her, we are of all time and no time.[1]

The mysterious circumstances surrounding the dramatic "transit" of fifty-three members of the Order of the Solar Temple (OTS, *Ordre du Temple Solaire*) in Switzerland and in Québec in October 1994 have spawned an unprecedented wave of public speculation and conspiracy mongering. The subsequent death of sixteen people in France in December 1995 and of five more in Québec in March 1997 have only added to these conspiratorial speculations. Ironically, Joseph Di Mambro, Luc Jouret, and those who, over the course of months, methodically prepared their own deaths and the deaths of dozens of others were quite concerned about the impact their departure would have on the public mind and spent many hours creating a kind of legend that would survive their earthly exit. Why else would they have felt the need to send manifestos justifying *post mortem* their decision not only to other members but also to television stations, newspapers, and some other correspondents (including the author of this article)? The Swiss investigators found a tape, dating probably from the spring of 1994, in which one can hear the core group discuss the "departure." There is a telling exchange between Joseph Di Mambro and Luc Jouret:

JDM: People have beaten us to the punch, you know.
LJ: Well, yeah. Waco beat us to the punch.
JDM: In my opinion, we should have gone six months before them . . . what we'll do will be even more spectacular . . .[2]

"More spectacular": such are the words used by Joseph Di Mambro himself. A movement such as the Solar Temple cannot escape its media-saturated era. It worries about its public image until the very hour of the "crowning of the work," to use its own vocabulary. Many fringe movements tend to cultivate a very high estimation of their own importance, and the OTS was no exception. The core members of the group understood themselves as an elect people who had incarnated periodically on Earth since ancient times in order to fulfill a cosmic mission. They had gathered together for that purpose and were ready to sacrifice their lives for its sake. Especially toward the end, some internal texts disclose these grandiose perspectives:

Do you understand what we represent? We are the promise that the R[osy] C[ross] made to the Immutable. We are the Star Seeds that guarantee the perennial existence of the universe, we are the hand of God that shapes creation. We are the Torch that Christ must bring to the Father to feed the Primordial Fire and to reanimate the forces of Life, which, without our contribution, would slowly but surely go out. We hold the key to the universe and must secure its Eternity.[3]

In reality, like so many other movements that see themselves on the cutting edge of cosmic progress and who assign to minor events in their own history a global significance, the Solar Temple was in fact a tiny (and actually declining) group whose claim to cosmic importance would have been viewed as dubious by most commentators. But through a sensational act of self-immolation that compelled the attention of both popular and academic observers, the leaders of the Solar Temple came close to creating a durable legend for their esoteric order.

Unfortunately for the order's leaders, documents exist which, when analyzed carefully, begin to deconstruct this legend. If everything had worked as Di Mambro planned, no trace would have remained. Nothing, not even the bodies themselves, would have been recovered: "We will not let our bodies dissolve according to nature's slow alchemy, because we don't want to run the risk that they become soiled by frantic lunatics."[4] The Solar Temple's thorough preparation for their mysterious exit, however, could not take into account certain technical problems: some of the devices intended to start the fire did not function properly, which made it possible for the investigators to seize a large number of written documents (in part found on computers that survived the fires relatively unscathed) as well as video and audio cassettes belonging to the group's archives. It is upon these sources that this article is in large part based.[5]

Joseph Di Mambro, the Golden Way Foundation, and the Neo-Templar Movement

Joseph Di Mambro was born in Pont-Saint-Esprit, in the French department of Gard, 19

August 1924. At the age of sixteen, he began an apprenticeship as a watchmaker and jeweler and very soon became fascinated with esotericism. In January 1956, he joined the Ancient and Mystical Order Rosae Crucis (AMORC), to which he would belong until at least 1968. In the 1960s, he apparently established links with several persons who would later play a role in OTS history, including Jacques Breyer, the initiator of a "Templar resurgence" in France in 1952 to which several groups, including Di Mambro's OTS, trace part of their roots.

Several major points of doctrine, as well as an embryonic circle of disciples, began crystallizing during the 1960s. After visiting Israel and dealing with legal problems in Nîmes in 1971 related to swindling and writing bad checks, Di Mambro set himself up in Annemasse, near the Swiss border. In 1973, he became president of the Center for the Preparation of the New Age, which was presented as a "cultural center for relaxation" and a yoga school. The center became a full-time job by 1976. That same year, eight people (seven of whom resided at a common address) formed a building society and purchased a house named "The Pyramid" at Collonges-sous-Salève, close to Geneva. Of these eight people, four would lose their lives in October 1994. The building society in fact sheltered an esoteric activity: the consecration of the Temple of the Great White Universal Lodge, Pyramid Sub-Lodge, was celebrated on 24 June 1976. Internal documents show that, of the fifty-three believers who died in October 1994, at least twelve already belonged to the group by the end of 1977.

The next step commenced on 12 July 1978 with the creation of the Golden Way Foundation in Geneva. This foundation would remain at the very heart of activities undertaken by Di Mambro's various groups over the ensuing years. Thanks to substantial financial sacrifices made by several members, the foundation bought an attractive property in a suburb of Geneva that was the site of meetings open to nonmembers. The Golden Way Foundation was above all a front for a nucleus of people called simply the "Fraternity,"[6] who took part in esoteric rites in a communitarian setting. This communitarian ideal played a role in attracting people to the group and also led later to disappointments when the gap between the ideal and the reality of everyday life became untenable for certain members. People belonging to the "Fraternity" held all assets in common; along with them lived people belonging to what was called the "Community," who kept their income, paid a rent, and bought tickets for food and beverages. In the context of the 1970s, it was only one attempt among many others at developing an ideal communal life. Indeed, one member who joined at that time had lived in the New Age community of Findhorn, Scotland, and was hoping to find something similar in the Golden Way.

Excerpts from an account given at a 1994 OTS meeting provide us with retrospective (and no doubt idealized) glimpses into the experiences of the pioneer members of the brotherhood:

Meeting at first in a house which they called "the Pyramid," where every evening was devoted to rituals and meditation, they later moved near Geneva, to a large property which was discovered to be an ancient Templar command post . . . There, living in a perfect fraternity where all was equally shared – salaries were put into a common fund and everyone received in return an equal share – they devoted all their free time to the cause of spirituality. Daily ceremonies quickly became operational at the highest degree, even more so because hermeticists, alchemists, and spiritually elevated people joined in. The Masters of the beyond regularly manifested themselves, with a presence visible, audible, and olfactory.

The Golden Way Foundation had impressive headquarters, but in order to spread its ideas on a larger scale the group needed a communicator. Enter a Belgian homeopathic physician, Luc Jouret (born 18 October 1947), who was likely introduced to Di Mambro by one of the victims of October 1994. On 30 May 1982, Jouret and his then wife[7] were "accepted in the Golden Way" and took the

oath of "Knights of the Rosy Cross." Di Mambro confided to some members at the time that Jouret had charisma and, being a physician, would be taken seriously; therefore, he should be pushed into the limelight, while Di Mambro would remain discretely backstage.

From that moment on, Luc Jouret became the propagandist for the group. Beginning in 1983, he gave lectures in Switzerland, France, and Canada. Cultural clubs were created and, from 1984 to 1990, the organization operated as a tripartite structure involving (1) public lectures and seminars given by Jouret and a few others under the label of Amenta; (2) an exoteric structure, the Archedia Clubs, for those wishing to go further; and finally, for a limited number of candidates, (3) an initiatory order (organized as the esoteric counterpart of the clubs) called the "International Order of Chivalry, Solar Tradition."[8] Obviously, the group hoped to attract a wider audience, and it thus prepared structures meant for a much larger movement than it ever became. The success of Luc Jouret, a gifted speaker who easily attracted hundreds to his lectures, could only add fuel to the fire of such hopes. The fact that Jouret was able to draw such large audiences to his lectures is proof that the topics he was dealing with were of interest to at least a part of the cultic milieu of the time.[9] However, because of the seeker's mentality typical of the cultic milieu, most of those who came to Jouret's lectures did not want to commit themselves on a firm basis and, despite the lecturer's success, significant growth for the OTS in terms of committed membership never materialized.

The group's Templar activities[10] had their roots in a 1952 "resurgence" in which the French esoteric author Jacques Breyer (1922–96) played a central role. While reluctant to take upon himself any administrative responsibility in those Templar circles claiming some link with the "resurgence," Breyer enjoyed the role of an elder adviser to whom those groups turned at crucial times in order to ask his opinion. Di Mambro did so several times.

Although Di Mambro's OTS considered the 1952 resurgence as a "first impulse," the real resurgence began for them on 21 March 1981. On that day, "knights" met at the Golden Way Foundation headquarters "to renew their oath of alegiance to the Order of the Temple and to the XXIIIrd Occult Grand Master to come."[11] One of the goals of the meeting was to achieve "Templar unity," and for this purpose the heads of two Neo-Templar Orders had been invited – Jean-Louis Marsan, Grand Master of the OSTS (*Ordre Souverain du Temple Solaire*, i.e., Sovereign Order of the Solar Temple) and Julien Origas, Grand Master of the ORT (*Ordre Rénové du Temple*, i.e., Renewed Order of the Temple). Like Di Mambro, both Origas and Marsan had been connected with the resurgence initiated by Breyer. "Templar unity" was not achieved, but such meetings show that members of these neo-Templar groups were partly interacting in the same milieu, with each group maintaining its specific features. For instance, the ORT was originally sponsored by Raymond Bernard (born in 1923), head of AMORC for French-speaking countries, who functioned for a time as the secret Grand Master of the ORT.[12]

After the death of Julien Origas (1920–83), Luc Jouret briefly took control of the ORT as Grand Master, but immediately found himself confronted with opposition from Origas's wife and daughter. At the same time, some Canadians linked to the ORT expressed a strong interest in Jouret's message. During this period of crisis (March 1984), Luc Jouret, Joseph Di Mambro, and a Canadian member went to consult Jacques Breyer. Breyer told them that he thought it possible to develop something out of the small Canadian nucleus through restructuring the local groups and transferring the center of the OTS's activities to Canada. Breyer's advice was connected to apocalyptic considerations typical of his way of thinking: the "age of plagues," needed to open people up spiritually, was about to come because of the earth's growing corruptions. The area around Toronto, Breyer claimed, would experience less upheaval during this time of troubles. In 1984, the Golden Way Foundation financed Joseph and Jocelyne Di Mambro's emigration to Canada; according to Breyer's advice, the Di Mambros first moved

to Toronto. And Breyer himself, at a conclave of ORT officers during Easter 1984 in Geneva, informed the gathered people that the deposit was "to be transported to Canada" where a "Noah's ark" was to be built.[13]

From 1984 forward, the movement had two centers of activity – French-speaking Europe and Québec. The presence in Canada was also meant to reach the English-speaking world, mainly the United States:

The Executive Council of this New Order decided that, in line with the historic destiny of the Order of the Temple, the headquarters of the Order should be located somewhere on the North America continent. The reason for this decision is simple. North America has become the source of most of the new impulses which determine the way life evolves on this planet. It is therefore fitting that the modern Knight Templar of the old continent should play his part in the Age of Aquarius by adding his inspiration to that which his counterparts in the New World will bring to the planet.[14]

However, despite the beginning of a translation project designed to make certain rules and ritual texts available to English-speaking audiences, the order never had more than a handful of isolated members in the United States. In January 1989, at the height of its development and before internal turmoil took its toll on membership, OTS had 442 members, of which 90 were in Switzerland (monthly revenues: $12,600), 187 in France ($12,700), 53 in Martinique ($3,400), 16 in the United States ($1,125), 86 in Canada ($7,000) and 10 in Spain.

From Survivalism to Self-Destruction

In addition to these revenues, several well-endowed members donated large sums that amounted to hundreds of thousands (and up to millions) of US dollars over the years. These donors hoped that their generosity would permit the financing of "life centers" on farms acquired in Canada and in Cheiry, Switzerland, in 1990. But the group's leaders diverted part of these donations into other areas, including their own travel expenses and living costs for community members with no external means of support. The constant need for funds led to financial problems, which were perhaps not entirely unrelated to the events of 1994.

Beginning in the 1990s, several members began distancing themselves from the order. Important donors among these members wanted to recoup at least some of their money, and the group's revenues began to decline. Di Mambro had long pretended (since at least the late 1970s) to represent the "Mother Lodge" and to receive his orders from mysterious "Masters" in Zurich. The theme of "Unknown Superiors" is a commonplace of occult movements such as Rosicrucianism, Theosophy, and the I AM Activity. However, around 1990, Di Mambro's son Elie (1969–94) began seriously to doubt the existence of the "Masters" of Zurich and discovered that fakery had been practiced by his father to produce the illusion of spiritual phenomena during the ceremonies celebrated in the order's sanctuaries. These phenomena – which included apparitions of spiritual entities – had been a major reason why several members had accepted Di Mambro as what he claimed to be. Even today, several leading former members remain convinced that, notwithstanding occasional fakery, some of the phenomena were authentic. Elie spoke openly about what he had discovered, which led to the departure of fifteen members. In 1993, there was a wave of resignations of French members who saw that their donations ended up as home improvements for their leader's residence. In February 1994, two members from Geneva sent an open letter to announce their decision to leave the movement, because "real fraternity [did] not exist in this structure, as extolled in the teachings." They were also worried about what happened to their contributions, observing the absence of the "life centers" which were supposed to be created.[15] And these were not the only examples of defections.

Throughout the years, according to explanations provided by former members, Di Mambro had grown more authoritarian. He no longer helped with the daily chores, as he had in the original community.[16] He wanted to gather bright people around him, but probably was also afraid of potential competitors. There was never any attempt at a takeover, but there were rivalries among Di Mambro's underlings, and some people felt that he was playing a game of divide and rule while expecting unconditional obedience from all members.[17] When speaking to the police, a Canadian member who broke with the Solar Temple in 1993 summarized the feelings of many defectors: "I did not feel that the people were living what they preached. And I was tired of the infighting and never being able to find out what was going on, so I left."[18]

A report on the organization's situation in Europe written to Di Mambro on 10 December 1993 by a Swiss OTS officer reflects the growing dissent that was affecting the group at this time. The document also shows how a longtime follower who had developed serious doubts about Di Mambro's honesty nevertheless wanted to persevere in serving the ideal he had dedicated his life to for so many years. This loyalty had tragic consequences, as he was murdered in October 1994 as he was about to leave the farm where he lived with other members. The report states,

Rumors about embezzlement and various [forms of] skullduggery are propagated by influential ex-members. Many members ... have left or are leaving. They feel their ideals have been betrayed ... It is even said that you have fallen because of money and women, and you're no longer credible. This is very serious for the Order's mission.

There are even more serious grumblings, and you know them. Here they are: everything that we saw and heard in certain places has been a trick. I have known this for some time. Tony [Dutoit][19] has been talking about this for years already ... I have always refused to pay attention to these rumors, but the evidence is growing, and questions are being asked. This calls into question many things I've seen, and messages. I would be really upset if I had to conclude that I had sincerely prostrated myself in front of an illusion!!! . . . There is enough stuff here to send less committed people packing. And all the resignations and departures of recent times just confirm it.

I don't want to analyze the reasons that could lead to such trickery, which was motivated by good intentions no doubt, but which transgressed the rules of common sense, when we see the mess we're in now. It's also been said that Zurich has never existed, that it's pure fantasy . . .

As for myself, I believe in the cosmic law. I believe in the message received 2000 years ago by which I aim to live. I believe in the life ethic which my parents taught me and which I aim to apply. I believe in a conscience which I aim to find within myself. If I go down this path, I cannot be wrong. And no rumor, true of false, could deter me from what I have to do. I will continue to work in the Order and for the mission as long as you need me and as long as I can do it.[20]

These controversies were not confined to the OTS sanctuaries. During the 1980s, the Solar Temple had more or less escaped anti-cult polemics. Jouret had two lines written about him in an entry on the ORT in a booklet put out by a French anti-cult group in 1984,[21] but in the 1987 edition, both he and the ORT were left unmentioned. Oddly enough, in the end critical coverage did not come from Europe or Canada, but from the island of Martinique: on 10 September 1991, Lucien Zécler, president of the local branch of the Association for the Defense of Families and Individuals (ADFI), the leading anti-cult movement in France, sent a letter to several associations and centers in Québec, asking for information on the OTS. The request followed the decision of several citizens of Martinique to sell their worldly goods, leave their families, and move to Canada to escape coming disasters. At the end of 1992, a former member of the OTS went to Martinique to publicly denounce the Solar Temple, which provoked local media coverage.

Not long after, Luc Jouret ran afoul of law enforcement officials in Québec after he encouraged trusted members to buy guns illegally. The police were investigating anonymous threats from an unknown terrorist group at the time and, when tipped off by an informer about the attempt by an inexperienced OTS member to get three guns with silencers, began to watch several members of the group. The members were arrested in March 1993. The Canadian media reported the story and published extracts from police wiretaps revealing the homeopath's unusual interest in firearms. This gave the OTS more unwanted publicity and cooled the enthusiasm of several members, even though Jouret and two of his followers were given the relatively mild sentence of one year of unsupervised probation and a fine of one thousand Canadian dollars (to be paid to the Red Cross) for buying prohibited arms.

These problems, internal and external, are crucial in understanding the OTS's gradual distortion and disintegration. Di Mambro had gathered around him a group that lent an appearance of reality to the fictions he created. And now this imaginary universe began to come under critical scrutiny. The head of the Solar Temple apparently decided to respond by taking himself and his followers away from the scene altogether.

Throughout the 1980s, the Solar Temple's doctrine had grown increasingly apocalyptic. Even in his public meetings, Luc Jouret frequently alluded to cataclysmic upheavals that threatened the planet with imminent destruction. The apocalyptic thinking of the Solar Temple had clear ecological connotations, and Jouret's lectures often described the earth as a holistic living entity who could no longer endure what humankind was inflicting on her.[22] The concern of the leaders for the environmental situation seems to have been a sincere one: Di Mambro kept several video recordings of TV reports about ecological problems; in his home, investigators also found a testament showing that Di Mambro and his wife had considered listing ecological organizations in their will.

The Solar Temple's message was survivalist as well. We have already seen that this had caused the group to establish a base in Canada, which was considered to be a safer place. In 1986, the temple published in Toronto two volumes under the title, *Survivre à l'An 2000* (*Survival beyond the Year 2000*). The first volume was mostly doctrinal. The second dealt with the subject in a very practical way, establishing guidelines as to what provisions to store in order to survive a disaster that would destroy all essential technologies and what to do to survive atomic, bacteriological, or chemical warfare. In addition, it provided a detailed first aid manual. Nothing in these volumes would lead one to suspect suicidal tendencies; to the contrary, it seemed as if the adepts hoped to find themselves among those who survived the apocalypse unscathed.

How, then, can one explain the reversal that led a core of members to choose collective self-immolation? Besides survivalism, there were other latent themes, always on the same apocalyptic foundation, which had the potential to encourage somewhat different pursuits in the group.[23] In a certain way, the Solar Temple's goals were classically gnostic in that they ultimately aimed at "the release of the 'inner man' from the bonds of the world and his return to his native realm of light."[24] The manifesto-testaments sent just prior to the events of October 1994 echo such feelings: "We, Servants of the Rosy Cross, forcefully reaffirm that we are not of this world and we know perfectly well the coordinates of our Origins and our Future."[25] "Always belonging to the Reign of the Spirit, incarnating the subtle link between Creature and Creator, we rejoin our Home."[26] The most devoted Solar Temple adepts would push this reasoning to its extreme logical consequences.

According to several testimonies gathered by the investigators, the theme of "transit" began to be evoked by Di Mambro in 1990 or 1991. It meant a voluntary departure or a consent to bring the germ of life to another planet. It was necessary to be ready to leave at any time in response to the call. Di Mambro said he did not yet know what the mode of transit would be: he presented the metaphor of a passage across a mirror and evoked the possibility of the coming of a flying saucer to take faithful members to another world. On this last point, it is worth noting that, at some of Luc Jouret's seminars which I attended in 1987, a comic strip called *Timeless Voyage* was on sale.[27] This strip tells the story of a group of UFO believers who, before the imminent "great mutation," are brought on board a "cosmic vessel" to "Vessel-Earth."[28] Solar Temple members were thus already familiar with this type of scenario well before 1990. An ex-member explained to the investigators that talks about transit never implied suicide, but rather the idea of being saved from disasters. Perhaps the theme of "transit," rather than marking a break with survivalism, should be interpreted as a reorientation towards a survival in other dimensions following the irreversible worsening of the situation on this planet.[29]

If we believe their declarations to the police after the events of 1994, most of those members who had heard about the idea of "departure" or "transit" considered it as rather nebulous or interpreted it innocuously as a departure to other geographical locations (for example, leaving Geneva). When members wanted to know more, they sometimes received evasive answers:

Transit was the return to the Father, the return to the Unity, after having left Earth . . . Two or three years before October 1994, I discussed with —— what was meant by the concept. She told me that I shouldn't worry, that I wouldn't realize, that we would all leave together, as one. At the time, naively, I never thought that meant collective suicide.[30]

Some members had known a little more precisely how things would happen. One remembers that Di Mambro "started talking about transit to another world. He said that this would be accomplished by a shift in consciousness and we wouldn't be aware of it."[31] But this operation presupposed a certain degree of preparation:

[Di Mambro] explained to us that one day we'd all be called to a meeting at which a transit would be accomplished. It had to do with a mission, with a departure towards Jupiter . . . He said to his listeners that they had to be on call twenty-four hours a day so as not to miss the departure and that once the order was given, we would have to move quickly.[32]

This helps to explain the speed with which some of the victims suddenly abandoned everything to head to their mysterious demise. But if this confirms the emergence of the idea of "transit" well before October 1994, it does not explain the reasoning that led Di Mambro toward this plan of action. Outside of possible explanations linked to Di Mambro's mental state, it seems likely that criticism by ex-members, episodic public exposure in Martinique and Québec, and disappointed hopes for success led the Solar Temple's leadership to revise their view of the future. In addition, the wiretaps of Luc Jouret made by the police in Québec during the 1993 investigation reveal that the charismatic physician was in a depressed mood, constantly complaining about feeling tired and expressing eagerness to leave the world. Still, no one factor is sufficient in and of itself, especially since the collective self-immolation involved not just one individual but the order's entire core group. We cannot rule out the possibility that some elements in the decision still remain unknown to us.

The first known version of a text explaining "departure" had been written by February 1993. This coincides with the opening of the investigation into the group by Québec police on 2 February 1993; since some sources suggest that Jouret may have gotten word of the investigation before the police interventions of 8 March 1993, we do not know with absolute certainty whether the text was written without knowledge of the investigation in progress.[33] At any rate, even if the problems in Martinique and in Québec confirmed Di Mambro and his close associates in their plan to leave a world perceived as unjust and doomed, these events did not initiate the idea of departure: the attempt at buying guns indicates that the idea was already under consideration prior to these investigations.

Passing the Torch

The fact that texts trying to explain and justify the "transit" (including two of the four which were sent to the media in October 1994) were written by 1993 reveals that a group of people methodically prepared for their deaths over a period of many months. To be ready for the passage to other spheres, the most dedicated members progressively severed all ties with the outside world. Messages received from other dimensions came to bolster them in their resolve to quit this planet. For example, a series of five messages collected under the title, "The Polestar," and supposedly delivered by "the Lady of Heaven," were received between 24 December 1993 and 17 January 1994. The first message calls on the recipients to root out their "terrestrial attraction" and talks about Jupiter as their "Next Home." The second message exhorts them to "put [their] last things in order to leave Earth free and clear." The third message declares, "We want you free to rejoin us, without feeling constrained, without feeling pressure, but of your own free will," and warns, "If you do not try your hardest to escape the attraction of this Earth, woe is you!" The fourth message repeats, "It is now time to leave humanity to its deadly destiny, you are done with it. Don't look in the world for whomever or whatever to save. Close the door on humans." As for the fifth message, it announces in a solemn tone that "no Light will stay on Earth" and can be summed up by the sentence, "Retire, let go of this Earth without remorse."[34]

It no doubt took a great deal of persuasion to convince a nucleus of members to accept such a radical step. Some documents reflect the hesitation that was probably expressed and the arguments used to reassure and maintain adherence to the plan. A few of these arguments were in keeping with classic themes of millenarian literature not otherwise found in the group's teachings:

The idea of the passage from one world to another might worry some of you. I assure you that you are going towards a marvelous world which could not be, in any case, any worse than the one you are leaving.

Know from now on that after the passage, you will have a body of glory but you will still be recognizable. You will no longer need to eat but if you want to eat, you will be able to do it without earning your bread with the sweat of your brow.

Your eternal body will be subject neither to aging nor to pain nor to sickness.[35]

According to Solar Temple beliefs, the departure was only possible because on 6 January 1994 the mysterious "Elder Brothers of the Rosy Cross" "effected their Transit for an Elsewhere that only the initiates know and serve."[36] Taking off towards superior dimensions, the "Brothers" in some way carried Solar Temple members in their wake, allowing those who were worthy to ascend to a higher level. Significant allusions to this subject can be read in notes found on a diskette in one of the chalets in Salvan (Switzerland): "Take the place of the E[lder] B[rothers] on Venus, so that later on J[upiter?], we will be reunited. They will precede us, make room for us, show us the way and we will follow them." According to the declarations of a witness who later perished during the second "transit" in December 1995, Jouret, at a small gathering just before the events of October 1994, explained that if the leadership would cross a new step in effecting a passage from matter to essence, all the subsequent levels would automatically progress one degree.

Even within this perspective of escape from worldly catastrophes and transit to a better world, however, the order's leaders deemed it fitting to leave something behind for posterity. Only this desire to leave a legacy can explain why the leadership continued to be as active as ever while making preparations for their exit. The exact date of "departure" was probably decided on short notice: the outline of the internal monthly instructions meant for distribution to the members, which was found by police in the chalets in Salvan, continued until May 1995. These instructions were prepared by Jocelyne Di Mambro, who knew

about the self-destruction project. If the day or the month had been set a long time in advance, she would certainly not have taken the time to prepare instructions for the period after the set date. The will to leave a legacy and a following behind after the "transit" also shows itself in the initiative of summer 1994 (and up to the eve of the events) to start up a new organization, the Rosicrucian Alliance (*Alliance Rose-Croix*, ARC).

Over the years, it appears the group devoted a great deal of energy to organizing and reorganizing its various subsidiaries. As early as 1991, documents had suggested that the Templar Order should soon make room for "a new Rosicrucian Fraternity"; but there was resistance to this idea in some OTS sectors by believers who were attached to the Templar form. Although there is no real historical connection between the medieval Templar Order and Rosicrucian doctrines, the conjoining of the Temple and the Rosy Cross was nothing new, since such theories had originally appeared in Western occult circles during the eighteenth century.[37] According to the teachings of the Solar Temple, "the true Order of the Rosy Cross is . . . the Order of the Temple in its center . . . More than an esoteric institution at the heart of the Order, it was and it is in truth its secret Church."[38]

At a first meeting in Avignon on 9 July 1994, 95 out of the 118 people present responded positively to the proposition to create a new association. The ARC's constituent assembly, a purely administrative operation, met with a few people present in Montreux on 13 August 1994. Of the four committee members elected that day, two were found dead in October. The real launching of the ARC took place at a second meeting in Avignon on 24 September 1994, with the theme "The new mission of the Rosy Cross"; the invitation described the new order as "the natural successor to the OTS."[39] One hundred people were present, including 88 dues-paying members plus some of Di Mambro's entourage. The documents revealed a desire to simplify the organizational structure. Participants had the feeling of a new beginning; the notebook of one of the participants had listed under 24 September, "Meeting of the New Alliance in Avignon."

A Persecution Mania

Many of those present on 24 September 1994 were not aware that the hour of the "departure" was approaching. Joseph Di Mambro and those close to him were becoming more and more discouraged, as an audio cassette from spring 1994 in which several core members of the group discussed their "departure" demonstrates. Di Mambro is heard saying,

We are rejected by the whole world. First by the people, the people can no longer withstand us. And our Earth, fortunately she rejects us. How would we leave [otherwise]? We also reject this planet. We wait for the day we can leave . . . life for me is intolerable, intolerable, I can't go on. So think about the dynamic that will get us to go elsewhere.

Compared with other controversial groups, the Solar Temple encountered very modest opposition; it would be excessive to use the term "persecution," despite what the group's spiritual testament would have us believe. In fact, Di Mambro's loss of a sense of reality made any opposition or criticism intolerable. The legal problems encountered by Jouret and others in Québec in 1993 did nothing to assuage his growing sense of paranoia. After all, the press had reported that several members of the group had been subjected to official surveillance and wiretapping.[40] This led the core leadership to believe themselves the object of omnipresent police control and the victims of traitors who had infiltrated the movement.

Jocelyne Di Mambro's difficulties in getting her passport renewed only exacerbated these suspicions. This and the fact that Di Mambro sent a posthumous letter to Charles Pasqua (then French minister of the Interior) gave rise to speculation concerning a mysterious political or criminal background for the OTS's leader. The explanation is simpler. Di Mambro

had traveled several times to Australia, where he attempted to create a "life center." Suspicious international monetary transfers drew the attention of the Australian police: during the month of October 1993, Di Mambro received on three separate occasions 100,000 dollars from Switzerland, money which was then deposited into bank accounts he had opened in Sydney. Canberra Interpol asked the French police for information regarding Di Mambro, who had no known resources. The French police squad in charge of financial improprieties wondered if it might be a case of illegal trafficking in foreign currency.

The French consulate in Montreal also became suspicious of the Di Mambros. In March 1994, the French Ministry of Foreign Affairs asked the Ministry of the Interior to advise whether it should extend Jocelyne Di Mambro's passport, as the family was unable to provide proof of their residence in Canada and had changed residence five times in five years. Even stranger, Joseph Di Mambro had obtained no less than five passports in seven years, and his visas showed he had made numerous short international trips, including several to Malaysia. By October 1994, the inquiry headed by the financial squad of the French judicial police was still ongoing. As for Jocelyne Di Mambro's passport, the French embassy in Ottawa finally renewed it, but only for three months, and this gave rise to a strange incident. Jocelyne Di Mambro hired a Montreal lawyer to defend her interests in the passport renewal affair. Through an unknown channel (perhaps simply the French consulate?), the lawyer heard about the investigation of his client and her husband and seems to have become reluctant to be associated with the couple and their possibly questionable business affairs. He wrote to Jocelyne Di Mambro on 25 August 1994 to explain to her that the affair had implications that were "political as much as they were legal," and that the non-renewal decision came from the French Ministry of the Interior and was linked "to a police investigation of a criminal matter." Even as he told his client that he would no longer be representing her interests, he advised her to "take very seriously the results of the investigation by the French authorities."[41]

In point of fact, during the investigations following the events of October 1994, nothing came to light confirming a surveillance of the group during this period.[42] Not only did the financial investigations squad of the French police likely have more urgent business to attend to, but the matter appears to have been related only to unexplained financial transfers by an individual French citizen and not by the leader of a small apocalyptic order. The police in Québec ceased their surveillance of the Solar Temple after the incident with the illegal gun purchase in 1993, and the French *Renseignements généraux* (political police), which also keep an eye on religions and "cults," knew little about the Solar Temple. But one can imagine what the lawyer's statement could have meant for an increasingly paranoid leadership, which now believed that its worst suspicions were confirmed. It is significant that the document sent in October 1994 to Charles Pasqua (enclosed with the Di Mambros' passports) was written on a computer at Salvan on 30 August 1994 – just after the Di Mambros received the letter from their Montreal lawyer. As Minister of the Interior, Pasqua was held personally responsible for the problems they encountered: "We accuse you of deliberately wanting to destroy our Order and having done so for reasons of state."[43] Such writings confirm the Di Mambros' growing persecution paranoia, but lend no credibility to the theories linking the letter to Pasqua with mysterious underworld connections.

Another text found on Jocelyne Di Mambro's computer and written after a conversation with an unknown speaker adds further evidence of a growing sense of persecution:

We are far from knowing the whole truth about the surveillance. Police all over the world are concentrating on us. Our file is coded, nobody has access except the leaders (it is on Pasqua's desk).

We don't know when they might close the trap on us . . . a few days? a few weeks?

We are being followed and spied upon in our every move. All the cars are equipped with tracing and listening devices.

All of their most sophisticated techniques are being used on us. While in the house, beware of surveillance cameras, lasers, and infra-red.

Our file is the hottest on the planet, the most important of the last ten years, if not of the century.

However that may be, as it turns out, the concentration of hate against us will give us enough energy to leave.[44]

The alleged surveillance was construed as one more proof that the group was really what it claimed to be, the vehicle of a mission of cosmic magnitude. The previous document also mentions two members (one of whom died in Switzerland and the other a year later in France) suspected of infiltrating the movement. Several texts written during that period warn against "traitors," and the group believed in the right of applying "justice and sentence" to those who showed disloyalty. In a videotape dated September 1994, Di Mambro explains that "justice and sentence" are the equivalent of "vengeance," but in an impersonal sense. In the spring 1994 audio track about the "departure," Di Mambro talks about those "who had committed themselves and then no longer wanted to remain involved. That changes nothing about their commitment . . . You'll see, you'll see how things will go for them." The letter to Charles Pasqua is explicit:

If we must apply our justice ourselves, it is because of the fact that yours is rotten and corrupt . . . It behooves us, before we leave these stinking terrestrial planes, to reduce certain traitors to silence, which you and your agencies have directly or indirectly manipulated . . . to destroy our honor and our actions.[45]

While it cannot be doubted that the external opposition encountered by the Solar Temple strengthened the resolve of its leaders to depart for a higher plane of existence,[46] the root of Di Mambro's decision to launch the process which led to the "transit" is most closely connected to internal dissent (the theoretical idea of the possibility of having to "depart" having already been present longer in the ideology of the group, as we have seen). Di Mambro nourished a deep resentment toward critical members and former members, although these dissidents had kept their criticism within the confines of the group and had not gone public – except for the ex-member who spoke with the media in Martinique in December 1992 and who had repeated her accusations to the Canadian media in March 1993.[47] In the important tape recording (mentioned earlier) of a discussion within the core group in spring 1994, Di Mambro declared to his most trusted disciples,

There are people who claim that I have taken everything for me . . . what I have taken, I haven't taken it for me, since I leave everything behind. But I will leave nothing, I will leave ashes, I will leave nothing to the bastards who have betrayed us. The harm they have done to the Rosy Cross, that I cannot forgive; what they have done to me, it doesn't matter. But the harm they have done to the Rosy Cross, I won't forgive it. I cannot.[48]

Di Mambro still harbored feelings of betrayal and resentment during the final hours of his life. On 3 October 1994, when the "transit" had begun and a number of victims had in all likelihood already lost their lives, Di Mambro (or one of his assistants) wrote two drafts of letters to a general attorney which accused two former members of blackmailing him and of tarnishing the Temple's reputation.[49]

The Creation of a Legend

As already asserted, however, it was not just a matter of "leaving" and punishing "traitors," but of accomplishing these ends in such a manner as to leave behind an enduring legend. The group was convinced that it belonged to "the pivotal elite" which "has been removed from the collective by superhuman effort." The temple "did not recognize" itself "as belonging to the human world, but to the race of Gods."[50]

The leaders of the Solar Temple explained their actions in the texts sent to the media from a Geneva post office on 5 October 1994, and in three videocassettes which were shipped to a French OTS member by another trusted member at the same time. Two of these cassettes are titled "Testament of the Rosy Cross," and the third is titled "Joseph of Arimathea – Messages."

The lengthy recording of the "Testament of the Rosy Cross" opens with the symbol of ARC (a double-headed eagle behind a rose with a cross). On the screen a seated woman appears[51] who reads a text; in the background, a rose emerges from a misty landscape; as background music, the Grail theme from Richard Wagner's opera *Lohengrin* plays throughout the entire lecture.[52] The lengthy "testament" is read with a growing exaltation; there are several mentions of "departure." This "Testament of the Rosy Cross" is most interesting because of its synthesis of Solar Temple beliefs on the eve of the group's self-immolation.

The testament first underlines man's mission as mediator between God and the Earth: "We are the focalization on which the Creator rests . . . Today, we are in the final cycle of conscious creation; we must be able to control these bodies . . . and, with full maturity, to leave the mother [i.e. the Earth] . . . We must not bring back consciousness to the state before the fall, but become aware of this state, enrich it with the painful experience of the fall and redeem our being, so that we could continue after the fall with a capital of enriched consciousness-energy-love." In this way, the spirit is able to follow its route across the sublimation of matter and, enriched by its experience in matter, "start up a superior cycle of evolution."[53]

According to the testament, 26,000 years ago the Blue Star (related to Sirius's energy) left on the earth "Sons of the One"; it appears in the sky every time its help is needed and responds to magnetization when humanity undergoes its crises of transmutation. The years 1950 to 1960 saw a growing change in the consciousness of human beings. Humanity is passing through periods of preparation called "tribulations," successive cycles of seven years which end in 1998. The circumstances of the "departure" are then explained:

In the 1980s, the Sons of the One called the Blue Star. With man's consciousness still too fragmented, it was asked of the spiritual forces to intervene and to allot an additional period of time to move back the date, to slow down the irrevocable changes on Earth . . . The Earth was given an additional seven years to prepare . . . This delay acts like a rubber band which, when stretched to its limit, becomes unstable and too powerful. This limit has been reached . . . and we still need more time. But this delay given to us has nonetheless allowed beings to hear the message, to prepare and to participate with full consciousness in this unique event which we call the passage. The passage, which is also the gathering of the Sons of the One. The Blue Star has come to magnetize the last workers and bring them back towards those of the first hour. The time of return is at hand and the astrological influences are affecting all the physical and non-physical planes. They work on the hearts and spirits of all those who accept their divine origin and are ready to play their part until the end. At the moment of passage, the Blue Star . . . will instantly transform in a flash the carriers of life and of the consciousness.

The Star will unleash its influence on the earth, and there man, the unbeliever, remaining on Earth, will hope for death. The Blue Star will leave, he will feel abandoned and he will be right, but it will be too late. The radiant Star will be gone, bringing with it every chance at redemption. Yet, if man had wanted to remember, wanted to hear, wanted to see . . . Why did he not seize his last chance, brought by the Blue Star?[54]

The third cassette is a composite of four elements: three messages received from above by one of the members and a strange sequence that Di Mambro wanted to leave to posterity. In a room that looks like a church crypt, we see through a doorway, in front of a large pillar, people's profiles, one by one, whom it is not possible to identify because they are dressed in ample capuchin capes pulled around their faces. They process in a slow and untiring march, each holding in both hands a lit candle. This mysterious procession is commented on by the voice of Joseph Di Mambro and a member of the fraternity:

JDM: Space is curved, time comes to an end . . . Our cycle is over, these images tell all.
F: On 6 January 1994, at 0 h 15 m, the Elder Brothers of the Rosy Cross left their terrestrial planes, preceded by entities from the Great Pyramid who have gone back to their original planes. Programmed for all eternity, this unique event in history confirms the truth and the actualization of the prophecies that warned man that one day, because of [mankind's] disdain for the Word, the Gods would leave the earth . . . A unique time is coming to an end as these knights, anonymous by choice, last carriers of the original fire, prepare in their turn to proceed, by their own means, with the liberation of the capital of energy-consciousness which the Rosy Cross bequeathed to them until the completion of the work.
JDM: The good-hearted man can live in this precise second . . . a sublime event: the passage of the cycle of Adamic man towards a new cycle of evolution, programmed on another earth, an earth prepared to receive the stored vibrations enriched by the authentic servants of the Rosy Cross.[55]

This solemn scene is meant to symbolize the final procession of the Knights of the Solar Temple, who are leaving this Earth: "Noble travelers, we are of no era, of no place."[56] If there were still a need to demonstrate that Di Mambro planned to create and leave behind a grand legend concerning his order's transit, this "choreography" offers persuasive evidence.

The End of the Solar Temple

On 4 October 1994, at 1:40 p.m. (Swiss time), Canadian police intervened at a fire in Morin Heights and discovered two adult corpses. On

6 October, the corpses of two parents who had been savagely murdered were found with their baby child hidden in a closet. It was later discovered that the murders had occurred on 30 September and that the perpetrators had subsequently flown back to Switzerland. Also on 4 October, a little before midnight, residents of the small Swiss village of Cheiry noticed that a fire had started at the La Rochette farm in the heights around the village. On Wednesday, 5 October, around 3 a.m., three chalets were in flames at another place in Switzerland, Granges-sur-Salvan. Twenty-three corpses were discovered at Cheiry, twenty-five at Salvan. In Cheiry, most of the victims had apparently been called to a meeting on Sunday and were probably already dead on Monday, 3 October. A total of sixty-five bullets were found in their heads, and most of the victims had absorbed a strong soporific before being shot. No firearm had been used at Salvan, where only members of the core group lived; they had been injected with a poisonous substance provided by Jouret.

It has been clearly established that some of the fifty-three victims were murdered, while others submitted to execution voluntarily. However, even if their deaths were technically assassinations (bullets in the head), we will never know with absolute certainty how many victims volunteered for their "departure" or how many realized beforehand that the fabulous voyage to another planet they had been hoping for would take such brutal form.

The fact that members who were fully cognizant of the macabre details of this "departure" and who were deeply affected by the loss of long-standing friends nevertheless decided, in December 1995, to themselves "leave" (again using firearms) in a clearing in French Vercors left many observers in such a state of incredulity that a number of journalists advanced the hypothesis of external intervention. But no such trace has been found (which would have been easy, since the area was snowy), and without ruling out the possibility that some victims did not fully consent or wanted to back out at the last minute, the deeds of these members are explicable without the intervention of a third party. It is true that several OTS survivors (including victims of the December 1995 "transit") were troubled over the methods used in October 1994. However, this discomfort did not stop a few of them from recognizing that they would have responded to the call if it had been addressed to them, or indeed from feeling a little disappointed not to have been invited to participate.

Several testimonies collected by the Swiss police after the event of December 1995 show that a process of reinterpretation was quickly elaborated among the core of the surviving believers, leading to the conclusion that what happened was in fact positive and that those who departed had sacrificed to save the consciousness of the planet and to pave the way for others. In their eyes, the "departure" conjoined the horrible and the sublime in a strange harmony. They came to the decision to follow the same path, probably convinced that the first group was waiting for them.[57] The death of five more persons in Québec in March 1997 follows the same pattern, and the letter sent to the media by this handful of hardliners articulates their doubts that there remain other people ready to follow the same path after them.[58]

Scholarly observers have advanced varied interpretations of the Solar Temple's saga.[59] Whatever the primary cause of the "transit," it was not a hasty decision, and the core group took time and care to legitimate ideologically the suicides and murders. This process probably also helped them reinforce each other in their choices, which had to be agreed upon collectively. Moreover, they likely celebrated ceremonies that ritualized their beliefs concerning the act they were about to commit near the time of the final departure. Texts detailing these ceremonies were discovered at Di Mambro's residence at Salvan. They strikingly illustrate the mind-set of the core group with regard to the coming transit:

Brothers and Sisters of the First and of the Last Hour . . .
Today . . . as we are gathered here in this Holy Place . . .
The Great Terrestrial Cycle is closing in on itself.

Alpha and Omega are fusing [to initiate] a
new Creation.
The Time of the Great Gathering is proclaiming the Departure of the Sons of
Heaven.

In the Name of a Will above mine . . .
I am handing the seed of our Immortality and
of our Transcendent Nature to the Infinite
Worlds . . .
At this Supreme Moment . . .
The ruby power of the Work should free itself
and rejoin the Levels of the Future . . .
So that, engendered by ourselves . . .
Like the Phoenix . . .
We might be reborn from our ashes.
Through the Sword of Light . . .
Raised toward the Levels Above, what is
refined should depart from the world of
density . . .
And ascend toward its Point of Origin.

Our Terrestrial Journey is coming to an end
. . .
The Work is being completed.
Everyone must return to their position on the
Great Celestial Chessboard.[60]

We have to consider seriously the OTS's
beliefs. Di Mambro acted at times like a
common swindler, but he very likely remained
convinced of his message and mission until the
end. Certainly, internal dissent and outside
criticism helped to convince hesitant members
of the core group that radical methods were
needed in order to leave Earth. But, although
we will never know for sure, it seems doubtful that a lesser degree of public exposure
would have prevented the "transit." Even if he
was able to hide such feelings when it was
needed, Di Mambro had reached the point
that he could no longer accept questioning of
or disagreement with his views. Convinced of
their own superiority and insulated psychologically from countervailing perspectives, the
leadership came to view any dissonant voice as
unbearable.

Finally, the transit presented an attractive
response to the movement's decline: the
temple needed to be "re-dynamized" periodically. The transit also allowed the group to
escape from perceived threats and offered a

way to assert dramatically its claims before the
entire world. Creators of their own legend, the
core members of the Solar Temple considered
themselves as an elect circle, heirs to an
uncommon destiny who were invested with a
cosmic task to fulfill. Believing that they would
become gods, they followed the flute player in
a dance of death and paid the ultimate price.

Notes

1 Concluding text from two videocassettes
titled, "Testament of the Rosy Cross," sent
from Geneva to a member of the OTS on 5
October 1994.

2 This quote is excerpted from a tape transcript
made for the use of the police investigation. All
documents without specific indication of
source belong to the material gathered by the
police and kept either in Fribourg or in
Martigny (Switzerland). These documents are
not individually numbered, and they are not
presently accessible to researchers; the author
has been able to use them solely because of his
participation in the official police investigation
of the Solar Temple case. Regarding quotes
from interrogations conducted by the police
with witnesses, they can be included only if the
anonymity of the individuals quoted remains
fully protected. For this reason, it is not possible to provide references in the usual way.

3 Taken from a document dated 28 May 1994
found on one of the order's computers. Rituals
celebrated toward the end, especially one
called "The Return of the Fire," develop such
ideas and show how the core members had the
feeling of being in control of events when
committing suicide and returning to their original home after having been enriched through
their experiences.

4 "Transit to the Future," one of four texts delivered to several dozen recipients on 5 October
1994. All the (unpublished) internal documents of OTS quoted in these notes were
written in French, but their titles are translated
here into English.

5 An original, longer version of this study was
published in French as *Les Mythes du temple
solaire* (Geneva: Georg, 1996). A revised and
updated Italian translation was published the
following year as *Il Tempio Solare* (Leumann
[Turin]: Editrice Elle Di Ci, 1997). There is

also an updated and extended German version, *Der Sonnentempel: Die Tragödie einer Sekte* (Freiburg: Paulusverlag, 1998). The English version has been rewritten to a large extent and also contains several passages and quotes which are not found in the previous versions. The author thanks the three anonymous reviewers for their critical comments: he has tried to take several of their remarks into consideration. Comparisons with other cases of suicide or violent action by religious groups, however, will be kept for a future article. This one concentrates exclusively upon the OTS case.

6 There were always people who belonged to the inner "Fraternity' around Di Mambro and never to OTS itself. Hence the use of "OTS" as a generic label can be misleading.

7 He divorced his first wife in January 1985, but she continued to follow the group and was found dead at Cheiry in October 1994.

8 Although it is used here generically for describing the group, the name "Order of the Solar Temple" was only one label among several and was not always in use between 1970 and 1994.

9 Some attendees with whom the author spoke did not like Jouret's apocalyptic leanings. He sometimes conveyed the ambiguous impression that he was possessed of both charm and fanaticism.

10 An overview of the various (and sometimes unconnected) movements with reference to the Neo-Templar tradition is provided in the first part of an article by Massimo Introvigne, "Ordeal by Fire: The Tragedy of the Solar Temple," *Religion* 25 (1995): 267–83.

11 Gaetan Delaforge, *The Templar Tradition in the Age of Aquarius* (Putney, VT: Threshold Books, 1987), 136. 'Gaetan Delaforge" is the pseudonym of a North American OTS member (who is still alive).

12 See Serge Caillet, *L'Ordre rénové du temple. Aux racines du temple solaire* (paris: Dervy, 1997). There is no relation between the French citizen Raymond Bernard and his American homonym who wrote books on the "hollow earth" theory and other topics popular in some segments of the cultic milieu; according to information provided by Joscelyn Godwin, the (late) American Raymond Bernard's real name was Walter Siegmeister (Joscelyn Godwin, *Arktos: The Polar Myth in Science, Symbolism, and Nazi Survival* [London: Thames and Hudson, 1993], 122).

13 Tape of conclave of ORT officers, Easter 1984, Geneva, Switzerland, found in personal archives of Joseph Di Mambro.

14 Delaforge, *The Templar Tradition*, 138.

15 Open Letter, February 1994. See note 2.

16 However, there were several other members who remained totally devoted to Joseph Di Mambro, as their decision to follow him in death demonstrates. Regarding the question of the nature of Di Mambro's charisma, see Jean-François Mayer, "Les Chevaliers de l'Apocalypse: l'Ordre du Temple Solaire et ses adeptes," in *Sectes et démocratie*, ed. Françoise Champion and Martine Cohen (Paris: Seuil, 1999), 205–23. The article also examines the interaction between affiliations with the Solar Temple and previous backgrounds in the cultic milieu.

17 He justified this demand by claiming that he was only relaying the orders from the "Mother Lodge."

18 Interrogation of former member by Canadian police, 28 December 1994. See note 2.

19 Tony Dutoit, his wife, and their baby child were the first victims of the carnage of 1994, savagely murdered in Morin Heights (Québec).

20 Report to Joseph Di Mambro by OTS officer, Switzerland, 10 December 1993. See note 2.

21 *Les Sectes: que sont-elles? comment agissent-elles? comment s'en défendre? ce qu'il faut en savoir* (Paris: Centre de Documentation, d'Education et d'Action contre les Manipulations Mentales, 1984), 49. In 1987, during a discussion with the author, Jouret did not hide his irritation concerning those two lines.

22 For more details about the ecological concern behind the apocalpytic views of the Solar Temple, see Mayer, "Les Chevaliers de l'Apocalypse." 211–14.

23 See also the interesting observations by Susan Palmer, "Purity and Danger in the Solar Temple," *Journal of Contemporary Religion* 11 (1996): 303–18.

24 Hans Jonas, *The Gnostic Religion* (Boston, MA: Beacon press, 1958), 67. "The reawakening of the gnostic conscience in a few human beings is considered as the sign that the diffuse parcels of light dispersed in the world will reunite and that apocalyptic events are imminent" (Massimo Introvigne, *Il ritorno dello gnosticismo* [Milan: SugarCo, 1993], 15–16).

25 "To those who can still hear the voice of wisdom . . . we send this final message," Manifesto-testament of OTS, 1994, 2.

26 "Transit to the future," Manifesto-testament of OTS, 1994, 5.

27 Appel Guery and Sergio Macedo, *Voyage intemporel* (Grenoble, France: Glénat, 1983). There exists an English translation, *Timeless Voyage* (Papeete, Tahiti: Transtar Pacific, 1987).

28 This is not merely a comic strip, because it carries the message of a French UFO group which really exists.

29 "The current planetary situation is irreversibly escaping all human control . . . All creative and positive forces are strangled . . . we refuse to participate in the assassination of our carrier the Earth, we leave this world where our voices can no longer be heard" ("Transit to the Future"). "Once the time of the Great gathering will have come and the Sons of the One will withdraw, . . . the North and South Poles, deprived of their magnetic balance which had until now been kept by the conscious carriers, will give birth to cataclysms and final destruction. This is the Third secret of Our Lady of Fatima, which is revealed here" (from a document dated 28 April 1994 found on a computer in Salvan, Switzerland).

30 From interrogation of former OTS member by Swiss police, 18 January 1996. See note 2.

31 Ibid, 22 January 1996.

32 Ibid.

33 John R. Hall and Philip Schuyler, "The Mystical Apocalypse of the Solar Temple," in *Millenium, Messiahs, and Mayhem; Contemporary Apocalyptic Movements*, ed. Thomas Robbins and Susan J. Palmer (London: Routledge, 1997), 300.

34 "The Polestar," a series of five OTS messages founds at Salvan, Switzerland, December 1993–January 1994. See note 2.

35 "Last Voyage," document found at Salvan, Switzerland, 1993. See note 2.

36 Message dated 28 January 1994.

37 See René Le Forestier, *La Franc-Maçonnerie occultiste et templière aux XVIIIe et XIXe soècles*, 2nd edn., 2 vols. (Paris: La Table d'Emeraude, 1987).

38 "Epistle/Archives ZZA-4," OTS teaching material sent to members, n.d. See note 2.

39 OTS invitation to meeting, 24 September 1994. See note 2.

40 This wiretapping was conducted over several weeks spanning February and March 1993.

41 Letter from Di Mambro's Lawyer in Montreal, 25 August 1994. See note 2.

42 It should, however, be mentioned that the French embassy in Washington, DC sent a request to law enforcement agencies in Canada in early 1994 requesting information concerning possible involvement of Joseph Di Mambro in money laundering. It is not known if active investigations were undertaken following this request.

43 Letter sent by Di Mambro to French Interior Minister charles Pasqua in October 1994. See note 2.

44 Untitled document found on computer at Salvan, Switzerland. See note 2.

45 Letter sent by Di Mambro to French Interior Minister Charles Pasqua in October 1994. See note 2.

46 In a recent article, two American scholars have very pointedly observed that the "critical issue seems to concern whether the group's principals can legitimate to their followers the claim of persecution by apostates and other external opponents as the basis of their troubles." See John R. Hall and Philip Schuyler, "Apostasy, Apocalyse, and Religious Violence: An Exploratory Comparison of Peoples Temple, the Branch Davidians, and the Solar Temple," in *The Politics of Religious Apostasy: The Role of Apostates in the Transformation of Religious Movements*, ed. David G. Bromley (London: Praeger, 1998), 168.

47 In a few cases, dissidents were threatening to go public with their criticisms in an attempt to recoup financial contributions.

48 Transcript of tape, spring 1994. See note 2.

49 For unknown reasons, the letters were never completed or mailed.

50 From a document entitled "Exit toward the light," end of 1993. See note 2.

51 The woman was one of Joseph Di Mambro's most convinced followers. In the spring 1994 audiocassette, already cited several times, this woman is shown as one of those most in favor of the idea of a "departure": "Yes, I have asked for that for a long time, I think I will have no regrets . . . I think I will have no doubts or fears . . . I am ready to leave."

52 Di Mambro enjoyed Wagner's music, which was often used in OTS ceremonies.

53 Excerpt from two videocassettes called "Testament of the Rosy Cross." See note 1.

54 Ibid.

55 Excerpt from third videocassette sent with "Testament of the Rosy Cross." See note 1.

56 Sometimes used by OTS members, this phrase

is actually borrowed from the famous occultist and adventurer, Cagliostro, whose real name was Giuseppe Balsamo (1743–95). Di Mambro considered himself a reincarnation of Cagliostro. The author wishes to thank Massimo Introvigne for bringing the original author of this phrase to his attention.

57 Internal documents show that the leadership was considering the possibility (and hoping) that other people would follow at a later stage. The manifesto "To those who can still hear the voice of wisdom" conludes with the following sentence: "From where we will be, we will always hold our arms toward those who will be worthy of joining us." It is difficult to establish accurately how far the media harassment and the wild theories spread about the group contributed to the resolve of surviving OTS members to "leave" in December 1995 and March 1997. The conclusions of the French investigation have not yet been made public at the time of the last revisions to this article (November 1998).

58 Letter sent 21 March 1997 to leading newspapers in Québec including *La Presse*, *Le Devoir*, and *Le Soleil*.

59 For an overview of the various interpretive categories, see Massimo Introvigne, *Les Veilleurs de l'apocalypse: Millénarisme et nouvelles religions au seuil de l'an 2000* (Paris: Claire Vigne, 1996), 223–45.

60 Ritual entitled "The Return of the Fire," n.d., found at Salvan, Switzerland, with manuscript corrections. See note 2.

VII

Sex and Gender Issues and New Religious Movements

As researchers began to acquire a better grasp of the details of life in many NRMs it became apparent that men and women often are attracted to these groups for different reasons and their experiences in them differ in important ways as well. Some of the differences simply emerged from in-depth interviews with the participants in various groups. Women, for example, have expressed either their satisfaction or irritation, depending on the circumstances, with their fate as mothers in different NRMs. In many groups the duties of motherhood exclude them from achieving spiritual authority (e.g., Krishna Consciousness), while in others it garners honor and is beneficial (e.g., the Unification Church). But regrettably attention has also been drawn to the issue of gender differences by the sexual scandals and accusations of abuse that have been leveled at some movements. As each of the readings in this section discuss, the bond between the leaders of NRMs and their followers is very intense and personal. Sometimes, whether intentionally or unintentionally, students and teachers also become lovers. More often than not the teachers in NRMs are male, while the students are female. In some traditions, or under some circumstances, this development is not necessarily problematic and no one is hurt. But at other times the sexual intimacy either contravenes the dictates of the religion, impairs the spiritual development of the devotee, or disrupts the social harmony of the group. In some religious traditions sexual energies are enlisted as natural aids in the pursuit of spiritual wisdom or other religious goals, but for most of the major religions of the world the sexual appetites of humanity are viewed with suspicion. They are manifestations of our baser natures, and associated with volatile and distracting emotions that must be transcended to achieve peace and enlightenment. In all the situations, however, the sexual relationships happen within the confines of a larger and imbalanced relationship of power that places the student at a disadvantage. From a psychological and sociological perspective there are intrinsic problems with such relationships. But we must be cautious in considering accusations of abuse or harm since, as demonstrated in chapter 6, it is common for the opponents of new religions to use claims of some kind of sexual deviance, whether justified or not, to discredit these movements.

In NRMs, as in contemporary society in general, gender and sexual relations are contentious. But the concern with issues of sex, affection, and intimacy in NRMs is not accidental. Gender is what sociologists call a "master status," and in modern Western societies the private spheres of live in which gender identities are shaped and primarily exercised are being "de-institutionalized"(see Hunter 1981). Where once there were clear social rules about dating, marriage, and child-rearing (i.e., with regard to who could or should do what with whom and how), now there is a greater freedom of expression that creates ambiguity. For some individuals, the level of ambiguity is disconcerting and concern about these issues plays a key role in why some people join NRMs. Religions have always been sites of meaning, order, and controlled experimentation with aspects of sexual and family life (see Dawson 2000). Religions anchor the moral regulation of our private lives – so important to our sense of security and worth – in the natural or transcendent order of things. The new religions reassert the certainty of this ordered and meaningful life, giving a cosmic significance to personal relationships. For some individuals in our increasingly secularized societies, particularly women, who by nature or socialization are typically more concerned with these matters, this increased certainty is appealing (e.g., Rose 1987; Davidman 1990).

In these and many other ways discussed in the readings of this section, the issues of sex and gender go to the heart of a sound understanding of both the emergence and functioning of NRMs and the controversy swirling around them (see Dawson 1998: 94–101). In chapter 14, "Women in New Religious Movements," Elizabeth Puttick provides an excellent overview of the research findings on the topic, highlighting the issues of access to power, sexual abuse, alternative conceptions of the relationship of sexuality and spirituality, and the experience of motherhood in different NRMs. Like Susan Palmer (chapter 15), Puttick notes the important role played by different interpretive orientations in this research. For some observers the experience of women in NRMs is empowering, while for others it is regressive and repressive. For other observers it is empowering in some cases (e.g., Wicca) and regressive in others (e.g., Krishna Consciousness). The judgment will depend on the interpretive perspective brought to bear on the situation (e.g., conservative Christian or feminist). But in other cases, the same situation (e.g., involvement in the Rajneesh/Osho movement) can be seen as both empowering and regressive depending on which aspects of the situation are emphasized. The issues are

complex, but one thing is clear: there are a greater variety of attitudes to women and experiences of women in NRMs than is commonly appreciated. Still, in the end, Puttick presents most NRMs as essentially patriarchical, either because they continue to place a higher priority on male spiritual development and authority, even if they honor a feminine ideal of spirituality, or because they may grant women real positions of power but in accordance with a feminine ideal that is very traditional and restrictive. There are some signs, however, of the emergence of a more "postmodernist, post-feminist, and androgynous style of leadership" that Puttick thinks is preferable, and potentially more revolutionary.

In chapter 15, "Women's 'Cocoon Work' in New Religious Movements: Sexual Experimentation and Feminine Rites of Passage," Susan Palmer presents a more optimistic view of the experience of women. Palmer focuses more attention on what actually happens to women in NRMs, stressing in particular the fact that most people stay involved for only a short period of time (less than two years; see chapter 11). Even more than Puttick she emphasizes the diversity of women's roles in different NRMs, noting that at least three quite distinct models of gender relations can be found: sex complementarity, sex polarity, and sex unity. She further suggests that many women are using their time in NRMs to experiment with new identities, to "find themselves" in an alternative and supportive social context. "By temporarily inhabiting the stylized feminine roles in NRMs and submitting to their leaders' erotic/ascetic ordeals," Palmer argues, "members appear to undergo a self-imposed psychological metamorphosis, or 'cocoon work,' which in many ways resembles the ritual process found in feminine rites of passage in traditional sociaties."

NRMs have good reason to experiment with alternative sexual practices as a way of accessing and reforming the most personal and significant motivations and self-conceptions of their members, and rupturing their habitual bonds to the supposedly misguided or even sinful customs and goals of conventional society. The realm of sexuality has long been a theater of operation in the war to save souls. There are also organizational motivations for wishing to change and regulate the sexual behavior of members, since the obligations associated with romantic love relationships may run counter to the demands for group solidarity. But as the old adage says, "What is one man's poison, is another's meat or drink," and in most instances there is no clear way to define religiously sanctioned forms of sexuality as deviant without at least implicitly invoking and accepting some other religious preference as normative, and that choice poses ethical and legal problems in our increasingly pluralistic societies (see Dawson 2000).

References

Davidman, Lynn 1990: Women's Search for Family and Roots: A Jewish Religious Solution to a Modern Dilemma. In T. Robbins and D. Anthony (eds.), *In Gods We Trust: New Patterns of Religious Pluralism in America*, 2nd edn. New Brunswick, NJ: Transaction Books, 385–407.

Dawson, Lorne L. 1998: *Comprehending Cults: The Sociology of New Religious Movements.* Toronto: Oxford University Press.

——2000: Religious Cults and Sex. In C. D. Bryant (ed.), *The Encyclopedia of Criminology and Deviant Behavior.* New York: Taylor and Francis, 323–6.

Hunter, James D. 1981: The New Religions: Demodernization and the Protest Against Modernity. In B. Wilson (ed.), *The Social Impact of New Religious Movements.* New York: Rose of Sharon Press, 1–19.

Rose, Susan 1987: Woman Warriors: The Negotiation of Gender in a Charismatic Community. *Sociological Analysis* 48 (3): 245–58.

CHAPTER FOURTEEN

Women in New Religious Movements

Elizabeth Puttick

Gender Roles in NRMs

The position of women in religion is paradoxical. On the one hand they are the primary
'consumers' of religion who fill the churches,
keep the ritual fire burning, venerate and
adorn statues of divinities. On the other hand,
in most of the world's religions they are
debarred from playing an active role and
sometimes even from entering places of
worship. Women are sometimes perceived as
having an affinity with the numinous, possessing qualities of devotion, compassion, intuition and receptivity that are often associated
with religiosity. Yet they may also be condemned as spiritually inferior, weak, fallen,
polluted, incapable of attaining enlightenment, even literally soul-less. Accordingly, in
most religions their role has been limited
to the menial: arranging flowers on the altar,
sweeping the temple floor, but not preaching
or teaching.

Despite the enormous range of experimentation in belief and practice in NRMs, until
recently there has been depressingly little evidence of significant changes in gender roles.
This is mainly because most NRMs are based
on world religions and tend to reflect their traditional values. Accordingly, most research on
gender has found an across-the-board subordination of women, even where the ideology was non-discriminatory, especially within
Christian NRMs such as the Jesus Movement

and the New Christian Right. Despite some
questioning of gender roles resulting in theoretical equality, in practice women are socialized into rigidly submissive roles in relation to
their husbands and pastors.[1]

Asian religions have also tended to view
women as spiritually inferior and deny them
power and status, and Eastern-based NRMs
tend to continue this tradition. In the Eastern
groups she studied, Aidala found that ideologically, 'No differences were seen in the
abilities of men and women to attain self
perfection or "higher consciousness" which
was held to be the only relevance in life'.
However, translated into daily life, 'Concern
for such mundane matters as the tendency
of male members of the commune to avoid
household chores was scorned as evidence of
wrong or limited consciousness'. In other
words, 'The quest for personal transcendence
in such groups most often resulted in the
reproduction of traditional patterns of gender
relations, however refurbished with spiritual
explanations'.[2]

Kim Knott, discussing the low status of
women in ISKCON, suggests that it is unfair
to make comparisons with the ideal of gender
roles in liberated American society.[3] ISKCON
is unliberated even by Indian standards; educated Indian women do not follow the policy
of standing separately from men during
temple functions. But the main criticism of
Knott's position is that to set different

standards and criteria, making a special case of religion, is to marginalize these movements even further, as well as setting dangerous precedents that can be used to maintain women's inferiority. Furthermore, it leaves open the risk of such arguments being reapplied from religious to secular life, as has happened so often historically.

The only Hindu-based NRM that directly challenges misogyny is the Brahma Kumaris movement, which Skultans describes as 'without doubt a movement where women control men. Women occupy positions of power and status, whereas men, both in their secular and religious roles, are subordinate to women'.[4] In some respects it offers a complete role reversal: 'Men look after the practical aspects of living thus freeing women for higher spiritual duties.' In other words, they 'appear to be playing the role of wives'. This leads to the interesting and rare phenomenon that 'male pupil and female mentor is a typical combination'. Although Skultans does not explicitly term it a feminist movement, her study makes it clear that there is an implicit feminist ideology. This is admitted by some of the women leaders, but they prefer to emphasize their role in promoting peace and environmental concerns.

Buddhism presents the interesting paradox that despite its original freedom from doctrinal inequality, patriarchy arose and turned the religion into an overwhelmingly male-dominated institution where women were perceived as profane and polluted. This reversal was exemplified by the eight extra rules for ordained women, which are still imposed in the Theravada tradition. Buddhist misogyny has been vigorously challenged both in writing and practice, particularly in America.[5] The Friends of the Western Buddhist Order (FWBO) in Britain share in this questioning, though perhaps less radically than their American counterparts. The official line is that 'men and women enjoy equal "status" and have access to the same opportunities and facilities for serious Dharma practice', via a 'middle way between the traditional subordination of women within the sangha . . . and a demand for equality in a purely secular sense'.[6]

Again, the practice does not always match the theory, and some members express disquiet at the under-representation of women in the higher echelons and the perceived reluctance of the movement's leader Sangharakshita to ordain women.

Research since the mid-1980s presents a more positive picture of gender roles, probably reflecting the impact of feminism throughout Western society. In some NRMs, particularly of the counter-cultural variety, women may be liberated, empowered and fulfilled. Women are more numerous in this kind of NRM, and may outnumber men by as much as 2 to 1. This is the case in the Osho movement, the Brahma Kumaris, many Wiccan, goddess-worshipping and other Pagan groups, whereas in the more traditional, authoritarian Christian sects and NRMs such as the Unification Church and ISKCON, men are in the majority.[7] This finding is important in countering the popular perception of women as brainwashed victims of patriarchal authority, demonstrating that they tend to choose movements offering greater scope for their abilities, while the minority who choose conservative groups may derive other benefits (see below).

Women in Power in the Osho Movement

The Osho movement is the only movement, apart from the Brahma Kumaris, that has a female majority in leadership and administrative roles. Although the teachings of the leader, Osho, promoted an ideal of female discipleship that emphasized traditional feminine attributes (see below), he also advocated an equal opportunities vision of woman freed of the shackles of centuries-old conditioning, reclaiming her power:

My own vision is that the coming age will be the age of the woman. Man has tried for five thousand years and has failed. Now a chance has to be given to the woman. Now she should be given the reins of all the powers. She should be given an opportunity to bring her feminine energies to function, to work.[8]

This ideology was reflected in the social organization. Osho was always clearly in the position of ultimate authority, but about 80 per cent of the top jobs were held by women. His explanation for this positive discrimination was inspirational: 'I want [the commune] to be run by the heart, because to me, to be feminine is to become vulnerable, to become receptive . . . Yes, the ashram is run by women because I want it run by the heart.'[9] However, it can also be argued that it was logical to put women in charge of what was in effect a feminized workplace: where decision-making processes were based on intuition rather than empiricism; caring was given a higher value than efficiency; devotion and meditation were higher goals than productivity and profitability; competition was renounced in favour of co-operation.

Most of the female co-ordinators exemplified this management style, which was claimed to work well until the appointment of Sheela as Osho's deputy, who ran the American commune of Rajneeshpuram until its demise in 1985. At the time Sheela attracted great admiration and devotion from sannyasins for her energy, drive and charisma, but her ruthlessness made her increasingly tyrannical and she was largely responsible for the totalitarian regime that developed, resulting in a débâcle that brought down the whole community, including Sheela herself who served a prison sentence. It is clear that Osho bears some responsibility, at least for the choice of an unsuitable deputy if not for active collaboration, but it was an unfortunate outcome of a grand vision of female potential. However, most sannyasins felt that the experiment had been largely successful, particularly in the earlier and later phases of the movement, as a successful antidote to the technological and left-brained bias of the modern Western approach to work and the bureaucratization of modern life.

Discipleship: The Path of Feminine Spirituality?

There are very few role models for women's spirituality. They may sometimes become nuns, although usually with lower status than monks and heavily constrained by extra rules, particularly in Buddhism. Religious titles betray this bias, either possessing no female equivalent or a debased meaning: priest, master, guru, pope. Only priest has the counterpart priestess, but overlaid by pagan antinomian connotations. The women's spirituality movement has revived and created a mythology of pagan priestesses, but in most religions women's priestly role is severely limited or proscribed.

One of the main paths of spiritual growth is discipleship, but in most religious traditions it has been mainly or wholly confined to men. Yet in many ways it is a highly feminine path, with its emphasis on receptivity, love and devotion to the guru and God. This is partly recognized in the Hindu bhakti tradition, which encourages the devotee to develop a feminine psychology, visualizing himself as a woman and sometimes practising transvestism.[10] Some NRMs have developed this potential into a path of feminine spirituality.

ISKCON can be seen as a transitional movement in this respect, in that Prabhupada allowed women disciples but was ambivalent about their status, alternating between a mystical concept of spiritual equality with male disciples and a conservative Vedic-based belief in female inferiority. Krishna Consciousness itself is 'a feminine approach to spirituality' in that it consists of 'surrender and service to others', and ultimately to Krishna, who represents the masculine polarity.[11] Women are perceived as better socialized to practise this path, but the misogyny sometimes displayed by the movement's leader Prabhupada and his chief male disciples has resulted in lower status for women. Women also had restricted access to Prabhupada, chopping vegetables while the male devotees accompanied him on his morning walks.

Osho was clearly drawing on the bhakti tradition, taking the next logical step: if 'feminine' devotion to a male god is the primary characteristic of devotional religion, it is easier, more natural, for women to be devotees of a male god – or male master. His definitions of masculine and feminine qualities were fairly traditional, in line with Jungian psychology: emotional and intuitive attributes were seen as feminine, whereas strength, decisiveness, objectivity and the intellect itself were seen as masculine. However, the ideal that sannyasins strive towards is androgyny: a balance and integration between the qualities so misleadingly termed feminine and masculine, which is becoming increasingly commended in the New Age. Feminine qualities were also seen as central in discipleship, and women were perceived as superior in this respect: 'The disciple needs receptivity; he has to receive. Even the male disciple has to function almost in a feminine way . . . Hence the woman proves to be the perfect disciple.'[12]

The women's movement has been highly critical of the master–disciple relationship for its encouragement of female submissiveness to a male master. The requirement to wear a mala[13] was a particularly regressive symbol to feminists, who singled out the Osho movement for criticism on this score. Yet a number of women sannyasins had been in the women's movement prior to joining. One former leading feminist whom I interviewed answered the question of how taking on a male master connected to her feminist principles:

It didn't strike me with much difficulty, but it did to a lot of my friends – a man's picture around my neck! But I'd been moving away for some time from feminism. I found that it was restricting me and my development spiritually. And also when I looked at the truth of my life, I found that the people who really mattered to me were my son and my lover. Feminism didn't give me a framework to explain this.

Most sannyasins found discipleship a positive and fulfilling spiritual path. The master–disciple relationship is based on deep love. Osho often used erotic imagery to convey the ecstasy of the experience: 'The disciple and teacher must become deep lovers. Only then can the higher, the beyond, be expressed.'[14] Such experiences and images are sanctified in the devotional traditions of all religions, particularly in 'marriage mysticism',[15] but is also encountered in more austere traditions such as Buddhism. One of Boucher's respondents described a 'psychic merging' with her teacher whereby she became 'so close to this person that I was really fused with him in a way that my identity was submerged. That's part of Dharma transmission, to become one with your teacher so that you can see through their eyes.'[16] However, the emphasis on 'falling in love' with the master in a kind of spiritualized version of a romantic love affair carries particular dangers for women; in the context of the intensity and intimacy of the master–disciple relationship such love may easily slide into sexuality, and thence into sexual abuse.

Sexual Abuse: The Shadow Side of the Master–Disciple Relationship

Nowadays, one of the main issues for feminists regarding charismatic authority is sexual abuse, which is widespread in old and new religions within the context of general patriarchal abuse of power. It is the shadow side of the master–disciple relationship, which has darkened the reputation of a number of NRMs and the lives of their members. In the past it has often been perceived as a problem of Asian gurus encountering more permissive Western societies. However, within the last ten years, Christianity's moral hegemony has been undermined by a series of scandals regarding love affairs between evangelical preachers or priests and their parishioners, who have often been abandoned when pregnant while the priest is moved on to a new parish. One recent Christian scandal in Britain partook of all the features usually associated with charismatic leaders of NRMs. It featured Chris Brain, vicar and former leader of the 9 O'Clock Service in Sheffield. In November 1995 he admitted having had improper sexual relations with twenty of his female parishioners, as a result of which he resigned. His ministry had formerly been greatly admired by the Anglican establishment, who had therefore speeded up his ordination. He had also been endorsed by the well-known American religious teacher and writer Matthew Fox, whose Creation

Spirituality rituals he had adapted in his own services. Women who complained to their local bishop were dismissed as troublemakers, and 'rubbished very effectively' by Brain and his staff, although following his exposure he was condemned as a 'cult leader'.

The most wide-scale example of sexual abuse in an NRM is another Christian movement, the Children of God (COG) also known as The Family. David Berg, the leader, had multiple sexual relationships with his female followers and encouraged the membership to follow his example. The practice for which the movement is most notorious is 'flirty fishing', a recruitment technique devised by Berg and his wife for female members to bring in potential converts through prostitution. At the peak of this phase in the late 1970s, the practice spread throughout the movement's international communes, and women were working two to five nights a week. It died down because of the spread of sexually transmitted diseases, combined with the strain on family life and the increasing demands of childcare, and in 1987 the practice was stopped altogether in response to the AIDS epidemic.[17]

The abuses within the COG have been exposed, but feminist research raises further issues about the presentation and interpretation of such contentious material. One concern is the 'sexual objectification' that results from the imposition of so-called value-free, scientific methodology. Janet Jacobs particularly highlights Wallis's research on the COG as typifying 'those studies that fail to question the norms of patriarchal control that lead to the sexual exploitation of female devotes'.[18] She accuses him of dehumanizing them by describing them as the group's sexual resources and not investigating or even acknowledging their responses. Jacobs herself has undertaken the most extensive research on the abuse of women by male religious leaders.[19] She describes an 'economy of love', a process of affiliation in which the female devotee hopes to be emotionally 'rescued' and loved by the guru in return for her devotion. Unfortunately, the exchange tends to break down because of the unequal power relations whereby a large number of women are competing for the love of one man and are subjected to neglect, rejection and abuse. As a result many of them leave, bitter and disillusioned by the confusion between sexual and spiritual fulfilment and the resulting exploitation.

Many gurus have been accused of sexual abuse, including Maharishi Mahesh Yogi, Muktananda, Da Avabhasa and Swami Rama. Buddhism in the West has been shaken by a number of scandals, mainly exposed through the vociferous protests of Buddhist women.[20] In particular, Chogyam Trungpa was notorious for his many sexual partners called 'consorts', as well as his alcoholism. He was exposed after his death, having chosen as his dharma heir Osel Tendzin, who died of AIDS after allegedly infecting his many partners without telling them. Sogyal Rinpoche was a protégé of Trungpa and is the best-known Tibetan lama in the West apart from the Dalai Lama. He was recently sued for $10 million by an American ex-devotee claiming sexual and physical abuse. The case was finally settled out of court, but since then there have been numerous other allegations of abuse by his female disciples.

Trungpa and Sogyal, among others, have justified sexual relationships with their students on the basis of Tantra or 'crazy wisdom', as a means of spiritual growth. Anthony and Wilber, both experienced meditators as well as academics, censure such attempts as 'a rationalization for flamboyant acting-out and impulsivity', leading to exploitation, deep psychological wounding and spiritual disillusion.[21] Traditional Tantra at least regulates such relationships through strict ethical codes, but these are absent in most NRMs.

The women involved are not always passive victims. They may fall in love with their gurus and even actively attempt to seduce them. However, such situations are largely the result of harem-style structures where women attain power and status by being the guru's lover and are encouraged to compete for his favours. In return they are often promised special transmissions and teachings, promises which may not always be fulfilled. In addition, the qualifications for such attentions may not be spiritual. As the teacher Andrew Cohen recently commented, 'Isn't it interesting how only the youngest and prettiest women are chosen?'

Altogether, the evidence suggests that when the powerful energy of sexuality is harnessed to the drive for power and the search for enlightenment, the results are pain and disillusion for the victims, and loss of reputation for the perpetrators, which sometimes reflects on the whole tradition. Tantra may have worked in the past as a framework for such relationships and may have potential for the present under very carefully regulated conditions, but the examples of most NRMs in this tradition show that the dangers far outweigh the benefits.[22] The Dalai Lama has said that the true Tantric master is capable of drinking urine or alcohol with complete equanimity, and that the path is so difficult and demanding that there is probably nobody alive capable of walking it.

For the future it is important that sexuality in the religious context, particularly within the master–disciple relationship, is addressed, preferably by NRMs themselves. If dysfunctional family dynamics and organizational politics preclude this, abuse needs to be publicly denounced. Chris Brain was exposed after a group of his women parishioners met and agreed: 'This is not just a sex scandal, but an abuse of religious power.' Richard Baker was thrown out of San Francisco Zen Center following a mass rebellion after he was discovered to be sleeping with a trustee's wife. On a wider scale, public awareness of the extent of abuse within Buddhism emerged following the first conference on Women and Buddhism in America in 1983. The Sogyal Rinpoche case is significant partly because it established a precedent for legal action. Above all, there is a need for teachers not to exploit their position, and for women to empower themselves and take action against sexual abuse.

Sexuality and Marriage in NRMs

Historically, sects and 'cults' tend towards extremism – either asceticism or antinomianism – and contemporary NRMs continue this trend. Another option sometimes encountered – which does not stand out historically because it reflected social norms but is contentious in the modern West – is arranged or controlled marriage. The Brahma Kumaris are probably the most extreme and uncompromising example of the Eastern-based NRMs advocating celibacy, at least in Britain. The Osho movement, particularly in the 1970s, exemplifies the 'free love' ethic of the counterculture. The 'Moonie mass marriage' provides the most dramatic example of arranged marriage.

Whatever pattern is followed, the beliefs and behaviours of religions regarding sexuality correlate with their ideas about women and femininity. Most organized religions and many NRMs are ambivalent or condemnatory about sex, leading to a polarized model of (celibate) holiness as male and (sexual) sinfulness as female. Religions that equate celibacy with purity invariably promote a dualistic, body-rejecting and misogynistic philosophy in which women are seen as Evil Temptresses whose only hope for salvation (if any exists) is to become a nun.

Free love and hedonism as spiritual path

The predominant media image of the Osho movement during Osho's lifetime was of a 'sex cult' led by a 'sex guru'. However, his aim was to create a scientific yet sacramental sexuality based on a synthesis between Tantra and Reichian psychotherapy. The main lines of his teachings on sex were established in a series of lectures in Bombay in 1968, published as *From Sex to Superconsciousness*:

All our efforts to date have borne wrong results because we have not befriended sex but have declared war on it; we have used suppression and lack of understanding as ways of dealing with sex problems . . . And the results of repression are never fruitful, never pleasing, never healthy.[23]

In contrast to most religions, including NRMs, which are hostile or ambivalent towards sexuality, Osho taught that it is our most powerful natural energy with three levels of potential. It begins as a biological method of procreation (animal), develops into a source of pleasure and intimacy (human), and ultimately a means to self-realization (divine). He emphasized women's potential, through their capacity for multiple orgasms, to become Tantric adepts and attain enlightenment, providing a range of techniques for the purpose.

Although the 'free love ethic' was normative in the Osho movement, sexual behaviour was as varied as elsewhere in Western society, and serial monogamy was the predominant pattern, especially among long-term sannyasins. Osho's statements on marriage are mainly critical, although he would sometimes commend its potential as 'a deep spiritual communion'. In Poona there was no encouragement for sexual partners to marry, although the 'religion' of Rajneeshism later included a marriage ceremony. Nowadays, as a response to the AIDS crisis, there is a growing emphasis on monogamy.

The main source of Pagan beliefs and practices on sexuality is the mythology of the goddess: 'Sexuality is sacred because it is a sharing of energy, in passionate surrender to the power of the Goddess, immanent in our desire. In orgasm, we share in the force that moves the stars.'[24] Much interest has focused on the Great Rite: ritual sex between the high priest and priestess in pagan rituals, but the evidence suggests that it is more often symbolic than actual. Witches do tend to worship 'sky-clad' (naked), but 'as a way of establishing closeness and dropping social masks, because power is most easily raised that way, and because the human body is itself sacred'.[25] Paganism particularly affirms the female body and provides rituals for celebrating 'women's mysteries', such as menstruation and childbirth.

The English Wiccan high priestess Vivianne Crowley perceives that the 'negative attitude to women displayed in Christianity has derived largely from negative attitudes to sex',[26] particularly following the glorification of celibacy. She describes Pagan sexual morality as simple:

there are no barriers to sexual activity with other unattached adults; but we are expected to have regard to the consequences of our actions and to ensure that we do not cause unwanted pregnancy, spread sexual disease, or mislead others as to our level of commitment to the relationship.

This means that 'For unattached adults, there are no barriers to sexual activity with other unattached adults' (although attitudes to homosexuality vary between different groups), but extra-marital sex is forbidden if it causes hurt, while rape and child – adult sex are 'anathema'.[27]

Pagans are uninterested in marriage as a legal institution, seeing it as a device to protect property and dominate women. However, a loving monogamous relationship is seen as a personal contract to be honoured. As Starhawk puts it: 'Marriage is a deep commitment, a magical, spiritual, and psychic bond. But it is only one possibility out of many for loving, sexual expression.'[28] Various Pagan groups have created colourful wedding rituals, sometimes called 'handfasting', which are often celebrated at a seasonal festival, such as the spring festival of Beltain. Alternative marriages are increasing in Britain by about 50 per cent a year, including among non-Pagans, in reaction to the outdatedness and sexism of the Judaeo-Christian rituals and the unspirituality of the civil ceremony.[29]

The path of purity and celibacy

In contrast to sannyasin and Pagan attitudes to sexuality as gift and spiritual path, the Brahma Kumaris see it as an obstacle to enlightenment. The main method for counteracting this 'greatest vice' is to cultivate a dualistic attitude, exemplified by their mantra: 'I am a soul, my body is a garment.' The movement appears to attract people who are uninterested in sex and for whom celibacy therefore has a positive appeal. Unusually among non-monastic movements, they require celibacy for their core members, even between husbands and wives. As long as chastity is maintained, marriage and family life are allowed, even encouraged (perhaps to avoid the accusation of breaking up families). However, the married women I interviewed had been married for many years, and one admitted that this might have been a factor in easing the move into celibacy:

Possibly our relationship had come to brother and sister anyway. He's a very modest person, and he loved it. I never told him about celibacy, I just moved out of the bedroom one day. He must have wondered, but he never said anything ... I think we have a much better relationship now, it's great.

Buddhism, like Catholicism, has a developed monastic tradition. In the West, discipline tends to be looser, but Theravada and some Zen groups impose celibacy on the monks, sometimes accompanied by misogynistic attitudes. It is less usual to find women advocating celibacy in Buddhism, although the Zen teacher Kennett Roshi believes it is a precondition to attain enlightenment:

If you're married, the singleness of mind, the devotion, the oneness with that eternal can't take place, because you're dividing it off for a member of the opposite sex ... If you're going to follow the eternal, *he's* the one you're gonna be fond of. He-she-it. [30]

Witnessing sexual energy without repression or indulgence is a subtle and arduous process, and may work more effectively with older, serious adepts. Most women who choose to become celibate Buddhist nuns are older and have fully experienced relationships previously. In the FWBO celibacy is practised in the long term more by older women. An 86-year-old nun at the Tibetan monastery of Samye-Ling in Scotland had been ordained in her sixties, and felt that this was a more sensible age to begin, as did a 52-year-old woman at the Theravada community of Amaravrati. A former nun in a Korean Zen monastery highlighted lack of affection as a much harder problem for women than lack of sex, and stressed the importance of clarity regarding the aim of celibacy: that it should be under-

taken only as an aid to practice and not to repress the body and one's full humanity.

Spiritually arranged marriages

Arranged marriages were sacralized by all the world's religions during periods when they were the cultural norm, and they still take place in some conservative sects of Western religions. Some women prefer arranged marriage with its accompanying clarity of family and gender role, despite the price of sexual restraint. There is some evidence that the women who join fundamentalist movements have suffered childhood abuse and/or broken homes, often followed by victimaization in their own relationships, which predisposes them to sacrifice freedom for stability. Some women claim that not being treated as a sex object is a benefit of such customs as covering hair and body, but the religion itself traditionally interprets them in terms of purity and pollution. In fundamentalist Christian NRMs such as the London Church of Christ, marriages are not usually formally arranged but often rely on the advice and consent of the pastor, and divorce is forbidden except for adultery. The Jesus Army is more extreme, perceiving marriage as the 'lower way', inferior to celibacy, which is promoted in *Celibate Cutting Edge*, their 'inspirational bulletin of celibacy'. In this respect the movement may be perceived as a militant version of the men's movement in which the men give up being 'feminized' and don combat gear as warriors for Jesus, also displaying misogynistic attitudes.

Eastern-based NRMs may encourage or impose arranged marriage. The 'Moonie mass marriage' is the most dramatic example, in which 2,000 or more couples may be married in one ceremony or 'Blessing', often without having even met each other beforehand. These marriages are preceded by at least six years' celibacy, followed by three years' celibacy in which the partners strive to become the Ideal Man and Woman (as exemplified by Mr and Mrs Moon) before consummation is allowed. Finally, in a three-day ceremony following a seven-day fast, the marriage is consummated in a ritual that aims to reverse the Fall precipitated by Adam and Eve's premature sexual relationship. Women may thereby attain equal or greater spiritual status than men as 'creatures of the heart' but at the price of total submission to husband and guru. It is possible to refuse these marriages, but few do.

ISKCON also favours arranged marriage, though couples may come to a private understanding beforehand, and women may actively select their husband. However, they then need permission to marry from the temple president. Marital sex is permitted but only for the purpose of procreation, hedged around with restrictions. Marriage improves the social and spiritual status of women but not men, who are held to be superior to women on all levels, particularly when celibate. A woman may be perceived as 'a temptress first and a devotee second', and excluded from sharing power with the men so as not to 'sexually agitate them'.[31] However, the situation is beginning to improve now, as a result partly of the high failure rate of the marriages,[32] partly of women's greater power in the movement.

NRMs offer women a wide range of choices regarding sexuality as with other aspects of life, but it is important to recognize the consequences of some of these choices. Some women are attracted to the certainty and stability of arranged marriage and are prepared to sacrifice freedom and status, but may also suffer abuse from their husbands. Celibacy only works for a few exceptional women, and denies the affective needs. Both these solutions are associated with misogyny. Free love worked in the Osho movement partly because there was enough encouragement of monogamy to produce stability, whereas in the more extreme and authoritarian Children of God it caused great suffering. The more world-accepting middle way of Pagan sexuality also offers a successful model, a sacralized form of the serial monogamy predominant in Western society. Most of the support for holistic spirituality, in all religions, is from women, and it may be that body-positive immanence is inherently more female, celibate transcendence more male. The main condition for success and happiness is that women should be in control of their own sexuality and fertility.

Motherhood and Community: Beyond the Nuclear Family

One of the main accusations against NRMs, especially from the ACM, is that they break up families.[33] Given the small numbers of people involved in NRMs and the range of beliefs and practices regarding the family, this is an exaggerated reproach. However, as on other social issues, these experimental groups provide an interesting commentary and critique on the state of family and community. As with sexual practices, the conservative NRMs attempt to revive traditional, patriarchal family structures, whereas the counter-cultural movements experiment with alternative forms, particularly the commune.

It is particularly within marriage and motherhood that feminists see woman's 'self' as most at risk of being negated. Patriarchy demands that women should sacrifice their own needs and demands to their family, valuing selflessness over self-realization, caring for others over creation of self. Most religions sanctify motherhood as a woman's destiny and true vocation, especially the more patriarchal traditions such as Roman Catholicism, the more fundamentalist movements within all three Western religions, and NRMs like the Unification Church where Mrs Moon as a 'devoted wife and mother' is a role model for Unificationist women. Women who are themselves conservative, internalizing and upholding these beliefs, may be drawn to such religions.[34] The benefits are clearly defined gender roles and stable families, but the downside is a rigid control of sexuality, work and worship by husband and elders, loss of status and opportunities for direct spiritual advancement, and a high incidence of wife and child abuse.

Conservative Christianity is now the main preserver and legitimator of traditional family values in the West, and herein lies the appeal for certain kinds of women, looking for discipline and stability in contrast to the 'decadent experiments' of secular life. The women may find it hard to give up their autonomy to a husband, particularly given 'the lack of strong sensitive men to head the godly institutions of church and family in a loving and responsible manner'. Yet this requirement is enshrined in the social organization, as in all patriarchal society, here upheld by the Director of Counselling at Thomas Road Baptist Ministries: 'The Bible clearly states that the wife is to submit to her husband's leadership. Two-headed households are as confusing as they are clumsy.'[35] The women finally made this sacrifice, deciding 'they would rather follow than be left behind to struggle with their own individual identities'. Rose concludes: 'While they may be relatively content in their relationships with their men, their bench mark is embedded in the old system of patriarchy which continues to perpetuate the costly contradictions that trap both men and women.'[36]

The one interesting exception to this pattern of patriarchal dominance over women and children is the women's spirituality movement, where there has been a resacralization of motherhood similar to the revival in secular society. The dangers of reverting to biological determinism through overemphasizing and romanticizing female bodily existence have been incisively analysed by Ursula King as 'a form of retraditionalization' at the expense of 'a wider human experience of self-development'.[37]

The Osho movement was the most militantly anti-family of all NRMs in the 1970s. Like R. D. Laing and other radical psychologists of the time, Osho believed the family was 'outdated', 'the most hindering phenomenon for human progress' and 'the root cause of all our neurosis'. Nevertheless, he would sometimes describe motherhood as potentially the peak of female creativity and responsibility: 'becoming the mother of a Buddha'. However, his main emphasis was firmly on self-realization for women: 'A woman is not only capable of giving birth to children, she is also capable of giving birth to herself as a seeker of truth. But that side of woman has not been explored at all.'[38] Osho discouraged women from having children on the basis (a)

that most people were incapable of positive parenting, and (b) that children were a distraction from the spiritual growth that was the main purpose of being there. The main problem for sannyasins who did have children was that the commune was set up primarily as a kind of monastery, for childless adults choosing to pursue spiritual development as the main priority. Traditionally, seekers have been required to sacrifice everything, including family life, for this goal.[39] Women with children were committed to 'giving birth to themselves as seekers of truth', but also, naturally, to their children. As with sexual relationships, family life in a monastic setting can be highly problematic, setting up conflicts with the spiritual objectives. Having made the choice to be in effect a working mother, women had less time for their children and some later regretted the missed joys of motherhood. But the consensus was that even if the children had been somewhat neglected, they had still been better off in a commune than a single-parent family. Some women found motherhood and personal development compatible. One woman had found motherhood 'one of the greatest gifts that's ever happened in my life', and managed to combine it easily with meditation and communal living.

Buddhist monasteries have the same dilemma. The FWBO has experimented with various community structures and found that single-sex ones work best, reducing the psychological dependence, conflict and entanglements of family life. In America, on the other hand, there is a growing tendency for Buddhist monasteries to be non-segregated, combining single and married practitioners, sometimes including children. Mothers report a variety of experience – bitterness at the neglect of their needs; guilt at their own inadequacies; and the joys of motherhood as a path.[40]

As with other social and spiritual issues, NRMs offer women a range of options from the traditional nuclear family to childless freedom. The choices and experiences of women regarding religion have close parallels with their secular equivalents. Women who accept motherhood as their vocation and are looking for a stable, secure family life therefore tend to be drawn to conservative old and New Religious Movements. The price of these benefits, as with non-working mothers but to a greater degree, is a loss of liberty, self-determination and other possibilities for growth. Women who prefer to focus on their personal development tend to choose religions such as Buddhism, the Osho movement and Paganism. The price paid by women with children in these movements, as with career women, is the stress of combining motherhood with an often arduous regime of work and spiritual practice. However, the commune is widely endorsed as a form of social organization offering many of the benefits of the extended family such as childcare, a stimulating environment for adults and children, the opportunity for women to be mothers without sacrificing their own development. As such, it might well be acknowledged and developed as a viable model for an increasingly single-parent society.

Female Spiritual Leadership in NRMs

Stark and Bainbridge postulate that 'one of the things that attracts particularly ambitious women to cults is the opportunity to become leaders or even founders of their own religious movements'.[41] Most such women will have been frustrated, but a few have succeeded. The lack of opportunity within their own religion will sometimes drive women to convert to completely different traditions, as happened with a well-known Zen master:

The only reason she turned away from Christianity, Roshi Kennett told me, was her incredibly deep calling to become a priest. And, as a woman, 'there was no way I could become a priest in Christianity.' It was the sexism of the Church of England that compelled her to cut loose from Christianity and finally become a monk in a foreign country, in a foreign religion, in a foreign language.[42]

The priestly role is debarred to women in many Asian religions, as in Christianity. In ISKCON conditions are improving to the point where women may now theoretically become gurus, but none have so far, intimidated by the lack of respect and role models. In the Osho movement women held most of the secular power, but Osho believed that women's spirituality lay in their capacity for discipleship rather than teaching, and that they could not become masters. This was partly because he believed women were emotionally centred, whereas men had superior minds which made it hard for them to surrender as disciples but gave them an advantage as teachers. Another reason why 'only the male mind can be a master' was: 'To be a Master means to be very aggressive. A woman cannot be aggressive. Woman, by her very nature, is receptive. A woman is a womb, so the woman can be the very best disciple possible.'[43]

The Brahma Kumaris present a similar pattern of a founder who favoured and promoted women, and has been run mainly by women since his death. In some respects the role reversal is more complete than in the Osho Movement, since women are teachers as well as administrators, and there is a very clear doctrine on gender equality. They are concerned with women's issues and spiritual leadership. However, as with sannyasins, Brahma Kumaris women become core members by being fully 'surrendered', and their prominence derives from their mediumistic capacities, channelling *murlis* (sermons) from their dead founder. As a result, 'their power is veiled . . . through the device of possession. Women, even when they possess power, cannot be seen to wield it. Hence, the importance of spirit possession where women are the instruments or mouthpieces of a male spirit.'[44]

There are a few contemporary Indian women gurus teaching in their own right, such as Amritanandamayi, known as Ammachi or 'the hugging guru', and Mother Meera who now lives in Germany. However, these women have not founded large organizations or left bodies of teaching. This is probably largely owing to their lack of education, in contrast to the male gurus who are often highly educated – both Osho and Prabhupada were professors of philosophy. The women are bhakti gurus, but for their devotees this simplicity may be an advantage in contrast to the perceived arid intellectuality of Western religion and culture.

One of the very few women who adheres to the male style of charismatic leadership is Nirmala Devi, known as Mataji, founder of Sahaj Yoga. What in interesting is that she began as a disciple of Osho and in setting up as a guru in her own right has imitated his style, although she is publicly critical of him as he sometimes was of her. Osho claims that after they had visited Muktananda together and been unimpressed, the idea entered Nirmala's head: 'If such a fool like Muktananda can become a saint, then why can't I become a saint?'[45] Like Osho – and Gurumayi, the female successor to Muktananda – she is anti-feminist, fearing that if women behave like men they will lose their femininity. Her teaching on gender is as traditional as ISKCON's, endorsing the ideal of the Indian wife, submissive to her husband, and advocating clearly defined, traditional gender roles.

Western religion has an underground history of female leadership in sects, particularly in America where Mother Anne Lee became leader of the Shakers, Mary Baker Eddy founded Christian Science, and Ellen White founded Seventh-day Adventism. Among contemporary NRMs, the Church Universal and Triumphant was originally founded by a man, but on his death in 1973 the leadership was taken over by his wife, Elizabeth Clare Prophet, known to her followers as Guru Ma. Spiritualism has been dominated by women in America and Britain, as is channelling, its New Age derivation. The New Age itself has been created and shaped at least as much by women as men, such as Helena Blavatsky, co-founder of Theosophy, and Alice Bailey who created the Arcane School. Many of the leading figures in the turn-of-the-century occult revival were women, such as the British magician Dion Fortune. In Paganism, women are generally perceived as equal if not superior to men. Feminist witchcraft obviously has a female leadership, while most Wiccan covens have a high priest and a high priestess as equals. The best-known Pagan writers are women, such as Margot Adler and Starhawk in America and Vivianne Crowley in Britain.

Most women in Christian and Eastern religion hitherto have acquired the titles Mother, Ma or Mataji. Women who positively identify with motherliness will tend towards a more feminine style of leadership. Receptivity is the most-cited quality to epitomize both femininity and spirituality, particularly in movements based on discipleship or mediumship, and the women leaders of such NRMs tend to emphasize its importance along with softness, kindness and intuition. Other qualities that women leaders have exemplified as positively feminine and beneficial for authority are practicality, intuition, tenderness, body-affirmation, caring, healing, devotion, forgiveness, holism, social engagement and social mysticism.

Probably the most flexible and relevant model of female leadership for the future is of a more androgynous kind, which steers a middle path between imitating the traditional masculine models, with the danger of taking on their flaws to an even greater degree, or adhering too closely to a feminine model, which lacks toughness in a confrontation or crisis. Osho offered women techniques and opportunities to experiment with this approach, which some adapted more successfully than others. The Brahma Kumaris also promote this kind of integration as a leadership quality, as do many Buddhist teachers. Particularly within the meeting between East and West taking place in America, with its scope for experimentation and fruitful confrontation, many women teachers in Buddhism and other religions are leading the way towards a postmodernist, post-feminist, androgynous style of leadership.

A New Typology of Spiritual Needs and Values

As has been demonstrated, the position and status of women vary considerably between different NRMs. The differences correlate with my new typology of religion based on Abraham Maslow's 'hierarchy of needs'.[46] The typology classifies new religions into five groups or levels according to the needs and values of their members: survival; safety; esteem; belongingness and love; self-actualization. I then combine these five levels into two broad groupings: traditionalism (levels 1–2) and personal development (levels 3–5). I would argue that the traditionalist movements share a focus on conservative or traditional values, whereas those in levels 3–5 may be understood in terms of a spectrum of personal development from simple self-improvement to spirituality. Each level also represents clear differences in beliefs and practices regarding gender.[47]

Traditionalist movements (levels 1–2) are the most conservative, reactionary and hierarchical, comprising fundamentalist NRMs and sects within world religions. Their main appeal is to women who are confused and frightened by the complexity of the modern world. In contrast, they offer clearly defined gender roles and stable family life. They thus fulfil security needs, though often at a price of limitation and oppression. Some of these NRMs, such as ISKCON, are responding to the advances of feminism as their women members find their voices and demand greater equality. However, it is significant that these movements tend to have a male majority, sometimes 2 to 1 or higher, whereas in more liberal NRMs the ratio is typically reversed.

The appeal of NRMs focused on personal development lies in their great scope for self-expression, exploration and empowerment, sometimes beyond what is available in secular life. They attract, on the one hand, counter-cultural seekers, on the other hand women who have achieved secular/professional success and are now looking for spiritual growth. Their beliefs and practice on gender are more fluid and flexible, sometimes with a focus on androgyny, and usually including women in leadership positions. NRMs such as the Osho movement, the Brahma Kumaris, and many Buddhist and Pagan groups offer equal opportunities with no glass ceiling, and possibilities for women to combine work, marriage and motherhood with spiritual growth.

Notes

1 Mary Harder, 'Sex Roles in the Jesus Movement', *Social Compass*, 21 (3), 1974, pp. 345–53; Susan Rose, 'Women Warriors: the Negotiation of Gender in a Charismatic Community', *Sociological Analysis*, 48 (3), 1987, pp. 245–58.

2 Angela Aidala, 1985, 'Social Change, Gender Roles, and New Religious Movements', *Sociological Analysis*, 46 (3), 1985, 295. Similar conclusions were reached by Janet Jacobs, 'The Economy of Love in Religious Commitment', *Journal for the Scientific Study of Religion*, 23 (2), 1984, pp. 155–71.

3 Kim Knott, 'Men and Women, or Devotees?', in Arvind Sharma (ed.), *Women in the World's Religions, Past and Present*, New York: Paragon House, 1987.

4 Vieda Skultans, 'The Brahma Kumaris and the Role of Women', in Elizabeth Puttick and Peter Clarke (eds), *Women as Teachers and Disciples in Traditional and New Religions*, Lewiston, NY: Edwin Mellen Press, 1993.

5 Sandy Boucher, *Turning the Wheel*, Boston, MA: Beacon Press, 1988, and Lenore Friedman, *Meetings with Remarkable Women*, Boston, MA: Shambhala, 1987, based their books on extensive research into the growing number of women teachers in America, who are introducing many changes through their questioning and pragmatic attitudes towards the tradition.

6 Cited in the official FWBO magazine *The Golden Drum*, November 1989–January 1990, an issue devoted to the discussion of women's issues.

7 For general research on women in NRMs see Susan Palmer, *Moon Sisters, Krishna Mothers, Rajneesh Lovers*, Syracuse, NY: Syracuse University Press, 1994; Elizabeth Puttick, *Women in New Religions*, London: Macmillan, 1996; on the women's spirituality movement see Mary Bednarowski, 'The New Age and Feminist Spirituality', in J. R. Lewis and J. Gordon Melton (eds), *Perspectives on the New Age*, New York: SUNY, 1992; Nancy Finley, 'Political Activism and Feminist Spirituality', *Sociological Analysis*, 52 (4), 1991, pp. 349–62; Susan Greenwood, 'Feminist Witchcraft', in Nickie Charles and Felicia Hughes-Freeland (eds), *Practising Feminism*, London: Routledge, 1995; Mary Neitz, 'In Goddess We Trust', in T. Robbins and D. Anthony (eds), *In Gods*

We Trust, New Brunswick, NJ: Transaction, 1990.

8   Osho, *A New Vision of Women's Liberation*, Cologne: Rebel Press, 1987.

9   Cited by Judith Thompson and Paul Heelas, *The Way of the Heart*, Wellingborough: Aquarian, 1986, p. 93. They appear to endorse this statement, quoting a Medina sannyasin in support.

10 Katherine Young, 'Hinduism', in Arvind Sharma (ed.), *Women in World Religions*, New York: SUNY, 1987; Wendy O'Flaherty, *Women, Androgynes and Other Mythical Beasts*, Chicago, IL: Chicago University Press, 1980.

11 Kim Knott, 'The Debate about Women in the Hare Krishna Movement', *Journal of Vaishnava Studies*, 3 (4), 1995, pp. 85–109.

12 Osho, *Theologia Mystica*, Poona: Rajneesh Foundation International, 1983, p. 266.

13 A necklace of wooden beads with a locket containing Osho's photo.

14 *The Book of the Secrets*, vol. 1, Poona: Rajneesh Foundation, 1974, p. 5.

15 R. W. Hood and J. R. Hall, 'Gender Differences in the Description of Erotic and Mystical Experiences', *Review of Religious Research*, 21 (2), 1980, pp. 195–207; Kees Bolle, 'Hieros Gamos', in Mircea Eliade (ed.), *Encyclopedia of Religion*, New York: Macmillan, 1987, pp. 317–21.

16 Boucher, op. cit., pp. 218–19.

17 See Gordon Melton, 'Sexuality and the Maturation of "the Family"', unpublished paper presented at the Federal University of Pernambuco, Brazil, 1994, for an extended account of sexuality in the COG.

18 'Gender and Power in New Religious Movements', *Religion*, 21, 1991, pp. 345–56.

19 Jacobs, 1984, op. cit.

20 See in Boucher, op. cit.; Friedman, op. cit.

21 Dick Anthony, Bruce Ecker and Ken Wilber (eds), *Spiritual Choices: The Problem of Recognizing Authentic Paths to Inner Transformation*, New York: Paragon House, 1987, P. 67.

22 John Stevens, *Lust for Enlightenment*, Boston, MA: Shambhala, 1990; Miranda Shaw, *Passionate Enlightenment*, Princeton, NJ: Princeton University Press, 1994, give accounts of the Tantric tradition and the high status of women.

23 Osho, *From Sex to Superconsciousness*, Poona: Rajneesh Foundation, 1978, p. 89.

24 Starhawk, *The Spiral Dance*, San Francisco, CA: HarperSanFrancisco, 1989, 2nd edn, p. 208.

25 Ibid., p. 97.

26 *The Phoenix from the Flame*, London: Aquarian, 1994, p. 116.

27 Ibid., pp. 163–4.

28 Op. cit., p. 27.

29 This trend has attracted media attention in national newspapers and magazines, for example 'Pagans of Suburbia' in *Elle*, February 1994, and articles on alternative weddings in the *Independent*, 13 February 1995 and 24 December 1995. Even *Hello!* magazine has featured a celebrity handfasting. Graham Harvey has written a chapter on Handfastings in Druidry in Phillip Carr-Gomm (ed.), *The Druid Renaissance*, London: Thorsons, 1996.

30 Boucher, op. cit., p. 143.

31 ISKCON's official magazine *Back to Godhead*, 1991, issues 1 and 2, in which a selection of women devotees express their views.

32 One informant estimated that 50 per cent ISKCON marriages had failed.

33 Eileen Barker, *New Religious Movements: A Practical Introduction*, London: HMSO, 1989; Bryan Wilson, *The Social Dimensions of Sectarianism*, Oxford: Clarendon Press, 1990.

34 For example, approximately 80 per cent of white converts to Islam in Britain and America are women, who appear to be largely attracted by the high value placed on motherhood as well as the moral certainties and clearly defined gender roles.

35 Rose, op. cit., pp. 247–8.

36 Ibid., p. 257.

37 *Women and Spirituality*, London: Macmillan, 1989, p. 80.

38 Osho, 1987, op. cit. This concept is based on the Hindu doctrine that the goal of the religious life is to become *dwija*, twice-born, a rebirth into the spiritual Self.

39 Baker makes this point, citing scriptural references to Jesus's and Buddha's exhortations to their disciples (op. cit., p. 87).

40 Boucher, op. cit.

41 Rodney Stark and William Bainbridge, *The Future of Religion*, Berkeley: University of California Press, 1985, p. 414.

42 Friedman, op. cit., p. 173.

43 Osho, *The Path of Love*, Poona: Rajneesh Foundation, 1978, p. 44.

44 Skultans, op. cit., p. 52.

45 Osho, *Philosophia Perennis*, Poona: Rajneesh Foundation, 1981, p. 318.

46 Elizabeth Puttick, 'A New Typology of Religion Based on Needs and Values', *Journal of Beliefs and Values*, 18 (2), 1997, pp. 133–45.

47 It should be emphasized that while levels 3–5 appear to represent 'higher' needs, no value judgement is implied. The categories are less fixed than the typology suggests; in practice most people's needs continuously fluctuate between levels, and NRMs correspondingly contain elements of all levels. See my article cited in note 46 for a fuller discussion of these issues.

CHAPTER FIFTEEN

Women's "Cocoon Work" in New Religious Movements: Sexual Experimentation and Feminine Rites of Passage

SUSAN J. PALMER

In contrast to the depth of interest shown by historians and anthropologists in women's participation in utopias (Foster 1981; Kern 1981; Moore 1977), ecstatic cults (Cohn 1970; Lewis 1971), and Christian heresies (Pagels 1988; Reuther 1983), the issue of women's experiences in contemporary non-conventional religions has not been adequately addressed. Fieldwork in the area of NRM sex roles is limited (Wagner 1982; Wallis 1982; Richardson, Stewart, and Simmonds 1979; Wessinger 1993), and only a few "gendered" approaches to "cult conversion" processes (Grace 1985; Rochford 1985; Barker 1984) have been written. Thus, the appeal for women of communities practicing spiritually based forms of celibacy, polygamy, eugenics, or "free love" remains enigmatic.

Robbins (1988) identifies a rift between those scholars who stress the *empowerment* of women in unconventional spiritual groups (Babb 1986; Bednarowski 1980; Haywood 1983; Neitz 1988) and an opposing "camp" (Aidala 1985; Davidman 1991; Rose 1987) who portray NRMs as a *backlash* against the feminist movement and a retreat into conservative family patterns within enclaves of patriarchy. Jacobs's (1984) study of women's defection from NRMs, for example, presents NRMs as magnifying the patriarchal patterns of authority found in mainstream religions. Since social control in charismatic communities is greater, Jacobs (1984: 158) argues, "the overall effect is a system in which men are dominant, women are submissive and the exercise of male power leads to almost total subordination of the female devotees." Interestingly, scholars of nineteenth-century "new religions" tend to find their women "empowered," whereas studies of contemporary NRMs (with the notable exception of Wicca) often stress the theme of feminine degradation, a view reflected in literature of the anticult movement (Ritchie 1991) and in the press – as summed up by the *Guardian* (Women and abuse in cults 1991: 33): "The degrading treatment of women in many religious cults today reads like a chapter from the dark ages. Yet 200 years ago, women were leaders of a number of sects, asserting feminine equality (and even superiority) within them. What went wrong?"

Perhaps the most objective and comprehensive analysis of the relationship between current gender ambiguities and youth's conversion to NRMs appears in Aidala's (1985) seminal study. Aidala argues that communal NRMs are responding to the erosion of norms regulating gender roles occurring in the larger society. She demonstrates that members of religious communes (as opposed to secular ones) exhibit a low tolerance for the shifting interpretations of masculinity and femininity. She proposes an "elective affinity" between the clear-cut sex roles found in charismatic groups and the need perceived in contemporary youth to resolve gender-related ambiguities. She finds that, unlike the individualistic experimentation occurring in secular communes, where the rules governing sexual behavior are ill-defined, religiously based gender roles are rigid and absolute. While Aidala (1985: 297) notes among her groups "a great diversity in sexual and gender role ideology," she emphasizes their universal patriarchal character. In her view, joining religious communes represents a *flight* from feminism, modernity, and the moral ambiguity that characterizes our pluralistic society. The static, rigid quality of new religious sex roles, therefore, she interprets as a *rejection of* or *reaction against* the more fluid and experimental approaches prevailing in the secular sphere.

In this study I propose a "gendered" specification and modification of Aidala's central argument: that communal NRMs provide ideological resolutions to moral ambiguity and gender confusion. First, evidence shows that new religious sex roles are considerably more diverse than Aidala acknowledges, challenging previous classifications as "patriarchal" or "feminist." Second, they are more *fluid* in their patterns of gender and authority than Aidala's more static portrait suggests – and, if observed over a period of time, exhibit flexibility and a commitment to experimentation. Third, given the high attrition rates found in NRMs, and striking affinities between the "liminal period" (Turner 1968) and new religious sexual experiments, I argue that the "cult experience," for most female participants, can best be understood as fulfilling a similar function to the feminine rites of passage found in traditional societies.

This study will demonstrate the wide variety of feminine roles available in NRMs, and will analyze the various routes to resolving gender ambiguity outlined in these movements. Eight groups were selected for study, as examples of NRMs in which women's roles were radically alternative, highly developed, and mutually contrasting:

The International Society for Krishna Consciousness (ISKCON)

The Unification Church (UC)

The Rajneesh Movement (currently known as Osho Friends International)

The Institute for the Harmonious Development of the Human Being (IHDHB)

The Raëlian Movement International

The Northeast Kingdom Community Church (NEKC)

The Ansaaru Allah Community (AAC)

The Institute of Applied Metaphysics (LAM)

Information on their gender roles was gathered from a variety of sources, including NRM literature, videocassettes of leaders' discourses, field research, and over 150 interviews with members and ex-members.

The Diversity of New Religious Women's Roles

Aidala (1985: 297) insists that "in none of the religious communes did ideological formulation or practice pose a direct challenge to the traditional allocation of greater social and economic power to men. Many groups actively promoted traditional inequalities. Those that did not denied the reality of inequalities which allowed traditional patterns to continue." Many of the groups studied here challenge this statement. The Raëlian Movement, for example, deliberately encourages homosexual and bisexual expression (Palmer 1992). Rajneesh and Brahmakumari leaders are overwhelmingly female (Babb 1986; Barker 1991; Gordon 1986). Leaders' speeches conveying notions of radical or conservative romantic feminism (Reuther 1983), denouncing men as world spoilers and exalting women as world saviors, appear in such NRM literature as *A New Vision of Woman's Liberation* (Rajneesh 1987), *Adi Dev, the First Man* (Chander 1981), and *Sensual Meditation* (Vorilhon 1986).

The most striking feature of women's roles in new religious movements, besides their diversity, is their clarity and simplicity. This clarity seems to be achieved by emphasizing *one* role and de-emphasizing or rejecting others. Krishna-conscious women, for example, are defined as "mothers" by title and by occupation, even if unmarried or childless (Knott 1987; Rochford 1985). The sexually expressive Rajneeshee is a "lover" in relation to Bhagwan Shree Rajneesh (metaphorically speaking) and to the male disciples; but she was not permitted to give birth or raise her existing children during the communal phase, and the role of "wife" is still considered demeaning (Belfrage 1981; Milne 1986). Women in the Raëlian Movement are defined as sensually aware, bisexual "playmates" and tend to reject marriage in favor of "free love," and avoid procreating in anticipation of being cloned by extraterrestrials (Vorilhon 1986; Palmer 1992).

Even many NRMs that appear to foster "traditional" roles deviate widely from the mainstream (and from each other) in their interpretations of woman's domestic role. Exemplary "wives" in the Institute of Applied Metaphysics are postmenopausal, childless "handmaidens" and work partners to their considerably younger "lords" (Morris 1986). "Wives" in the Ansaaru Allah Community are heavily veiled and come in sets of four, since the Nubian household should (ideally) feature a Domestic Wife, a Cultured Wife, an Educated Wife, and a Companion Wife (As Sayyid 1988). In their role of "breeder," AAC women are exhorted to usher in the 144,000 pure Nubian children to "rapture" their parents when the satanic reign of the "paleman" ends in the cataclysm of 2000 (As Sayyid 1987). In spite of this literary emphasis on the ideal Muslim family, real-life Ansaars live in same-sex dormitories, separated from their children, and are permitted to cohabit with their spouses once every three months in the "Green Room," in accordance with their founder's racialist eugenics theory (Philips 1988). Unificationist women have opted for a wider range of roles – but only one role at a time. They begin their careers in the movement as celibate "sisters," and then become "daughters" of Reverend Moon when he blesses them in marriage to one of their "brothers." These marriages remain unconsummated for three or more years, during which time the "wives" strive to mature into "The Ideal Woman" (Grace 1985).

Thus, a survey of a corner of the "spiritual supermarket" suggests that a contemporary North American woman who is seeking alternative spiritual, sexual, and social experiences is presented with a remarkable range of possibilities. She can be a celibate "sister," a devoted "wife," a domineering "lover," a veiled "Nubian Bride," an immortal "Yin-Yang Unit," a "breeder" of the perfect race, an ageless, celibate "daughter" with magical powers, a "quadrasexual playmate," or an asexual shaman.

New religious models of gender also vary widely. Aidala (1985: 294) found three basic approaches to understanding gender relations: "biblically based understandings of patriarchy, bio-mystical complementarity and subjectivist denials of gender differences." These three approaches apply to the eight groups explored here and correspond to Allen's typology (1987: 21) of sex polarity/sex complementarity/sex unity, describing three philosophical notions of sex identity developed within Christendom. Some elaboration is required in order to increase the relevance of this model to eclectic and "oriental import" NRMs, as follows[1]:

Sex Complementarity groups endow each sex with unique spiritual qualities, and emphasize marriage as the union of spiritual opposites in order to from a whole androgyne. Gender and marriage continue in the afterlife, marriage to the dead is possible, and weddings and procreation assist in ushering in the Millennium. A dual or androgynous godhead overshadows these communities. The Unification Church, Northeast Kingdom, and Institute of Applied Metaphysics conform to this view.

Sex Polarity groups regard the sexes as spiritually different, and as useless or obstructive to the other's salvation. The notion of sex pollution is importantly present and the sexes are segregated so as to avoid weakening each other's spiritual resolve. Levels of salvation might be quite different for men and women since they are unequal. ISKCON and the Ansaars espouse this view, whereas the

Rajneeshee and the Brahmakumaris might be described as "reverse sex polarity" groups, where women are vaunted as spiritually more powerful than men.

Sex Unity groups view the body and its gender as a superficial layer of false identity obscuring the immortal, asexual spirit. Groups espousing this view might adopt "unisex" clothing and cultivate androgynous social *personae*, or they might "play act" traditional sex roles while maintaining a psychological detachment from these roles. In shamanistic or gnostic groups there is often the notion that by transcending the limits of social/sexual identity, the adept can release the powerful spiritual potentialities. The IHDHB, Scientology, and the Raëlians espouse this view.

While these models are not necessarily unique to NRMs, and feminist theorists like Mary Daly, Dana Densmore, and Valerie Solanas have articulated versions of androgyny and sex polarity that are no less radically alternative (Castro 1984), new religions appear to offer more scope for collective and individual experimentation in praxis. Women in secular society, whether they define themselves as lesbian feminists or as Real Women, must confront conflicting notions of gender in moving from the private through the different sectors of the public sphere. The secretary, for example, will expect sex unity in her paycheck, will "act out" sex polarity in the synagogue or the YMCA locker room – but might yearn for sex complementarity in the course of her Friday night dinner date. Elaborate "face-work" is required in our pluralistic society as women move from one arena to the next (Goffman 1959; Westley 1983). Within intentional communities, however, *one* model of gender prevails. Dress codes, rituals, work roles, and authority patterns tend to reflect a single, clear-cut model of male–female relations.

Creation myths educate new religious women in the mysteries of sexuality and offer theodicies to explain the ongoing war between the sexes that is waging outside their utopias. These myths convey clear-cut models of gender – as, for example, when the 3,500-year-old warrior Ramtha (channeled by J. Z.

Knight) relates the myth of how one god, Duvall-Debra, split into male and female and how the two became enemies "through jealousy, possessiveness and . . . superiority" (*Ramtha Intensive: Soulmates*, 1987). The notion of sex unity is dramatized in the *Creation Story Verbatim* (Gold 1973) when "god" recalls how he sent a spaceship to save human specimens when Atlantis was flooded, and how the ship's captain "goofed" by rescuing two males, so that one of them had to undergo a sex-change operation, and then even god couldn't tell which was which.

New feminine archetypes hold out keys to understanding – or at least testing – who woman is and what her potential might be. These narratives establish the guidelines for courtship rituals, marital relations, and sexual ethics in spiritual communities. Informants described the therapeutic and empowering effects of inhabiting these roles. One ex-Ansaar observed, "I felt superior wearing the veil, because it was not easy . . . I had to put away western ideas of beauty and fashion and become a Muslim . . . It made me feel godly. It made me feel like Eve when I learned that Eve dressed this way after the world got populated . . . Also, Sarah, Abraham's wife – and all the other righteous women in the Bible." Unificationist women are encouraged to relate their own sad experiences of the "abuse of love" with Eve's tragic seduction at the hands of Satan. Participants in the 1983 "Conference on Eve," held at Barrytown, New York even described encountering Eve and conversing with her during their "travels in the spirit world."[2] Within these carefully supervised playing fields, women can explore the potential and limitations of new religious models of gender in their daily life.

The Experimental Quality of NRM Patterns of Gender

A striking feature of new religions, when observed over a period of time, is their flexibility in trying out different patterns of authority and gender. This experimentation occurs on two levels: the collective and the individual.

Collective experiments

A close study of NRMs' short histories reveals a tendency to "flip-flop" in policies for awarding leadership posts determined by gender. Two outstanding examples of this pattern are the Institute of Applied Metaphysics (IAM) and the Rajneesh movement. In the early days of IAM (1963–75) women were leaders, but after the "Yin-Yang units" were formed, husband and wife were defined as equal halves of a whole person, and took part in ritual and work life as a team. Women's authority began to plummet in 1983 after the founder Winifred Barton was deposed by her husband (Morris 1986). A similar mood of experimentation can be found throughout the history of the Rajneesh Movement. During the 1981–5 communal phase in Rajneeshpuram, women were conspicuous in leadership positions. After the "Sheela scandal" in 1985, however, the group became disillusioned with the utopian notion that women were less aggressive than men, and the international communes began to appoint male leaders. This experiment was abandoned after the group settled back in Poona, and women took over the reins again.

Even "patriarchal" groups fostering nostalgic recreations of perfect families from a mythic golden age are wont to improvise. The acephalous Northeast Kingdom Community will occasionally modify its conservative gender roles, as when the women in Island Pond put aside their head coverings during working days, in response to a collective revelation received by the elders in Boston in April, 1991.[3] The AAC leader, As Sayyid as Imaam Isa, after instructing women since 1969 to wear a face veil, accept polygamy, and devote their energies to housework, suddenly announced in the January 1992 *Nubian Village Bulletin* his change of title to "The Lamb, Liberator of Women," and advised women to discard the veil, wear "pantoons,' and embrace monogamy. Today women are permitted (in theory) to "peddle" crafts on public streets, drive cars, and preach in the mosque.

Exercises permitting members to "play-act" the opposite sex are found in several therapeutically oriented NRMs. The Raëlians hold a transvestite banquet dance on the final night of the Sensual Meditation Camp, and, as one member put it, "We show the opposite sex what we don't like about the way they treat us!" The Rajneesh hold a "Sexual Fantasies" party at the end of their "Tantra" therapy groups in Poona, and one participant described how one man dressed as a prostitute, another dressed as Lolita, and one woman came as a male "flasher." The IHDHB practice "gender-erasing" in the "Daysnap" exercise, which requires participants to vocally assume the personalities of "Helpful Herbie," "Gross-out Gertrude," "Doubtful Danny," or "Condescending Connie" (Palmer 1976). Est trainees "make asses of themselves" in a role-playing exercise described by Rhinehart (1976: 150–1):

> In two of the most difficult roles, women are asked to play the role of a loud, stupid, blustering drunk, and men are asked to play a "cute" ten-year-old girl reciting a silly flirtatious poem about herself: the women being asked to be aggressively masculine, the men pertly feminine.

Individual experimentation

The experimentation in gender and sexual mores found in NRMs can also be observed taking place on the individual level. As Robbins and Bromley (1992: 3) pointed out, new members who "adopt the convert role and collaborate in the process of self-reconstruction often conceive of themselves as engaged in experimentation." Several informants for this study described conversion careers in which they had moved through a series of spiritual movements, assuming serial feminine identities and experimenting with various forms of celibacy, polygamy, and/or pantagamy.

The interview data and sex ratio surveys challenge prevailing notions that "cult-women" are the passive victims of the ineluctable forces of charisma, "brainwashing," or "patriarchal authority," who will submit to whatever sexual excesses emanate from the leader's dark libido. Our informants made it clear they chose *which* experiment to participate in, and for specific personal reasons. The interviews suggest that women are drawn to groups that offer them the roles they feel comfortable inhabiting, an escape route from the too-demanding roles in the modern family, or an initiation into a longed-for role that eluded them in secular life. A comparison of sex ratios indicates that some movements hold a stronger appeal for one sex than for the other. Men outnumber women two to one in the Unificationist Church (Barker 1984; Grace 1985), whereas women outnumber men by a considerable margin in the Brahmakumaris (Babb 1986), and by a slight margin in the Rajneesh Movement (Braun 1984; Gordon 1986; Milne 1986). Groups that espouse the "reverse sex polarity" view and promote feminine leadership appear to attract more women than men.

Contributing to the argument that women select NRMs that serve their particular needs is evidence that different age sets are represented in different movements, as are specific classes of women. The great majority of women attending Spiritualist seances are in late middle age or elderly (Haywood 1983), whereas the mean age of women in the Rajneesh Movement is between 31 and 35 (Braun 1984; Carter 1987). ISKCON, however, appeals to girls in their late teens and early twenties (Judah 1974). Studies of the Rajneesh have consistently shown that the disciples tend to be highly educated professionals from the middle- to upper-middle class (Wallis 1982). Women in the AAC are recruited from the middle- to lower-middle classes and are exclusively black (Philips 1988). Single mothers appear to find the Northeast Kingdom Community attractive, whereas many of the Rajneesh and Raëlian women interviewed had postponed or rejected childbearing in favor of a career, and had lived out of wedlock with a number of men before joining the movement.

New religious sexual experiments might be seen as a *series*, dedicated to solving specific sets of social problems confronted by contemporary women. NRM literature offers theodicies that account for the failure of marriage in the secular realm, and advertise spiritual solutions to problems of intimacy that resonate with different audiences. A Krishna devotee, for example, described her parents' brutality throughout her childhood, and claimed that the male authority in ISKCON offered women a benign "protection," because it was based on a "spiritual line of discipline succession." A *chela* of Elizabeth Clare Prophet described how she had suffered during divorce, and how "Guru Ma made me understand that my former marriage was only a *karmic* relationship – something we had to work out from our previous lives." Having recently married a celibate "soulmate" in the Church Universal and Triumphant, she happily anticipated her eventual reunion with her "twin flame" into an androgynous, enlightened being. A Rajneesh "lover" recounted her pain in losing her two-year-old daughter to leukemia, and her relief in joining the Rajneesh commune, where motherhood was not an option, and where she could "surrender to Bhagwan" and assuage her grief through short-term, pluralistic love affairs with the "beautiful, soft swamis."

The "Cult Experience" and Contemporary Rites of Passage

Aidala's study does not address the issue of defection. While my findings corroborate her observations concerning the appeal of the ideological certainty of new religious gender roles to youth, it appears significant that between 80 percent and 90 percent of members participate in these alternative patterns of sexuality for one, two, or even three years – and then leave. Sociologists consistently have maintained that NRMs exhibit high rates of voluntary defection and that the average length of membership is less than two years (Barker 1984; Judah 1974; Ofshe 1976; Skonovd 1983; Wright 1988). Bird and Reimer (1982) found that in the Unification Church at least 80 percent of members defected within two years. In ISKCON less than 600 disciples out of the original 10,000 initiated under Swami Prabhupada have remained in the movement.[4] The Rajneesh Foundation International claimed 250,000 members in 1985, but Belfrage (1981) described a common pattern of defection by Poona visitors, following their impulsive decision to "take sannyas" (initiation). Of the Ansaar's leader, Philips (1988: 37) noted, "every two or three years he has a major turnover of followers."

"The temporality of membership should alter dramatically the way in which unconventional religious movements are perceived," noted Wright (1988: 163). The high attrition rate suggests that joining spiritual families rarely turns out to be a satisfactory solution to the ambiguity surrounding gender issues, but rather that NRMs in general (and their sexual innovations in particular) provide laboratories for individual and collective social experimentation. This interpretation, however, cannot be applied to lifelong participants who commit themselves to furthering the group's collective goals. When Unificationist couples remain together to raise their "perfect children," and aging Brahmakumari leaders maintain their vows of celibacy as they instruct future generations in the *gyan*, these members have evidently rejected the experimental mode to forge as new culture.

The theory that NRMs provide experiences analogous to those found in traditional rites of passage has been convincingly argued by a number of scholars. As Melton and Moore (1982: 46) wrote, "the phenomenon of the 'cult experience'. . . must be seen within the context of states of transition – particularly the transition from adolescence to young adulthood." Turner (1968) pointed to the hippie movement, and Levine (1984) to "radical groups" as fulfilling a function similar to traditional rites of passage. Prince (1974) pursued a similar line of argument, but adopted the metaphor of "cocoon work," suggesting a process of psychological healing and maturation.

These authors point to a *lacuna* in our society, which has set individuals adrift as the role of public ritual has declined in the wake of secularization. "Instead of having one's change in situation acknowledged clearly and publicly with social support and with knowledgeable ritual elders to usher one through the limbo of the transition state," Melton and Moore (1982: 50) noted, "in modern culture one is all too often left to one's own devices, having to seek out social support and 'ritual elders' wherever they may be found." Rites of passage are an urgent imperative in our pluralistic society, they insist, if only because the coming of age in America involves confronting so many complex and depressingly insoluble problems. One of the major dilemmas, they agree, is that of choosing one's sexual orientation and code of sexual ethics. Prince (1974: 271) asked, "What is it to be a man, or a woman, a father, or a mother? Educated side by side and equipped for identical roles in the same universities, how can male and female find differences and sexual identity?" He described the pessimism of contemporary youth at the prospect of adopting their parents' way of life, which they seem to feel is "a blueprint for disaster."

Aidala (1985: 289) accounts for this attitude as follows: "As horizons expand beyond the family unit, traditional gender roles into which they have been socialized . . . fail to resonate with emerging social-cultural realities." It seems fair to assert that woman's coming of age today is even more problematic than man's, requiring not only the initiation into women's mysteries, but also into the public realm of professional life – until recently an almost exclusively male domain. Toffler (1974) spoke of "overchoice," and Glendon (1985) deplored women's "role overload" in the "New Family." For women facing pluralistic and open sets of possibilities, their gender identities must be "accomplished" (McGuire 1992) and sexual relationships "negotiated" (Rose 1987).

It might be argued that new religious founders play a role comparable to traditional societies' "ritual elders" in youth's search for authority – for some authentic voice to outline the true shape of their sexuality which reflects the divine cosmos. The certainty of charismatic *gurus* on matters of sexual morality contrasts sharply with the rather "wishy-washy" stances of mere priestly authorities (Bibby 1987: 164), rendering them attractive to disoriented youth. While Turner (1968) and Foster (1981) insisted that the distinctive features of the liminal period of individual rites of passage can also be seen in larger, more complex social transitions, it is, however, important to distinguish between the two contexts. In contrast to the approved shamans or priestly authorities, the well-established social statuses, and the predictable ceremonies of long traditions, Foster (1981: 9) observed,

the prophet-founders of millennial movements face a more difficult task. They must begin to create a new way of life and status relationships at the very same time that they are trying to initiate individuals into those not yet established roles. In short, the desired end point is often unclear.

None of these theorists has addressed the issue of whether these ritual processes are different for men than they are for women – an oversight that apparently also exists in anthropological literature, where "discussions of female initiation ceremonies are fewer by far [than of male] and often their function is clear: a severe suppression of female sexuality and symbolic expression of female inferiority" (Myerkoff 1982: 123). An exception is found in Lincoln (1991: 101), who argued that Van Gennep's *rite de passage* model is based on a study of male initiations, and proposes a trope of insect metamorphosis as more descriptive of women's initiations. Lincoln (1991) suggested that female rites of passage follow a tripartite structure of enclosure, magnification, and emergence, and that these dramas celebrate woman's new reproductive function and invest sacred power in her body, thus ensuring the future of her society. Women's roles in NRMs, which are usually far more stylized and confining than the roles of men (Aidala 1985: 311), might be analyzed within this framework. For the collective, woman's body is often

a symbol of the commune, the maternal womb from whence the "New Man" will emerge. The Lamb eloquently expresses this notion:

We are the caterpillar that crawled around on the ground alongside the snake in America . . . We metamorphosed step by step into a perfect being. We wore all kinds of African attire . . . like bones in our ears . . . The destination of the caterpillar was he would be painted by the hand of the Artist of the Universe . . . So we walked around cloaked in our cocoon (the veil, Jallaabiyah) awaiting the great day when we would unfold the cocoon and come forth in our beauty as a nation. (*Nubian Village Bulletin*, 1992, Ed. 1: 15)

On the individual level, women experience the "enclosure" of a stiff, cocoon-like group identity, and give birth to a new feminine identity – which is frequently better suited to living in the larger society. Studying the progress of Ansaar apostates, one might argue that they retreat behind the veil so as to undergo a period of racial deconditioning and psychological metamorphosis, until they are ready to expand beyond the boundaries of the sect; and they emerge perhaps better equipped to cope with the problems of being an African-American woman in a white society.

Sexual innovations and liminality

Some of the more singular features of NRM sex roles – their ideological rigidity, their surrealism or postmodernist qualities – can be better understood within the framework of Turner's thoughts on liminality. Turner (1968) outlined Van Gennep's three stages, and expands upon the second. The initial "separation" stage involves a symbolic death of the novice to his or her former sociocultural state, and the third stage of "reaggregation" involves rejoining the community. The second "liminal" period is found to be the most central to the ritual process. Described as a "social limbo" of ritual time and space, the liminal period has three major components: the communication of *sacra*, the encouragement of *ludic recombination*, and the fostering of *communitas*.

The communication of *sacra* can be observed in the instruction female novices receive in new religious narratives, creation myths, and iconography of female saints or deities. Besides these exhibitions, there are ritual actions, stylized postures and greetings, and community dances that reflect sacred models of sex identity.

Some of the more outrageous sexual innovations found in these groups begin to "make sense" if considered as *ludic recombination*. NRM courting rituals – the Rajneesh "Tantric" exercises, the Raëlian transvestite balls, the IDHHB "Objective Sex" workshops, the "Moonie" matchings and mass marriages – might strike the outsider as extreme versions – even parodies – of "mainstream" American courting rituals, and many of them imply harsh critiques of the poorly organized and minimally supervised "dating game" practiced in secular society. These playful recombinations of American cultural traits resemble the "unusual, even bizarre and monstrous configurations . . . masks, images, contraptions, costumes" found in traditional rites of passage.

The clear-cut, spiritually based gender roles outlined in new religious literature invite participation in *communitas*, the "direct, spontaneous and egalitarian mode of social relationship, as against hierarchical relationships among occupants of structural status-roles" (Turner and Turner 1982: 202). A recurring theme in interviews was woman's hope of rebuilding better relationships with men, based on the mutual recognition of each other's essential spiritual status – which outweighed the sexual element. One Krishna-conscious "widow" noted, "When I talk to my godbrothers and godsisters, there's a special understanding. We all know we are spirit-souls and have lived on this earth in many different bodies for hundreds of thousands of years. We know our godbrothers respect us and would never treat us as instruments of sense gratification." A Rajneesh "supermom" explained the "heart connection" she felt with the male sannyasins in a commune, which enabled her to navigate the emotional pitfalls of a "free love" lifestyle:

The swamis here are more available than most men. You can confront them, pour your guts out and they don't just walk away. That's because they're coming from the heart space, they have a commitment to the spiritual search, so they are more vulnerable . . . and not afraid to show their emotional side.

What these women appear to be describing is the experience of *communitas*, a generic bond outside the limits of social structure; a transient condition that liberates them from conformity to general norms, and opens a space for experimentation.

I would argue that the deceptively conservative roles of "wife" or "mother" present opportunities for a process of self-reconstruction that is no less radical than that observed in "feminist" groups; that some of these "traditional" roles, on closer examination, appear no less deviant than those found in "free love" NRMs; and that their stiff, stylized quality suggests that the women who inhabit them are not embracing a permanent lifestyle, but rather trying on a modern version of the ritual mask. "Wives" in the Ansaars, ISKCON, Unification Church, and CUT might dress up and play the role with gusto, but in most cases are not actually permitted to live with, sleep with, clean up after, or cook for their "husbands."

Whether the group espouses sex unity, complementarity, or polarity, a common thread running through their rhetoric is the notion of the androgyne. Women and men, whether they practice monogamy, celibacy, or "free love," set aside their individuality and strive to build a collective identity, to experience "communion" (Kanter 1972) with the opposite sex, and to merge into an undifferentiated whole. Rejecting hierarchical relationships and social status, initiates embrace the symbolism of totality, the presexuality of childhood innocence or the perfection of androgyny. New religions function as protective microsocieties where women can recapture a sense of innocence, and slowly recapitulate the stages of their sexual/social development in a new cultural setting. These "traditional" women, therefore, also seek "empowerment," albeit of another kind. As Gross (1987) observed, societies that segregate the sexes through gender-based work roles and dress codes seem to be particularly successful in conjuring up an aura of mystery, charm, and taboo around the opposite sex. For this reason, the phenomenon of modern women choosing to inhabit the stylized roles in NRMs might be better understood *not* as a rejection of pluralism and contemporary experimentation (Aidala 1985), nor as a lifelong choice to opt for traditional family values in the face of gender uncertainty in the larger society (Davidman 1991), but rather as the ancient and familiar search for the powerful religious and social epiphanies available within the ritual passage.

Conclusion

This study has endeavored to prove that one of the significant cultural contributions of NRMs is their provision of a modern equivalent to the feminine rites of passage found in traditional societies, which allow women to engage in an intensive process of self-reconstruction. While utopian sexual innovations have usually been interpreted as collective rites of passage (Foster 1981), or as "commitment mechanisms" (Kanter 1972) designed to bind members to the whole community to become the hierophants or parents of the next generation, there is evidence to show that the majority of members eventually reject the authority of their ad hoc "ritual elders" and instead use these rites of passage for individual ends. The significance of our apostates' erotic/ascetic ordeals, whether in retrospect they found them to be repressive or empowering, resides in their ritual aspects. Thus, while NRMs are obviously not indistinguishable from tráditional rites of passage, but rather might be seen as near substitutes, the experiences of their women – while perhaps not authentically "liminal" – at least are "liminoid."

The data suggest that the innovations in sex roles and sexual mores presently developing in NRMs, far from representing a conservative reaction against "mainstream" experimentation and feminism, might more accurately be characterized as offering even *more* extreme, intensified, and diverse versions of the ongoing experimentation already occurring outside these utopias. The highly organized and strictly supervised group experiments occurring in NRMs appeal to prospective members as safe havens in which they might engage in more radical forms of experimentation than are possible in the secular sphere. Our informants appeared to be reacting not so much to gender ambiguity *per se* (Aidala 1985: 287), but rather to the disorganized and haphazard ways in which "sexual experiments" were being conducted in the larger society.

While inhabiting these new, postmodernist Eves, Sitas, and Fatimahs, if only for a few months or years, these women apostates had found an arena for the symbolic and ritual expression of their own half-formulated and conflicting notions of sexuality, and its place in the divine cosmos. For the researcher, investigating these alternative and sacred patterns of sexuality tends to confirm Durkheim's theory on religion's representational and interpretive function (Durkheim 1964). By replicating, resolving, and even parodying the pluralistic approaches towards sexuality prevailing in our transitional age, new religious Eves and Adams hold up fragments of a mirror, inviting society to see itself and to become self-conscious.

Notes

1 These categories also overlap with Rosemary Reuther's (1983: 199) typology of eschatological, liberal, and romantic feminism.
2 "Conference on Eve" materials from Unificationist women's conference at Barrytown seminary, April 3, 1983.
3 This innovation was explained during a visit to the Island Pond Community in April 1991.
4 This estimate was communicated by a former temple president in Canada, who had been initiated by Prabhupada in 1968.

References

Aidala, Angela 1985: Social change, gender roles, and new religious movements. *Sociological Analysis* 46: 287–314.

Allen, Prudence, RSM. 1987: Two medieval views on woman's identity: Hildegard of Bingen and Thomas Aquinas. *Studies in Religion* 16: 21–36.

As Sayyid as Imaam Isa as Haadi al Mahdi 1987: *The Paleman.* Brooklyn NY: The Tents of Kedar.

——1988: *Hadrat Faatimah, the Daughter of the Prophet Muhammad (PBUH).* Brooklyn NY: The Tents of Kedar.

Babb, Lawrence 1986: The Brahmakumaris: History as movie. In *Redemptive Encounters: Three Modern Styles in the Hindu Tradition,* edited by Lawrence Babb, 110–55. Berkeley: University of California Press.

Barker, Eileen 1984: *The Making of a Moonie: Choice or Brainwashing?* New York: Blackwell.

——1991 *New Religious Movements: A Practical Introduction.* London: HMSO.

Bednarowski, Mary Farrell 1980: Outside the mainstream: women's religion and women religious leaders in nineteenth century America. *Journal of the American Academy of Religion* 48: 207–31.

Belfrage, Sally 1981: *Flowers of Emptiness.* New York: Dial Press.

Bibby, Reginald W. 1987: *Fragmented Gods: The Poverty and Potential of Religion in Canada.* Richmond Hill: Irwin.

Bird, Frederick and William Reimer 1982: Participation rates in new religious movements an para-religious movements. *Journal for the Scientific Study of Religion* 21: 1–14.

Braun, Kirk 1984: *Rajneeshpuram: The Unwelcome Society.* West Linn, OR: Scouts Creek Press.

Carter, Lewis 1987: The new renuciates of Bhagwan Shree Rajneesh. *Journal for the Scientific Study of Religion* 26: 148–72.

Castro, Ginette 1984: *Radioscope du feminism americain.* Paris: Presses de la Fondation Nationale des Sciences Politiques.

Chander, Jagdish 1981: *Adi Dev, the First Man.* Prajapita Brahma Kumaris World Spiritual University. Singapore, Malaysia: Kim Hup Lee Printing.

Cohn, Norman 1970: *The Pursuit of the Millennium.* New York: Oxford University Press.

Davidman, Lynn 1991: *Tradition in a Rootless World: Women Turn to Orthodox Judaism.* Berkeley: University of California Press.

Durkheim, Emile 1964 (1912): *The Elementary Forms of Religious Life.* New York: Free Press.

Foster, Lawrence 1981: *Religion and Sexuality: Three American Communal Experiments of the Nineteenth Century.* New York: Grove Press.

Glendon, Mary Ann 1985: *The New Family and the New Property.* Toronto: Butterworth.

Goffman, Erving 1959: *The Presentation of Self in Everyday Life.* Garden City, NY: Doubleday Anchor.

Gold E. J. 1973: *The Creation Story Verbatim: The Autobiography of God.* No. 64 of 200 copies bound by Djinn and Eddin, Crestline, California: IDHHB Publishing.

Gordon, James 1986: *The Golden Guru.* Lexington, KY: Stephen Greene Press.

Grace, James H. 1985: *Sex and Marriage in the Unification Church.* Lewiston, NY: Edwin Mellen Press.

Gross, Rita 1987: Tribal religions: Aboriginal Australia. In *Women in World Religions,* edited by Arvind Sharma, 37–58. Albany: State University of New York Press.

Haywood, Carol L. 1983: The authority and empowerment of women among spiritualist groups. *Journal for the Scientific Study of Religion* 22: 156–66.

Jacobs, Janet 1984: The economy of love in religious commitment: The deconversion of women from non-traditional movements. *Journal for the Scientific Study of Religion* 13: 155–71.

Judah Stillson J. 1974: *Hare Krishna and the Counterculture.* New York: Haworth.

Kanter, Rosabeth Moss 1972: *Commitment and Community: Communes and Utopias in a Sociological Perspective.* Cambridge, MA: Harvard University Press.

Kern, Louis 1981: *An Ordered Love.* Chapel Hill: University of North Carolina Press.

Knott, Kim 1987: Men and women or devotees? In *Women in World's Religions, Past and Present,* edited by Ursula King, 112–16. New York: Paragon House.

Levine, Saul 1984: *Radical Departures: Desperate Detours to Growing Up.* Toronto: Harcourt Brace Jovanovich.

Lewis, I. M. 1971: *Ecstatic Religion: An Anthropological Study of Spirit Possession and Shamanism.* Harmondsworth: Penguin.

Lincoln, Bruce 1991: *Emerging from the Chrysalis: Rituals of Women's Initiation.* New York: Oxford University Press.

McGuire, Meredith 1992: Gendered spirituality and quasi-religious ritual. Paper presented at the Society for the Scientific Study of Religion in Washington, DC.

Melton, Gordon and Robert L. Moore 1982: *The Cult Experience: Responding to the New Religious Pluralism.* New York: Pilgrim Press.

Milne, Hugh 1986: *Bhagwan the God that Failed.* London: Caliban Books.

Moore, Lawrence R. 1977: *In Search of White*

Crows: Spiritualism, Parapsychology and American Culture. New York: Oxford University Press.

Morris, Madeline 1986: IAM: A group portrait. Unpublished senior essay, Yale University.

Myerkoff, Barbara 1982: Rites of passage: Process and paradox. In Celebration: Studies in Festivity and Ritual, edited by Victor Turner, 109–35. Washington, DC: Smithsonian Institute Press.

Neitz, Mary Jo 1988: Sacremental sex in modern witchcraft. Paper presented at the Midwest Sociological Society, Minneapolis.

Nubian Village Bulletin 1992: Shahru Yahshua 21, A. T. Brooklyn: The Tents of Kedar.

Ofshe, Richard 1976: Synanon: The people's business. In The New Religious Consciousness, edited by Charles Glock and Robert Bellah, 116–37. Berkeley: University of California Press.

Pagels, Elaine 1988: Adam, Eve and the Serpent. New York: Random House.

Palmer, Susan J. 1976: Shakti! The spiritual science of DNA. Unpublished Masters thesis. Concordia University, Montreal.

——1992: Playmates in the Raëlian movement: Power and pantagamy in a UFO cult. SYZYGY: Journal of Alternative Religion and Culture (1): 227–45.

Philips, Abu Ameenah Bilal 1988: The Ansar Cult in America. Riyadh, Saudi Arabia: Tawheed.

Prince, Raymond 1974: Cocoon work: Contemporary youth's concern with the mystical. In Religious Movements in Contemporary America, edited by Irving Zaretsky and Mark P. Leone, 255–74. Princeton, NJ: Princeton University Press.

Rajneesh, Bhagwan Shree 1987: A New Vision of Women's Liberation. Poona, India; Rebel Press.

Ramtha Intensive: Soulmates 1987: Eastsound, WA: Sovereignty Inc.

Reuther, Rosemary Radford 1983: Sexism and God Talk. Boston, MA: Beacon Press.

Rhinehart, Luke 1976: The Book of Est. New York: Holt, Rinehart and Winston.

Richardson, James T., Mary W. Stewart, and Robert Simmonds 1979: Organized Miracles: A Study of a Contemporary Youth Communal, Fundamentalist Organization. New Brunswick, NJ: Transaction Books.

Ritchie, Jean 1991: The Secret World of Cults. London: Angus and Robertson.

Robbins, Tom 1988: Cults, Converts and Charisma. London: Sage.

Robbins, Tom and David Bromley 1992: Social experimentation and the significance of American new religions: A focused review essay. In Research in the Social Scientific Study of Religion, vol. 4, edited by Monty Lynn and David Moberg. Greenwich, CT: JAI Press.

Rochford, Burke, Jr. 1985: The Hare Krishna in America. New Brunswick, NJ: Rutgers University Press.

Rose, Susan 1987: Women warriors: The negotiation of gender in a charismatic community. Sociological Analysis 48: 245–58.

Skonovd, L. Norman 1983: Leaving the cultic milieu. In The Brainwashing Deprogramming Controversy: Sociological, Psychological, Legal and Historical Perspectives, edited by David Bromley and James Richardson, 91–106. Lewiston, NY: Edwin Mellen Press.

Toffler, Alvin 1974: Future Shock. New York: Bantam Books.

Turner, Victor 1968: The Ritual Process. Chicago, IL: Aldine.

Turner, Victor and Edith Turner 1982: Religious celebrations. In Celebrations: Studies in Festivity and Ritual, edited by Victor Turner, 201–19. Washington, DC: Smithsonian Institute Press.

Vorilhon, Claude (Raël) 1986: Sensual Meditation. Tokyo: AOM Corporation.

Wagner, Jon (ed.) 1982: Sex Roles in Contemporary Communes. Bloomington: Indiana University Press.

Wallis, Roy 1982: Millennialism and Charisma. Belfast: Queen's University Press.

Wessinger, Catherine 1993: Women's Leadership in Marginal Religions: Explorations Outside the Mainstream. Urbana: University of Illinois Press.

Westley, Frances 1983: The Complex Forms of Religious Life: A Durkheimian View of New Religious Movements. Chico, CA: Scholars Press.

Women and abuse in cults 1991: Guardian, 9 May: 33.

Wright, Stuart 1988: Leaving new religions: Issues, theories and research. In Falling from the Faith: Causes and Consequences of Religious Apostasy, edited by David G. Bromley, 143–65. Sage, CA: Newbury Park.

VIII

New Religious Movements
and the Future

In recent years the public controversy over "cults" has waned in North America, though bitter struggles continue in Europe, China, and elsewhere. But we have little reason to believe that the number and variety of NRMs coming into being in modern Western societies will wane. As the influence of the dominant religious traditions of the past dissipates in these societies, under the pressures of secularization and globalization, the environment for religious innovation improves. It is clear that NRMs will be a permanent feature of our societies for the foreseeable future. It is far less clear, however, just what form these new religions will take. The NRMs that emerged in North America and Europe since the 1960s have been highly resourceful in adapting to changes in the social and technological conditions of their host societies. Still, they may all fade in the presence of other NRMs yet to be born or studied.

Having observed the changes many NRMs go through, and the tendency for most groups to stagnate or fail, in the first essay in this section, the American sociologist Rodney Stark tries to explain why a handful of groups have managed to succeed (in terms of their growth, geographic distribution, increased material assets, social influence, and legitimacy). Is there a recipe for success? In "Why Religious Movements Succeed or Fail: A Revised General Model" Stark comes close to providing one. He delineates ten theoretical

propositions about what contemporary groups must do, as well as what they must be lucky enough to experience, to repeat the success of older NRMs like the Mormons and the Jehovah's Witnesses. His analysis is unique, concise, and thought provoking.

In formulating his theory Stark demonstrates the cumulative character of research on NRMs – a key indicator of "scientific" credibility and success. His analysis integrates a rich body of data derived from numerous studies, by the author and others, into sets of general and clear theoretical propositions. The propositions demonstrate the ways in which careful study of the NRMs of the recent past have yielded valuable and systematic insights into the future prospects of these and other NRMs. In other words, they add a predictive component to the sociology of NRMs – yet another traditional hallmark of successful "scientific" research. His propositions offer interrelated and testable hypotheses that can be used to ground reliable comparative analyses of multiple aspects of NRMs and their interactions with the rest of society. In the process he introduces some substantive concerns not previously addressed in this reader.

In the second reading in this section our attention is turned even more emphatically to the future, exploring the impact of the communications revolution launched by the Internet on the nature and spread of new religious groups. In one of the first papers published on the topic, the Canadian sociologists Lorne Dawson and Jenna Hennebry examine the promises and the perils of the new medium. NRMs were quick to seize the advantages offered by the Internet. Small or large, they have made their presence known on the world wide web, but so have a large number of anticult organizations. Today the Internet provides one of the quickest and most worthwhile ways of acquiring information about an ever widening array of "cults." Great care must be exercised, however, in dealing with this unregulated environment, since prejudicial statements are readily presented as the unalloyed truth and ignorance masquerades as wisdom. "New Religions and the Internet: Recruiting in a New Public Space" give us a taste of the new religious life online. Its primary purpose, however, is to refute the common fear and misconception that the Internet will provide NRMs with an unprecedented opportunity to recruit new and unsuspecting members. Employing the lessons learned from previous research about who joins NRMs, how, and why (see chapters 7 and 8), Dawson and Hennebry argue that the Internet is unlikely to swell the ranks of the new religions that go online. Ready access to so much religious information, however, is likely to have a favorable impact on their public relations, as millions of surfers may learn about their beliefs and practices. Moreover, the Internet, as a distinct kind of medium of mass communication, may well introduce other unanticipated changes in the very conception and expression of religious aspirations, bringing a whole new style of religiosity into being. Dawson and Hennebry, for example, examine the possibility of strictly online religions. The systematic investigation, however, of the ramifications of computer mediated communications for the experience of religion has just begun (see, for example, O'Leary 1996; Dawson 2000, 2001a, 2001b, 2002; Brasher 2001).

References

Brasher, Brenda 2001: *Give Me That Online Religion*. San Francisco, CA: Jossey-Bass.

Dawson, Lorne L. 2000: Researching Religion in Cyberspace: Issues and Strategies. In J. K. Hadden and D. Cowan (eds.), *Religion on the Internet* (Religion and the Social Order, vol. 8). New York: JAI Press, 25–54.

——2001a: Doing Religion in Cyberspace: The Promise and the Perils. *The Council of Societies for the Study of Religion Bulletin* 30 (1): 3–9.

——2001b: Invited Keynote Address, "The Mediation of Religious Experience in Cyberspace: A Preliminary Analysis." Religious Encounters in Digital Networks, University of Copenhagen, Nov. 1 (forthcoming in M. Hojsgaard and M. Warburg, eds., *Religion in Cyberspace*, a book being developed from the conference papers).

——2003: Religion and the Internet: Presence, Problems, and Prospects. In P. Antes, A. Geertz, and R. Warne (eds.), *New Approaches to the Study of Religion*. Berlin: Verlag de Gruyter.

O'Leary, Stephen D. 1996: Cyberspace as Sacred Space: Communicating Religion on Computer Networks. *Journal of the American Academy of Religion* 64 (4): 781–808.

CHAPTER SIXTEEN

Why Religious Movements Succeed or Fail: A Revised General Model

RODNEY STARK

Introduction

This year, hundreds of new religious movements will appear on earth. Some will be formed by disgruntled members who withdrew from older religious bodies. Others will be born because someone created or discovered a new religious culture and convinced others of its authenticity. However, whatever their origins, virtually every new group will have one thing in common: eventual failure. Although it is impossible to calculate the actual rate of success, probably no more than one religious movement out of 1,000 will attract more than 100,000 followers and last for as long as a century. Even most movements that achieve these modest results will become no more than a footnote in the history of religions.

Given such harsh realities, one would suppose that efforts to distinguish between the occasional success and the mass of failures would have very high intellectual priority. Not so. When I published an initial version of a theoretical model of how new religions succeed (Stark 1987), I could find virtually nothing to cite. And, aside from an essay from Bryan Wilson (1987) – published in the same volume as was my model – that remains true. Although the model was very well-received and widely cited (cf. Johnson 1987; Robbins 1988), it has not yet influenced the case study literature as I had hoped it would. In particu-

lar, it has failed to cause field researchers to address issues concerning the success or failure of the groups they study. Yet, if this literature is to become of real comparative value, it will need to address *sets* of *common issues* in the same way that a common research agenda has facilitated the construction of massive cross-cultural data sets from anthropological field work. For lack of such an agenda, social scientific studies of new religious movements support little comparison, being quite idiosyncratic as to content and often being focused on the odd and exotic. Thus, studies of the Children of God (now known as The Family) are almost certain to discuss 'flirty-fishing', but are unlikely to try to explain why the movement grew rapidly to about 10,000 members and then stagnated.

By identifying a set of propositions to explain why religious movements succeed or fail, I had hoped to encourage those involved in case studies to investigate these issues and consequently to begin an accumulation of comparable data. Looking back, it probably was a mistake to publish such an essay in an edited volume that soon became difficult to find, rather than in an easily available journal. Now, having extensively revised and broadened the scope of the theory, it seems appropriate to try again.

My original version of the theory excluded sect movements, being limited to new religions (cult movements) and was especially concerned with the rise of Christianity, Islam and the contemporary success of Mormonism. I wanted to identify the factors that separated these rare winners from the thousands of losers among movements based on new religions, as opposed to new religious movements (most of which are sects). I subsequently recognized that with slight modification the theory could be applied to all religious movements, thus greatly increasing its scope and utility. It is this revised and expanded version that follows.

The theory itself consists of ten propositions which attempt to specify the necessary and sufficient conditions for the success of religious movements. Before turning to these it will be useful to define religion and religious movements and to distinguish these from magic and magical movements.

Religion and Magic

'Religion' refers to any system of beliefs and practices concerned with ultimate meaning and which assumes the existence of the supernatural. 'Religious movements' are social enterprises whose primary purpose is to create, maintain and supply religion to some set of individuals. This definition excludes both secular social movements and movements based primarily upon magic.

Social movements concerned with such things as achieving political utopia or with averting environmental disaster are not religious movements regardless of their capacity to inspire intense commitment. Lack of a supernatural assumption makes all non-religious movements vulnerable to empirical disconfirmations. Attempts to create a classless society can fail and be seen to fail, for such a goal must be achieved in this world – which is precisely why the dozens of attempts to sustain secular utopian communities during the nineteenth century were so short-lived (Stark and Bainbridge 1996a). In similar fashion, widely publicized predictions made during the early 1970s (Meadows and Meadows 1972) that the world would run out of most primary mineral resources by 1990 are now known to

have been foolish. However, predictions to be realized in another world are beyond empirical inspection and, therefore, religious movements may rely on non-empirical claims, or at least claims without empirical implications in this world. The promise of eternal life in heaven, for example, cannot be observed to fail, whereas the promise of eternal life here on earth can be. That is a key difference between religion and magic.

As Durkheim (1915: 44) noted, magic does not address ultimate questions (has no theology), but attempts to provide desired rewards within an empirical context. What distinguishes it from science or technology is that *magic is utilized without regard for evidence concerning the effectiveness of the means employed*. Thus, magic can be (and often is) observed to fail. In our deductive theory of religion Bainbridge and I (Stark and Bainbridge 1996a [originally published in 1987]) traced several major implications of the contrast between magic and religion. First, being vulnerable to disproof, magic is risky goods and therefore the roles of priest and magician will tend to be differentiated, and successful religious movements will, over time, reduce the amount of magic they provide. Secondly, to obtain the rewards promised by religion it usually will be necessary to maintain a long-term exchange relationship with the divine and this enables religious movements to require long-term, stable patterns of participation. In contrast, as Durkheim (1915: 44) noted when he asserted 'There is no church of magic', magicians offer specific, short-term results and, thus, are unable to require long-term commitments – magicians will have clients, not followers.

These differences between religion and magic are important because, especially in Western societies, religion and magic are not always clearly differentiated. Thus, to the extent that a religious movement also offers magic, it will risk losses of credibility when its magic is seen to fail. Moreover, to the extent that a movement relies primarily on magic rather than religion, it will fail to gather a committed membership, as demonstrated by various New Age 'audiences'.

Conservation of Cultural Capital

It is axiomatic in the social sciences that, within the limits of their information and available choices, guided by their preferences and tastes, humans will tend to maximize – to attempt to acquire the most while expending the least. Put another way, humans will seek to conserve their capital. When economists apply this principle, they concentrate on efforts to acquire and retain capital of the monetary variety, but the same principles hold when applied to *cultural* capital.

Cultural capital is the result of socialization and education. When we are socialized into a particular culture, we also are investing in it – expending time and effort in learning, understanding and remembering cultural material. For example, persons raised to be Christians have accumulated a substantial store of Christian culture – a store that can be conceived of as cultural capital. When faced with the option of shifting religions, the maximization of cultural capital leads people to prefer to save as much of their cultural capital as they can and to expend as little investment in new capital as possible (Stark and Bainbridge 1996a: 220; Iannaccone 1990; Sherkat and Wilson 1995).

Stated as a proposition: *People will be more willing to join a religious group to the degree that doing so minimizes their expenditure of cultural capital.* An example may be helpful. A young person from a Christian background and living in a Christian society is deciding whether to join the Mormons or the Hare Krishnas. By becoming a Mormon, this person retains his or her entire Christian culture and simply adds to it. The Mormon missionaries, noting that the person has copies of the Old Testament and the New Testament, suggest that an additional scripture, The Book of Mormon, is needed to complete the set. In contrast, the Hare Krishna missionaries note that the person has the wrong scriptures and must discard the Bible in exchange for the Bhagavad Gita. The principle of the conservation of cultural capital predicts (and explains) why the overwhelming majority of converts within a Christian context select the Mormon

rather than the Hare Krishna option, with the reverse being the case in a Hindu context.

In the form stated above, the principle of the conservation of cultural capital explains individual behavior *vis-à-vis* conversion. Since my concern here is with the fate of religious movements, a macro-level form of the proposition is needed and becomes the first of the ten propositions comprising the theory: (1) *New religious movements are likely to succeed to the extent that they retain cultural continuity with the conventional faith(s) of the societies in which they seek converts.* i.e. Christianity → mormon

I now must distinguish two basic forms of religious movements, each rather differently positioned in terms of cultural continuity.

The *sect* is a religious movement in a state of relatively high tension with its sociocultural environment (Johnson 1963). The life history of a sect typically begins when a religious movement (usually a quite successful one) starts to reduce its degree of tension with the world. As this occurs, not everyone approves and eventually, as the group continues to reduce its tension, the dissenters organize and eventually withdraw to form their own group: a sect. Because sects split off from a conventional religious body, they are born with a very substantial level of cultural continuity. Thus, when the Methodists broke away from the Anglicans they took their entire Christian culture with them – indeed, they claimed greater continuity with historic Christian teachings than, in their view, could their parent body. Thus, sects reaffirm the conventional religious culture(s) of the society in which they appear.

While sects are new religious organizations rooted in the traditional faith, some religious movements are based on *new* religions which, with no invidious judgements implied, sometimes are referred to as cult movements. These groups often add a substantial amount of new culture to the conventional religious culture(s) of the society in which they appear – Christians, Muslims, Mormons and Christian Scientists being examples – and in that way retain a substantial amount of cultural continuity. Others involve religious culture entirely different from the conventional culture. This can occur because someone creates or discovers new religious ideas, or because alien religious culture is imported from another society. While new religions may differ greatly in their degree of cultural continuity, they are always lacking somewhat in this regard compared with sects. Thus, within a Christian society, other things being equal, conservation of cultural capital favours the Jehovah's Witnesses over the Mormons. This explains why the current rates of Witness growth in European nations far exceed that of the Mormons – in 1994 there were 1,200,000 Witnesses in Europe compared with 350,000 Mormons.

However, when faiths travel abroad, sects can become cults – indeed, even the most conventional religious bodies of one society will be defined as cults if they attempt to operate in a society having a different religious culture. Thus, for example, Catholic missionaries in India represent a cult, as do Episcopalians in Japan and Hindus in the United States. Hence, in Asia the Jehovah's Witnesses have no advantage over the Mormons in terms of cultural capital – both are cults in that context – and the two movements are doing about equally well in this region (each with about 250,000 members).

If Prophecy Fails

As noted earlier, the immense advantage religious movements have *vis-à-vis* secular movements is their capacity to avoid empirical disconfirmations. Religious movements need not deliver on their promises in this world – their most valuable rewards are to be obtained in a reality beyond inspection. Although, in principle, all religious movements have this option, not all of them take it. Some make important empirical assertions – for example, that the world will soon end. Others offer an extensive array of magic and must deal with frequent disconfirmations. Elsewhere, I have discussed at some length the problems faced by the medieval Catholic Church because of its extensive reliance on magic (Stark and Bainbridge 1985).

Other things being equal, failed prophesies are harmful for religious movements. Although prophesies may arouse a great deal of excitement and attract many new followers beforehand, the subsequent disappointment usually more than offsets these benefits. Indeed, the Jehovah's Witnesses suffered a very marked decline in missionary activity, as well as in conversion rates for several years after their 1975 expectation of the end went unfulfilled (Singelenberg 1989; Stark and Iannaccone 1997).

This discussion leads to the second proposition in the theory: (2) *New religious movements are likely to succeed to the extent that their doctrines are non-empirical.*

[handwritten: not guided from experience? not based on empirical evidence – faith driven]

Medium Tension (Strictness)

In order to grow, a religious movement must offer a religious culture that sets it apart from the general, secular culture. That is, movements must be distinctive and impose relatively strict moral standards. Stated as a proposition: (3) *New religious movements are likely to succeed to the extent that they maintain a medium level of tension with their surrounding environment – are strict, but not too strict.*

In its initial form, the proposition made no mention of strictness, although that was part of what I intended. However, the implications of the proposition are more fully revealed if the theoretical work on 'strictness' is made an explicit part (Kelley 1972; Iannaccone 1992, 1994, 1995a, 1995b; Stark and Iannaccone 1993). Strictness refers to the degree that a religious group maintains 'a separate and distinctive lifestyle or morality in personal and family life, in such areas as dress, diet, drinking, entertainment, uses of time, sex, child rearing and the like', or a group is not strict to the degree that it affirms 'the current . . . mainline lifestyle in these respects' (Iannaccone 1994: 1190).

To anticipate the argument, strictness makes religious groups strong by screening out free riders and thereby increasing the average level of commitment in the group. This, in turn, greatly increases the credibility of the religious culture (especially promises concerning future benefits, since credibility is the result of high levels of consensus), as well as generating a high degree of resource mobilization (see below).

Free-rider problems are the Achilles' heel of collective activities. Other things being equal, people will not contribute to a collective enterprise, when they can fully share in the benefits without contributing. This is called free riding and the collective consequence of free riding is that insufficient collective goods are created because too few contribute. Everyone suffers, but those who give most generously suffer the most. Because religion must involve collective action and all collective action is potentially subject to exploitation by free riders, religious groups must confront free riding.

One need not look far to find examples of anemic congregations plagued by free-rider problems – a visit to the nearest liberal Protestant church will usually suffice to discover 'members' who draw upon the group for weddings, funerals, holiday celebrations, daycare and even counselling, but who provide little or nothing in return. Even if they do make substantial financial contributions, they weaken the group's ability to create collective religious goods because their inactivity devalues the religious capital and reduces the 'average' level of commitment. However, strictness in the form of costly demands offers a solution to this problem.

At first glance it would seem that costly demands must always make a religion less attractive. Indeed, the economists' law of demand predicts just that, *other things remaining equal*. However, it turns out that other things do not remain equal when religions impose these kinds of costs on their members. To the contrary, costly demands strengthen a religious group in two ways. First, they create a barrier to group entry. No longer is it possible merely to drop in and reap the benefits of membership. To take part at all you must qualify by accepting the sacrifices demanded from everyone. Thus, high costs tend to *screen out* free riders – those potential members whose commitment and participation would otherwise be low. The costs act as non-

refundable registration fees which, as in secular markets, measure seriousness of interest in the product. Only those willing to pay the price qualify.

Secondly, high costs tend to *increase* participation among those who do join by increasing the rewards derived from participation. It may seem paradoxical that when the cost of membership increases, the net gains of membership increase too. However, this is necessarily the case with collectively produced goods. For example, an individual's positive experience of a worship service increases to the degree that the church is full, the members participate enthusiastically (everyone joins in the songs and prayers) and others express very positive evaluations of what is taking place. Thus, as each member *pays* the costs of membership, each gains from higher levels of production of collective goods.

Furthermore, for a religious group, as with any organization, *commitment is energy.* That is, when commitment levels are high, groups can undertake all manner of collective actions and these are in no way limited to the psychic realm. This is well illustrated by early Christianity. Because of their capacity to generate very high levels of commitment, the early Christian communities were bastions of mutual aid. As Paul Johnson (1976: 75) pointed out, the early church 'ran a miniature welfare state in an empire which for the most part lacked social services'. Thus, the fruits of this faith were not limited to the realm of the spirit, but offered much to the flesh as well – members were greatly rewarded here and now for belonging. Thus, while membership in the early church was expensive, it was, in fact, a bargain (Stark 1996).

This line of analysis leads to a critical insight, perhaps *the* critical insight: membership in a strict (costly) religion is, for many people, a 'good bargain'. Conventional cost-benefit analysis alone suffices to explain the continued attraction of strict religions.

Obviously, there are *limits* to how much tension or strictness is beneficial. One easily notices groups too strict to expect growth – indeed, most sects never grow at all and their initial level of strictness seems to be the primary reason (Stark and Bainbridge 1985). Strictness must be sufficient to exclude potential free riders and doubters, but it must also be sufficiently low not to drive away everyone except a few misfits and fanatics.

Legitimate Authority

While it is convenient to speak of organizations doing this or that, we must always keep in mind that, in fact, organizations never do anything. Only people ever act and individual actions can be interpreted as on behalf of an organization only to the extent that they are co-ordinated and directed. That is, all successful social movements require effective leadership and this, in turn, requires that the authority of the leaders is seen as legitimate. Put as a complex proposition: (4) *Religious movements will succeed to the extent that they have legitimate leaders with adequate authority to be effective.* This, in turn, will depend upon two factors. The first is: (4a) *Adequate authority requires clear doctrinal justifications for an effective and legitimate leadership.* The second is: (4b) *Authority is regarded as more legitimate and gains in effectiveness to the degree that members perceive themselves as participants in the system of authority.*

There are many bases for legitimate authority within organizations, depending on factors such as whether members are paid to participate and/or whether special skills and experience are recognized as vital qualifications to lead. However, when organizations stress doctrine, as all religious movements do, these doctrines must define the basis of leadership. Who may lead and how is leadership obtained? What powers are granted to leaders? What sanctions may leaders impose? These are vital matters, brought into clear relief by the many examples of groups that failed (or are failing) for lack of doctrines defining a legitimate basis for effective leadership.

That doctrines can directly cause ineffective leadership is widely evident in contemporary New Age and 'metaphysical' groups. If everyone is a 'student' and everyone's ideas and

insights are equally valid, then no one can say what must be done or who is to do what, when. The result is the existence of virtual non-organizations – mere affinity or discussion groups incapable of action (Wagner 1983). In similar fashion, the early Christian gnostics could not sustain effective organizations because their fundamental doctrines prevented them from ever being anything more than a loose network of individual adepts, each pursuing secret knowledge through private, personal means (Pagels 1979). In contrast, from the start Christianity had doctrines appropriate for an effective structure of authority, since Christ himself was believed to have selected his successors as head of the church.

Control of access to divine inspiration can also be a major factor in determining the authority of leaders. If the religious culture legitimates revelations or if its religious practices include trance states or speaking in tongues, these always pose a potential challenge to authority. As James S. Coleman noted:

> . . . one consequence of the 'communication with God' is that every[one] who so indulges . . . can create a new creed. This possibility poses a constant threat of cleavage within a religious group. (Coleman 1986: 49–50)

Therefore, even religious movements founded on revelations will soon attempt to curtail revelations or at least prevent novel (heretical) revelations. Max Weber's (1947, 1963) work on the routinization of charisma obviously applies here. Weber regarded charismatic authority as suited only for 'the process of originating' religious movements and as too unstable to sustain an organized social enterprise. Moreover, upon the death or disappearance of the prophet, a new basis for authority is required in any event. Several options exist. The movement can take the position that the age of revelations is ended, for all necessary truths have been told. This has been the usual Protestant stance. Or the capacity to reveal new truths may be associated with the leadership role – the charisma of the prophet is replaced by charisma of office, in Weber's terms. This has been the Roman Catholic and the Mormon choice. In either case, however, doctrine is stabilized sufficiently to sustain a changeover from prophetic to administrative leadership.

Whatever the justifications for authority, an additional source of legitimacy is the extent to which the rank-and-file feel enfranchised – believe that they have some impact on the decisions. As the examples of the Mormons, Jehovah's Witnesses and Soka Gakkai demonstrate, religious movements based on a lay clergy have particularly high levels of rank-and-file enfranchisement, even when they have also very strongly centralized authority. In contrast, sect movements often erupt precisely because members felt they lacked impact on decisions made by the parent body. Of course, people are far more likely to feel enfranchised when, in fact, they are.

A Religious Labour Force

In order to grow, religious movements need missionaries. Other things being equal, the more missionaries there are seeking converts, and the harder these missionaries work, the faster a religious movement will grow.

In addition to missionizing, a large, volunteer religious labour force contributes to the strength of religious movements in other important ways (Iannaccone et al. 1995). For example, labour often can be substituted for capital. Thus, while many of the so-called 'mainline' churches must not only pay their clergy, they must also pay for all their clerical, cleaning and maintenance services, and hire contractors to build new churches. In contrast, some movements (the Jehovah's Witnesses and the Mormons, for example) can rely entirely on volunteer labour to provide most or all these things.

To sum up this discussion: (5) *Religious movements will grow to the extent that they can generate a highly motivated, volunteer, religious labour force, including many willing to proselytize.*

Rapidly growing religious movements rely on their rank-and-file members to gather in the converts. If, during the next few years, you were to keep track of which religious groups have showed up at your door and how often, you would have a very accurate picture of who is growing and who is not. *(i.e Jehovas witness)*

Adequate Fertility

turnover rates

In order to succeed, (6) *Religious movements must maintain a level of fertility sufficient to at least offset member mortality.* If a religious movement's appeal is too narrow, this may result in a demographic composition incapable of sustaining its ranks. If a group is unable to replace itself through fertility, then when the initial generation of converts begins to die, their rising rate of mortality may cancel a substantial rate of conversion. In contrast, a religious movement can sustain substantial growth through fertility alone. For example, the Amish have not attracted converts for several centuries and in each generation there is substantial defection. Yet, at the end of each year the number of Amish is greater than before due to their normal demographic composition and a high fertility rate.

Religious movements typically over-recruit women (Stark and Bainbridge 1985; Cornwall 1988; Thompson 1991; Miller and Hoffman 1995; Stark 1996). However, this does not seem to matter unless it reduces fertility. Thus, the early Christian communities had a substantial excess of females, but Christian women probably had higher rates of fertility than did pagan women (Stark 1996). However, when movements greatly over-recruit women who are beyond their childbearing years, that is quite another matter. For example, by greatly over-recruiting older women, Christian Science soon faced the need for very high rates of conversion merely to offset high rates of mortality (Stark and Bainbridge 1985). Thus, what had been a very rapidly growing movement suddenly ceased to grow and soon entered a period of accelerating decline.

A Favourable Ecology

To the extent that a community is crowded with effective and successful religious organizations, it will be hard for new movements to make headway (Stark 1985, 1993; Stark and Bainbridge 1980b, 1985, 1996a; Stark and Iannaccone 1993, 1994). Stated as a proposition: (7) *Other things being equal, new religious movements will prosper to the extent that they compete against weak, local conventional religious organizations within a relatively unregulated religious economy.* Put another way, new religious organizations will do best where conventional religious mobilization is low – at least to the degree that the state gives new groups a chance to exist. Thus, we ought to find that where conventional church membership and church attendance rates are low, the incidence of new religious movements will be high. Initially, I argued that only cult movements would thrive where the conventional religious bodies were weak and that sects would cluster where conventional religious bodies were strong (Stark and Bainbridge 1980b, 1985). Subsequently, I realized that this conclusion was based on faulty theoretical reasoning and that *all* new religious movements must contest for a market share. Moreover, subsequent research finds that cult and sect movements are equally responsive to the strength of established competitors (as shown below and also in Nock 1987).

The individual-level form of this proposition is that *converts to religious groups will come primarily from the ranks of the religiously inactive*, in that people involved in a religious body will be relatively unlikely to switch. Moreover, this tendency will be maximized for groups lacking cultural continuity since the irreligious will possess little religious cultural capital and, consequently, it will not be costly for them to accept a faith outside the conventional religious culture.

There has been a considerable amount of research sustaining both the macro- and the micro-level versions of the proposition (Stark and Bainbridge 1980b, 1985, 1996a; Stark 1996; Nock 1987). Table 16.1 offers an addi-

Table 16.1 The ecology of success: 25 Canadian metropolitan areas (1991)

Membership rates	Correlations (r) with % giving their religious affiliation as none
Jehovah's Witnesses	0.61**
Mormons	0.60**
Para-religions[1]	0.82**

** $P < 0.01$.

[1] Statistics Canada created this category by combining all persons who gave their religious affiliation as Scientology, New Age, New Thought, Metaphysical, Kalabarian, Pagan, Rastafarian, Theosophical, Satanic or one of several other smaller groups of a similar nature.

tional test, based on the 1991 Census of Canada (Statistics Canada 1993). Using the 25 Canadian Metropolitan Areas as the units of analysis, the data show strong, very significant correlations between the percentage of the population reporting their religious preference as 'none' and membership rates for the Jehovah's Witnesses, Mormons and a cluster of 'para-religions' – so defined by Statistics Canada. That is, these groups are meeting with greater success where conventional religious bodies are weaker.

Network Ties

Religious commitment is sustained by interpersonal attachments. People value their religion more highly to the extent that a high value is communicated to them by those around them. Moreover, social relationships are part of the tangible rewards of participating in a religious movement – affection, respect, sociability and companionship being vital exchange commodities. Therefore, religious movements lacking strong internal networks of social relationships – being made up of casual acquaintances – will be notably lacking in commitment as they will also be lacking in the capacity to reward members.

Weak internal networks have doomed many religious movements. I have already noted how doctrines and practices leading to singularity have impeded authority; they also undercut network ties within groups such as the gnostics or various New Age movements. Moreover, I suspect that all movements lacking in strictness will also be lacking in network ties, for there is nothing about their religion that sets them apart from the general public. Liberal Protestant denominations illustrate this principle. Their congregations are more like theatre audiences than groups, for only small minorities of liberal Protestants report having close personal friends among members of their local congregation. In contrast, large majorities of members of Protestant sects report that most or all of their best friends are members of their congregation (Stark and Glock 1968).

On the other hand, many religious movements also are doomed because of internal networks that are too all-embracing, thus making it difficult and often impossible for members to maintain or form attachments with outsiders. When that is the case, conversion is impossible. People do not join religious groups because they suddenly found the doctrines appealing. They convert when their ties to members outweigh their ties to nonmembers – for most people, conversion consists of aligning their religious behaviour with that of their friends (Lofland and Stark 1965; Stark and Bainbridge 1980a, 1985, 1996a; Kox et al. 1991). When members do not have outside friends, such realignments do not occur. Hence, this proposition: (8) *New religious movements will succeed to the extent that they sustain strong internal attachments, while remaining an open social network, able to maintain and form ties to outsiders.*

Early Christians sustained very strong network ties within the group, but never did they allow these to result in a 'social implosion' (Bainbridge 1978), wherein members restricted their social relationships to one another. Had they done so, they would have remained obscure. Instead, Christians continued to grow because they managed to form bonds to pagans and these often allowed the movement to spread through new networks of pre-existing attachments. Intermarriage, especially between Christian women and pagan men, was a frequent mode of forming attachments to new pagan networks (Stark 1995, 1996). In similar fashion, the ability of the Mormons to maintain open networks has been remarked (Stark and Bainbridge 1980a, 1985). In contrast, many religious movements fail from the inability of members to form and maintain outside social ties.

Staying Strict

If strictness is the key to high morale and rapid growth, then (9) *Religious movements will continue to grow only to the extent that they maintain sufficient tension with their environment – remain sufficiently strict.*

Speaking precisely to this proposition, the leader of a rapidly growing evangelical Protestant group noted that it was not only necessary to keep the front door of the church open, but that it was necessary to keep the back door open, too. That is, growth not only depends upon bringing people in, but in letting go of those who don't fit in. The alternative is to modify the movement in an effort to satisfy those who are discontented, which invariably means to reduce strictness. People whose retention depends on reduced costs are 'latent free riders', and to see the full implications of accommodating them, simply reverse the discussion of strictness developed earlier in this essay.

This is not to say that successful religious movements never compromise with the world. However, these compromises must not cause too great a reduction in the degree of tension between the movement and the surrounding society. One factor that helps successful movements is a rather high rate of defection, not only by subsequent generations, but by new converts as well. A second factor is simply rapid growth, because even were there no defectors, the majority of members of a relatively rapidly growing religious group will, at any given moment, be recent converts. For example, in an ordinary year the Mormons baptize four times as many converts as they do infants born to members and, consequently, the average Mormon is a first generation convert. The same is true for the Jehovah's Witnesses and Soka Gakkai.

Studies of the transformation of sects from higher to lower tension have long recognized the central role played by second and third generation members in this process. As Bryan Wilson put it, 'There is certainly a difference between those who are converted to a sect, and those who accept adventist teachings at their mother's knee' (Wilson 1966: 207). When groups do not grow or grow very slowly, they will soon be made up primarily of those who did not choose to belong, but simply grew up belonging. Conversion selects people who find the current level of a movement's 'strictness' to be satisfactory. However, socialization will not 'select' nearly so narrowly. Therefore, unless most who desire reduced costs defect (which tends to be the case for encapsulated groups such as the Amish), the larger the proportion of socialized members, the larger the proportion who wish to reduce strictness.

Effective Socialization

To succeed, (10) *Religious movements must socialize the young sufficiently well as to minimize both defection and the appeal of reduced strictness.* As mentioned, many groups have perished for lack of fertility. A sufficiently high rate of defection by those born into the faith amounts to the same thing as low fertility. That is, much conversion is needed simply to offset mortality since so much fertility is cancelled by defection. However, the retention of offspring is not favourable to continued growth, if it causes the group to reduce its strictness, as noted above.

In subsequent work I will examine specific mechanisms by which successful movements effectively socialize their children. To anticipate these discussions it may be useful to note that each successful movement for which data exist finds important things for young people to *do* on behalf of their faith –

ways in which youth can exhibit and build commitment. Hence, movements get more from their young people to the extent that they ask more of them. Here, too, higher costs pay off.

Conclusion

This essay has necessarily been somewhat abstract. In it I have tried to sketch a theoretical model of the success or failure of religious movements – a set of ten propositions or rules governing their fate. I think a strong case can be made for each proposition. However, I also think it likely that while these may be necessary conditions for success, they may not be the sufficient conditions. That is, more propositions may need to be added. The only way to discover such omissions is to apply the theory to a number of groups to see if it accurately separates the successes from the failures. This is a task to which I plan to devote substantial future effort, but my effort will count for little unless I can tempt others to take part.

For ease of reference, the ten propositions are listed below.

Other things being equal, religious movements will succeed to the degree that:

1 They retain cultural continuity with the conventional faiths of the societies within which they seek converts.
2 Their doctrines are non-empirical.
3 They maintain a medium level of tension with their surrounding environment – are strict, but not too strict.
4 They have legitimate leaders with adequate authority to be effective.
   (4a) Adequate authority requires clear doctrinal justifications for an effective and legitimate leadership.
   (4b) Authority is regarded as more legitimate and gains in effectiveness to the degree that members perceive themselves as participants in the system of authority.
5 They can generate a highly motivated, volunteer, religious labour force, including many willing to proselytize.

6 They maintain a level of fertility sufficient to at least offset member mortality.

7 They compete against weak, local conventional religious organizations within a relatively unregulated religious economy.

8 They sustain strong internal attachments, while remaining an open social network, able to maintain and form ties to outsiders.

9 They continue to maintain sufficient tension with their environment – remain sufficiently strict.

10 They socialize the young sufficiently well as to minimize both defection and the appeal of reduced strictness.

References

Bainbridge, W. S. 1978: *Satan's Power*. Berkeley: University of California Press.

Coleman, J. S. 1986: Social Cleavage and Religious Conflict. *Journal of Social Issues* 12, 5: 44–56.

Cornwall, M. 1988: The Influence of Three Agents on Religious Socialization: Family, Church, and Peers, in Darwin, T. ed. *The Religion and Family Connection*. Provo, UT: Religious Studies Center, Brigham Young University, 207–31.

Durkheim, E. 1915: *The Elementary Forms of the Religious Life*. London: George Allen and Unwin.

Iannaccone, L. R. 1990: Religious Practice: A Human Capital Approach. *Journal for the Scientific Study of Religion* 29, 287–314.

——1992: Sacrifice and Stigma: Reducing Free Riding in Cults, Communes, and Other Collectives. *Journal of Political Economy* 100, 271–91.

——1994: Why Strict Churches Are Strong. *American Journal of Sociology* 99, 1180–1211.

——1995a: Risk, Rationality, and Religious Portfolios. *Economic Inquiry* 33, 285–96.

——1995b: Voodoo Economics? Reviewing the Rational Choice Approach to Religion. *Journal for the Scientific Study of Religion* 34, 76–88.

——Olson D. and Stark, R. 1995: Religious Resources and Church Growth. *Social Forces* 74, 709–31.

Johnson, B. 1963: On Church and Sect. *American Sociological Review* 28, 539–49.

——1987: A Sociologist of Religion Looks at the Future of New Religious Movements, in Bromley, D. and Hammond, P. E. eds. *The Future of New Religious Movements*. Macon, GA: Mercer University Press, 251–60.

Johnson, P. 1976: A *History of Christianity*. New York: Atheneum.

Kelley, D. M. 1972: *Why Conservative Churches are Growing*. New York: Harper and Row.

Kox, W., Wim, M. and 't Hart, H. 1991: Religious Conversion of Adolescents: Testing the Lofland and Stark Model of Religious Conversion. *Sociological Analysis* 52, 227–40.

Lofland, J. and Stark, R. 1965: Becoming a World-Saver: A Theory of Conversion to a Deviant Perspective. *American Sociological Review* 30, 862–75.

Meadows, D. and Meadows, D. 1972: *The Limits to Growth: A Report for the Club of Rome's Projection on the Predicament of Mankind*. New York: Universe Books.

Miller, A. S. and Hoffman, J. P. 1995: Risk and Religion: An Explanation of Gender Differences in Religiosity. *Journal for the Scientific Study of Religion* 34, 63–75.

Nock, D. A. 1987: Cult, Sect, and Church in Canada: A Reexamination of Stark and Bainbridge. *Canadian Review of Sociology and Anthropology* 24, 514–25.

Pagels, E. 1979: *The Gnostic Gospels*. New York: Random House.

Robbins, T. 1988: *Cults, Converts and Charisma*. Beverly Hills, CA: Sage Publications.

Sherkat, D. E. and Wilson, J. 1995: Preferences, Constraints, and Choices in Religious Markets: An Examination of Religious Switching and Apostasy. *Social Forces* 73, 993–1026.

Singelenberg, R. 1989: 'It Separated the Wheat from the Chaff': The '1975' Prophesy and its Impact on Dutch Jehovah's Witnesses. *Sociological Analysis* 50, 23–40.

Stark, R. 1985: Europe's Receptivity to Religious Movements, in Stark R. ed. *New Religious Movements: Genesis, Exodus, and Numbers*. New York: Paragon, 301–43.

——1987: How New Religions Succeed: A Theoretical Model, in Bromley, D. and Hammond, P. E. eds. *The Future of New Religious Movements*. Macon, GA: Mercer University Press, 11–29.

——1993: Europe's Receptivity to New Religious Movements: Round Two. *Journal for the Scientific Study of Religion* 32, 397–8.

——1995: Reconstructing the Rise of Christianity: The Role of Women. *Sociology of Religion* (formerly *Sociological Analysis*) 56, 229–44.

——1996: *The Rise of Christianity: A Sociologist Reconsiders History*. Princeton, NJ: Princeton University Press.

——and Bainbridge, W. S. 1980a: Networks of

Faith: Interpersonal Bonds and Recruitment to Cults and Sects. *American Journal of Sociology* 85, 1376–95.

—— 1980b: Secularization, Revival, and Cult Formation. *Annual Review of the Social Sciences of Religion*, 4, 85–119.

—— 1985: *The Future of Religion: Secularization, Revival, and Cult Formation*. Berkeley: University of California Press.

—— 1996a: *A Theory of Religion*. New Brunswick, NJ: Rutgers University Press.

—— 1996b: *Religion, Deviance, and Social Control*. New York: Routledge.

Stark, R. and Glock, C. Y. 1968: *American Piety*. Berkeley: University of California Press.

Stark, R. and Iannaccone, L. R. 1993: Rational Choice Propositions and Religious Movements, in Bromley, D. G. and Hadden, J. K. eds. *Religion and the Social Order: Handbook on Cults and Sects in America*. Greenwich, CT: JAI Press, 109–25.

—— 1994: A Supply-Side Reinterpretation of the 'Secularization' of Europe. *Journal for the Scientific Study of Religion* 33, 230–52.

—— 1997: Why the Jehovah's Witnesses are Growing so Rapidly: A Theoretical Application. *Journal of Contemporary Religion* 12 (2): 133–57.

Statistics Canada 1993: *Religions in Canada: The Nation*. Ottawa: Statistics Canada.

Thomspon, E. H. 1991: Beneath the Status Characteristic: Gender Variations in Religiousness. *Journal for the Scientific Study of Religion* 30, 381–94.

Weber, M. 1947: *The Theory of Social and Economic Organization*. Glencoe, IL: Free Press.

—— 1963: *The Sociology of Religion*. Boston, MA: Beacon Press.

Wagner, M. B. 1983: Spiritual Frontiers Fellowship, in Fichter, J. H. ed. *Alternatives to American Mainline Churches*. New York: Rose of Sharon Press.

Wilson, B. 1966: *Religion in Secular Society*. London: C. A. Watts.

—— 1987: Factors in the Failure of New Religious Movements, in Bromley, D. and Hammond, P. E. eds. *The Future of New Religious Movements*. Macon, GA: Mercer University Press, 30–45.

CHAPTER SEVENTEEN

New Religions and the Internet: Recruiting in a New Public Space

LORNE L. DAWSON AND JENNA HENNEBRY

Concerns After Heaven's Gate

Twice in the last year (1998) the first author of this paper[1] has been asked to speak to groups in our community about the presence of "cults"[2] on the world wide web, and the threat they might pose. These talks were prompted, undoubtedly, by the tragic death of the 39 members of Heaven's Gate at Rancho Sante Fe, California, on March 26, 1997. To the surprise of many it seems, the media reports of this strange and ceremonious mass suicide revealed a group with its own elaborate web page (see figure 17.1). What is more, this new religion designed sophisticated web pages for other organizations. In fact, it received much of its income from a company called Higher Source, operated by its members. Heaven's Gate had been using the Internet to communicate with some of its followers and to spread its message for several years. This news generated a special measure of curiosity and fear from some elements of the public.[3] This reaction stemmed, we suspect, from the coincidental confluence of the misunderstanding and consequent mistrust of both the new technology and of cults.

Despite the ballyhoo recently accorded the launch of the "information superhighway" (by the government, the computer industry, and the media), the Internet is still only used, with any regularity, by a relatively small percentage of the population.[4] In the absence of personal experience, the web is popularly thought to be the creature of those believed to be its primary users: large corporations on the one hand (from Microsoft to Nike), and isolated "computer nerds" on the other. Most certainly, religious organizations are not commonly associated in the public perception with such leading-edge technologies (despite the omni-presence of televangelists on the American airwaves). For most North Americans in fact, the topic of religion calls to mind churches, and the churches are associated with traditionalism, if not with an element of hostility to the cultural influence of developments in science and technology. New religious movements, in addition, are still rather crudely seen as havens for the socially marginal, and perhaps even personally deficient individuals – those least likely or capable of mastering the social and technical demands of a new world order. The image, then, of cultists exploiting the web seemed incongruous to many. Combined with the established suspicion of "cults" (e.g., Pfeifer 1992; Bromley and Breschel 1992) and the almost mystical power often attributed to the Internet itself, the example set by Heaven's Gate seemed ominous.

When compared with the familiar media used to distribute religious views, like books, videos, tapes, radio and television programs, Internet sites are easily accessible and in many respects more economical to produce and operate. With the appropriate knowledge and

Figure 17.1   Front page, Heaven's Gate website

minimal computer hardware and software, anyone can sample a wide array of alternative religious views, and, if they so choose, just as easily hide their exposure or consumption of such views from the prying eyes of others (e.g., parents, partners, friends, or employers). In fact, the net opens surprising new opportunities to even start one's own religion (as will be discussed below).

Have cults found in the Internet, then, a new and more effective means to recruit members? If so, has the world wide web changed the playing field, so to speak, allowing quite small and unusual groups unprecedented access to a new and impressionable audience of potential converts and supporters?

Most scholars of new religious movements would be skeptical, we think, that the advent of the world wide web offered any reason for renewed concern about the presumed threat posed by "cults" to mainstream society. Within days of the Heaven's Gate deaths, however, several media stories appeared in prominent sources (e.g., *The New York Times*, *Time* magazine, *Newsweek*, and CNN), each raising the prospect of "spiritual predators" on the net. In the words of George Johnson in *The New York Times*:

In the public mind – moulded by news reports on the old media, which are still more powerful and pervasive than anything on-line – the Internet is starting to seem like a scary place, a labyrinth of electronic tunnels as disturbing and seedy as anything Thomas Pynchon has dreamed up for the bizarre worlds in such works as *Gravity's Rainbow*, *V* and *Vineland*. The Heaven's Gate suicides can only amplify fears that, in some quarters, may be already bordering on hysteria. The Internet, it seems, might be used to lure children not only to shopping malls, where some "sicko" waits, but into joining UFO cults. (See the version reprinted in Canada's national newspaper, *The Globe and Mail*, April 5, 1997: C27)

CNN's online news magazine carried these suspicions further (http://cnn.com/TECH/9703/27/techno.pagans/index.html), citing comments from presumed experts on the web, like Erik Davis of *Wired* magazine, and "experts" on cults, like Margaret T. Singer. A story, posted under the heading "The Internet as a God and Propaganda Tool for Cults," sought to create the impression that "computer nerds" and other compulsive denizens of the net, might be particularly susceptible to cult recruitment (and hence eventually to abuse). In Davis's view, "identifying more and more of your life with what's happening on the other side of the [computer] screen . . ." can have a "very dissociative effect," increasing the risk of cult conversion. What is more, Singer assures us, the cults are targeting these very people:

What the cults want to recruit are average, normal, bright people and especially, in recent years, people with technical skills, like computer skills. And often, they haven't become street smart. And they're too gullible.

Wisely, the stories in *The New York Times* and *Time* magazine (April 7, 1997) both seek to cast doubt on such scare mongering. They each seek to do so, however, by defending the integrity of the world wide web and not the cults. Their pointed concern is to disassociate the net as a neutral means of communication from its use by religions (i.e., don't confuse the medium with the message). No effort is made to even begin to address the realities of cult recruitment in general, let alone their actual use of the net.

So what do we know about cult recruitment and the world wide web? Do we have reason to believe that the Internet either has or someday could become a significant source of new converts? Is there something to worry about? A recent survey of adult Canadians reported that 12 percent claim they use the Internet for "religious purposes."[5]

This essay examines and compares what we know about the presence of new religious movements on the Internet and how people come to join these groups. The most reliable results of decades of research into religious conversions cast doubt on the special utility of the world wide web as a mechanism of recruitment. Face-to-face social interactions and networks of personal relationships play too large a role in the data about conversions collected by scholars. Further, previous studies suggest that such "disembodied appeals" as religious advertisements, radio shows, and televangelism, have little significant effect on rates of religious recruitment (Lofland 1966; Shupe

1979; Snow, Zurcher, and Ekland-Olson 1980; Rochford 1982; Hoover 1988). But these are broadcast media, and largely under the control of a relatively small elite. Might things be different within the interactive and more democratic, even anarchic, conditions of cyberspace? At present we cannot say, because there is little reliable information and because it is too soon. Discussions of the nature and impact of the new public space opened up by the Internet, however, suggest that the emergence of the world wide web may be changing the conditions of new religious life in our societies in significant ways. There are both promise and peril in the new technologies of cyberspace for the future of religion.

Internet Surveys

Our analysis of these matters is augmented with insights drawn from two surveys: our own survey of the "web meisters" of several new religious movements, and an online profile of Internet users. Some interesting problems with the first survey will be discussed before proceeding with the analysis.

In the late spring of 1998, we surveyed the web page creators of thirty groups by e-mail (see table 17.1). The brief survey asked 23 questions delving into such matters as the origins of their web pages, whether professional help was used in their design or updating, whether the pages were official or unofficial in status, the primary purposes of the web pages, their level of satisfaction with the web pages and what measures of success they used, the mechanisms used for inviting feedback (if at all), the nature of the feedback received and the responses given, any knowledge of whether people had become affiliated with their groups as a result of contact with the web page, and their views on whether and how the world wide web should be regulated.

The groups and individuals approached were selected according to three criteria: (1) they represented relatively well-known new religious movements; (2) they represented a fairly reasonable cross-section of the kinds of groups active in North America; (3) they were

Table 17.1 Survey sample – new religious movements on the Internet

Group	Site name	URL site location
ARE	ARE Inc.	http://www.are-cayce.com/
Aumism	Aumism – Universal Religion	http://www.aumisme.org/gb/
BOTA	BOTA Home page (Builders Of The Atydum)	http://www.atanda.com/bota/default.html
Brahma Kumaris	Brahma Kumaris WSO	http://www.rajayoga.com/
	Brahma Kumaris WSO	http://www.bkwsu.com
Church Universal and Triumphant	Our Church (Church Universal and Triumphant)	http://www.tsl.org/intro/church.html
Churches of Christ	Boston Church of Christ	http://www.bostoncoc.org/
	International Churches of Christ	http://www.intlcc.com/
Covenant of the Goddess	Covenant of the Goddess	http://www.canjure.com
Eckankar	Eckankar	http://www.eckankar.org
Foundation for Inner Peace (ACIM)	A Course in Miracles – ACIM	http://www.acim.org/
	Miracles web site	http://www.miraclesmedia.org/
International Society for Krishna Consciousness	ISKCON.NET A Hare Krishna Network	http://iskcon.net
Meher Baba Group	Meher Baba Group	http://davey.sunyerie.edu/mb/html
MSIA	MSIA – Movement of Spiritual Inner Awareness	http://www.msia.com/
Ordo Templi Orientis	Hodos Chamelionis Camp of the Ordo Templi Orientis Thelema	http://pw2.netcom.com/~bry-guy/hcc-oto.html
		http://www.crl.com?~thelema.home.html
Osho	Meditation: The Science of the Inner	http://www.osho.org/homepage.html
Raëlians	International Rëalian Movement	http://www.rael.org/
Rosicrucian Order	Rosicrucian Order (English) AMORC Home Page	http://www.rosicrucian.org/
	AMORC International	http://www.amorc.org
School of Wisdom	School of Wisdom Home Page	http://ddi.digital.net/~wisdom/school/welcome.html
Scientology	Scientology: SCIENTOLOGY HOME PAGE	http://www.scientology.org/

Shambhala	Welcome to Shambhala	http://www.shambhala.org/
Shirdi Sai Baba	Shirdi Sai Baba	http://www.saiml.com
Sikh Dharma (3H)	International Directory of Kundalini Yoga Centers (3HO)	http://www.sikhnet.com
Soka Gakkai	Soka Gakkai International Public Info Site	http://www.sgi.org
	Soka Gakkal International-USA (SGI-USA)	http://www.sgi-usa.org/
Subud	SUBUD: The World Subud Association Website	http://www.subud.org/english.menu.html
Quest For Utopia (Koufuku no kagaku)	Quest for Utopia	http://www.quest-utopia.com
	Institute Research Human Happiness (Koufuku no Kagaku)	http://www.quest-utopia.com/info/irh.html
Temple of Set	Temple of Set	http://www.xeper.org/pub/tos/noframe.htm
	Balanone: Temple of Set Information	http://www.geocities.com
The Family	The Family – An International Christian Fellowship	http://www.thefamiiy.org/
TM	Complete Guide to the Transcendental Meditation	http://www.TM.org/
Unification Church	Unification Church Home Page	http://www.unification.org/
Urantia	Urantia Foundation	http://www.urantia.org
Wicca	Wiccan Church of Canada Home Page	http://www.wcc.on.ca/
	Welcome to Daughters of the Moon (Dianic Wicca)	http://www.wco.com/~moonwmyn/index.html

already known to be operating fairly sophisticated web pages. In administering the survey by e-mail we had hoped to garner a higher rate of return from these "computer savvy" individuals and groups, thinking many might be able to respond almost immediately by return e-mail (as requested). To our surprise, however, the rate of return was very low: seven surveys or 23.3 percent.[6] Why the low rate of return? We are not sure, although we have some ideas. Using the Internet to do surveys would seem to be a subject in need of systematic investigation itself.[7]

All the same, some information from our seven respondents will be introduced here, for strictly illustrative purposes, since this is the only empirical data currently available. Moreover, the seven respondents happen to represent several of the more prominent new religions and an interesting, if highly limited, cross-section of the kinds of new religions available (neo-pagan, Christian, Hindu, Buddhist, and psychotherapeutic).[8]

The information derived from the other survey of Internet users, on which we are calling, is more straightforward and based on a large, if perhaps not completely reliable, sample (N = 9,529) collected by the Inter Commerce Corporation and made available to all on the net at http://www.survey.net (see table 17.2).[9]

Better data on both counts would assist future investigations of the issues raised by this essay. But a timely, appropriate, and significant response can be made with the data and theoretical insights at hand. Research into the nature, social and religious functions, and consequences of the Internet is only beginning and the issues raised in this discussion help to explain why we need to do more.

New Religions on the Net

To date we do not know much about how surfing the web may have contributed to anyone joining a new religious movement. With the exception of the brief forays undertaken by Cottee, Yateman, and Dawson (1996: 459–68) and Bainbridge (1997:

149–55), we know of no specific studies, popular or academic, of this subject. The journalist Jeff Zaleski has written an interesting book about religion and the Internet called *The Soul of Cyberspace* (Zaleski 1997). It contains some fascinating interviews with religious figures from many of the world's religions that have already heavily invested in the Internet as a tool of religious discourse (from the Chabad-Lubavitch Jews of New York, at http://www.chabad.org, to Zen Buddhists, at http://wwwl.mhv.net/~dharmacom/1htmlmro.htm). It also contains some equally intriguing conversations with a few of the founding or influential figures of cyberspace and virtual reality about the possible interface of religion and cyberspace. Zaleski's attention, however, is directed to discerning if anyone thinks that religious services can be performed authentically over the web and how. Can the spiritual essence of religion, the subtle energies of *prana*, as he calls it, be adequately conveyed by the media of cyberspace? Or will such hyper-real simulations always be inadequate to the task? The question of recruitment arises in his discussions, but it is never explored in any detail. On the contrary, in his comments on Heaven's Gate and the threat posed by "cults" on the Internet, Zaleski displays a level of prejudice and misunderstanding that is out of keeping with the rest of his book:

> Those most vulnerable to a cult's message – the lonely, the shy, misfits, outcasts – are often attracted to the Net, relishing its power to allow communion with others while maintaining anonymity. While the Net offers an unprecedented menu of choice, it also allows budding fanatics to focus on just one choice – to tune into the same Web site, the same newsgroup, again and again, for hours on end, shut off from all other stimuli – to isolate themselves from conflicting beliefs. Above all, the headiness of cyberspace, its divorce from the body and the body's incarnate wisdom, gives easy rise to fantasy, paranoia, delusions of grandeur. (Zaleski 1997: 249)

In echoing the comments of Davis and Singer, Zaleski is rather unreflexive about his own

Table 17.2 Internet user statistics (1997–8) [http://www.wisdom.con/sv/sv-inetl.htm]

Age		Sex	
26–30 yrs. old	25.40%	Female	28.40%
22–25	16.50%	Male	71.50%
31–35	13.00%		
41–50	12.90%		
19–20	9.10%	Education	
36–40	9.00%	College	34.00%
51–60	4.60%	College Graduate	30.10%
13–16	4.00%	Masters Degree	18.20%
17–18	4.00%	Some High School	6.70%
61–70	0.90%	High School Graduate	6.60%
under 12	0.30%	Ph.D. +	4.10%
over 71	0.20%	Ph.D. Student	0.30%
Occupation		Industry	
Professional	59.20%	Education/Student	37.10%
Student	34.30%	Service	23.60%
Blue Collar	4.50%	Publishing	12.20%
Retired	1.90%	Other/Unemployed	7.10%
		Sales	6.30%
Occupation associated		Government	5.10%
w/computers	39.40%	Manufacturing	5.10%
		Arts/Creative	3.40%
Primary Use of the Internet			
Research	44.50%		
Entertainment	24.50%		
Communication	15.90%		
Sales/Marketing	9.70%		
Education	5.30%		

Source: Inter Commerce Corporation, "SURVEY.NET."

and other' fascination with religion on the Internet.

Reports on the web say that Heaven's Gate did contact people by e-mail and through conversations tried to involve them in their activities, even encouraged them to leave home and join the main group in California. One particular conversation between a member of the group and an adolescent in Minnesota has been recorded (we are told), and it does not seem unreasonable to presume that there were more. How many? How successful were these contacts? Who knows? Reports in the news of the past lives of some of the 39 people who died indicated that a few of the members first contacted the group through the Internet.[10] But we lack details of how and of what happened. Did these people know of the group before or not? Had they been involved in similar groups before? Did the Internet contact play a significant or a merely peripheral role in the decisions they made about joining Heaven's Gate? There are a lot of important questions that have yet to be answered.

Was the recruiting done over the Internet part of a fully sanctioned and prepared strategy of Heaven's Gate or something simply done by enthusiastic members – like an evangelist in any tradition, taking advantage of opportunities as they arise? At present we do not know. We briefly describe the presence of new religions on the Internet. Then we place our discussion in context by looking at the scholarly record about who joins new religious movements and how, to see how this data fits with the results of our survey of the creators of web pages for the new religious movements and the survey of the users of the net.

Heaven's Gate did have a relatively flashy website (for its time), making a lot of information available, although it was of variable quality. The site employed many colorful graphics, but in the main it consisted of programmatic statements of the group's beliefs, focused on the role played by aliens from space in the past, present, and future life of humankind. Undergirding all was the warning that a great change was at hand: "The earth's present 'civilization' is about to be recycled – spaded under. Its inhabitants are refusing to evolve. The 'weeds' have taken over the garden and disturbed its usefulness beyond repair." In the days immediately preceding the mass suicide of the group, their web page declared: "Red Alert. HALE-BOPP Brings Closure." It was time for the loyal followers of their leader Do to abandon their earthy "containers" in preparation for being carried off by a UFO, thought to be accompanying the comet Hale-Bopp, to a new home at "The Evolutionary Level Beyond Human" somewhere else in the galaxy. Few if any people, it now seems clear, were listening or chose to take their warnings seriously – an interesting indicator of the real limits on the vaunted power of the web as a means of religious "broadcasting."

Apart from the imminent character of its apocalyptic vision, the Heaven's Gate website is fairly representative of the presence of new religious movements on the Internet. Most of the better known new religions (e.g., Scientology, Krishna Consciousness, the Unification Church, Soka Gakkai, the Church Universal and Triumphant, Eckankar, Osho, Sri Sai Baba) have had websites of some sophistication (in graphics, text, and options) for several years (see table 17.1). The respondents to our survey said their sites were launched in 1995 or very early in 1996, when the world wide web was still more or less in its infancy. In addition, there are literally hundreds of other sites for more obscure religious or quasi-religious groups. Most of these sites are official, in some sense, although some are privately run by devotees and others. Most of these sites simply replicate, in appearance and content, the kind of material available in other publications by these groups, and the web materials are often meant to be down-loaded as a ready substitute for more conventional publications. Most of these sites offer ways of establishing further contact to obtain more materials (e.g., pamphlets, books, tapes, and videos) and to access courses, lectures, and other programs, either by e-mail, telephone numbers, or mailing addresses. All of our respondents indicated that this was an important feature of their sites, most claiming that they respond to several messages every day, and one award-winning site claiming to receive "about 100 messages per day." Similar comments can be found in the conversations Zaleski had with other religious web masters. A few of the more elaborate sites (e.g., Scientology, Eckankar) offer virtual tours of the interiors of some of their central facilities and temples. Many offer music and sound bites in real audio (e.g., messages from their founders and other inspirational leaders). None of our respondents claimed that their websites had been professionally designed or altered. The individuals or groups had done the work themselves. Three of the respondents indicated, however, that they have since become engaged, to some extent, in the professional creation of web pages for other groups within their own organization or tradition, as well as other clients altogether.

The primary use of the web is clearly a way to advertise the groups and to deliver information about them cheaply. Most respondents stressed how ideal the medium was for the dissemination of their views (see also Zaleski 1997: 73, 75, 125). To this end, many of the new religions operate multiple pages with slightly different foci, all "hot-linked" to one another, to maximize the chances of a browser stumbling across one of the pages. Similarly, these pages are often launched with unusually long and diverse lists of "key word" search terms, assuring that their address will appear when requests are made through search engines for all kinds of information that may be only tangentially related to the religious beliefs or mission of the group in question (see also Zaleski 1997: 105; see table 17.3).[11] In these ways, the websites act as a new and relatively effective means of outreach to the larger community. They undoubtedly enhance the public profile of each of these religions and add to the revenues obtained by the sale of books, tapes, and other paraphernalia. In fairness most of the literature available through the web is offered free of charge – to spread the word.[12]

The Internet and Recruitment

The popular stereotypes of recruits to NRMs are that they are young, naive, and duped, or that they are social losers and marginal types seeking a safe haven from the real world. In an inconsistent and opportunistic manner, some members of the anti-cult movement (e.g., Singer 1995) have recently claimed that everyone is susceptible to being recruited. The comments of Erik Davis and Margaret Singer in the CNN story on cults and the Internet, and those of Zaleski in *The Soul of Cyberspace*, manage to combine all three points of view. Heavy users of computers and hence often the world wide web are presumed to be "social nerds" and thus more vulnerable to the "loving" outreach of online cult recruiters. Is this the case? The evidence at hand shows that the situation is probably much more complex.

In the first place, the data acquired by sociologists over the last twenty or more years about who joins NRMs and how they join tends not to support the popular supposition (see the summaries and references provided in Dawson 1996, 1998). It is true, as studies reveal, that "cult involvement seems to be strongly correlated with having fewer and weaker extra-cult social ties . . . [as well as] fewer and weaker ideological alignments." In the terms of reference of Rodney Stark and William Sims Bainbridge (1985), the "unchurched" are more likely to join (Dawson 1996: 149; 1998: 70–1). If heavy users of the net are indeed social isolates, then in at least one respect they may appear to be at greater risk of being persuaded to join an NRM.

But there are three other propositions about who joins NRMs and how, with significantly greater empirical substantiation, that off-set this impression:

1 "Studies of conversion and case studies of specific groups have found that recruitment to NRMs happens primarily through preexisting social networks and interpersonal bonds. Friends recruit friends, family members each other, and neighbours recruit neighbours." (Dawson 1996: 147; 1998: 68)

2 "In general, case studies of individuals who joined NRMs or of the groups themselves commonly reveal the crucial role of affective bonds with specific members in leading recruits into deeper involvements." (Dawson 1996: 148; 1998: 69–70)

3 "Equally strongly, from the same studies it is clear that the intensive interaction of recruits with the rest of the existing membership of the group is pivotal to the successful conversion and maintenance of new members." (Dawson 1996: 149; 1998: 70)

First and foremost, the process of converting to an NRM is a social process. If the denizens of cyberspace tend in fact to be socially isolated, then it is unlikely that they will be recruited through the web or otherwise. What is more, there is little reason to think that the Internet, in itself, ever will be a very effective, means of recruitment. As the televangelists learned some time ago (Hoover 1988), the initial provision of information is unlikely to produce any specific commitments, unless it is followed up by much more personal and complete forms of interaction, by phone and in person. Therefore, most of the successful televangelists run quite extensive "para-church" organizations to which they try to direct all their potential recruits. The religious web masters, as Zaleski's interviews reveal (Zaleski

Table 17.3 Inventory of new religious movements on the Internet, detailed

Group	Site characteristics				Communications		
	Keywords	Design	Interactiveness	Special features	e-mail	Phone	Mail
ARE	13	advanced	high	audio, links, books	×	×	×
Aumism	*93	average	med-high	petition	×	×	×
BOTA	*34	advanced	high (Java)	multi-language, regional, free brochure	×	×	×
Brahma Kumaris	7	advanced	med	books, regional links	×	×	×
Church Universal and Triumphant	*49	average	low	regional links, multi-language	×	×	×
Churches of Christ (Boston)	—	advanced	med	regional links, directory	×		×
Covenant of the Goddess	5	average	med-low	webring, regional links	×		
Eckankar	*20	advanced	med	free books		×	×
Foundation for Inner Peace (ACIM)	—	basic	low	catalog, mailing list	×	×	×
International Society for Krishna Consciousness	49	advanced	high (Java)	audio, site host, search engine, international	×		×
Meher Baba Group	—	average	low	products, organization links	×		
Movement of Spiritual Inner Awareness	*19	advanced	med	multi-language	×		
Ordo Templi Orientis	—	basic	low	links to other Thelemic sites	×		
Osho	*14	advanced	high	audio talks, online shopping	×	×	×
Quest for Utopia (Koufuku no Kagaku)	—	average	high (Java)	audio, languages (Japanese)	×		
Raëlians	—	advanced	low	multi-language, multi-geographical, counter	×		

Organization	Keywords	Website	Interactivity	Features			
Rosicrucian Order	—	basic	med-low	free booklet, counter	X	X	X
School of Wisdom	11	average	high (Java)	guestbook		X	X
Scientology	*31	advanced	high (Java)	free info, film, search engine, multi-language	X	X	X
Shambhala	*32	advanced	med	international server		X	X
Sikh Dharma (3HO)	*39	advanced	high	chat room, search engine, international	X	X	X
Shirdi Sai Baba	—	advanced	high (Java)	multi-links	X	X	X
Soka Gakkai	—	advanced	med	international		X	X
Subud	15	basic	med	international	X	X	X
Temple of Set	—	advanced	med	mailing list, language	X	X	X
The Family	*26	advanced	med-high	audio, free info, music		X	X
TM	*78	advanced	med-high	video, links, online books		X	X
Unification Church		advanced	med-high	online bookstore, online newsletter, reading list	X	X	X
Urantia	4	advanced	med-high	international, online catalog	X	X	X
Wiccan Church of Canada	—	average	low	regional links	X	X	X

* Keywords were not specific to organization.

Summary statistics: 47% used detailed keyword searches, with 10 keywords or more; 30% high interactivity; 40% medium interactivity; 63% advanced websites; 97% provided e-mail addresses; 40% provided e-mail, telephone, and mailing addresses.

1997: 63, 73, 75, 125), do the same, pressing interested individuals to visit the nearest center or temple. As the creator of one site, Christian Web, states:

Internet ministries are never meant to be a replacement for the real church. It is impossible for anyone to develop a personal relationship with God without being around His people, His church. These Internet works are nothing more than something to draw in people who may otherwise not want to know anything about Jesus or not want to visit a church for fear of the unknown. For some reason, people find it less intimidating if they can sit at home in the privacy of their own room asking questions about the church and the Bible and God that they have always wanted to ask but never quite feel comfortable enough in the real church to do so. (Zaleski 1997: 125)

Approaching the same question from another angle, can we learn anything from a comparison of the social profiles that we have of Internet users and the members of NRMs (see table 17.1 and Dawson 1996: 152–7; 1998: 74–9)? Both groups tend to be drawn disproportionately from the young adult population, to be educated better than the general public, and they seem to be disproportionately from the middle to upper classes. In the case of the Internet users, the latter conclusion can only be inferred from their levels of education and occupations. But it is fair to say that the fit between this profile and the stereotypes of cult converts is ambiguous at best. By conventional social inferences, it would seem to be inappropriate to view these people as social losers or marginal. Nor clearly do they constitute "everybody." Are they more naive and prone to being duped or manipulated? That would be difficult to determine. But we do not have any reliable evidence to believe such is the case, certainly not for Internet users. On average, they are not as young as most converts to NRMs, even better educated, and overwhelmingly from professional occupations (or so they report). Given the extent of their probable involvement in computer technology, surfing the web, and the real world of

their professions, it is more plausible to speculate that they will be more skeptical, questioning, and worldly-wise (in at least a cognitive sense) than other segments of the population.

But even if we were to somehow learn that this is not the case, there are other issues to be explored that raise doubts about the soundness of the popular fear of cult recruitment through the net. The common complaint of educators, parents, and spouses is that those drawn to the web for hours on end are simply riding on the surface of things (surfing). They have substituted the vicarious life of the web for real life commitments. In this they call to mind certain individuals whom Eileen Barker (1984: 194–8, 203; see also Dawson 1998: 108) noted in her comprehensive study of the Moonies. These are people who seem to fit the profile of potential recruits delineated by the anti-cult movement, yet in fact attend a few lectures with some enthusiasm, only to drop-out in pursuit of some other novel interest on the horizon.

On the other hand, following the logic of the argument advanced by Stark and Bainbridge (1996: 235–7) for the involvement of social elites in cults, we can speculate that there are special reasons why a certain percentage of heavy Internet users may be interested in cult activities and why NRMs may have a vested interest in recruiting these people. "In a cosmopolitan society which inflicts few if any punishments for experimentation with novel religious alternatives," Stark and Bainbridge propose, "cults may recruit with special success among the relatively advantaged members of society" (Stark and Bainbridge 1996: 235). Even within elites, they point out, there is an inequality in the division of rewards and room for individuals to be preoccupied with certain relative deprivations (Glock 1964) not adequately compensated for by the power of the elite (e.g., concerns about beauty, health, love, and coping with mortality). In fact, the very material security of this group may well encourage their preoccupation with these other less fundamental concerns. People moved by these relative deprivations are unlikely to be drawn to religious sects to alleviate their needs, because the sects are much more likely to be opposed in principle to "the exact rewards the elite possesses as a class" (Stark and Bainbridge 1996: 236). Alternatively, Stark and Bainbridge stipulate:

... an innovative cult ... can offer a set of compensators outside the political antagonisms which divide the elite from other citizens, and focus instead on providing compensators for particular sets of citizens with a shared set of desires that wish to add something to the power of the elite while preserving it. (Stark and Bainbridge 1996: 236)

In addition, "in a cosmopolitan society ... in which the elite accepts and supports cultural pluralism and thus encourages cultural novelty," certain religious innovations may hold a special appeal because they are emblematic of "progress." Cults are often associated with the transmission of "new culture" and as such may have a certain appeal in terms of the cultural capital of the elite. More mundanely, of course, there is also the fact that the elite are the ones "with both the surplus resources to experiment with new explanations and, through such institutions as higher education, the power to obtain potentially valuable new explanations before others do" (Stark and Bainbridge 1996: 236–7).

From the perspective of the NRMs, members of an elite are particularly attractive candidates for recruitment, not just because of the resources they can donate to the cause, but because they are more likely to be involved in the kind of wide-ranging social networks essential for the dissemination of a new cultural phenomenon. "Since networks are composed of interlocking exchange relationships," Stark and Bainbridge reason, "a network will be more extensive, including more kinds of exchanges for more valued rewards, if its members possess the power to obtain the rewards" (Stark and Bainbridge 1996: 236). Recruitment from the elites of society can be instrumental in the success of a new religion.

Whether any of this is relevant in this context is a matter for empirical investigation.

The survey of Internet users does suggest, however, that the web provides a convenient point of access to a seemingly elite segment of our society. Access to computing technology and to the Internet, as well as sufficient time and knowledge to use these resources properly, is still largely a luxury afforded the better-off segments of our society.

The conclusions we can draw about the threat posed by "cults" on the Internet are limited, yet important. First, while the Internet does make it cheaper for NRMs to disseminate their beliefs over a larger area and to a potentially much larger audience, it is unlikely that it has intrinsically changed the capacity of NRMs to recruit new members. In the first place, Web pages, at present at least, differ little in content or function from more traditional forms of religious publication and broadcasting. Secondly, we have no real evidence that Internet users are any more prone to convert to a new religion than other young and well-educated people in our society. All the same, there are other reasons for wondering if the world wide web is changing the environment in which NRMs operate in fundamental and perhaps even dangerous ways.

The Perils and Promise of the New Public Space

We are starting to be inundated with discussions of the wonders and significance of cyberspace. Much of the dialogue is marked by hyperbole and utopian rhetoric that leaves scholars cold. A few key insights, however, warrant further investigation. Most fundamentally, it is important to realize that it may be best to think of the Internet as a new environment or context in which things happen rather than just another new tool or service. As David Holmes (1997) observes (citing Mark Poster 1997):

The virtual technologies and agencies ... cannot be viewed as instruments in the service of pre-given bodies and communities, rather they are themselves contexts which bring about new corporealities and new politics corresponding to space-worlds and time-worlds that have never before existed in human history. (Holmes 1997: 3)

When religion, like anything else, enters these new worlds, there are both anticipated and unanticipated consequences. The new religious "web meisters" we questioned seemed to approach the Internet simply as a tool and showed little or no appreciation of the potential downside of their efforts. But in thinking about these matters, two disparate sociological observations by Anthony Giddens and James Beckford came to mind and we began to wonder about a connection.

With the advent of the technologies of modernity, Giddens (1990) argues, time has become separated from space and space from place, giving rise to ever more "disembedded social systems." Social relations have been lifted out of local contexts of interaction and restructured across "indefinite spans of time-space" (Giddens 1990: 21). Writing, money, time-clocks, cars, freeways, television, computers, ATMs, walkmans, electronic treadmills for running, shopping malls, theme parks and so on, have all contributed to the transformation of the human habitat, incrementally creating "successive levels of 'new nature' " for humanity (Holmes 1997: 6). As sociologists since Marx (1846) have realized, new technologies bring about new forms of social interaction and integration that can change the taken-for-granted conditions of social life. This is especially true of communications technologies. Relative to our ancestors, we have become like gods in our powers of production, reconstruction, and expression. Yet the price may have been high. Even these pre-virtual technologies have changed our environments in ways that detrimentally standardize, routinize, and instrumentalize our relations with our own bodies and with other people. As we have refashioned our world, we have in turn been remade in the image of techno-science (see, for example, McLuhan 1964; Ellul 1964; Marcuse 1966; Baudrillard 1970; Foucault 1979; Postman 1985). Does the advent of the Internet typify, or even magnify,

these and other undesirable social trends? Some keen observers of the sociological implications of the Internet, like Holmes (1997), seem to think it does. If so, what unanticipated consequences might stem from the attempt of religions to take advantage of the disembedded freedom of cyberspace? A clue is provided by an observation by Beckford.

Beckford has intriguingly proposed that it might be better to conceptualize religion in the contemporary Western world as "a cultural resource . . . than as a social institution" (Beckford 1992: 23; see also Beckford 1989: 171). The social structural transformations wrought by the emergence of advanced industrial societies have undermined the communal, familial, and organizational bases of religion. As a consequence, while "religious and spiritual forms of sentiment, belief and action have survived as relatively autonomous resources . . . retain[ing] the capacity to symbolize . . . ultimate meaning, infinite power, supreme indignation and sublime compassion," they have "come adrift from [their] former points of social anchorage." Now "they can be deployed in the service of virtually any interest-group or ideal: not just organizations with specifically religious objectives" (Beckford 1992: 22–3). Is this an apt description for what the Internet may be doing to religion? Like any "environment," the web acts back upon its content, modifying the form of its users or inhabitants. Is the "disembedded" social reality of life in cyberspace contributing to the transformation of religion into a "cultural resource" in a postmodern society? If it is, what would be the consequences for the future form and function of religion? Perhaps developments in religion on the web will provide some initial indications. After examining the pitfalls of life on the web, we will briefly comment on one such development: the creation of truly "churchless religions."

With these conjectures in mind, we briefly itemize and counterpoise some of the noted benefits and liabilities of life on the Internet.[13] On the positive side, much has been made of the net as an electronic meeting place, a new public space for fashioning new kinds of communities (Shields 1996; Holmes 1997; Zaleski

1997). The defining features of these new communities are the various freedoms allowed by the technology. The Internet allows freedom from "the constraints of the flesh" (Holmes 1997: 7), from the limitations of interaction within Cartesian space and the natural cycles of time. It allows a greater measure of freedom from traditional forms of social control, both formal and informal. It allows for the "breakdown of hierarchies of race, class, and gender." It allows for "the construction of oppositional subjectivities hitherto excluded from the public sphere" (ibid: 13). It allows people, seemingly, to "bypass or displace institutional politics" (ibid: 19). The bottom line, we are told by the hardcore denizens and promoters of the net, is that the Internet constitutes a new and freer community of speech, transcending conventional institutional life.

All of these presumed freedoms, each as yet a worthy subject of empirical investigation (see, for example, Shields 1996; Holmes 1997), rest upon the anonymity and fluidity of identity permitted and sometimes even mandated by life on the Internet. The technology of the net allows, and the emergent culture of the net fosters, the creative enactment of pluralism, at the individual or psychological level as well as the social, cultural, and collective level. This unique foundation of freedom, however, comes at a price that may vitiate the creation of any real communities, of faith or otherwise.

As noted, there is a marked tendency for life on the net to be fashioned in the image of the current techno-science, with its new possibilities and clear limitations. This environmental influence on social relations is likely to spill out of the confines of the computer into the stream of everyday life – much like the virtual realities of television that influence the social ontologies of North America, Britain, Japan, and much of Europe. Part of this new standardization, routinization, and instrumentalization of life is the further commodification of human needs and relations. The pitch for the creation of new virtual communities bears the hallmarks of the emergence of "community" as a new commodity of advanced capitalism – a product which is marketed in ways that induce the felt need for a convenient substitute for an increasingly problematic reality.

But do "communities" shaped by the Internet represent real communities any more than shopping malls? Are the possibilities of interaction and exchange sufficient in kind, number, and quality to replicate and possibly even to replace the social relationships born of more immediate and spatially and temporally uniform kinds of communal involvement? There is good reason to be skeptical, for as Holmes notes:

. . . technologies of extension [like the Internet or freeways] . . . characteristically attenuate presence by enabling only disembodied and abstract connections between persons, where the number of means of recognizing another person declines. In the "use" of these technologies . . . the autonomy of the individual is enhanced at the point of use, but the socially "programmed" nature of the technology actually prohibits forming mutual relations of reciprocity outside the operating design of the technological environment. (Holmes 1997: 6–7)

Sharpening the critique, Holmes further cites the views of Michele Willson (1997: 146):

. . . the presence of the Other in simulated worlds is more and more being emptied out to produce a purely intellectual engagement, and possibilities of commitment to cooperative or collective projects become one-dimensional, or, at best, self-referential. "Community is then produced as an ideal, rather than as a reality, or else it is abandoned altogether." (Holmes 1997: 16)

In like manner, Willson (1997) points out, the Internet seemingly allows us to celebrate and extend social pluralism. But appearances can be deceiving. In the first place, the largely ungrounded and potentially infinite multiplicity of the net is often little more than "a play of masks," which serves more to desensitize us to the real and consequential differences between us. Secondly, the medium simultaneously and paradoxically tends to "compartmentalize populations" and physically isolate individuals, while also "homogenizing" them (Holmes 1997: 16–17). As in the rest of our consumer culture, the market of the Internet tends to favor standardization with marginal differentiation. Consequently, with Holmes we find that dialogues on the net tend to be "quite transient and directionless, seldom acquiring a substantive enough history to constitute a political [or religious] movement" (ibid: 18).

To the extent that any of this is true, and speculation far out-strips sound empirical research at this point, it is clear that the side-effects of involvement in the net could be quite deleterious for religions, new and old. The lauded freedom of the net merely compounds the difficulties, since the producers of content have little control over the dissemination and use of their material once launched. Things may be repeated out of context and applied to all manner of ends at odds with the intentions of the original producers. The Internet, as Zaleski says,

> is organized laterally rather than vertically or radially, with no central authority and no chain of command. (Individual webmasters have power over Web sites, as do . . . system operators . . . over bulletin board systems, and moderators over Usenet groups, but their influence is local and usually extremely responsive to the populations they serve.) (Zaleski 1997: 111)

There is little real regulation of the Internet and to date, only a few organizations have been able to enforce some of their intellectual property rights (most notably, some software producers and the Church of Scientology – see Frankel 1996; Grossman 1998). The sheer speed and scope of the Internet and the complexity of possible connections can frustrate any attempts to control the flow of information. As several of the web masters we surveyed stated, any attempt to regulate the net would likely violate the freedom of speech and religion guaranteed by the United States constitution and in the process render the net itself ineffective.

However, this state of affairs can have a number of other unanticipated consequences for religions venturing onto the Internet that our web masters did not seem to realize:

> Because the medium influences the message, it's possible that in the long run the Internet will favour those religions and spiritual teachings that tend toward anarchy and that lack a complex hierarchy. Even now, those who log on to cyberspace may tend to gravitate to religious denominations that emphasize centrifugal rather than centripetal force, just as the medium that is carrying them does. Authority loses its trappings and force on the Net. (Zaleski 1997: 111–12)

This reality of the world of the Internet might well pose serious problems for religions that have historically stressed the role of a strong central authority, like the Roman Catholic Church or Scientology.

> As public information sources multiply through the Internet, it's likely that the number of sites claiming to belong to any particular religion but in fact disseminating information that the central authority of that religion deems heretical also will multiply. (ibid: 108)

When everyone can potentially circumvent the filters of an ecclesial bureaucracy and communicate directly and *en masse* with the leadership in Rome, Los Angeles, or wherever, there will be a shift in power towards the grassroots (ibid: 112). The internet could have a democratizing effect on all religions and work against those religions that resist this consequence.

The elaborate theorizing of Stark and Bainbridge (1996) and their colleagues (e.g., Innaccone 1995) suggests, however, another somewhat contrary unanticipated consequence of the emergence of the world wide web for new religions. As Stark points out in his discussion of the rise of Christianity, the way had been cleared for the phenomenal triumph of Christianity in the Greco-Roman world by the "*excessive* pluralism" (Stark 1996: 197) of paganism. The massive influx of new cults into the Roman empire in the first century created "what E. R. Dodds called 'a bewildering mass of alternatives. There were too many cults, too many mysteries, too many philosophies of life to choose from'" (ibid: 197). This abundance of choice had at least two consequences with parallel implications for the fate of new religions on the Internet.

In the first place, it assured that only a truly different religion, one that was favored by other circumstances largely beyond its control, was likely to emerge from the crowd. For excessive pluralism, as Stark argues, "inhibits the ability of new religious firms to gain a market share" (ibid: 195), since the pool of potential converts is simply spread too thin. The competition for this pool, moreover, is likely to drive the competing new religions into ever new radical innovations to secure a market edge.

Secondly, as Stark and Bainbridge argue elsewhere (Stark and Bainbridge 1985, 1996; see also Stark 1996: ch. 8), if many of the religious choices people have are "nonexclusive," as was the case in the Roman Empire and seems to be the case on the Internet – there is no way of demanding or assuring that people hold to only one religion at a time – then, given the inherent risks of religious commitment (i.e., choosing the wrong salvific investment), people "will seek to diversify" (Stark 1996: 204). The most rational strategy in the face of such structurally induced uncertainty will be to maintain a limited involvement in many competitive religions simultaneously – quite possibly to the long-term detriment of all. Stark, Bainbridge, and Innaccone suggest that true religious "movements" are much more likely to emerge from new religions that demand an exclusive commitment. As a medium, however, the Internet carries a reverse bias.[14]

This bias is reflected most clearly in some new religions to which the Internet itself has given birth – communities of belief that exist only, or at least primarily, on the net. The ones people are most likely to know are intentional jokes, blatant parodies like the Church of the Mighty Gerbil (http://www.gerbilism.snpedro.com) or the First Presbyterian Church of Elvis the Divine (http://chelsea.ios.com/~hkarlinl/welcome.html). But there are other more problematic instances as well, one of which we have begun to study: Thee Church ov MOO (http://members.xoom.com/gecko23/moo). This new religion was invented, almost by accident, by a group of gifted students interacting on an Internet bulletin board in Ottawa, Canada, sometime in the early 1990s. Today many of these same people operate a sophisticated website with over eight hundred pages of fabricated religious documents covering a sweeping range of religious and pseudo-religious subjects. A visit to the website reveals an elaborate development of alternative sets of scriptures, commandments, chronicles, mythologies, rituals, and ceremonies. Much of this material reads like a bizarre religious extension of *The Hitch Hiker's Guide to the Galaxy*. It is irreverent and playful, alternately verging on the sophomoric and the sophisticated. Many of the texts of the Church ov MOO seem to have been devised with a keen awareness of religious history, comparative beliefs and practices, and some real knowledge of the philosophy, anthropology, and sociology of religion. The site records a great many hits every day, we are told, and about ten thousand people have applied for membership.

Several of the key figures are currently pursuing training or careers in physics, mathematics, computer science, and the other so-called hard sciences. With MOOism they are attempting to devise a self-consciously postmodern, socially constructed, relativist, and self-referenial system of religious ideas, purposefully and paradoxically infused with humor, irony, and farce, as well as a serious appreciation of the essentially religious or spiritual condition of humanity. In a typically postmodernist manner, the conventions we normally draw between academic reflection and religious thought are flaunted. An unsolicited essay we received from one of the church leaders on "MOOism, Social Constructionism, and thee Origins ov Religious Movements" characteristically begins with the following note:

Thee language ov this essay conforms to TOPY standards ov language discipline. Thee purpose ov this is twofold: first, to prevent thee reader from forgetting that E am not attempting to separate this sociological comment from religious text; second, to prevent thee writer from forgetting thee same thing. These ideas should be taken neither too lightly nor too seriously.

Similarly, the MOO homepage declares:

Among other things, MOOism has been called the Negativland of religion. Not only does it irreverently (and sometimes irrelevantly) sample innumerable other religious traditions, it uses recontextualization and paradoxical framing techniques to prevent minds from settling into orthodoxy. Paradox and radical self-contradiction are, in the postmodern context, the most reasonable way to approach the Absolute.

MOOIsm is certainly about having "fun" with religion. But the objective does seem to be to encourage and facilitate the rise of a new conceptual framework and language for religious experience suited to the changed environmental conditions of postmodern society. The "religion" seems to be influenced significantly by neo-paganism and is representative of what is coming to be called Technopaganism. (But it is also influenced by such earlier and quite sophisticated joke religions as Discordianism and the Church of the SubGenius.) In line with many aspects of that movement it is seeking to provide an intellectual and social forum for fostering the king of human imagination and creativity that empowers people to override the public demise of spiritual life or "realities" in our time (see Luhrmann 1989). But unlike many other forms of neo-paganism, this "religion" is well suited, in form and function, to life on the net, perhaps because it is in many respects the witting and unwitting mirror reflection of the sensibilities of the Internet culture in which it developed. But, in truth, we do not know as yet whether MOOism is a "religious" movement or just a most elaborate hoax. The Church solicited our attention and its web page currently carries the

disclaimer: "This page is in the progress of being altered to mislead *Lorne Dawson*. It may therefore seem disjointed and confused." If it is all a joke, then one must marvel at the time and energy invested in its creation and perpetuation. In conversations, however, we have been led to believe that the originators of MOOism are beginning to have an ambiguous understanding of their creation and are seeking some assistance in thinking through the significance of MOOism as a social phenomenon. One thing is clear, without the Internet, this phenomenon is unlikely to have developed or exercised the influence it undoubtedly has on some people. But is it reflective of the future of religion in some regard? Joke or not, it may be similar to other current or future religious phenomena on the net that are of a more serious intent. The Church ov MOO does appear to embody elements of both Beckford's conception of religion as a "cultural resource" and Stark and Bainbridge's speculations about the special appeal of cult innovations to elites.[15]

At present, most of the virtual communities of the net are much less intriguing and problematic. Most new religions seem content to use the net in quite limited and conventional ways. But the web masters we surveyed are uniformly intent on constantly improving their web pages in visual, auditory, and interactive technology. So we must be careful not to underestimate what the future may hold. There is merit, we think, in the metaphorical conclusion of Zaleski:

Virtual and physical reality exert a gravitational pull on one another. At present, virtuality is the moon to the real world, bound by its greater mass, but just as the moon influences tides, spiritual work in the virtual communities is influencing and will continue to influence that work in real-world communities. (Zaleski 1997: 254)

The new religious uses of the Internet are likely to exercise an increasingly determinant, if subtle, effect on the development of all religious life in the future (Lövheim and Linderman 1998).

Notes

1 This paper was first presented to a special seminar on "New and Marginal Religions in the Public Space" held in Montreal on July 25, 1998, organized by Pauline Coté.

2 The term "cults" is so strongly associated with negative images in the popular mind that academics have long preferred to use such terms as "new religions" or "new religious movements" (see, for example, Richardson 1993). The word will be used, nonetheless, at various points in this essay to call to mind the fears giving rise to this discussion in the first place.

3 "Web of Death" was the *double entendre* used as the headline of a *Newsweek* cover story on the Heaven's Gate suicide.

4 In 1997, Statistics Canada reported that of all the homes in Canada with some type of facility to access the Internet, only 13 percent have made use of the opportunity. Reginald Bibby (1995) reported that 31 percent of Canadians had some contact with the Internet, ranging from daily to hardly ever. The rate of growth of the net, however, is exponential and quite phenomenal. It is estimated that the world wide web is growing at a rate, of close to 10 percent per month. Zaleski (1997: 136) notes, for example: "In 1993, the year the Web browser Mosaic was released, the Web proliferated a 341,634 percent annual growth rate of service traffic."

5 This finding, from a more general survey by the Barna Research Group in February, 1997, is reported in *Maclean's* magazine (May 25, 1998: 12).

6 Five groups (potentially another 16.6 percent) informed us that our request had been passed along to higher authorities, but at the time this paper was submitted, a later reminder notice had merely earned us a reiteration of this reply. Another five groups or individuals declined to participate in our survey, for a variety of reasons: several complained that they are simply not religions; one pointed out that they do not wish to be associated with the subject of cults in any way; and two said that they receive too many surveys and now refuse to respond to them. Thirteen groups or 43.3 percent of the sample simply did not respond. (None of the messages were returned as undeliverable.)

7 The questionnaire and accompanying information letter of our survey were reviewed by two other experienced survey researchers, as well as by the ethics review board for research with human subjects of our university. Nonetheless, some mistakes may have been made with regard to the sensitivity of these groups to outside investigations of any sort. Undoubtedly many new religions are wary about cooperating with any requests for information about their operations. Others are simply ignorant of the real nature of sociological research and mistrustful of the unknown in their own right. Further, it has been our experience that some of these groups are by no means as organized and professional in their activities as many exponents of the anti-cult movement would have us believe. It is likely that some of our surveys have simply been overlooked or "trashed." Contrary to our expectations, in each regard, the immediacy and the anonymity of the Internet may actually have worked against us. Our colleague Dr. John Goyder of the University of Waterloo Survey Research Institute told us of two other e-mail surveys in which he participated that resulted in similarly disappointing rates of return (about 33 percent). These were, however, surveys of university faculty, which were dealing with relatively noncontroversial subjects. In one instance, when the first survey was followed by a mailed questionnaire to all non-respondents, the overall rate of return was doubled. It is possible that the Internet is already a saturated medium and not well suited for survey research. However, research into these matters has just begun (see, for example, Bedell 1998).

8 Respondents to the survey were offered anonymity and most of the seven groups and individuals who did respond requested that they not be identified or quoted directly without permission. The groups will therefore not be named in this essay.

9 We wish to thank Jeff Miller for calling our attention to this data in his Senior Honours Essay (Sociology, University of Waterloo 1998) on "Internet Subcultures."

10 As Zaleski reports (1997: 249) and we recall from the news: "At least one of the suicides, 39-year-old Yvonne McCurdy-Hill of Cincinnati, a post-office employee and mother of five, initially encountered the cult in cyberspace and decided to join in response to its online message."

11 For example, the web page for Osho actually employs a set of "key words" for each page of its very large site and many of these search

terms are very general: meditation, Christianity, brainwashing, deprogramming, relaxation, self-esteem, sadness, depression, tensions, and so on.

12 Of course, the web has offered new opportunities to the opponents of new religions as well. Entering the term "cults" in any search engine will produce a surfeit of sites dedicated to so-called watch dog organizations or the home pages of disgruntled ex-members (e.g., American Religion Information Center, http://www.fopc.org/ARIC_home.html; Watcher, http://www.marsweb.com/~watcher/cult.html; Operation Clambake – The Fight Against Scientology on the Net, http://www.xenu.net).

13 These reflections are strongly influenced by the ideas discussed by David Holmes in the introduction to his book on identity and community in cyberspace, *Virtual Politics* (1997).

14 Zaleski points out that the websites of the Holy See (http://www.vatican.va) and the Church of Jesus Christ of Latter Day Saints (http://www.lds.org) both characteristically commit what in cyberspace are two "cardinal sins." The sites offer no links to other sites, giving lie to the notion of Internet and world wide web, and they seek to misuse the net as a broadcast medium since no e-mail or other facility is provided for interactivity.

15 This is not the only net-created religion of which we are aware. A student is currently doing research on the Otherkin – a "religious movement" which, at least in some of its forms, largely exists only on the net. The Otherkin believe they are reincarnated elves, dwarfs, and other mythical and mystical creatures.

References

Barker, E. 1984: *The Making of a Moonie: Choice or Brainwashing.* Oxford: Blackwell.

Bainbridge, W. 1997: *The Sociology of Religious Movements.* New York: Routledge.

Baudrillard, J. 1970: *La société de consommation.* Paris: Editions Denoel. Translated and republished as *The Consumer Society.* London: Sage, 1998.

Beckford, J. 1989: *Religion in Advanced Industrial Society.* London: Unwin Hyman.

Beckford, J. 1992: "Religion, Modernity and Post-modernity." In Wilson, B. ed. *Religion: Contemporary Issues,* London: Bellew, 11–23.

Bedell, K. 1998: "Religion and the Internet: Reflections on Research Strategies." Paper presented to the Society for the Scientific Study of Religion, Montreal.

Bibby, R. W. 1995: *The Bibby Report: Social Trends Canadian Style.* Toronto: Stoddart.

Bromley, D. G. and Breschel, E. 1992: "General Population and Institutional Elite Support for Social Control of New Religious Movements: Evidence From National Survey Data *Behavioural Sciences and the Law* 10, 39–52.

Cottee, T., Yateman, N., and Dawson, L. 1996: "NRMs, the ACM, and the WWW: A Guide for Beginners." In Dawson, L. ed. *Cults in Context: Readings in the Study of New Religious Movements.* Toronto: Canadian Scholars Press (published in the United States by Transaction Pub.), 453–68.

Dawson, L. L. 1996: "Who Joins New Religious Movements and Why: Twenty Years of Research and What Have We Learned?" *Studies in Religion* 25 (2), 193–213. [chapter 7, this volume]

——1998: *Comprehending Cults: The Sociology of New Religious Movements.* Toronto and New York: Oxford University Press.

Ellul, J. 1964: *The Technological Society.* New York: Alfred A. Knopf.

Foucault, M. 1979: *Discipline and Punish.* New York: Vintage Books.

Frankel, A. 1996: "Making Law, Making Enemies." *American Lawyer* 3, March; downloaded from: http://www2.thecia.net/users/rnewman/scientology/media/amlawyer-3.36.html.

Giddens, A. 1990: *The Consequences of Modernity.* Cambridge: Polity Press.

Glock, C. Y. 1964: "The Role of Deprivation in the Origin and Evolution of Religious Groups." In Lee, R. and Marty, M., eds. *Religion and Social Conflict.* New York: Oxford University Press, 24–36.

Grossman, W. M., 1998: "alt.scientology.war" from Wired Magazine, downloaded from: http://www.wired.com/wired/3.12/features/alt.scientology.war.html.

Holmes, D. 1997: *Virtual Politics: Identity and Community in Cyberspace.* London: Sage.

Hoover, S. 1988: *Mass Media Religion.* Thousand Oaks, CA: Sage.

Innaccone, L. R. 1995: "Risk, Rationality, and Religious Portfolios." *Economic Inquiry* 33, 285–95.

Lofland J. 1966: *Doomsday Cult.* Englewood Cliffs, NJ: Prentice-Hall.

Lövheim M. and Linderman, A. 1998: "Internet –

A Site for Religious Identity Formation and Religious Communities?" Paper presented to the Society for the Scientific Study of Religion, Montreal.

Luhrmann, T. M. 1989: *Persuasions of the Witch's Craft: Ritual Magic in Contemporary England.* Cambridge, MA: Harvard University Press.

Marcuse, H. 1966: *One Dimensional Man.* Boston, MA: Beacon Press.

Marx, K. and Engels, F. 1970 [1846]: *The German Ideology.* New York: International Publishers.

McLuhan, M. 1964: *Understanding Media.* New York: McGraw-Hill.

Miller, J. 1998: "Internet Subcultures." Senior Honours Essay, Department of Sociology, University of Waterloo, Ontario, Canada.

Pfeifer, J. E. 1992: "The Psychological Framing of Cults: Schematic Representations and Cult Evaluations." *Journal of Applied Social Psychology* 22 (7), 513–44.

Postman, N. 1985: *Amusing Ourselves to Death.* New York: Penguin Books.

Poster, M. 1997: "Cyberdemocracy: The Internet and the Pubic Sphere." In Holmes, D., ed. *Virtual Politics. London:* Sage, 212–28.

Richardson, J. 1993: "Definitions of Cult: From Sociological–Technical to Popular–Negative." *Review of Religious Research* 34 (4), 348–56.

Rochford, E. B., Jr. 1982: "Recruitment Strategies, Ideology and Organization in the Hare Krishna Movement." *Social Problems* 29, 399–410.

Shields, R. (ed.) 1996: *Cultures of the Internet: Virtual Spaces, Real Histories, Living Bodies.* London: Sage.

Shupe, A. D. 1979: ' "Disembodied Access' and Technological Constraints on Organizational Development: A Study of Mail-Order Religions." *Journal for the Scientific Study of Religions* 15, 177–85.

Singer, M. T. 1995: *Cults in our Midst: The Hidden Menace in our Everyday Lives.* San Francisco, CA: Jossey–Bass.

Snow, D. A., Zurcher, L. A., Jr., and Ekland-Olson, S. 1980: "Social Networks and Social Movements: A Microstructural Approach to Differential Recruitment."*American Sociological Review* 45 (5), 787–801.

Stark, R. 1996: *The Rise of Christianity: A Sociologist Reconsiders History.* Princeton, NJ: Princeton University Press.

Stark, R. and Bainbridge, W. S. 1985: *The Future of Religion: Secularization, Revival and Cult Formation.* Berkeley: University of California Press.

——1997: A *Theory of Religion.* New Brunswick, NJ: Rutgers University Press. (Originally published by Peter Lang, 1987.)

Willson, M. 1997: "Community in the Abstract: A Political and Ethical Dilemma?" In Holmes, D., ed. *Virtual Politics.* London: Sage, 145–62.

Zaleski, J. 1997: *The Soul of Cyberspace: How New Technology is Changing Our Spiritual Lives.* New York: HarperCollins.

Index

Adler, Margot, 241
Aetherius Society, 56
affective ties, and joining cults, 119, 279
Aidala, Angela, 230, 245–7, 250–1
Alcoholics Anonymous, 89
Allen, Prudence, 247
American Protective Association, 76
Amish, 265, 268
Amritanandamayi, 240
Anabaptists
  the group, 74
  and Munster, 74, 77
androgyny, 233, 241–2, 247, 250, 253
Angelou, Maya, 102
Ansaaru Allah Community (AAC), 246–53
Anthony, Dick, 167, 184, 234
anti-cult movement (ACM), 2, 6, 10, 15–16,
    44, 114, 238
  and the Internet, 258, 290n.
  in the nineteenth century, 75–85
  and Peoples Temple, 196–7
  and Solar Temple, 213
apocalyptic
  and Jonestown, 188, 192
  and Solar Temple, 213–16
  thought, 77, 184, 192
Arica, 51
audience cults, 64
auditing, 49–50
Aum Shinrikyo, 26, 181, 182
authoritarianism, 44

baby boomers, 90, 114
  and social and religious change, 103–4
Back, Kurt, 49, 52

Bainbridge, William Sims, 27, 34, 114, 120–4,
    240, 276, 279, 282–3, 286–8
  and his theory of religion, 59–60, 260
Baker, Richard, 235
Barker, Eileen, 7–24, 119, 121–6, 163, 282
Barthes, Roland, 187
Beckford, James, 26–34, 167, 284, 288
Bellah, Robert, 102
Berg, David (Moses David, Mo), 36–7, 41, 43,
    234
Bhaktivedenta, Swami Prabuphada, 36–7, 240
  and women, 232
Bird, Frederick, 250
Blavatsky, Helena P., 79, 83, 241
Bonhoffer, Dietrich, 102
Brahma Kumaris, 231, 235–6, 240–2, 246, 248,
    250–1
brainwashing, 2, 16, 18, 27–8, 105, 113–14, 117,
    119, 143–5, 160–5, 167–77, 193, 206, 250
  critique of, 160–78
  description and application to cults, 147–59
  ethical concerns, 161–5
  and the law, 143, 161
  and Peoples Temple, 196–7, 203, 206
  and physical coercion, 149, 160
  and popular acceptance, 161
  rhetoric of, 171–2
  themes of, 154–7
  three stages of, 157–8
Branch Davidians, 26–7, 116, 126, 181–2, 186
Breyer, Jacques, 210–11
Bromley, David G., 125, 164, 167, 175, 184, 249
Brown, Norman O., 102
Bry, Adelaide, 52
Buddha, 1, 83, 103

Buddhism, 53, 71, 123, 231–5, 237, 239, 241–2
  and Theosophy, 83
  Zen Buddhism, 104–5, 237, 240

Canada
  and Solar Temple, 211
  statistics on new religions, 266
Carter, Lewis, 122
Catholic Church, 71, 73, 262, 265, 286
  abuses in, 26
  anti-Catholic propaganda, 75–6
  and patriarchy, 238
celibacy, 235–8, 245, 247, 249, 253
charisma
  and authority, 233, 250, 264
  and leadership, 73, 75, 184, 193, 210
  routinization of, 264–5
charismatic movement, 55–6, 120, 164
  see also Pentecostalism
Children of God (The Family), 114, 134, 142
  abnegation of self, 43–4
  and the anti-cult movement, 71
  patterns of growth, 259
  recruitment, 119, 164
  and sexual deviance, 234, 238
  world-rejecting cult, 36–42
Chogyam Trungpa, 234
Christian Science, 61, 84, 123, 241, 261, 265
Christianity
  early Christian community, 263–5, 267, 286
  and sexual abuse, 233
  and women, 230–1, 239, 247, 260, 261
Church Fathers, 74
Church of Bible Understanding, 174
Church Universal and Triumphant (CUT),
  120–3, 241, 250, 253, 278
CIA, and Jonestown, Peoples Temple, 205
civil rights movement, 94–6
client cults, 64
coercive persuasion, 143, 147, 167, 170–2
  see also brainwashing
Cohen, Albert K., 67
Cohen, Andrew, 235
Coleman, James S., 264
Committee for the Future, 68
communists
  and China, 148, 154, 160
  and North Korea, 148, 154, 160
  and the Soviet Union, 148, 160
communitas, 252
Concerned Relatives, 186–7, 199–201, 203–5
con-game, and new religions, 147, 149–50, 157
Constitution of the United States, and religious
  freedom, 143, 145, 168

consumerism
  expansion after 1960, 98
  and the Internet, 285–6
  and religious change, 98
conversion, 114, 118–21, 131–42, 144, 154,
  160–5, 173–5, 249, 261, 266–8
  medicalization of, 168, 176
  problems with accounts, 170–1
Cox, Harvey, 102, 104
Crowley, Vivianne, 236, 241
cult movements, 64, 261
cult scare, 78–9
cult typologies, 33–4
cultural capital, and success of new religions, 261
cultural diversity, 102, 105

Dalai Lama, 235
Daly, Mary, 248
Danites (Destroying Angels), 79–80
Davis, Erik, 272–3, 279
Dawson, Lorne, 114, 116–30, 183, 258, 271–90,
  276
deception
  heavenly deception, 154
  and new religions, 169, 173–6, 177n., 178n.
defection from new religions, 164, 250–1, 267–8
Delgado, Richard, 163, 174, 175, 178n.
demonization, 27–8, 161, 206
deprogramming, 161, 164, 168–9, 174
deviance amplification, 15, 181
Di Mambro, Joseph, 208–15, 217–20, 222
Dianectics, 49, 51, 61
discipleship, 233, 241
discipline, 41, 45
Discordianism, 288
dissatisfaction
  with conventional religion, 103–4
  with "living for today," 106–7
Divine Light Mission, 136, 142, 164, 173
Dobbelaere, Karel, 118–20, 122–3
doubling of identity, 158–9
Dowie, John Alexander, 84
Durkheim, Emile, 254, 260
Dyer, Mary, 78

Eckancar, 122, 125, 278
Eddy, Mary Baker, 61, 69, 241
education, 30
  changing patterns, 99
  of converts, 122
Edwards, Thomas, and *Gangraena*, 74
elites and new religions, 282–3
Ellwood, Robert, 48
entrepreneurship and new religions, 63–6

est (Erhard Seminars Training), 45, 47–53, 66, 90, 249
evil
  social confrontation with, 100–1
  and spirituality, 101, 107
exit counseling, 159

failed prophecies, 262
family life
  changes, 98
  and religious changes, 98–9
Father Divine, 190
femininity, 241
feminism and religious change, 97
fertility and success of new religions, 265, 268
Fichter, Joseph, 55–6
flirty fishing, 40, 234, 259
Foster, Lawrence, 252
Fox, Margaret, 82–3
fraud
  and new religions, 64–5, 74, 82–3
  and Solar Temple, 212–13
free love, 245, 247, 253
  and Osho, 235–6
free rider problem, 262–3, 267
freedom
  American conceptions, 92–3
  changing conceptions, 93–5, 107
  and spirituality, 102
Freemasons (Masons), 71, 73, 75–6
Friends of the Western Buddhist Order (FWBO), 231, 237, 239
fundraising (funding)
  and new religions, 39–40, 53
  and Peoples Temple, 191–2
  and Solar Temple, 211–12

Galanter, Marc, 163
Gardner, Martin, 61
gender issues and new religions, 227–8, 238, 241, 245–6, 248, 251, 253–4
Giddens, Anthony, 284
God, conceptions of, 36, 48
Golden Way Foundation, 209–10
Great Awakenings, 75
Greil, Arthur, 118, 164
Gross, Rita, 254
Gunther, Bernard, 51

Hall, John R., 182–3, 184–206
Harris, Thomas Lake, and Brotherhood of the New Life, 81–2
Hawthorne, Geoffrey, 204
Healthy Happy Holy Organization (3HO), 131–2

Hearst, Patricia, 148, 150
Heaven's Gate, 26, 182, 271–2, 276–8
Heirich, Max, 164
Hinduism, 53–4, 123, 232
  and Theosophy, 83
Holmes, David, 283–6, 290n.
hostility towards new religions, 161, 168, 176–7
House of David, 85
Hubbard, L. Ron, 16, 49, 61, 64–5, 135
Human Potential Movement, 47–8, 51, 53, 104
Hunter, Edward, and *Brainwashing in Red China*, 148

individualism, religious emphasis on, 48–9
identity
  crises, 131–42
  new identities, 158
  pseudo identities, 158
INFORM (Information Network Focus on Religious Movements), 10–11, 18
Inner Peace Movement, 50, 53
Insight, 52
Institute of Applied Metaphysics (IAM), 246–7, 249
Institute for the Harmonious Development of Human Being (IHDHB), 246, 248–9, 253
Internet, 257
  Internet surveys, 273–6
  and new religions, 271–90
  social dangers of, 284–6
Islam, 71, 260

Jackins, Harvey, and *The Human Side of Human Beings*, 51–2
Jacobs, Janet, 119, 234, 245
Jefferson, Thomas, 92–3
Jehovah's Witnesses, 26, 113, 257, 262, 265, 268
  and Watch Tower Society, 84
Jenkins, Philip, 71
Jesus, 1, 37, 83
Jesus Army, 237
Jews, 132
  and recruitment to new religions, 123
John-Rogers, 116
joining
  new religions, 118–21, 131–42, 144, 160–5, 173–5
  theories of, 124–5
Jones, Jim, 38, 69, 74, 105, 182–3, 186–206
  see also Peoples Temple; Jonestown
Jonestown, 27, 37, 39–41, 43, 105, 117, 126, 182–3, 186–206
  inception of, 196–8
  see also Peoples Temple

Jouret, Luc, 208, 210–11, 213, 215, 217

Kennett, Roshi, 237
Kerouac, Jack, 95, 99
Kilbourne, Brock, 163
King, Martin Luther, Jr., 94–5
  assassination, 100
King, Ursula, 239
Knights Templar, 183, 209–11, 216
Kontt, Kim, 230
Koresh, David, 74, 116
Kox, Willem, 118
Krishna Consciousness (International Society for Krishna Consciousness, ISKCON), 9, 44, 90, 114, 119–23, 136, 142, 196, 203, 261
  anti-cult movement, 71, 73
  deception, 174
  gender issues, 227–8, 230–2, 238, 240–2, 246–7, 253
  and the Internet, 278
  reasons for persecuting, 168
  recruitment, 173, 177n., 250–1
  relative size, 164
  world-rejecting cult, 36–41
Ku Klux Klan, 76

La Barre, Weston, 62–3
Latkin, Carl, 122–3, 161
law
  and brainwashing, 143–4, 161, 167, 169–70, 178n.
  and Branch Davidians, 181
  and new religions, 17–18, 143–5
Lemert, Edwin, 62
Levine, Saul, 114, 124–6, 131–42, 251
Lévi-Strauss, Claude, 63
Lewis, James R., 164
Lifton, Robert J., 151, 154–7, 162, 172
liminality, 246, 252, 254
Lincoln, Bruce, 252
Lofland, John, 118–20, 125, 171–2
love-bombing, 170–1
Love Family, 62, 155, 203

McCutchan, Robert, 54
McGuire, Meredith, 55, 163
Machalek, Richard, 122
McVeigh, Timothy, 186
magic, as differentiated from religion, 260
Maharishi Mahesh Yogi, 45, 48, 234
Maharji Ji, 136, 173
Malcomson, Scott, 186
Manson, Charles, 38, 41–3, 148

marketing and religion, 52–3
marriage
  arranged, 235, 237–8
  and Brahma Kumaris, 236–7
  and Krishna Consciousness, 238
  and Osho, 236
  and paganism, 236
  and Unification Church, 237–8, 247
Marx, Karl, 92, 194, 284
Maslow, Abraham, 241
Matthews, Robert, 77
Mayer, Jean-François, 183, 208–22
media
  and Heaven's Gate, 271
  and new religions, 1, 6, 16–17, 28, 83–5, 181, 187
  and Peoples Temple, 197, 205
  and Solar Temple, 208
Melton, J. Gordon, 251
mental illness
  and conversion, 176
  and religious innovation, 60–3
Mesmer, Franz Anton, 65
Mesmerist movement, 77–8
methodology (social scientific) and study of new religions, 11–15, 18–19
Millar, Robert G., 186
mind-control, 143, 160, 167, 169, 170–1, 173–4, 176
  see also brainwashing
misogyny, 237–8
modernity
  anonymity of, 92
  and new religions, 27–9
  religious clash with, 6
Mohammed, 1, 76
MOO, Church of, 287–8
Moon, Sun Myung, 16, 21, 36, 38, 161, 175, 196, 237
Moore, Robert L., 251
Mormons (Church of Latter Day Saints), 26, 71, 73–6, 205, 257, 260–2, 265, 267–8
  anti-Mormonism, 76–7, 78–81, 205
  and the Internet, 290n.
Mother Meera, 240
motherhood
  and new religions, 227, 238–40
  and Osho, 239
Movement of Spiritual Inner Awareness, 48
Muktananda, 241

Native American religion, 78
Nichiren Shoshu (Soka Gakkai), 177n., 265, 268
  adaptation to West, 56

Nichiren Shoshu (Soka Gakkai) (cont'd)
  and the Internet, 278
  joining, recruitment, 118–19, 122–5
  world-affirming cult, 46, 48–9, 54
Nirmala Devi, 241
Norris, Kathleen, 101
Northeast Kingdom Community Church
  (NEKC), 246–7, 249–50
Novak, Michael, 97
Noyes, John Humphrey, 61, 77, 81

Oneida Community, 61, 77, 81
Osho see Rajneesh, Bhagwan Shree

paganism, 236, 238, 240–2
Palmer Susan, 122–3, 125, 128, 228,
  245–54
Parsons, Arthur, 125
patriarchy and new religions, 230–5, 238–9, 240,
  245–6, 250
Pentecostalism, 55, 188–9
Peoples Temple, 27, 37, 39–41, 43, 69, 182,
  186–206
  see also Jonestown; Jones, Jim
Phillips, Cynthia, 118, 120
Pilarzyk, Thomas, 164
politics
  and new religions, 38, 145, 167
  and Peoples Temple, 194
polygamy
  campaign against, 78–81
  and new religions, 249
Popper, Karl, 7–8, 11
Power, The, 68–9
Prince, Raymond, 251
Prophet, Elizabeth Clare, 241, 250
prosperity, American changes in, 99
Puttick, Elizabeth, 228, 230–43
  theory of types of religion, 241–2

Quakers (Friends), 71, 74

Raëlian Movement International, 14, 246–50,
  253
Rajneesh, Bhagwan Shree (Osho), 16, 235
  and the Internet, 278
  sex and gender issues, 228, 231–3, 235–6,
  238–42, 246–51, 253
  social attributes of members, 122–3
Rajneeshpuram, 232, 249
Ramtha, 248
recruitment
  and the Internet, 271–3, 279–83
  see also conversion

Re-evaluation Counseling, 50, 52
Reich, Charles, 104
Reimer, William, 250
religion, Stark's definition of, 260
religious background and joining new religions,
  123–4
renunciation, 42–4
revolutionary suicide, 195, 199, 202
Reynolds v. US, 80
Richardson, James T., 117, 120, 144, 160–5
Riesman, David, and Lonely Crowd, 92
rites of passage, 246, 250–4
Robbins, Thomas, 125, 144, 164, 167–78, 184,
  249
Rochford, E. Burke, 120, 122–3
Rosicrucianism (AMORC), 66, 123, 209,
  211–12, 216
Rosy Cross, 208, 210, 214, 216, 219–20
  see also Rosicrucianism; Solar Temple
Roszak, Theodore, 104
Rudy, David, 118, 164
Ryan, Leo (Congressman), 186, 200–2, 205

Sargent, William, 172
Satanism, and ritual abuse, 18
Schein, Edgar, 151, 157–8, 162, 172
Scientology, 90, 125, 135, 155, 248
  fit with models of cult creation, 61, 64–6
  and the Internet, 278, 286
  reasons for persecuting, 168
  social attributes of members, 121–3
  world-affirming cult, 48–54
Scott, Gina Graham, 50, 53
Second Coming (of Jesus), 37–8, 39
Second Vatican Council, 90, 108
sects, 265, 267, 268
  Stark's definition of, 261
seekership, 120, 123, 163
Seth, 91
Seventh Day Adventist Church, 113, 241
sexual abuse, 27, 193, 227–8, 233–5
sexual deviance, accusations of, 73, 75–6, 81, 84,
  228–9
sexual ethics, 41–2, 229, 236, 248, 251
sexuality, changes in, 99, 245–6
Shakers, 73–4, 203, 241
  anti-Shaker views, 77–8
Shapiro, Robert, 169
Shupe, Anson, Jr., 167, 175
Silva Mind Control, 44, 48
Silverman, Julian, 62
Singer, Margaret T., 119, 143–4, 147–59, 162,
  172, 272–3, 279
  Singer's six conditions of brainwashing, 151–4

sixties (1960s), 89–94
  and changes in spirituality, 102, 105, 107
Skonovd, Norman, 171–2
Snow, David, 46, 56, 118, 120, 122
social attributes of converts to new religions, 121–4
social change and new religions, 72
social control and Peoples Temple, 193
social implosion, 267
  and cult formation, 68–9
social mobility, changes in, 99
social networks and joining new religions, 119, 266–7, 279
socialization and the success of new religions, 268
Society for Psychical Research, 79, 82
Sogyal Rinpoche, 234–5
Soka Gakkai see Nichiren Shoshu
Solar Temple, 116, 126, 144, 182–3, 208–22
Solomon, Trudy, 164
Somit, Albert, 172
Spiritualism, 77, 79, 81, 241, 250
  anti-spiritualism, 82–3
spirituality
  changing American kinds, 89–108
  contrast with religion, 102–3
  feminine, 232–3
Starhawk, 236, 241
Stark, Rodney, 34, 114, 120, 122–5, 240, 257, 259–69, 279, 282–3, 286–8
  theory of conversion, 118–20
  theory of religion, 59–60, 260
  theory of success of new religions, 259–69
stereotypes
  of conversion, 114
  of deceptive cults, 175
  of joiners, 113, 117
Stone, Donald, 48, 54
Strauss, Roger, 164
strictness and the success of new religions, 262–3, 267–8
Subud, 56
success of new religions, 257, 259–69
suicide
  and Peoples Temple, 199–200, 202–5
  religious, 26, 214–15
  and Solar Temple, 208–22
Symbionese Liberation Army, 148
Synanaon, 41–2, 54, 68
Szasz, Thomas, 167

Tantra, 234–6, 249
taxes and new religions, 29
Technopaganism, 288
Teed, Cyrus R., 84

Theosophy, 79, 83, 85, 113, 123, 212, 241
thought reform, 143, 147, 150–9, 172
  see also brainwashing
Tipton, Steven, 120, 123, 125
Toennies, Ferdinand, 92
Transcendental Meditation (TM), 44–5, 47–9, 53–4, 104
transit, the, and Solar Temple, 214–16, 219–22
Turner, Victor, 251–3

Unification Church (Moonies), 9–10, 133, 196, 282
  and the anti-cult movement, 71, 73–4, 116
  and Booneville Farm, 175–6
  and the brainwashing debate, 163–4, 171–5
  and the Internet, 278
  joining and recruitment, 118–21, 125
  Molko and Leal v. Holy Spirit Association for the Unification of World Christianity, 178n.
  reasons for persecuting, 168
  sex and gender issues, 227, 231, 235, 237–8, 246–8, 250–1
  social attributes of members, 123–5
  world-rejecting cult, 36–7, 39–41, 44

Van Driel, Barend, 117
Van Gennep, Arnold, 252
violence (religious), 26–7
  causes of, 181–4, 202–6, 215–20
  and Garfield assassination, 81
  and Jonestown, 184–207
  and Solar Temple deaths, 208–22
  and Solar Temple murders, 218, 220–1

Wallace, Anthony F. C., 62
Wallis, Roy, 33–4, 36–69, 120–3
Washington, Joseph, Jr., 95
Weber, Max, 264
White, Ellen, 241
Whyte, William, and Organization Man, 92
Wicca, 228, 231, 236, 241, 245
  see also paganism
Wilber, Ken, 234
Wilson, Bryan, 118–23, 268
Willson, Michele, 285
Winter, Gibson, 104
women and new religions, 227–56
world rejection and new religions, 36–44
Wright, Stuart, 164, 251
Wuthnow, Robert, 8, 72, 89–111

Yogi Bhajan, 132

Zaleski, Jeff, 276, 278–9, 286, 288, 290n.
Zinzendorf, Count, 75